PAGES 154–65
*Street Finder maps
5, 6, 12*

PAGES 250–55
*Street Finder maps
5, 6*

PAGES 64–75
*Street Finder maps
5, 12*

PAGES 166–75
*Street Finder maps
5, 6*

Via Veneto

Quirinal

Esquiline

PAGES 76–95
*Street Finder maps
5, 8, 9, 12*

itol

Forum

Palatine

Lateran

PAGES 96–101
Street Finder map 8

nfine

Caracalla

0 metres	500
0 yards	500

PAGES 188–97
*Street Finder maps
8, 9*

PAGES 176–87
*Street Finder maps
6, 9, 10*

EYEWITNESS TRAVEL

ROME

EYEWITNESS TRAVEL
ROME

LONDON, NEW YORK,
MELBOURNE, MUNICH AND DELHI
www.dk.com

PROJECT EDITOR Fiona Wild
ART EDITOR Annette Jacobs
EDITORS Ferdie McDonald, Mark Ronan, Anna Streiffert
DESIGNER Lisa Kosky
DESIGN ASSISTANT Marisa Renzullo
PICTURE RESEARCH Catherine O'Rourke
RESEARCH IN ROME Sam Cole
DTP EDITOR Siri Lowe

MAIN CONTRIBUTORS
Olivia Ercoli, Ros Belford, Roberta Mitchell

PHOTOGRAPHERS
John Heseltine, Mike Dunning, Kim Sayer

ILLUSTRATORS
Studio Illibill, Kevin Jones Associates,
Martin Woodward, Robbie Polley

This book was produced with the assistance of
Websters International Publishers.

Reproduced by Colourscan, Singapore
Printed and bound by South China Printing Co. Ltd., China

First published in Great Britain in 1993
by Dorling Kindersley Limited
80 Strand, London WC2R 0RL

Reprinted with revisions 2001, 2002, 2003, 2004, 2005, 2006, 2007,
2008, 2009, 2010, 2011 (001)

Copyright 1993, 2011 © Dorling Kindersley Limited, London
A Penguin Company

ALL RIGHTS RESERVED. NO PART OF THIS PUBLICATION MAY BE
REPRODUCED, STORED IN A RETRIEVAL SYSTEM, OR TRANSMITTED IN
ANY FORM OR BY ANY MEANS, ELECTRONIC, MECHANICAL,
PHOTOCOPYING, RECORDING OR OTHERWISE, WITHOUT THE PRIOR
WRITTEN PERMISSION OF THE COPYRIGHT OWNER.

A CIP catalogue record is available from the British Library.

ISBN: 978-1-40534-837-9

FLOORS ARE REFERRED TO THROUGHOUT IN
ACCORDANCE WITH EUROPEAN USAGE; IE THE "FIRST FLOOR"
IS THE FLOOR ABOVE GROUND LEVEL.

Front cover main image: St Peter's Basilica at sunset

MIX
Paper from
responsible sources
FSC
www.fsc.org   FSC™ C018179

**The information in this
DK Eyewitness Travel Guide is checked annually.**
Every effort has been made to ensure that this book is as up-
to-date as possible at the time of going to press. Some details,
however, such as telephone numbers, opening hours, prices,
gallery hanging arrangements and travel information, are
liable to change. The publishers cannot accept responsibility
for any consequences arising from the use of this book, nor
for any material on third party websites, and cannot guarantee
that any website address in this book will be a suitable source
of travel information. We value the views and suggestions
of our readers very highly. Please write to: Publisher, DK
Eyewitness Travel Guides, Dorling Kindersley, 80 Strand, London
WC2R 0RL, Great Britain, or email: travelguides@dk.com.

CONTENTS

Colosseum

INTRODUCING ROME

Moses by Michelangelo in
San Pietro in Vincoli

◁ St Peter's Square with crowds

Fresco in Villa Farnesina

ROME
AREA BY AREA

The Tempietto

Arch of Titus

TRAVELLERS'
NEEDS

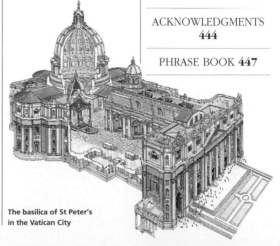

The basilica of St Peter's
in the Vatican City

Mosaic in Santa Prassede

SURVIVAL GUIDE

Roman antipasto

HOW TO USE THIS GUIDE

This Eyewitness Travel Guide helps you get the most from your stay in Rome with the minimum of practical difficulty. The opening section, *Introducing Rome*, locates the city geographically, sets modern Rome in its historical context and explains how Roman life changes through the year. *Rome at a Glance* is an overview of the city's attractions. The main sightseeing section, *Rome Area by Area*, starts on page 62.

It describes all the important sights with maps, photographs and detailed illustrations. In addition, nine planned walks take you to parts of Rome you might otherwise miss.

Carefully researched tips for hotels, shops and markets, restaurants and cafés, sports and entertainment are found in *Travellers' Needs*, and the *Survival Guide* has advice on everything from posting a letter to catching the Metro.

FINDING YOUR WAY AROUND THE SIGHTSEEING SECTION

Each of the sixteen sightseeing areas in the city is colour-coded for easy reference. Every chapter opens with an introduction to the part of Rome it covers, describing its history and character, followed by a Street-by-Street

map illustrating the heart of the area. Finding your way around each chapter is made simple by the numbering system used throughout. The most important sights are covered in detail in two or more full pages.

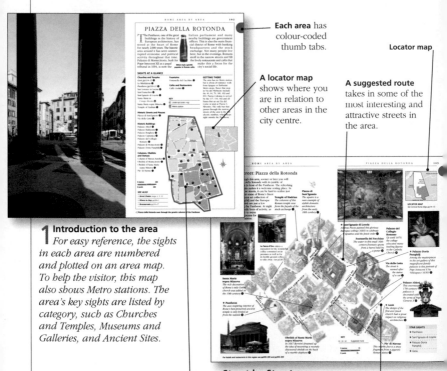

Each area has colour-coded thumb tabs.

Locator map

A locator map shows where you are in relation to other areas in the city centre.

A suggested route takes in some of the most interesting and attractive streets in the area.

1 Introduction to the area
For easy reference, the sights in each area are numbered and plotted on an area map. To help the visitor, this map also shows Metro stations. The area's key sights are listed by category, such as Churches and Temples, Museums and Galleries, and Ancient Sites.

The area covered in greater detail on the *Street-by-Street Map* is shaded pink.

2 Street-by-Street map
This gives a bird's-eye view of interesting and important parts of each sightseeing area. The numbering of the sights ties in with the area map and the fuller description of the entries on the pages that follow.

Stars indicate the sights that no visitor should miss.

ROME AREA MAP
The coloured areas shown on this map *(see inside front cover)* are the sixteen main sightseeing areas of Rome – each covered in a full chapter in *Rome Area by Area (pp62–255)*. They are highlighted on other maps throughout the book. In *Rome at a Glance (pp42–57)*, for example, they help locate the top sights. They are also used to help you find the position of the nine guided walks *(p273)*.

Numbers refer to each sight's position on the area map and its place in the chapter.

Practical information provides everything you need to know to visit each sight. Map references pinpoint the sight's location on the *Street Finder map (see pp396–419)*.

The façade of each major sight is shown to help you spot it quickly.

The visitors' checklist gives all the practical information needed to plan your visit.

3 Detailed information
All the important sights in Rome are described individually. They are listed in order following the number-ing on the area map at the start of the section. Practical information includes a map reference, opening hours and telephone numbers. The key to the symbols is on the back flap.

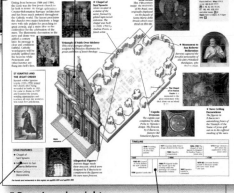

4 Rome's major sights
Historic buildings are dissected to reveal their interiors; museums and galleries have colour-coded floorplans to help you find the most important exhibits.

The list of star sights indicate the best features and works of art.

A timeline charts the key events in the history of the building.

INTRODUCING ROME

FOUR GREAT DAYS IN ROME

Rome wasn't built in a day but you can just about see all its highlights in four. Its history can be traced in the crumbling columns of the ancient empire, the medieval alleys lined with Renaissance palaces and Baroque fountains splashing on elegant piazzas. Rome has dozens of

The Mouth of Truth – no place for liars

museums, from the vast Vatican to compact collections like the Galleria Borghese. There are hundreds of art-stuffed churches too, from tiny chapels to the great basilicas and St Peter's itself. These itineraries offer you a taste of it all. The price guides include cost of travel, food and admission fees.

Teatro di Marcello and the trio of standing columns

ANCIENT ROME

- **Explore the Republic**
- **Lunch in medieval ambience**
- **Absorb Imperial grandeur**
- **See how the Caesars lived**

TWO ADULTS allow at least €150

Morning

Cram highlights of the 1,000-year history of ancient Rome's Republic and Empire into one very full day. Start at its heart, the **Roman Forum** *(see pp76–91)*, then spend an hour or so perusing some of its treasures inside the **Capitoline Museums** *(see pp70–3)*. Stroll over to Largo della Torre Argentina to gaze upon the remains of three Republican-era temples and the crumbling brick steps of the 55 BC Baths of Pompey, where Julius Caesar was murdered, ending the Republican era. The Baths of Pompey complex included a theatre that has now vanished but some of its vaults survive in the foundations of the Campo de' Fiori area's

medieval buildings – including the basement rooms of **Ristorante Da Pancrazio** *(see p320)*, which serves excellent pasta.

Afternoon

Return to the core of ancient Rome past the Teatro di Marcello – model for the Colosseum – and the two tiny **Temples of the Forum Boarium** *(see p203)* in Piazza della Bocca della Verità. Nip up Via del Velabro to the Forum's back entrance and cut through to Via dei Fori Imperiali to explore the ruins of Rome's Imperial era – the **Market and Forum of Trajan** *(see pp88–9)*, and the **Forums of Caesar**, **Augustus**, and **Nerva** *(see pp90–91)*. At the end, you can admire the **Domus Aurea** (Nero's Golden House) *(see p175;* closed at present) and the nearby **Colosseum** *(see pp92–3)*, built over Nero's former artificial lake. Stroll up the Via Sacra to roam the **Palatine Hill** *(see pp97–101;* entry included on Colosseum ticket), peppered with original palatial homes.

CHRISTIAN ROME

- **The Vatican Museums**
- **Picnic on the Piazza**
- **Mosaics and a Mithraic temple**
- **Holy (dinner) orders**

TWO ADULTS allow at least €185

Morning

Exploring the **Vatican Museums** *(see pp234–47)* can easily occupy a full morning. When you're hungry, leave the museum and walk four streets up Via Tunisi to shop for goodies at the outdoor market on Via Andrea Doria. Take them back to picnic on Piazza San Pietro.

Afternoon

Pop into **St Peter's Basilica** *(see pp230–33)* to marvel at this capital of Christendom, then head to admire the glittering mosaics of **Santa Maria Maggiore** *(see pp172–3)*. Afterwards, visit **San Clemente** *(see pp186–7)*, a gorgeous 12th-century church built atop a 4th-century one, which stands on an ancient Mithraic temple. You will find important works by Raphael,

Detail of the mosaics in Santa Maria Maggiore

Dolce & Gabbana store window in Piazza di Spagna

Bernini, Caravaggio and Bramante in the church of **Santa Maria del Popolo** (see pp138–9). Enjoy the evening *passeggiata* – Rome's see-and-be-seen stroll along the Via del Corso – with a drink at one of the busy cafés flanking the piazza. Round off by eating in one of two restaurants run by nuns: the simple, family-style **Fraterna Domus** (see p317), or the exotic but pricey **L'Eau Vive** (see p316).

ART AND SHOPPING

- Fountains and piazzas
- National Gallery treasures
- Temples and boutiques
- Spanish Steps and the Trevi

TWO ADULTS allow at least €25

Morning
Start at the fruit and flower market of **Campo de' Fiori** (see pp143–53), located around a statue of Giordano Bruno, who was burned at the stake in the Middle Ages. **Piazza Navona** (see p116–27), with its Baroque fountains and excellent cafés, owes its oval shape to the ancient stadium beneath (a fragment is visible at its north end). Visit the collections of the National Gallery in the **Palazzo Altemps** (see p127). Peek into the church of **San Luigi dei Francesi** (see p122) for the early Caravaggios,

then duck into Corso del Rinascimento 40 to see the hidden fantasy façade on **Sant'Ivo alla Sapienza** (see p122). Do not miss Rome's **Pantheon** (see pp110–11), an ancient temple (now church), and **Santa Maria sopra Minerva** (see p108), for its art. Try the cappuccinos at **Caffè Sant'Eustachio** (see p330).

Afternoon
Cross the Via del Corso, and enjoy an afternoon's shopping in the chic boutiques of **Via Condotti** (see p133) and its tributaries fanning out from the base of the **Spanish Steps** (see pp134–5). To end the day treat yourself to one of Rome's best ice creams at **San Crispino** (see p330), and wander over to the nearby **Trevi Fountain** (see p159) before it melts.

A FAMILY DAY

- Cycle in Villa Borghese park
- See puppets, creatures and creepy crypts
- Cross the Tiber for medieval alleys and panoramic views

FAMILY OF 4 allow at least €185

Morning
Rent bikes in **Villa Borghese** park (see pp258–9) where, as well as exploring, you can visit the Etruscan Museum in **Villa Giulia** (see pp262–3) or the excellent **Galleria**

Borghese (see pp260–61; book ahead). If the kids need less art and more fun, take in Rome's zoo, the **Bioparco** (see p259). If it's a Sunday, stop at **Pincio Gardens** (see pp136–7) for an open-air carousel and the San Carlino, one of Rome's few remaining puppet theatres that puts on Pulcinella shows from 11am.

Afternoon
Return the bikes and stroll past the top of the **Spanish Steps** (see pp134–5) down Via Gregoriana, looking out for the Palazzetto Zuccari at number 28, whose windows and doors are shaped into hideous creatures. Below Via Veneto's **Santa Maria della Concezione** (see p254) lies the creepy Capuchin Crypts, which are covered in mosaics made from the bones of monks. (Cappuccino coffee was named after the colour of these friars' robes.)

At Piazza della Bocca della Verità, on the porch of **Santa Maria in Cosmedin** (see p202), sits the Mouth of Truth, an ancient drain cover carved as a monstrous face. The story goes that if you tell a lie with your fingers in the mouth, it will bite them off. Head across the river to **Trastevere** (see pp207–13), an area of twisting medieval alleys. Climb **Janiculum hill** (see pp215–17) to enjoy the sweeping views of the city. Descend to Trastevere for a pizza at **Pizzeria Ivo** (see p328).

View of Via Condotti from the top of the Spanish Steps

Putting Rome on the Map

Since its foundation over 2,750 years ago on seven hills near the banks of the River Tiber, Rome has grown into a city of three million people covering 1,500 sq km (580 sq miles) of central Italy. Within this area is the independent Vatican City State. Rome was made capital of the newly united Italy in 1870. It is about 28 km (17 miles) from the sea and has good rail and road links to many other historic Italian towns and cities.

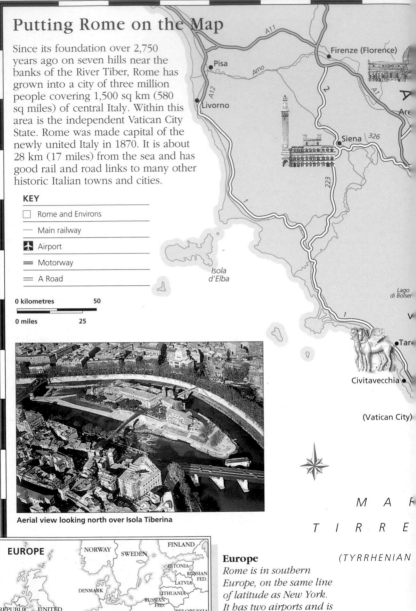

KEY

☐ Rome and Environs

— Main railway

✈ Airport

═ Motorway

═ A Road

0 kilometres   50

0 miles   25

Pisa
Livorno
Firenze (Florence)
Siena
Isola d'Elba
Lago di Bolser
Civitavecchia
(Vatican City)
Tar

Aerial view looking north over Isola Tiberina

M A R
T I R R E
(TYRRHENIAN

Europe

Rome is in southern Europe, on the same line of latitude as New York. It has two airports and is about 2½ hours' flying time from London. Rome is also linked to the rest of Europe by road and rail. It is about 15 hours from Paris by train. It is also at the centre of Italy's main road network, parts of which follow the routes of ancient Roman roads.

EUROPE
NORWAY SWEDEN FINLAND
ESTONIA
RUSSIAN FED.
LATVIA
DENMARK LITHUANIA
RUSSIAN FED.
REPUBLIC OF IRELAND UNITED KINGDOM BELORUSSIA
NETHERLANDS POLAND
BELGIUM GERMANY
LUXEMBOURG CZECH REPUBLIC UKRAINE
FRANCE SLOVAKIA
AUSTRIA HUNGARY
SWITZERLAND SLOVENIA CROATIA ROMANIA
ITALY BOSNIA AND HERZEGOVINA SERBIA
MONTENEGRO BULGARIA
Rome
SPAIN GREECE
PORTUGAL
ALGERIA TUNISIA

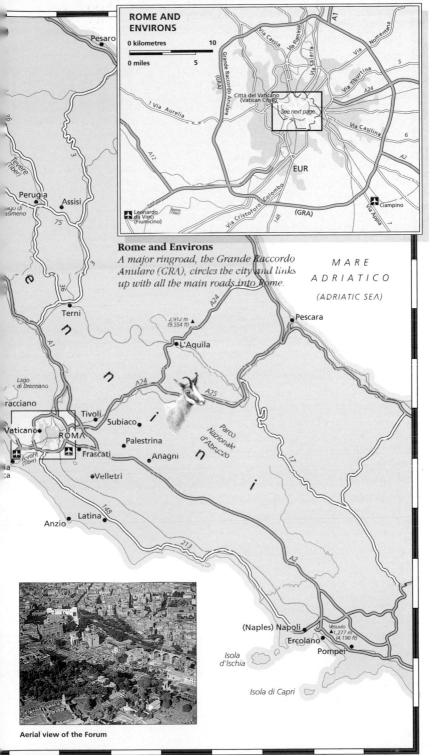

ROME AND ENVIRONS

0 kilometres 10

0 miles 5

Via Cassia
Via Flaminia
Via Salaria
Via Nomentana
A1
Via Tiburtina
A24
Via Casilina
6
A2
Via Appia
7
Ciampino
EUR
(GRA)
Grande Raccordo Anulare (GRA)
1 Via Aurelia
Citta del Vaticano (Vatican City)
See next page
A12
Via Cristoforo Colombo
148
Leonardo da Vinci (Fiumicino)
Tevere (Tiber)

Rome and Environs

A major ringroad, the Grande Raccordo Anularo (GRA), circles the city and links up with all the main roads into Rome.

MARE ADRIATICO
(ADRIATIC SEA)

Pesaro

Tevere (Tiber)

26

3

Perugia

Assisi

ago di asimeno

75

3

36

e

n

n

Terni

A1

2,912 m (9,554 ft)

L'Aquila

Lago di Bracciano

A24

Pescara

racciano

Vaticano

Tivoli

Subiaco

ROMA

Palestrina

Parco Nazionale d'Abruzzo

A25

Tevere (Tiber)

ia

a

Frascati

Anagni

Velletri

n

17

Latina

148

Anzio

213

A2

(Naples) Napoli

Ercolano

Vesuvio 1,277 m (4,190 ft)

Pompei

Isola d'Ischia

Isola di Capri

Aerial view of the Forum

Central Rome

This book divides central Rome into 16 areas and has further sections for sights on the outskirts of the city, including some day trips, as well as some suggested walks. Each of the main areas has its own chapter and contains a selection of sights that convey some of its history and distinctive character. The Forum will give you a glimpse of ancient Rome, while the Capitol, Piazza della Rotonda and Piazza Navona represent the historic centre. If you are interested in Renaissance palaces, make a point of visiting the fine examples in Campo de' Fiori. In Piazza di Spagna, you can find designer shops and hints of the Grand Tour. A stop at the Vatican will reveal the impressive St Peter's and the heart of Roman Catholicism.

Pantheon
Fronted by lofty granite column the Pantheon was built as a Roman temple of "all the gods (see pp110–11).

KEY

▮	Star sights
Ⓜ	Metro station
▤	Train station
🚌	Main bus terminal
🚊	Tram terminal
ℹ	Tourist information
—	City Wall

Vatican Museums
This vast complex of buildings holds one of the world's greatest collections of Classical and Renaissance art (see pp234–47).

Colosseum
One of Rome's most famous landmarks, the Colosseum (see pp92–5) was the venue for gladiatorial and animal fights. These provided a gory spectacle for Rome's citizens, up to 55,000 of whom would cram into the amphitheatre at one time.

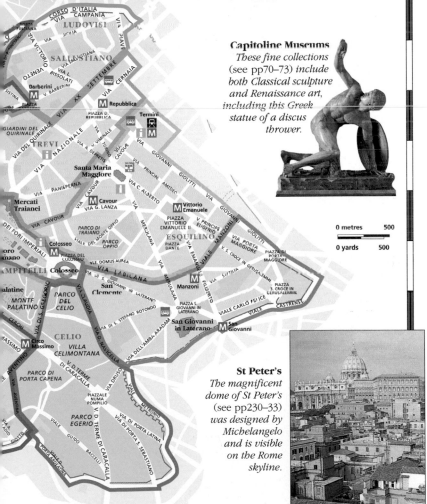

Capitoline Museums
These fine collections (see pp70–73) include both Classical sculpture and Renaissance art, including this Greek statue of a discus thrower.

| 0 metres | 500 |
| 0 yards | 500 |

St Peter's
The magnificent dome of St Peter's (see pp230–33) was designed by Michelangelo and is visible on the Rome skyline.

THE HISTORY OF ROME

One of the most ancient cities in Europe, Rome was founded over 2,750 years ago. Since then it has been continuously inhabited, and, as the headquarters first of the Roman Empire and then of the Catholic Church, it has had an immense impact on the world. Many European languages are based on Latin; many political and legal systems follow the ancient Roman model; and buildings all round the world utilize styles and techniques perfected in ancient Rome. The city itself retains layers of buildings spanning over two millennia. Not surprisingly, all this history can seem a little overwhelming.

**Roman eagle
(2nd century AD)**

Rome began as an Iron Age hut village, founded in the mid-8th century BC. In 616, the Romans' sophisticated Etruscan neighbours seized power, but were ousted in 509, when Rome became a Republic. It conquered most of the rest of Italy, then turned its attentions overseas, and by the 1st century BC ruled Spain, North Africa and Greece. The expansion of the Empire provided opportunities for power-hungry individuals, and the clashing of egos led to the collapse of democracy. Julius Caesar ruled for a time as dictator, and his nephew Octavian became Rome's first emperor, assuming the title Augustus. During the reign of Augustus, Christ was born, and though Christians were persecuted until the 4th century AD, the new religion took hold and Rome became its main centre.

Even though it was the seat of the papacy, during the Middle Ages Rome went into decline. The city recovered spectacularly in the mid-15th century, and for over 200 years was embellished by the greatest artists of the Renaissance and the Baroque. Finally, in 1870, Rome became the capital of the newly unified Italy.

**15th-century map
of Rome from the north**

◁ Detail from 2nd-century AD Roman mosaic from the Temple of Fortune in Palestrina

Rome's Early Development

According to the historian Livy, Romulus founded Rome in 753 BC. Sometime later, realizing his tribe was short of females, he invited the neighbouring Sabines to a festival, and orchestrated the mass abduction of their women. Although Livy's account is pure legend, there is evidence that Rome was founded around the middle of the 8th century BC, and that the Romans and Sabines united shortly afterwards. Historical evidence also gives some support to Livy's claim that after Romulus's death Rome was ruled by a series of kings, and that in the 7th century BC it was conquered by the Etruscans and ruled by the Tarquin family. Last of the dynasty was Tarquinius Superbus (Tarquin the Proud). His despotic rule led to the Etruscans being expelled and the founding of a Republic run by two annually elected consuls. The uprising was led by Lucius Junius Brutus, the model of the stern, patriotic Roman Republican.

EXTENT OF THE CITY

■ 750 BC   □ Today

Ceremonial trumpets

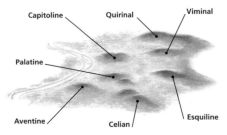

Capitoline   Quirinal   Viminal

Palatine

Aventine   Celian   Esquiline

The Seven Hills of Rome
By the 8th century BC, shepherds and farmers lived on four of Rome's seven hills. As the population grew, huts were built in the marshy valley later occupied by the Forum.

Iron Age Hut
Early settlers lived in wattle and daub huts. Traces of their foundations have been found on the Palatine.

Augur, digging foundation

TEMPLE OF JUPITER
This Renaissance painting by Perin del Vaga shows Tarquinius Superbus founding the Temple of Jupiter on the Capitol, the sacred citadel of Rome.

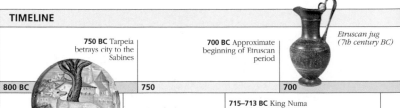

TIMELINE

750 BC Tarpeia betrays city to the Sabines

700 BC Approximate beginning of Etruscan period

Etruscan jug *(7th century BC)*

800 BC   750   700

Romulus and Remus

753 BC Legendary founding of Rome by Romulus, first of seven kings

715–713 BC King Numa Pompilius establishes 12-month calendar

659 BC Romans destroy rival city, Alba Longa

The Legend of the She-Wolf
The evil king of Alba threw his baby nephews, Romulus and Remus, into the Tiber but they were washed ashore, and suckled by a she-wolf.

Raven, guardian of the citadel

Apollo of Veio
Etruscan culture and religion were influenced by the Greeks. This 5th- or 6th-century statue of the Greek god Apollo comes from Veio, a powerful, wealthy Etruscan city.

King Tarquin, holding stone worshipped as a thunderbolt

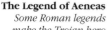

The Legend of Aeneas
Some Roman legends make the Trojan hero Aeneas the grandfather of Romulus and Remus.

WHERE TO SEE ETRUSCAN ROME

The Cloaca Maxima sewer still functions, but there are few other traces of Etruscan Rome. Most finds come from Etruscan sites outside Rome like Tarquinia, with its tomb paintings of sumptuous banquets *(see p271)*, but there are major collections in the Villa Giulia *(pp262–3)* and Vatican Museums *(p238)*. The most famous object, however, is a bronze statue of the legendary she-wolf in the Capitoline Museums *(p73)*. The Antiquarium Forense *(p87)* displays objects from the necropolis which once occupied the site of the Roman Forum.

Funeral urns shaped like huts were used for cremation from the mid-8th century BC.

Etruscan jewellery, like this 7th-century BC gold filigree brooch, was lavish. Treasures of this kind have given the Etruscans a reputation for luxurious living.

578 BC Servius Tullius Etruscan king

600 BC Possible date of construction of Cloaca Maxima sewer

616 BC Tarquinius Priscus, first Etruscan king. Forum and Circus Maximus established

L J Brutus

565 BC Traditional date of the Servian Wall around Rome's seven hills

Statue of Jupiter

534 BC King Servius murdered

509 BC L J Brutus expels Etruscans from Rome and founds the Republic

510 BC Temple of Jupiter consecrated on the Capitoline hill

507 BC War against Etruscans. Horatius defends wooden bridge across Tiber

600 | 550 | 500

Kings, Consuls and Emperors

Rome had over 250 rulers in the 1,200 years between its foundation by Romulus and AD 476, when the last emperor was deposed by the German warrior Odoacer. Romulus was the first of seven kings, overthrown in 509 BC when Rome became a Republic. Authority was held by two annually elected consuls, but provision was made for the appointment of a dictator in times of crisis. In 494 BC, the office of Tribune was set up to protect the plebeians from injustice at the hands of their patrician rulers. Roman democracy, however, was always cosmetic. It was discarded completely in 27 BC, when absolute power was placed in the hands of the emperor.

70–63 BC Pompey

107–87 BC Marius is consul seven times

205 BC Scipio Africanus

218 BC Quintus Fabius Maximus

Romulus, his twin Remus and the she-wolf who suckled them

c.753–715 BC Romulus

456 BC Lucius Quintus Cincinnatus

800 BC	700	600	500	400	300	200	
SEVEN KINGS			REPUBLIC				
800 BC	700	600	500	400	300	200	

c.715–673 BC Numa Pompilius

396 BC Marcus Furius Camillus

133 BC Tiberius Gracchus

c.673–641 BC Tullus Hostilius

c.509 BC Lucius Junius Brutus and Horatius Pulvillus

122–121 BC Gaius Gracchus

c.641–616 BC Ancus Marcius

c.534–509 BC Tarquinius Superbus

82–80 BC Sulla

c.579–534 BC Servius Tullius

63 BC Cicero

616–579 BC Tarquinius Priscus

60–50 BC Triumvira of Julius Caes Pompey and Crass

45–44 BC Ju Caesar is sole re

Tarquinius Priscus consulting an augur

Julius Caesar, whose rise to power marked the end of the Roman Republic

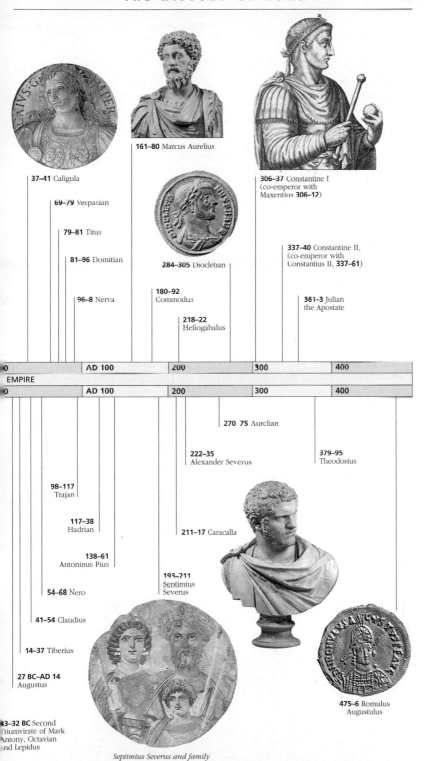

37–41 Caligula

69–79 Vespasian

79–81 Titus

81–96 Domitian

96–8 Nerva

161–80 Marcus Aurelius

284–305 Diocletian

180–92 Commodus

218–22 Heliogabalus

306–37 Constantine I (co-emperor with Maxentius **306–12**)

337–40 Constantine II, (co-emperor with Constantius II, **337–61**)

361–3 Julian the Apostate

AD 100   200   300   400

EMPIRE

AD 100   200   300   400

270 75 Aurelian

222–35 Alexander Severus

379–95 Theodosius

98–117 Trajan

117–38 Hadrian

211–17 Caracalla

138–61 Antoninus Pius

193–211 Septimius Severus

54–68 Nero

41–54 Claudius

14–37 Tiberius

27 BC–AD 14 Augustus

43–32 BC Second Triumvirate of Mark Antony, Octavian and Lepidus

Septimius Severus and family

475–6 Romulus Augustulus

The Roman Republic

By the mid-2nd century BC, Rome controlled the western Mediterranean, policing and defending it with massive armies. The troops had more loyalty to the generals than to distant politicians, giving men like Marius, Sulla, Pompey and Caesar the muscle to seize political power. Meanwhile, peasants, whose land had been destroyed during the invasion of Hannibal in 219 BC, had flooded into Rome. They were followed by slaves and freedmen from conquered lands such as Greece, swelling the population to half a million. There was plenty of work for immigrants, constructing roads, aqueducts, markets and temples, financed by taxes on Rome's expanding trade.

Bronze coin, showing Temple of Vesta (c.57 BC)

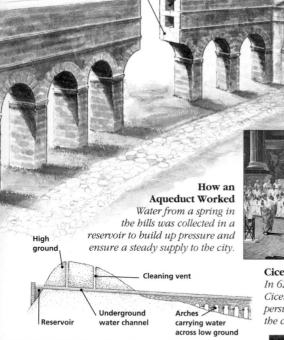

Cut stone blocks

Covered water channels

Arch spanning road

The gradient of an aqueduct was about 1 in 1,000.

How an Aqueduct Worked
Water from a spring in the hills was collected in a reservoir to build up pressure and ensure a steady supply to the city.

High ground

Cleaning vent

Reservoir

Underground water channel

Arches carrying water across low ground

Cicero Denounces Catiline
In 62 BC Catiline planned a coup. Cicero discovered the plot and persuaded the Senate to condemn the conspirators to death.

TIMELINE

499 BC Battle against Latin tribes; Temple of Castor and Pollux built to commemorate the victory

396 BC Definitive victory over rival Etruscan city, Veio

380 BC Servian Wall rebuilt

Via Appia

312 BC Construction of Via Appia and Rome's first aqueduct, the Aqua Appia

500 BC	450 BC	400 BC	350 BC	30

Relief of Capitoline geese

390 BC Rome invaded by Celtic Gauls: quacking geese on Capitoline hill warn of impending attack

264–241 BC Fir Punic War (agains Carthage

Roman Street
In the 1st century BC, most buildings in Rome were made from brick and concrete. Only a few public buildings used marble.

WHERE TO SEE REPUBLICAN ROME

This fresco depicting a gang of slaves building a wall can be seen at the Museo Nazionale Romano (*see p163*).

AQUEDUCT (2ND CENTURY BC)
Rome owed much of her prosperity to her skilled civil engineers. When the city's wells were no longer sufficient, aqueducts were built to bring water from surrounding hills. Some were over 80 km (50 miles) long.

Arches for maintaining a constant gradient over low-lying land

The Temple of Saturn, first built in 497 BC, now consists of eight majestic columns overlooking the Forum at the end of the Via Sacra (*see p83*).

Rome's loveliest Republican buildings are the two Temples of the Forum Boarium (*see p203*). Four more temples can be seen in the Area Sacra of Largo Argentina (*p150*). Most monuments from this period, however, lie underground. Only a few, like the Tomb of the Scipios (*p195*), have been excavated. One of the bridges leading to Tiber Island (*p153*), the Ponte Fabricio, dates from the 1st century BC and is still used by pedestrians.

Temple of Juno
The ruins of this 197 BC temple are embedded in the church of San Nicola in Carcere (see p151). Romans consulted their gods before all important ventures.

Scipio Africanus
In 202 BC the Roman general Scipio defeated Hannibal. Rome replaced Carthage as master of the Mediterranean.

250 BC	200 BC	150 BC	100 BC
220 BC Via Flaminia built, linking Rome to the Adriatic coast	**168 BC** Victory in Macedonian War completes Roman conquest of Greece	**133–120 BC** Gracchi brothers killed for trying to introduce land reforms	**51 BC** Caesar conquers Gaul
218–202 BC Second Punic War; Scipio Africanus defeats Carthaginians	**149–146 BC** Third Punic War; Carthage destroyed	**71 BC** Spartacus's slave revolt crushed by Crassus and Pompey	**60 BC** Rome has three joint rulers: Pompey, Crassus and Caesar

Ponte Fabricio, built in 62 BC

Hannibal

Imperial Rome

Statue of Bacchus, god of wine

In 44 BC Caesar became dictator for life, only to be assassinated a month later. The result was 17 years of civil war, which ended only in 27 BC when Augustus became Rome's first emperor. The Empire expanded in fits and starts, but by the late 3rd century was so huge that Diocletian decided to share it between four emperors. Thanks to trade and taxes from its vast domains, Rome was the most magnificent city in the world, studded with the lavish buildings of emperors keen to advertise their civic munificence and military triumphs.

EXTENT OF THE CITY

☐ AD 250   ☐ Today

Cross-vaulted ceiling with mosaic decoration

Natatio (swimming pool)

Apotheosis of Augustus
The first and perhaps the greatest Roman emperor, Augustus ruled for 27 years and was deified by the Senate after his death.

ROMA CAPVT MVNDI

The baths could hold up to 3,000 people. They met to gossip in the central *frigidarium* (cold room).

Area for exercise and gymnastics

The Roman Empire under Trajan
By the 2nd century AD, the Roman Empire stretched from Britain to Syria, and Rome was known as the Caput Mundi, the head of the world.

TIMELINE

Emperor Nero

Statue of St Peter in San Paolo fuori le Mura

49 BC Caesar crosses the Rubicon and takes Rome

27 Augustus becomes first emperor

64 Fire during Nero's rule destroys much of city

65 First persecution of Christians under Nero

72 Colosseum begun

50 BC	0	AD 50	100

44 Caesar becomes dictator for life, and is murdered by Brutus and Cassius

13 Ara Pacis is erected to celebrate the peace Augustus has secured in the Empire

AD 42 St Peter the Apostle comes to Rome

67 St Peter is crucified and St Paul executed in Rome

Roman Revelry
Banquets could last for up to 10 hours, with numerous courses, between which guests would retire to a small room to relax.

WHERE TO SEE IMPERIAL ROME

There are relics of Imperial Rome throughout the city centre, some hidden below churches and palazzi, others like the Forum *(see pp76–87)*, the Palatine *(pp97–101)* and the Imperial Fora *(pp88–91)*, fully excavated. The magnificence of the era, however, is best conveyed by the Pantheon *(pp110–11)* and the Colosseum *(pp92–5)*.

BATHS OF DIOCLETIAN (AD 298)
Rome's public baths were not just places to keep clean. They also had bars, libraries, barbers' shops, brothels and sports facilities.

The Arch of Titus *(p87)*, erected in the Forum in AD 81, commemorates Emperor Titus's sack of Jerusalem in AD 70.

Tepidarium (warm room)

Virgil (70–19 BC)
Virgil was Rome's greatest epic poet. His most famous work is the Aeneid, *the story of the Trojan hero Aeneas's journey to the future site of Rome.*

A relief of Mithras, a popular Persian god (3rd century AD), can be seen beneath the church of San Clemente *(pp186–7)*.

164–180 Plague rages in Roman Empire

212 Citizenship granted to virtually all inhabitants of the Empire

270 Aurelian Wall begun

Section of Aurelian Wall

150	200	250

125 Hadrian redesigns the Pantheon

Mosaic from the Baths of Caracalla

216 Baths of Caracalla completed

247 Rome's Millennium is celebrated

284 Empire divided into West and East

Early Christian Rome

Crucifixion in Santa Maria Antiqua

In the 1st century AD, during the reign of Tiberius, a rebellious pacifist was crucified in a distant corner of the Empire. This was nothing unusual, but within a few years Jesus Christ and his teachings became notorious in Rome, his followers were perceived as a threat to public order, and many were executed. This was no deterrent, and the new religion spread through all levels of Roman society. When the Apostles Peter and Paul arrived in Rome there was already a small Christian community, and in spite of continued persecution by the state, Christianity flourished. In AD 313 the Emperor Constantine issued an edict granting freedom of worship to Christians, and soon after founded a shrine on the site of St Peter's tomb. This secured Rome's position as a centre of Christianity, but in the 5th century the political importance of Rome declined and the city fell to Goths and other invaders.

EXTENT OF THE CITY

⬛ AD 395   ☐ Today

St Paul

Youthful, beardless representation of Christ

4TH-CENTURY MOSAIC, SANTA COSTANZA
Beautiful mosaics, often with palm trees and other oriental motifs suggesting Jerusalem, helped spread the message of early Christianity.

Classical-style border decorated with fruit

Santo Stefano Rotondo
This 17th-century engraving shows how a Roman temple (top) might have been transformed (above) into the 5th-century round church of Santo Stefano.

The Good Shepherd
The pagan image of a shepherd sacrificing a lamb became a Christian symbol.

TIMELINE

Gold solidus of Theodosius

Battle of the Milvian Bridge

300	350	400	45(

c.320 Building of first St Peter's

356 Legendary founding of Santa Maria Maggiore

410 Rome sacked by Alaric's Goths

455 Rome sacked again by Vandals

312 Control of Empire won by Constantine after battle at Milvian Bridge

380 Emperor Theodosius makes Christianity the official religion of the Roman Empire

395 Division of the Empire between Ravenna and Constantinople

422 Founding of Santa Sabina

Epigraph of Peter and Paul
This is one of hundreds of early Christian graffiti housed in the Lapidary Gallery of the Vatican (see p237).

Crucifixion, Santa Sabina
This 5th-century panel on the door of Santa Sabina (see p204) *is one of the earliest known representations of the Crucifixion. Interestingly, Christ's cross is not actually shown.*

St Peter receiving peace from the Saviour

Lambs symbolizing the Christian flock

Constantine's Cross
Constantine's vision of the True Cross during the Battle of the Milvian Bridge made him convert to Christianity.

WHERE TO SEE EARLY CHRISTIAN ROME

There are traces of early Christianity all over Rome. Many ancient churches were built over early Christian meeting places and sites of martyrdoms: among them San Clemente *(see pp186–7)*, Santa Pudenziana *(p171)* and Santa Cecilia *(p211)*. Outside the walls of the old city are miles of underground catacombs *(pp265–6)*, many decorated with Christian frescoes, while the Vatican's Pio-Christian Museum *(p240)* has the best collection of early Christian art.

This statuette, carved out of bone, is embedded in the rock of the Catacombs of San Panfilo, just off the Via Salaria (**map** 2 F4).

The Cross of Justin, in the Treasury of St Peter's *(p232)*, was given to Rome by the Emperor Justin II in AD 570.

The Papacy

The Pope is considered Christ's representative on earth, claiming his authority from St Peter, the first Bishop of Rome. Though some popes have been great thinkers and reformers, the role has rarely been purely spiritual. In the Middle Ages, many popes were involved in power struggles with the Holy Roman Emperor. Renaissance popes like Julius II and Leo X, the patrons of Raphael and Michelangelo, lived as luxuriously as any secular prince. The popes listed here include all those who exercised significant political or religious influence, up as far as the end of the Counter-Reformation, when the power of the papacy began to wane.

St Ludovic Kneels before Boniface VIII *by Simone Martini*

314–35 St Sylvester I

222–30 St Urban I

217–22 St Callixtus I

590–604 St Gregory the Great

496–8 Anastasius II

Gregory the Great leading a procession to end the plague

931–5 John XI

891–6 Formosus

955–64 John XII

1227–41 Gregory IX

1216–27 Honorius III Savelli

0	200	400	600	800	1000	120

PAPACY BASED IN ROME

0	200	400	600	800	1000	120

336 Mark

352–66 Liberius

c.88–97 St Clement

c.42–67 St Peter

579–90 Pelagius II

608–15 St Boniface IV

731–41 St Gregory III

772–95 Adrian I

1032–44, 1047–8 Benedict IX

1073–85 St Gregory VII

1099–1118 Paschal II

1130–43 Innocent II

1154–9 Adrian IV

847–55 St Leo IV

817–24 St Paschal I

1198–1216 Innocent III

St Peter, *from a mosaic in Santa Prassede* (see p171)

795–816 St Leo III

Innocent III's Vision of the Church, *from a fresco by Giotto*

Portrait of Gregory XIII
by Lavinia Fontana

1560–65 Pius IV Medici

1555–9 Paul IV

1523–34
Clement VII Medici

1513–21 Leo X Medici

1492–1503
Alexander
VI Borgia

1572–84 Gregory XIII Boncompagni

1294–1303
Bonifacc VIII

1484–92
Innocent VIII Cybo

1670–76 Clement X Altieri

1667–9 Clement IX

1471–84 Sixtus IV della Rovere

1655–67
Alexander VII Chigi

1464–71 Paul II Barbo

1605 Leo XI
Medici

1458–64
Pius II Piccolomini

1700–21 Clement XI

| 1300 | 1400 | 1500 | 1600 | 1700 |

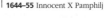
AVIGNON | PAPACY AGAIN BASED IN ROME

| 1300 | 1400 | 1500 | 1600 | 1700 |

1417–31
Martin V Colonna

1644–55 Innocent X Pamphilj

1447–55
Nicholas V

1585–90
Sixtus V

1623–44 Urban VIII Barberini

Nicholas V Receiving a
Book, *illustration from a
contemporary manuscript*

1592–1605
Clement VIII
Aldobrandini

1503–13 Julius II della Rovere

1605–21 Paul V
Borghese

Urban VIII Approving a Building
Project *in the Vatican's Gallery
of Tapestries* (see p241)

Raphael's portrait of Julius II

1534–49 Paul III Farnese

Paul III Gives His Approval to
the Capuchin Order *by
Sebastiano Ricci*

Medieval Rome

Mosaic, San Clemente

Supplanted by Constantinople as capital of the Empire in the 4th century, Rome was reduced to a few thousand inhabitants by the early Middle Ages, its power just a memory. In the 8th and 9th centuries, the growing importance of the papacy revived the city and made it once more a centre of power. But continual conflicts between the pope and the Holy Roman Emperor soon weakened the papacy. The 10th, 11th and 12th centuries were among the bleakest in Roman history: violent invaders left Rome poverty-stricken and the constantly warring local barons tore apart what remained of the city. Despite this, the first Holy Year was declared in 1300 and thousands of pilgrims arrived in Rome. But by 1309 the papacy was forced to move to Avignon, leaving Rome to slide into further squalor and strife.

EXTENT OF THE CITY

▓ *1300*   ☐ *Today*

Charlemagne Crowned in St Peter's
On Christmas Day in 800, Charlemagne was made "emperor of the Romans", ruler of a new Christian dominion to replace that of ancient Rome.

San Giovanni in Laterano

Aurelian Wall

Trajan's Column

Column of Marcus Aurelius

Madonna and Child Mosaic
The Chapel of St Zeno (817–24) in the church of Santa Prassede (see p171) has some of the best examples of Byzantine mosaics in Rome.

MEDIEVAL PLAN OF ROME
Maps like this one, illustrating the principal features of the city, were produced for pilgrims, the tourists of the Middle Ages.

TIMELINE

Emperor Otto I

700	800	900	10
725 King Ine of Wessex founds the first hostel for pilgrims in the Borgo	**852** The Vatican is fortified with walls following a raid by Saracens		**961** King Otto the Great of Germany becomes first Holy Roman Emperor
778 Charlemagne, King of the Franks, conquers Italy	**800** Charlemagne crowned emperor in St Peter's	**880–932** Rome is ruled by two women, Theodora and then her daughter, Marozia	

Stefaneschi Triptych *(1315)*
Giotto and his pupils painted this triptych for Cardinal Stefaneschi as an altarpiece for St Peter's. It is now in the Vatican Museums (see p240).

WHERE TO SEE MEDIEVAL ROME

Among the most interesting churches of the period are San Clemente, with a fine apse mosaic and Cosmati floor *(see pp186–7)*, Santa Maria in Trastevere *(pp212–13)* and Santa Maria sopra Minerva, Rome's only Gothic church *(p108)*. Santa Cecilia in Trastevere *(p211)* has a Cavallini fresco, and there is fine Cosmati work in Santa Maria in Cosmedin *(p202)*.

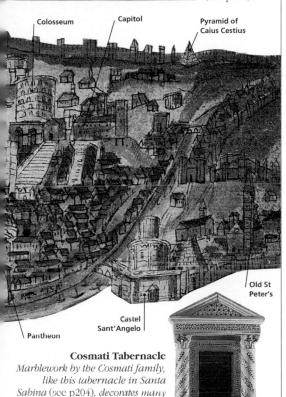

Colosseum · Capitol · Pyramid of Caius Cestius · Old St Peter's · Castel Sant'Angelo · Pantheon

Charlemagne's Dalmatic in the Treasury of St Peter's *(p232)* was supposedly worn by the emperor at his coronation in 800. In fact the richly embroidered vestment probably dates from the 14th century.

Cosmati Tabernacle
Marblework by the Cosmati family, like this tabernacle in Santa Sabina (see p204), decorates many of Rome's medieval churches.

Santa Sabina *(p204)* on the Aventine Hill has a medieval bell tower.

1084 Rome is attacked by Normans

1108 San Clemente is rebuilt

1200 Rome is an independent commune under Arnaldo di Brescia

1309 Pope Clement V moves the papacy to Avignon

1300 First Holy Year proclaimed by Pope Boniface VIII

1348 Black Death strikes Rome

1100 · **1200** · **1300**

Mosaic façade, Santa Maria in Trastevere (pp212–13)

1232 Cloister of San Giovanni in Laterano completed

1140 Santa Maria in Trastevere is restored

Cola di Rienzo

1347 Cola di Rienzo – an Italian patriot – tries to restore the Roman Republic

Renaissance Rome

Detail of Botticelli's *Youth of Moses* (1480s)

Pope Nicholas V came to the throne in 1447 determined to make Rome a city fit for the papacy. Among his successors, men like Julius II and Leo X eagerly followed his lead, and the city's appearance was transformed. The Classical ideals of the Renaissance inspired artists, architects and craftsmen, such as Michelangelo, Bramante, Raphael and Cellini, to build and decorate the churches and palaces of a newly confident Rome.

EXTENT OF THE CITY

▨ 1500	☐ Today

Hemispherical dome

Balustrade of small columns

Classical colonnade of 16 Doric columns

School of Athens by Raphael
In this fresco (see p243) Raphael complimented many of his peers by representing them as ancient Greek philosophers. The building shown is based on a design by Bramante.

THE TEMPIETTO
The Tempietto (1502) at San Pietro in Montorio (see p219) was one of Bramante's first works in Rome. A simple, perfectly proportioned miniature Classical temple, it is a model of High Renaissance architecture.

Cosmati-style mosaic floor

Palazzo Caprini
Bramante's design had a strong influence on later Renaissance palazzi. Parts of the building survive in Palazzo dei Convertendi (see p227).

TIMELINE

1377 Papacy returns to Rome from Avignon under Pope Gregory XI

1409–15 Papacy moves to Pisa

1452 Demolition of old St Peter's basilica begins

1444 Birth of Bramante

1350	1400	145

1378–1417 The Great Schism, a division in the papacy in Avignon

1417 Pope Martin V ends the Great Schism in the papacy

Pope Martin V, reigned 1417–31

Sack of Rome
In 1527, the unruly troops of Charles V of Spain pillaged the city, destroying countless works of art. Pope Clement VII took refuge in Castel Sant'Angelo.

Pope Nicholas V
Nicholas ordered the demolition of the old St Peter's.

Statue of St Peter, believed to have been crucified on this site

Underground chapel

WHERE TO SEE RENAISSANCE ROME

The Campo de' Fiori area *(see pp142–53)* is full of grand Renaissance palazzi, especially along Via Giulia *(pp276–7)*. Across the river stands the delightful Villa Farnesina *(pp220–21)*. The most typical church of the period is Santa Maria del Popolo *(pp138–9)*, and the best collection of Renaissance art is in the Vatican Museums *(pp234–47)*. These include the Sistine Chapel *(pp244–7)* and the Raphael Rooms *(pp242–3)*.

The Madonna di Foligno by Raphael (1511–12) is one of the fine Renaissance paintings in the Vatican Pinacoteca *(p241)*.

The Pietà, commissioned for St Peter's in 1501, was one of Michelangelo's first sculptures executed in Rome *(p233)*.

1483 Birth of Raphael

1486 Building of Palazzo della Cancelleria

1519 Frescoes completed in Villa Farnesina

1527 Troops of Emperor Charles V sack Rome

Emperor Charles V

1500

1550

1475 Birth of Michelangelo

1506 Pope Julius II orders start of work on new St Peter's

1508 Michelangelo begins painting the Sistine Chapel ceiling

Cumaean Sibyl, Sistine Chapel

1547 Pope Paul III appoints Michelangelo architect of St Peter's

Baroque Rome

Baroque putto

By the 16th century, the Catholic Church had become immensely rich – one of the chief criticisms of the Protestant reformers. The display of grandeur and extravagance by the papal court contrasted sharply with the poverty of the people, and wealthy Roman society was characterized by sumptuous luxury and a ceaseless round of entertainment. To make the Catholic faith more appealing than Protestantism, scores of churches were built and monuments and fountains were erected to glorify the Holy See. The finest architects in the ornate, dramatic style of the Baroque were Bernini and Borromini.

EXTENT OF THE CITY

■ 1645   □ Today

Gian Lorenzo Bernini *(1598–1680)*
The favourite artist of the papacy, Bernini transformed Rome with his churches, palaces, statues and fountains.

Ceiling portraying heavenly scenes

Monument to Pope Alexander VII
This Bernini tomb in St Peter's (pp230–33) includes a skeleton brandishing an hour-glass.

Holy Family fresco

Tapestry of Pope Urban VIII
Bernini's most devoted patron, Pope Urban VIII Barberini (1623–44), is shown here receiving the homage of the nations.

A marble rose marks the best place to stand to appreciate the illusion of space created by the artist.

TIMELINE

1568 The Jesuits build the Gesù, prototypical church of the early Baroque

Altar carving from the Gesù

1595 Annibale Carracci begins to fresco Palazzo Farnese

1624 Bernini's sculpture of *Apollo and Daphne*

1626 Work on St Peter's is completed

1550	1575	1600	1625

1571 Birth of Caravaggio

1585 Pope Sixtus V plans new streets

1600 Philosopher Giordano Bruno is burned at the stake for heresy

Galileo

1633 Galileo condemned to house arrest for heresy

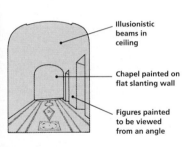

Illusionistic
beams in
ceiling

Chapel painted on
flat slanting wall

Figures painted
to be viewed
from an angle

Queen Christina of Sweden
*In a coup for Catholicism, Christina
renounced Protestantism and abdicated
her throne. In 1655 she moved to Rome,
where she became the centre of a
lively literary and scientific circle.*

St Ignatius,
founder of
the Jesuits

Francesco Borromini
*(1599–1667)
In the many churches
he built in Rome,
Borromini made
use of revolutionary
geometric forms.*

POZZO CORRIDOR
*The use of perspective
to create an illusion of
depth and space was a
favourite Baroque device.
Andrea Pozzo painted
this illusionistic corridor
in the 1680s in the Rooms
of St Ignatius near the
Gesù (see pp114–15).*

**San Carlo alle
Quattro Fontane**
*One of Borromini's
most influential designs
was this tiny oval
church (see p161) on
the Quirinal hill.*

1651 Bernini
redesigns
much of
Piazza
Navona

*Bernini's Fontana
dei Fiumi in
Piazza Navona*

1694 Palazzo di
Montecitorio is
completed

1735 Spanish Steps are designed

1732 Work starts on
the Trevi Fountain

1650	1675	1700	1725

1657 Borromini completes
Sant'Agnese in Agone

*Bonnie Prince
Charlie, pretender
to the throne
of England*

1721 Bonnie
Prince Charlie
is born in
Rome

1734 Clement XII
makes Palazzo
Nuovo world's first
public museum

1656 Work starts on Bernini's
colonnade for St Peter's Square

Understanding Rome's Architecture

Arch of Titus

The architecture of Imperial Rome kept alive the Classical styles of ancient Greece, at the same time developing new, uniquely Roman forms based on the arch, the vault and the dome. The next important period was the 12th century, when many Romanesque churches were built. The Renaissance saw a return to Classical ideals, inspired by the example of Florence, but in the 17th century Rome found a style of its own again in the flamboyance of the Baroque.

The entablature above these columns has both straight and arched sections (Hadrian's Villa).

CLASSICAL ROME

Most Roman buildings were of concrete faced with brick, but from the 1st century BC, the Romans started to imitate earlier Greek models, using marble to decorate temples and other public buildings.

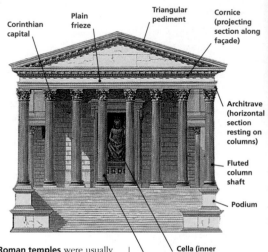

Corinthian capital · Plain frieze · Triangular pediment · Cornice (projecting section along façade) · Architrave (horizontal section resting on columns) · Fluted column shaft · Podium · Cella (inner sanctuary) · Colonnade enclosing portico

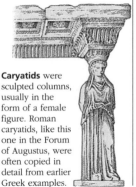

Caryatids were sculpted columns, usually in the form of a female figure. Roman caryatids, like this one in the Forum of Augustus, were often copied in detail from earlier Greek examples.

Roman temples were usually built on a raised dais or podium, to make them prominent. Many were fronted by a portico, a roofed porch with columns.

The orders of Classical architecture were building styles, each based on a different column design. The three major orders were borrowed by the Romans from the Greeks.

Doric order

Ionic order

Corinthian order

Aedicules were small shrines, framed by two pillars, usually containing a statue of a god.

Coffers were decorative sunken panels that reduced the weight of domed and vaulted ceilings.

EARLY CHRISTIAN AND MEDIEVAL ROME

The first Christian churches in Rome were based on the basilica: oblong, with three naves, each usually ending in an apse. From the 10th to the 13th centuries, most churches were built in the Romanesque style, which used the rounded arches of ancient Rome.

The triumphal arch divides the nave of a church from the apse. Here, in San Paolo fuori le Mura, it is decorated with mosaics.

A tabernacle is used to house the Sacrament for the mass. This 13th-century Gothic wall tabernacle is in San Clemente.

Basilicas in Rome have, in most cases, kept their original rectangular shape. The nave of San Giovanni in Laterano retains its 4th-century floorplan.

RENAISSANCE AND BAROQUE ROME

Renaissance architecture (15th–16th centuries) drew its inspiration directly from Classical models. It revived the use of strict geometric proportions. The Baroque age (late 16th–17th centuries) broke many established rules, favouring grandiose decoration over pure Classical forms.

A baldacchino is a canopy, supported on columns, rising over the main altar. This Baroque example is in St Peter's.

Putti were a popular decorative feature in the Baroque. A putto is a painting or a sculpture of a child like a Cupid or cherub.

A loggia is an open-sided gallery or arcade. It may be a separate structure or part of a building, as here at San Saba.

Rusticated masonry decorates the exterior of many Renaissance palazzi. It consists of massive blocks divided by deep joints.

COSMATESQUE SCULPTURE AND MOSAICS

The Cosmati family, active in Rome during the 12th and 13th centuries, have given their name to a particularly Roman style of decoration. They worked in marble, producing all kinds of fittings for churches, including cloisters, episcopal thrones, tombs, pulpits, fonts and candlesticks. These were often decorated with

Cosmatesque floor, Santa Maria in Cosmedin

bands of colourful mosaic. They also left many fine floor mosaics, usually of white marble with an inlay of red and green porphyry. Ancient Roman columns were cut up to provide the materials. Several other families of stonemasons used a similar style, and their work is also described as Cosmatesque.

Rome during Unification

Under Napoleon, Italy had a brief taste of unity, but by 1815 it was once more divided into many small states and papal rule was restored in Rome.

Over the next 50 years, patriots, led by Mazzini, Garibaldi and others, struggled to create an independent, unified Italy. In 1848 Rome was briefly declared a Republic, but

Garibaldi in his distinctive red shirt

Garibaldi's forces were driven out by French troops. The French continued to protect the pope, while the rest of Italy was united as a kingdom under Vittorio Emanuele of Savoy. In 1870, troops stormed the city, and Rome became capital of Italy.

EXTENT OF THE CITY

☐ 1870   ☐ Today

Allegory of Italy's Liberty
This patriotic poster from 1890 shows the king, his chief minister Cavour, Garibaldi and Mazzini. The woman in red represents Italy.

Vittorio Emanuele II
Vittorio Emanuele of Savoy became the first King of Italy in 1861.

Porta Pia

Tricoloured flag of the new Italian kingdom

Plumed hat of the Bersaglieri, crack troops from Savoy

ROYALISTS STORM PORTA PIA
On 20 September 1870, troops of the kingdom of Italy put an end to the papal domination of Rome. They breached the city walls near Porta Pia; the pope retreated and Rome was made the Italian capital.

TIMELINE

Napoleon Bonaparte

1751 Piranesi's *Views of Rome* revive interest in Classical ruins

1762 Trevi Fountain is completed

1797 Napoleon captures Rome

1799 Napoleon expelled from Italy by Austrians and Russians

1750	1775	1800

Piranesi etching of Trajan's Forum

1792 Canova creates the Tomb of Pope Clement XIII, St Peter's

1800–1 Napoleon takes Italy again

1807 Birth of Garibaldi

Garibaldi and Rome

The charismatic leader Giuseppe Garibaldi had taken much of Italy from foreign rule by 1860. Rome still remained a crucial problem. Here he declares "O Roma o morte" (Rome or Death).

Giuseppe Verdi

(1813–1901)
Verdi, the opera composer, supported unification and in 1861 became a member of Italy's first national parliament.

Villa Paolina

Breach in
Aurelian Wall

A Freed City

This marble plaque was set up at Porta Pia to commemorate the liberation of Rome.

Victor Emmanuel Monument

A vast monument to Italy's first king (see p74) stands in Piazza Venezia.

> S · P · Q · R ·
> VRBE · ITALIAE · VINDICATA
> INCOLIS · FELICITER · AVCTIS
> GEMINOS · FORNICES · CONDIDIT

816 Work begins on Piazza del Popolo

Fountain in Piazza del Popolo

1848 Nationalist uprising in Rome. Pope flees and a Republic is formed

1860 Garibaldi and his 1,000 followers take Sicily and Naples

1870 Royalist troops take Rome, completing the unification of Italy

1825

1850

1820 Revolts throughout Italy

1821 English poet Keats dies in Piazza di Spagna

1849 Pope is restored to power, protected by a French garrison

Pope Pius IX

1861 Kingdom of Italy founded with capital in Turin

Modern Rome

The Fascist dictator Mussolini dreamed of recreating the immensity, order and power of the old Roman Empire: "Rome", he said, "must appear wonderful to the whole world". He began to build a grandiose new complex, EUR, in the suburbs, and razed 15 churches and many medieval houses to create space for wide new roads. Fortunately most of the old centre has survived, leaving the city with one of Europe's most picturesque historic cores. To mark the Holy Year and the new millennium, many crumbling churches, buildings and monuments were given a thorough facelift.

World Cup mania

EXTENT OF THE CITY

▨ *1960s*   ☐ *Today*

Mussolini's Plans for Rome
This propaganda poster reflects Mussolini's grandiose projects such as Via dei Fori Imperiali in the Forum area (see p76), and EUR (p266).

Pope Benedict XVI
The German cardinal Joseph Ratzinger became Pope Benedict XVI in 2005. The Pope exerts a tremendous influence on the lives of the world's Catholics.

JUBILEE CELEBRATIONS
Jubilee Years are usually celebrated every quarter of a century. Millions of Catholics visited Rome to celebrate the year 2000.

TIMELINE

1915 Italy enters World War I

1929 Lateran Treaty creates a separate Vatican state

1926 Opposition parties banned

1944 Allies liberate Rome from Germans

1946 National referendum establishes Italy as a Republic; King Umberto II exiled

1900	1915	1930	1945

1911 Victor Emmanuel Monument is completed

1922 Fascists march on Rome. Mussolini becomes prime minister

Poster for EUR

1940 Italy enters World War II; work begins on EUR zone

1957 Treaty of Rome initiates European Common Market

Three Tenors Concert (1990)
Combining Italy's love for music and football, this opera recital at the Baths of Caracalla was broadcast live during the World Cup.

Poster for La Dolce Vita
In the 1950s and 1960s Rome was Europe's Hollywood. Ben-Hur, Quo Vadis? *and* Cleopatra *were made at the Cinecittà studios, as well as Italian films like Fellini's* La Dolce Vita.

Valentino Model
While not as important as Milan for fashion, Rome is still home to some of the industry's leading designers.

City-Centre Traffic
Rome's streets are congested, and many buildings have been damaged by pollution. There are plans to close the historic centre to traffic.

Olympic es are in Rome

1978 Premier Aldo Moro kidnapped, then killed, by Red Brigades; Karol Wojtyla is elected Pope John Paul II

1990 Rome hosts soccer World Cup finals

2004 EU constitution signed in Rome

2005 Pope John Paul II dies in Rome; he is succeeded by Benedict XVI

| 1975 | 1990 | 2005 | 2020 |

1962 Second Vatican Council brings about Church reforms

1981 Assassination attempt on Pope John Paul II in St Peter's Square

1993 Frances-co Rutelli becomes Rome's first elected mayor

2000 Rome enters the 21st century with millions of pilgrims celebrating the Holy Year – the Jubilee

2009 Rome hosts the World Swimming Championships

ROME AT A GLANCE

From its early days as a settlement of shepherds on the Palatine hill, Rome grew to rule a vast empire stretching from northern England to North Africa. Later, after the empire had collapsed, Rome became the centre of the Christian world and artists and architects flocked to work for the popes. The legacy of this history can be seen all over the city. The following pages are a time-saving summary of some of the best Rome has to offer. There are sections on churches, museums and galleries, fountains and obelisks, and celebrated artists and writers in Rome. Below are the top attractions that no visitor should miss.

ROME'S TOP TOURIST ATTRACTIONS

Capitoline Museums
See pp70–73.

Colosseum
See pp92–5.

Sistine Chapel
See pp244–7.

Spanish Steps
See p134.

Raphael Rooms
See pp242–3.

Trevi Fountain
See p159.

Castel Sant'Angelo
See pp248–9.

Pantheon
See pp110–11.

St Peter's
See pp230–33.

Roman Forum
See pp78–87.

Piazza Navona
See p120.

◁ Interior of the Pantheon, by Giovanni Paolo Pannini (1691–1765)

Rome's Best: Churches and Temples

As the centre of Christianity, Rome has a
vast wealth of beautiful and interesting
churches. These range from magnificent great
basilicas, built to assert the importance of
the medieval and Renaissance Catholic church,
to smaller, humbler buildings where the first
Christians gathered, often in secret. Among
the most fascinating early churches are those
converted from ancient Roman
temples. Additions to these
over the years have resulted in
some intriguing, many-layered
buildings. A more detailed
historical overview of
Rome's churches is on
pages 46–7.

Pantheon
*This monumental 2,000-year-old
building is one of the largest
surviving temples of ancient Rome.*

St Peter's
At 136 m (450 ft) high,
Michelangelo's dome is
the tallest in the world.
Sadly, the artist died
before seeing his work
completed.

**Santa
Maria
in Trastevere**
*Built over a very early
Christian foundation, this
church is famous for its
ornate mosaics.*

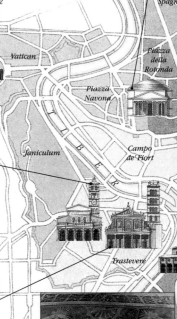

Santa Cecilia in Trastevere
*This statue of Cecilia, showing her as she
lay when her tomb was uncovered, was
sculpted in 1599 by Stefano Maderno.*

Santa Maria in Cosmedin
*The decorations in this 6th-century church are
12th-century and earlier. A restored painting
in the apse shows the Virgin, Child and saints.*

Santa Maria Maggiore
Rich mosaics and relics contrast with the sober interior form of Santa Maria Maggiore. Among its treasures are vestments bearing the Borghese coat of arms.

Sant'Andrea al Quirinale
Bernini made maximum use of strong, dynamic curves in this oval interior (1658–70), creating a small masterpiece of the Roman Baroque.

Santa Prassede
Magnificent Byzantine mosaics cover the walls and ceilings of this 9th-century church. This Christ with Angels is in the Chapel of St Zeno.

Santa Croce in Gerusalemme
Saints adorn the façade of Santa Croce. Inside are relics of the Cross, brought from Jerusalem by St Helena.

Via Veneto

Quirinal

Forum

Palatine

Esquiline

Lateran

Caracalla

| 0 metres | 500 |
| 0 yards | 500 |

San Clemente
Different archaeological layers lie beneath the 12th-century church. This sarcophagus dates from the 4th century.

San Giovanni in Laterano
The original church was built by Constantine, the first Christian emperor. The Chapel of St Venantius mosaics include the figure of St Venantius himself.

Exploring Churches and Temples

There are more churches in Rome than there are days of the year, so you'll have to be selective. Catholic pilgrims have always been drawn to the seven major basilicas: **St Peter's**, the heart of the Roman Catholic church, **San Giovanni in Laterano**, **San Paolo fuori le Mura**, **Santa Maria Maggiore**, **Santa Croce in Gerusalemme**, **San Lorenzo fuori le Mura** and **San Sebastiano**. These have a wealth of relics, tombs and magnificent works of art from many different periods. Smaller churches can be equally fascinating, especially those that have preserved their original character.

ANCIENT TEMPLES

One pagan temple survives virtually unaltered since it was erected in the 2nd century AD. The **Pantheon**, "Temple of all the Gods", has a domed interior quite different in structure from any other church in Rome. It was reconsecrated as a Christian church in the 7th century.

Other Roman temples have been incorporated into Christian churches at various times. Two of these are in the Forum; **Santi Cosma e Damiano** was established in the Temple of Romulus in 526, while San Lorenzo in Miranda was built on to the ruins of the **Temple of Antoninus and Faustina** in the 11th century. The Baroque façade, built in 1602, looms behind the columns of the temple.

Another church that clearly shows its ancient Roman origins is **Santa Costanza**, built as a mausoleum for Constantine's daughter. It is a round church with some splendid 4th-century mosaics.

13th-century fresco by Pietro Cavallini in Santa Cecilia

EARLY CHRISTIAN AND MEDIEVAL CHURCHES

Some early basilicas – the 5th-century **Santa Maria Maggiore** and **Santa Sabina**, for example – retain much of their original structure. Other, even earlier, churches such as the 4th-century **San Paolo fuori le Mura** and **San Giovanni in Laterano** still preserve their original basilica shape. San Paolo was rebuilt after a fire in 1823 destroyed the original building, and the San Giovanni of today dates from a 1646 reconstruction by Borromini. Both these churches still have their medieval cloisters.

The impressive domed interior of the Pantheon, which became a church in 609

Santa Maria in Trastevere and **Santa Cecilia in Trastevere** were built over houses where the earliest Christian communities met and worshipped in secret to avoid persecution. One church where the different layers of earlier structures can clearly be seen is **San Clemente**. At its lowest level, it has a Mithraic temple of the 3rd century AD. Other early churches include **Santa Maria in Cosmedin**, with its impressive Romanesque bell tower, and the fortified convent of **Santi Quattro Coronati**. Many Roman churches, most notably **Santa Prassede**, contain fine early Christian and medieval mosaics.

Cloister of San Giovanni in Laterano

UNUSUAL FLOORPLANS

The design of Rome's first churches was based on the ancient basilica, a rectangular building divided into three naves. Since then there have been many bold departures from this plan, including round churches, square churches based on the shape of the Greek cross, as in Bramante's plan for St Peter's, and, in the Baroque period, even oval and hexagonal ones.

Pantheon (2nd century)

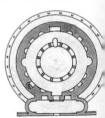
Santa Costanza (4th century)

RENAISSANCE

The greatest undertaking of the Renaissance popes was the rebuilding of **St Peter's**. Disagreements on the form it should take meant that, although work started in 1506, it was not completed until well into the 17th century. Fortunately, this did not prevent the building of Michelangelo's great dome. As well as working on St Peter's, Michelangelo also provided the **Sistine Chapel** with its magnificent frescoes.

On a completely different scale, another key work of Renaissance architecture is Bramante's tiny **Tempietto** (1499) on the Janiculum. **Santa Maria della Pace** has a Bramante cloister, some frescoes by Raphael and a charming portico by Pietro da Cortona. Also of interest is Michelangelo's imaginative use of the great vaults of the Roman Baths of Diocletian in the church of **Santa Maria degli Angeli**.

There are other churches worth visiting for the sake of

Michelangelo's dramatic dome crowning the interior of St Peter's

their outstanding paintings and sculptures. **Santa Maria del Popolo**, for example, has two great paintings by Caravaggio, the Chigi Chapel designed by Raphael, and a series of 15th-century frescoes by Pinturicchio. **San Pietro in Vincoli**, besides having the chains with which St Peter was bound in prison, also has Michelangelo's awe-inspiring statue of Moses, while **San Luigi dei Francesi** has three Caravaggios depicting St Matthew and frescoes by Domenichino.

BAROQUE

Interior of Rosati's dome in San Carlo ai Catinari (1620)

The Counter-Reformation inspired the exuberant, lavish style of churches such as the **Gesù** and **Sant' Ignazio di Loyola**. The best loved examples of Roman Baroque are the later works associated with Bernini, such as the great colonnade and baldacchino he built for **St Peter's**. Of the smaller churches he designed, perhaps the finest is **Sant' Andrea al Quirinale**, while **Santa Maria della Vittoria** houses his truly astonishing Cornaro Chapel with its sculpture of the *Ecstasy of St Teresa*. The late Baroque was not all Bernini, however. You should also look out for churches such as **San Carlo**

ai Catinari with its beautiful dome by Rosato Rosati and the many churches by Bernini's rival, Borromini. **Sant'Agnese in Agone** and **San Carlo alle Quattro Fontane** are famed for the dramatic concave surfaces of their façades, while the complex structure of **Sant'Ivo alla Sapienza** makes it one of the miniature masterpieces of the Baroque.

WHERE TO FIND THE CHURCHES

Bramante's St Peter's (1503)

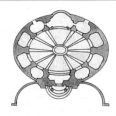

Sant'Andrea al Quirinale (1658)

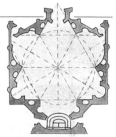

Sant'Ivo alla Sapienza (1642)

Rome's Best: Museums and Galleries

The museums of Rome are among the richest in the world; the Vatican alone contains incomparable collections of Egyptian, Etruscan, Greek, Roman and Early Christian artifacts, as well as frescoes by Michelangelo and Raphael, priceless manuscripts and jewels. Excavations in the 19th century added treasures from ancient Rome which are now on show in museums throughout the city. The finest Etruscan collections in the world can be enjoyed in the Villa Giulia. More details of Rome's museums and galleries are given on pages 50–51.

Vatican Museums
The galleries and long corridors hold priceless artifacts such as this 9th-century mosaic showing scenes from the life of Christ.

Villa Giulia
Etruscan treasures from Rome's early history are displayed in this beautiful Renaissance villa.

| 0 metres | 500 |
| 0 yards | 500 |

Vatican

Piazza Navona

Galleria Spada
This collection's strength lies in its 17th- and 18th-century paintings. Earlier works include a Visitation *by Andrea del Sarto (1486–1530).*

Campo de' Fio

Janiculum

Palazzo Corsini
Included here are works by Caravaggio, Rubens and Van Dyck, as well as a painting of the Baroque sculptor Bernini – a rare portrait by Il Baciccia (1639–1709).

Trastevere

Galleria Doria Pamphilj
Most of the great names of the Renaissance are represented on this gallery's crowded walls. Titian (1485–1576) painted Salome *early in his career.*

Museo e Galleria Borghese
The ground-floor museum houses ancient Greek and Roman sculpture as well as early Bernini masterpieces such as his David (1619). Upstairs are paintings by Titian, Rubens and other masters.

Museo Nazionale Romano
This fresco, from Livia's Villa (1st century AD) outside Rome, is one of a huge collection of finds from archaeological sites throughout the city.

Palazzo Barberini
The works of art here date mainly from the 13th to the 16th centuries. This figure of Providence comes from Pietro da Cortona's The Triumph of Divine Providence (1633–9).

Palazzo Venezia
The highlights of Rome's most important museum of decorative arts are its Byzantine and medieval collections, including this Byzantine enamel of Christ dating from the 13th century.

Via Veneto

Quirinal

Esquiline

Forum

Palatine

Caracalla

Lateran

Capitoline Museums: Palazzo dei Conservatori
Pietro da Cortona's Rape of the Sabine Women (1629) is one of many Baroque paintings in the picture gallery.

Capitoline Museums: Palazzo Nuovo
Among the sculptures is this head of Giulia Domna (wife of Septimius Severus) from the 2nd century AD.

Exploring Museums and Galleries

Rome's museums and galleries have two major strengths: Greek and Roman archaeological treasures, and paintings and sculptures of the Renaissance and the Baroque. The Vatican Museums have superb collections of both, as do, on a smaller scale, the Capitoline Museums. Fine paintings can also be found scattered throughout Rome in museums, galleries and churches *(see pp46–7).*

Etruscan clay head, Villa Giulia

ETRUSCAN ARTIFACTS

5th-century BC Etruscan gold plate with inscription, Villa Giulia

The Etruscans inhabited an area stretching from Florence to Rome from the 8th century BC, and ruled Rome from the late 7th century BC *(see pp18–19).* It was the Etruscan custom to bury the dead along with their possessions, and as a result Etruscan artifacts have been excavated from tombs all over central Italy. Three main collections can be seen in Rome. The **Villa Giulia** has been the home of the Museo Nazionale Etrusco since 1889. The villa, designed by Vignola for Pope Julius III for summer outings, is one of Rome's prettiest Renaissance buildings. Its gardens contain a reconstructed Etruscan temple. Not

Victory banner, Museo della Civiltà Romana

all objects here are Etruscan, however; some of the pottery, statuettes and artifacts are relics of the Faliscans, Latins and other tribes who inhabited central Italy before the Romans.

The Gregorian Etruscan Museum in the **Vatican Museums** was opened in 1837 to house Etruscan finds from tombs on Church-owned land. The Museo Barracco in the **Piccola Farnesina** has statues from the much older civilizations of ancient Egypt and Assyria.

ANCIENT ROMAN ART

The archaeological zone in Rome forms a huge open-air museum of evidence of ancient Roman life, while the porticoes and cloisters of the city's churches are filled with ancient sarcophagi and fragments of statuary. The largest important collection can be seen in the **Museo Nazionale Romano** at the Baths of Diocletian and its new branch Palazzo Massimo. The museum's many ancient artifacts include, most notably, a sarcophagus from Livia's Villa at Prima Porta just north of Rome. Also on display are some wonderfully well-preserved mosaics. The museum's great collection of Roman statues is now housed in the recently restored **Palazzo Altemps**. The most important statues are in the **Vatican Museums**, which also have the best of the great Greek works, such as the *Laocoön,* brought to Rome around

the 1st century AD. It had tremendous influence on the subsequent development of Roman art. Splendid copies of Greek originals can be seen in the **Capitoline Museums**.

In the Forum, occupying two floors of the church of Santa Francesca Romana, is the **Antiquarium Forense** with restored finds from the excavations. For those who enjoy history, the large scale model at the **Museo della Civiltà Romana** in EUR gives an excellent idea of what ancient Rome looked like in the 4th century AD.

Centurion's breast plate, Museo della Civiltà Romana

ART GALLERIES

Muses in Raphael's *Parnassus* (1508–11), Vatican Museums

In the past, many of Rome's great aristocratic families owned magnificent private collections of paintings and sculpture. Some of these are still housed in ancestral palazzi, which are open to the public. One is the **Galleria Doria Pamphilj**, which has the greatest concentration of paintings of any palazzo in Rome. It's well worth searching through the various rooms to find the pearls of the collection, which include works by Raphael,

Filippo Lippi, Caravaggio, Titian and Claude Lorrain, and a portrait of Pope Innocent X Pamphilj by the Spanish artist Velázquez. The **Galleria Spada** collection, begun by Bernardino Spada in 1632, is still housed in the fine original gallery built for it. The paintings demonstrate 17th-century Roman taste and include works by Rubens, Guido Reni, Guercino and Jan Brueghel the Elder. The **Galleria Colonna** contains a collection of art dating from the same period.

Hellenistic faun, Museo Borghese

Other old family residences are now showcases for state art collections. The Galleria Nazionale d'Arte Antica is divided between **Palazzo Barberini** and **Palazzo Corsini**. Palazzo Barberini, built between 1625 and 1633 by Bernini and others for the Barberini family, houses paintings from the 13th to the 16th centuries. It also has *objets d'art* acquired by the state from various private collections. At some future date, the 17th- and 18th-century paintings exhibited in the Palazzo Corsini, on the south side of the Tiber, will

be transferred to join the Palazzo Barberini collection. Another wonderful private collection was that of the Borghese family, also now managed by the state. The **Museo e Galleria Borghese** contains a sculpture collection, including the technically amazing *Apollo and Daphne* by the youthful genius Bernini and the famous statue of Pauline Borghese by Canova. On the first floor is the picture collection with paintings by Titian, Correggio and others.

The **Capitoline Museums** hold collections that were gifts of the popes to the people of Rome. The Pinacoteca (art gallery) in the **Palazzo dei Conservatori** contains works by Titian, Guercino and Van Dyck. There is an art gallery at the **Vatican Museums**, but lovers of Renaissance art will head straight for the Sistine Chapel and the Raphael Rooms. Rome's main modern art collection is in the **Galleria Nazionale d'Arte Moderna**.

SMALLER MUSEUMS

The most important of the smaller collections is the beautifully laid-out medieval museum in **Palazzo Venezia**, with exhibits ranging from ceramics to sculpture. Rome has a wealth of specialist museums like the **Museum of Musical Instruments**, the **Museo di Roma in Trastevere**, with tableaux showing life in Rome during the last century, and the **Burcardo Theatre Museum**. For those with an interest in the English Romantic poets who lived in Rome in the 19th century, there is the **Keats-Shelley Memorial House**, a museum in the house where John Keats died. Focusing on the French Empire, the **Museo Napoleonico** has relics and paintings

Laocoön (1st century AD) in the Vatican's Pio-Clementine Museum

of Napoleon and members of his family, many of whom came to live in Rome.

Portrait of Pauline Borghese painted by Kinson (c.1805), now in the Museo Napoleonico

The Deposition (1604) by Caravaggio, the Vatican

Rome's Best: Fountains and Obelisks

Rome has some of the loveliest fountains in the world.
Many of them are the work of the greatest sculptors of the
Renaissance and Baroque. Some fountains are flamboyant
displays, others restful trickles of water. Many are simply
drinking fountains, while a few cascade from the sides
of buildings. Obelisks date from far earlier in the city's
history. Although some of them were commissioned
by Roman emperors, many are even older and were
brought to Rome by triumphant, conquering armies.
A more detailed overview of Rome's fountains and
obelisks is on pages 54–5.

Piazza San Pietro
*Twin fountains give
life to the splendid
monumental piazza
of St Peter's. Maderno
designed the one on
the Vatican side in
1614; the other was
later built to match.*

Piazza del Popolo
*Nineteenth-century
marble lions and
fountains surround an
ancient obelisk in the
centre of the piazza.*

Fontana dei Quattro Fiumi
*The fountain of the four
rivers is the work of
Bernini. The four figures
represent the Ganges, the
Plate, the Danube and
the Nile.*

**Obelisk of Santa Maria
sopra Minerva**
*The Egyptian obelisk,
held up by Bernini's
marble elephant, dates
from the 6th century BC.*

Fontana delle Tartarughe
*One of Rome's more secret fountains,
this jewel of Renaissance sculpture
shows youths helping tortoises into a basin.*

Fontana della Barcaccia
This elegant fountain of 1627 is probably the work of Pietro Bernini, father of the more famous Gian Lorenzo.

Trevi Fountain
The Trevi, inspired by Roman triumphal arches, was designed by Nicola Salvi in 1732. Tradition has it that a coin thrown into the water guarantees a visitor's return to Rome.

0 metres 500
0 yards 500

Fontana delle Naiadi
When this fountain was unveiled in 1901, the realistically sensual bronze nymphs caused a storm of protest.

Obelisk of Piazza San Giovanni in Laterano
The oldest obelisk in Rome dates from the 14th century BC. It came to Rome in AD 357, brought here on the orders of Constantine II.

Piazza della Bocca della Verità Fountain
In this 18th-century fountain, built by Carlo Bizzaccheri for Pope Clement XI, water spills over a craggy rock formation where two Tritons hold aloft a large shell.

Exploring Fountains and Obelisks

Fountain of the Amphorae (1920s)

The popes who restored the ancient Roman aqueducts used to build fountains to commemorate their deeds of munificence. As a result, fountains of all sizes and shapes punctuate the city, drawing grateful crowds on hot summer days. Ancient obelisks provide powerful reminders of the debt Roman civilization owed to the Egyptians. Architects have learnt to incorporate them into Roman piazzas in fascinating ways.

The Pantheon Fountain

FOUNTAINS

The Trevi fountain is one of the most famous of all. It is a *mostra*, a monumental fountain built to mark the end of an aqueduct – in this case the Acqua Vergine, built by Marcus Agrippa in 19 BC, although the Trevi itself was only completed in 1762. Other *mostre* are the **Fontana dell'Acqua Paola**, built for Pope Paul V in 1612 on the Janiculum, and the **Moses Fountain**, commemorating the opening of the Acqua Felice by Pope Sixtus V in 1587.

Almost all Rome's famous piazzas have fountains. In **Piazza San Pietro** there is a matching pair of powerful fountains. Piazza Navona has Bernini's wonderful Baroque **Fontana dei Quattro Fiumi** (fountain of the four rivers) as its main attraction. The fountain's four figures each represent one of the principal rivers of the four continents then known. To the south of this is the smaller **Fontana del Moro** (the Moor), also by Bernini, showing an Ethiopian struggling with a dolphin. At the north end, Neptune

wrestles with an octopus on a 19th-century fountain. In Piazza Barberini is the magnificent Bernini creation of 1642–3: the **Fontana del Tritone** with its sea god blowing through a shell.

More recently, large piazzas have been redesigned around fountains. Valadier's great design for **Piazza del Popolo** (1816–20) has marble lions and fountains surrounding the

Fountain of the four tiaras located behind St Peter's

central obelisk plus two more fountains on the east and west sides of the square. The early 20th century saw the opening of the **Fontana delle Naiadi** (nymphs) in Piazza della Repubblica; its earthy figures caused great scandal at the time. The highly original **Fountain of the Amphorae** (map 8 D2) was erected in Piazza dell'Emporio during the 1920s. The same designer, Pietro Lombardi, also created the **Fountain of the Four Tiaras** (map 3 C3) behind the colonnade of St Peter's.

The city also has a number of smaller, and often very charming, fountains. At the foot of the Spanish Steps is the **Fontana della Barcaccia** (the leaking boat) of 1627; the **Fontana delle Tartarughe**

Fontana dei Cavalli Marini

THE TREVI FOUNTAIN

Appropriately for a fountain resembling a stage set, the theatrical Trevi has been the star of many films set in Rome, including romantic films like *Three Coins in a Fountain* and *Roman Holiday*, but also *La Dolce Vita*, Fellini's satirical portrait of Rome in the 1950s. Whatever liberties Anita Ekberg took then, paddling in the fountains of Rome is now forbidden, however tempting it could be in the summer heat.

Anita Ekberg in *La Dolce Vita* (1960)

(the tortoise fountain) has been in the tiny Piazza Mattei since 1581, and by Santa Maria in Domnica is the **Fontana della Navicella** (little boat), created out of an ancient Roman sculpture in the 16th century. In the forecourt of **Santa Sabina** (map 8 D2) water gushes from a huge mask set in an ancient basin. The **Pantheon Fountain** (map 4 F4), from 1575, is by Jacopo della Porta. **Le Quattro Fontane** (four fountains) have stood at the Quirinal hill crossroads since 1593.

Fountains in parks and gardens include the **Galleon Fountain** (1620–21) at the Vatican, and the **Fontana dei Cavalli Marini** (seahorses), of 1791, at Villa Borghese. The somewhat decayed 16th-century terraced gardens of the **Villa d'Este**, with their display of over 500 fountains, are still worth the journey.

Piazza Navona with Fontana dei Quattro Fiumi, by Pannini (1691–1765)

The Ovato fountain at Villa d'Este

OBELISKS

The most ancient and tallest of Rome's obelisks is the **Obelisk of Piazza di San Giovanni in Laterano**. Built of red granite, 31 m (100 ft) high, it came from the Temple of Amon at Thebes, erected in the 14th century BC. It was brought to Rome in AD 357 by the order of Constantine II and put up in the Circus Maximus. In 1587 it was rediscovered, broken into three pieces, and was re-erected in the following year. Next in age is the obelisk in **Piazza del Popolo**, from the 13th or 12th century BC. It was

brought to Rome in the time of Augustus and also erected in the Circus Maximus. The slightly smaller **Obelisk of Piazza Montecitorio** was another of Augustus's trophies. The bronze ball and spike at the top recall its past use as a gnomon for a sundial of vast proportions.

Other obelisks, such as the one at the top of the Spanish Steps, are Roman imitations of Egyptian originals. The **Obelisk of Piazza dell' Esquilino** and the one in **Piazza del Quirinale** (map 5 B4) first stood at the entrance to the Mausoleum of Augustus. When re-erected, most obelisks were mounted on decorative bases, often with statues and fountains at their foot. Others became parts of sculptures. Bernini

Obelisk in Piazza del Popolo

was the creator of the marble elephant balancing the Egyptian **Obelisk of Santa Maria sopra Minerva** on its back, and the **Fontana dei Fiumi**, with an obelisk from the Circus of Maxentius. Another obelisk was added to the remodelled Pantheon Fountain in 1711. The obelisk in **Piazza San Pietro** is Egyptian but does not have the usual hieroglyphics.

Wall fountain at Villa d'Este

WHERE TO FIND THE FOUNTAINS AND OBELISKS

Artists and Writers Inspired by Rome

Artists and writers have been attracted to Rome since Classical times. Many came to work for the emperors; the poets Horace, Virgil and Ovid, for example,

all enjoyed the patronage of Emperor Augustus. Later on, especially in the Renaissance and Baroque periods, the greatest artists and architects came to Rome to compete for commissions from the popes. However, patronage was not the only magnet. Since the Renaissance, Rome's Classical past and its picturesque ruins have drawn artists, architects and writers from all over Italy and abroad.

The prolific love poet Ovid (43 BC–AD 17)

Self-portrait by the 18th-century artist Angelica Kauffmann, c.1770

PAINTERS, SCULPTORS AND ARCHITECTS

Diego Velázquez, one of many great 17th-century artists to visit Rome

In the early 16th century, artists and architects were summoned from all parts of Italy to realize the grandiose building projects of the popes. From Urbino came Bramante (1444–1514) and Raphael (1483–1520); from Perugia Perugino (1450–1523); from Florence Michelangelo (1475–1564) and many others. They worked in the Vatican, on the new St Peter's and the decoration of the Sistine Chapel. Artists were often well rewarded, but they also lived in dangerous times. Florentine sculptor and goldsmith Benvenuto Cellini (1500–71) helped defend Castel Sant' Angelo (see pp248–9) during the Sack of Rome (1527), but was later imprisoned there and made a dramatic escape. His memoirs tell the story.

Towards the end of the 16th century Church patronage was generous to the

Milanese-born Caravaggio (1571–1610) despite his violent character and unruly life. The Carracci family from Bologna also flourished – especially brothers Annibale (1560–1609) and Agostino (1557–1602).

The work of Gian Lorenzo Bernini (1598–1680) can be seen all over Rome. He succeeded Carlo Maderno (1556–1629) as architect of St Peter's, and created its great bronze baldacchino, the splendid colonnade (see pp230–31) and numerous fountains, churches and sculptures. His rival for the title of leading architect of the Roman Baroque was Francesco Borromini (1599–1667), whose highly original genius can be appreciated in many Roman churches and palazzi.

In the 17th century it became more common for artists from outside Italy to come and work in Rome. Diego Velázquez (1599–1660), King Philip IV of Spain's court painter, came in 1628 to study

the art treasures of the Vatican. Rubens (1577–1640) came from Antwerp to study, and carried out various commissions. The French artists Nicolas Poussin (1594–1665) and Claude Lorrain (1600–82) lived here for many years.

The Classical revival of the 18th century attracted artists to Rome in unprecedented numbers. From Britain came the Scottish architect Robert Adam (1728–92) and the Swiss artist Angelica Kauffmann (1741–1807), who settled here and was buried with great honour in Sant'Andrea delle Fratte. After the excesses of the Baroque, sculpture also turned to the simplicity of Neo-Classicism. A leading exponent of this movement was Antonio Canova (1757–1821). Sculptors from all over Europe were influenced by him, including the Dane Bertel Thorvaldsen (1770–1844) who lived in Rome for many years.

Claude Lorrain's view of the Forum, painted in Rome in 1632

WRITERS

Dante (1262–1321) visited Rome during his exile from Florence and in the *Inferno* describes the great influx of pilgrims for the first Holy Year (1300). The poet Petrarch (1304–74), born in Arezzo, came to the city in much happier circumstances to be crowned with laurels on the Capitol in 1341. The poet Torquato Tasso (1544–95), from Sorrento, was invited to receive a similar honour, but died soon after his arrival. He is buried in Sant'Onofrio (*see p219*) on the Janiculum.

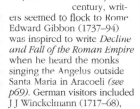

Torquato Tasso

Two of the first writers from abroad to visit Rome were the French essayist Montaigne (1533–92) and English poet John Milton (1608–74). Then, by the early 18th century, writers seemed to flock to Rome. Edward Gibbon (1737–94) was inspired to write *Decline and Fall of the Roman Empire* when he heard the monks singing the Angelus outside Santa Maria in Aracoeli (*see p69*). German visitors included J J Winckelmann (1717–68),

who wrote influential studies of ancient art, and the poet J W von Goethe (1749–1832).

In the Romantic period Rome teemed with English writers: poets Keats, Shelley and Byron, followed by the Brownings and the novelist Charles Dickens. Travel writers in the 19th century included Augustus Hare (1834–1903) and the German historian Ferdinand Gregorovius (1821–91). Much of *The Portrait of a Lady* by American Henry James (1843–1916) is set in Rome.

Modern life in Rome is brilliantly captured by the Roman novelist and short-story writer Alberto Moravia (1907–90).

Portrait of the poet John Keats painted by his friend Joseph Severn in 1819

MUSICIANS

Giovanni Luigi da Palestrina (1525–94), from the town of that name, became choirmaster and organist to the Vatican and composed some of the greatest unaccompanied choral music ever written. In 1770 the 14-year-old Mozart heard Gregorio Allegri's unpublished *Miserere* in the Sistine Chapel and wrote it down from memory. Arcangelo Corelli (1653–1713), the great violinist and composer of the Baroque age, worked in Rome under the patronage of Cardinal Ottoboni. One of his first commissions was to provide a festival of music for Queen Christina of Sweden.

During the 19th century the Prix de Rome brought many French musicians to study here at the Villa Medici (*see p135*). Hector Berlioz (1803–69) owed the inspiration for his popular *Roman Carnival*, the overture to his opera *Benvenuto Cellini*, to his two-year stay in Rome. Georges Bizet (1838–75) and Claude Debussy (1862–1918) were also Prix de Rome winners. Franz Liszt (1811–86), after his 50th year, settled in Rome, took minor orders and became known as Abbé Liszt. He wrote *Fountains of the Villa d'Este* while staying at the villa in Tivoli.

Giacomo Puccini

Twentieth-century musical associations with Rome include the popular works by Ottorino Respighi (1870–1936): *The Fountains of Rome* and *The Pines of Rome*, while Giacomo Puccini (1858–1924) used Roman settings when creating his dramatic, tragic opera *Tosca*.

ROMAN CINEMA

The Cinecittà studios, built in 1937 just outside Rome, are most famous for the films made here in the 1940s – classics of Italian Neo-Realism such as Roberto Rossellini's *Roma Città Aperta* and Vittorio De Sica's *Sciuscià* and *Ladri di Biciclette*. The director most often linked with Roman cinema is Federico Fellini, through films like *La Dolce Vita* (1960) and *Roma* (1972). However, perhaps the most famous artist associated with Rome is the controversial writer-turned-film-maker Pier Paolo Pasolini (1922–75), widely known for his films *Teorema* (1968) and *Il Decamerone* (1971).

Since the 1950s, Rome and Cinecittà have also been much used for foreign films: from *Ben-Hur* and *Spartacus* in the 1950s through to *Gladiator* and Scorsese's *Gangs of New York*.

Pier Paolo Pasolini

ROME THROUGH THE YEAR

The best times to visit Rome are spring and autumn when the weather is usually warm, and sometimes even hot enough to sunbathe and swim at the beaches and lakes outside the city. In the winter months, the weather tends to be grey and wet, while in high summer, most people (including Romans, who leave the city in their droves) find the heat unbearable. Easter and Christmas are obviously very special in Rome, but there are other religious festivals worth seeing at other times in the year, as well as some enjoyable secular events like the Festa de' Noantri in Trastevere and the Flower Festival in Genzano. In villages outside Rome, local celebrations are held to welcome new crops such as strawberries and beans in the spring, and grapes and truffles in the autumn.

SPRING

Easter, falling in March or April, marks the official beginning of the tourist season in Rome. Catholics from all over the world flock into the city to make their pilgrimages to the main basilicas and to hear the Pope's Easter Sunday address outside St Peter's, while the less devout come simply to take advantage of the mild weather. Meanwhile, Romans pile into their cars and head for the coast and countryside, so you can expect the roads, beaches and restaurants of the Castelli Romani and Lake Bracciano to be busy.

Temperatures tend to be around 18° C (66° F), but can hit 28° C (82° F), so by mid-May it is usually possible to lunch and dine outside. However, there can still be sudden downpours and temperature swings, so do bring warm clothes and an umbrella.

Crowds gathering in St Peter's Square at Easter

In April tubs full of colourful azaleas are ranged on the Spanish Steps and along Via Veneto, and once the roses start to flower in the city's Rose Garden overlooking the Circus Maximus, it is opened to the public.

For a fortnight from mid-May Via dei Coronari is lit by candles, lined with plants and hung with banners for the street's antiques fair, while Via Margutta hosts an outdoor art show. In the first week of May the International Horse Show is held in the Villa Borghese. Also usually in May, many world-class tennis players flock to Rome to compete in the International Tennis Championships held annually at the Foro Italico.

EVENTS

Festa di Santa Francesca Romana *(9 March)*, Santa Francesca Romana. Blessing of the city's vehicles *(see p87)*.
Festa di San Giuseppe *(19 March)*, in the Trionfale area. St Joseph's (and Father's) Day celebrated in the streets.
Rome Marathon *(late March)*, through the city *(see p367)*.
Good Friday *(March/April)*, Colosseum. Procession of the Cross at 9pm led by the Pope.
Easter Sunday *(March/April)*, St Peter's Square. Address made by the Pope *(see p231)*.
Rome's Birthday *(21 April)*, Piazza del Campidoglio and elsewhere.
Festa della Primavera *(March/April)*, Spanish Steps and Trinità dei Monti. Azaleas in the street and concerts.
Art exhibition *(April/May)*, Via Margutta *(see p353)*.
International Horse Show *(early May)*, Villa Borghese *(see p366)*.
Antiques Fair *(mid–late May)*, Via dei Coronari *(see p336)*.
International Tennis Championships *(usually May)*, Foro Italico *(see p366)*.

International Horse Show in Villa Borghese in May

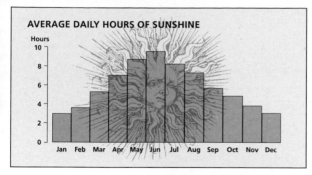

AVERAGE DAILY HOURS OF SUNSHINE

Hours

| Jan | Feb | Mar | Apr | May | Jun | Jul | Aug | Sep | Oct | Nov | Dec |

Sunshine Chart
Rome is famous for its light. June is the sunniest month but it is also very dry, and without the odd shower the bright heat can feel intense. In autumn, Rome's southerly position means that the sun can still be enjoyably warm at midday.

SUMMER

In June a season of concerts begins, with performances in some of the city's most beautiful palaces, churches and courtyards. In July and August opera and drama are staged at Ostia Antica (*see pp270–71*) and in various outdoor locations. During the summer there are also contemporary cultural events – film, music of all kinds, dance and theatre. On midsummer evenings there are stalls and amusements on the Tiber embankments by Castel Sant'Angelo, while in the last two weeks of July Trastevere becomes an open-air party as the Noantri festival is celebrated with trinket stalls, dining in the street and fireworks.

Flower-carpeted streets in Genzano

In August, when the temperature often soars to over 40° C (104° F), virtually all Romans flee the city for the seaside, meaning that many cafés, shops and restaurants close for the entire month.

EVENTS

Flower Festival (*June, the Sunday after Corpus Domini*), Genzano, Castelli Romani, south of Rome. Streets are carpeted with flowers.
Festa di San Giovanni (*23–24 June*), Piazza di Porta San Giovanni. Celebrated with meals of snails in tomato sauce, suckling pig, a fair and firework display.
Festa di Santi Pietro e Paolo (*29 June*), many churches. Celebrations mark the feast of SS Peter and Paul.
Tevere Expo (*end June–mid-July*), along the Tiber. Crafts,

food and wine, music and fireworks (*see p353*).
Festa de' Noantri (*last two weeks in July*), the streets of Trastevere. Food and entertainment (*see p353 and p355*).
Alta Moda Fashion Show (*usually mid- to late July*), Spanish Steps (*see p353*).
Estate Romana (*July/August*), Villa Ada, Ostia Antica, in parks, by the Tiber. Opera, concerts, drama, dance and film (*see p355*).
Festa della Madonna della Neve (*5 August*), Santa Maria Maggiore. Fourth-century snowfall re-enacted with white flower petals (*see p172*).
Ferragosto (*15 August*), Santa Maria in Trastevere. Midsummer holiday. Almost everything closes down. Celebrations are held for the Feast of the Assumption.

Summer vegetables

The sales (*saldi*) begin in mid-July, and the relatively new Alta Moda Fashion Show is usually held mid- to late July at the Spanish Steps.

Many Romans leave the city at the end of June, when schools close, but as June and July are peak tourist months, hotels, cafés, restaurants and all the main places of interest and other attractions are packed out.

The heat of an August afternoon in front of St Peter's

AVERAGE MONTHLY RAINFALL

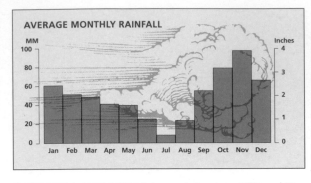

MM												Inches
100												4
80												3
60												2
40												1
20												0
0	Jan Feb Mar Apr May Jun Jul Aug Sep Oct Nov Dec											

Rainfall Chart
Autumn is Rome's rainiest season, with heavy downpours, sometimes lasting for days, especially in November. Rain in summer tends to come in violent – but often extremely refreshing – storms. In winter and early spring expect a few dull, drizzly days.

AUTUMN

September and October are the best – and among the most popular – months to visit Rome. The fiery heat of July and August will have cooled a little, but midday can be very hot, and you can still eat and drink outside without feeling chilly until late at night. Visiting Rome in November is not recommended: it is the wettest month of the year and Roman rainstorms are often very strong and heavy.

At the beginning of October an artisans' fair is held on Via dell'Orso and adjacent streets, while nearby the antiques galleries of Via dei Coronari hold open house. There are also October antiques fairs in Orvieto and Perugia, two of the loveliest Umbrian hill towns, which are about an hour's drive north of Rome. In November, there's yet another prestigious antiques fair at the papal palace of Viterbo, 65 km (40 m) north of Rome *(see p271)*.

Autumn is the season of harvest festivals, so head out to the small towns around Rome to sample delicacies such as local cheeses, sausages, chestnuts and mushrooms.

MARRONI

A roast chestnut stall in autumn

Another reason for taking a trip out of Rome is the wine festival in Marino, in the Castelli Romani, south of the city. There are many opportunities to sample the wines of this region that was once the home to luxurious 16th- and 17th-century country residences but now is renowned particularly for its white wines.

Throughout the autumn and winter in Rome freshly roasted chestnuts can be bought from vendors on street corners, and occasionally there is a stand on Campo de' Fiori where you can sample *vino novello*, the new season's wine. On All Saints' and All Souls' Days, which fall on 1 and 2

November respectively, the Romans make pilgrimages to place chrysanthemums on the tombs of relatives who are buried in the two main cemeteries of Prima Porta and Verano. On a much happier note, the classical concert and opera seasons begin again in October and November.

Details of performances can be found in listings magazines such as *Trova-Roma* and *Roma c'è (see p354)*, in daily newspapers, such as *La Repubblica (see p383)*, and on posters around the city.

EVENTS

RomaEuropa *(autumn)*. Films, dance, theatre and concerts around Rome *(see p355)*.
La Notte Bianca *(September)*. Free entry to museums and galleries all night one Saturday.
Art fair *(September)*, Via Margutta *(see p353)*.
Crafts fair *(last week September/first week October)*, Via dell'Orso *(see p353)*.
International Festival of Cinema *(October)*. New screenings and stars aplenty *(see p360)*.
Marino Wine Festival *(first Sunday in October)*, Marino. Celebrations include tastings and street entertainment.
Antiques Fair *(mid-October)*, Via dei Coronari *(see p353)*.
All Saints' and All Souls' Days *(1, 2 November)*, Prima Porta and Verano cemeteries. The Pope usually celebrates Mass in the Verano cemetery.
Festa di Santa Cecilia *(22 November)*, Santa Cecilia in Trastevere and Catacombs of San Callisto.

Autumn in the Villa Doria Pamphilj park

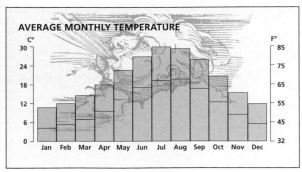

AVERAGE MONTHLY TEMPERATURE

Temperature Chart
The chart shows the average minimum and maximum monthly temperatures. July and August can be unbearably hot, making sightseeing a chore. The fresher days of spring and autumn are ideal to visit Rome, but there are some dull and rainy spells.

WINTER

During the winter Rome is bracingly chilly but the temperature rarely drops below freezing. Not all buildings are centrally heated so if you are staying in a small hotel bring warm clothes and request extra blankets as soon as you arrive, as they can be in short supply. Warm up in cafés with hot chocolate and cappuccino.

The run-up to Christmas is great fun in Rome, especially if you have children. Manger scenes, *presepi*, are set up in many churches, piazzas and public places and from mid-December to Twelfth Night

Rome during one of its rare snowfalls

parties and parades along Via Nazionale, Via Cola di Rienzo and the Pincio. Keep out of the way of teenagers with shaving-cream spray cans and water-filled balloons.

EVENTS

Festa della Madonna Immacolata *(8 December)*, Piazza di Spagna. In the Pope's presence, firemen climb up a ladder to place a wreath on the statue of the Virgin Mary.
Christmas Market *(mid-December – 6 January)*, Piazza Navona. Christmas and children's market *(see p120)*.
Nativity scenes *(mid-December – mid-January)*, many churches. Life-size scene in St Peter's Square, collection at Santi Cosma e Damiano.
Midnight Mass *(24 December)*, at most churches.
Christmas Day *(25 December)*, St Peter's Square. Blessing by the Pope.
New Year's Eve *(31 December)*, all over city. Firework displays, furniture thrown out.
La Befana *(6 January)*, all over city. Parties for children.

Market on Piazza Navona

Piazza Navona hosts a market where you can buy manger scenes, decorations and toys. Unless you have friends in Rome, Christmas itself can be rather lonely, as it is very much a family event. On New Year's Eve, however, everyone is out on the street to drink sparkling wine and let off fireworks.

La Befana, on 6 January, is a traditional holiday when a witch, called La Befana, delivers sweets to children.

The Carnival season runs from late January through to February, celebrated largely by children with fancy-dress

PUBLIC HOLIDAYS

New Year's Day (1 Jan)
Epiphany (6 Jan)
Easter Monday
Liberation Day (25 Apr)
Labour Day (1 May)
Republic Day (2 Jun)
SS Peter & Paul (29 Jun)
Ferragosto (15 Aug)
All Saints' Day (1 Nov)
Immaculate Conception (8 Dec)
Christmas Day (25 Dec)
Santo Stefano (26 Dec)

Via Condotti at Christmas

Fontana delle Naiadi in Piazza della Repubblica ▷

ROME AREA BY AREA

CAPITOL

The temple of Jupiter on the Capitol, the southern summit of the Capitoline hill, was the centre of the Roman world. Reached by a zig-zag path up from the Forum, the temple was the scene of all the most sacred religious and political ceremonies. The hill and its temple came to symbolize Rome's authority as *caput mundi*, head of the world, and the Capitol gave its name to the seat of the US Congress. Throughout the city's history, the Capitol (Campidoglio), has remained the seat of municipal government. Today's city council, the

Hand of colossal statue in Palazzo dei Conservatori

Comune di Roma, meets in the Renaissance splendour of Palazzo Senatorio. The Capitol also serves as Rome's Registry Office. Rome's position as a modern capital is forcefully expressed in the enormous Victor Emmanuel Monument, which unfortunately blots out the view of the Capitol from Piazza Venezia. The present arrangement on the hill dates from the 16th century, when Michelangelo created a beautiful piazza reached by a flight of steps, the Cordonata. Two of the buildings around the piazza now house the Capitoline Museums.

SIGHTS AT A GLANCE

Churches and Temples
San Marco ⑫
Santa Maria in Aracoeli ⑦
Temple of Jupiter ⑧

Museums and Galleries
Capitoline Museums:
Palazzo dei Conservatori
pp72–3 ②
Capitoline Museums:
Palazzo Nuovo pp70–71 ①
Palazzo Venezia
and Museum ⑪

Historic Buildings
Roman *Insula* ⑤

Historic Streets and Piazzas
Aracoeli Staircase ⑥
Cordonata ④
Piazza del Campidoglio ③

Ancient Sites
Tarpeian Rock ⑨

Monuments
Victor Emmanuel
Monument ⑩

GETTING THERE
All the sights in this area are within walking distance of Piazza Venezia. Bus routes converge here from all parts of the city, as do many thousands of motorists. From Termini station you can catch the 40, 64, or 170; from Piazza Barberini the 63 or 95. From St Peter's and the Vatican the only buses are the 40, 62 and 64. Piazza Venezia is also a stopping-off point for the 110 tourist bus.

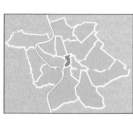

0 metres 200
0 yards 200

KEY
Street-by-Street map

SEE ALSO
• *Street Finder,* maps 5, 12

◁ Statue of Marcus Aurelius on Michelangelo's Piazza del Campidoglio

Street-by-Street: The Capitol and Piazza Venezia

The Capitol, citadel of ancient Rome, is a must for every visitor. A broad flight of steps (the Cordonata) leads up to Michelangelo's spectacular Piazza del Campidoglio. This is flanked by the Palazzo Nuovo and Palazzo dei Conservatori, housing the Capitoline Museums with their fine collections of sculptures and paintings. The absence of cars makes the hill a welcome retreat from the squeal of brakes below, but you should brave the traffic to visit Palazzo Venezia and its museum.

Victor Emmanuel Monument
This huge white marble monument to Italy's first king was completed in 1911 **⑩**

San Marco
The church of the Venetians in Rome has a fine 9th-century apse mosaic **⑫**

Palazzo Venezia
The museum's finest exhibits, such as this 13th-century gilded angel decorated with enamel, date from the late Middle Ages **⑪**

Roman *Insula*
This is a ruined apartment block dating from Imperial Rome **⑤**

Cordonata
Michelangelo's great staircase changed the orientation of the Capitol towards the west **④**

Aracoeli Staircase
When it was built in 1348, the staircase became a centre for political debate **⑥**

PIAZZA VENEZIA

PIAZZA VENEZIA

VIA DEL TEATRO DI MARC

KEY

— — — Suggested route

| 0 metres | 75 |
| 0 yards | 75 |

★ Palazzo dei Conservatori
In this part of the Capitoline Museums a fine series of reliefs from the Temple of Hadrian (see p106) is displayed in the courtyard **②**

Santa Maria in Aracoeli
The treasures hidden behind the church's brick façade include this 15th-century fresco of the Funeral of St Bernardino by Pinturicchio ❼

LOCATOR MAP
See Central Rome Map pp14–15

★ Palazzo Nuovo
This bust of Augustus in the Hall of the Emperors is one of many fine Classical sculptures in the Capitoline Museums ❶

Palazzo Senatorio was used by the Roman Senate from about the 12th century. It now houses the offices of the mayor.

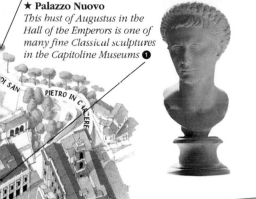

★ Piazza del Campidoglio
Michelangelo designed both the geometric paving and the façades of the buildings ❸

Temple of Jupiter
This artist's impression shows the gold and ivory statue of Jupiter that stood in the temple ❿

Tarpeian Rock
In ancient Rome traitors were thrown to their death from this cliff on the Capitol ❾

STAR SIGHTS

★ Palazzo dei Conservatori

★ Palazzo Nuovo

★ Piazza del Campidoglio

Capitoline Museums: Palazzo Nuovo ❶

See pp70–71.

Capitoline Museums: Palazzo dei Conservatori ❷

See pp72–3.

Piazza del Campidoglio ❸

Map 5 A5 & 12 F5. 🚌 *See **Getting There** p65.*

When Emperor Charles V visited Rome in 1536, Pope Paul III Farnese was so embarrassed by the muddy state of the Capitol that he asked Michelangelo to draw up plans for repaving the piazza, and for renovating the façades of the Palazzo dei Conservatori and Palazzo Senatorio.

Michelangelo proposed adding the Palazzo Nuovo to form a piazza in the shape of a trapezium, embellished with Classical sculptures chosen for their relevance to Rome. Building started in 1546 but progressed so slowly that Michelangelo only lived to oversee the double flight of steps at the entrance of Palazzo Senatorio. The piazza was completed in the 17th century,

the design remaining largely faithful to the original. Pilasters two storeys high and balustrades interspersed with statues link the buildings thematically. The piazza faces west towards St Peter's, the Christian equivalent of the Capitol. At its centre stands a replica of a statue of Marcus Aurelius. The original is in the Palazzo dei Conservatori *(see pp72–3).*

Cordonata ❹

Map 5 A5 & 12 F5. 🚌 *See **Getting There** p65.*

From Piazza Venezia, the Capitol is approached by a gently rising, subtly widening ramp – the Cordonata. At the foot is a pair of granite Egyptian lions, and on the left a 19th-century monument to Cola di Rienzo, close to where the dashing 14th-century tyrant was executed. The top of the ramp is guarded by restored Classical statues of the Dioscuri – Castor and Pollux.

Roman *Insula* ❺

Piazza d'Aracoeli. **Map** 5 A5 & 12 F4. **Tel** 06-0608. 🚌 *See **Getting There** p65. **Open** by appt only: telephone first.*

Two thousand years ago the urban poor of Rome used to make their homes in *insulae* – apartment blocks. These

A statue of one of the Dioscuri at the top of the Cordonata

were often badly maintained by landlords, and expensive to rent in a city where land costs were high. This 2nd-century AD tenement block, of barrel-vault construction, is the only survivor in Rome from that era. The fourth, fifth and part of the sixth storey remain above current ground level.

In the Middle Ages, a section of these upper storeys was converted into a church; its bell tower and 14th-century Madonna in a niche are visible from the street.

During the Fascist years, the area was cleared, and three lower floors emerged. Some 380 people may have lived in the tenement, in the squalid conditions described by the 1st-century AD satirical writers Martial and Juvenal. The latter mentions that he had to climb 200 steps to reach his garret.

This *insula* may once have had more storeys. The higher you lived, the more dismal the conditions, as the poky spaces of the building's upper levels testify.

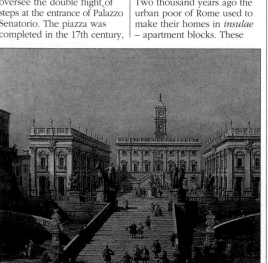

The Cordonata in an 18th-century painting by Antonio Canaletto

Aracoeli Staircase ❻

Piazza d'Aracoeli. **Map** 5 A5 & 12 F4. See **Getting There** p65.

The Aracoeli Staircase numbers 124 marble steps (122 if you start from the right) and was completed in 1348, some say in thanks for the passing of the Black Death, but probably in view of the 1350 Holy Year.

The 14th-century tribune-turned-tyrant Cola di Rienzo used to harangue the masses from the Aracoeli Staircase; in the 17th century foreigners used to sleep on the steps, until Prince Caffarelli, who lived on the hill, scared them off by rolling barrels filled with stones down them.

Popular belief has it that by climbing the steps on your knees you can win the Italian national lottery. From the top there is a good view of Rome, with the domes of Sant' Andrea della Valle and St Peter's slightly to the right.

Aracoeli Staircase

Santa Maria in Aracoeli ❼

Piazza d'Aracoeli (entrances via Aracoeli Staircase and door behind Palazzo Nuovo). **Map** 5 A5 & 12 F4. **Tel** 06-6976 38 39. See **Getting There** p65. **Open** summer: 9am–12.30pm, 3–6.30pm daily; winter: 9am–12.30pm, 2.30–5.30pm daily.

Dating from at least the 6th century, the church of Santa Maria in Aracoeli, or St Mary of the Altar in the Sky, stands on the northern summit of the

Ceiling commemorating Battle of Lepanto in Santa Maria in Aracoeli

Capitoline, on the site of the ancient temple to Juno. Its 22 columns were taken from various ancient buildings; the inscription on the third column to the left tells us that it comes "a cubiculo Augusto-rum" – from the bedroom of the emperors.

The church of the Roman senators and people, Santa Maria in Aracoeli has been used to celebrate many triumphs over adversity. Its ceiling, with naval motifs, commemorates the Battle of Lepanto (1571), and was built under Pope Gregory XIII Boncompagni, whose family crest, the dragon, can be seen towards the altar end.

Many other Roman families and individuals are honoured by memorials in the church. To the right of the entrance door, the tombstone of arch-deacon Giovanni Crivelli, rather than being set into the floor of the church, stands eternally to attention, partly so that the signature "Don-atelli" (by Donatello) can be read at eye-level.

The frescoes in the first chapel on the right, painted by Pinturicchio in the 1480s in the beautifully clear style of the early Renaissance, depict St Bernardino of Siena. On the left wall, the perspective of *The Burial of the Saint* slants to the right, taking into account the position of the viewer just outside the chapel.

The church is most famous, however, for an icon with apparently miraculous powers, the *Santo Bambino*, a 15th-century olive-wood figure of the Christ Child which was carved out of a tree from the garden of Gethsemane. Its powers are said to include resurrecting the dead, and it is sometimes summoned to the bedsides of the gravely ill. The original figure was stolen in 1994 but has been replaced by a replica.

At Christmas the Christ Child takes its place in the centre of a picturesque crib (second chapel to the left) but is usually to be found in the sacristy, as is the panel of the *Holy Family* from the workshop of Giulio Romano.

The miraculous olive-wood Christ Child at Santa Maria in Aracoeli

Capitoline Museums: Palazzo Nuovo ❶

A collection of Classical statues has been kept on the Capitoline hill since the Renaissance. The first group of bronze sculptures was given to the city by Pope Sixtus IV in 1471 and more additions were made by Pope Pius V in 1566. The Palazzo Nuovo was designed by Michelangelo as part of the renovation of the Piazza del Campidoglio, and after its completion in 1655, a number of the statues were transferred here. In 1734 Pope Clement XII Corsini decreed that the building be turned into the world's first public museum.

★ **Capitoline Venus**
This marble statue of Venus dating from around AD100–150, is a Roman copy of the original carved in the 4th century BC by the Greek sculptor Praxiteles. The statue is prized for its striking beauty.

MUSEUM GUIDE

The Palazzo Nuovo is devoted chiefly to sculpture, and most of its finest works, such as the Capitoline Venus, are Roman copies of Greek masterpieces. For visitors keen to identify the philosophers and poets of ancient Greece and the rulers of ancient Rome, there are collections of busts assembled in the 18th century. Admission price also includes entry to the Palazzo dei Conservatori opposite. A gallery below Piazza del Campidoglio links the two buildings.

Portrait of a Flavian Lady
The woman wears the fanciful and elaborate hairstyle popular among the female aristocracy of the 1st century AD.

First floor

Courtyard

Hall of the Philosophers
The hall contains a rich mix of portraits of Greek politicians, scientists and literary figures.

Ground floor

The façade of Palazzo Nuovo was designed by Michelangelo, but the work was actually finished in 1655 by the brothers Carlo and Girolamo Rainaldi.

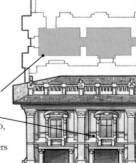

STAR SCULPTURES

★ Capitoline Venus

★ Discobolus

★ Dying Galatian

KEY TO FLOORPLAN

▨ Non-exhibition space

☐ Exhibition space

Mosaic of the Doves
This charming, naturalistic mosaic once decorated the floor of Hadrian's Villa at Tivoli (see p269). It shows doves drinking water from a vase.

VISITORS' CHECKLIST

Musei Capitolini, Piazza del Campidoglio. **Map** 5 A5 & 12 F5. **Tel** 06-0608. 63, 70, 75, 81, 87, 95, 160, 170, 204, 628, 716 and many other routes to Piazza Venezia. **Open** 9am–8pm Tue–Sun (last adm 7pm). **Closed** 1 Jan, 1 May, 25 Dec. **Adm charge** Tickets are valid for the whole complex. Note that the main entrance is through Palazzo dei Conservatori.
www.museicapitolini.org

★ Discobolus
The twisted torso was part of a Greek statue of a discus thrower. An 18th-century French sculptor, Monnot, made the additions that turned him into a wounded warrior.

Stairs to ground floor

2

7   8

Stairs to galleries below the Senate and connecting with Palazzo dei Conservatori

Stairs to first floor

Red Faun
Found at Tivoli, the famous red marble satyr is a 2nd-century AD version of a Greek original – an example of Hadrian's fondness for all things Greek.

★ Dying Galatian
Great compassion is conveyed in this Roman copy of an original Greek work of the 3rd century BC.

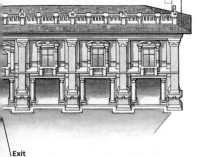

Alexander Severus as Hunter
In this marble of the 3rd century AD, the emperor's pose is a pastiche of Perseus, holding up the head of Medusa the Gorgon after he had killed her in her sleep.

Exit

Capitoline Museums: Palazzo dei Conservatori ②

The Palazzo dei Conservatori was the seat of the city's magistrates during the late Middle Ages. Its frescoed halls are still used occasionally for political meetings and the ground floor houses the municipal register office. The palazzo was built by Giacomo della Porta who carried out Michelangelo's designs for the Piazza del Campidoglio in the mid-16th century. While much of the palazzo is given over to sculpture, the art galleries on the second floor hold works by Veronese, Guercino, Tintoretto, Rubens, Caravaggio, Van Dyck and Titian.

Façade of Palazzo dei Conservatori
Work began on this Michelangelo design in 1563, the year before his death.

MUSEUM GUIDE

The museum is being reorganized, so some items might move. The first-floor rooms have original 16th- and 17th-century decoration and Classical statues. The second-floor gallery holds paintings and a porcelain collection. Rooms 10 and 11 are used as temporary exhibition space.

Burial and Glory of St Petronilla
This huge Baroque altarpiece was painted in 1622–3 by Guercino to hang in St Peter's.

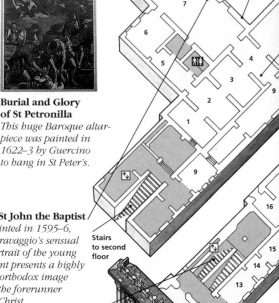

Second-floor art gallery

Stairs to second floor

Stairs to first floor

Main entrance

★ **St John the Baptist**
Painted in 1595–6, Caravaggio's sensual portrait of the young saint presents a highly unorthodox image of the forerunner of Christ.

The Horatii and Curatii
D'Arpino's fresco was painted in 1613 and depicts a duel taken from early Roman legend.

KEY TO FLOORPLAN

☐ Exhibition space

▨ Non-exhibition space

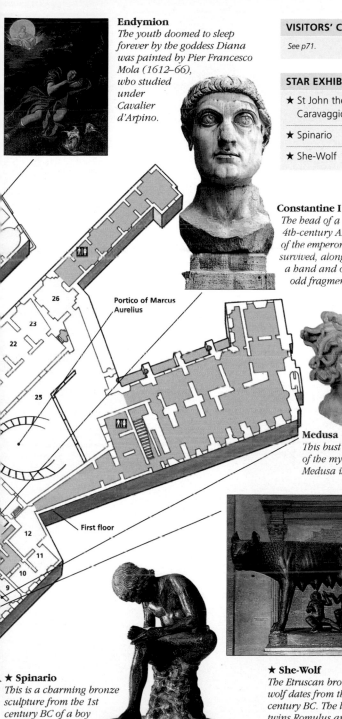

Endymion
The youth doomed to sleep forever by the goddess Diana was painted by Pier Francesco Mola (1612–66), who studied under Cavalier d'Arpino.

VISITORS' CHECKLIST

See p71.

STAR EXHIBITS

★ St John the Baptist by Caravaggio

★ Spinario

★ She-Wolf

Constantine I
The head of a colossal 4th-century AD statue of the emperor has survived, along with a hand and other odd fragments.

Portico of Marcus Aurelius

Medusa
This bust by Bernini of the mythological Medusa is in Room 5.

First floor

★ **Spinario**
This is a charming bronze sculpture from the 1st century BC of a boy trying to remove a thorn from his foot.

★ **She-Wolf**
The Etruscan bronze of the wolf dates from the early 5th century BC. The legendary twins Romulus and Remus (see pp18–19) were probably added in the 15th century.

Temple of Jupiter ⑧

Via del Tempio di Giove. **Map** 5 A5 & 12 F5. 🚌 See **Getting There** p65.

The temple of Jupiter, the most important in ancient Rome, was founded in honour of the arch-god around 509 BC on the southern summit of the Capitoline hill. From the few traces that remain, archaeologists have been able to reconstruct the rectangular, Greek appearance of the temple as it once stood. In places you can see remnants of its particularly Roman feature, the podium. Most of this lies beneath the Museo Nuovo wing of the Palazzo dei Conservatori *(see pp72–3).*

By walking around the site, from the podium's south-western corner in Via del Tempio di Giove to its south-eastern corner in Piazzale Caffarelli, you can see that the temple was about the same size as the Pantheon.

Ancient coin showing the Temple of Jupiter

Tarpeian Rock ⑨

Via di Monte Caprino and Via del Tempio di Giove. **Map** 5 A5 & 12 F5. 🚌 See **Getting There** p65.

The southern tip of the Capitoline is called the Tarpeian Rock (Rupe Tarpea), after Tarpeia, the young daughter of Spurius Tarpeius, defender of the Capitol in the 8th-century BC Sabine War.

The Sabines, bent on vengeance for the rape of their women by Romulus and

Sabine soldiers crushing the treacherous Tarpeia with their shields

his men, bribed Tarpeia to let them up on to the Capitol. As the Augustan historian Livy records, the Sabines used to wear heavy gold bracelets and jewelled rings on their left hands, and Tarpeia's reward for her treachery was to be "what they wore on their shield-arms".

The Sabines kept to the letter of the bargain if not to its spirit – they repaid Tarpeia not with their jewellery but by crushing her to death between their shields. Tarpeia was possibly the only casualty of her act of treachery – as the invading warriors met the Roman defenders, the Sabine women leapt between the two opposing armies, forcing a reconciliation. Traitors and other condemned criminals were subsequently executed by being thrown over the sheer face of the rock.

The place has been considered dangerous and used to be fenced off, but restoration work is now under way.

Victor Emmanuel Monument ⑩

Piazza Venezia. **Map** 5 A5 & 12 F4. **Tel** 06-699 17 18. 🚌 See **Getting There** p65. **Open** 9.30am–4pm daily (to 5pm summer).

Known as Il Vittoriano, this monument was begun in 1885 and inaugurated in 1911 in honour of Victor Emmanuel II of Savoy, the first king of a unified Italy. The king is depicted here in a gilt bronze equestrian statue, oversized like the monument itself – the statue is 12 m (39 ft) long.

The edifice also contains a museum of the Risorgimento, the events that led to unification *(see pp38–9).* Built in austere white Brescian marble, the "wedding cake" or "typewriter" (two of the many insulting nicknames given to this white elephant) will never mellow into the ochre tones of surrounding buildings. It is widely held to be the epitome of self-important, insensitive architecture, though the views that it offers are spectacular.

Victor Emmanuel Monument in Piazza Venezia

Palazzo Venezia and Museum

Via del Plebiscito 118. **Map** 5 A4
& 12 E4. **Tel** 06-6999 4319.
See **Getting There** p65.
Open 9am–7pm Tue–Sun
(last adm: 1 hour before closing).
Closed 1 Jan, 1 May, 25 Dec.
Adm charge. **Temporary
exhibitions**.

The arched windows and
doors of this Renaissance
civic building are so
harmonious that
the façade was
once attributed to
the great Humanist
architect Leon
Battista Alberti
(1404–72). It
was more
probably
built by
Giuliano da
Maiano, who is
known to have carved the
fine doorway on to the piazza.

Pope Paul II

Palazzo Venezia was built
in 1455–64 for the Venetian
cardinal Pietro Barbo, who
later became Pope Paul II.
It was at times a papal
residence, but it also served
as the Venetian Embassy to
Rome before passing into
French hands in 1797. Since
1916 it has belonged to the
state, in the Fascist era
Mussolini used it as his headquarters and addressed crowds
from the central balcony.

The interior is best seen by
visiting the Museo del Palazzo
Venezia, Rome's most
underrated museum. It holds
first-class collections of early
Renaissance painting; painted
wood sculptures and
Renaissance chests from Italy;
tapestries from all of Europe;
majolica; silver; Neapolitan
ceramic figurines; Renaissance
bronzes; arms and armour;
Baroque terracotta sculptures
by Bernini, Algardi and
others; and 17th- and 18th-
century Italian painting. There
is a marble screen from the
Aracoeli convent, destroyed to
make way for the Victor
Emmanuel Monument, and a
bust of Paul II, showing him
to rank with Martin V and Leo
X among the fattest-ever popes.
The building also hosts major
temporary exhibitions.

Palazzo Venezia with Mussolini's balcony in the centre

San Marco

Piazza San Marco 48. **Map** 5 A4 &
12 F4. **Tel** 06-679 52 05. See
Getting There p65. **Open** 8:30am–
noon Tue–Sun, 4–6:30pm Mon–Sat,
9am–1pm, 4–8pm Sun.

The church of San Marco
was founded in 336 by Pope
Mark, in honour of St Mark
the Evangelist. The Pope's
relics lie under the altar. The
church was restored by
Pope Gregory IV in
the 9th century –
the magnificent
apse mosaics date
from this period.

Further major
rebuilding took
place in 1455–71,
when Pope Paul II
Barbo made San
Marco the church
of the Venetian
community in Rome.

**Coat of arms of
Pope Paul II**

The blue and gold coffered
ceiling is decorated with Pope
Paul's heraldic crest, the lion
rampant, recalling the lion of
St Mark, the patron saint of
Venice. The appearance of the
rest of the interior, with its
colonnades of Sicilian jasper,
was largely the creation of
Filippo Barigioni in the 1740s.
Complemented by an
interesting array of funerary
monuments in the aisles, the
style is typical of the late
Roman Baroque.

Leon Battista
Alberti, whose
name is also
mentioned
tentatively in
connection with
Palazzo Venezia,
may have been the
architect of the
elegant travertine
arcade and loggia
of the façade.

San Marco's apse mosaic of Christ, with Gregory IV on the far left

FORUM

The Forum was the centre of political, commercial and judicial life in ancient Rome. The largest buildings were the basilicas, where legal cases were heard. According to the playwright Plautus, the area teemed with "lawyers and litigants, bankers and brokers, shopkeepers and strumpets, good-for-nothings waiting for a tip from the rich". As Rome's population boomed, the Forum became too small. In 46 BC Julius Caesar built a new one, setting a precedent that was followed by emperors from Augustus to Trajan. As well as the Imperial Fora, emperors also erected triumphal arches to themselves, and just to the east Vespasian built the Colosseum, centre of entertainment after the business of the day.

Figure of barbarian on the Arch of Constantine

SIGHTS AT A GLANCE

Churches and Temples
Santa Francesca Romana ⑭
Temple of Antoninus and Faustina ⑪
Temple of Castor and Pollux ⑧
Temple of Romulus and Santi Cosma e Damiano ⑫
Temple of Saturn ⑤
Temple of Venus and Rome ⑰
Temple of Vesta ⑨

Historic Buildings
Basilica Aemilia ①
Basilica of Constantine and Maxentius ⑬
Basilica Julia ⑦

Casa dei Cavalieri di Rodi ㉑
Colosseum pp92–5 ㉗
Curia ②
House of the Vestal Virgins ⑩
Mamertine Prison ㉔
Torre delle Milizie ⑳
Trajan's Markets pp88–9 ⑱

Museums
Antiquarium Forense ⑮

Arches and Columns
Arch of Constantine ㉖
Arch of Septimius Severus ④
Arch of Titus ⑯
Column of Phocas ⑥
Trajan's Column ⑲

Ancient Sites
Forum of Augustus ㉒
Forum of Caesar ㉓
Forum of Nerva ㉕
Rostra ③

GETTING THERE
The simplest way is by Metro to Colosseo on line B. The main entrance to the Forum is on Via dei Fori Imperiali, served by buses 75, 85, 87, 117, 175, 186, 810 and 850. It is also a short walk from Piazza Venezia. For Trajan's Markets, the best buses are the 64 and 70 which stop in Via IV Novembre.

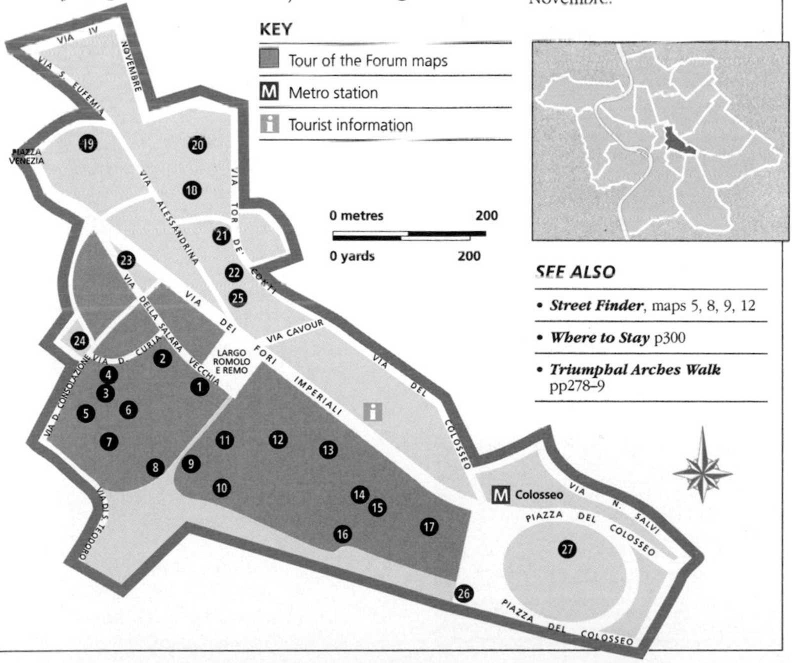

KEY
Tour of the Forum maps
M Metro station
i Tourist information

0 metres 200
0 yards 200

SEE ALSO
• *Street Finder*, maps 5, 8, 9, 12
• *Where to Stay* p300
• *Triumphal Arches Walk* pp278–9

◁ **View of the Forum with the Colosseum rising behind the bell tower of Santa Francesca Romana**

A Tour of the Roman Forum: West

To appreciate the layout of the Forum before visiting its confusing patchwork of ruined temples and basilicas, it is best to view the whole area from above, from the back of the Capitol. From there you can make out the Via Sacra (the Sacred Way), the route followed through the Forum by religious and triumphal processions towards the Capitol. Up until the 18th century when archaeological excavations began, the Arch of Septimius Severus and the columns of the Temple of Saturn lay half-buried underground. Excavation of the Forum continues, and the ruins uncovered date from many different periods of Roman history.

The Temple of Vespasian was the point from where Piranesi made this 18th-century engraving of the Forum. Its three columns were then almost completely buried.

Temple of Concord

Portico of the Dii Consentes

Temple of Saturn
The eight surviving columns of this temple stand close by the three columns of the Temple of Vespasian **5**

Rostra
These are the ruins of the platform used for public oratory in the Forum **3**

Basilica Julia
Named after Julius Caesar, who ordered its construction, the basilica housed important law courts **7**

Column of Phocas
One of the very last monuments erected in the Forum, this single column dates from AD 608 **6**

★ Arch of Septimius Severus
A 19th-century engraving shows the arch after the Forum was first excavated ❹

Santi Luca e Martina was an early medieval church, but was rebuilt in 1635–64 by Pietro da Cortona.

The Forum included the area under Via dei Fori Imperiali. More parts have now been made public.

LOCATOR MAP
See Central Rome Map pp14–15

STAR SIGHT

★ Arch of Septimius Severus

Curia
This 3rd-century rebuilding of the Curia was greatly restored in 1937 ❷

KEY

– – – Suggested route

| 0 metres | 75 |
| 0 yards | 75 |

Basilica Aemilia
This large meeting hall was razed to the ground in the 5th century AD ❶

VIA DELLA CURIA

VIA DELLA SALARA VECCHIA

VIA DEI FORI IMPERIALI

Entrance to Forum

The Temple of Julius Caesar was erected in his memory by Augustus on the spot where Caesar's body was cremated after his assassination in 44 BC.

Julius Caesar

To Roman Forum:
East
See pp80–81

Temple of Castor and Pollux
A temple to the twin brothers (of whom only Pollux was fathered by Jupiter) stood on this spot from the 5th century BC. This section of cornice and its supporting columns date from the rebuilding of AD 6 ❽

A Tour of the Roman Forum: East

The eastern end of the Roman Forum is dominated by the massive barrel-vaulted ruins of the Basilica of Constantine. To picture the building as it was in the 4th century AD, you must imagine marble columns, floors and statues, and glittering tiles of gilt bronze. The remains of the other important buildings are scanty, though the garden and ponds in the centre of the House of the Vestal Virgins make it a very attractive spot. The two churches in this part of the Forum cannot be reached from within the archaeological area, but are accessible from the road outside.

The Regia was the office of the Pontifex Maximus, the chief priest of ancient Rome.

To Forum entrance

Temple of Antoninus and Faustina
The portico of this temple, built in AD 141, has been incorporated in the church of San Lorenzo in Miranda ⑪

An early Iron Age necropolis was found here in 1902. Finds from it, such as this burial urn, are on view in the Antiquarium.

Temple of Vesta
Partly reconstructed, this tiny temple to the goddess of the hearth was one of ancient Rome's most sacred shrines ⑨

VIA SACRA

Temple of Romulus
This domed building from the 4th century AD has survived as part of the church of Santi Cosma e Damiano ⑫

★ House of the Vestal Virgins
The priestesses who tended the sacred flame in the Temple of Vesta lived here. The house was a large rectangular building around a central garden ⑩

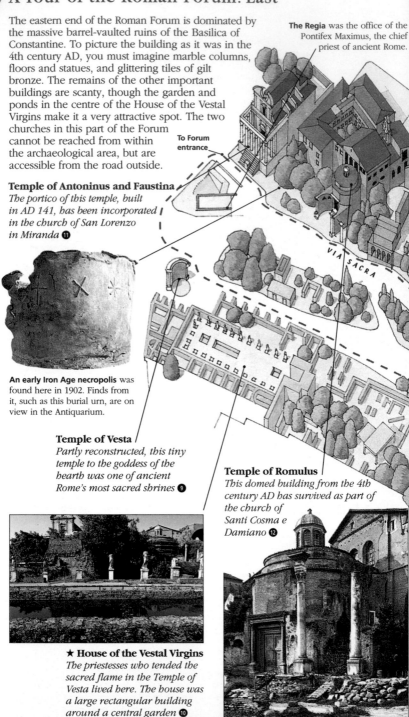

★ Basilica of Constantine and Maxentius
The stark remains of the basilica's huge arches and ceilings give some idea of the original scale and grandeur of the Forum's public buildings ⑬

LOCATOR MAP
See Central Rome Map pp14–15

Santa Francesca Romana
The church takes its name from a saint who cared for the Roman poor in the 15th century ⑭

VIA DEI FORI IMPERIALI

Antiquarium Forense
A small museum houses archaeological finds made in the Forum. They include this frieze of Aeneas and the Founding of Rome from the Basilica Aemilia ⑮

Colonnade surrounding Temple of Venus and Rome

Temple of Venus and Rome
These extensive ruins are of a magnificent temple, built here in AD 121 by the Emperor Hadrian, largely to his own design ⑰

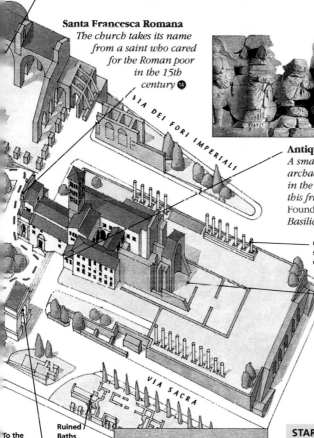

VIA SACRA

To the Palatine

Ruined Baths

Arch of Titus
This 19th-century reconstruction shows how the arch may have looked when it spanned the flagstoned roadway of the Via Sacra ⑯

STAR SIGHTS

★ House of the Vestal Virgins

★ Basilica of Constantine

KEY

‑ ‑ ‑ Suggested route

| 0 metres | 75 |
| 0 yards | 75 |

VISITORS' CHECKLIST

Entrances: Via della Salara
Vecchia 5/6. **Map** 5 B5 & 8 F1.
Tel 06-3996 7700. 🚌 85, 87,
117, 175, 186, 810, 850.
🚃 3. Ⓜ Colosseo. **Open**
8.30am–1 hour before sunset
daily (last adm: 1 hour before
closing). **Closed** 1 Jan, 25 Dec.
Adm charge (includes entry
to Colosseum and Palatine).

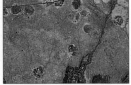

**Melted coins embedded in the floor
of the Basilica Aemilia**

Basilica Aemilia ❶

See Visitors' Checklist.

Originally this building was a
rectangular colonnaded hall,
with a multicoloured marble
floor and a bronze-tiled roof.
It was built by the consuls
Marcus Aemilius Lepidus and
Marcus Fulvius Nobilor in 179
BC. The two consuls, who
were elected annually,
exercised supreme power
over the Republic.

Basilicas in ancient Rome
served no religious purpose;
they were meeting halls for
politicians, moneylenders and
publicani (businessmen
contracted by the state to
collect taxes). A consortium
agreed to hand over a specified
sum to the state, but its
members were allowed to
collect as much as they
could and keep the difference.
This is why tax-collectors in
the Bible were so loathed.

The basilica was
rebuilt many times; it
was finally burned
down when the Visi-
goths sacked Rome in
AD 410. Business
seems to have carried
on until the last
moment, for the pave-
ment is splashed with
tiny lumps of coins
that melted in the fire.

Curia ❷

See Visitors' Checklist.

A modern restoration now
stands over the ruins of the
hall where Rome's Senate
(chief council of state) used
to meet. The first Curia stood
on the site now occupied
by the church of Santi
Luca e Martina, but
after the building
was destroyed by
fire in 52 BC, Julius
Caesar built a new
Curia at the edge
of the Forum. This
was restored by
Domitian in AD 94
and, after another
fire, rebuilt by
Diocletian in the 3rd
century. The building you see
today is a 1937 restoration of
Diocletian's Curia. Inside are
two relief panels commissioned
by Trajan to decorate the
Rostra. One shows Trajan
destroying records of unpaid
taxes to free citizens from debt;
in the other he sits on a throne
receiving a mother and child.

The Curia today

Rostra ❸

See Visitors' Checklist.

Ruins of the Imperial Rostra

Speeches were delivered from
this dais, the most famous –
thanks to Shakespeare –
being Mark Antony's "Friends,
Romans, Countrymen" oration
after the assassination of Julius
Caesar in 44 BC. Caesar
himself had just reorganized
the Forum and this speech
was made from the newly
sited Rostra, where the
ruins now stand. In
the following year
the head and
hands of Cicero
were put on show
here after he had
been put to death
by the second
Triumvirate
(Augustus, Mark
Antony and Marcus
Lepidus). Fulvia,
Mark Antony's
wife, stabbed the great
orator's tongue with a hairpin.
It was also here that Julia,
Augustus's daughter, was said
to have played the prostitute –
one of many scandalous acts
that led to her banishment.

The dais took its name from
the ships' prows *(rostra)* with
which it was decorated.
Sheathed in iron (for ramming
enemy vessels), these came
from ships captured at the
Battle of Antium in 338 BC.

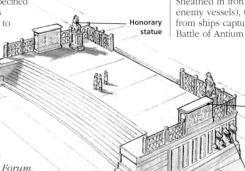

Honorary
statue

Relief panel
in balustrade,
showing
Trajan's acts
of charity

Prows of ships
(rostra)

Rostra
*This reconstruction
shows the platform for
public speaking in the Forum,
as it looked in Imperial times.*

Arch of Septimius Severus ❹

See Visitors' Checklist.

This triumphal arch, one of the most striking and best preserved monuments of the Forum, was erected in AD 203 to celebrate the tenth anniversary of the accession of Septimius Severus. The relief panels – largely eroded – celebrate the emperor's victories in Parthia (modern-day Iraq and Iran) and Arabia. Originally, the inscription along the top of the arch was to Septimius and his two sons, Caracalla and Geta, but after Septimius died Caracalla murdered Geta, and had his brother's name removed. Even so the holes into which the letters of his name were pegged are still visible.

Barbarian captives, Arch of Severus

During the Middle Ages the central arch, half buried in earth and debris, was used to shelter a barber's shop.

Triumphal arch of the Emperor Septimius Severus

Temple of Saturn ❺

See Visitors' Checklist.

The most prominent of the ruins in the fenced-off area between the Forum and the Capitoline hill is the Temple of Saturn. It consists of a high platform, eight columns and a section of entablature. There was a temple dedicated to

Ionic capitals on the surviving columns of the Temple of Saturn

Saturn here as early as 497 BC, but it had to be rebuilt many times and the current remains date only from 42 BC.

Saturn was the mythical god-king of Italy, said to have presided over a prosperous and peaceful Golden Age from which slavery, private property, crime and war were absent. As such, he appealed particularly to the lower and slave classes. Every year, between 17 December and 23 December, Saturn's reign was remembered in a week of sacrifices and feasting, known as the Saturnalia.

As long as the revels lasted, the normal social order was turned upside down. Slaves were permitted to drink and dine with (and sometimes even be served by) their masters. Senators and other high ranking Romans would abandon the aristocratic togas that they usually wore to distinguish themselves from the lower classes and wear more democratic, loose-fitting gowns. During the holidays, all the courts of law and schools in the city were closed. No prisoner could be punished, and no war could be declared.

People also celebrated the Saturnalia in their own homes: they exchanged gifts, in particular special wax dolls and wax tapers, and played light-hearted gambling games, the stakes usually being nuts, a symbol of fruitfulness. Much of the spirit and many of the rituals of the festival have been preserved in the Christian celebration of Christmas.

Column of Phocas ❻

See Visitors' Checklist.

This column, 13.5 m (44 ft) high, is one of the few to have remained upright since the day it was put up. Until 1816, when an inquisitive Englishwoman, Lady Elizabeth Foster, widow of the fifth Duke of Devonshire, decided to excavate its pedestal, nobody knew what it was. It turned out to be the youngest of the Forum's monuments, erected in AD 608 in honour of the Byzantine emperor, Phocas, who had just paid a visit to Rome. The column may have been placed here as a mark of gratitude to Phocas for giving the Pantheon to the pope *(see pp110–11).*

Slender, fluted Column of Phocas

Remains of the Basilica Julia, a Roman court of civil law

Basilica Julia ⑦

See Visitors' Checklist, p82.

This immense basilica, which occupied the area between the temple of Saturn and the temple of Castor and Pollux, was begun by Julius Caesar in 54 BC and completed after his death by his great-nephew Augustus. It was damaged by fire almost immediately afterwards in 9 BC, but was subsequently repaired and dedicated to the emperor's grandsons, Gaius and Lucius.

After numerous sackings and pilferings, only the steps, pavement and column stumps remain. Nevertheless the ground plan is fairly clear. The basilica had a central hall, measuring 80 m by 18 m

(260 ft by 59 ft), surrounded by a double portico. The hall was on three floors, while the outer portico had only two.

The Basilica Julia was the seat of the *centumviri*, a body of 180 magistrates who tried civil law cases. They were split into four chambers of 45 men, and unless a case was particularly complicated they would all sit separately.

The four courts were, however, divided only by screens or curtains, and the voices of lawyers and cheers and boos of spectators in the upper galleries echoed through the building. Lawyers used to hire crowds of spectators, who would applaud every time the lawyer who was paying them made a point and jeer at his opponents. The clappers and booers must have had a good deal of time on their hands: scratched into the steps are chequerboards where they played dice and other gambling games to while away the time between cases.

Temple of Castor and Pollux ⑧

See Visitors' Checklist, p82.

The three slender fluted columns of this temple form one of the Forum's most beautiful ruins. The first temple here was probably dedicated in 484 BC in honour of the mythical twins and patrons of horsemanship, Castor and Pollux. During the battle of Lake Regillus (499 BC) against the ousted Tarquin kings, the Roman dictator Postumius promised to build a temple to the twins if the Romans were victorious. Some said the twins appeared on the battlefield, helped the Romans to victory and then materialized in the Forum – the temple marks the spot – to announce the news.

The temple, like most buildings in the Forum, was rebuilt many times. The three surviving columns date from the last occasion on which it was rebuilt – by the future Emperor Tiberius after a fire in AD 6. For a long period the temple housed the city's office of weights and measures, and it was also used at times by a number of bankers.

Corinthian columns of the Temple of Castor and Pollux

Temple of Vesta ⑨

See Visitors' Checklist, p82.

The Forum's most elegant temple, a circular building originally surrounded by a ring of 20 fine fluted columns, dates from the 4th century AD, though there had been a temple on the site for far longer. It was partially reconstructed in 1930.

The cult of the Vestals was one of the oldest in Rome, and centred on six Vestal Virgins, who were required to

TEMPLE OF VESTA
The temple preserved the shape of an original primitive structure made of wooden posts with a thatched roof.

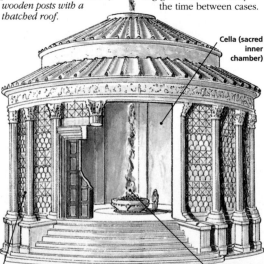

Cella (sacred inner chamber)

Ring of Corinthian columns

Sacred flame

keep alight the sacred flame of Vesta, the goddess of the hearth. This responsibility was originally entrusted to the daughters of the king, but it then passed to the Vestals, the only group of women priests in Rome. It was no easy task, as the flame was easily blown out. Any Vestal who allowed the flame to die was whipped by the high priest (Pontifex Maximus) and dismissed.

The girls, who had to belong to noble families, were selected when they were between 6 and 10 years old. They served for 30 years: the first ten were spent learning their duties, the next ten performing them and the final ten teaching novices. They enjoyed high status and financial security, but had to remain virgins. The penalty for transgressing was to be buried alive, although only ten Vestals are recorded as ever having suffered this fate. The men concerned were whipped to death. When Vestals retired, they were free to live the rest of their lives as ordinary citizens. If they wished they could marry, but few ever did.

Another of the Vestals' duties was to guard the Palladium, a sacred statue of the goddess Pallas Athenae. The irreverent Emperor Heliogabalus burgled the temple in the 3rd century AD. He thought he had succeeded in stealing the Palladium, but the Vestals had been warned of his intention and had replaced it with a replica.

Restored section of Temple of Vesta

Central courtyard of the House of the Vestal Virgins

House of the Vestal Virgins ❿

See Visitors' Checklist, p82.

As soon as a girl became a Vestal she came to live in the House of the Vestal Virgins. Originally this was an enormous complex with about 50 rooms on three storeys. The only substantial remains today are some of the rooms around the central courtyard. This space is perhaps the most evocative part of the Forum. Overlooking ponds of water lilies and plump goldfish is a row of eroded, and mostly headless, statues of senior Vestals, dating from the 3rd and 4th

Honorary statue of a Vestal Virgin

centuries AD. The better-preserved examples were transferred to the Museo Nazionale Romano (see p163). On one of the pedestals the inscription has been removed because the Vestal in question suffered some disgrace. It is thought she may have been a certain Claudia, known to have betrayed the cult by converting to Christianity.

Though many of the rooms surrounding the courtyard are well preserved – some even retain flights of steps leading to an upper floor – you are not allowed inside them. If you peep into the series of rooms along the south side, however, you might be able

to see the remains of a mill, used for grinding the grain with which the Vestals made a special sacrificial cake. The bakery was next door.

Temple of Antoninus and Faustina ⓫

See Visitors' Checklist, p82.

One of the Forum's oddest sights is the Baroque façade of the church of San Lorenzo in Miranda rising above the porch of a Roman temple. First dedicated in AD 141 by the Emperor Antoninus Pius to his late wife Faustina, the temple was rededicated to them both on the death of the emperor. In the 11th century it was converted into a church because it was believed that San Lorenzo (St Lawrence) had been condemned to death there. The current church dates from 1601.

Temple of Antoninus and Faustina

Temple of Romulus and Santi Cosma e Damiano ⑫

See Visitors' Checklist, p82.
Santi Cosma e Damiano
Tel 06-692 0441.
Open 9am–1pm, 3–7pm daily.
Crib closed Mon–Thu.
Adm charge for crib. 🚻 ♿

No one is sure to whom the Temple of Romulus was dedicated, but it was probably to the son of Emperor Maxentius, and not to Rome's founder.

The temple is a circular brick building, topped by a cupola, with two rectangular side rooms and a concave porch. The heavy, dull bronze doors are original.

Since the 6th century the temple has acted as a vestibule to the church of Santi Cosma e Damiano, which itself occupies an ancient building – a hall in Vespasian's Forum of Peace. The entrance to the church is on Via dei Fori Imperiali. The beautiful carved figures of its 18th-century Neapolitan *presepio* (crib or Nativity scene) are back on view now, and the church has a vivid Byzantine apse mosaic with Christ pictured against orange clouds.

Roof of the Temple of Romulus

Basilica of Constantine and Maxentius ⑬

See Visitors' Checklist, p82.

The basilica's three vast, coffered barrel vaults are powerful relics of what was the largest building in the Forum. Work began in AD 308 under the Emperor Maxentius. When he was deposed by Constantine after the Battle of the Milvian Bridge in AD 312, work on the massive project continued under the new regime. The building, which, like other Roman basilicas, was used for the administration of justice and for carrying on business, is often referred to simply as the Basilica of Constantine.

The area covered by the basilica was roughly 100 m by 65 m (330 ft by 215 ft). It was originally designed to have a long nave and aisles running from east to west, but Constantine switched the axis around to create three short broad aisles with the main entrance in the centre of the long south wall. The height of the building was 35 m (115 ft). In the apse at the western end, where it could be seen from all over the building, stood a 12-m (39-ft) statue of the emperor, made partly of wood and partly of marble. The giant head, hand and foot are on display in the courtyard of the Palazzo dei Conservatori *(see pp72–3)*. The roof of the basilica glittered with gilded tiles until the 7th century when they were stripped off to cover the roof of the old St Peter's.

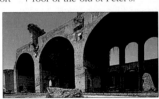

The three barrel-vaulted aisles of the basilica were used as law courts.

The octagonal coffers in the vaulted ceiling were originally faced with marble.

The main entrance was added by Constantine in AD 313.

The roof was supported by eight massive Corinthian columns. One now stands in Piazza Santa Maria Maggiore *(see p173)*.

Santa Francesca Romana

Piazza di Santa Francesca Romana. **Map** 5 B5. *Tel* 06-679 5528. 85, 87, 117, 175, 810. 3. Colosseo. **Open** 10.30am–noon, 4.30–5.30pm daily (times may vary).

Every year on 9 March devout Roman drivers try to park as close as possible to this Baroque church with a Romanesque bell tower. The aim of their pilgrimage is to have their vehicles blessed by Santa Francesca Romana, the patron saint of motorists. During the 15th century, Francesca of Trastevere founded a society of pious women devoted to helping the less fortunate. After her canonization in 1608 the church, originally named Santa Maria Nova, was rededicated to Francesca.

Bell tower of Santa Francesca

The most curious sight inside the church is a flagstone with what are said to be the imprints of the knees of St Peter and St Paul. A magician, Simon Magus, decided to prove that his powers were superior to those of the Apostles by levitating above the Forum. As Simon was in mid-air, Peter and Paul fell to their knees and prayed fervently for God to humble him, and Simon immediately plummeted to his death.

Antiquarium Forense

See Visitors' Checklist, p82.

The former convent of Santa Francesca Romana is now occupied by the offices in charge of the excavations of the Forum and a small museum. The latter is currently being reorganized, and only a couple of rooms are open. They contain Iron Age burial urns, graves and their skeletal occupants along with some ancient bric-a-brac exhumed from the Forum's drains. When the reorganization is complete you should be able to see fragments of statues, capitals, friezes and other architectural decoration taken from the Forum's buildings.

Frieze of Aeneas in the Antiquarium Forense

Arch of Titus

See Visitors' Checklist, p82.

This triumphal arch was erected in AD 81 by the Emperor Domitian in honour of the victories of his brother, Titus, and his father, Vespasian, in Judaea. In AD 66 the Jews, weary of being exploited by unscrupulous Roman officials, rebelled. A bitter war broke out which ended four years later in the fall of Jerusalem and the Jewish Diaspora.

Although the reliefs inside the arch are badly eroded, you can make out a triumphant procession of Roman soldiers carrying off spoils from the Temple of Jerusalem. The booty includes the altar, silver trumpets and a golden seven-branched candelabrum.

Temple of Venus and Rome

See Visitors' Checklist, p82.

The emperor Hadrian designed this temple to occupy what had been the vestibule to Nero's Domus Aurea (see p175). Many of the columns have been re-erected, and though there is no access, there is a good view as you leave the Forum and from the upper tiers of the Colosseum. The temple, the largest in Rome, was dedicated to Roma, the personification of the city, and to Venus because she was the mother of Aeneas, father of Romulus and Remus. Each goddess had her own *cella* (shrine). When the architect Apollodorus pointed out that the seated statues in the niches were too big (had they tried to "stand" their heads would have hit the vaults), Hadrian had him put to death.

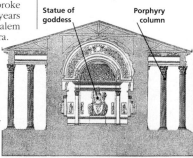
Statue of goddess — Porphyry column
Cross-section of Temple of Venus and Rome

Dedication to Titus and Vespasian on the Arch of Titus

Trajan's Markets ⑱

Originally considered among the wonders of the Classical world, Trajan's Markets now show only a hint of their former splendour. Emperor Trajan and his architect, Apollodorus of Damascus, built this visionary new complex of 150 shops and offices (probably used for administering the corn dole) in the early 2nd century AD. It was the ancient Roman equivalent of the modern shopping centre, selling everything from silks and spices imported from the Middle East to fresh fish, fruit and flowers.

The Markets Today
Above the façade stands the 13th-century Torre delle Milizie, built for defensive purposes.

Cross vaulting

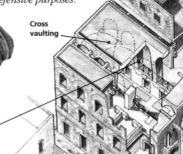

Trajan
The emperor was a benevolent ruler and a successful general.

Main Hall
Twelve shops were built on two floors, and the corn dole was shared out on the upper storey. This was a free corn ration given to Roman men to prevent hunger.

Via Biberatica
The main street which runs through the market is named after the drinking inns which once lined it.

Small semicircle of shops

Staircase

TIMELINE

AD 100–112 Building of Trajan's Markets	**472** Invasion by Ricimer the Suevian. Some of his Germanic troops stationed here	**1200s** Torre delle Milizie built on top of the markets	**1572** Convent of Santa Caterina da Siena built over part of markets	**1924** Many medieval houses demolished

AD 100	AD 500	1000	1300		1800	1950

AD 117 Death of Trajan	**552** Byzantine takeover of Rome. Markets occupied and fortified by the army	**1300s** Annibaldi and Caetani families vie for control of the area	**1828** First tentative excavations, but value of site not recognized	**1911–14** Convent demolished
AD 98 Trajan succeeds Nerva as emperor				**1930–33** Markets finally excavated

VISITORS' CHECKLIST

Mercati Traianei, Via IV Novembre.
Map 5 B4.
Tel 06-6992 3521.
64, 70, 170 and many routes to Piazza Venezia.
Open 9am–6.45pm.
Closed 1 Jan, 25 Dec.
Last adm: 45 mins before closing. 🚻 ♿

The Markets in the 16th Century
This fanciful fresco depicts a gladiatorial combat taking place in front of the partly buried remains of Trajan's Markets.

A Market Shop
Shops were built with arched entrances, with jambs and lintels creating rectangular portals and windows. A wooden mezzanine was used for storage.

Upper Corridor
Shops on this upper level were thought to have sold wine and oil, since a number of storage jars were discovered here.

The terrace over the archway spanning Via Biberatica has a good view of the Forum of Trajan below.

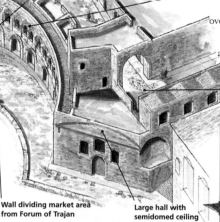

Wall dividing market area from Forum of Trajan

Large hall with semidomed ceiling

Forum of Trajan, built in front of the markets in AD 107–113, was flanked by the Basilica Ulpia. The basilica, measuring 170 m (558 ft) by 60 m (197 ft), was the largest in Rome. A small portion of the Forum has been excavated; unfortunately, however, the rest of it remains buried beneath modern Rome's busy city streets.

MARKET SHOPPING

Shops opened early and closed about noon. The best ones were decorated with mosaics of the goods they sold. Almost all the shopping was done by men, though women visited the dressmaker and cobbler. The tradesmen were almost all male. In employment records for the period AD 117–193, the only female shopkeepers mentioned are three wool-sellers, two jewellers, a greengrocer and a fishwife.

Fish mosaic

Trajan's Markets ⑱

See pp88–9.

Trajan's Column ⑲

Via dei Fori Imperiali. **Map** 5 A4 &
12 F4. *See Visitors' Checklist for
Trajan's Markets, p89.*

Detail of Trajan's Column

This elegant marble column
was inaugurated by Trajan in
AD 113, and celebrates his
two campaigns in Dacia
(Romania) in AD 101–3 and
AD 107–8. The column, base
and pedestal are 40 m (131 ft)
tall – precisely the same height
as the spur of the Quirinal hill
which was excavated to make
room for Trajan's Forum.
Spiralling up the column are
minutely detailed scenes from
the campaigns, beginning with
the Romans preparing for war
and ending with the Dacians
being ousted from their
homeland. The column is
pierced with small windows
to illuminate its internal spiral
staircase (closed to the public).
If you wish to see the reliefs
in detail there is a complete
set of casts in the Museo
della Civiltà Romana at EUR
(see p266).
When Trajan died in AD 117
his ashes, along with those of
his wife Plotina, were placed
in a golden urn in the column's
hollow base. The column's
survival was largely thanks
to the intervention of Pope
Gregory the Great (reigned
590–604). He was so moved
by a relief showing Trajan
helping a woman whose son
had been killed that he begged
God to release the emperor's
soul from hell. God duly

appeared to the pope to say
that Trajan had been rescued,
but asked him not to pray for
the souls of any more pagans.
According to legend, when
Trajan's ashes were exhumed
his skull and tongue were not
only intact, but his tongue
told of his release from hell.
The land around the column
was then declared sacred and
the column itself was spared.
The statue of Trajan remained
on top of the column until
1587, when it was replaced
with one of St Peter.

Torre delle Milizie ⑳

Mercati Traianei, Via IV Novembre.
Map 5 B4. **Tel** 06-679 0048.
Closed to the public.

For centuries this massive
brick tower was thought to
have been the one in which
Nero stood watching Rome
burn, after he had set it alight
to clear the city's slums. It is
uncertain whether arson was
among Nero's crimes, but it is
certain that he did not watch
the fire from this tower – it
was built in the 13th century.

Casa dei Cavalieri di Rodi ㉑

Piazza del Grillo 1. **Map** 5 B5. **Tel**
06-0608. 🚌 84, 85, 87, 117, 175,
186, 810, 850. **Open** Tue am, Thu
am (by appt only, well in advance).

Loggia, Casa dei Cavalieri di Rodi

Since the 12th century the
crusading order, the Knights of
St John, also known as the
Knights of Rhodes (Rodi) or
Malta, have had their priorate
in this medieval house above
the Forum of Augustus. If you
are lucky enough to get
inside, ask to see the beautiful
Cappella di San Giovanni
(Chapel of St John).

Forum of Augustus ㉒

Piazza del Grillo 1. **Map** 5 B5 & 12 F5.
*See Trajan's Markets' Visitors' Checklist,
p89.* **Tel** 06-0608. **Open** by appt.

**Podium of the Temple of Mars in
the Forum of Augustus**

The Forum of Augustus
was built to celebrate
Augustus's victory over Julius
Caesar's assassins, Brutus and
Cassius, at the Battle of
Philippi in 41 BC. The temple
in its centre was dedicated to
Mars the Avenger. The forum
stretched from a high wall at
the foot of the sleazy Suburra
quarter to the edge of the
Forum of Caesar. At least half
of it is now concealed below
Mussolini's Via dei Fori
Imperiali. The temple is easily
identified, with its cracked
steps and four Corinthian
columns. Originally it had a
statue of Mars which looked
very like Augustus. In case
anyone failed to notice the
resemblance, a giant statue of
Augustus himself was placed
against the Suburra wall.

Forum of Caesar ㉓

Via del Carcere Tulliano. **Map** 5 A5.
Tel 06-0608. 🚌 84, 85, 87, 175,
186, 810. 850. **Open** to research
scholars by appt only.

The first of Rome's Imperial
fora was built by Julius
Caesar. He spent a fortune –
most of it booty from his
conquest of Gaul – buying up
and demolishing houses on
the site. Pride of place went
to a temple dedicated in 46
BC to the goddess Venus
Genetrix, from whom Caesar
claimed descent. The temple
contained statues of Caesar
and Cleopatra as well as of
Venus. All that remains of this
temple to vanity is a platform

and three Corinthian columns. The forum was enclosed by a double colonnade which sheltered a row of shops, but this burned down in AD 80 and was rebuilt by Domitian and Trajan. Trajan also added the Basilica Argentaria and a heated public lavatory.

The forum is only open to the public by appointment, but parts are visible from above in Via dei Fori Imperiali.

Mamertine Prison ❷

Clivo Argentario 1. **Map** 5 A5. **Tel** 06-679 2902. 84, 85, 87, 175, 186, 810, 850. **Closed** for restoration; call 06-0608 for information.

19th-century engraving of guards visiting prisoners in the Mamertine

Below the 16th-century church of San Giuseppe dei Falegnami (St Joseph of the Carpenters) is a dank dungeon in which, according to Christian legend, St Peter was imprisoned. He is said to have caused a spring to bubble up into the cell, and used the water to baptize his guards.

The prison, also known as Tullianum, was in an old cistern with access to the city's main sewer (the Cloaca Maxima). The lower cell was used for executions and bodies were thrown into the sewer. Among the enemies of Rome to be executed here was the Gaulish leader Vercingetorix, defeated by Julius Caesar in 52 BC.

17th-century view of the ruined Forum of Nerva

Forum of Nerva ❷

Piazza del Grillo 1 (reached through Forum of Augustus). **Map** 5 B5. **Tel** 06-0608. 84, 85, 87, 175, 186, 810, 850. **Open** by appt only.

The Forum of Nerva was begun by his predecessor, Domitian, and completed in AD 97. Little more than a long corridor with a colonnade along the sides and a Temple of Minerva at one end, it was also known as the Forum Transitorium because it lay between the Forum of Peace built by the Emperor Vespasian in AD 70 and the Forum of Augustus. Vespasian's forum is almost completely covered by Via dei Fori Imperiali, as is much of the Forum of Nerva itself. Excavations have unearthed Renaissance shops and

taverns, but only part of the forum can be seen, including the base of the temple and two columns that were part of the original colonnade. These support a relief of Minerva above a frieze of young girls learning to sew and weave.

Arch of Constantine ❷

Between Via di San Gregorio and Piazza del Colosseo. **Map** 8 F1. 75, 85, 87, 175, 673, 810. 3. Ⓜ Colosseo.

This triumphal arch was dedicated in AD 315 to celebrate Constantine's victory three years before over his co-emperor, Maxentius. Constantine claimed he owed his victory to a vision of Christ, but there is nothing Christian about the arch – in fact, most of the medallions, reliefs and statues were scavenged from earlier monuments.

There are statues of Dacian prisoners taken from Trajan's Forum and reliefs of Marcus Aurelius, including one where he distributes bread to the poor. Inside the arch are reliefs of Trajan's victory over the Dacians. These were probably by the artist who worked on Trajan's Column.

Medallion on the Arch of Constantine

Colosseum ❷

See pp92–5.

North side of the Arch of Constantine, facing the Colosseum

Colosseum ㉗

Rome's greatest amphitheatre was commissioned by the Emperor Vespasian in AD 72 on the marshy site of a lake in the grounds of Nero's palace, the Domus Aurea *(see p175).* Deadly gladiatorial combats and wild animal fights were staged free of charge by the emperor and wealthy citizens for public viewing. The Colosseum was built to a practical design, with its 80 arched entrances allowing easy access to 55,000 spectators, but it is also a building of great beauty. The drawing here shows how it looked at the time of its opening in AD 80. It was one of several similar amphitheatres built in the Roman Empire, and some survive at El Djem in North Africa, Nîmes and Arles in France, and Verona in northern Italy. Despite being damaged over the years by neglect and theft, it remains a majestic sight.

Outer Wall of the Colosseum
Stone plundered from the façade in the Renaissance was used to build several palaces, bridges and parts of St Peter's.

The Founder of the Colosseum
Vespasian was a professional soldier who became emperor in AD 69, founding the Flavian dynasty.

The outer walls are made of travertine.

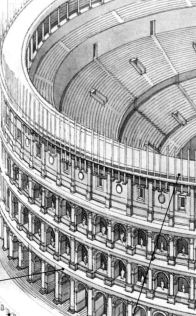

FLORA OF THE COLOSSEUM

By the 19th century the Colosseum was heavily overgrown. Different micro-climates in various parts of the ruin had created an impressive variety of herbs, grasses and wild flowers. Several botanists were inspired to study and catalogue them and two books were published, one listing 420 different species.

Borage, a herb

The bollards anchored the velarium.

The velarium was a huge awning which shaded spectators from the sun. Supported on poles fixed to the upper storey of the building, it was then hoisted into position with ropes anchored to bollards outside the stadium.

TIMELINE

80 Vespasian's son, Titu stages inaugural festival in the amphitheatre. It lasts 100 days

AD 70		10⬤
72 Emperor Vespasian begins work on the Colosseum	**81–96** Amphi-theatre complete in reign Domitiar	

Internal Corridors
These were designed to allow the large and often unruly crowd to move freely and to be seated within ten minutes of arriving at the Colosseum.

The **vomitorium** was the exit used from each numbered section.

Brick formed the inner walls.

VISITORS' CHECKLIST

Piazza del Colosseo. **Map** 9 A1.
Tel 06-3996 7700. 🚌 75, 81, 85, 87, 117, 175, 673, 810. 🚊 3 to Piazza del Colosseo. Ⓜ Colosseo. **Open** 8.30am–1 hour before sunset daily. **Closed** 1 Jan, 25 Dec. **Adm charge** *(includes the Palatine & Forum)*. ♿ limited. 🎦 📷 📖 **Beware** of "gladiators" who will charge you for photographs.

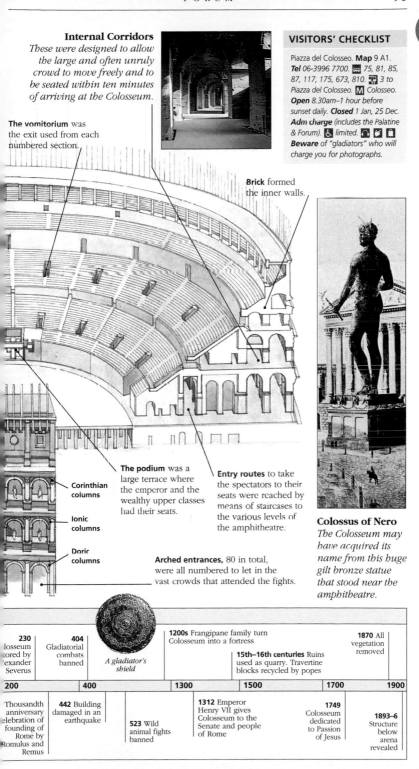

Corinthian columns

Ionic columns

Doric columns

The podium was a large terrace where the emperor and the wealthy upper classes had their seats.

Entry routes to take the spectators to their seats were reached by means of staircases to the various levels of the amphitheatre.

Arched entrances, 80 in total, were all numbered to let in the vast crowds that attended the fights.

Colossus of Nero
The Colosseum may have acquired its name from this huge gilt bronze statue that stood near the amphitheatre.

A gladiator's shield

230 Colosseum restored by Alexander Severus	**404** Gladiatorial combats banned		**1200s** Frangipane family turn Colosseum into a fortress			**1870** All vegetation removed
				15th–16th centuries Ruins used as quarry. Travertine blocks recycled by popes		
200	**400**	**1300**	**1500**		**1700**	**1900**
Thousandth anniversary celebration of founding of Rome by Romulus and Remus	**442** Building damaged in an earthquake	**523** Wild animal fights banned	**1312** Emperor Henry VII gives Colosseum to the Senate and people of Rome		**1749** Colosseum dedicated to Passion of Jesus	**1893–6** Structure below arena revealed

How Fights were Staged in the Arena

The emperors held shows here which often began with animals performing circus tricks. Then on came the gladiators, who fought each other to the death. When one was killed, attendants dressed as Charon, the mythical ferryman of the dead, carried his body off on a stretcher, and sand was raked over the blood ready for the next bout. A badly wounded gladiator would surrender his fate to the crowd. The "thumbs up" sign from the emperor meant he could live, "thumbs down" that he die, and the victor became an instant hero. Animals were brought here from as far away as North Africa and the Middle East. The games held in AD 248 to mark the thousandth anniversary of Rome's founding saw the death of a host of lions, elephants, hippos, zebras and elks.

Beneath the Arena
Late 19th-century excavations exposed the network of underground rooms where the animals were kept.

Interior of the Colosseum
The amphitheatre was built in the form of an ellipse, with tiers of seats around a vast central arena.

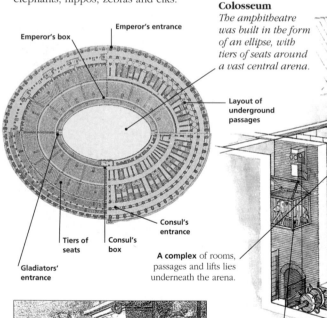

Emperor's box

Emperor's entrance

Layout of underground passages

Tiers of seats

Consul's box

Consul's entrance

Gladiators' entrance

A complex of rooms, passages and lifts lies underneath the arena.

Dramatic Entrances
Below the sand was a wooden floor through which animals, men and scenery appeared in the arena.

Roman Gladiators
These were usually slaves, prisoners of war or condemned criminals. Most were men, but there were a few female gladiators.

The Colosseum by Antonio Canaletto
This 18th-century view of the Colosseum shows the Meta Sudans fountain (now demolished). Water "sweated" from a metal ball on top of its brick cone.

Metal fencing kept animals penned in, while archers stood by just in case any escaped.

Seating was tiered, and different social classes were segregated.

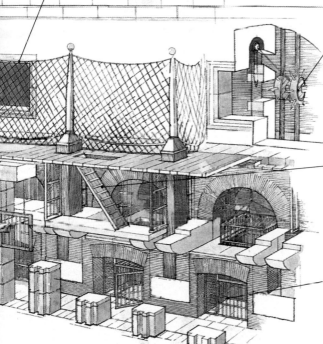

A winch brought the animal cages up to arena level when they were due to fight.

A ramp and trap door enabled the animal to reach the arena after walking along a corridor.

Cages were like three-sided lifts which went up to the next level where the animals were released.

SEA BATTLES IN THE ARENA

The historian Dion Cassius, writing in the 4th century AD, relates how, 150 years earlier, the Colosseum's arena was flooded to stage a mock sea battle. Scholars now believe that he was mistaken. The spectacle probably took place in the Naumachia of Augustus, a water-filled arena situated across the Tiber in Trastevere.

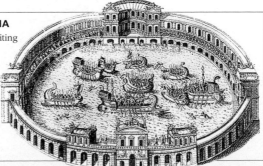

PALATINE

According to legend, Romulus and Remus were brought up here by a wolf in a cave. Traces of Iron Age huts, dating from the 9th century BC, have been found on the Palatine hill, providing archaeological support for the area's legendary links with the founding of Rome. The Palatine was a very desirable place to live, becoming home to some of the city's most famous inhabitants. The great orator Cicero had a house here, as did the lyric poet Catullus. Augustus was born on the hill and continued to live here in very modest

Fresco of mask in the House of Augustus

circumstances even when he became emperor. The two buildings identified as the House of Augustus and the House of Livia, his wife, are among the best preserved here. The first emperor's example of frugality was ignored by his successors, Tiberius, Caligula and Domitian, who all built extravagant palaces here. The ruins of Tiberius's palace lie beneath the 16th-century Farnese Gardens. The most extensive ruins are those of the Domus Augustana and Domus Flavia, the two wings of Domitian's palace, and the later extension built by Septimius Severus.

SIGHTS AT A GLANCE

Temples
Temple of Cybele ⑥

Historic Buildings
Domus Augustana ③
Domus Flavia ①
House of Livia ⑤

Ancient Sites
Cryptoporticus ②
Huts of Romulus ⑦
Stadium ④

Parks and Gardens
Farnese Gardens ⑧

SEE ALSO
• *Street Finder*, map 8

GETTING THERE
There are two ways of getting on to the Palatine hill; either through the Roman Forum (from Via dei Fori Imperiali) or through the entrance in Via di San Gregorio. A separate ticket for the Palatine is needed, even if you come through the Forum. The best buses are the 75, 85, 87, 117, 175, 186, 810, 850; all stop in Via dei Fori Imperiali near the main entrance. Tram 3 and Colosseo Metro station are also handy.

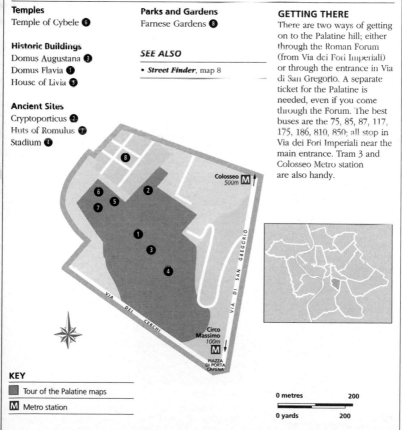

KEY

▉	Tour of the Palatine maps
Ⓜ	Metro station

0 metres 200
0 yards 200

◁ **Towering ruins of the Palace of Septimius Severus on the Palatine hill**

A Tour of the Palatine

Shaded on its lower slopes with pines, and scattered in spring with wild flowers, the Palatine is the most pleasant and relaxing of the city's ancient sites. You can reach the hill by walking up from the Roman Forum *(see pp76–7)*. The area is dominated by the ruins of the Domus Flavia and the Domus Augustana, two parts of Domitian's huge palace built at the end of the 1st century AD. What you are able to see depends on where excavations are taking place at the time.

Huts of Romulus
These are traces of a 9th-century BC village on the Palatine ⑦

To Farnese Gardens
See p101

House of Augustus

Temple of Cybele
Also known as the Temple of the Magna Mater, this was the centre of an important fertility cult ⑥

★ House of Livia
Many of the wall paintings have survived in the house where Augustus lived with his wife Livia ⑤

STAR SIGHTS

★ House of Livia

★ Domus Flavia

KEY

– – – Suggested route

| 0 metres | 75 |
| 0 yards | 75 |

★ Domus Flavia
This oval fountain was designed to be seen from the dining hall of the palace ①

Domus Augustana
The Roman emperors lived in this part of the palace, while the Domus Flavia was used for public functions ③

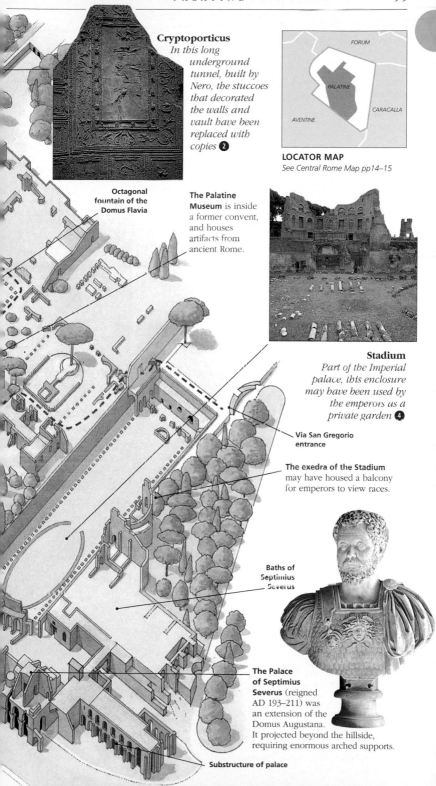

Cryptoporticus
In this long underground tunnel, built by Nero, the stuccoes that decorated the walls and vault have been replaced with copies **2**

LOCATOR MAP
See Central Rome Map pp14–15

Octagonal fountain of the Domus Flavia

The Palatine Museum is inside a former convent, and houses artifacts from ancient Rome.

Stadium
Part of the Imperial palace, this enclosure may have been used by the emperors as a private garden **4**

Via San Gregorio entrance

The exedra of the Stadium may have housed a balcony for emperors to view races.

Baths of Septimius Severus

The Palace of Septimius Severus (reigned AD 193–211) was an extension of the Domus Augustana. It projected beyond the hillside, requiring enormous arched supports.

Substructure of palace

VISITORS' CHECKLIST

Entrances & ticket kiosks: Via
di San Gregorio 30.
Map 8 E1–8 F1. **Tel** 06-3996
7700. 75, 85, 87, 117, 175,
186, 810, 850 to Via dei Fori
Imperiali. 3. M Colosseo.
Open 8.30am–1 hour before
sunset daily; last adm: 1 hour
before closing. **Closed** 1 Jan,
25 Dec. **Adm charge** (includes
entry to the Palatine Museum,
the Forum & the Colosseum)
(see pp92–5).

Domus Flavia ❶

See Visitors' Checklist.

**Marble pavement in the courtyard
of the Domus Flavia**

In AD 81 Domitian, the third
of the Flavian dynasty of
emperors, decided to build a
splendid new palace on the
Palatine hill. But the western
peak, the Germalus, was
covered with houses and temples, while the eastern peak,
the Palatium, was very steep.
So the emperor's architect,
Rabirius, flattened the
Palatium and used the soil to
fill in the cleft between the
two peaks, burying (and
preserving) a number of
Republican-era houses.

The palace had two wings –
one official (the Domus
Flavia), the other private (the
Domus Augustana). It was the
main Imperial palace for 300
years. At the front of the
Domus Flavia, the surviving
stubs of columns and fragments of walls trace the
shapes of three adjoining
rooms. In the first of these, the
Basilica, Domitian dispensed
his personal brand of justice.

The central Aula Regia was a
throne room decorated with
12 black basalt statues. The
third room (now covered
with corrugated plastic) was
the Lararium, a shrine for the
household gods known as
Lares (usually the owner's
ancestors). It may have been
used for official ceremonies
or by the palace guards.

Fearing assassination,
Domitian had the walls of the
courtyard covered with shiny
marble slabs designed to act
as mirrors so that he could
see anyone lurking behind
him. In the event, he was
assassinated in his bedroom,
possibly on the orders of his
wife, Domitia. The courtyard
is now a pleasant place to
pause; the flower beds in the
centre follow the maze pattern
of a sunken fountain pool.

Cryptoporticus ❷

See Visitors' Checklist.

The Cryptoporticus, a series
of underground corridors,
was built by Nero to connect
his Domus Aurea *(see p175)*
with the palaces of earlier
emperors on the Palatine. A
further branch leading to the
Palace of Domitian was added
later. Its vaults are decorated
with delicate stucco reliefs –
copies of originals now kept
in the Palatine's museum.

Domus Augustana ❸

See Visitors' Checklist.

This part of Domitian's
palace was called the Domus
Augustana because it was
the private residence of the
"august" emperors. On the
upper level a high brick wall

remains, and you can make
out the shape of its two
courtyards. The far better-
preserved lower level is closed
to the public, though you can
look down on its sunken
courtyard with the geometric
foundations of a fountain in
its centre. Sadly, you can't see
the stairs linking the two levels
(once lit by sunlight falling
on a mirror-paved pool),
nor the surrounding rooms,
paved with coloured marble.

Stadium ❹

See Visitors' Checklist.

Stadium viewed from the south

The Stadium on the Palatine
was laid out at the same time
as the Palace of Domitian. It
is not clear whether it was a
public stadium, a private track
for exercising horses, or
simply a large garden. The
alcove in the eastern wall
looks as though it may have
held a box from which the
emperor could have watched
races. It is, however, known
that the Stadium was used for
foot races by the Ostrogothic
king, Theodoric, in the 6th
century – he added the small
oval-shaped enclosure at the
southern end of the site.

Remains of the Domus Augustana and the Palace of Septimius Severus

House of Livia

See Visitors' Checklist. If closed, apply to custodian.

Fresco in the House of Livia

This house dating from the 1st century BC is one of the best preserved on the Palatine. It was probably part of the house in which the Emperor Augustus and his wife Livia lived. Compared with later Imperial palaces, it is a relatively modest home. According to Suetonius, the biographer of Rome's early emperors, Augustus slept in the same small bedroom for 40 years on a low bed which had "a very ordinary coverlet".

Detail of floor mosaic

A flight of steps leads down to a mosaic-paved corridor into a courtyard. Its imitation-marble wall frescoes have been detached in order to preserve them, but they still hang in situ. They are faded, but you can still make out the veining patterns. Off the courtyard are three small reception rooms. The frescoes in the central one include a faded scene of Hermes coming to the rescue of Zeus's beloved Io, who is guarded by the 100-eyed Argos. In the left-hand room are frescoed figures of griffins and other beasts, while the decor in the right-hand room includes landscapes and cityscapes.

In the nearby House of Augustus are four excavated rooms (entrance hall, dining room, bedroom and study) of what is believed to have been Augustus' original home before becoming

emperor. Dating from c. 30 BC, they are brilliantly frescoed with geometric designs and *trompe l'oeil* effects. Only five visitors at a time are allowed.

Temple of Cybele

See Visitors' Checklist.

Other than a platform with a few column stumps and capitals, there is little to see of the Temple of Cybele, a popular fertility goddess imported to Rome from Asia. The priests of the cult castrated themselves in the belief that if they sacrificed their own fertility it would guarantee that of the natural world.

The annual festival of Cybele, in early spring, culminated with frenzied eunuch-priests slashing their bodies to offer up their blood to the goddess, and the ceremonial castration of novice priests.

Statue of the goddess Cybele

Huts of Romulus

See Visitors' Checklist.

According to legend, after killing his brother Remus, Romulus founded a village

on the Palatine. In the 1940s a series of holes was found filled with earth lighter in colour than the surrounding soil. Archaeologists deduced that these holes must originally have held the supporting poles of three Iron Age huts – the first foundations of Rome (*see pp18–19*).

Farnese Gardens

See Visitors' Checklist.

In the mid-16th century Cardinal Alessandro Farnese, grandson of Pope Paul III, bought the ruins of Tiberius's palace on the Palatine. He filled in the ruined building and had Vignola, architect of the interior of the Gesù church, design a garden for him. The result was one of the first botanical gardens in Europe, its terraces linked by steps stretching from the House of Vestal Virgins in the Forum to the Palatine's Germalus peak. The gardeners introduced a number of plants to Italy and Europe, among them *Acacia farnesiana*. Farnese was at the centre of a glittering set which included a number of courtesans, so the parties here are likely to have been somewhat unholy.

The area was dug up during the excavation of the Palatine and relandscaped afterwards. Nevertheless the tree lined avenues, rose gardens and glorious views still make it an ideal place to unwind.

Farnese pavilions, relics of the age when the Palatine was a private garden

PIAZZA DELLA ROTONDA

The Pantheon, one of the great buildings in the history of European architecture, has stood at the heart of Rome for nearly 2,000 years. The historic area around it has seen uninterrupted economic and political activity throughout that time. Palazzo di Montecitorio, built for Pope Innocent XII as a papal tribunal in 1694, is now the Italian parliament and many nearby buildings are government offices. This is also the main financial district of Rome with banking headquarters and the stock exchange. Not many people live here, but in the evenings, Romans stroll in the narrow streets and fill the lively restaurants and cafés that make this a focus for the city's social life.

Bitter-style apéritif, popular in Roman cafés

SIGHTS AT A GLANCE

Churches and Temples
Gesù pp114–15 **9**
La Maddalena **15**
Pantheon pp110–11 **13**
San Lorenzo in Lucina **20**
Sant'Eustachio **14**
Sant'Ignazio di Loyola **3**
Santa Maria in
  Campo Marzio **18**
Santa Maria sopra Minerva **11**
Temple of Hadrian **1**

Historic Streets and Piazzas
Piazza di Sant'Ignazio **2**
Via della Gatta **7**

Historic Buildings
Palazzo Altieri **8**
Palazzo Baldassini **17**
Palazzo Borghese **19**
Palazzo Capranica **24**
Palazzo del Collegio
  Romano **4**
Palazzo di Montecitorio **21**
Palazzo Doria Pamphilj **6**

Columns, Obelisks and Statues
Column of Marcus Aurelius **23**
Obelisk of Montecitorio **22**
Obelisk of Santa Maria
  sopra Minerva **12**
Pie' di Marmo **10**

Fountains
Fontanella del Facchino **5**

Cafés and Restaurants
Caffè Giolitti **16**

KEY
■ Street-by-Street map
Ⓜ Metro station

GETTING THERE
The area has no Metro station, but is about 20 minutes' walk from Spagna or Barberini Metro stops. Buses that stop in Via del Plebiscito include the 46, 64, 70, 186, 492 and 810. Piazza Colonna is served by the 117, 119, 492 and all buses that go up Via del Corso or stop at Piazza S. Silvestro. The only bus that passes through the narrow streets of the area is the 116 electric minibus, which stops right outside the Pantheon.

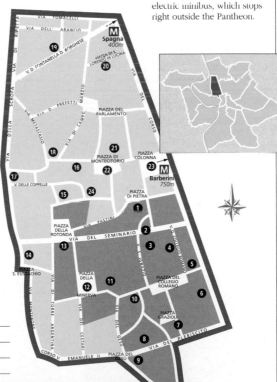

```
0 metres        200
0 yards         200
```

SEE ALSO

◁ **Piazza della Rotonda seen through the granite columns of the Pantheon**

Street-by-Street: Piazza della Rotonda

If you wander through this area, sooner or later you will emerge into Piazza della Rotonda with its jumble of open-air café tables in front of the Pantheon. The refreshing splash of the fountain makes it a welcome resting place. In this warren of narrow streets, it can be hard to realize just how close you are to some of Rome's finest sights. The magnificent art collection of Palazzo Doria Pamphilj and the Baroque splendour of the Gesù are just a few minutes' walk from the Pantheon. At night there is always a lively buzz of activity, as people dine in style or enjoy the coffee and ice creams for which the area is famous.

Temple of Hadrian
The columns of this Roman temple now form the façade of the stock exchange ❶

Piazza di Sant'Ignazio
The square is a rare example of stylish domestic architecture from the early 18th century ❷

La Tazza d'Oro enjoys a reputation for the wonderful coffee consumed on its premises as well as for its freshly ground coffee to take away. *(See p330.)*

Santa Maria sopra Minerva
The rich decoration of Rome's only Gothic church was added in the 19th century ⓫

★ **Pantheon**
The awe-inspiring interior of Rome's best-preserved ancient temple is only hinted at from the outside ⓭

Obelisk of Santa Maria sopra Minerva
In 1667 Bernini dreamed up the idea of mounting a recently discovered obelisk on the back of a marble elephant ⓬

LOCATOR MAP
See Central Rome Map pp14–15

★ **Sant'Ignazio di Loyola**
Andrea Pozzo painted this glorious Baroque ceiling (1685) to celebrate St Ignatius and the Jesuit order ❸

Palazzo del Collegio Romano
Up until 1870, the college educated many leading figures in the Catholic Church ❹

Fontanella del Facchino
The water in this small 16th-century fountain spurts from a barrel held by a porter ❺

★ **Palazzo Doria Pamphilj**
Among the masterpieces in the art gallery of this magnificent family palazzo is this portrait of Pope Innocent X by Velázquez (1650) ❻

Via della Gatta
The street is named after the statue of a cat ❼

Palazzo Altieri
This enormous 17th-century palazzo is decorated with the arms of Pope Clement X ❽

★ **Gesù**
The design of the first-ever Jesuit church had a great impact on religious architecture ❾

Pie' di Marmo
This marble foot is a stray fragment from a gigantic Roman statue ❿

KEY

- - - Suggested route

0 metres 75
0 yards 75

STAR SIGHTS

★ Pantheon

★ Sant'Ignazio di Loyola

★ Palazzo Doria Pamphilj

★ Gesù

Temple of Hadrian ❶

La Borsa, Piazza di Pietra. **Map** 4 F3 &
12 E2. 🚌 *117, 119, 492 and routes
along Via del Corso or stopping at Piazza
S. Silvestro.* **Open** *for exhibitions.*

This temple honours the
emperor Hadrian as a god
and was dedicated by his son
and successor Antoninus Pius
in AD 145. The remains of the
temple are visible on the
southern side of Piazza di
Pietra, incorporated in a 17th-
century building. This was
originally a papal customs
house, completed by Carlo
Fontana and his son in the
1690s. Today the building
houses the Roman stock
exchange (La Borsa).

Eleven marble Corinthian
columns 15 m (49 ft) high
stand on a base of *peperino*, a
volcanic rock quarried from
the Alban hills to the south of
Rome. The columns decorated the northern flank of the
temple enclosing its inner
shrine, the *cella*. The *peperino*
wall of the *cella* is still visible
behind the columns, as is part
of the coffered portico ceiling.

A number of reliefs from
the temple, representing conquered Roman provinces, are
now in the courtyard of the
Palazzo dei Conservatori
(see pp72–3). They reflect the
mostly peaceful foreign policy
of Hadrian's reign.

Remains of Hadrian's Temple

Piazza di Sant'Ignazio ❷

Map 4 F4 & 12 E3. 🚌 *117, 119,
492 and routes along Via del Corso or
stopping at Piazza S. Silvestro.*

One of the major works of
the Roman Rococo, the piazza
(1727–8) is Filippo Raguzzini's
masterpiece. It offsets the
imposing façade of the church
of Sant'Ignazio with the

Illusionistic ceiling in the crossing of Sant'Ignazio

intimacy of the houses
belonging to the bourgeoisie.
The theatrical setting, the cur-
vilinear design and the playful
forms of its windows, balconies
and balusters mark the piazza
as one of a highly distinct group
of structures. Along with Palazzo
Doria Pamphilj (1731), the
façade of La Maddalena (1735)
and the aristocratic Spanish
Steps (1723), it belongs to the
moment when Rome's bubbly
Rococo triumphed over conservative Classicism.

Sant'Ignazio di Loyola ❸

Piazza di Sant'Ignazio. **Map** 4 F4 &
12 E3. **Tel** *06-679 4406.* 🚌 *117,
119, 492 and along Via del Corso.*
Open *7.30am–7pm daily.* 🚹

The church was built by Pope
Gregory XV in 1626 in
honour of St Ignatius of
Loyola, founder of the Society
of Jesus and the man who
most embodied the zeal of
the Counter-Reformation.

Together with the Gesù *(see
pp114–15),* Sant'Ignazio forms
the centre of the Jesuit area in
Rome. Built in Baroque style,
its vast interior, lined with
precious stones, marble,
stucco and gilt, creates a
sense of theatre. The church
has a Latin-cross plan, with an
apse and many side chapels.

A cupola was planned but
never built, so the space it
would have filled was covered
by a fake perspective painting.
The piers built to uphold the
cupola support the observatory of the Collegio Romano.

Palazzo del Collegio Romano ❹

Piazza del Collegio Romano. **Map** 5 A4
& 12 E3. 🚌 *117, 119, 492 and along
Via del Corso or stopping at Piazza
Venezia.* **Not open** *to the public.*

On the same block as the
church of Sant'Ignazio is the
palazzo used by Jesuits as a
college where many future
bishops, cardinals and popes
studied. The college was con-
fiscated in 1870 and turned
into an ordinary school. The
portals bear the coat of arms
of its founder, Pope Gregory
XIII of Boncompagni (reigned
1572–85). The façade is also
adorned with a bell, a clock,
and two sundials. On the right
is a tower built
in 1787 as a
meteorological
observatory. Un-
til 1925 its time
signal regulated
all the clocks
within the city.

**Portal of the
Collegio Romano**

Fontanella del Facchino ❺

Via Lata. **Map** 5 A4 & 12 E3. 🚌 *64, 81, 85, 117, 119, 492 and many other routes.*

Il Facchino (the Porter), once in the Corso, now set in the wall of the Banco di Roma, was one of Rome's "talking statues" like Pasquino *(see p124)*. Created around 1590, the fountain may have been based on a drawing by painter Jacopino del Conte. The statue of a man holding a barrel most likely represents a member of the Università degli Acquaroli (Fraternity of Water-carriers), though it is also said to be of Martin Luther, or of the porter Abbondio Rizzio, who died carrying a barrel.

The Facchino drinking fountain

Palazzo Doria Pamphilj ❻

Via del Corso 305. **Map** 5 A4 & 12 E3. **Tel** 06-679 7323. 🚌 *64, 81, 85, 117, 119, 492 and many other routes.* **Open** *10am–5pm daily.* **Closed** *1 Jan, Easter Sun, 1 May, 15 Aug, 1 Nov, 25 Dec.* **Adm charge.** ♿ 📷 *for private apartments.* 🔊 📱 💻 **Concerts** www.doriapamphilj.it

Palazzo Doria Pamphilj is a great island of stone in the heart of Rome, the oldest parts dating from 1435. Through the Corso entrance you can see the 16th-century porticoed courtyard with the coat of arms of the della Rovere family. The Aldobrandini were the next owners. Between 1601 and 1647 the mansion acquired a second courtyard and flanking wings at the expense of a public bath that stood nearby.

When the Pamphilj family took over, they completed the Piazza del Collegio Romano façade and the Via della Gatta wing, a splendid chapel and a theatre inaugurated by Queen Christina of Sweden in 1684.

In the first half of the 1700s, Gabriele Valvassori created the gallery above the courtyard and a new façade along the Corso, using the highly decorative style of the period known as the *barocchetto*, which now dominates the building. The stairways and salons, the Mirror Gallery and the picture gallery all radiate a sense of light and space.

The family collection in the Doria Pamphilj gallery has over 400 paintings dating from the 15th to the 18th century, including the famous portrait of Pope Innocent X Pamphilj by Velázquez. There are also works by Titian, Caravaggio, Lorenzo Lotto and Guercino. The rooms in the private apartment have many of their original furnishings, including splendid Brussels and Gobelin tapestries. Occasionally, the gallery hosts concerts and evening visits of the collection.

Via della Gatta ❼

Map 5 A4 & 12 E3. 🚌 *62, 63, 64, 70, 81, 87, 186, 492 & routes along Via del Plebiscito & Corso Vittorio Emanuele II.*

This narrow street runs between the Palazzo Doria Pamphilj and the smaller Palazzo Grazioli. The ancient marble sculpture of a cat *(gatta)* that gives the street its name is on the first cornice on the corner of Palazzo Grazioli.

Via della Gatta's marble cat

Palazzo Altieri ❽

Via del Gesù 93. **Map** 4 F4 & 12 E3. 🚌 *46, 62, 63, 64, 70, 81, 87, 186, 492 and routes along Via del Plebiscito and Corso Vittorio Emanuele II.* 🚋 *8.*

The Altieri family is first mentioned in Rome's history in the 9th century. This palazzo was built by the last male heirs, the brothers Cardinal Giambattista di Lorenzo Altieri and Cardinal Emilio Altieri, who later became Pope Clement X (reigned 1670–76). Many surrounding houses had to be demolished, but an old woman called Berta refused to leave, so her hovel was incorporated in the palazzo. Its windows are still visible on the west end of the building.

Gesù ❾

See pp114–15.

Caravaggio's *Rest during the Flight into Egypt* in Palazzo Doria Pamphilj

Marble foot from a Roman statue

Pie' di Marmo ⑩

Via Santo Stefano del Cacco. **Map** 4
F4 & 12 E3. 🚌 62, 63, 64, 70, 81,
87, 116, 186, 492 and other routes
along Via del Corso, Via del Plebiscito
and Corso Vittorio Emanuele II.

It was popularly believed in
the Middle Ages that half the
population of ancient Rome
was made up of bronze and
marble statues. Fragments of
these giants, usually gods or
emperors, are scattered over
the city. This piece, a marble
foot *(pie' di marmo)*, comes
from an area dedicated to the
Egyptian gods Isis and Serapis
and was probably part of a
temple statue. Statues were
painted and covered with
jewels and clothes given by the
faithful – a great fire risk with
unattended burning tapers.

Santa Maria sopra Minerva ⑪

Piazza della Minerva 42. **Map** 4 F4
& 12 E3. **Tel** 06-679 3926.
🚌 116 and along Via del Corso,
Via del Plebiscito and Corso Vittorio
Emanuele II. **Open** 7am–7pm
Mon–Sat, 8am–1pm, 4–7pm Sun.
Cloister closed for restoration –
call for details. 🚹 🔇 **Concerts**.

Few other churches display
such a complete and im-
pressive record of Italian art.
Dating from the 13th century,
the Minerva is one of the few
examples of Gothic architecture in Rome. It was the
traditional stronghold of the
Dominicans, whose anti-
heretical zeal earned them the
nickname of *Domini Canes*
(the hounds of the Lord).
  Built on ancient ruins,
supposed to have been the
Temple of Minerva, the
simple T-shaped vaulted
building acquired rich chapels

and works of art by which its
many patrons wished to be
remembered. Note the Cosmatesque 13th-century tombs and
the exquisite works of 15th-
century Tuscan and Venetian
artists. Local talent of the
period can be admired in
Antoniazzo Romano's
Annunciation, featuring
Cardinal Juan de
Torquemada, uncle of the
infamous Spanish Inquisitor.
  The more monumental style
of the Roman Renaissance is
well represented in the tombs
of the 16th-century Medici
popes, Leo X and his cousin
Clement VII, and in the richly
decorated Aldobrandini
Chapel. Near the steps of
the choir is the celebrated
sculpture of the *Risen Christ*,
started by Michelangelo but
completed by Raffaele da
Montelupo in 1521. There
are also splendid works of
art from the Baroque
period, including a tomb
and a bust by Bernini.
  The church is also
visited because it
contains the tombs of
many famous Italians:
St Catherine of Siena,
who died here in 1380;
the Venetian sculptor
Andrea Bregno (died
1506); the Humanist
Cardinal Pietro Bembo
(died 1547); and Fra
Angelico, the Dominican
friar and painter, who
died in Rome in 1455.

Obelisk of Santa Maria sopra Minerva ⑫

Piazza della Minerva. **Map** 4 F4 & 12
D3. 🚌 116 and routes along Via del
Corso and Corso Vittorio Emanuele II.

Originally meant to decorate
Palazzo Barberini as a joke,
this exotic elephant and
obelisk sculpture is typical
of Bernini's inexhaustible
imagination. (The elephant was
actually sculpted by Ercole
Ferrata to Bernini's design.)
When the ancient obelisk
was found in the garden
of the monastery of Santa
Maria sopra Minerva, the
friars wanted the monument
erected in their piazza. The
elephant was provided with
its enormous saddle-cloth
because of a friar's insis-
tence that the gap under
the animal's abdomen
would undermine its
stability. Bernini knew
better: you need
only look at the
Fontana dei
Quattro Fiumi *(see
p120)* to appreciate
his use of empty
space. The elephant,
an ancient symbol
of intelligence and
piety, was chosen as
the embodiment of
the virtues on which
Christians should
build true wisdom.

**Bernini's Egyptian
obelisk and
marble elephant**

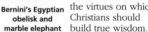

Nave of Santa Maria sopra Minerva

Pantheon ⓭

See pp110–11.

Sant'Eustachio ⓮

Piazza Sant'Eustachio. **Map** 4 F4 & 12 D3. **Tel** 06-686 5334. 🚌 116 and routes along Corso Vittorio Emanuele II. **Open** 9am–noon, 4–7.30pm daily. 🚹

The origins of this church date to early Christian times, when it offered relief to the poor. In medieval times, many charitable brotherhoods elected Sant'Eustachio as their patron and had chapels here.

The Romanesque bell tower is one of the few surviving remains of the medieval church, which was completely redecorated in the 17th and 18th centuries.

Nearby is the excellent Caffè Sant'Eustachio *(see p330)*.

Bell tower of Sant'Eustachio

La Maddalena ⓯

Piazza della Maddalena. **Map** 4 F3 & 12 D2. **Tel** 06-899 281. 🚌 116 and many routes along Via del Corso and Corso Vittorio Emanuele II. **Open** 8am–noon, 5–8pm daily (from 9.30am Sat & Sun). 🚹

Situated in a small piazza near the Pantheon, the Maddalena's Rococo façade, built in 1735, epitomizes the love of light and movement of the late Baroque. Its curves are reminiscent of Borromini's San Carlo alle Quattro Fontane *(see p161)*. The façade has been lovingly restored, although diehard Neo-Classicists dismiss its painted stucco as icing sugar.

The small size of the Maddalena did not deter

The old-fashioned *salone* of the Caffè Giolitti

the 17th- and 18th-century decorators who filled the interior with ornaments from the floor to the top of the elegant cupola. The organ loft and choir are particularly powerful examples of the Baroque's desire to fire the imagination of the faithful.

Many of the paintings and sculptures adopt the Christian imagery of the Counter-Reformation. In the niches of the nave, the statues are personifications of virtues such as Humility and Simplicity. There are also scenes from the life of San Camillo, who died in the adjacent convent in 1614. The church belonged to his followers, the Camillians, a preaching order active in Rome's hospitals. Like the Jesuits, they commissioned powerful works of art to convey the force of their religious message.

La Maddalena's stuccoed façade

Caffè Giolitti ⓰

Via degli Uffici del Vicario 40. **Map** 4 F3 & 12 D2. **Tel** 06-699 1243. 🚌 116 and many routes along Via del Corso and Corso Rinascimento. **Open** 7am–1am daily.

Founded in 1900, the Caffè Giolitti is the heir to the *Belle Époque* cafés that lined the nearby Via del Corso in Rome's first days as capital of the new Italian state. Its *salone* holds tourists in summer and Roman families at weekends, and on weekdays is frequented by local workers from a wide range of industries. Its ice creams are especially good.

Palazzo Baldassini ⓱

Via delle Coppelle 35. **Map** 4 F3 & 12 D2. 🚌 116 and many routes along Via del Corso and Corso Rinascimento. **Not open** to the public.

Melchiorre Baldassini commissioned Antonio da Sangallo the Younger to build his home in Florentine Renaissance style in 1514–20. With its cornices marking the different floors and wrought-iron window grilles, this is one of the best examples of an early 16th-century Roman palazzo. It stands in the part of Rome still known as the Renaissance Quarter, which flourished around the long straight streets such as Via di Ripetta and Via della Scrofa built at the time of Pope Leo X (reigned 1513–21).

Pantheon ⑬

In the Middle Ages the Pantheon, the Roman temple of "all the gods", became a church; in time this magnificent building with its awe-inspiring domed interior became a symbol of Rome itself. The rectangular portico screens the vast hemispherical dome: only from inside can its true scale and beauty be appreciated. The rotunda's height and diameter are equal: 43.3 m (142 ft). The hole at the top of the dome, the *oculus*, provides the only light. We owe this marvel of Roman engineering to the emperor Hadrian, who designed it (AD 118–125) to replace an earlier temple built by Marcus Agrippa, son-in-law of Augustus. The shrines that now line the wall of the Pantheon range from the Tomb of Raphael to those of the kings of modern Italy.

★ Interior of the Dome
The dome was cast by pouring concrete mixed with tufa and pumice over a temporary wooden framework.

The portico, enclosed by granite columns

The walls of the drum supporting the dome are 6 m (19 ft) thick.

The immense portico is built on the foundations of Agrippa's temple.

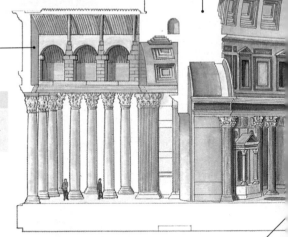

STAR FEATURES

★ Interior of the Dome

★ Tomb of Raphael

Bell Towers
This 18th-century view by Bernardo Bellotto shows Bernini's much-ridiculed turrets, which were removed in 1883.

Floor Patterning
The marble floor, restored in 1873, preserves the original Roman design.

RAPHAEL AND LA FORNARINA

Raphael, at his own request, was buried here when he died in 1520. He had lived for years with his model, La Fornarina (*see p210*), seen here in a painting by Giulio Romano, but she was excluded from the ceremony of his burial. On the right of his tomb is a memorial to his fiancée, Maria Bibbiena, niece of the artist's patron, Cardinal Dovizi di Bibbiena.

VISITORS' CHECKLIST

Piazza della Rotonda. **Map** 4 F4 & 12 D3. **Tel** 06-6830 0230. 116 and routes along Via del Corso, Corso Vittorio Emanuele II & Corso del Rinascimento. **Open** 8.30am–7.30pm Mon–Sat, 9am–6pm Sun, 9am–1pm pub hols. **Closed** 1 Jan, 1 May, 25 Dec.

Oculus

Coffering
Constructing the dome from hollow decorative coffers reduced its weight.

Relieving Arches
Brick arches embedded in the structure of the wall act as internal buttresses, distributing the weight of the dome.

★ **Tomb of Raphael**
The artist's body rests below a Madonna by Lorenzetto (1520).

TIMELINE

Inscription on pediment

30 BC	AD 100	600	1100	1600

27–25 BC Marcus Agrippa builds first Pantheon

735 Gregory III roofs the Pantheon in lead

1309–77 While papal seat is in Avignon, Pantheon is used as a fortress and poultry market

1888 Tomb of King Vittorio Emanuele II completed

118–25 Hadrian builds new Pantheon

609 Pope Boniface IV consecrates Pantheon as church of Santa Maria ad Martyres

663 Byzantine Emperor Constans II strips gilded tiles from the roof

1632 Urban VIII melts down bronze from portico for Bernini's baldacchino in St Peter's

Bernini's curving southern façade of Palazzo di Montecitorio

Santa Maria in Campo Marzio ⑱

Piazza in Campo Marzio 45. **Map** 4 F3 & 12 D2. **Tel** 06-679 4973. 🚌 116 and many routes on Via del Corso and Corso Rinascimento. **Open** for services 8am Mon–Sat, 10.30am Sun.

Around the courtyard through which you enter the church, there are fascinating remnants of medieval houses, once the property of the original monastery. The church itself was rebuilt in 1685 by Antonio de Rossi, using a square Greek-cross plan with a cupola. Above the altar is a 12th-century painting of the Madonna, after which the church is named.

Palazzo Borghese ⑲

Largo della Fontanella di Borghese. **Map** 4 F3 & 12 D1. 🚌 81, 117, 492, 628. **Closed** to the public.

The palazzo was acquired in about 1605 by Cardinal Camillo Borghese, just before he became Pope Paul V. Flaminio Ponzio was hired to enlarge the building and give it the grandeur appropriate to the residence of the pope's family. He added a wing overlooking Piazza Borghese and the delightful porticoed courtyard inside. Subsequent enlargements included the building and decoration of a great *nymphaeum* known as the Bath of Venus. For more than two centuries this palazzo housed the Borghese family's renowned collection of paintings, which was bought

by the Italian state in 1902 and transferred to the Galleria Borghese *(see pp260–61)*.

Pope Paul V, who commissioned Palazzo Borghese for his family

San Lorenzo in Lucina ⑳

Via in Lucina 16A. **Map** 4 F3 & 12 E1. **Tel** 06-687 1494. 🚌 81, 117, 492, 628. **Open** 8:30am–8pm daily. 🔲

The church is one of Rome's oldest Christian places of worship, and was probably built on a well sacred to Juno, protectress of women. It was rebuilt during the 12th century, and today's external appearance is quite typical of the period featuring a portico with reused Roman columns crowned by medieval capitals, a plain triangular pediment and a Romanesque bell tower with coloured marble inlay.
    The interior was totally rebuilt in 1856–8. The old basilical plan was destroyed and the two side naves were replaced

by Baroque chapels. Do not miss the fine busts in the Fonseca Chapel, designed by Bernini, or the *Crucifixion* by Guido Reni above the main altar. There is also a 19th-century monument honouring French painter Nicolas Poussin, who died in Rome in 1655 and was buried in the church.

Palazzo di Montecitorio ㉑

Piazza di Montecitorio. **Map** 4 F3 & 12 E2. 🚌 116 and all routes along Via del Corso or stopping at Piazza S. Silvestro. **Open** 10am–6.30pm, usually 1st Sun each month (except Aug). **Tel** 06-676 01. **www**.camera.it

The palazzo's first architect, Bernini, got the job after he presented a silver model of his design to the wife of his patron, Prince Ludovisi. The building was completed in 1694 by Carlo Fontana and became the Papal Tribunal of Justice. In 1871 it was chosen to be Italy's new Chamber of Deputies and by 1927 it had doubled in size with a second grand façade. The 630 members of parliament are elected by a majority system with proportional representation.

The church of San Lorenzo in Lucina

Emperor Augustus's obelisk

Obelisk of Montecitorio ②

Piazza di Montecitorio. **Map** 4 F3 & 12 E2. 🚌 116 and routes along Via del Corso or to Piazza S. Silvestro.

The measurement of time in ancient Rome was always a rather hit-and-miss affair: for many years the Romans relied on an imported (and therefore inaccurate) sundial, a trophy from the conquest of Sicily. In 10 BC the Emperor Augustus laid out an enormous sundial in the Campus Martius. Its centre was roughly in today's Piazza di San Lorenzo in Lucina. The shadow was cast by a huge granite obelisk that he had brought back from Heliopolis in Egypt. Unfortunately this sundial too became inaccurate after only 50 years, possibly due to subsidence.

The obelisk was still in the piazza in the 9th century, but then disappeared until it was rediscovered lying under medieval houses in the reign of Pope Julius II (1503–13). The pope was intrigued, because Egyptian hieroglyphs were thought to hold the key to the wisdom of Adam before the Fall, but it was only under Pope Benedict XIV (reigned 1740–58) that the obelisk was finally unearthed. It was erected in its present location in 1792 by Pope Pius VI.

Column of Marcus Aurelius ㉓

Piazza Colonna. **Map** 5 A3 & 12 E2. 🚌 116 and routes along Via del Corso or to Piazza S. Silvestro.

Clearly an imitation of the Column of Trajan (see p90), this monument was erected after the death of Marcus Aurelius in AD 180 to commemorate his victories over the barbarian tribes of the Danube. The 80-year lapse between the two works produced a great artistic change: the wars of Marcus Aurelius are rendered with simplified pictures in stronger relief, sacrificing Classical proportions for the sake of clarity and immediacy. The spirit of the work is more akin to the 4th-century Arch of Constantine (see p91) than to Trajan's monument. Gone are the heroic qualities of the Roman soldiers, by now mostly barbarian mercenaries, and a sense of respect for the vanquished. A new emphasis on the supernatural points to the end of the Hellenistic tradition and the beginning of Christianity.

Composed of 28 drums of marble, the column was restored in 1588 by Domenico Fontana on the orders of Pope Sixtus V. The emperor's statue on the summit was replaced by a bronze of St Paul. The 20 spirals of the low relief chronicle the German war of AD 172–3, and (above) the Sarmatic war of AD 174–5. The column is almost 30 m (100 ft) high and 3.7 m (12 ft) in diameter. An internal spiral staircase leads to the top. The easiest way to appreciate the sculptural work, however, is to visit the Museo della Civiltà Romana at EUR (see p266) and study the casts of the reliefs.

Palazzo Capranica ㉔

Piazza Capranica. **Map** 4 F3 & 12 D2. 🚌 116 and routes along Via del Corso or to Piazza S. Silvestro.

Windows of Palazzo Capranica

One of Rome's small number of surviving 15th-century buildings, the palazzo was commissioned by Cardinal Domenico Capranica both as his family residence and as a college for higher education. Its fortress-like appearance is a patchwork of subsequent additions, not unusual in the late 15th century, when Rome was still hovering between medieval and Renaissance taste. The Gothic-looking windows on the right of the building show the cardinal's coat of arms and the date 1451 is inscribed on the doorway underneath. The palazzo now houses a conference centre.

Relief of the emperor's campaigns on the Column of Marcus Aurelius

Gesù ⑨

Dating from between 1568 and 1584, the Gesù was the first Jesuit church to be built in Rome. Its design epitomizes Counter-Reformation Baroque architecture and has been much imitated throughout the Catholic world. The layout proclaims the church's two major functions: a large nave with side pulpits for preaching to great crowds, and a main altar as the centrepiece for the celebration of the mass. The illusionistic decoration in the nave and dome was added a century later. Its message is clear and confident: faithful, Catholic worshippers will be joyfully uplifted into the heavens while Protestants and other heretics are flung into hell's fires.

★ Chapel of Sant'Ignazio
Above its altar is a statue of the saint, framed by gilded lapis lazuli columns. The chapel was built in 1696–1700 by Andrea Pozzo, a Jesuit artist.

Triumph of Faith Over Idolatry
This vivid Baroque allegory sculpted by Théudon illustrates the great ambition of Jesuit theology.

ST IGNATIUS AND THE JESUIT ORDER

Spanish soldier Ignatius Loyola (1491–1556) joined the Church after being wounded in battle in 1521. He came to Rome in 1537 and founded the Jesuits, sending missionaries and teachers all over the world to win souls for Catholicism.

Main entrance

STAR FEATURES

★ Chapel of Sant'Ignazio

★ Monument to San Roberto Bellarmino

★ Nave Ceiling Decorations

Allegorical Figures
Antonio Raggi made these stuccoes, which were designed by Il Baciccia to complement the figures on his own nave frescoes.

Madonna della Strada

This 15th-century image, the Madonna of the Road, was originally displayed on the façade of Santa Maria della Strada which once stood on this site.

VISITORS' CHECKLIST

Piazza del Gesù.
Map 4 F4 & 12 E4. **Tel** 06-697 001. H, 46, 62, 64, 70, 81, 87, 186, 492, 628, 810 and other routes. 8.
Open 7am–12.30pm (7.30am–1pm Sun), 4–7.45pm daily.

★ Monument to San Roberto Bellarmino

Bernini captured the forceful personality of this anti-Protestant theologian, who died in 1621.

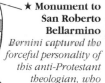

The Chapel of St Francis Xavier is a memorial to the great missionary who died alone on an island off China in 1552.

Cupola Frescoes

The cupola was completed by della Porta to Vignola's design. The frescoes, by Il Baciccia, feature Old Testament figures.

★ Nave Ceiling Decorations

The figures in Il Baciccia's astonishing fresco of the Triumph of the Name of Jesus *spill out on to the coffered vaulting of the nave.*

TIMELINE

1540 Founding of the Society of Jesus (the Jesuits)	**1571** Giacomo della Porta's design chosen for the façade	**1696–1700** The Chapel of Sant' Ignazio is designed by Andrea Pozzo, a Jesuit artist	**1773** Pope Clement XIV orders the suppression of the Jesuit order
	1584 Church's consecration		
1500	**1600**		**1700**
1545–63 Council of Trent defines the new Catholic orthodoxy	**1568–71** Vignola builds the church up to the crossing under the patronage of Cardinal Alessandro Farnese		**1670–83** Giovanni Battista Gaulli (Il Baciccia) paints the nave vault, dome and apse
1556 Ignatius Loyola dies		**1622** Ignatius Loyola is canonized	

PIAZZA NAVONA

The foundations of the buildings surrounding the elongated oval of Piazza Navona were the ruined grandstands of the vast Stadium of Domitian. The piazza still provides a dramatic spectacle today with the obelisk of the Fontana dei Quattro Fiumi in front of the church of Sant' Agnese in Agone as its focal

Lion on Fontana dei Quattro Fiumi

point. The predominant style of the area is Baroque, many of its finest buildings dating from the reign of Innocent X Pamphilj (1644–55), patron of Bernini and Borromini. Of special interest is the complex of the Chiesa Nuova, headquarters of the Filippini, the order founded by San Filippo Neri, the 16th-century "Apostle of Rome".

SIGHTS AT A GLANCE

Churches and Temples
Chiesa Nuova ⑮
Oratorio del Filippini ⑯
San Luigi dei Francesi ⑦
San Salvatore in Lauro ⑳
Sant'Agnese in Agone ④
Sant'Andrea della Valle ⑩
Sant'Ivo alla Sapienza ⑨
Santa Maria dell'Anima ⑤
Santa Maria della Pace ⑥

Museums
Museo Napoleonico ㉑
Palazzo Braschi ⑫

Historic Buildings
Palazzo Altemps ㉓
Palazzo del Banco
   di Santo Spirito ⑱
Palazzo Madama ⑧
Palazzo Massimo
   alle Colonne ⑪
Palazzo Pamphilj ③
Torre dell'Orologio ⑰

Fountains and Statues
Fontana dei Quattro Fiumi ①
Pasquino ⑬

Historic Streets and Piazzas
Piazza Navona ②
Via dei Coronari ⑲
Via del Governo Vecchio ⑭

Restaurants
Hostaria dell'Orso ㉒

SEE ALSO

• *Street Finder*, maps 4, 11, 12

• *Where to Stay* p301

• *Restaurants* pp317–18

GETTING THERE
This central area is within walking distance of many parts of the city and it is easily reached by bus. The principal routes along Corso Vittorio Emanuele II are the 64 from Termini station to St Peter's and the 46. Corso del Rinascimento, which runs parallel to Piazza Navona, is served by several useful routes, including the 70, 81, 116, 186 and 492.

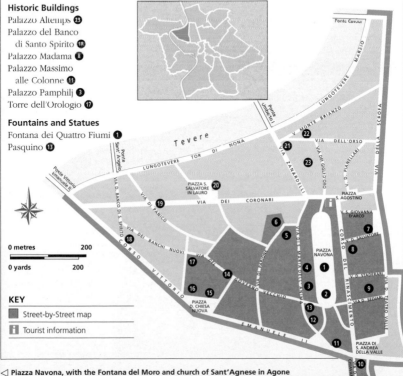

KEY

▨	Street-by-Street map
ℹ	Tourist information

◁ **Piazza Navona, with the Fontana del Moro and church of Sant'Agnese in Agone**

Street-by-Street: Piazza Navona

No other piazza in Rome can rival the theatricality of Piazza Navona. Day and night there is always something going on in the pedestrian area around its three flamboyant fountains. The Baroque is also represented in many of the area's churches. To discover an older Rome, walk along Via del Governo Vecchio to admire the façades of its Renaissance buildings and browse in the fascinating antiques shops.

Oratorio dei Filippini
The musical term oratorio comes from this place of informal worship ⑯

Torre dell' Orologio
This clock tower by Borromini (1648) is part of the Convent of the Filippini ⑰

VIA DEL CORALLO

VIA DEL GOVERNO VECCHIO

VIA DI PARIONE

Chiesa Nuova
This church was rebuilt in the late 16th century for the order founded by San Filippo Neri ⑮

To Corso Vittorio Emanuele II

Via del Governo Vecchio
This street preserves a large number of fine Renaissance houses ⑭

CORSO VITTORIO

EMANUELE II

PIAZZA DI PAS

Pasquino
Romans hung satirical verses and dialogues on this weather-beaten statue ⑬

Palazzo Pamphilj
This grand town house was built for Pope Innocent X and his family in the mid-17th century ③

PIAZZA DI SAN PANTALEO

Santa Maria della Pace
This medallion shows Pope Sixtus IV who reigned 1471–84 and under whose orders the church was built ⑥

Palazzo Braschi
A late 18th-century building with a splendid balcony, the palazzo houses the Museo di Roma ⑫

STAR SIGHTS

★ San Luigi dei Francesi

★ Piazza Navona

★ Sant'Andrea della Valle

Palazzo Massimo alle Colonne
The magnificent curving colonnade (1536) is by Baldassarre Peruzzi ⑪

KEY

– – – Suggested route

| 0 metres | 75 |
| 0 yards | 75 |

Sant'Agnese in Agone
Borromini's startling concave façade (1657) dominates one side of Piazza Navona ❹

Santa Maria dell'Anima
For four centuries this has been the German church in Rome ❺

Fontana dei Quattro Fiumi
This fountain supporting an Egyptian obelisk was designed by Bernini ❶

Palazzo Madama
A spread-eagled stone lion skin decorates the central doorway of the palazzo, now the Italian Senate ❽

LOCATOR MAP
See Central Rome Map pp14–15

MARIA DELL'ANIMA

PIAZZA NAVONA

CORSIA AGONALE

CORSO DEL RINASCIMENTO

VIA DEL SALVATORE

VIA DEGLI STADERARI

VIA DEI SEDIARI

PIAZZA DI SANT'ANDREA DELLA VALLE

★ **San Luigi dei Francesi**
An 18th-century statue of St Louis stands in a niche in the façade ❼

★ **Piazza Navona**
This unique piazza owes its shape to a Roman racetrack and its stunning decor to the genius of the Roman Baroque ❷

The Fontana del Moro was remodelled in 1653 by Bernini, who designed the central sea god.

Sant'Ivo alla Sapienza
This tiny domed church is one of Borromini's most original creations. He worked on it between 1642 and 1650 ❾

★ **Sant'Andrea della Valle**
The church, with its grandiose façade by Carlo Rainaldi (1665), has gained fame outside Rome as the setting of the first act of Puccini's Tosca ❿

To Campo de' Fiori

Fontana dei Quattro Fiumi ❶

Piazza Navona. **Map** 4 E4 & 11 C3.
🚌 46, 62, 64, 70, 81, 87, 116, 492, 628.

Built for Pope Innocent X Pamphilj, this magnificent fountain in the centre of Piazza Navona was unveiled in 1651. The pope's coat of arms, the dove and the olive branch, decorate the pyramid rock formation supporting the Roman obelisk, which once stood in the Circus of Maxentius on the Appian Way. Bernini designed the fountain, which was paid for by means of taxes on bread and other staples. The great rivers – the Ganges, the Danube, the Nile and the River Plate – are represented by four giants. The Nile's veiled head symbolizes the river's unknown source, but there is also a legend that the veil conveys Bernini's dislike for the nearby Sant'Agnese in Agone, designed by his rival Borromini. Similarly, the

Palazzo Pamphilj, the largest building in Piazza Navona

athletic figure of the River Plate, cringing with arm upraised, is supposed to express Bernini's fear that the church will collapse. Sadly, these widely believed stories can have no basis in fact: Bernini had completed the fountain before Borromini started work on the church.

Piazza Navona ❷

Map 4 E3 & 11 C2. 🚌 46, 62, 64, 70, 81, 87, 116, 492, 628.

Rome's most beautiful Baroque piazza follows the shape of Domitian's Stadium which once stood on this site – some of its arches are still visible below the church of Sant'Agnese in Agone. The *agones* were athletic contests held in the 1st-century stadium, which could seat 33,000 people. The word "Navona" is thought to be a corruption of *in agone*. The piazza's unique appearance

and atmosphere were created in the 17th century with the addition of the Fontana dei Quattro Fiumi. The other fountains date from the previous century but have been altered several times since. The basin of the Fontana di Nettuno, at the northern end, was built by Giacomo della Porta in 1576, while the statues of Neptune and the Nereids date from the 19th century. The Fontana del Moro, at the southern end, was also designed by della Porta, though Bernini altered it later, adding a statue of a Moor fighting a dolphin.

Up until the 19th century, Piazza Navona was flooded during August by stopping the fountain outlets. The rich would splash around in carriages, while street urchins paddled after them. Today, with its numerous shops and cafés, the piazza is a favourite in all seasons. In summer it is busy with street entertainers, while in winter it fills with colourful stalls selling toys and sweets for the feast of the Befana.

Palazzo Pamphilj ❸

Piazza Navona. **Map** 4 E4 & 11 C3.
🚌 46, 62, 64, 70, 81, 87, 116, 492, 628. **Not open** to the public.

Family dove and olive branch on façade of Palazzo Pamphilj

In 1644 Giovanni Battista Pamphilj became Pope Innocent X. During his 10-year reign, he heaped riches on his own family, especially his domineering sister-in-law, Olimpia Maidalchini. The "talking statue" Pasquino (*see p124*) gave her the nickname "Olim-Pia", Latin for "formerly virtuous". She lived in the grand Palazzo Pamphilj, which has frescoes by Pietro da Cortona and a gallery by Borromini. The building is now the Brazilian embassy and cultural centre.

Symbolic figure of the River Ganges in the Fontana dei Quattro Fiumi

Sant'Agnese in Agone ❹

Piazza Navona. **Map** 4 E4 & 11 C3.
Tel 06-6819 2134. 🚍 46, 62, 64,
70, 81, 87, 116, 492, 628.
Open 9.30am–12.30pm, 4–7pm
Tue–Sun. 🕇 🕭

This church is believed to
have been founded on the
site of the brothel where, in
AD 304, the young St Agnes
was exposed naked to force
her to renounce her faith. A
marble relief in the crypt
shows the miraculous growth
of her hair, which fell around
her body to protect her
modesty. She was martyred
on this site and is buried
in the catacombs that bear
her name along the Via
Nomentana *(see p264)*.

Today's church was
commissioned by Pope
Innocent X in 1652. The first
architects were father and
son, Girolamo and Carlo
Rainaldi, but they were
replaced by Borromini
in 1653. He stuck
more or less to the
Rainaldi scheme
except for the
concave façade
designed to
emphasize the
dome. A statue
of St Agnes on the
façade is said to
be reassuring
the Fontana dei
Quattro Fiumi's
statue of the River
Plate that the
church is stable.

**Statue of St Agnes
on façade of Sant'
Agnese in Agone**

Carlo Saraceni's *Miracle of St Benno and the Keys of Meissen Cathedral*

tomb by Baldassarre Peruzzi
in Santa Maria dell'Anima. It
stands to the right of
Giulio Romano's
damaged altarpiece and
is redolent of the
pagan Renaissance
spirit the pope had so
condemned during
his brief, rather
gloomy reign, when
patronage of the arts
ground to a halt. Santa
Maria dell'Anima is
the German church in
Rome and some of its
paintings, such as the
Miracle of St Benno by
Carlo Saraceni (1618),
illustrate events connected
with the history of Germany.

Santa Maria dell'Anima ❺

Via Santa Maria dell'Anima 66.
Map 4 E4 & 11 C2. *Tel* 06-682
8181. 🚍 46, 62, 64, 70, 81, 87,
116, 492, 628. **Open** 3–7pm daily
(9am–1pm Thu–Tue). 🕇 🕭

Pope Adrian VI (reigned
1522–3), son of a ship-builder
from Utrecht, was the last
non-Italian pope before
John Paul II. He would have
disapproved of his superb

Santa Maria della Pace ❻

Vicolo dell'Arco della Pace 5.
Map 4 E3 & 11 C2. *Tel* 06-686
1156. 🚍 46, 62, 64, 70, 81, 87,
116, 492, 628. **Open** 9am–noon
Mon, Wed, Sat. 🕇 🕭 2 steps.
Exhibitions, concerts.

A drunken soldier allegedly
pierced the breast of a
painted Madonna on this site,

causing it to bleed. Pope
Sixtus IV della Rovere
(reigned 1471–84) placated
the Virgin by ordering Baccio
Pontelli to build her a church
if she would bring the war
with Turkey to an end. Peace
was restored and the church
was named Santa Maria della
Pace (St Mary of Peace).

The cloister was added by
Bramante in 1504. As in his
famous Tempietto *(see p219)*,
he scrupulously followed
Classical rules of proportion
and achieved a monumental
effect in a relatively small
space. Pietro da Cortona
may have had Bramante's
Tempietto in mind when he
added the church's charming
semi-circular portico in 1656.
The interior, a short nave
ending under an octagonal
cupola, houses Raphael's
famous frescoes of four *Sybils*,
and four *Prophets* by his pupil
Timoteo Viti, painted for the
banker Agostino Chigi in
1514. Baldassarre Peruzzi also
did some work in the church
(fresco in the first chapel on
the left), as did the architect
Antonio da Sangallo the
Younger, who designed the
second chapel on the right.

San Luigi dei Francesi ❼

Piazza di San Luigi dei Francesi 5.
Map 4 F4 & 12 D2. **Tel** 06-688 271.
🚌 70, 81, 87, 116, 186, 492, 628.
Open 10am–12.30pm, 4–7pm daily.
Closed Thu pm. 🚹 🚻 📷

The French national church
was founded in 1518, but it
took until 1589 to complete,
with contributions by Giacomo della Porta and Domenico
Fontana. The church serves as
a last resting place for many
illustrious French people,
including Chateaubriand's
lover Pauline de Beaumont.

Three Caravaggios hang in
the fifth chapel on the left, all
dedicated to St Matthew.
Painted between 1597 and
1602, these were Caravaggio's
first great religious works: the
Calling of St Matthew, the
Martyrdom of St Matthew and
St Matthew and the Angel.
The first version of this last
painting was rejected because
of its vivid realism; never
before had a saint been
shown as a tired
old man with
dirty feet. All
three works
display very
disquieting
realism and
a highly
dramatic use
of light.

Caravaggio, whose paintings of St Matthew hang in San Luigi dei Francesi

**Shield linking symbols of France
and Rome on façade of San Luigi**

Palazzo Madama ❽

Corso del Rinascimento. **Map** 4 F4
& 12 D3. **Tel** 06-670 61. 🚌 70, 81,
87, 116, 186, 492, 628. **Open**
10am–6pm first Sat of month
(except Aug). **www**.senato.it

This 16th-century palazzo was
built for the Medici family,
who had owned a bank here
in the previous century. It
was the residence of Medici
cousins Giovanni and Giuliano,
both of whom became popes:
Giovanni as Leo X and Giuliano as Clement VII. Caterina
de' Medici, Clement VII's niece,
also lived here before she was
married to Henry, son of King
Francis I of France, in 1533.

The palazzo takes its name
from Madama Margherita of
Austria, illegitimate daughter
of Emperor Charles V, who
married Alessandro de' Medici
and, after his death, Ottavio
Farnese. Thus part of the art
collection of the Florentine
Medici family was inherited
by the Roman Farnese family.

The spectacular façade was
built in the 17th century by
Paolo Maruccelli. He gave it an
ornate cornice and whimsical
decorative details on the roof.
Since 1871 the palazzo has
been the seat of the upper
house of the Italian parliament.

Cornice of Palazzo Madama

Sant'Ivo alla Sapienza ❾

Corso del Rinascimento 40.
Map 4 F4 & 12 D3. **Tel** 06-361
2562. 🚌 40, 46, 64, 70, 81,
87, 116, 186, 492, 628.
Open 9am–noon Sun. 🚹

The church's lantern
is crowned with a
cross on top of a
dramatic twisted
spiral – a highly
distinctive land-
mark from
Rome's roof
terraces. No
other Baroque
church is
quite like this   **Lantern and spire**
one, made   **of Sant'Ivo**
by Borro-
mini. Based on a ground
design of astonishing
geometrical complexity, the
walls are a breathtaking
combination of concave and
convex surfaces. The church
stands in the small courtyard
of the Palazzo della Sapienza,
seat of the old University of
Rome from the 15th century
until 1935.

Sant'Andrea della Valle ⑩

Piazza Sant'Andrea della Valle.
Map 4 E4 & 12 D4. **Tel** 06-686
1339. 🚌 H, 40, 46, 62, 64, 70,
81, 87, 116, 186, 492, 628.
🚋 8. **Open** 7.30am– noon,
4.30–7.30pm daily. ✝

Dome of Sant'Andrea della Valle

The church is the scene of
the first act of Puccini's opera
Tosca, though opera fans
will not find the Attavanti
chapel, a poetic invention.
The real church has much
to recommend it – the
impressive façade shows the
flamboyant Baroque style at
its best. Inside, a golden light
filters through high windows,
showing off the gilded interi-
or. Here lie the two popes
of the Sienese Piccolomini
family: on the left of the
central nave is the tomb of
Pius II, the first Humanist
pope (reigned 1458–64);
Pope Pius III lies opposite –
he reigned for less than a
month in 1503.

The church is famous for its
beautiful dome, the largest in
Rome after St Peter's. It was
built by Carlo Maderno in
1622–5 and was painted
with splendid frescoes by
Domenichino and Giovanni
Lanfranco. The latter's
extravagant style, to be seen
in the dome fresco *Glory of
Paradise*, won him most of
the commission, and the
jealous Domenichino is said
to have tried to kill his
colleague. He failed, but
Domenichino's jealousy was
unnecessary, as shown by
his two beautiful paintings

of scenes from the life of St
Andrew around the apse and
altar. In the Strozzi Chapel,
built in the style of
Michelangelo, the altar has
copies of the *Leah* and *Rachel*
by Michelangelo in San Pietro
in Vincoli *(see p170)*.

Palazzo Massimo alle Colonne ⑪

Corso Vittorio Emanuele II 141.
Map 4 F4 & 11 C3. 🚌 40, 46, 62,
64, 70, 81, 87, 116, 186, 492, 628.
Chapel open 7am–noon 16 Mar.

Roman column, Palazzo Massimo

During the last two years of
his life, Baldassarre Peruzzi
built this palazzo for the
Massimo family, whose home
had been destroyed in the
1527 Sack of Rome. Peruzzi
displayed great ingenuity in
dealing with an awkwardly
shaped site. The previous
building had stood on the
ruined Theatre of Domitian,
which created a curve in the
great processional Via Papalis.
Peruzzi's convex colonnaded
façade follows the line of the
street. His originality is also
evident in the small square
upper windows, the court-
yard and the stuccoed
vestibule. The Piazza de'
Massimi entrance has
a Renaissance-style,
frescoed façade. A
single column from
the theatre has been
set up in the piazza.

The Massimo family
traced its origins to
Quintus Fabius
Maximus, conqueror
of Hannibal in the 3rd
century BC, and their

coat of arms is borne by an
infant Hercules. Over the years
the family produced many
great Humanists, and in the
19th century, it was a Massimo
who negotiated peace with
Napoleon. On 16 March each
year the family chapel opens
to the public to commemorate
young Paolo Massimo's resur-
rection from the dead by San
Filippo Neri in 1538.

Palazzo Braschi ⑫

Piazza San Pantaleo 10. **Map** 4 E4
& 11 C3. **Tel** 06-6710 8346. 🚌 40,
46, 62, 64, 70, 81, 87, 116, 186,
492, 628. **Open** 9am–7pm Tue–Sun
(ticket office closes at 6.30pm). ♿
📷 🏛 🛍

On one side of Piazza San
Pantaleo is the last Roman
palazzo to be built for the
family of a pope. Palazzo
Braschi was built in the late
18th century for Pope Pius
VI Braschi's nephews by the
architect Cosimo Morelli. He
gave the building its imposing
façade which looks out on
to the piazza.

The palazzo now houses the
municipal Museo di Roma. It
holds collections of pictures,
drawings and
everyday objects
illustrating life in
Rome from medi-
eval times to the
19th century.

**Angel with raised wing by Ercole Ferrata,
flanking the façade of Sant'Andrea della Valle**

Pasquino ⑬

Piazza di Pasquino. **Map** 4 E4 & 11 C3. 🚌 *40, 46, 62, 64, 70, 81, 87, 116, 492, 628.*

Pasquino, the most famous of Rome's satirical "talking statues"

This rough chunk of marble is all that remains of a Hellenistic group, probably representing the incident in Homer's *Iliad* in which Menelaus shields the body of the slain Patroclus. For years it lay as a stepping stone in a muddy medieval street until it was erected on this corner in 1501, near the shop of an outspoken cobbler named Pasquino. Freedom of speech was not encouraged in papal Rome, so the cobbler wrote out his satirical comments on current events and attached them to the statue.

Other Romans followed suit, hanging their maxims and verses on the statue by night to escape punishment. Despite the wrath of the authorities, the sayings of the "talking

statue" (renamed Pasquino) were part of popular culture up until the 19th century. Other statues started to "talk" in the same vein; Pasquino used to conduct dialogues with the statue Marforio in Via del Campidoglio (now in the court-yard of Palazzo Nuovo, *see pp70–71*) and with the Babuino in Via del Babuino *(see p135)*. Pasquino still speaks on occasion and Rome's English-language cinema is named after him *(see p361)*.

Via del Governo Vecchio ⑭

Map 4 E4 & 11 B3. 🚌 *40, 46, 62, 64.*

The street takes its name from Palazzo del Governo Vecchio, the seat of papal government in the 17th and 18th centuries. Once part of the Via Papalis, which led from the Lateran to St Peter's, the street is lined with 15th- and 16th-century houses and small workshops. Particularly interesting are those at No. 104 and No. 106. The small palazzo at No. 123 was once thought to have been the home of Bramante.

Opposite is Palazzo del Governo Vecchio. It is also known as Palazzo Nardini, from the name of its founder, which is inscribed on the first-floor windows along with the date 1477.

Via del Governo Vecchio

Chiesa Nuova ⑮

Piazza della Chiesa Nuova. **Map** 4 E4 & 11 B3. **Tel** 06-687 52 89. 🚌 *40, 46, 62, 64.* **Open** *8am–noon (to 1pm Sun), 4.30–7pm daily.* ✝

Façade of the Chiesa Nuova

San Filippo Neri (St Philip Neri) is the most appealing of the Counter-Reformation saints. A highly unconventional reformer, he required his noble Roman followers to humble themselves in public. He made aristocratic young men parade through the streets of Rome in rags or even with a fox's tail tied behind them, and set noblemen to work as labourers building his church. With the help of Pope Gregory XIII, his church was built in place of an old medieval church, Santa Maria in Vallicella, and it has been known ever since as the Chiesa Nuova (new church).

Begun in 1575 by Matteo da Città di Castello and continued by Martino Longhi the Elder, it was consecrated in 1599 (although the façade, by Fausto Rughesi, was only finished in 1606). Against San Filippo's wishes, the interior was decorated after his death; Pietro da Cortona frescoed the nave, dome and apse, taking nearly 20 years. There are also three paintings by Rubens: *Madonna and Angels* above the altar, *Saints Domitilla, Nereus and Achilleus* on the right of the altar, and *Saints Gregory, Maurus and Papias* on the left. San Filippo is buried in his own chapel, to the left of the altar.

Borromini's façade of the Oratorio

Oratorio dei Filippini 16

Piazza della Chiesa Nuova.
Map 4 E4 & 11 B3. 📷 46, 62, 64. **Closed** for restoration.

With the adjoining church and convent, the oratory formed the centre of Filippo Neri's religious order, which was founded in 1575. Its members are commonly known as Filippini. The musical term "oratorio" (a religious text sung by solo voices and chorus) derives from the services that were held here.

Filippo Neri came to Rome aged 18 to work as a tutor. The city was undergoing a period of religious strife and an economic slump after the Sack of Rome in 1527. There was also an outbreak of the plague. It was left to newcomers like Neri and Ignazio di Loyola to revive the spiritual life of the city.

Neri formed a brotherhood of laymen who worshipped together and helped pilgrims and the sick (see Santissima Trinità dei Pellegrini p147). He founded the Oratory as a centre for religious discourse. Its conspicuous curving brick façade was built by Borromini in 1637–43.

Torre dell' Orologio 17

Piazza dell'Orologio. **Map** 4 E4 & 11 B3. 📷 40, 46, 62, 64.

Borromini built this clock tower to decorate one corner of the Convent of the Oratorians of San Filippo Neri in 1647–9. It is typical of Borromini in that the front and rear are concave and the sides convex. The mosaic of the Madonna beneath the clock is by Pietro da Cortona, while on the corner of the building is a small tabernacle to the Madonna flanked by angels in the style of Bernini.

Pietro da Cortona (1596–1669)

Palazzo del Banco di Santo Spirito 18

Via del Banco di Santo Spirito.
Map 4 D4 & 11 A2. 📷 40, 46, 62, 64. **Open** normal banking hours.

Formerly the mint of papal Rome, this palazzo is often referred to as the Antica Zecca (old mint). The upper storeys of the façade, built by Antonio da Sangallo the Younger in the 1520s, are in the shape of a Roman triumphal arch. Above it stand two Baroque statues symbolizing Charity and Thrift, and in the centre of the arch above the main entrance an inscription records the founding of the Banco di Santo Spirito by Pope Paul V Borghese in 1605.

Pope Paul was a very shrewd financier and he encouraged Romans to deposit their money at the bank by offering the vast estates of the Hospital of Santo Spirito (see p226) as security. The system catered only for the rudimentary banking requirements of the population, but business was brisk as people deposited money here safe in the knowledge that they could get it out simply by presenting a chit. The hospital coffers also gained from the system. The Banco di Santo Spirito still exists, but is now part of the Banca di Roma.

Façade of the Banco di Santo Spirito, built to resemble a Roman arch

Via dei Coronari ⑲

Map 4 D3 & 11 B2. 🚌 *40, 46, 62, 64, 70, 81, 87, 116, 186, 280, 492.*

Large numbers of medieval pilgrims making their way to St Peter's walked along this street to cross over the Tiber at Ponte Sant'Angelo. Of the businesses that sprang up to try to part the pilgrims from their money, the most enduring was the selling of rosaries, and the street is still named after the rosary sellers *(coronari)*. The street followed the course of the ancient Roman Via Recta (straight street), which originally ran from today's Piazza Colonna to the Tiber.

Making one's way through the vast throng of people in Via dei Coronari could be extremely hazardous. In the Holy Year of 1450, some 200 pilgrims died, crushed by the crowds or drowned in the Tiber. Following the tragedy, Pope Nicholas V demolished the Roman triumphal arch that stood at the entrance to Ponte Sant'Angelo. In the late 15th century, Pope Sixtus IV encouraged the building of private houses and palaces along the street.

Although the rosary sellers have been replaced by antiques dealers, the street still has many original buildings from the 15th and 16th centuries. One of the earliest, at Nos. 156–7, is known as the House of Fiammetta, the mistress of Cesare Borgia.

Antiques shop, Via dei Coronari

Cloister, San Salvatore in Lauro

San Salvatore in Lauro ⑳

Piazza San Salvatore in Lauro 15. **Map** 4 E3 & 11 B2. **Tel** *06-687 5187.* 🚌 *70, 81, 87, 116, 186, 280, 492.* **Open** *9am–noon, 4–6pm daily.* ✝

The church is named "in Lauro" after the laurel grove that grew here in ancient times. The church standing here today was constructed at the end of the 16th century by Ottaviano Mascherino. The bell tower and sacristy were 18th-century additions by Nicola Salvi, famous for the Trevi Fountain *(see p159)*.

The church contains the first great altarpiece by the 17th-century artist Pietro da Cortona, *The Birth of Jesus*, in the first chapel to the right.

The adjacent convent of San Giorgio, to the left, has a pretty Renaissance cloister, a frescoed refectory and the monument to Pope Eugenius IV (reigned 1431–47), moved here when the old St Peter's was pulled down. An extravagant Venetian, Eugenius would willingly spend thousands of ducats on his gold tiara, but requested a "simple, lowly burial place" near his predecessor Pope Eugenius III. His portrait, painted by Salviati, hangs in the refectory.

In 1669 San Salvatore in Lauro became the seat of a pious association, the Confraternity of the Piceni, who were inhabitants of the Marche region. Fanatically loyal to the pope, the Piceni were traditionally employed as papal soldiers and tax collectors.

Museo Napoleonico ㉑

Piazza di Ponte Umberto 1. **Map** 4 E3 & 11 C1. **Tel** *06-6880 6286.* 🚌 *70, 81, 87, 116, 186, 280, 492.* **Open** *9am–7pm Tue–Sun.* **Closed** *1 Jan, 1 May, 25 Dec.* **Adm charge.** 🗸 🖬 🖬

This museum contains memorabilia and portraits of Napoleon Bonaparte and his family. Personal relics of Napoleon himself include an Indian shawl he wore during his exile on St Helena.

After his death in 1821, the pope allowed many of the Bonaparte family to settle in Rome, including his mother Letizia, who lived in Palazzo Misciattelli on Via del Corso, and his sister Pauline who married the Roman Prince Camillo Borghese. The museum has a cast of her right breast, made by Canova in 1805 as a study for his statue of her as a reclining Venus, now in the Museo Borghese *(see p261)*. Portraits and personal effects of other members of the family are on display, including uniforms, court dresses, and a penny-farthing bicycle that belonged to Prince Eugène, the son of Emperor Napoleon III.

The last male of the Roman branch of the family was Napoleon Charles, portrayed in a late 19th-century painting by Guglielmo de Sanctis. The collection was assembled in 1927 by the Counts Primoli, the sons of Charles's sister, Carlotta Bonaparte.

Façade of San Salvatore in Lauro

The palace next door, in Via Zanardelli, houses the Racolta Praz, an impressive selection of over a thousand *objets d'art,* paintings and pieces of furniture. Dating from the 17th and 18th centuries, they were collected by the art historian and literary critic Mario Praz.

Side relief of the Ludovisi Throne, Palazzo Altemps

Entrance to Museo Napoleonico

Hostaria dell'Orso ㉒

Via dei Soldati 25. **Map** 4 E3 & 11 C2. 🚌 *70, 81, 87, 116, 186, 204, 280, 492, 628.* **Open** 8pm–1am Mon–Sat.

This ancient inn *(see p318)* has a 15th-century portico and loggia built with columns from Roman ruins. Visitors to the inn included the 16th-century French writers Rabelais and Montaigne. Dante is also said to have stayed here.

Palazzo Altemps ㉓

Piazza Sant'Apollinare 46. **Map** 4 E3 & 11 C2. **Tel** 06-3996 7700. 🚌 *70, 81, 87, 116, 280, 492, 628.* **Open** 9am–7.45pm Tue–Sun (last adm: 1 hour before closing.) **Closed** 1 Jan, 25 Dec. **Adm charge.** 🚻 🎦 📷

An extraordinary collection of Classical sculpture is housed in this branch of the Museo Nazionale Romano.

Restored as a museum during the 1990s, the palazzo was originally built for Girolamo Riario, nephew of Pope Sixtus IV in 1480. The Riario coat of arms can still be seen in the janitor's room. In the popular uprising that followed the pope's death in 1484, the building was sacked and Girolamo fled the city.

In 1568 the palazzo was bought by Cardinal Marco Sittico Altemps. His family was of German origin – the name is an Italianization of Hohenems – and influential in the church. The palazzo was renovated by Martino Longhi the Elder in the 1570s. He added the great belvedere, crowned with obelisks and a marble unicorn. The Altemps family were ostentatious collectors; the courtyard and its staircase are lined with ancient sculptures. These form part of the museum's collection, together with the Ludovisi collection of ancient sculptures, which was previously housed in the Museo Nazionale Romano in the Baths of Diocletian *(see p163).* Located on the ground floor is the Greek statue of Athena Parthenos and the Dionysius group, a Roman copy of

the Greek original. On the first floor, at the far end of the courtyard, visitors can admire the Painted Loggia, dating from 1595. The Ludovisi throne, a Greek original carved in the 5th century BC, is on the same floor. It is decorated with reliefs, one of which shows a young woman rising from the sea, who is thought to represent Aphrodite. In the room which is known as the Salone del Camino is the powerful statue *Galatian's Suicide,* a marble copy of a group originally made in bronze. Nearby is the Ludovisi Sarcophagus, dating from the 3rd century AD.

Galatian's Suicide in the Palazzo Altemps

PIAZZA DI SPAGNA

By the 16th century, the increase in numbers of visiting pilgrims and ecclesiastics was making life in Rome's already congested medieval centre unbearable. A new triangle of roads was built, still in place today, to help channel pilgrims as quickly as possible from the city's north gate, the Porta del Popolo, to the Vatican. By the 18th century hotels had sprung up all over

Lion fountain in Piazza del Popolo

the district. Today this attractive area offers much more: the superb works of Renaissance and Baroque art in Santa Maria del Popolo and Sant' Andrea delle Fratte, the magnificent reliefs of the restored Ara Pacis, art exhibitions in the Villa Medici, fine views of the city from the Spanish Steps and the Pincio Gardens and Rome's most famous shopping streets, centred around Via Condotti.

SIGHTS AT A GLANCE

Churches
All Saints ⑫
San Rocco ㉑
Sant'Andrea delle Fratte ①
Santa Maria dei Miracoli and
　Santa Maria in Montesanto ⑭
Santa Maria del
　Popolo pp138–9 ⑰
Santi Ambrogio e Carlo
　al Corso ㉒
Trinità dei Monti ⑩

Museums and Galleries
Casa di Goethe ⑬
Keats-Shelley
　Memorial House ⑦

Historic Buildings
Palazzo di Propaganda
　Fide ②
Villa Medici ⑪

Arches, Gates and Columns
Colonna dell'Immacolata ③
Porta del Popolo ⑱

Historic Streets and Piazzas
Piazza del Popolo ⑯
Piazza di Spagna ⑥

Spanish Steps ⑨
Via Condotti ④

Monuments and Tombs
Ara Pacis ⑲
Mausoleum of Augustus ⑳

Parks and Gardens
Pincio Gardens ⑮

Cafés and Restaurants
Babington's Tea Rooms ⑧
Caffè Greco ⑤

0 metres 300
0 yards 300

GETTING THERE
For Piazza di Spagna and the shops around Via Condotti, Spagna Metro station on line A is more convenient than the main bus routes along Via del Corso and Via del Tritone. Stay on until Flaminio Metro if you wish to visit Piazza del Popolo. For getting around locally, the 116 and 117 minibuses are very handy.

KEY
▨ Street-by-Street map
Ⓜ Metro station
— City Wall

SEE ALSO
- *Street Finder*, maps 4, 5
- *Where to Stay* pp301–3
- *Restaurants* pp318–19
- *Shops* pp334–51

◁ The Spanish Steps leading up to the church of Trinità dei Monti

Street-by-Street: Piazza di Spagna

The network of narrow
streets between Piazza di
Spagna and Via del Corso is
one of the liveliest areas in
Rome, drawing throngs of
tourists and Romans to its
discreet and elegant shops.
In the 18th century the area
was full of hotels for frivol-
ous English aristocrats doing
the Grand Tour, but there
were also artists, writers and
composers, who took the
city's history and culture
more seriously.

Caffè Greco
*Busts and portraits
recall the café's former
artistic patrons* ⑤

★ Piazza di Spagna
*For almost three centuries
the square with its curious
Barcaccia fountain in the
centre has been the chief
meeting place for
visitors to Rome* ⑥

**Via delle
Carrozze** took its
name from the
carriages of wealthy
tourists that used to
queue up here for
repairs.

Via Condotti
*This shadowy,
narrow street
has the smartest
shops in one
of the smartest
shopping areas
in the world* ④

Bulgari sells
very expensive
jewellery behind
an austere
shopfront in Via
Condotti.

| 0 metres | 75 |
| 0 yards | 75 |

KEY

- - - Suggested route

Ⓜ Metro station

Trinità dei Monti
This 16th-century church has a spectacular setting and some of the finest views in Rome ⑩

Babington's Tea Rooms
English tourists are catered for in the style of the 1890s ⑧

LOCATOR MAP
See Central Rome Map pp14–15

Colonna dell'Immacolata
A Roman column supports a statue of the Virgin Mary ③

Palazzo di Propaganda Fide
This façade (1665) was one of the last works of the great Francesco Borromini ②

Sant'Andrea delle Fratte
Pasquale Marini painted The Redemption *to decorate the interior of Borromini's high dome in 1691* ①

★ Keats-Shelley Memorial House
The library is part of the small museum established in the house where the English poet Keats died in 1821 ⑦

★ Spanish Steps
Even obscured by crowds, the steps are one of the glories of late Baroque Rome ⑨

STAR SIGHTS

★ Piazza di Spagna

★ Keats-Shelley Memorial House

★ Spanish Steps

Sant'Andrea delle Fratte ❶

Via Sant'Andrea delle Fratte 1. **Map** 5 A3. **Tel** 06-679 3191. 🚍 116, 117. Ⓜ Spagna. **Open** 6.30am–noon, 4–7pm daily (4.30–7.30pm summer). ✝

When Sant'Andrea delle Fratte was built in the 12th century, this was the northernmost edge of Rome. Though the church is now firmly embedded in the city, its name (*fratte* means thickets) recalls its original setting.

The church was completely rebuilt in the 17th century, partly by Borromini. His bell tower and dome, best viewed from the higher ground further up Via Capo le Case, are remarkable for the complex arrangement of concave and convex surfaces. The bell tower is particularly fanciful, with angel caryatids, flaming torches, and exaggerated scrolls like semi-folded hearts supporting a spiky crown.

In 1842, the Virgin Mary appeared in the church to a Jewish banker, who promptly converted to Christianity and became a missionary. Inside, the chapel of the Miraculous Madonna is the first thing you notice. The church is better known, however, for the angels that Borromini's rival, Bernini, carved for the Ponte Sant'Angelo. Pope Clement IX declared they were too lovely to be exposed to the weather, so they remained with Bernini's family until 1729, when they were moved to the church.

Palazzo di Propaganda Fide ❷

Via di Propaganda 1. **Map** 5 A2. **Tel** 06-6987 9299. **Fax** 06-6988 0246. 🚍 116, 117. Ⓜ Spagna. **Open** by appt (via fax).

The powerful Jesuit Congregation for the Propagation of the Faith was founded in 1622. Their headquarters had to be a remarkable building, and Bernini was commissioned. But Innocent X, who became pope in 1644, preferred the style of Borromini who was asked to continue. His extraordinary west façade, completed in 1662, must have outstripped everyone's expectations. It is striped with broad pilasters, between which the first-floor windows bend in, and the central bay bulges. A rigid band divides its floors, and the cornice above the convex central bay swerves inwards. The more you look at it, the more restless it seems; a sign perhaps of the increasing unhappiness of the architect who committed suicide in 1667.

Angel by Bernini, Sant'Andrea delle Fratte

Entrance to the Jesuit College

Colonna dell'Immacolata ❸

Piazza Mignanelli. **Map** 5 A2. 🚍 116, 117. Ⓜ Spagna.

Inaugurated in 1857, the column commemorates Pope Pius IX's proclamation of the doctrine of the Immaculate Conception, holding that the Virgin Mary was the only human being ever to have been born "without the stain of original sin". The column itself dates from ancient, pagan Rome but is crowned with a statue of the Virgin Mary.

On 8 December the Pope, assisted by the fire brigade, places a wreath around the head of the statue (*see p61*).

Portrait of Pope Pius IX (reigned 1846–78)

Via Condotti ❹

Map 5 A2. 🚌 81, 116, 117, 119, 492 and many routes along via del Corso or stopping at Piazza S. Silvestro. Ⓜ Spagna. See **Shops and Markets** pp333–45.

Named after the conduits that carried water to the Baths of Agrippa near the Pantheon, Via Condotti is now home to the most traditional of Rome's designer clothes shops. Stores selling shoes and other leather goods are also well represented. The street is extremely popular for early evening strolls, when elegant Italians mingle with tourists in shorts and trainers.

Slightly younger designers such as Laura Biagiotti and the Fendi sisters have shops on the parallel Via Borgognona, while Valentino and Giorgio Armani both have shops on Via Condotti itself. Valentino has a second branch on Via Bocca di Leone, which crosses Via Condotti just below Piazza di Spagna, and Versace also has a shop here. Giorgio Armani has a second store on nearby Via del Babuino, among the discreet art galleries, exclusive antique shops and furnishing stores.

View along Via Condotti towards the Spanish Steps

Caffè Greco ❺

Via Condotti 86. **Map** 5 A2. **Tel** 06-67 91 700. 🚌 81, 116, 117, 119, 492. Ⓜ Spagna. **Open** 9am–7pm daily. **Closed** 1 Jan, 14 & 15 Aug. ♿

This café was opened by a Greek (hence greco) in 1760, and throughout the 18th

Caffè Greco, over 240 years old

century it was a favourite meeting place for foreign artists. Writers such as Keats, Byron and Goethe and composers like Liszt, Wagner and Bizet all breakfasted and drank here. So too did Casanova, and mad King Ludwig of Bavaria. Today, Italians stand in the crowded foyer to sip a quick espresso coffee, and foreigners sit in a cosy back room, whose walls are studded with portraits of the café's illustrious customers.

Piazza di Spagna ❻

Map 5 A2. 🚌 116, 117, 119. Ⓜ Spagna.

Shaped like a crooked bow tie and surrounded by tall, shuttered houses painted in muted shades of ochre, cream and russet, Piazza di Spagna (Spanish square) is crowded all day and (in summer) most of the night. It is the most famous square in Rome, and has long been the haunt of foreign visitors and expatriates.

In the 17th century Spain's ambassador to the Holy See had his headquarters on the square, and the area around it was deemed to be Spanish territory. Foreigners who unwittingly trespassed were liable to be dragooned into the Spanish army. In the 18th and 19th centuries Rome was almost as popular with

visitors as it is today, and the square stood at the heart of the city's main hotel district. Some of the travellers came in search of knowledge and artistic inspiration, but most were more interested in gambling, collecting ancient statues and conducting love affairs with Italian women.

Not surprisingly, the wealthy travellers attracted hordes of beggars, who were usually supplied with tear-jerking letters by scribes who worked in the square.

The Fontana della Barcaccia in the square is the least showy of Rome's Baroque fountains, and it is often completely screened from view by people resting on its rim. It was designed either by the famous Gian Lorenzo Bernini or by his father Pietro. Because the pressure from the aqueduct that feeds the fountain is extremely low there are no spectacular cascades or spurts of water. Instead, Bernini constructed a leaking boat – barcaccia means useless, old boat – which lies half submerged in a shallow pool.

Pope Urban VIII's arms, with the Barberini bees

The bees and suns that decorate the Fontana della Barcaccia are taken from the family coat of arms of Pope Urban VIII Barberini, who commissioned the fountain.

The Fontana della Barcaccia at the foot of the Spanish Steps

Bust of Shelley by Moses Ezekiel

Keats-Shelley Memorial House ❼

Piazza di Spagna 26. **Map** 5 A2.
Tel 06-678 4235. 🚌 116, 117, 119.
Ⓜ Spagna. **Open** 10am–1pm,
2–6pm Mon–Fri, 11am–2pm, 3–6pm
Sat. **Closed** at Christmas and
New Year. **Adm charge**. 📷
📹 book in advance. 🔲
www.keats-shelley-house.org

In November 1820 the English
poet John Keats came to stay
with his friend, the painter
Joseph Severn, in a dusty
pink house, the Casina
Rossa, on the corner of the
Spanish Steps. Suffering from
consumption, Keats had been
sent to Rome by his doctor, in
the hope that the mild, dry
climate would help the young
man's recovery. Depressed
because of scathing criticism of
his work and tormented by his
love for a young girl named
Fanny Brawne, Keats died the
following February, aged 25.

His death inspired fellow
poet Percy Bysshe Shelley
to write the poem *Mourn
not for Adonais*. In July 1822
Shelley himself was drowned
in a boating accident in the
Gulf of La Spezia off the
coast of Liguria. Keats,
Shelley and Severn are all
buried in Rome's Protestant
Cemetery (*see p205*).

In 1906 the house was
bought by an Anglo-American
association and preserved as
a memorial and library in
honour of English Romantic

poets. The relics include a
lock of Keats's hair, some
fragments of Shelley's bones
in a tiny urn and a garish
carnival mask picked up by
Lord Byron as a souvenir of
a trip to Venice. You can visit
the room where Keats died,
though all the original
furniture was burnt after
his death, on papal orders.

Babington's Tea Rooms ❽

Piazza di Spagna 23. **Map** 5 A2. **Tel**
06-678 6027. 🚌 116, 117, 119. Ⓜ
Spagna. **Open** 9am–8.15pm
daily. **Closed** 25 Dec. ♿

These august, old-fashioned
tea rooms were opened in
1896 by two Englishwomen,
Anna Maria and Isabel Cargill
Babington, to serve homesick
British tourists with scones,
jam and pots of Earl Grey tea.
The food remains homely –
shepherd's pie and chicken
supreme for lunch, muffins
and cinnamon toast for tea –
although these days the menu
offers pancakes with maple
syrup for breakfast as well as
the traditional bacon and egg.

**Purveyors of English breakfasts to
homesick exiles since 1896**

Spanish Steps ❾

Scalinata della Trinità dei Monti,
Piazza di Spagna. **Map** 5 A2. 🚌
116, 117, 119. Ⓜ Spagna.

In the 17th century the French
owners of Trinità dei Monti
decided to link the church
with Piazza di Spagna by
building a magnificent new
flight of steps. They also
planned to place an equestrian
statue of King Louis XIV at the
top. Pope Alexander VII Chigi
was not too happy at the

The Spanish Steps in spring with azaleas in full bloom

prospect of erecting a statue of a French monarch in the papal city, and the arguments continued until the 1720s when an Italian architect, Francesco de Sanctis, produced a design that satisfied both parties. The steps, completed in 1726, combine straight sections, curves and terraces to create one of the city's most dramatic and distinctive landmarks.

When the Victorian novelist Charles Dickens visited Rome, he reported that the Spanish Steps were the meeting place for artists' models, who would dress in colourful traditional costumes, hoping to catch the attention of a wealthy artist. The steps are now a popular place to sit, write postcards, take photos, flirt, busk or watch the passers-by, but eating here is not allowed.

Trinità dei Monti ⑩

Piazza della Trinità dei Monti. **Map** 5 A2. **Tel** 06-679 4179. 116, 117, 119. M Spagna. **Open** 9am–1pm, 3–7pm Tue–Sun.

Trinità dei Monti's bell towers

The views of Rome from the platform in front of the twin bell-towered façade of Trinità dei Monti are so beautiful that the church itself is often ignored. It is, however, unusual for Rome, for it was founded by the French in 1495, and although it was later badly damaged, there are still traces of attractive late Gothic latticework in the vaults of the transept. The interconnecting side chapels are decorated with Mannerist paintings, including two fine works by Daniele da Volterra.

19th-century engraving of the inner façade of the Villa Medici

A pupil of Michelangelo, Volterra had to paint clothes on the nudes in the *Last Judgment* in the Sistine Chapel, in response to the objections of Pope Pius IV.

Michelangelo's influence is obvious in the powerfully muscled bodies shown in the *Deposition* (second chapel on the left). The circles of gesturing figures and dancing angels surrounding the Virgin Mary in the *Assumption* (third chapel on the right) have more in common with the graceful style of Raphael.

Villa Medici ⑪

Accademia di Francia a Roma, Viale Trinità dei Monti 1. **Map** 5 A2. **Tel** 06-676 11. 117, 119. M Spagna. **Open** for exhibitions and concerts. **Gardens open** for visits at 10.30am, 11.45am, 2pm & 3.15pm daily. **Adm charge.**

Superbly positioned on the Pincio hill above Piazza di Spagna, this 16th-century villa has kept the name it assumed when Cardinal Ferdinando de' Medici bought it in 1576. From the terrace you can look across the city to Castel Sant'Angelo, from where Queen Christina of Sweden is said to have fired the large cannon ball which now sits in the basin of the fountain.

The villa is home to the French Academy. This was founded by Louis XIV in 1666 to give a few select painters the chance to study in

Fontana del Sileno, on Via del Babuino since 1957

Rome. Nicolas Poussin was one of the first advisers to the Academy, Ingres was a director and ex-students include Jean-Honoré Fragonard and François Boucher.

After 1803 when the French Academy moved to the Villa Medici, musicians were also admitted; both Berlioz and Debussy came to Rome as students of the Academy.

All Saints ⑫

Via del Babuino 153B. **Map** 4 F2. **Tel** 06-3600 1881. 117, 119. **Open** 8am–4pm daily.

In 1816 the Pope gave English residents and visitors the right to hold Anglican services in Rome, but it wasn't until the early 1880s that they acquired a site to build their own church. The architect was G E Street, best known in Britain for his Neo-Gothic churches and the London Law Courts. All Saints is also built in Victorian Neo-Gothic, and the interior, though splendidly decorated with different coloured Italian marbles, has a very English air. Street also designed St-Paul's-within-the-Walls in Via Nazionale, whose interior is a jewel of British Pre-Raphaelite art.

The street on which All Saints stands got its name from the Fontana del Sileno, known as Babuino (baboon) due to the sad condition in which it was found.

Casa di Goethe ⑬

Via del Corso 18. **Map** 4 F1. **Tel** *06-3265 0412.* 🚌 *95, 117, 119, 490, 495, 628, 926.* 🚊 *2.* Ⓜ *Flaminio.* **Open** *10am–6pm Tue–Sun.* **Adm charge.** ♿ ✏ ◻ **www**.casadigoethe.it

The German poet, dramatist and novelist Johann Wolfgang von Goethe (1749–1832) lived in this house from 1786 until 1788 and worked on a journal that eventually formed part of his travel book *The Italian Journey*. Rome's noisy street life irritated him, especially during Carnival time. He was a little perturbed by the number of murders in his neighbourhood, but Rome energized him and his book became one of the most influential ever written about Italy.

Santa Maria dei Miracoli and Santa Maria in Montesanto ⑭

Piazza del Popolo. **Map** 4 F1. 🚌 *95, 117, 119, 490, 495, 628, 926.* 🚊 *2.* Ⓜ *Flaminio.* **Santa Maria dei Miracoli Tel** *06-361 0250.* **Open** *7am–1pm, 4–7.30pm Mon–Sat, 8am–1pm, 4.30–7.30pm Sun & public hols.* ✝ ♿ **Santa Maria in Montesanto Tel** *06-361 0594.* **Open** *4–7pm Mon–Sat, 11am–12.30pm Sun.*

The two churches at the south end of Piazza del Popolo were designed by the architect Carlo Rainaldi (1611–91), proof that he could be as ingenious as his peers, Bernini and Borromini. To provide a focal point for the piazza, the churches had to appear

Portrait of Goethe in the Roman countryside by Tischbein (1751–1821)

symmetrical, but the site on the left was narrower. So, Rainaldi gave Santa Maria dei Miracoli (on the right) a circular dome and Santa Maria in Montesanto an oval one to squeeze it into the narrower site, while keeping the sides of the supporting drums that face the piazza identical.

Pincio Gardens ⑮

Il Pincio. **Map** 4 F1. 🚌 *95, 117, 119, 490, 495, 628, 926.* 🚊 *2.* Ⓜ *Flaminio.*

The Pincio Gardens lie above Piazza del Popolo on a hillside that has been so skilfully terraced and richly planted with trees that, from below, the zig-zagging road climbing to the gardens is virtually invisible. In ancient Roman times, there were magnificent gardens on the Pincio hill, but the present gardens were designed in the early 19th century by Giuseppe Valadier (who also redesigned the Piazza

The Pincio Gardens water clock

del Popolo). The broad avenues, lined with umbrella pines, palm trees and evergreen oaks soon became a fashionable place to stroll, and even this century such diverse characters as Gandhi and Mussolini, Richard Strauss and King Farouk of Egypt patronized the Casina Valadier, an exclusive café and restaurant in the grounds.

From the Pincio's main square, Piazzale Napoleone I, the panoramic views of Rome stretch from the Monte Mario to the Janiculum. For full effect, approach the gardens from the grounds of Villa Borghese *(see pp258–9)* above the Pincio, or along Viale della Trinità dei Monti.

The twin churches of Santa Maria in Montesanto (left) and Santa Maria dei Miracoli in a 19th-century view of Piazza del Popolo

The panorama is particularly beautiful at sunset, the traditional time for tourists to take a stroll in the gardens.

One of the most striking features of the park itself is an Egyptian-style obelisk which Emperor Hadrian erected on the tomb of his favourite, the beautiful male slave Antinous. After the slave's premature death (according to some accounts he died saving the emperor's life), Hadrian deified him.

The 19th-century water clock on Via dell'Orologio was designed by a Dominican monk. It was displayed at the Paris Exhibition of 1889.

The Casina Valadier restaurant in the Pincio Gardens

Piazza del Popolo ⓰

Map 4 F1. 🚌 95, 117, 119, 490, 495, 926. 🚎 2. Ⓜ Flaminio.

A vast cobbled oval standing at the apex of the triangle of roads known as the Trident, Piazza del Popolo forms a grand symmetrical antechamber to the heart of Rome. Twin Neo-Classical façades stand on either side of the Porta del Popolo; an Egyptian obelisk rises in the centre; and the matching domes and porticoes of Santa Maria dei Miracoli and Santa Maria in Montesanto flank the beginning of Via del Corso.

Although it is now one of the most unified squares in Rome, Piazza del Popolo evolved gradually over the centuries. In 1589 the great town-planning pope, Sixtus V, had the obelisk erected in the centre by Domenico Fontana.

Traditional carnival band in Piazza del Popolo

Over 3,000 years old, the obelisk was originally brought to Rome by Augustus to adorn the Circus Maximus after the conquest of Egypt. Almost a century later Pope Alexander VII commissioned Carlo Rainaldi to build the twin Santa Marias.

In the 19th century the piazza was turned into a grandiose oval by Giuseppe Valadier, the designer of the Pincio Gardens. He also encased Santa Maria del Popolo in a Neo-Classical shell to make its south façade fit in better with the overall appearance of the piazza.

In contrast to the piazza's air of ordered rationalism, many of the events staged here were barbaric. In the 18th and 19th centuries, public executions were held in Piazza del Popolo, often as part of the celebration of Carnival. Condemned men were sometimes hammered to death by repeated blows to the temples. The last time a criminal was executed in this way was in 1826, even though the guillotine had by then been adopted as a more scientific means of execution.

The riderless horse races from the piazza down Via del Corso were scarcely more humane: the performance of the runners was enhanced by feeding the horses stimulants, wrapping them in nail-studded ropes, and letting off fireworks at their heels.

Santa Maria del Popolo ⓱

See pp138–9.

Porta del Popolo ⓲

Between Piazzale Flaminio and Piazza del Popolo. **Map** 4 F1. 🚌 95, 117, 119, 490, 495, 926. 🚎 2. Ⓜ Flaminio.

The Via Flaminia, built in 220 BC to connect Rome with Italy's Adriatic coast, enters the city at Porta del Popolo, a grand 16th-century gate built on the orders of Pope Pius IV Medici. The architect, Nanni di Baccio Bigio, modelled it on a Roman triumphal arch. The outer face has statues of St Peter and St Paul on either side and a huge Medici coat of arms above.

A century later, Pope Alexander VII commissioned Bernini to decorate the inner face to celebrate the arrival in Rome of Queen Christina of Sweden. Lesser visitors were often held up while customs officers rifled their luggage. The only way to speed things up was with a bribe.

Porta del Popolo's central arch

Santa Maria del Popolo ⑰

One of Rome's greatest stores of artistic treasures, this early Renaissance church was commissioned by Pope Sixtus IV della Rovere in 1472. Among the artists who worked on the building were Andrea Bregno and Pinturicchio. Later additions were made by Bramante and Bernini. Many illustrious families have chapels here, all decorated with appropriate splendour. The Della Rovere Chapel has delightful Pinturicchio frescoes, the Cerasi Chapel has two Caravaggio masterpieces, *The Conversion of St Paul* and *The Crucifixion of St Peter*, but the finest of all is the Chigi Chapel designed by Raphael for his patron, the banker Agostino Chigi. The most striking of the church's many Renaissance tombs are the two by Andrea Sansovino behind the main altar.

★ Chigi Chapel
Raphael designed this chapel, which has an altarpiece by Sebastiano del Piombo. Niches on either side of the altar house sculptures by Bernini and Lorenzetto. Mosaics in the dome show God as creator of the seven heavenly bodies.

Kneeling Skeleton
This floor mosaic of the figure of death was added to the Chigi Chapel in the 17th century.

NERO'S GHOST

Nero lived on in the imagination of the people long after the fall of the Roman Empire. In the Middle Ages a legend arose that a walnut tree growing here on the spot where his ashes were buried was haunted by the emperor. Ravens roosting in the tree were thought to be demons tormenting him for his hideous crimes. When the first church was built here in 1099 by Pope Paschal II, the tree was cut down, supposedly putting an end to the supernatural events that had terrified local people.

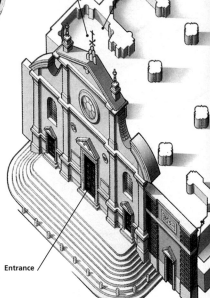

Entrance

Cybo
Chapel

STAR FEATURES

★ Chigi Chapel

★ Caravaggio Paintings in Cerasi Chapel

★ Delphic Sibyl

Della Rovere Chapel
Pinturicchio painted the frescoes in the lunettes and the Nativity above the altar in 1490.

VISITORS' CHECKLIST

Piazza del Popolo 12. **Map** 4 F1.
Tel 06-361 0836. 🚌 95, 117,
119, 490, 495, 926. 🚊 2. Ⓜ
Flaminio. **Open** 7.30am–noon,
4–7pm Mon–Sat, 7.30am–
1.30pm, 4.30–7.30pm Sun. ✝

★ Caravaggio Paintings in Cerasi Chapel

One of two Caravaggios in the Cerasi Chapel, The Crucifixion of St Peter uses dramatic fore-shortening to highlight the sheer effort involved in turning the saint's crucifix upside down.

The altarpiece of *The Assumption* is by Annibale Carracci (1540–1609).

Stained Glass

In 1509 French artist Guillaume de Marcillat was invited to provide Rome's first two stained-glass windows.

The Tomb of Ascanio Sforza, who died in 1505, is by Andrea Sansovino.

★ Delphic Sibyl

This is one of a series of frescoes by Pinturicchio, some Classical and others Biblical, painted in 1508–10 to decorate the ceiling of the apse.

The altar houses the 13th-century painting known as the *Madonna del Popolo.*

The Tomb of Giovanni della Rovere (1483) is by pupils of Andrea Bregno.

TIMELINE

	1213–27 Church enlarged under Gregory IX	*Pinturicchio (c.1454–1513)*		**1485–9** Della Rovere Chapel painted by Pinturicchio	**1513–16** Raphael designs and executes Chigi Chapel
1090	**1200**	**1300**	**1400**	**1500**	
1099 Paschal II builds chapel over tombs of the Domitia family (which included Nero) in honour of the Madonna		*Pope Paschal II (reigned 1099–1118)* **1473** Main altar built	**1472–8** Sixtus IV builds church (one of the first Renaissance churches in Rome)		**1530–34** Chigi Chapel altarpiece built by Sebastiano del Piombo

Ara Pacis ⑲

Lungotevere in Augusta. **Map** 4 F2.
Tel 06-0608. 🚌 70, 81, 117, 119,
186, 628. **Open** 9am–7pm Tue–Sun
(last adm: 6pm). **Closed** 1 Jan, 1 May,
25 Dec. 🎫 ♿ 📷

Frieze on south wall showing procession with the family of Augustus

Reconstructed at considerable expense over many years, the Ara Pacis (Altar of Peace) is one of the most significant monuments of ancient Rome. It celebrates the peace created throughout the Mediterranean area by Emperor Augustus after his victorious campaigns

Marcus Agrippa (right)

in Gaul and Spain. The monument was commissioned by the Senate in 13 BC and completed four years later. It was positioned so that the shadow of the huge obelisk sundial on Campus Martius *(see p113)* would fall upon it on Augustus' birthday. It is a square enclosure on a low platform with the altar in the centre. All surfaces are decorated with magnificent friezes and reliefs carved in Carrara marble. The reliefs on the north and south walls depict a procession that took place on 4 July 13 BC,

in which the members of the emperor's family can be identified, ranked by their position in the succession. At the time the heir apparent was Marcus Agrippa, husband of Augustus's daughter Julia. All the portraits in the relief are carved with extraordinary realism, even the innocent toddler clinging to his mother's skirts.

The tale of the rediscovery of the Ara Pacis dates back to the 16th century, when the first panels were unearthed. One section ended up in Paris, another in Florence. Further discoveries were made in the late 19th century, when archaeologists finally realized

just what they had found. What we see today has all been pieced together since 1938, in part original, in part facsimile. In 1999 the architect Richard Meier designed a building to house the monument.

Livia (right), Augustus's wife and the mother of Tiberius, with an unidentified member of the family

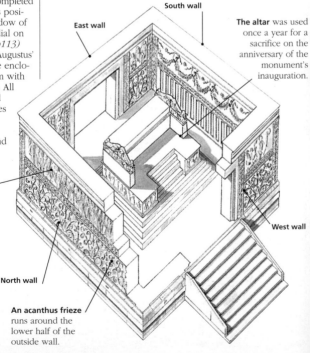

South wall

East wall

The altar was used once a year for a sacrifice on the anniversary of the monument's inauguration.

West wall

North wall

An acanthus frieze runs around the lower half of the outside wall.

Augustus's young grandson, Lucius

Mausoleum of Augustus ⑳

Piazza Augusto Imperatore.
Map 4 F2. **Tel** 06-0608. 81, 117, 492, 628, 926. **Open** by appt only (see p383).

Now just a weedy mound ringed with cypresses and sadly strewn with litter, this was once the most prestigious burial place in Rome. Augustus had the mausoleum built in 28 BC, the year he became sole ruler, as a tomb for himself and his descendants. The circular building was 87 m (285 ft) in diameter with two obelisks (now in Piazza del Quirinale and Piazza dell'Esquilino) at the entrance.

Inside were four concentric passageways linked by corridors where the urns containing the ashes of the Imperial family were placed. The first to be buried here was Augustus's favourite nephew, Marcellus, who had married Julia, the emperor's daughter. He died in 23 BC, possibly poisoned by Augustus's second wife Livia, who felt that her son, Tiberius, would make a more reliable emperor. When Augustus died in AD 14, his ashes were placed in the mausoleum, Tiberius duly became emperor, and dynastic poisonings continued to fill the family vault with urns.

This sinister monument was later used as a medieval fortress, a vineyard, a private garden, and even, in the 18th century, as an auditorium and a theatre.

Augustus, the first Roman emperor

Madonna, San Rocco and Sant'Antonio with Victims of the Plague by Il Baciccia (1639–1709)

San Rocco ㉑

Largo San Rocco 1. **Map** 4 F2. **Tel** 06-689 6416 81, 117, 492, 628, 926. **Open** 7.30–9.15am, 4.30–8pm Mon–Sat, 8.30am–1pm Sun. **Closed** 17–31 Aug

This church, with a restrained Neo-Classical façade by Giuseppe Valadier, the designer of Piazza del Popolo, began life as the chapel of a 16th-century hospital with beds for 50 men – San Rocco was a healer of the plague-stricken. A maternity wing was added for the wives of Tiber bargees to save them from having to give birth in the insanitary conditions of a boat. The hospital came to be used by unmarried mothers, and one section was set aside for women who wished to be unknown. They were even permitted to wear a veil for the duration of their stay. Unwanted children were sent to an orphanage, and if any mothers or children died they were buried in anonymous graves. The hospital was abandoned in the early 20th century, and demolished in the 1930s during the excavation of the Mausoleum of Augustus.

The church sacristy is an interesting Baroque altarpiece (c.1660) by Il Baciccia, the artist who decorated the ceiling of the Gesù *(see pp114–15)*.

Santi Ambrogio e Carlo al Corso ㉒

Via del Corso 437. **Map** 4 F2. **Tel** 06-682 8101. 81, 117, 492, 628, 926. **Open** 7am–7pm daily.

This church belonged to the Lombard community in Rome, and is dedicated to two canonized bishops of Milan, Lombardy's capital. In 1471, Pope Sixtus IV gave the Lombards a church which they dedicated to Sant'Ambrogio, who died in 397. Then in 1610, when Carlo Borromeo was canonized, the church was rebuilt in his honour. Most of the new church was the work of father and son, Onorio and Martino Longhi, but the fine dome is by Pietro da Cortona. The altarpiece by Carlo Maratta (1625–1713) is the *Gloria dei Santi Ambrogio e Carlo*. An ambulatory leads behind the altar to a chapel housing the the heart of San Carlo in a richly decorated reliquary.

Statue of San Carlo by Attilio Selva (1888–1970) behind the apse of Santi Ambrogio e Carlo

CAMPO DE' FIORI

Between Corso Vittorio Emanuele II and the Tiber, the city displays many distinct personalities. The open-air market of Campo de' Fiori preserves the lively, bohemian atmosphere of the medieval inns that once flourished here, while the area also contains Renaissance palazzi, such as Palazzo Farnese and Palazzo Spada, where powerful Roman families built

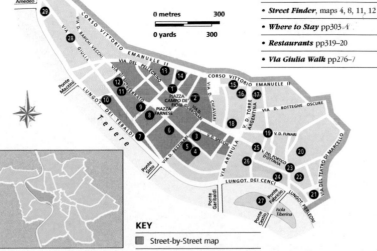

18th-century Madonna in Campo de' Fiori

their fortress-like houses near the route of papal processions. Close by, overlooking the picturesque Tiber Island, lies the former Jewish Ghetto, where many traces of daily life from past centuries can still be seen. The Portico of Octavia and the Theatre of Marcellus are spectacular examples of the city's many-layered history, built up over the half-ruined remains of ancient Rome.

SIGHTS AT A GLANCE

Churches and Temples
San Carlo ai Catinari ⑱
San Giovanni dei Fiorentini ㉙
San Girolamo della Carità ⑨
San Nicola in Carcere ㉑
Sant'Eligio degli Orefici ⑩
Santa Maria dell'Orazione
   e Morte ⑦
Santa Maria in Campitelli ⑳
Santa Maria in Monserrato ⑪
Santissima Trinità
   dei Pellegrini ⑤

Museums and Galleries
Burcardo Theatre Museum ⑮
Palazzo Spada ⑥
Piccola Farnesina ⑭

Historic Buildings
Casa di Lorenzo Manilio ㉕
Palazzo Cenci ㉖
Palazzo del Monte di Pietà ③
Palazzo della Cancelleria ⑬
Palazzo Farnese ⑧
Palazzo Pio Righetti ②
Palazzo Ricci ⑫

Fountains
Fontana delle Tartarughe ⑲

Historic Streets and Piazzas
Campo de' Fiori ①
Ghetto and Synagogue ㉔
Tiber Island ㉗
Via Giulia ㉘

Famous Theatres
Teatro Argentina ⑯

Ancient Sites
Area Sacra dell'Argentina ⑰
Portico of Octavia ㉓
Sotterranei di San Paolo
   alla Regola ④
Theatre of Marcellus ㉒

GETTING THERE
Only bus 116 can manage the narrow streets around Campo de' Fiori, but many routes, including the 40, 46, 62 and 64, and tram 8, converge on Largo Argentina. This is a useful starting point for exploring the area. Only the 40, 46, 62 and 64 run the full length of Corso Vittorio Emanuele II while 23 and 280 run along Lungotevere.

SEE ALSO

0 metres 300
0 yards 300

KEY

☐ Street-by-Street map

◁ **Fruit stalls surrounding the statue of Giordano Bruno in the Campo de' Fiori market**

Street-by-Street: Campo de' Fiori

This fascinating part of Renaissance Rome is also an exciting area for shopping and night life, centred on the market square of Campo de' Fiori. Its stalls supply many nearby restaurants, and young people shop for clothes in Via dei Giubbonari. Popular restaurants keep the area alive late into the night, when overcrowding and drunks can become problems. By day there are great buildings to admire, though few are open to the public. Two exceptions are the Piccola Farnesina, with its collection of Classical statues, and Palazzo Spada, home to many important paintings.

Sant'Eligio degli Orefici
A small Renaissance church designed by Raphael is concealed behind a later façade **⑩**

Palazzo Ricci
Painted Classical scenes were a favourite form of decoration for the façades of Renaissance houses **⑫**

San Girolamo della Carità
The chief attraction of this church is Borromini's fabulous Spada Chapel **⑨**

Santa Maria in Monserrato
This church, which has strong connections with Spain, houses a Bernini bust of Cardinal Pedro Foix de Montoya **⑪**

Santa Maria dell'Orazione e Morte
A pair of dramatic winged skulls flank the doorway to this church dedicated to the burial of the dead **⑦**

KEY

– – – Suggested route

0 metres	75
0 yards	75

Palazzo Farnese
Michelangelo and other great artists helped create this monumental Renaissance palazzo **⑧**

Palazzo della Cancelleria
The papal administration ran the affairs of the Church from this vast building **13**

Piccola Farnesina
This plaque honours Giovanni Barracco. His sculpture collection is housed in the palazzo **14**

LOCATOR MAP
See Central Rome Map pp14–15

PIAZZA DELLA CANCELLERIA

VIA DEI BAULLARI

PIAZZA CAMPO DE' FIORI

VIA DEI GIUBBONARI

VIA CAPO DI FERRO

PIAZZA DEL MONTE DI PIETÀ

VIA DEGLI SPECCHI

I PETTINARI

★ **Campo de' Fiori**
This colourful market makes Piazza Campo de' Fiori one of Rome's most entertaining squares **1**

Palazzo Pio Righetti
Heraldic eagles stare down from the pediments of the palazzo's windows **2**

Palazzo del Monte di Pietà
This was a papal institution, where the poor pawned their possessions in order to borrow small sums of money **3**

Sotterranei di San Paolo alla Regola
Remains of a Roman house have survived in the basement of an old palace **4**

★ **Palazzo Spada**
The picture gallery houses a collection started by two wonderfully eccentric 17th-century cardinals **6**

Santissima Trinità dei Pellegrini
The principal role of this church was one of charity, looking after poor pilgrims arriving in Rome **5**

STAR SIGHTS

★ Campo de' Fiori

★ Palazzo Spada

Campo de' Fiori ❶

Piazza Campo de' Fiori. **Map** 4 E4 & 11 C4. 🚌 116 and routes to Largo di Torre Argentina or Corso Vittorio Emanuele II. See **Markets** p352.

The Campo de' Fiori (field of flowers), once a meadow, occupies the site of the open space facing the Theatre of Pompey. Cardinals and noble-men used to rub shoulders with fishmongers and foreign-ers in the piazza's market, making it one of the liveliest areas of medieval and Renais-sance Rome. Today's market retains much of the traditional lively atmosphere.

In the centre of the square is a statue of the philosopher Giordano Bruno, burnt at the stake for heresy here in 1600. The hooded figure is a grim reminder of the executions that were held here.

The piazza was surrounded by inns for pilgrims and other travellers. Many of these were once owned by the successful 15th-century courtesan, Vannozza Catanei, mistress of Pope Alexander VI Borgia. On the corner between the piazza and Via del Pellegrino you can see Catanei's shield, which she had decorated with her own coat of arms and those of her husband and her lover, the Borgia pope.

Market stalls in Campo de' Fiori

Palazzo Pio Righetti ❷

Piazza del Biscione 89. **Map** 4 E5 & 11 C4. 🚌 116 and routes to Largo Torre Argentina or Corso Vittorio Emanuele II. **Not open** to the public.

The vast 17th-century Palazzo Pio Righetti was built over the ruined Theatre of Pompey.

Window pediment with heraldic lion and pine cones, Palazzo Pio Righetti

The windows of the palazzo are decorated with lions and pine cones from the coat of arms of the Pio da Carpi family who lived here.

The curve of the Theatre of Pompey, completed in 55 BC, is followed by Via di Grotta Pinta. Rome's first permanent theatre was built of stone and concrete and in the basement of the Pancrazio restaurant you can see early examples of *opus reticulatum* – small square blocks of tufa (porous rock) set diagonally as a facing for a concrete wall.

Palazzo del Monte di Pietà ❸

Piazza del Monte di Pietà 33. **Map** 4 E5 & 11 C4. **Tel** 06-6844 2001. 🚌 116 and routes to Largo di Torre Argentina or Corso Vittorio Emanuele II. 🚊 8. **Chapel open** only by appt. Ring well in advance between 9am and noon.

The Monte, as it is known, is a public institution, founded in 1539 by Pope Paul III Farnese as a pawnshop to staunch the usury then ram-pant in the city. The building still has offices and auction rooms for the sale of unre-deemed goods.

The stars with diagonal bands on the huge central plaque decorating the façade are the coat of arms of Pope Clement VIII Aldobrandini, added when Carlo Maderno enlarged the palace in the 17th century. The clock on the left was added later.

Within, the chapel is a jewel of Baroque architecture, adorned with gilded stucco, marble panelling and reliefs. The decoration makes a per-fect setting for the sculptures by Domenico Guidi – a bust of San Carlo Borromeo and a relief of the *Pietà*. There are also splendid reliefs by Gio-vanni Battista Théudon and Pierre Legros of biblical scenes illustrating the charita-ble nature of the institution.

Relief by Théudon of *Joseph Distributing Grain to the Egyptians* in Palazzo del Monte di Pietà

Sotterranei di San Paolo alla Regola ❹

Via di San Paolo alla Regola. **Map** 11 C5. **Tel** 06-0608. 🚌 23, 116, 280 and routes to Largo di Torre Argentina. 🚊 8. **Open** by appt only; permit needed (see p383).

An old palace hides the per-fectly conserved remains of an ancient Roman house, dat-ing from the 2nd–3rd centu-ries. Restoration works are being carried out in order to open this site to the public, but at present it is only possi-ble to visit by special arrangement.

A ramp leads down well below today's street level, to reveal the locations of shops of the time. One level above is the Stanza della Colonna, at one time an open courtyard, with traces of frescoes and mosaics on its walls.

Guido Reni's *Holy Trinity*, in Santissima Trinità dei Pellegrini

Santissima Trinità dei Pellegrini ❺

Piazza della Trinità dei Pellegrini. **Map** 4 E5 & 11 C5. **Tel** 06-686 8451. 🚍 23, 116, 280 and routes to Largo di Torre Argentina. 🚊 8. **Open** 4.30– 7.15pm daily (also 8.30am–1pm Sun).

The church was donated in the 16th century to a charitable organization founded by San Filippo Neri to care for the poor and sick, in particular the thousands of paupers who flocked in pilgrimage to Rome during the special holy years known as Jubilees. The 18th-century façade has niches with statues of the Evangelists by Bernardino Ludovisi. The interior, with Corinthian columns, ends in a horseshoe vault and apse, dominated by Guido Reni's striking altarpiece of the Holy Trinity (1625). The frescoes in the lantern are also by Reni. Other interesting paintings include *St Gregory the Great Freeing Souls from Purgatory,* by Baldassarre Croce (third chapel to the left); Cavalier d'Arpino's *Virgin and Saints* (second chapel to the left); and a painting by Borgognone (1677) of the Virgin and recently canonized saints, including San Filippo Neri. In the sacristy are depictions of the nobility washing the feet of pilgrims, a custom which was started by San Filippo.

Palazzo Spada ❻

Piazza Capo di Ferro 13. **Map** 2 F5. **Tel** 06-686 1158 (Palazzo) or 06-32 810 (Galleria). 🚍 23, 116, 280 and routes to Largo di Torre Argentina. 🚊 8. **Galleria Spada Open** 8.30am– 7.30pm Tue–Sun (last adm: 7pm). **Closed** 1 Jan, 25 Dec. **Adm charge**. 🚫 ♿ 📷 🏛

This majestic palazzo, built around 1550 for Cardinal Capo di Ferro, has an elegant stuccoed courtyard and façade decorated with reliefs evoking Rome's glorious past.

Cardinal Bernardino Spada, who lived here in the 17th century with his brother Virginio (also a cardinal), hired architects Bernini and Borromini to work on the building. The brothers' whimsical delight in false perspectives resulted in a colonnaded gallery by Borromini that appears four times longer than it really is.

The cardinals also amassed a superb private collection of paintings, which is now on display in the Galleria Spada. The collection features a wide range of artists, including Rubens, Dürer and Guido Reni. The most important works on display include *The Visitation* by Andrea del Sarto (1486–1530), *Cain and Abel* by Giovanni Lanfranco (1582–1647) and *The Death of Dido* by Guercino (1591–1666).

Santa Maria dell'Orazione e Morte ❼

Via Giulia 262. **Map** 4 E5 & 11 B4. **Tel** 06-6880 2715. 🚍 23, 116, 280. **Open** for 6pm mass Sun. ✝

A pious confraternity was formed here in the 16th century to collect the bodies of the unknown dead and give them a Christian burial. The theme of death is stressed in this church, dedicated to St Mary of Prayer and Death. The doors and windows of Ferdinando Fuga's dramatic Baroque façade are decorated with winged skulls. Above the central entrance there is a *clepsydra* (an ancient hourglass) – symbolic of death.

Offertory box in Santa Maria dell'Orazione e Morte

Palazzo Farnese ❽

Piazza Farnese. **Map** 4 E5 & 11 B4. 🚍 23, 116, 280 and routes to Corso Vittorio Emanuele II. **Not open** to the public.

The prototype for numerous princely palaces, the imposing Palazzo Farnese was originally built for Cardinal Alessandro Farnese (who became Pope Paul III in 1534). He commissioned the greatest artists to work on it, starting with Antonio da Sangallo the Younger as architect in 1517. Michelangelo, who took over after him, contributed the great cornice and central window of the main façade, and the third level of the courtyard.

Michelangelo had a plan for the Farnese gardens to be connected by a bridge to the Farnese home in Trastevere, Villa Farnesina *(see pp220– 21)*. The elegant arch spanning Via Giulia belongs to this sadly unrealized scheme. The palazzo was completed in 1589, on a less ambitious scale, by Giacomo della Porta. It is now the home of the French Embassy, which moved in as early as 1635.

Majestic façade of Palazzo Farnese

Spada Chapel in San Girolamo

San Girolamo della Carità **9**

Via di Monserrato 62A.
Map 4 E5 & 11 B4.
Tel 06-687 9786.
🚌 23, 40, 46, 62, 64, 116, 280.
Open 10.30–11.30am Sun. ✝

The church was built on a site incorporating the home of San Filippo Neri, the 16th-century saint from Tuscany who renewed Rome's spiritual and cultural life by his friendly, open approach to religion. He would have loved the frolicking putti shown surrounding his statue, in his chapel, reminding him of the Roman urchins he had cared for during his lifetime.

The breathtaking Spada Chapel was designed by Borromini, and is unique both as a work of art and as an illustration of the spirit of the Baroque age. All architectural elements are concealed so that the space of the chapel's interior is defined solely by decorative marblework and statues. Veined jasper and precious multicoloured marbles are sculpted to imitate flowery damask and velvet hangings. Even the altar rail is a long swag of jasper drapery held up by a pair of kneeling angels with wooden wings.

Although there are memorials to former members of the Spada family, oddly there is no indication as to which of the Spadas was responsible for endowing the chapel. It was probably art-lover Virgilio Spada, a follower of San Filippo Neri.

Sant'Eligio degli Orefici **10**

Via di Sant'Eligio 8A. **Map** 4 D4 & 11 B4. *Tel* 06-686 8260. 🚌 23, 40, 46, 62, 64, 116, 280. **Open** 9.30am–1pm Mon–Fri (call first at Via di Sant'Eligio 7). **Closed** Aug. ✝

The name of the church still records the fact that it was commissioned by a rich corporation of goldsmiths (*orefici*) in the early 16th century. The original design was by Raphael, who, like his master Bramante, had acquired a sense of the grandiose from the remains of Roman antiquity. The influence of some of Bramante's works, such as the choir of Santa Maria del Popolo (*see pp138–9*), is evident in the simple way the arches and pilasters define the structure of the walls.

The cupola of Sant' Eligio is attributed to Baldassarre Peruzzi, while the façade was added in the early 17th century by Flaminio Ponzio. Among the various 16th-century painters who decorated the interior was Taddeo Zuccari, who worked on Palazzo Farnese (*see p147*).

Statue of San Filippo Neri by Pierre Legros

Santa Maria in Monserrato **11**

Via di Monserrato. **Map** 4 E4 & 11 B3. *Tel* 06-686 5865. 🚌 23, 40, 46, 62, 64, 116, 280. **Open** for mass only, 10am–1.30pm Sun. ✝

An early bust by Bernini of Cardinal Pedro Foix de Montoya

The origins of the Spanish national church in Rome go back to 1506, when a hospice for Spanish pilgrims was begun by a brotherhood of the Virgin of Montserrat in Catalonia. Inside is Annibale Carracci's painting *San Diego de Alcalà* and, in the third chapel on the left, a copy of a Sansovino statue of St James. Some beautiful 15th-century tombs by Andrea Bregno and Luigi Capponi are in the courtyard and side chapels. Don't miss Bernini's bust of Pedro Foix de Montoya, the church's benefactor, in the annexe.

***San Diego** by Annibale Carracci*

Palazzo Ricci **⑫**

Piazza de' Ricci. **Map** 4 D4 & 11 B4.
🚌 *23, 40, 46, 62, 64, 116, 280, 870.*
Not open to the public.

Palazzo Ricci was famous for its frescoed façade – now rather faded – originally painted in the 16th century by Polidoro da Caravaggio, a follower of Raphael.

In Renaissance Rome it was common to commission artists to decorate the outsides of houses with heroes of Classical antiquity. A fresco by a leading artist such as Polidoro, reputedly the inventor of this style of painting, was a conspicuous status symbol, in the nobility's attempts to outshine each other with their palazzi.

Part of the frescoed façade of Palazzo Ricci

Palazzo della Cancelleria **⑬**

Piazza della Cancelleria.
Map 4 E4 & 11 C3. **Tel** *06-6989 3405.* 🚌 *40, 46, 62, 64, 70, 81, 87, 116, 492.* **Open** by appointment only, Tue pm & Sat am.

The palazzo, a supreme example of the confident architecture of the Early Renaissance, was begun in 1485. It was financed partly with the gambling winnings of Cardinal Raffaele Riario. Roses, the emblem of the Riario family, adorn the vaults and capitals of the beautiful Doric courtyard. The palazzo's interior was decorated after the Sack of Rome in 1527. Giorgio Vasari boasted that he had completed work on one enormous room in just 100 days; Michelangelo allegedly retorted: "It looks like it." Other Mannerist artists, Perin del Vaga and Francesco Salviati, frescoed the rooms of the cardinal in charge of the Papal Chancellery, the office that gave the palazzo its name when it was installed here by Pope Leo X. On the right of the main entrance is the unobtrusive and rather quaint church of San Lorenzo in Damaso, founded by Pope Damasus

Lily on façade of the Piccola Farnesina

(reigned 366–84). It was reconstructed in 1495 and although Bernini made alterations to the transept and apse in 1638, it was later restored to its 15th-century lines. Its porticoes housed libraries for the first Papal Archives.

Piccola Farnesina **⑭**

Corso Vittorio Emanuele II 168.
Map 4 E4 & 11 C3.
Tel *06-6880 6848.* 🚌 *40, 46, 62, 64, 70, 81, 87, 116, 492.*
Open *9am–7pm Tue–Sun.*

This delightful miniature palazzo acquired its name from the lilies decorating its cornices. These were mistakenly identified as part of the Farnese family crest. In fact they were part of the coat of arms of a French clergyman, Thomas Le Roy, for whom the palazzo was built in 1523.

The entrance is in a façade built to overlook Corso Vittorio Emanuele II when the road was constructed at the start of the 20th century. The original façade on the left of today's entrance is attributed to Antonio da Sangallo the Younger. Note the asymmetrical arrangement of its windows and ledges. The elegant central courtyard also retains its original appearance. The Piccola Farnesina now houses the Museo Barracco, a collection of ancient sculpture assembled during the last century by the politician Baron Giovanni Barracco. A bust of the baron can

be seen in the courtyard. The collection includes an ancient Egyptian relief of the scribe Nofer, some Assyrian artifacts and, among the Etruscan exhibits, a delicate ceramic female head. On the first floor is the Greek collection with a head of Apollo.

Inner courtyard, Piccola Farnesina

Burcardo Theatre Museum **⑮**

Via del Sudario 44. **Map** 4 F4 & 12 D4. **Tel** *06-681 9471.* 🚌 *40, 46, 62, 64, 70, 81, 186, 492.* 🚋 *8.* **Museum and library Open** *9am–1.30pm Mon–Fri.* **Closed** Aug. 🎫 www.burcardo.org

This late 15th-century house once belonged to Johannes Burckhardt, chamberlain to Pope Alexander VI Borgia and author of a diary of Rome under the Borgias. His house now holds Rome's most complete collection of theatre literature, plus Chinese puppets and comic masks from the various regions of Italy.

Teatro Argentina ⑯

Largo di Torre Argentina 56. **Map** 4 F4 & 12 D4. **Tel** 06-684 000 311. ▦ 40, 46, 62, 64, 70, 81, 87, 186, 492, 810. ▦ 8. **Plays** performed Oct–Jun. See **Entertainment** pp360–61. **www**.teatrodiroma.net

One of the city's most important theatres was founded by the powerful Sforza Cesarini family in 1732, though the façade dates from a century later. Many famous operas, including those of Verdi, were first performed here. In 1816, the theatre saw the ill-fated début of Rossini's *Barber of Seville*, during which the composer insulted the unappreciative audience, who then pursued him, enraged, through the streets of Rome.

Detail of façade, Teatro Argentina

Area Sacra dell'Argentina ⑰

Largo di Torre Argentina. **Map** 4 F4 & 12 D4. ▦ 40, 46, 62, 64, 70, 81, 87, 186, 492, 810. ▦ 8. **Open** by appt only (call 06-0608).

The remains of four temples were discovered here in the 1920s. Dating from the Republican era, they are among the oldest in Rome. They are known as A, B, C and D. The oldest (temple C) dates from the early 3rd century BC. It was placed on a high platform preceded by an altar and is typical of Italic plans. Temple A is from later in the 3rd century BC. In medieval times the church of San Nicola de' Cesarini was built over its podium: remains of its two apses are still visible. The north column stumps belonged to a great portico, the Hecatostylum (portico of 100 columns). In

San Carlo at Prayer by Guido Reni

Imperial times two marble lavatories were built here – the remains of one are visible behind temple A. Behind temples B and C are remains of a great platform of tufa blocks identified as part of the Curia of Pompey – a rectangular building with a statue of Pompey. It was here that the Senate met and Julius Caesar was murdered on 15 March 44 BC. At the southwest corner of the site is a cat sanctuary, home to Rome's abandoned felines (open afternoons).

Area Sacra, with circular ruins of temple B in the foreground

San Carlo ai Catinari ⑱

Piazza B Cairoli. **Map** 4 F5 & 12 D4. **Tel** 06-6880 3554. ▦ see Area Sacra. ▦ 8. **Open** 4–7pm daily, also 7.30am–noon Mon–Sat & 9.30am–12.30pm Sun). ☐

In 1620, Rome's Milanese congregation decided to honour Cardinal Carlo Borromeo with

this great church. It was called "ai Catinari" on account of the bowl-makers' *(catinari)* shops in the area. The solemn travertine façade was completed in 1638 by the Roman architect Soria. The 16th-century basilican plan is flanked by chapels. The St Cecilia chapel was designed and decorated by Antonio Gherardi, who added a family portrait. The church's paintings and frescoes by Pietro da Cortona and Guido Reni are mature works of the Counter-Reformation, depicting the life and acts of the recently canonized San Carlo.

The ornate crucifix on the sacristy altar, inlaid with marble and mother-of-pearl, is by the 16th-century sculptor, Algardi.

Sacristy altar, San Carlo ai Catinari

Fontana delle Tartarughe ⑲

Piazza Mattei. **Map** 4 F5 & 12 D4. ▦ 46, 62, 63, 64, 70, 87, 186, 492, 810. ▦ 8.

The delightful Fontana delle Tartarughe (*tartarughe* are tortoises) was commissioned by the Mattei family to decorate "their" piazza between 1581 and 1588. The design was by Giacomo della Porta, but the fountain owes much of its charm to the four bronze youths each resting one foot on the head of a dolphin, sculpted by Taddeo Landini. Nearly a century after the fountain was built an

Della Porta's graceful Fontana delle Tartarughe

unknown sculptor added the struggling tortoises to complete the composition.

Santa Maria in Campitelli ⑳

Piazza di Campitelli 9.
Map 4 F5 & 12 E5. **Tel** 06-6880 3978. 🚌 40, 46, 62, 63, 64, 70, 87, 186, 780, 810. **Open** 7.30am–12.30pm, 3.30–7pm daily. 🚹 🚻

In 17th-century Rome the plague could still strike fiercely and there were no reliable, effective remedies. Many Romans simply prayed for a cure to a sacred medieval icon of the Virgin, the Madonna del Portico. When a particularly lethal outbreak of plague abated in 1656, popular gratitude was so strong that a new church was built to house the icon.

Lavish altar tabernacle in Santa Maria in Campitelli

The church, designed by a pupil of Bernini, Carlo Rainaldi, was completed in 1667. The main elements of the lively Baroque façade are the graceful columns, symbolizing the supporters of the true faith.

Inside the church stands a fabulously ornate, gilded altar tabernacle with spiral columns which was designed by Giovanni Antonio de Rossi to contain the image of the Virgin. The side chapels are decorated by some of Rome's finest Baroque painters: Sebastiano Conca, Giovanni Battista Gaulli (known as Il Baciccia) and Luca Giordano.

Façade and medieval bell tower of San Nicola in Carcere

San Nicola in Carcere ㉑

Via del Teatro di Marcello 46.
Map 5 A5 & 12 E5. **Tel** 06-6830 7198. 🚌 44, 63, 81, 95, 160, 170, 628, 780, 781. **Open** 10.30am–6pm daily; recent excavations by appt. 🚹

The medieval church of San Nicola in Carcere stands on the site of three Roman temples of the Republican era which were converted into a prison (carcere) in the Middle Ages. The temples of Juno, Spes and Janus faced a city gate leading from the Forum Holitorium, the city's vegetable and oil market, to the road down to the port on the Tiber. The columns embedded in the walls of the church belonged to two flanking temples whose platforms are now marked by grass lawns. The church

was rebuilt in 1599 and restored in the 19th century, but the bell tower and Roman columns are part of the original design.

The Theatre of Marcellus by Thomas Hartley Cromek (1809–73)

Theatre of Marcellus ㉒

Via del Teatro di Marcello.
Map 4 A5 & 12 E5. **Tel** 06-0608. 🚌 44, 63, 81, 95, 160, 170, 628, 780, 781. **Open** 9am–6pm (to 7pm in summer) daily.

The curved outer wall of this vast amphitheatre has supported generations of Roman buildings. It was built by the Emperor Augustus (27 BC–AD 14), who dedicated it to Marcellus, his nephew and son-in-law, who had died aged 19 in 23 BC.

The Middle Ages were a turbulent time of invasions and local conflicts (see p30) and by the 13th century the theatre had been converted into the fortress of the Savelli family. In the 16th century Baldassarre Peruzzi built a great palace on the theatre ruins for the Orsini family. This included a garden that faced the Tiber. The lower arches were later occupied by humble dwellings and workshops.

Close to the theatre stand three beautiful Corinthian columns and a section of frieze. These are from the Temple of Apollo, which housed many great works of art that the Romans had plundered from Greece in the 2nd century BC.

Portico of Octavia ㉓

Via del Portico d'Ottavia.
Map 4 F5 & 12 E5. ▥ *46, 62, 63, 64, 70, 87, 186, 780, 810.*

Built in honour of Octavia (the sister of Augustus and the abandoned wife of Mark Antony), this is the only surviving portico of what used to be the monumental piazza of Circus Flaminius. The rectangular portico enclosed temples dedicated to Jupiter and Juno, decorated with bronze statues. The part we see today is the great central atrium originally covered with marble facings.

In the Middle Ages a great fish market and a church, Sant'Angelo in Pescheria, were built in the ruins of the portico. As the church was associated with the fishing activities of the nearby river port, aquatic flora and fauna feature in many of its inlays. Links with the Tiber are also apparent in the stucco façade on the adjacent Fishmonger's Oratory, built in 1689. The church has a fresco of the Madonna and angels by the school of Benozzo Gozzoli.

Narrow lane in the Jewish Ghetto

Ghetto and Synagogue ㉔

Synagogue, Lungotevere dei Cenci. **Map** 4 F5 & 12 E5. **Tel** *06-6840 0661.* ▥ *23, 63, 280, 780 and routes to Largo di Torre Argentina.* ▤ *8.* **Museum Open** *mid-Jun–mid-Sep: 10am–7pm Sun–Thu, 10am–4pm Fri; mid-Sep–mid-Jun: 10am–5pm Sun–Thu, 9am–2pm Fri.* **Closed** *on Jewish public hols.* **Adm charge.** ▨ ▣ ▣ **Ghetto**, main street is Via del Portico d'Ottavia.

The first Jews came to Rome as traders in the 2nd century BC and there has been a

Synagogue overlooking the Tiber

Jewish community in Rome ever since. Jews were much appreciated for their financial and medical skills during the time of the Roman Empire.

Systematic persecution began in the 16th century. From 25 July 1556 all Rome's Jews were forced to live inside a high-walled enclosure erected on the orders of Pope Paul IV. The Ghetto was in an unhealthy part of Rome. Inhabitants were only allowed out during the day, and on Sundays they were driven into the Church of Sant'Angelo in Pescheria to listen to Christian sermons – a practice abolished only in 1848.

Persecution started again in 1943 with the German occupation. Although many Jews were helped to escape or hidden by Roman citizens, thousands were deported to German concentration camps.

Today many Jews still live in the former Ghetto and the medieval streets retain much of their old character. The Synagogue on Lungotevere was completed in 1904 and houses a Jewish museum that describes the history of the community through plans, Torahs and other artifacts.

Casa di Lorenzo Manilio ㉕

Via del Portico d'Ottavia 1D.
Map 4 F5 & 12 D5. ▥ *46, 62, 63, 64, 70, 87, 186, 780, 810.* **Not open** to the public.

Before the Renaissance, most Romans had only vague ideas of their city's past, but the 15th-century revival of interest in the philosophy and arts of antiquity inspired some to build houses recalling the splendour of ancient Rome. In 1468 a certain Lorenzo Manilio built a great house for his family, decorating it with an

elegant Classical plaque. The Latin inscription dates the building according to the ancient Roman method – 2,221 years after the foundation of the city – and gives the owner's name. Original reliefs are embedded in the façades as well as a fragment of an ancient sarcophagus. The Piazza Costaguti façade's windows are inscribed *Ave Roma* (Hail Rome).

Balcony of Palazzo Cenci

Palazzo Cenci ㉖

Vicolo dei Cenci. **Map** 4 F5 &12 D5. ▥ *See Ghetto and Synagogue.* **Not open** to the public.

Palazzo Cenci belonged to the family of Beatrice Cenci, who was accused, together with her brothers and step-mother, of witchcraft and the murder of her tyrannical father. She was condemned to death and beheaded at Ponte Sant'Angelo in 1599.

Row of Roman busts decorating the Casa di Lorenzo Manilio

Tiber Island, with Ponte Cestio linking it to Trastevere

Most of the original medieval palazzo has been demolished, and the building you see today dates back to the 1570s, though its rather forbidding appearance seems medieval. Heraldic half-moons decorate the main façade on Via del Progresso while pretty balconies open on the opposite side where a medieval arch joins the palace to Palazzetto Cenci, designed by Martino Longhi the Elder. Inside is a traditional courtyard with an Ionic-style loggia; many of the rooms retain the original 16th-century decoration that the unfortunate Beatrice would have known as a child.

Tiber Island ㉗

Isola Tiberina. **Map** 8 D1 & 12 D5. 23, 63, 280, 780. 8.

In ancient times the island, which lay opposite the city's port, had large structures of white travertine at either end built to resemble the stern and prow of a ship.

Since 293 BC, when a temple was dedicated here to Aesculapius, the god of healing and protector against the plague, the island has been associated with the sick and there is still a hospital here.

San Bartolomeo all'Isola, the church in the island's central piazza, was built on the ruins of the Temple of Aesculapius in the 10th century. Its Romanesque bell tower is clearly visible from across the river.

From the Ghetto area you can reach the island by a footbridge, the Ponte Fabricio. The oldest original bridge over the Tiber still in use, it was built in 62 BC. In medieval times the Pierleoni,

and then the Caetani, two powerful families, controlled this strategic point by means of a tower, still in situ. The other bridge to the island, the Ponte Cestio, is inscribed with the names of the Byzantine emperors associated with its restoration in AD 370.

Via Giulia ㉘

Map 4 D4 & 11 A3. 23, 116, 280, 870.

This picturesque street was laid out by Bramante for Pope Julius II della Rovere. Lined with 16th–18th century aristocratic palazzi, as well as fine churches and antique shops, Via Giulia makes a fascinating walk (see pp276–7).

Mask fountain in Via Giulia

San Giovanni dei Fiorentini ㉙

Via Acciaioli 2. **Map** 4 D4 & 11 A2. **Tel** 06-6889 2059. 23, 40, 46, 62, 64, 116, 280, 870. **Open** 7.30am–noon, 4–7pm daily.

The church of St John of the Florentines was built for the large Florentine community living in this area. Pope Leo X wanted it to be an expression of the cultural superiority of Florence over Rome. Started in the early 16th century, the church took over a century to build. The principal architect was Antonio da Sangallo the Younger, but many others contributed before Carlo Maderno's elongated cupola was finally completed in 1620. The present façade was added in the 18th century.

The church was decorated mainly by Tuscan artists. One interesting exception is the 15th-century statue of San Giovannino by the Sicilian Mino del Reame in a niche above the sacristy. The spectacular high altar houses a marble group by Antonio Raggi, the *Baptism of Christ*. The altar itself is by Borromini, who is buried in the church along with Carlo Maderno.

This and San Lorenzo in Lucina (see p112) are the only churches in Rome which admit animals: the faithful can bring their pets, and an Easter lamb-blessing takes place.

Antonio Raggi's *Baptism of Christ* in San Giovanni dei Fiorentini

QUIRINAL

One of the original seven hills of Rome, the Quirinal was a largely residential area in Imperial times. To the east of the hill were the vast Baths of Diocletian, still standing in front of what is now the main rail station. Abandoned in the Middle Ages, the district returned to favour in the late 16th century. The prime site was taken by the popes for Palazzo del Quirinale. Great families such as the Colonna and the Aldobrandini had their palazzi lower down the hill. With the end of papal rule in 1870, the surrounding area, especially Via Nazionale, was redeveloped as the Quirinal became the residence of the kings of Italy, then of the Italian president.

1st-century BC stucco in the Museo Nazionale Romano

SIGHTS AT A GLANCE

Churches
San Carlo alle Quattro Fontane 12
San Marcello al Corso 5
Sant'Agata dei Goti 21
Sant'Andrea al Quirinale 11
Santa Maria degli Angeli 15
Santa Maria dei Monti 20
Santa Maria in Trivio 7
Santi Apostoli 4
Santi Domenico e Sisto 23
Santi Vincenzo e Anastasio 9

Museums and Galleries
Accademia Nazionale di San Luca 8
Museo delle Paste Alimentari 10
Museo Nazionale Romano (Palazzo Massimo) 16
Palazzo delle Esposizioni 19

Historic Piazzas
Piazza della Repubblica 18

Historic Buildings
Baths of Diocletian 17
Palazzo Colonna 3
Palazzo del Quirinale 2

Fountains and Statues
Castor and Pollux 1
Moses Fountain 14
Le Quattro Fontane 13
Trevi Fountain 6

Parks and Gardens
Villa Aldobrandini 22

GETTING THERE
The area has Metro stops at Repubblica and Cavour. Buses include the 40 (only one stop), 64 and 70 along Via Nazionale and the 71, 116T and 117, which go through the Traforo Umberto I tunnel. Many buses run along Via del Tritone but there is no bus to the top of the Quirinal. You have to walk up Via XXIV Maggio.

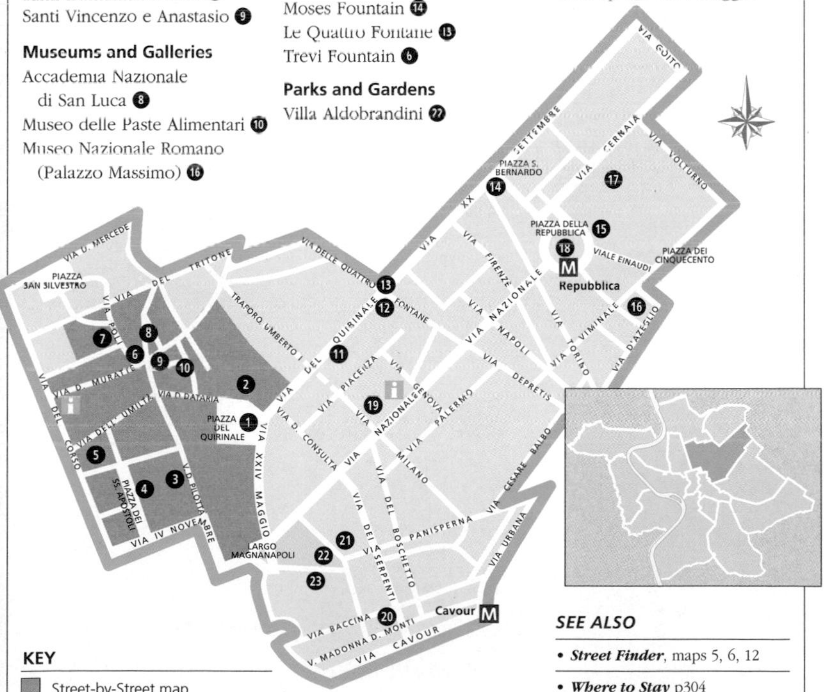

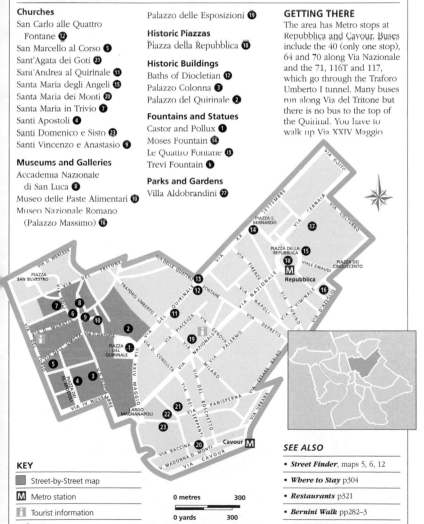

KEY
Street-by-Street map
Metro station
Tourist information

0 metres 300
0 yards 300

SEE ALSO

• ***Street Finder***, maps 5, 6, 12
• ***Where to Stay*** p304
• ***Restaurants*** p321
• ***Bernini Walk*** pp282–3

◁ **Fontana delle Naiadi in Piazza della Repubblica**

Street-by-Street: The Quirinal Hill

Even though Palazzo del Quirinale is usually closed to the public, it is well worth walking up the hill to the palace to see the giant Roman statues of Castor and Pollux in the piazza and enjoy fine views of the city. Come down the hill by way of the narrow streets and stairways that lead to one of Rome's unforgettable sights, the Trevi Fountain. Many small churches lie hidden away in the back streets. Towards Piazza Venezia there are grand palazzi, including that of the Colonna, one of Rome's most ancient and powerful families.

Santa Maria in Via is famous for its medieval well and miraculous 13th-century icon of the Madonna.

Santa Maria in Trivio
The attractive façade of this tiny church conceals a rich Baroque interior ❼

Accademia Nazionale di San Luca
The art academy has works by famous former members, such as Canova and Angelica Kauffmann ❽

★ Trevi Fountain
Rome's grandest and best-known fountain almost fills the tiny Piazza di Trevi ❻

Santi Vincenzo e Anastasio
The grand façade of this small Baroque church is on a corner facing the Trevi Fountain ❾

San Marcello al Corso
This stark Crucifixion by Van Dyck hangs in the sacristy of the church ❺

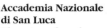

Palazzo Odescalchi has a Bernini façade from 1664, with a balustrade and richly decorated cornice. The building faces Santi Apostoli.

Museo delle Cere, a wax museum opened in 1953, places its emphasis on horror.

To Piazza Venezia

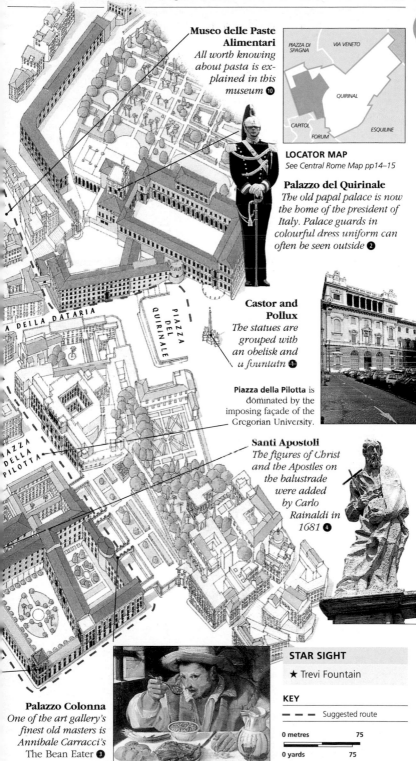

Museo delle Paste Alimentari
All worth knowing about pasta is explained in this museum ⑩

LOCATOR MAP
See Central Rome Map pp14–15

Palazzo del Quirinale
The old papal palace is now the home of the president of Italy. Palace guards in colourful dress uniform can often be seen outside ❷

A DELLA DATARIA

PIAZZA DEL QUIRINALE

Castor and Pollux
The statues are grouped with an obelisk and a fountain ❶

Piazza della Pilotta is dominated by the imposing façade of the Gregorian University.

PIAZZA DELLA PILOTTA

Santi Apostoli
The figures of Christ and the Apostles on the balustrade were added by Carlo Rainaldi in 1681 ❹

STAR SIGHT

★ Trevi Fountain

KEY

− − − Suggested route

0 metres	75
0 yards	75

Palazzo Colonna
One of the art gallery's finest old masters is Annibale Carracci's The Bean Eater ❸

Castor and Pollux ❶

Piazza del Quirinale. **Map** 5 B4.
🚌 H, 40, 64, 70, 170 and many
routes along Via del Tritone.

Quirinal fountain and obelisk with Roman statues of Castor and Pollux

Castor and Pollux – the patrons of horsemanship – and their prancing horses stand in splendour in the Piazza del Quirinale. Over 5.5 m (18 ft) high, these statues are huge Roman copies of 5th-century BC Greek originals. They once stood at the entrance to the nearby Baths of Constantine. Pope Sixtus V had them restored and placed here in 1588. Formerly known as the "horse tamers", they gave the square its familiar name of Monte Cavallo (horse hill).

The obelisk which stands between them was brought here in 1786 from the Mausoleum of Augustus. In 1818 the composition was completed by the addition of a massive granite basin, once a cattle trough in the Forum.

Palazzo del Quirinale ❷

Piazza del Quirinale. **Map** 5 B3. **Tel**
06-469 91. 🚌 H, 40, 64, 70, 170
and many routes along Via del
Tritone. **Open** 8.30am–noon Sun.
Closed public hols. **Adm charge**.
www.quirinale.it

By the 1500s, the Vatican had a reputation as an unhealthy location because of the high incidence of malaria, so Pope Gregory XIII chose this site on the highest of Rome's seven hills as a papal summer residence. Work began in 1573. Piazza del Quirinale has buildings on three sides while the fourth is open, with a splendid view of the city. Many great architects worked on the palace before it assumed its present form in the 1730s. Domenico Fontana designed the main façade, Carlo Maderno the huge chapel and Bernini the narrow wing on Via del Quirinale.

Following the unification of Italy in 1870, it became the official residence of the king, then, in 1947, of the president of the republic.

Just across the piazza are the Scuderie Papali, an exhibition space housed in the ex-stables of the Palazzo del Quirinale.

Canova's monument to Pope Clement XIV in Santi Apostoli, with figures of Humility and Modesty

Palazzo del Quirinale, official residence of the president of Italy

Palazzo Colonna ❸

Piazza SS. Apostoli 66. **Map** 5 A4 &
12 F3. **Tel** 06-679 4362. 🚌 H, 40,
64, 70, 170 and many routes to
Piazza Venezia. **Open** 9am–1.30pm
Sat only (last adm: 12.30pm). **Closed**
Aug & public hols. **Adm charge**. 🎫

Pope Martin V Colonna (reigned 1417–31) began building the palazzo, but most of the structure dates from the 18th century. The art gallery, built by Antonio del Grande between 1654 and 1665, is the only part open to the public. The pictures are numbered but unlabelled, so pick up a guide on the way in. Go up the stairs and through the antechamber leading to a series of three gleaming marble rooms with prominent yellow columns, the Colonna family emblem (*colonna* means column).

The ceiling frescoes celebrate Marcantonio Colonna's victory over the Turks at the Battle of Lepanto (1571). On the walls are 16th- to 18th-century paintings, including Annibale Carracci's *The Bean Eater (see p157)*. The room of landscape paintings, many by Poussin's brother-in-law Gaspare Dughet, reflects the 18th-century taste of Cardinal Girolamo Colonna. Beyond is a room with a ceiling fresco of *The Apotheosis of Martin V*. The throne room has a chair reserved for visiting popes and a copy of Pisanello's portrait of Martin V. The gallery also offers a fine view of the private palace garden, site of the ruined Temple of Serapis.

Santi Apostoli ❹

Piazza dei Santi Apostoli. **Map** 5 A4
& 12 F3. **Tel** 06-699 571. 🚌 H, 40,
64, 70, 170 and many other routes to
Piazza Venezia. **Open** 7am–noon,
4pm–7pm daily. ✝

The original 6th-century church on this site was rebuilt in the 15th century by Popes Martin V Colonna and Sixtus IV

della Rovere, whose oak-tree crest decorates the capitals of the late 15th-century portico. Inside the portico on the left is Canova's 1807 memorial to the engraver Giovanni Volpato. The church itself contains a much larger monument by Canova, his Tomb of Clement XIV (1789).

The Baroque interior by Francesco and Carlo Fontana was completed in 1714. Note the 3-D effect of Giovanni Odazzi's painted *Rebel Angels*, who really look as though they are falling from the sky. A huge 18th-century altarpiece by Domenico Muratori shows the martyrdom of the Apostles James and Philip, whose tombs are in the crypt.

Detail of Triton and "sea-horse" at Rome's grandest fountain, the Trevi

San Marcello al Corso ❺

Piazza San Marcello 5. **Map** 5 A4 & 12 F3. **Tel** 06-69 93 01. 🚌 62, 63, 81, 85, 95, 117, 119, 160, 175, 492, 628. **Open** 7am–noon (from 10am Sat, from 9am Sun), 4–7pm daily. ✝

This church was originally one of the first places of Christian worship in Rome, which were known as *tituli*. A later Romanesque building

Chapel in San Marcello al Corso, decorated by Francesco Salviati

burned down in 1519, and was rebuilt by Jacopo Sansovino with a single nave and many richly decorated private chapels on either side. The imposing travertine façade was designed by Fontana in late Baroque style.

The third chapel on the right has fine frescoes of the Virgin Mary by Francesco Salviati. The decoration of the next chapel was interrupted by the Sack of Rome in 1527. Raphael's follower Perin del Vaga fled, leaving the ceiling frescoes to be completed by

Daniele da Volterra and Pellegrino Tibaldi when peace returned to the city. In the nave stands a splendid Venetian-style double tomb by Sansovino, a memorial to Cardinal Giovanni Michiel (victim of a Borgia poisoning in 1503) and his nephew, Bishop Antonio Orso.

Trevi Fountain ❻

Fontana di Trevi. **Map** 5 A3 & 12 F2. 🚌 52, 53, 61, 62, 63, 71, 80, 95, 116, 119 and many other routes along Via del Corso and Via del Tritone.

Most visitors gathering around the coin-filled fountain assume that it has always been here, but by the standards of the Eternal City, the Trevi is a fairly recent creation. Nicola Salvi's theatrical design for Rome's largest and most famous fountain (*see p54*) was completed only in 1762. The central figures are Neptune, flanked by two Tritons. One struggles to master a very unruly "seahorse", the other leads a far more docile animal. These symbolize the two contrasting moods of the sea.

The site originally marked the terminal of the Aqua Virgo aqueduct built in 19 BC. One of the first-storey reliefs shows a young girl (the legendary virgin after whom the aqueduct was named) pointing to the spring from which the water flows.

Façade of Santa Maria in Trivio

Santa Maria in Trivio 7

Piazza dei Crociferi 49. **Map** 5 A3 & 12 F2. **Tel** 06-678 9645. 52, 53, 61, 62, 63, 71, 80, 95, 116, 119. **Open** 8am–noon, 4–7.30pm daily.

It has been said that Italian architecture is one of façades, and nowhere is this clearer than in the 1570s façade of Santa Maria in Trivio, delightfully stuck on to the building behind it. Note the false windows. There is illusion inside too, particularly in the ceiling frescoes, which show scenes from the New Testament by Antonio Gherardi (1644–1702).

The name of the tiny church probably means "St Mary-at-the-meeting-of-three-roads".

Accademia Nazionale di San Luca 8

Piazza dell'Accademia di San Luca 77. **Map** 5 A3 & 12 F2. **Tel** 06-679 8850. 52, 53, 61, 62, 63, 71, 80, 95, 116, 119 and many routes along Via del Corso and Via del Tritone. **Open** 10am–1pm Mon–Fri (some rooms may be closed due to ongoing restoration work).

St Luke is supposed to have been a painter, hence the name of Rome's academy of fine arts. Appropriately, the gallery contains a painting of *St Luke Painting a Portrait of the Virgin* by Raphael and his followers. The academy's heyday was in the 17th and 18th centuries, when many

members gave their work to the collection. Canova donated a model for his famous marble group, *The Three Graces*.

Of particular interest are three fascinating self-portraits painted by women: the 17th-century Italian Lavinia Fontana; the 18th-century Swiss Angelica Kauffmann, whose painting is copied from a portrait of her by Joshua Reynolds; and Elisabeth Vigée-Lebrun, the French painter of the years before the 1789 Revolution.

Santi Vincenzo e Anastasio 9

Vicolo dei Modelli 73. **Map** 5 A3 & 12 F2. **Tel** 331-284 5596. 52, 53, 61, 62, 63, 71, 80, 95, 116, 119. **Open** 10am–7.30pm daily.

Overlooking the Trevi Fountain (*see p159*) is one of the most over-the-top Baroque façades in Rome. Its thickets of columns are crowned by the huge coat of arms of Cardinal Raimondo Mazzarino, who commissioned Martino Longhi the Younger to build the church in 1650. The female bust above the door is of one

of the cardinal's famous nieces, either Louis XIV's first love, Maria Mancini (1639–1715), or her younger sister, Ortensia. In the apse, memorial plaques record the popes whose *praecordia* (a part of the heart) are enshrined behind the wall. This gruesome tradition was started at the end of the 16th century by Pope Sixtus V and continued until Pius X stopped it in the early 20th century.

Museo delle Paste Alimentari 10

Piazza Scanderbeg 117. **Map** 5 A3 &12 F2. **Tel** 06-699 1120. 52, 53, 61, 62, 63, 71, 80, 95, 116, 119. **Closed** for restoration (check website for information). www.museodellapasta.it

The role of pasta in Italian cuisine cannot be exaggerated, and this entertaining museum presents everything there is to know about the beloved staple. Its rooms focus on various aspects, such as the history of pasta, how it is made and the background of the different shapes, while others exhibit photography and art with a pasta theme.

Self-portrait by Lavinia Fontana in the Accademia Nazionale di San Luca

Interior of Bernini's oval Sant'Andrea al Quirinale

Sant'Andrea al Quirinale ⑪

Via del Quirinale 29. **Map** 5 B3.
Tel 06-474 4872. 116, 117
and routes to Via del Tritone.
Open 8.30am–noon, 3.30–7pm
daily.

Known as the "Pearl of the Baroque" because of its beautiful roseate marble interior, Sant'Andrea was designed by Bernini and executed by his assistants between 1658 and 1670. It was built for the Jesuits, hence the many IHS emblems (*Iesus Hominum Salvator* – Jesus Saviour of Mankind).

The site for the church was wide but shallow, so Bernini pointed the long axis of his oval plan not towards the altar, but towards the sides; he then leads the eye round to the altar end. Here Bernini ordered works of art in various media which function not in isolation, but together. The crucified St Andrew (Sant'Andrea) of the altarpiece

looks up at a stucco version of himself, who in turn ascends towards the lantern and the Holy Spirit.

The rooms of St Stanislas Kostka in the adjacent convent should not be missed. The quarters of the Jesuit novice, who died in 1568 aged 19, reflect not his own spartan taste, but the richer style of the 17th-century Jesuits. The Polish saint has been brilliantly immortalized in marble by Pierre Legros (1666–1719).

San Carlo alle Quattro Fontane ⑫

Via del Quirinale 23. **Map** 5 B3. *Tel*
06-488 3261. 116, 117 & routes
to Piazza Barberini. Barberini.
Open 10am–1pm, 3–6pm Mon–Fri;
10am–1pm Sat & Sun.

In 1634, the Trinitarians, a Spanish order whose role was to pay the ransom of Christian hostages to the Arabs, commissioned Borromini to design a church and convent at the Quattro Fontane cross-roads. The church, so small it would fit inside one of the piers of St Peter's, is also known as "San Carlino".

Although dedicated to Carlo Borromeo, the 16th-century Milanese cardinal canonized in 1620, San Carlo is as much a monument to Borromini. Both the façade and interior employ bold curves that give light and life to a small, cramped site. The oval dome and tiny lantern are particularly ingenious. The undulating lines of the façade are decorated with angels and a statue of San Carlo. Finished in 1667, the façade is one of Borromini's very last works.

There are further delights in the playful inverted shapes in the cloister and the stucco work in the refectory (now the sacristy), which houses a painting of San Carlo by Orazio Borgianni (1611).

In a small room off the sacristy hangs a portrait of Borromini himself wearing the Trinitarian cross. Borromini committed suicide in 1667, and in the crypt (which is now open to the public) a small curved chapel reserved for him remains empty.

Dome of San Carlo alle Quattro Fontane, lit by concealed windows

Fountain of Strength (or Juno)

Le Quattro Fontane ⑬

Intersection of Via delle Quattro Fontane and Via del Quirinale. **Map** 5 B3. 🚌 *Routes to Piazza Barberini or Via Nazionale.* Ⓜ *Barberini.*

These four small fountains are attached to the corners of the buildings at the intersection of two narrow, busy streets. They date from the great redevelopment of Rome in the reign of Sixtus V (1585–90). Each fountain has a statue of a reclining deity. The river god accompanied by the she-wolf is clearly the Tiber; the other male figure may be the Arno. The female figures represent Strength and Fidelity or the goddesses Juno and Diana.

The crossroads is at the highest point of the Quirinal hill and commands splendid views of three distant landmark obelisks: those placed by Sixtus V in front of Santa Maria Maggiore and Trinità dei Monti, and the one that stands in Piazza del Quirinale.

Moses Fountain ⑭

Fontana dell'Acqua Felice, Piazza San Bernardo. **Map** 5 C2. 🚌 *36, 60, 61, 62, 84, 175, 492.* Ⓜ *Repubblica.*

Officially known as the Fontana dell'Acqua Felice, this fountain owes its popular name to the grotesque statue of Moses in the central niche. The massive structure with its three elegant arches was designed by Domenico Fontana to mark the terminal of the Acqua Felice aqueduct, so called because it was one of the many great improvements commissioned by Felice Peretti, Pope Sixtus V. Completed in 1587, it brought clean piped water to this quarter of Rome for the first time.

The notorious statue of Moses striking water from the rock is larger than life and the proportions of the body are obviously wrong. Sculpted either by Prospero Bresciano or Leonardo Sormani, it is a clumsy attempt at recreating the awesome appearance of Michelangelo's Moses in the church of San Pietro in Vincoli *(see p170)*. As soon as it was unveiled, it was said to be frowning at having been brought into the world by such an inept sculptor.

Fontana's Moses Fountain

The side reliefs also illustrate water stories from the Old Testament: Aaron leading the Israelites to water and Joshua pointing the army towards the Red Sea. The fountain's four lions are copies of Egyptian originals (now in the Vatican Museums), which Sixtus V had put there for the public's "convenience" and "delight".

Gold coin with head of the Emperor Diocletian (AD 285–305)

Santa Maria degli Angeli ⑮

Piazza della Repubblica. **Map** 5 C3. **Tel** *06-488 0812.* 🚌 *36, 60, 61, 62, 64, 84, 90, 116, 170, 492, 910.* Ⓜ *Repubblica, Termini.* **Open** *7am–6.30pm daily.* 🚻 ♿ 🏛

Parts of the ruined Baths of Diocletian *(right)* provided building material and setting for this church, constructed by Michelangelo in 1563. The church was so altered in the 18th century that it has lost most of its original character.

An exhibition in the sacristy gives a detailed account of Michelangelo's original design.

Fidelity (or Diana) with her attendant dog, one of the Quattro Fontane

Museo Nazionale Romano (Palazzo Massimo) ⑯

Part of the Museo Nazionale Romano in the Baths of Diocletian

Palazzo Massimo, Largo di Villa Peretti 1. **Map** 6 D3. **Tel** 06-3996 7700. 🚍 36, 38, 40, 64, 86, 170, 175, H and other routes to Piazza dei Cinquecento. Ⓜ Repubblica, Termini. **Open** 9am–7.45pm Tue–Sun. **Closed** 1 Jan, 1 May, 25 Dec. **Adm charge** (the biglietto cumulativo gives entry to the museum's five branches). 🔾 🗶 🔾 🔾

Founded in 1889, the Museo Nazionale Romano holds most of the antiquities found in Rome since 1870 as well as pre-existing collections, and is one of the world's leading museums of Classical art. It now has five branches: its original site, occupying part of the Baths of Diocletian; the Palazzo Massimo; the Palazzo Altemps (see p127); the Aula Ottagona (near the Baths of Diocletian); and Crypta Balbi at Via delle Botteghe Oscure 31, excavated from the foyer of the theatre of Balbus (1st century BC) and housing findings from medieval Rome.

The Palazzo Massimo, built in 1883–7 on the site of a villa which belonged to Sixtus V, used to be a Jesuit college. In 1981–97 it was restored to house a significant proportion of the museum's collections. The exhibits, contained on four floors, are originals dating from the 2nd century BC to the end of the 4th century AD.

The basement contains an excellent display of ancient coins, precious artifacts and the only mummified child to be found in the ancient city. The ground floor is devoted to Roman statuary, with funeral monuments in Room 2 and Emperor Augustus in Pontifex Maximus guise in Room 5. Upstairs there are statues from Nero's summer villa in Anzio and Roman copies of famous Greek originals, such as the *Discobolos Ex-Lancellotti*. The real joy of the museum, however, is on the second floor, where entire rooms of wall paintings have been brought from various villas excavated in and around Rome. A guided tour of the wall paintings is necessary, which you can book at the museum entrance. The most incredible frescoes are from Livia's Villa at Prima Porta. Her triclinium (dining room) was decorated with an abundance of trees, plants and fruit, painted in a totally naturalistic style to fool guests that they were eating alfresco, rather than indoors. Other marvels include rooms brought from the first Villa Farnesina: the children's room has a predominantly white design, while the adults' bedroom is red, complete with erotic paintings. Equally impressive is the museum's display of mosaics on the same floor.

Baths of Diocletian ⑰

Terme di Diocleziano, Viale E de Nicola 79. **Map** 6 D3. **Tel** 06-3996 7700. 🚍 36, 60, 61, 62, 84, 90. Ⓜ Repubblica, Termini. **Open** 9am–7.45pm Tue–Sun.

Built in AD 298–306 under the infamous Emperor Diocletian, who murdered thousands of Christians, the baths (see pp24–5) were the most extensive in Rome and could accommodate up to 3,000 bathers at a time.

Part of the Museo Nazionale Romano, the complex houses a vast collection of Roman statues and inscriptions and incorporates a former Carthusian monastery which has a beautiful cloister designed by Michelangelo.

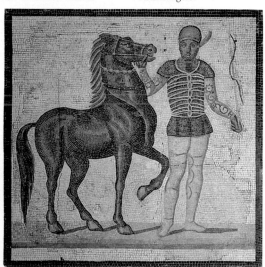

One of the Quattro Aurighe mosaics, Museo Nazionale Romano

Piazza della Repubblica ⑱

Map 5 C3. 🚌 *36, 60, 61, 62, 64, 84, 90, 170, 175, 492, 646, 910.* Ⓜ *Repubblica.*

Romans often refer to the piazza by its old name, Piazza Esedra, so called because it follows the shape of an *exedra* (a semicircular recess) that was part of the Baths of Diocletian. The piazza was part of the great redevelopment undertaken when Rome became capital of a unified Italy. Under its sweeping 19th-century colonnades there were once elegant shops, but they have been ousted by banks, travel agencies and cafés.

In the middle of the piazza stands the Fontana delle Naiadi. Mario Rutelli's four naked bronze nymphs caused something of a scandal when they were unveiled in 1901. Each reclines on an aquatic creature symbolizing water in its various forms: a seahorse for the oceans, a water snake for rivers, a swan for lakes, and a curious frilled lizard for subterranean streams. The figure in the middle, added in 1911, is of the sea god Glaucus, who represents man victorious over the hostile forces of nature.

Piazza della Repubblica and the Fontana delle Naiadi

Palazzo delle Esposizioni ⑲

Via Nazionale 194. **Map** 5 B4. **Tel** *06-489 411.* 🚌 *40, 60, 64, 70, 116T, 170.* **Open** *10am–8pm Tue–Thu & Sun, 10am–10.30pm Fri & Sat.* **Adm charge.** 🚫 ♿ *from Via Piacenza or Via Milano entrance.* 🍴 ▢ ▢ **www**.palazzoesposizioni.it

Façade of the Palazzo delle Esposizioni

This grandiose building, with wide steps, Corinthian columns and statues, was designed as an exhibition centre by the architect Pio Piacentini and built by the city of Rome in 1882 during the reign of Umberto I. The main entrance looks like a triumphal arch.

The restored palazzo is still used to house high-profile exhibitions of contemporary art. The exhibitions are changed every three months and include a variety of sculpture and paintings. Live performances, films and lectures also take place here *(see p360)*. Foreign films are usually shown in the original language.

Santa Maria dei Monti ⑳

Via Madonna dei Monti 41. **Map** 5 B4. **Tel** *06-48 55 31.* 🚌 *75, 84, 117.* Ⓜ *Cavour.* **Open** *7am–noon, 4.30–7.30pm Mon–Sat; 8.30am–1pm, 5–8pm Sun.* ✝ ♿

Designed by Giacomo della Porta, this church, dating from 1580, has a particularly splendid dome. Over the high altar is a stunning medieval painting of the Madonna, patroness of this quarter of Rome. The altar in the left transept houses the tomb and effigy of the unworldly French saint Benoît-Joseph Labre, who died here in 1783, having spent his life as a solitary pilgrim. He slept rough in the ruins of the Colosseum, gave away any charitable gifts he received, and came regularly to Santa Maria dei Monti to worship. His faith could not sustain his body: still in his mid-thirties, he collapsed and died outside the church. The foul rags he wore are preserved.

One of the bronze nymphs of the fountain in Piazza della Repubblica

Sant'Agata dei Goti ㉑

Via Mazzarino 16 and Via Panisperna 29. **Map** 5 B4. **Tel** 06-4879 3531.
🚌 40, 60, 64, 70, 71, 117, 170.
Open 7–9am, 4–7pm Mon–Sat, 9am–noon, 4–6pm Sun. 🚻 ♿

The Goths who gave their name to this church (*Goti* are Goths) occupied Rome in the 6th century AD. They were Aryan heretics who denied the divinity of Christ. The church was founded between AD 462 and 470, shortly before the main Gothic invasions, and the beautiful granite columns date from this period. The main altar has a well-preserved 12th-century Cosmatesque tabernacle, but the most delightful part of the church is the charming 18th-century courtyard built around an ivy-draped well.

Villa Aldobrandini ㉒

Via Panisperna. Entrance to gardens: Via Mazzarino 1. **Map** 5 B4.
🚌 40, 60, 64, 70, 71, 117, 170.
Gardens open dawn–dusk daily.
Villa not open to the public.

Built in the 16th century for the Dukes of Urbino, is closed to the public for his family by Pope Clement VIII Aldobrandini (reigned 1592–1605), the villa is now government property and houses an international law library.

The villa itself, decorated with the family's six-starred coat of arms, is closed to the public, but the gardens and terraces, hidden behind a high wall that runs along Via Nazionale, can be reached through an iron gate in Via Mazzarino. Steps lead up past 2nd-century AD ruins into the renovated gardens, highly recommended as an oasis of tranquillity in the centre of the city. Gravel paths lead between formal lawns and clearly marked specimen trees, and benches are provided for the weary. Since the garden is raised some 10 m (30 ft) above street level, the views are excellent.

18th-century courtyard of Sant'Agata dei Goti

Santi Domenico e Sisto ㉓

Largo Angelicum 1.
Map 5 B4. **Tel** 06-670 21.
🚌 40, 60, 64, 70, 71 117, 170.
Open 9am–noon Sat.

Chapel in Santi Domenico e Sisto

The church has a tall, slender Baroque façade rising above a steep flight of steps. This divides into two curving flights that sweep up to the terrace in front of the entrance. The pediment of the façade is crowned by eight flaming candlesticks.

The interior has a vaulted ceiling with a large fresco of *The Apotheosis of St Dominic* by Domenico Canuti (1620–84). The first chapel on the right was decorated by Bernini, who may also have designed the sculpture of Mary Magdalene meeting the risen Christ in the Garden of Gethsemane. This fine marble group was executed by Antonio Raggi (1649). Above the altar is a 15th-century terracotta plaque of the Virgin and Child. On the left over a side altar is a large painting of the Madonna from the same period, attributed to Benozzo Gozzoli (1420–97), a pupil of Fra Angelico.

Façade of Santi Domenico e Sisto

ESQUILINE

The Esquiline is the largest and highest of Rome's seven hills. In Imperial Rome the western slopes overlooking the Forum housed the crowded slums of the Suburra. On the eastern side there were a few villas belonging to wealthy citizens like Maecenas, patron of the arts and adviser to Augustus. The essential character of the place has persisted through two millennia; it is still one of the poorer quarters of the city.

Michelangelo's
Rachel **in San Pietro in Vincoli**

The area is now heavily built up, except for a rather seedy park on the Colle Oppio, a smaller hill to the south of the Esquiline, where you can see the remains of the Baths of Titus, the Baths of Trajan and Nero's Domus Aurea. The area's main interest, however, lies in its churches. Many of these were founded on the sites of private houses where Christians met to worship secretly in the days when their religion was banned.

SIGHTS AT A GLANCE

Churches
San Martino ai Monti ❶
San Pietro in Vincoli ❷
Santa Maria Maggiore
pp172–3 ❹
Santa Bibiana ❼
Santa Prassede ❺
Santa Pudenziana ❸

Museums
Museo Nazionale d'Arte
Orientale ❾

Historic Piazzas
Piazza Vittorio Emanuele II ❽

Ancient Sites
Auditorium of Maecenas ❿
Domus Aurea ⓬
Sette Sale ⓫

Arches
Arch of Gallienus ❻

GETTING THERE
This area is close to Termini station and has several other Metro stops: Vittorio Emanuele and Manzoni on line A, Cavour and Colosseo on line B. Bus routes here are a little confusing. Among the most useful are the 16, 75 and 714 from Stazione Termini and the 84. Tram 5 runs along Via Labicana.

SEE ALSO

- *Street Finder*, maps 5, 6
- *Restaurants* p322
- *Mosaics Walk* pp280–81

KEY

	Street-by-Street map
FS	Railway station
M	Metro station
i	Tourist information

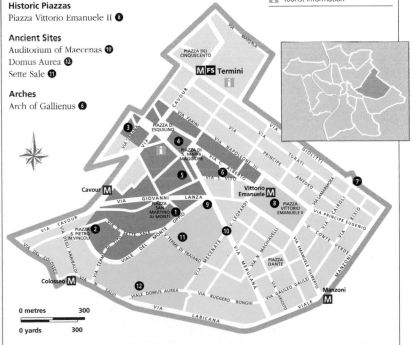

Street-by-Street: The Esquiline Hill

The sight that draws most people to this
rather scruffy part of Rome is the great basilica
of Santa Maria Maggiore. But it is also well
worth searching out some of the smaller
churches on the Esquiline: Santa Pudenziana
and Santa Prassede with their celebrated
mosaics, and San Pietro in Vincoli, home to
one of Michelangelo's most famous sculptures.
To the south, in the Colle Oppio park, are the
scattered remains of the Baths of Trajan.

Santa Pudenziana
*The apse of this
ancient church has
a magnificent 4th-
century mosaic of
Christ surrounded
by the Apostles* ❸

Piazza dell'Esquilino
was furnished with an
obelisk in 1587 by
Pope Sixtus V. This
helped to guide
pilgrims coming
from the north
to the important
church of
Santa Maria
Maggiore.

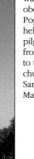

**To the
Colosseum**

VIA SFORZA

VIA DEI QUATTRO

VIA GIOVANNI LANZA

PIAZZA SA
MARTINO AI

VIA IN SELCI

PIAZZA DI
SAN PIETRO
IN VINCOLI

★ **San Pietro
in Vincoli**
*The church's
treasures include
Michelangelo's
Moses and the
chains that
bound St Peter* ❷

VIALE DEL MONTE

**Bat
Trajan**
109) wer
first to be bu
the massive scale
used in the Bat
Diocletian and of Cara

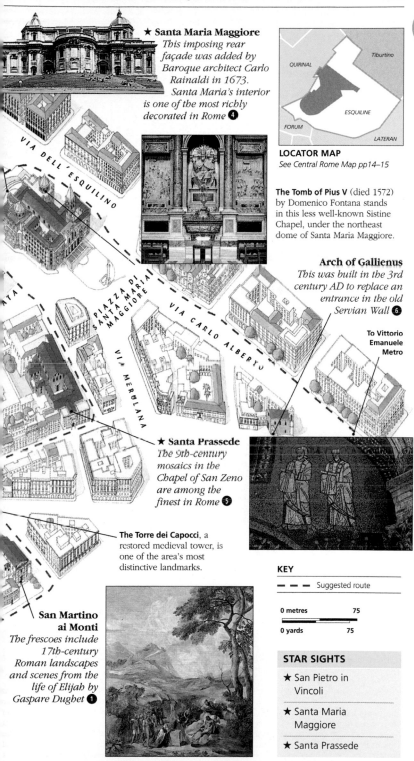

★ Santa Maria Maggiore
This imposing rear façade was added by Baroque architect Carlo Rainaldi in 1673. Santa Maria's interior is one of the most richly decorated in Rome ❹

LOCATOR MAP
See Central Rome Map pp14–15

The Tomb of Pius V (died 1572) by Domenico Fontana stands in this less well-known Sistine Chapel, under the northeast dome of Santa Maria Maggiore.

Arch of Gallienus
This was built in the 3rd century AD to replace an entrance in the old Servian Wall ❻

To Vittorio Emanuele Metro

★ Santa Prassede
The 9th-century mosaics in the Chapel of San Zeno are among the finest in Rome ❺

The Torre dei Capocci, a restored medieval tower, is one of the area's most distinctive landmarks.

San Martino ai Monti
The frescoes include 17th-century Roman landscapes and scenes from the life of Elijah by Gaspare Dughet ❶

KEY

– – – Suggested route

0 metres	75
0 yards	75

STAR SIGHTS

★ San Pietro in Vincoli

★ Santa Maria Maggiore

★ Santa Prassede

San Martino ai Monti ❶

Viale del Monte Oppio 28. **Map** 6 D5.
Tel 06-478 4701. 🚌 *16, 714.* Ⓜ
Cavour, Vittorio Emanuele. **Open**
*7.30–11.30am, 4–7pm Mon–Sat;
7am–noon, 4–7.30pm Sun.* 🚹 ♿

**Fresco of old San Giovanni in
Laterano in San Martino ai Monti**

Christians have been worship-
ping on the site of this church
since the 3rd century, when
they used to meet in the
house of a man named
Equitius. In the 4th century,
after Constantine had
legalized Christianity, Pope
Sylvester I built a church, one
of very few things he did
during his pontificate. In fact
he was so insignificant that
in the 5th century a more
exciting life was fabricated
for him – which included
tales of him converting
Constantine, curing him
of leprosy and forcing him
to close all pagan temples.
Pope Sylvester's fictional
life was further enhanced
in the 8th century, with the
forgery of a document in
which Constantine offered
him the Imperial crown.

Pope Sylvester's church
was replaced in about
AD 500 by St Symmachus,
rebuilt in the 9th century
and then transformed
completely in the 1630s.
The only immediate signs
of its age are the ancient
Corinthian columns dividing
the nave and aisles. The most
interesting interior features
are a series of frescoed
landscapes of the countryside
around Rome (*campagna
romana*) by the 17th-century

French artist Gaspare Dughet,
Poussin's brother-in-law, in
the right aisle. The frescoes
by Filippo Gagliardi, at either
end of the left aisle, show old
St Peter's and the interior of
San Giovanni in Laterano
before Borromini's redesign.
If you can find the sacristan,
you can go beneath the church
to see the remains of
Equitius's house.

San Pietro in Vincoli ❷

Piazza di San Pietro in Vincoli 4A. 🚌
75, 84, 117. Ⓜ *Cavour, Colosseo.*
Open *8am–12.30pm, 3–7pm
(Oct–Mar: 6pm) daily.* 🚹 ♿ 📷

According to tradition, the
two chains (*vincoli*) used to
shackle St Peter while he was
being held in the depths of

Reliquary with St Peter's chain

the Mamertine Prison (*see
p91*) were subsequently taken
to Constantinople. In the 5th
century, Empress Eudoxia
deposited one in a church in
Constantinople and sent the
other to her daughter Eudoxia
in Rome. She in turn gave hers
to Pope Leo I, who had this
church built to house it. Some
years later the second chain
was brought to Rome,
where it linked miraculously
with its partner.

The chains are still here,
displayed below the high
altar, but the church is now
best known for Michelangelo's
Tomb of Pope Julius II. When
it was commissioned in 1505,
Michelangelo spent eight
months searching for perfect
blocks of marble at Carrara in
Tuscany, but Pope Julius
became more interested in
the building of a new St
Peter's and the project
was laid aside. After the
pope's death in 1513,
Michelangelo resumed
work on the tomb, but
had only finished the
statues of *Moses* and
The Dying Slaves when Pope
Paul III persuaded him to
start work on the Sistine
Chapel's *Last Judgment*.
Michelangelo had planned
a vast monument with
over 40 statues, but the
tomb that was built –
mainly by his pupils –
is simply a façade with
six niches for statues.
The Dying Slaves are in
Paris and Florence, but
the tremendous bearded
Moses is here. The horns
on Moses' head should
really be beams of light
– they are the result of
the original Hebrew from
the Old Testament being
wrongly translated.

Michelangelo's *Moses* in San Pietro

Santa Pudenziana ❸

Via Urbana 160. **Map** 5 C4.
Tel 06-481 4622.
🚌 16, 75, 84, 105, 714.
Ⓜ *Cavour.* **Open** *9am–noon,
3–6pm daily.* ✝

Churches tend to be dedi-
cated to existing saints, but in
this case, the church, through
a linguistic accident, created a
brand new saint. In the 1st
century AD a Roman senator
called Pudens lived here, and,
according to legend, allowed
St Peter to lodge with him. In
the 2nd century a bath house
was built on this site and in
the 4th century a church was
established inside the baths,
known as the *Ecclesia
Pudentiana* (the church
of Pudens). In time it was
assumed that "Pudentiana"
was a woman's name and a
life was created for her – she
became the sister of Prassede
and was credited with caring
for Christian victims of
persecution. In 1969 both
saints were declared invalid,
though their churches both
kept their names.

The 19th-century façade of
the church retains an 11th-
century frieze depicting both
Prassede and Pudenziana
dressed as crowned Byzantine
empresses. The apse has
a remarkable 4th-century
mosaic, clearly influenced
by Classical pagan art in its
use of subtle colours. The
Apostles are represented as
Roman senators in togas but a
clumsy attempt at restoration
in the 16th century destroyed
two of the Apostles and left
other figures without legs.

Apse mosaics in Santa Prassede, showing the saint with St Paul

Santa Maria Maggiore ❹

See pp172–3.

Santa Prassede ❺

Via Santa Prassede 9A. **Map** 6 D4.
Tel 06-488 2456. 🚌 16, 70, 71,
75, 714. Ⓜ *Vittorio Emanuele.* **Open**
*7.30am–noon, 4pm–6.30pm daily
(afternoons only, Aug).* ✝ ♿

The church was founded by
Pope Paschal II in the 9th
century, on the site of a 2nd-
century oratory. Although the
interior has been altered and
rebuilt, the structure of the

original design of the 9th-cen-
tury church is clearly visible.
Its three aisles are separated
by rows of granite columns.
In the central nave, there is a
round stone slab covering the
well where, according to
legend, St Prassede is said
to have buried the remains
of 2,000 martyrs.

Artists from Byzantium
decorated the church with
glittering, jewel-coloured
mosaics. Those in the apse
and choir depict stylized
white-robed elders, the
haloed elect looking down
from the gold and blue walls
of heaven, spindly legged
lambs, feather-mop palm trees
and bright red poppies.

In the apse, Santa Prassede
and Santa Pudenziana stand
on either side of Christ, with
the fatherly arms of St Paul
and St Peter on their
shoulders. Beautiful mosaics
of saints, the Virgin and Christ
and the Apostles also cover
the walls and vault of the
Chapel of St Zeno, built as a
mausoleum for Pope Paschal's
mother, Theodora. Part of a
column brought back from
Jerusalem, allegedly the one
to which Christ was bound
and flogged, also stands here.

11th-century frieze and medallions on the façade of Santa Pudenziana

Santa Maria Maggiore ❹

Of all the great Roman basilicas, Santa Maria has the most successful blend of different architectural styles. Its colonnaded nave is part of the original 5th-century building. The Cosmatesque marble floor and delightful Romanesque bell tower, with its blue ceramic roundels, are medieval. The Renaissance saw a new coffered ceiling, and the Baroque gave the church twin domes and its imposing front and rear façades. The mosaics are Santa Maria's most famous feature. From the 5th century come the biblical scenes in the aisle and the spectacular mosaics on the triumphal arch. Medieval highlights include a 13th-century enthroned Christ in the loggia.

★ Cappella Paolina
Flaminio Ponzio designed this richly decorated chapel (1611) for Pope Paul V Borghese.

Obelisk in Piazza dell'Esquilino
The Egyptian obelisk was erected by Pope Sixtus V in 1587 as a landmark for pilgrims.

LEGEND OF THE SNOW

In 356, Pope Liberius had a dream in which the Virgin told him to build a church on the spot where he found snow. When it fell on the Esquiline, on the morning of 5 August in the middle of a baking Roman summer, he naturally obeyed. The miracle of the snow is commemorated each year by a service during which thousands of white petals float down from the ceiling of Santa Maria. Originally roses were used, but nowadays the petals are more usually taken from dahlias.

Coffered Ceiling
The gilded ceiling, possibly by Giuliano da Sangallo, was a gift of Alexander VI Borgia at the end of the 15th century. The gold is said to be the first brought from America by Columbus.

TIMELINE

Pope Gregory VII

356 Virgin appears to Pope Liberius

432–40 Sixtus III completes church

1347 Cola di Rienzo crowned Tribune of Rome in Santa Maria

1673 Carlo Rainaldi rebuilds apse

300 AD	600	900	1200	1500	1800

420 Probable founding date

1075 Pope Gregory VII kidnapped by opponents while saying Christmas mass in Santa Maria

1288–92 Nicholas IV adds apse and transepts

1743 Ferdinando Fuga adds main façade on orders of Benedict XIV

Coat of arms of Gregory VII

VISITORS' CHECKLIST

Piazza di Santa Maria Maggiore.
Map 6 D4.
Tel 06-6988 6800.
🚌 *16, 70, 71, 714.* 🚊 *14.*
Ⓜ *Termini, Cavour.*
Open *7am–6.45pm daily.*

★ **Coronation of the Virgin Mosaic**
*This is the central image of a series
of wonderful apse mosaics of the
Virgin by Jacopo Torriti (1295).*

Baldacchino *(1740s)
Its columns of red
porphyry and bronze
were the work of
Ferdinando Fuga.*

★ **Tomb of
Cardinal
Rodriguez**
*The Gothic
tomb (1299)
contains
magnificent
Cosmatesque
marblework.*

★ **Cappella Sistina**
*This Sistine Chapel was built
for Pope Sixtus V (1584–87)
by Domenico Fontana and
houses the pope's tomb.*

**Column in Piazza
Santa Maria Maggiore**
*A bronze of the Virgin and Child was
added to this ancient marble column
in 1615. The column came from the
Basilica of Constantine in the Forum.*

STAR FEATURES

★ Cappella Paolina

★ Coronation of the
   Virgin Mosaic

★ Tomb of Cardinal
   Rodriguez

★ Cappella Sistina

Arch erected in memory of Emperor Gallienus

Arch of Gallienus 6

Via Carlo Alberto. **Map** 6 D4. 🚌 16, 71, 714. Ⓜ Vittorio Emanuele.

Squashed between two buildings just off Via Carlo Alberto is the central arch of an originally three-arched gate erected in memory of Emperor Gallienus, who was assassinated by his Illyrian officers in AD 262. It was built on the site of the old Esquiline Gate in the Servian Wall, parts of which are visible nearby.

Santa Bibiana 7

Via Giovanni Giolitti 154. **Map** 6 F4. **Tel** 06-446 1021. 🚌 71. 🚊 5, 14. Ⓜ Vittorio Emanuele. **Open** 7.30–10am, 4.30–7.30pm daily. 🕇 ♿

The deceptively simple façade of Santa Bibiana was Bernini's first foray into architecture. It is a clean, economic design with superimposed pilasters and deeply shadowed archways. The church itself was built on the site of the palace belonging to Bibiana's family. This is where the saint was buried after being flogged to death with leaded cords during the brief persecution of the Christians in the reign of Julian the Apostate (361–3). Just inside the church is a small column against which Bibiana is said to have been whipped. Her remains, along with those of her mother Dafrosa and her sister Demetria, who also suffered martyrdom, are preserved in an alabaster urn below the altar. In a niche above the altar stands a statue of Santa Bibiana by Bernini – the first fully clothed figure he ever sculpted. He depicts her standing beside a column, holding the cords with which she was whipped, apparently on the verge of a deadly swoon.

Early sculpture by Bernini of the martyr Santa Bibiana (1626)

Piazza Vittorio Emanuele II 8

Map 6 E5. 🚌 4, 9, 71. 🚊 5, 14. Ⓜ Vittorio Emanuele. See **Markets** p352.

Piazza Vittorio, as it is called for short, was once one of the city's main open-air food markets, though now it has moved around the corner to new, covered premises. The arcaded square was built in the urban development undertaken after the unification of Italy in 1870. It was named after Italy's first king, but there is nothing regal about its appearance today.

However, the garden area in the centre of the square has been restored. It contains a number of mysterious ruins, including a large mound, part of a Roman fountain from the 3rd century AD and the Porta Magica, a curious 17th-century doorway inscribed with alchemical signs and formulae.

Museo Nazionale d'Arte Orientale 9

Via Merulana 248. **Map** 6 D5. **Tel** 06-4697 4831. 🚌 16, 70, 71, 714. Ⓜ Vittorio Emanuele. **Open** 9am–2pm Tue, Wed & Fri; 9am–7.30pm Thu, Sat & Sun. **Adm charge**. ♿ **www**. museorientale.beniculturali.it

The museum occupies part of the late 19th-century Palazzo Brancaccio, home of the Italian Institute of the Middle and Far East since 1957. The collection ranges from prehistoric Iranian ceramics, sculpture from Afghanistan, Nepal, Kashmir and India to 18th-century Tibetan paintings on vellum. From the Far East there are collections of Japanese screen paintings and Chinese jade.

The most unusual exhibits are the finds from the Italian excavation of the ancient

4th-century relief from Kashmir

Nepalese Bodhisattva in the Museo Nazionale d'Arte Orientale

civilization of Swat in northeast Pakistan. This fascinating Gandhara culture lasted from the 3rd century BC to about the 10th century AD. Its wonderfully exotic, sensual reliefs show an unusual combination of Hellenistic, Buddhist and Hindu influences.

Auditorium of Maecenas ❿

Largo Leopardi 2. **Map** 6 D5.
Tel 06-0608. 🚌 16, 714.
Ⓜ Vittorio Emanuele. **Open**
by appt; phone in advance. 📷 ♿

Maecenas, fop, gourmet and patron of the arts, was also an astute adviser and colleague of the Emperor Augustus. Fabulously rich, he created a fantastic villa and gardens on the Esquiline hill, most of which has long disappeared beneath the modern city. The partially reconstructed auditorium, isolated on a traffic island, is all that remains.

Inside, a semicircle of tiered seats suggests that it may have been a place for readings and performances. If it was, then Maecenas would have been entertained here by his protégés, the lyric poet Horace and Virgil, author of the *Aeneid*, reading their latest works. However, water ducts have also been discovered and it may well have been a *nympheum* – a kind of summerhouse – with fountains. Traces of frescoes

remain on the walls: you can make out garden scenes and a procession of miniature figures – including one of a characteristically drunken Dionysus (the Greek god of wine) being propped upright by a satyr.

Sette Sale ⓫

Via delle Terme di Traiano. **Map** 5 C5.
Tel 06-0608. 🚌 85, 87, 117, 186, 810, 850. 🚋 3. Ⓜ Colosseo. **Open**
by appt; phone in advance.

Not far from Nero's Domus Aurea is the cistern of the Sette Sale. It was built here to supply the enormous quantities of water needed for the Baths of Trajan. These were built for Emperor Trajan in AD 104 on parts of the Domus Aurea that had been damaged by a fire.

A set of stairs leads down into the cistern, well below street level. There is not much to see here now, but a walk through the huge, echoing cistern where light rays illuminate the watery surfaces is still an evocative experience. The nine sections, 30 m (98 ft) long and 5 m (16 ft) wide, had a capacity of eight million litres.

Domus Aurea ⓬

Viale della Domus Aurea.
Map 5 C5. **Tel** 06-0608.
🚌 85, 87, 117, 186, 810, 850
🚋 3. Ⓜ Colosseo. **Closed** to
public (call for further information).
📷 🎥 📷 📷

After allegedly setting fire to Rome in AD 64, Nero decided to build himself an outrageous new palace. The Domus Aurea (sometimes called Nero's Golden House) occupied part of the Palatine and most of the Celian and Esquiline hills – an area approximately 25 times the size of the Colosseum. The vestibule on the Palatine side of the complex contained a colossal gilded statue of Nero. There was an artificial lake, with gardens and woods where imported wild beasts were allowed to roam free.

According to Suetonius in his life of Nero, the palace walls were adorned with gold and mother-of-pearl, rooms were designed with ceilings that showered guests with flowers or perfumes, the dining hall rotated and the baths were fed with both sulphurous water and sea water.

Tacitus described Nero's debauched garden parties, with banquets served on barges and lakeside brothels serviced by aristocratic women, though as Nero killed himself in AD 68, he did not have long to enjoy his new home.

Nero's successors, anxious to distance themselves from the monster-emperor, did their utmost to erase all traces of the palace. Vespasian drained the lake and built the Colosseum (see pp92–5) in its place, Titus and Trajan each erected a complex of baths over the palace, and Hadrian placed the Temple of Venus and Rome (see p87) over the vestibule.

Rooms from one wing of the palace have survived, buried beneath the ruins of the Baths of Trajan on the Oppian hill. Excavations have revealed large frescoes and mosaics which are thought to be a panorama of Rome from a bird's-eye perspective. Currently closed for safety reasons, but hopefully more areas will open to the public when considered safe from landslides.

Frescoed room in the ruins of the Domus Aurea

LATERAN

In the Middle Ages the Lateran Palace was the residence of the popes, and the basilica of San Giovanni beside it rivalled St Peter's in splendour. After the return of the popes from Avignon at the end of the 14th century, the area declined in importance. Pilgrims still continued to visit San Giovanni and Santa

Cherub from San Giovanni in Laterano

Croce in Gerusalemme, but the area remained sparsely inhabited. Ancient convents slumbered amid gardens and vineyards until Rome became capital of Italy in 1870 and a network of residential streets was laid out here to house the influx of newcomers. Archaeological interest lies chiefly in the Aurelian Wall and the ruins of the Aqueduct of Nero.

SIGHTS AT A GLANCE

Churches

San Clemente pp186–7 ⑫
San Giovanni in Laterano pp182–3 ❶
Santa Croce in Gerusalemme ❺
Santi Quattro Coronati ⑪
Santo Stefano Rotondo ⑬

Shrines

Scala Santa and Sancta Sanctorum ❷

Arches and Gates

Porta Asinaria ❸
Porta Maggiore ❼

Ancient Sites

Amphiteatrum Castrense ❹
Aqueduct of Nero and the Freedmen's Tombs ❾
Baker's Tomb ❽

Museums

Museum of Musical Instruments ❻
Museo Storico della Liberazione di Roma ⑩

SEE ALSO

• *Street Finder,* maps 6, 9, 10

• *Restaurants* pp322–3

• *Mosaics Walk* pp280–81

GETTING THERE

San Giovanni Metro station on line A is just outside the city wall, but handy for many of the sights in the area. The 16, 81, 85, 87 and 186 are among the many buses to Piazza di San Giovanni in Laterano. This can also be reached by the 3 tram. This is slow, but its route makes it useful for exploring this part of Rome.

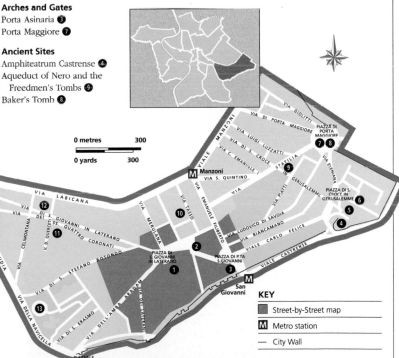

KEY

Street-by-Street map

Ⓜ Metro station

— City Wall

0 metres 300
0 yards 300

◁ **15th-century apse fresco in Santa Croce in Gerusalemme**

Street-by-Street: Piazza di San Giovanni

Both the Basilica of San Giovanni and the Lateran Palace look out over a huge open area, the Piazza di San Giovanni, laid out at the end of the 16th century with an Egyptian obelisk, the oldest in Rome, in the centre. Sadly the traffic streaming in and out of the city through Porta San Giovanni tends to detract from its grandeur. Across the square is the building housing the Scala Santa (the Holy Staircase), one of the most revered relics in Rome and the goal for many pilgrims. The area is also a venue for political rallies, and the feast of St John on 23 June is celebrated with a fair at which Romans consume roast *porchetta* (see p59).

The Chapel of Santa Rufina, originally the portico of the baptistry, has a 5th-century mosaic of spiralling foliage in the apse.

VIA DI SANTO STEFANO

VIA DELL'AMBA ARADAM

VIA DEI LATERANI

The Cloister of San Giovanni fortunately survived the two fires that destroyed the early basilica. A 13th-century masterpiece of mosaic work, the cloister now houses fragments from the medieval basilica.

Piazza di San Giovanni in Laterano boasts an ancient obelisk and parts of Nero's Aqueduct. This 18th-century painting by Canaletto shows how the piazza once looked.

STAR SIGHT

★ San Giovanni in Laterano

KEY

– – – Suggested route

0 metres 75

0 yards 75

The Chapel of San Venanzio is decorated with a series of 7th-century mosaics on a gold background. This detail from the apse shows one of the angels flanking the central figure of Christ. San Venanzio was an accomplished 6th-century Latin poet.

LOCATOR MAP
See Central Rome Map pp14–15

The Lateran Palace, residence of the popes until 1309, was rebuilt by Domenico Fontana in 1586.

★ San Giovanni in Laterano
Borromini's interior dates from the 17th century, but the grand façade by Alessandro Galilei, with its giant statues of Christ and the Apostles, was added in 1735 ❶

Scala Santa
This door at the top of the holy staircase leads to the Sancta Sanctorum ❷

The Triclinio Leoniano is a piece of wall and a mosaic from the dining hall of 8th-century Pope Leo III.

Porta Asinaria
This minor gateway, no longer in use, is as old as the Aurelian Wall, dating back to the 3rd century AD ❸

San Giovanni in Laterano ❶

See pp182–3.

Scala Santa and Sancta Sanctorum ❷

Piazza di San Giovanni in Laterano 14. **Map** 9 C1. **Tel** 06-772 6641. 🚌 16, 81, 85, 87, 186 and other routes to Piazza di San Giovanni in Laterano. 🚋 3. Ⓜ San Giovanni. **Open** 6.15am–noon, 3–6pm daily (3.30–6.30pm in summer). 🚻

Devout Christians climbing the Scala Santa on their knees

On the east side of Piazza di San Giovanni in Laterano, a building designed by Domenico Fontana (1589) houses two surviving parts of the old Lateran Palace. One is the Sancta Sanctorum, the other the holy staircase, the Scala Santa. The 28 steps, said to be those that Christ ascended in Pontius Pilate's house during his trial, are supposed to have been brought from Jerusalem by St Helena, mother of the Emperor Constantine. This belief, however, cannot be traced back any earlier than the 7th century.

The steps were moved to their present site by Pope Sixtus V (reigned 1585–90) when the old Lateran Palace was destroyed. No foot may touch the holy steps, so they are covered by wooden boards. They may only be climbed by the faithful on their knees, a penance that is performed especially on Good Friday. In the vestibule

there are various 19th-century sculptures including an *Ecce Homo* by Giosuè Meli (1874).

The Scala Santa and two side stairways lead to the Chapel of St Lawrence or Sancta Sanctorum (Holy of Holies), built by Pope Nicholas III in 1278. Decorated with fine Cosmatesque marble-work, the chapel contains many important relics, the most precious being an image of Jesus – the *Acheiropoeton* or "picture painted without hands", said to be the work of St Luke, with the help of an angel. It was taken on procession in medieval times to ward off plagues.

On the walls and in the vault, restoration work has revealed 13th-century frescoes which for 500 years had been covered by later paintings. The frescoes, representing the legends of St Nicholas, St Lawrence, St Agnes and St Paul, show signs of the style that would characterize the frescoes of Giotto in Assisi, made a few years later.

Porta Asinaria ❸

Between Piazza di Porta San Giovanni and Piazzale Appio. **Map** 10 D2. 🚌 16, 81, 85, 87. 🚋 3. Ⓜ San Giovanni. See **Markets** p353.

The Porta Asinaria (Gate of the Donkeys) is one of the minor gateways in the Aurelian Wall *(see p196)*. Twin circular

Porta Asinaria from inside the wall

towers were added and a small enclosure built around the entrance; the remains are still visible. From outside the walls you can see the gate's white travertine façade and two rows of small windows, giving light to two corridors built into the wall above the gateway. In AD 546 treacherous barbarian soldiers serving in the Roman army opened this gate to the hordes of the Goth Totila, who mercilessly looted the city. In 1084 the Holy Roman Emperor Henry IV entered Rome via Porta Asinaria with the antipope Guibert to oust Pope Gregory VII. The gate was badly damaged in the conflicts that followed.

The area close to the gate, especially in the Via Sannio, is the home of a popular flea-market *(see p353)*.

Amphiteatrum Castrense ❹

Between Piazza di Santa Croce in Gerusalemme and Viale Castrense. **Map** 10 E1. 🚌 649. 🚋 3. **Not open** to the public.

Columns and bricked-up arches of the Amphiteatrum Castrense

This small 3rd-century amphitheatre was used for games and baiting animals. It owes its preservation to the fact that it was incorporated in the Aurelian Wall *(see p196)*, which included several existing high buildings in its fortifications. The graceful arches framed by brick semicolumns were blocked up. The amphitheatre is best seen from outside the walls, from where there is also a good view of the bell tower of Santa Croce in Gerusalemme.

Discovery and Triumph of the Cross, attributed to Antoniazzo Romano, in Santa Croce in Gerusalemme

Santa Croce in Gerusalemme ❺

Piazza di Santa Croce in Gerusalemme 12. **Map** 10 E1. *Tel* 06-7061 3053. 🚌 16, 81, 649, 810 🚊 3 **Open** 7am–12.30pm, 2.30–7pm daily. 🕆 📷

Emperor Constantine's mother St Helena founded this church in AD 320 in the grounds of her private palace. Although the church stood at the edge of the city, the relics of the Crucifixion that St Helena had brought back from Jerusalem made it a centre of pilgrimage. Most important were the

pieces of Christ's Cross (*croce* means cross) and part of Pontius Pilate's inscription in Latin, Hebrew and Greek: "Jesus of Nazareth King of the Jews".

In the crypt is a Roman statue of Juno, found at Ostia (*see pp270–71*), transformed into a statue of St Helena by replacing the head and arms and adding a cross. The 15th-century apse fresco shows the medieval legends that arose around the Cross. Helena is shown holding it over a dead youth and restoring him to life. Another episode shows its recovery from the Persians by the Byzantine Emperor Heraclitus after a bloody battle. In the centre of the apse is a magnificent tomb by Jacopo Sansovino made for Cardinal Quiñones, Emperor Charles V's confessor (died 1540).

Museum of Musical Instruments ❻

Museo degli Strumenti Musicali, Piazza di Santa Croce in Gerusalemme 9a. **Map** 10 E1. *Tel* 06-701 4796. 🚌 16, 81, 649, 810. 🚊 3. **Open** 8.30am–7.30pm Tue–Sun. **Closed** 1 Jan, 25 Dec. **Adm charge**. 🛗 www.museostrumentimusicali.it

One of Rome's lesser-known museums, the building stands on the site of the Sessorianum, the great

Imperial villa belonging to Empress St Helena, later included in the Aurelian Wall. Opened in 1974, the museum has a collection of more than 3,000 instruments from all over the world, including instruments typical of the various regions of Italy, and wind, string and percussion instruments of all ages (including Egyptian, Greek and Roman). There are also sections dedicated to church and military music. The greater part of the collection is composed of Baroque instruments: don't miss the gorgeous Barberini harp, remarkably well-preserved, on the first floor in Room 13. There are spinets, harpsichords and clavichords, and one of the first pianos ever made, dating from 1722.

18th-century statue of St Helena on the façade of Santa Croce

Art Nouveau entrance to the Museum of Musical Instruments

San Giovanni in Laterano ●

Early in the 4th century, the Laterani family were disgraced and their land taken by Emperor Constantine to build Rome's first Christian basilica. Today's church retains the original shape, but has been destroyed by fire twice and rebuilt several times. Borromini undertook the last major rebuild of the interior in 1646, and the main façade is an 18th-century addition. Before the pope's move to Avignon in 1309, the adjoining Lateran Palace was the official papal residence, and until 1870 all popes were crowned in the church. The pope is the Bishop of Rome and here in the city's main cathedral he celebrates Maundy Thursday mass and attends the annual blessing of the people.

Cappella di San Venanzio
This chapel is attached to the baptistry and is decorated with 7th-century mosaics.

Entrance to museum

Apse

Papal Altar
Only the Pope can celebrate mass at this altar. The Gothic baldacchino, decorated with frescoes, dates from the 14th century.

★ Cloisters
Built by the Vassalletto family in about 1220, the cloisters are remarkable for their twisted twin columns and inlaid marble mosaics.

TIMELINE

AD 313 Constantine gives Laterani site to Pope Melchiades for a church		**1144** Church dedicated to San Giovanni in Laterano			**1646** Borromini rebuilds interior
314–18 Five-aisled basilical church is built	**896** Church damaged in earthquake	**1309** Papacy moves to Avignon	**1377** Return of popes from Avignon		

AD 300	800	1000	1400

324 Basilica consecrated by Pope Sylvester I and dedicated to the Redeemer	**904–911** Church rebuilt under Pope Sergius III	**1300** First Holy Year proclaimed	**1360** Church burnt down for second time	**1586** Domenico Fontana builds north façade
		1308 Church destroyed by fire		**1730–40** Alessandro Galilei constructs main façade

★ Baptistry
Though much restored, the domed baptistry dates back to Constantine's time. It assumed its present octagonal shape in AD 432 and the design has served as the model for baptistries throughout the Christian world.

VISITORS' CHECKLIST

Piazza di San Giovanni in Laterano 4. **Map** 9 C2. **Tel** 06-6988 6433. ▦ 16, 81, 85, 87, 186, 650, 850 and other routes to Piazza San Giovanni. Ⓜ *San Giovanni.* 🚊 3. **Church open** 7am–6.30pm daily. **Cloister open** 9am–6pm daily. **Museum open** 9am–1pm Mon–Sat. **Baptistry open** 8am–12.30pm, 4–7pm daily. **Adm charge** for museum and cloister. 🚻 🛗

STAR FEATURES

★ Baptistry
★ Cloisters

North Façade
This was added by Domenico Fontana in 1586. The pope gives his blessing from the upper loggia.

The original Lateran Palace was almost destroyed by the fire of 1308 which devastated San Giovanni. Pope Sixtus V commissioned Fontana to replace it in 1586.

Statues of Christ and the Apostles

Boniface VIII Fresco
This fragment showing the pope proclaiming the Holy Year of 1300 is attributed to Giotto.

A side door is opened every Holy Year.

The main entrance's bronze doors originally came from the Curia (*see p82*).

Corsini Chapel
This chapel was built in the 1730s for Pope Clement XII. The altarpiece is a mosaic copy of Guido Reni's painting of Sant'Andrea Corsini.

TRIAL OF A CORPSE

Fear of rival factions led the early popes to extraordinary lengths. An absurd case took place at the Lateran Palace in 897 when Pope Stephen VI tried the corpse of his predecessor, Formosus, for disloyalty to the Church. The corpse was found guilty, its right hand was mutilated and it was thrown in to the Tiber.
Pope Formosus

Porta Maggiore ❼

Piazza di Porta Maggiore. **Map** 6 F5.
🚌 105. 🚋 3, 5, 14, 19.

Originally the two arches of
Porta Maggiore were not part
of the city wall, but part of an
aqueduct built by the Emperor
Claudius in AD 52. They
carried the water of the Aqua
Claudia over the Via Labicana
and Via Prenestina, two of
ancient Rome's main southbound roads. You can still see
the original roadway beneath
the gate. In the large slabs of
basalt – a hard volcanic rock
used in all old Roman roads –
note the great ruts created by
generations of cartwheels.
On top of the arches separate
conduits carried the water of
two aqueducts: the Aqua
Claudia, and its offshoot, the
Aqueduct of Nero. They bear
inscriptions from the time of
the Emperor Claudius and
also from the reigns of
Vespasian and Titus, who
restored them in AD 71 and
AD 81 respectively. In all,
six aqueducts from different
water sources entered the city
at Porta Maggiore.

The Aqua Claudia was 68
km (43 miles) long, with over
15 km (9 miles) above ground.
Its majestic arches are a
notable feature of the Roman
countryside, and a popular
mineral water bears its name.
One stretch of the Aqua
Claudia had its arches bricked
up when it was incorporated
into the 3rd-century Aurelian
Wall *(see p196)*.

Relief showing breadmaking on the tomb of the baker Eurysaces

Baker's Tomb ❽

Piazzale Labicano. **Map** 6 F5.
🚌 105. 🚋 3, 5, 14, 19.

In the middle of the tram
junction near Porta Maggiore
stands the tomb of the rich
baker Eurysaces and his
wife Atistia, built in 30 BC.
Roman custom forbade
burials within city walls,
and the roads leading
out of cities became lined
with tombs and monu-
ments for the middle and
upper classes. This tomb
is shaped like a baking
oven: a low-relief frieze at
the top shows Eurysaces
presiding over his slaves
in the various phases
of breadmaking. The
inscription proudly asserts his
origins and reveals him as
a freed slave, probably of
Greek origin. Many men like
him saved money from their
meagre slave salaries to earn
their freedom and set up
businesses, becoming the
backbone of Rome's economy.

Aqueduct of Nero and the Freedmen's Tombs ❾

Intersection of Via Statilia and Via di
Santa Croce in Gerusalemme.
Map 10 D1. 🚌 105, 649. 🚋 3, 5,
14, 19. **Open** by appt only: call
06-0608.

The aqueduct was built by
Nero in the 1st century AD as
an extension of the Aqua
Claudia to supply Nero's

Golden House *(see p175)*.
It was later extended to the
Imperial residences on the
Palatine. Partly incorporated
into later buildings, the imposing arches make their way via
the Lateran to the Celian hill.
Along the first section of the
aqueduct, in
Via Statilia, is a
small tomb in
the shape of a
house, dating
from the 1st
century BC,
bearing the
names and
likenesses of a
group of freed
slaves. Their
name, Statilii,
indicates that
they had been
freed by the Statilii, the family
of Claudius's notorious wife
Messalina. Servants of families
often pooled funds in this way
to pay for a dignified burial in
a common resting place.

**Relief on the Tomb of
the Statilii freedmen**

**Well-preserved section of Nero's
Aqueduct near San Giovanni**

**Porta Maggiore, a city gate formed
by the arches of an aqueduct**

Museo Storico della Liberazione di Roma ⑩

Via Tasso 145. **Map** 9 C1. **Tel** 06-700 3866. Ⓜ *Manzoni, San Giovanni.* 🚌 3. **Open** 4–7pm Tue, Thu & Fri; 9.30am–12.30pm Tue–Sun.

This museum, dedicated to the resistance to the Nazi occupation of Rome, is housed in the ex-prison of the Gestapo. The makeshift cells with bricked-up windows and bloodstained walls make a strong impact *(see p266)*.

Santi Quattro Coronati ⑪

Via dei Santi Quattro Coronati 20. **Map** 9 B1. **Tel** 06-7047 5427. 🚌 85, 117, 850. 🚋 3. **Open** 6.30am–12.30pm, 3.30–7.45pm daily. ✝ ♿

Cloister of Santi Quattro Coronati

The name of this fortified convent (Four Crowned Saints) refers to four Christian soldiers martyred after refusing to worship a pagan god. For centuries it was the bastion of the pope's residence, the Lateran Palace. Its high apse looms over the houses below, while a Carolingian tower dominates the entrance. Erected in the 4th century AD, it was rebuilt after the invading Normans set fire to the neighbourhood in 1084. Hidden within is the garden of the delightful inner cloister (admission on request), one of the earliest of its kind, built c.1220.

The remains of medieval frescoes can be seen in the Chapel of Santa Barbara, but the convent's main feature is the Chapel of St Sylvester – its remarkable frescoes (1246) recount the legend of the conversion to Christianity of the Emperor Constantine by

Pope Sylvester I (reigned 314–35), then living as a hermit on Monte Soratte, north of Rome.

Stricken by the plague, Constantine is prescribed a bath in children's blood, to the horror of the matrons of Rome. Unable to bring himself to obey, Constantine is visited in a dream by St Peter and St Paul. They advise him to find Sylvester, who cures him and baptizes him. The final scene shows the emperor kneeling before the pope. The implied idea of the pope as heir to the Roman Empire would affect the whole course of medieval European history.

San Clemente ⑫

See pp186–7.

Santo Stefano Rotondo ⑬

Via di Santo Stefano Rotondo 7. **Map** 9 B2. **Tel** 06-42 11 99. **Fax** 06-4211 9125. 🚌 81, 117, 673. **Open** by appt (fax or email santo.stefano. rotondo@cgu.it to arrange). 📷

One of Rome's earliest Christian churches, Santo Stefano Rotondo was constructed between 468 and 483. It has an unusual circular plan with four chapels in

Distinctive circular outline of Santo Stefano Rotondo

the shape of a cross. The round inner area was surrounded by concentric corridors with 22 Ionic supporting columns. The high drum in the centre is 22 m (72 ft) high and just as wide. It is lit by 22 high windows, a few of them restored or blocked by restorations carried out under Pope Nicholas V (reigned 1447–55), who consulted the Florentine architect Leon Battista Alberti. The archway in the centre may have been added during this period.

In the 16th century the church walls were frescoed by Niccolò Pomarancio, with particularly gruesome illustrations of the martyrdom of innumerable saints. Some of the medieval decor remains: in the first chapel to the left of the entrance is a 7th-century mosaic of Christ with San Primo and San Feliciano.

Fresco of St Sylvester and Constantine in Santi Quattro Coronati

San Clemente

San Clemente provides an opportunity to travel back through three layers of history. At street level, there is a 12th-century church; underneath this lies a 4th-century church; and below that are ancient Roman buildings, including a Temple of Mithras. Mithraism, an all-male cult imported from Persia in the 1st century BC, was a rival to Christianity during the age of Imperial Rome.

The upper levels are dedicated to St Clement, the fourth pope, who was exiled to the Crimea and martyred by being tied to an anchor and drowned. His life is illustrated in some of the frescoes in the 4th-century church. The site was taken over in the 17th century by Irish Dominicans, who still continue the excavating work begun by Father Mullooly in 1857.

Entrance to the church is through a door in Via di San Giovanni in Laterano.

Paschal Candlestick
This 12th-century spiralling candlestick, striped with glittering mosaic, is a magnificent example of Cosmati work.

18th-century Façade
Twelfth-century columns were used in the arcade.

★ **Cappella di Santa Caterina**
The restored frescoes by the 15th-century Florentine artist, Masolino da Panicale, show scenes from the life of the martyred St Catherine of Alexandria.

12th-century church

4th-century church

Piscina
This deep pit was discovered in 1967. It could have been used as a font or fountain.

1st–3rd-century temple and buildings

TIMELINE

2nd century Site possibly used for secret Christian worship

Late 2nd century Temple of Mithras built

867 Reputed transfer of remains of San Clemente to Rome

1108 New church built over 4th-century church

1857 Original 4th-century church rediscovered by Father Mullooly

AD 10	500	1000	1500	1900

c.88–97 Papacy of St Clement

4th century First church built over courtyard of earlier Roman building

1667 Church and convent given to Irish Dominicans

AD 64 Nero's fire destroys area

1084 Church destroyed during Norman invasion led by Robert Guiscard

1861 Church is excavated. Roman ruins discovered

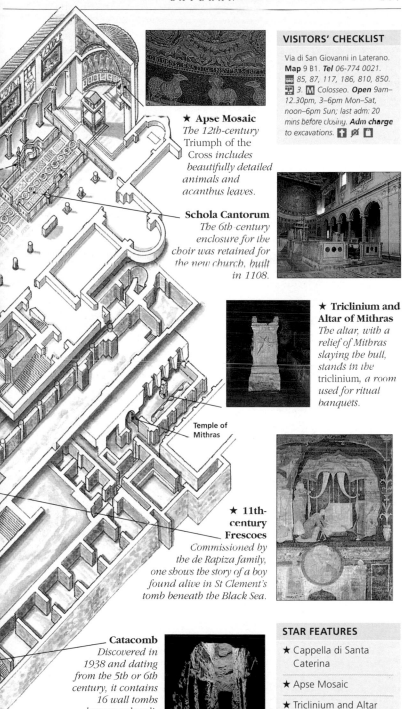

VISITORS' CHECKLIST

Via di San Giovanni in Laterano.
Map 9 B1. **Tel** 06-774 0021.
85, 87, 117, 186, 810, 850.
3. M Colosseo. **Open** 9am–
12.30pm, 3–6pm Mon–Sat,
noon–6pm Sun; last adm: 20
mins before closing. **Adm charge**
to excavations.

★ **Apse Mosaic**
The 12th-century
Triumph of the
Cross *includes
beautifully detailed
animals and
acanthus leaves.*

Schola Cantorum
*The 6th-century
enclosure for the
choir was retained for
the new church, built
in 1108.*

★ **Triclinium and
Altar of Mithras**
*The altar, with a
relief of Mithras
slaying the bull,
stands in the
triclinium, a room
used for ritual
banquets.*

Temple of
Mithras

★ **11th-
century
Frescoes**
*Commissioned by
the de Rapiza family,
one shows the story of a boy
found alive in St Clement's
tomb beneath the Black Sea.*

Catacomb
*Discovered in
1938 and dating
from the 5th or 6th
century, it contains
16 wall tombs
known as* loculi.

STAR FEATURES

★ Cappella di Santa
Caterina

★ Apse Mosaic

★ Triclinium and Altar
of Mithras

★ 11th-century
Frescoes

IOVINVSALVMNVS

CARACALLA

The Celian Hill over-looks the Colosseum, and takes its name from Caelius Vibenna, the legendary hero of Rome's struggle against the Tarquins *(see pp18–19)*. In Imperial Rome this was a fashionable place to live, and some of its vanished splendour is still apparent in the vast ruins of the Baths of Caracalla. Today, thanks to the

Capital from ruins of Baths of Caracalla

Archaeological Zone established at the beginning of the 20th century, it is a peaceful area, a green wedge from the Aurelian Wall to the heart of the city. Through it runs the cobbled Via di Porta San Sebastiano, part of the old Via Appia. This road leads to Porta San Sebastiano, one of the best-preserved gates in the ancient city wall.

SIGHTS AT A GLANCE

Churches
San Cesareo ⑧
San Giovanni a Porta Latina ⑨
San Giovanni in Oleo ⑩
San Gregorio Magno ②
San Sisto Vecchio ⑥
Santa Balbina ⑯
Santa Maria in Domnica ④
Santi Giovanni e Paolo ①
Santi Nereo e Achilleo ⑦

Arches and Gates
Arch of Dolabella ③
Arch of Drusus ⑬
Aurelian Wall and
   Porta San Sebastiano ⑭
Sangallo Bastion ⑮

Historic Buildings
Baths of Caracalla ⑰

Tombs
Columbarium of
   Pomponius Hylas ⑪
Tomb of the Scipios ⑫

Parks and Gardens
Villa Celimontana ⑤

GETTING THERE
Circo Massimo Metro station is handy if you are visiting the churches and parks on the Celian hill. For the Baths of Caracalla and other sights closer to Porta San Sebastiano, take the 628 along Viale delle Terme di Caracalla.

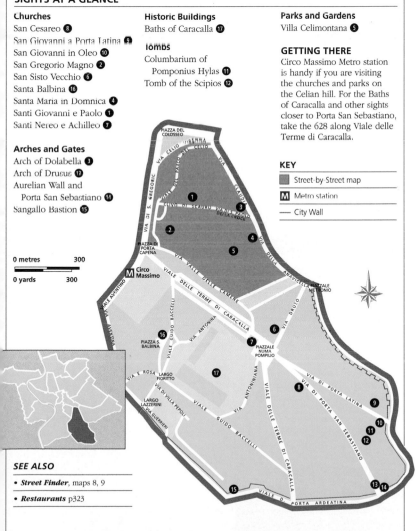

KEY

▨	Street-by-Street map
Ⓜ	Metro station
—	City Wall

0 metres   300
0 yards   300

SEE ALSO
• *Street Finder*, maps 8, 9
• *Restaurants* p323

◁ **Mosaic of an athlete from the Baths of Caracalla**

Street-by-Street: The Celian Hill

In the course of a morning exploring the green
slopes of the Celian hill, you will see a fascinating
assortment of archaeological remains and beautiful
churches. A good starting point is the church of San
Gregorio Magno, from where the Clivo di Scauro leads
up to the top of the hill. The steep narrow street passes
the ancient porticoed church of Santi Giovanni e Paolo
with its beautiful Romanesque bell tower soaring above
the surrounding medieval monastery buildings. Of the
parks on the hill, the best kept and most peaceful is the
Villa Celimontana with its formal walks and avenues.

It is a good place for a
picnic, as there
are few bars or
restaurants
in the area.

Clivo di Scauro, the Roman
Clivus Scauri, leads up to
Santi Giovanni e Paolo,
passing under
the flying buttresses
that support
the church.

VIA DI SAN GREGORIO

CLIVO DI SCAURO

To Circo
Massimo
Metro

La Vignola is a
delightful Renaissance
pavilion, reconstructed
here in 1911 after it
had been demolished
during the creation of
the Archaeological
Zone around the
Baths of Caracalla.

**San Gregorio
Magno**
*A monastery and
chapel were
founded here by
Pope Gregory the
Great at the end of
the 6th century* ❷

★ Santi Giovanni e Paolo
*The nave of the church, lit by a blaze
of chandeliers, has been restored
many times, assuming its present
appearance in the 18th century* ❶

★ Villa Celimontana
*The delightful 16th-
century villa built for the
Mattei family is now the
centre of a public park* ❺

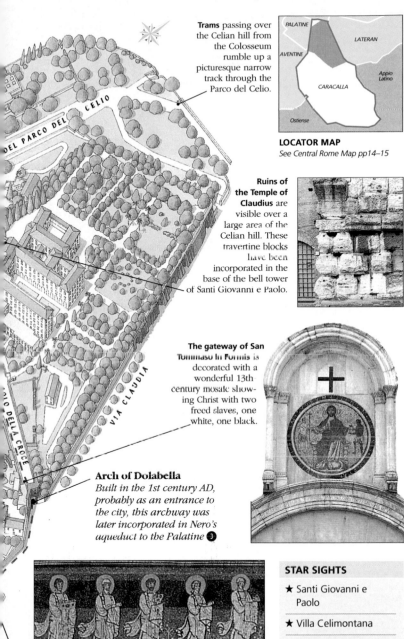

Trams passing over the Celian hill from the Colosseum rumble up a picturesque narrow track through the Parco del Celio.

LOCATOR MAP
See Central Rome Map pp14–15

Ruins of the Temple of Claudius are visible over a large area of the Celian hill. These travertine blocks have been incorporated in the base of the bell tower of Santi Giovanni e Paolo.

The gateway of San Tommaso in Formis is decorated with a wonderful 13th-century mosaic showing Christ with two freed slaves, one white, one black.

Arch of Dolabella
Built in the 1st century AD, probably as an entrance to the city, this archway was later incorporated in Nero's aqueduct to the Palatine ③

★ **Santa Maria in Domnica**
This church is famed for its 9th-century mosaics. These Apostles appear on the triumphal arch above the apse, flanking a medallion containing the figure of Christ ④

STAR SIGHTS

★ Santi Giovanni e Paolo

★ Villa Celimontana

★ Santa Maria in Domnica

KEY

– – – Suggested route

0 metres	75
0 yards	75

Santi Giovanni e Paolo ❶

Piazza Santi Giovanni e Paolo 13.
Map 9 A1. *Tel* 06-772 711.
🚌 75, 81, 117, 175, 673. 🚊 3.
Ⓜ *Colosseo or Circo Massimo.*
Church open 8.30am–noon,
3.30–6pm daily. **Roman houses** *Tel*
06-7045 4544. **Open** 10am–1pm,
3–6pm Thu–Mon. 🔼 ⓰
church only.

Santi Giovanni e Paolo is
dedicated to two martyred
Roman officers whose house
originally stood on this site.
Giovanni (John) and Paolo
(Paul) had served the first
Christian emperor, Constantine. When they were later
called to arms by the pagan
emperor Julian the Apostate,
they refused and were
beheaded and buried in
secret in their own house
in AD 362.

Built towards the end of the
4th century, the church
retains many elements of its
original structure. The Ionic
portico dates from the 12th
century, and the apse and bell
tower were added by
Nicholas Breakspeare, the
only English pope, who
reigned as Adrian IV
(1154–9). The base of the
superb 13th-century Romanesque bell tower was part of
the Temple of Claudius that
stood on this site. The interior,
which was remodelled in
1718, has granite piers and
columns. A tomb slab in the
nave marks the burial place of
the martyrs, whose relics are
preserved in an urn under the
high altar. In a tiny room near
the altar, a magnificent 13th-
century fresco depicts the
figure of Christ flanked by his
Apostles (ask the sacristan
who will be able to unlock
the door).

Excavations beneath the
church have revealed two 2nd-
and 3rd-century Roman houses
used as a Christian burial place.
These are well worth a visit.
The two-storey construction,
with 20 rooms and a labyrinth
of corridors, has well-preserved
pagan and Christian paintings.
The arches to the left of
the church were part of a
3rd-century street of shops.

Fresco of Christ and the Apostles in Santi Giovanni e Paolo

San Gregorio Magno ❷

Piazza di San Gregorio. **Map** 8 F2. *Tel*
06-700 8227. 🚌 75, 81, 117, 175,
673. 🚊 3. Ⓜ *Circo Massimo.* **Open**
9am–noon, 3.30–7pm daily. 🔼

Façade of San Gregorio Magno

To the English, this is one of
the most important churches
in Rome, for it was from here
that St Augustine was sent on
his mission to convert
England to Christianity. The
church was founded in AD 575
by San Gregorio Magno (St
Gregory the Great), who turned
his family home on this site into
a monastery. It was rebuilt in
medieval times and restored in
1629–33 by Giovanni Battista
Soria. The church is reached via
a flight of steps from the street.

The forecourt contains some
interesting tombs. To the left
is that of Sir Edward Carne,
who came to Rome several
times between 1529 and 1533
as King Henry VIII's envoy to
gain the pope's consent to the
annulment of Henry's mar-
riage to Catherine of Aragon.

The interior, remodelled by
Francesco Ferrari in the mid-
18th century, is Baroque, apart
from the fine mosaic floor and
some ancient columns. At the
end of the right aisle is the
chapel of St Gregory. Leading
off it, another small chapel, believed to have been the saint's
own cell, houses his episcopal
throne – a Roman chair of
sculpted marble. The Salviati
Chapel on the left contains a
picture of the Virgin said to
have spoken to St Gregory.

Outside, amid the cypresses
to the left of the church, stand
three small chapels, dedicated
to St Andrew, St Barbara and
St Sylvia (Gregory the Great's
mother). The restored
chapels contain frescoes by
Domenichino and Guido Reni.

**Marble throne of Gregory the Great
from the 1st century BC**

Arch of Dolabella

Via di San Paolo della Croce.
Map 9 A2. 🚌 81, 117, 673.
🚃 3. Ⓜ Colosseo.

The arch was built in AD 10 by consuls Caius Junius Silanus and Cornelius Dolabella, possibly on the site of one of the old Servian Wall's gateways. It was made of travertine blocks and later used to support Nero's extension of the Claudian aqueduct, built to supply the Imperial palace on the Palatine hill.

The restored Arch of Dolabella

Santa Maria in Domnica ❹

Piazza della Navicella 12.
Map 9 A2. **Tel** 06-7720 2685.
🚌 81,117, 673. 🚃 3. Ⓜ Colosseo.
Open 9am–noon, 3.30–7pm (to 6pm in winter) daily. 🔼 ♿

The church overlooks the Piazza della Navicella (little boat) and takes its name from the 16th-century fountain.

Dating from the 7th century, the church was probably built on the site of an ancient Roman firemen's barracks, which later became a meeting place for Christians. In the 16th century Pope Leo X added the portico and the coffered ceiling.

In the apse behind the modern altar is a superb 9th-century mosaic commissioned by Pope Paschal I. Wearing the square halo of the living, the pope appears at the feet of the Virgin and Child. The Virgin, surrounded by a throng of angels, holds a hand-kerchief like a fashionable lady at a Byzantine court.

Villa Celimontana ❺

Piazza della Navicella.
Map 9 A2. 🚌 81, 117, 673.
Park open 7am–dusk daily.

The Dukes of Mattei bought this land in 1553 and transformed the vineyards that covered the hillside into a formal garden. As well as palms and other exotic trees, the garden has its own Egyptian obelisk. Villa Mattei, built in the 1580s and now known as Villa Celimontana, houses the Italian Geographical Society.

The Mattei family used to open the park to the public on the day of the Visit of the Seven Churches, an annual event instituted by San Filippo Neri in 1552. Starting from the Chiesa Nuova (see p124), Romans went on foot to the city's seven major churches and, on reaching Villa Mattei,

were given bread, wine, salami, cheese, an egg and two apples. The garden, now owned by the city of Rome, still makes an ideal place for a picnic. In summer it hosts an excellent jazz festival (see p358).

Park of Villa Celimontana

San Sisto Vecchio ❻

Piazzale Numa Pompilio 8.
Map 9 A3. **Tel** 06-7720 5174.
🚌 160, 628, 671, 714. **Open** 9–11am, 3–5.30pm daily. 🚫

This small church is of great historical interest as it was granted to St Dominic in 1219 by Pope Honorius III. The founder of the Dominican order soon moved his own headquarters to Santa Sabina (see p204), San Sisto becoming the first home of the order of Dominican nuns. The church, with its 13th-century bell tower and frescoes, is also a popular place for weddings.

Apse mosaic of the Virgin and Child in Santa Maria in Domnica

Santi Nereo e Achilleo ❼

Via delle Terme di Caracalla 28. **Map** 9
A3. **Tel** 06-575 7996. 🚌 160, 628,
671, 714. **Open** Apr–Jul & Sep–Oct:
10am–noon, 4–6pm Thu–Mon (it is
advisable to call ahead). ♿

According to legend,
St Peter, after escap-
ing from prison,
was fleeing the
city when he
lost a bandage
from his
wounds. The
original church
was founded
here in the 4th
century on the
spot where the
bandage fell,
but later on it
was rededicated
to the 1st-century AD martyrs
St Nereus and St Achilleus.

**Detail of mosaic,
Santi Nereo e Achilleo**

Restored at the end of the
16th century, the church has
retained many medieval
features, including some fine
9th-century mosaics on the
triumphal arch. A magnificent
pulpit rests on an enormous
porphyry pedestal which was
found nearby in the Baths of
Caracalla. The walls of the side
aisles are decorated with
grisly 16th-century frescoes by
Niccolò Pomarancio, showing
in clinical detail how each of
the Apostles was martyred.

**Fresco by Niccolò Pomarancio of the *Martyrdom of
St Simon* in Santi Nereo e Achilleo**

San Cesareo ❽

Via di Porta San Sebastiano.
Map 9 A3. **Tel** 06-5823 0140.
🚌 218, 628. **Open** 10am–noon
Sun & by appt.

This splendid old church was
built over Roman ruins of the
2nd century AD. You can still
admire Giacomo della
Porta's fine Renaissance
façade, but by phoning
ahead to book a visit,
you can also see
Cosmatesque mosaic
work and carving
to rival that of any
church in Rome. The
episcopal throne, altar
and pulpit are decorated
with delightful birds
and beasts. The church
was restored in the
16th century by Pope
Clement VIII, whose coat of
arms decorates the ceiling.

San Giovanni a Porta Latina ❾

Via di San Giovanni a Porta Latina.
Map 9 B3. **Tel** 06-7740 0032. 🚌 218,
360, 628. **Open** 7.30am–12.30pm
(6.30am summer), 3–7pm daily. ✝ ♿

The church of "St John at the
Latin Gate" was founded in
the 5th century, rebuilt in 720
and restored in 1191. This is
one of the most picturesque
of the old Roman
churches. Classi-
cal columns sup-
port the medieval
portico, and the
12th-century bell
tower is superb.
A tall cedar tree
shades an ancient
well standing in
the forecourt.
The interior has
been restored,
but it preserves
the rare simplicity
of its early origins
with ancient
columns of
varying styles
lining the aisles.
Traces of early
medieval frescoes
can still be seen
within the church.
There are 12th-
century frescoes

showing 46 different biblical
scenes, from both the Old
and New Testaments, which
are among the finest of their
kind in Rome.

Fresco, San Giovanni a Porta Latina

San Giovanni in Oleo ❿

Via di Porta Latina. **Map** 9 C4. 🚌 628.
Adm ask at S. Giovanni a Porta Latina.

Frieze of San Giovanni in Oleo

The name of this charming
octagonal Renaissance chapel
means "St John in Oil". The
tiny building marks the spot
where, according to legend,
St John was boiled in oil –
and came out unscathed, or
even refreshed. An earlier
chapel is said to have existed
on the site; the present one
was built in the early 16th
century. The design has been
attributed to Baldassare Peruzzi
or Antonio da Sangallo the
Younger. It was restored by
Borromini, who altered the
roof, crowning it with a
cross supported by a sphere
decorated with roses. He also
added a terracotta frieze of
roses and palm leaves. The
wall paintings inside the
chapel include one of St John
in a cauldron of boiling oil.

Niches for funerary urns in the Columbarium of Pomponius Hylas

Columbarium of Pomponius Hylas ⓫

Via di Porta Latina 10. **Map** 9 B4.
🚌 218, 360, 628. **Open** by appt
only. call 06-0608.

Known as a columbarium because it resembles a dovecote (*columba* is the Latin word for dove), this kind of vaulted tomb was usually built by rich Romans to house the cremated remains of their freedmen. Many similar tombs have been uncovered in this part of Rome, which up until the 3rd century AD lay outside the city wall. This one, excavated in 1831, dates from the 1st century AD. An inscription informs us that it

Mosaic inscription in the Columbarium of Pomponius Hylas

is the Tomb of Pomponius Hylas and his wife, Pomponia Vitalinis. Above her name is a "V" which indicates that she was still living when the inscription was made. The tomb was probably a commercial venture. Niches in the interior walls of the columbarium were sold to people who could not afford to build vaults of their own.

Tomb of the Scipios ⓬

Via di Porta San Sebastiano 9.
Map 9 B4. **Tel** 06-0608.
🚌 218, 360, 628. **Closed** for restoration.

The Scipios were a family of conquering generals. Southern Italy, Corsica, Algeria, Spain and Asia Minor all fell to their victorious Roman armies. The most famous of these generals was Publius Cornelius Scipio Africanus, who defeated the great Carthaginian general Hannibal at the Battle of Zama in 202 BC (*see p23*). Scipio Africanus himself was not buried here in the family tomb, but at Liternum near Naples, where he owned a favourite villa.
The Tomb of the Scipios was discovered in 1780. It

contained various sarcophagi, statues and niches with terracotta burial urns. Many of the originals have now been moved to the Vatican Museums and copies stand in their place.
The earliest sarcophagus was that of Cornelius Scipio Barbatus, consul in 298 BC, for whom the tomb was built. Members of his illustrious family continued to be buried here up to the middle of the 2nd century BC. Excavations in the area have revealed a columbarium similar to that of Pomponius Hylas, a Christian catacomb and a three-storey house dating from the 3rd century AD, which was built over the Tomb of the Scipios.

Arch of Drusus ⓭

Via di Porta San Sebastiano.
Map 9 B4. 🚌 218, 360.

Arch of Drusus, part of the Aqua Antoniniana aqueduct

Once mistakenly identified as a triumphal arch, the so-called Arch of Drusus merely supported the branch aqueduct that supplied the Baths of Caracalla. It was built in the 3rd century AD, so had no connection with Drusus, a stepson of the Emperor Augustus. Its monumental appearance was due to the fact that it carried the aqueduct across the important route, Via Appia. The arch still spans the old cobbled road, just 50 m (160 ft) short of the gateway Porta San Sebastiano.

Aurelian Wall and Porta San Sebastiano ⑭

Museo delle Mura, Via di Porta San Sebastiano 18. **Map** 9 B4.
218, 360. **Tel** *06-7047 5284.*
Open *9am–2pm Tue–Sun.*
Last adm: 30 mins before closing.
Closed *1 Jan, 1 May, 25 Dec.*
Adm charge.

Most of the Aurelian Wall, begun by the emperor Aurelian (AD 270–75) and completed by his successor Probus (AD 276–82), has survived. Aurelian ordered its construction as a defence against Germanic tribes, whose raids were penetrating deeper and deeper into Italy. Some 18 km (11 miles) round, with 18 gates and 381 towers, the wall took in all the seven hills of Rome. It was raised to almost twice its original height by Maxentius (AD 306–12).

The wall was Rome's main defence until 1870, when it was breached by Italian artillery just by Porta Pia, close to today's British Embassy. Many of the gates are still in use, and although the city has spread, most of its noteworthy historical and cultural sights still lie within the walls.

Porta San Sebastiano, the gate leading to the Via Appia Antica *(see p284)*, is the largest and best-preserved gateway in the Aurelian Wall. It was rebuilt by Emperor Honorius in the 5th century AD. Originally the Porta Appia, in Christian times it gradually became known as the Porta San Sebastiano, because the Via Appia led to

the Basilica and Catacombs of San Sebastiano, which were popular places of pilgrimage.

It was at this gate that the last triumphal procession to enter the city by the Appian Way was received in state – that of Marcantonio Colonna after the victory of Lepanto over the Turkish fleet in 1571. Today the gate's towers house a museum with prints and models showing the walls' history. From here you can take a short walk along the restored walls. The views are spectacular.

Pope Paul III Farnese

Sangallo Bastion ⑮

Viale di Porta Ardeatina. **Map** 9 A4.
160. **Closed** *for restoration.*

Haunted by the memory of the Sack of Rome in 1527 and fearing attack by the Turks, Pope Paul III asked Antonio da Sangallo the Younger to reinforce the Aurelian Wall. Work on the huge projecting bastion began in 1537. For the moment its massive bulk can only be admired from outside.

The high altar of Santa Balbina

Santa Balbina ⑯

Piazza di Santa Balbina 8.
Map 8 F3. **Tel** *06-578 0207.*
160. *3.* Ⓜ *Circo Massimo.*
Open *12.30–1pm Mon–Fri; 10.30–11.30am Sun.*

Overlooking the Baths of Caracalla, this isolated church is dedicated to Santa Balbina, a 2nd-century virgin martyr. It is one of the oldest in Rome, dating back to the fifth century, and was built on the remains of a Roman villa. Consecrated by Pope Gregory the Great, in the Middle Ages Santa Balbina was a fortified monastery and over time has changed in appearance several times, regaining its Romanesque aspect in the 1920s.

From the piazza in front of the church, a staircase leads up to a three-arched portico. Inside, light streams in from a series of high windows along the length of the nave. The remains of St Balbina and her father, St Quirinus, are in an urn at the high altar, though the church's real treasure is situated in the far right-hand corner: the magnificent sculpted and inlaid tomb of Cardinal Stefanis de Surdis by Giovanni di Cosma (1303).

Other features worth noting are a 13th-century episcopal throne and various fragments of frescoes. These include a lovely *Madonna and Child*, an example of the school of Pietro Cavallini, in the second chapel on the left. Fragments of first-century Roman mosaics were also discovered in the 1930s. Depicting birds and signs of the zodiac, these are now set in the church floor.

Fortified gateway of Porta San Sebastiano

Baths of Caracalla ⑰

Viale delle Terme di Caracalla 52.
Map 9 A3. **Tel** 06-3996 7700. ▤
160, 628. ▣ 3. Ⓜ Circo Massimo.
Open 9am–1hr before sunset Tue–
Sun; 9am–2pm Mon. **Closed** 1 Jan,
25 Dec. **Adm charge.** ▣ ▣ ▣

Completed by Emperor
Caracalla in AD 217, the baths
functioned for about 300
years, until the plumbing was
destroyed by invading Goths.
Over 1,600 bathers at a time
could enjoy the facilities. A
Roman bath was a serious
business, beginning with a
sort of Turkish bath, followed
by a spell in the *caldarium*,
a large hot
room with
pools of water
to provide
humidity.
Then came
the lukewarm
tepidarium,
a visit to the
large central
meeting place,
known as the

**Fragment of
mosaic pavement**

frigidarium, and finally a
plunge into the *natatio*,
an open-air swimming
pool. For the rich,

Part of one of the gymnasia in the Baths of Caracalla

this was followed by a rub-
down with scented woollen
cloth. As well as the baths,
there were spaces for
exercise, libraries, art galleries
and gardens – a true
leisure centre. Most
of the rich marble
decorations of the baths
were removed by the
Farnese family in the
16th century to adorn
the interior of Palazzo
Farnese *(see p147)*.

Open-air operas are no longer
staged here because the vocal
exertions of the performers
are now thought to pose
a threat to the structure of
this ancient monument.

KEY

▢	Caldarium (very hot)
▢	Tepidarium (lukewarm)
▢	Frigidarium (cold)
▢	Natatio (pool)
▢	Garden

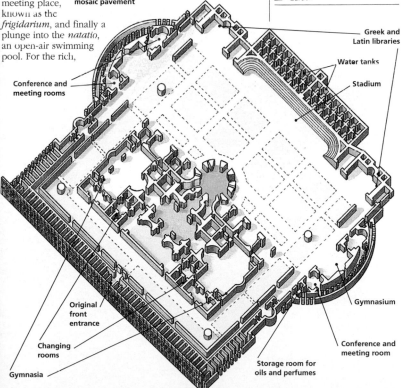

Greek and
Latin libraries

Water tanks

Stadium

Conference and
meeting rooms

Gymnasium

Original
front
entrance

Changing
rooms

Conference and
meeting room

Gymnasia

Storage room for
oils and perfumes

AVENTINE

This is one of the most peaceful areas within the walls of the city. Although it is largely residential, there are some unique historic sights. From the top of the Aventine hill, crowned by the magnificent basilica of Santa Sabina, there are fine views across the river to Trastevere and St Peter's. At the

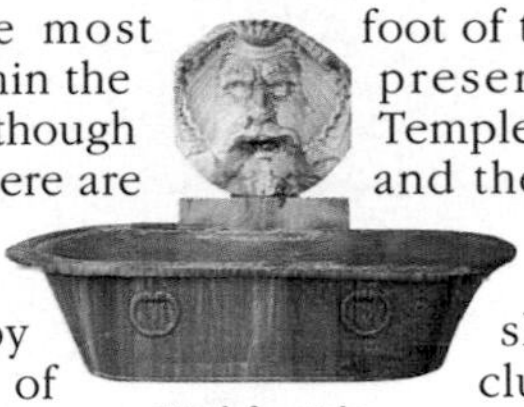

Mask fountain in courtyard of Santa Sabina

foot of the hill, ancient Rome is preserved in the two tiny Temples of the Forum Boarium and the Circus Maximus. The liveliest streets are in Testaccio, which has shops, restaurants and clubs, while to the south, beside Rome's solitary pyramid, the Protestant Cemetery is another oasis of calm.

SIGHTS AT A GLANCE

Churches and Temples
San Giorgio in Velabro ❸
San Giovanni Decollato ❻
San Saba ❺
San Teodoro ❹
Santa Maria della
  Consolazione ❺
Santa Maria in Cosmedin ❶
Santa Sabina ❾
Santi Bonifacio e Alessio ❿
Temples of the
  Forum Boarium ❽

Historic Buildings
Casa dei Crescenzi ❼

Arches
Arch of Janus ❷

Historic Streets and Piazzas
Piazza dei Cavalieri di Malta ⓫

Ancient Sites
Circus Maximus ⓰
Monte Testaccio ⓬

Monuments and Tombs
Protestant Cemetery ⓭
Pyramid of Caius Cestius ⓮

GETTING THERE
The quickest way is by Metro line B to Piramide or Circo Massimo. For a more interesting trip, take tram 3. Several buses go down from Piazza Venezia, including 81, 160 and 628, while 23 and 280 run along Via Marmorata to Piramide.

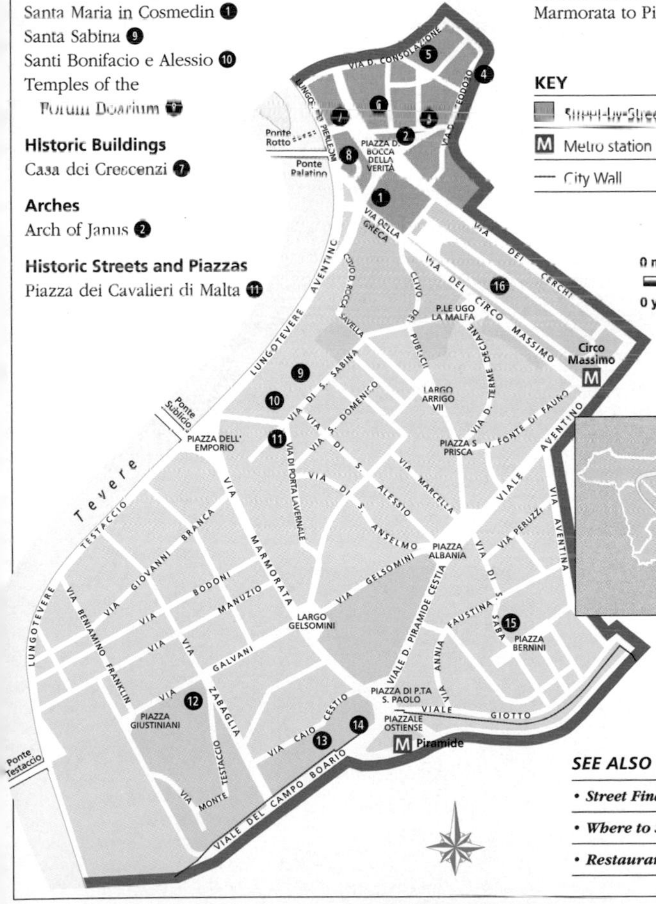

KEY

	Street-by-Street map
M	Metro station
—	City Wall

0 metres   300
0 yards   300

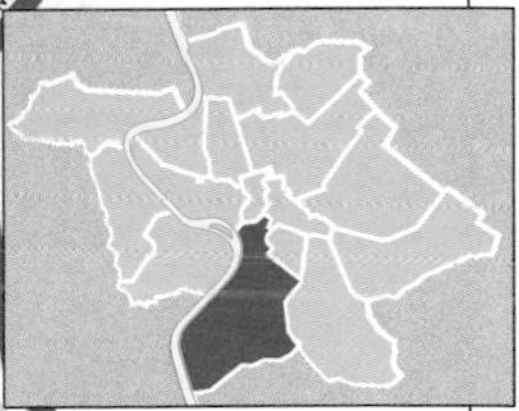

SEE ALSO
- *Street Finder*, maps 7, 8, 12
- *Where to Stay* p306
- *Restaurants* pp323–4

◁ Pines and orange trees on the Aventine hill with the dome of St Peter's in the distance

Street-by-Street: Piazza della Bocca della Verità

The area attracts visitors eager to place their hands inside
the Bocca della Verità (the Mouth of Truth) in the portico
of Santa Maria in Cosmedin. There are many other sights to
see in this quiet corner of the city beside the Tiber, which

was the site of ancient Rome's first port
and its busy cattle market. Substantial
Classical remains include two small
temples from the Republican age and
the Arch of Janus from the later Empire.
In the 6th century the area became
home to a Greek community from
Byzantium, who founded the churches
of San Giorgio in Velabro and Santa
Maria in Cosmedin.

Sant'Omobono
a late 16th-century
church, now stands
in isolation in the
middle of an
important
archaeological site.
The remains of
sacrificial altars and
two temples from the
6th century BC have
been discovered

Casa dei Crescenzi
*This 11th-century building
used columns and capitals
from ancient Roman
temples* ❼

Ponte Rotto, as this forlorn ruined
arch in the Tiber is called, means
simply "broken bridge". Built in the
2nd century BC, its original name
was Pons Aemilius.

LUNGOTEVERE DEI PIERLEONI

TEVERE

★ **Temples of the
Forum Boarium**
*The tiny round
Temple of Hercules
and its neighbour,
the Temple of
Portunus, are the
best preserved
of Rome's
Republican
temples* ❽

PONTE PALATINO

KEY

 — — — Suggested route

0 metres   75

0 yards   75

STAR SIGHTS

* ★ Santa Maria in
  Cosmedin

* ★ Temples of the Forum
  Boarium

★ **Santa Maria
in Cosmedin**
*This medieval church has a
fine marble mosaic floor and
a Gothic baldacchino* ❶

Santa Maria della Consolazione
This 16th-century church used to serve a hospital nearby ❺

San Teodoro
The 15th-century portal of this ancient round church is decorated with the insignia of Pope Nicholas V ❹

LOCATOR MAP
See Central Rome Map pp14–15

San Giovanni Decollato
The plain Renaissance façade was completed in about 1504 ❻

San Giorgio in Velabro
The simple 12th-century portico of Ionic columns was destroyed by a bomb in 1993 but has been restored ❸

Arch of Janus
This square structure with arches on each side dates from the 4th century AD ❷

The Arco degli Argentari, dedicated to the Emperor Septimius Severus in AD 204, is decorated with scenes of religion and war.

The Fontana dei Tritoni by Carlo Bizzaccheri was built here in 1715. The style shows the powerful influence of Bernini.

Bocca della Verità at
Santa Maria in Cosmedin

Santa Maria in Cosmedin ❶

Piazza della Bocca della Verità 18.
Map 8 E1. **Tel** 06-678 1419. 🚌 23,
44, 81, 95, 160, 170, 280, 628, 715,
716. **Open** summer: 9.30am–6pm
daily (to 5pm winter). 🔲 🔲 🔲

This beautiful unadorned
church was built in the 6th
century on the site of the
ancient city's food market.
The elegant Romanesque bell
tower and portico were added
during the 12th century. In the
19th century a Baroque façade
was removed and the church
restored to its original
simplicity. It contains many
fine examples of Cosmati work,
in particular the mosaic
pavement, the raised choir, the
bishop's throne and the canopy
over the main altar.

Set into the wall of the
portico is the Bocca della Verità
(Mouth of Truth). This may
have been a drain cover,
dating back to before the 4th
century BC. Medieval tradition
had it that the formidable
jaws would snap shut over
the hand of those who told
lies – a useful trick for testing
the faithfulness of spouses.

Arch of Janus ❷

Via del Velabro. **Map** 8 E1. 🚌 23,
44, 63, 81, 95, 160, 170, 280, 628,
715, 716, 780.

Probably dating from the
reign of Constantine, this
imposing four-faced marble
arch stood at the crossroads
on the edge of the Forum
Boarium, near the ancient

docks. Merchants did business
in its shade. On the keystones
above the four arches you
can see small figures of the
goddesses Roma, Juno, Ceres
and Minerva. In medieval
times the arch formed the
base of a tower fortress. It
was restored to its original
shape in 1827.

San Giorgio in Velabro ❸

Via del Velabro 19. **Map** 8 E1.
Tel 06-6920 4534. 🚌 23, 44, 63,
81, 95, 160, 170, 280, 628, 715, 716,
780. **Open** 8.30am–7pm daily.

San Giorgio in Velabro after its
restoration in 1999

In the hollow of the street
named after the Velabrum, the
swamp where Romulus and
Remus are said to have been
found by the she-wolf, is a
small church dedicated to St
George, whose bones lie
under the altar.

The 7th-century basilica has
suffered over the centuries
from periodic floods, and in
1993 a bomb caused exten-
sive damage to the front of
the church. Careful restoration
has, however, returned it to
its original appearance.

A double row of assorted
granite and marble columns
(taken from ancient Roman
temples) divides the triple
nave. The austerity of the
cool grey interior is relieved
by golden frescoes in the
apse (attributed to Pietro
Cavallini, 1295). The façade
and the bell tower date from
the 12th century.

San Teodoro ❹

Via di San Teodoro 7. **Map** 8 E1.
Tel 06-678 6624. 🚌 23, 44, 81,
95, 160, 170, 280, 628, 715, 716.
Open 9.30am–12.30pm Sun–Fri.

If you are in the area on a
Sunday morning, you will find
this small round 6th-century
church at the foot of the
Palatine a delight to visit for
the Greek Orthodox services.
Inside, the 6th-century mosaics
in the apse are breathtaking,
as is the Florentine cupola
dating from 1454. The fetching
outer courtyard was designed
by Carlo Fontana in 1705.

The church of San Teodoro, one of
Rome's hidden treasures

The Arch of Janus, where cattle dealers sheltered from the midday sun

Façade of Santa Maria della Consolazione

Santa Maria della Consolazione ❺

Piazza della Consolazione 84.
Map 5 A5. **Tel** 06-678 4654.
🚌 23, 44, 63, 81, 95, 160, 170, 280, 628, 715, 716, 780.
Open 6.30am–6pm daily. 🛉 ♿

The church stands near the foot of the Tarpeian Rock, the site of public execution of traitors since the time of the Sabine War (see p74).

In 1385, Giordanello degli Alberini, a condemned nobleman, paid two gold florins for an image of the Virgin Mary to be placed here, to provide consolation to prisoners in their final moments before execution. Hence the name of the church that was built here in 1470. It was reconstructed between 1583 and 1600 by Martino Longhi who provided the early Baroque façade.

The church's 11 side-chapels are owned by noble families and local crafts guild members. In the presbytery is the famed image of Mary, attributed to Antoniazzo Romano.

San Giovanni Decollato ❻

Via di San Giovanni Decollato 22.
Map 8 E1. **Tel** 06-679 1890.
🚌 23, 44, 63, 81, 95, 160, 170, 280, 628, 715, 716, 780. **Closed** for restoration.

The main altar is dominated by Giorgio Vasari's *The Beheading of St John* (1553) from which the church takes

its name, San Giovanni Decollato. In 1490 Pope Innocent VIII gave this site to build a church for a very specialized Florentine confraternity. Clad in black robes and hoods, their task was to encourage condemned prisoners to repent and to give them a decent burial after they had been hanged. In the cloisters there are seven manholes (one for women), which received the bodies.

The oratory contains a cycle of frescoes describing the life of St John the Baptist by the leading Florentine Mannerists, Jacopino del Conte and Francesco Salviati. In style the figures resemble some of those in the Sistine Chapel.

Casa dei Crescenzi ❼

Via Luigi Petroselli. **Map** 8 E1.
🚌 23, 44, 63, 81, 95, 160, 170, 280, 628, 715, 716, 780.

Studded with archaeological fragments, the house is what remains of an 11th-century tower fortress. The powerful Crescenzi family built it to keep an eye on the docks (now the site of the Anagrafe or Public Records Office) and on the bridge where they collected a toll.

Ancient Roman fragments in the Casa dei Crescenzi

Temples of the Forum Boarium ❽

Piazza della Bocca della Verità. **Map** 8 E1. 🚌 44, 81, 95, 160, 170, 628.

Temple of Portunus

These miraculously well-preserved Republican temples are particularly appealing by moonlight, in their grassy enclave under the umbrella pines beside the Tiber. They date from the 2nd century BC and were saved for posterity when they were reconsecrated as Christian churches in the Middle Ages. They offer rare examples of combined elements from Greek and Roman architecture.

The rectangular temple (formerly known as the Temple of Fortuna Virilis) was in fact dedicated to Portunus, the god of rivers and ports – a reference to the nearby port of ancient Rome. Set on a podium, it has four Ionic travertine columns fluted at the front and 12 half-columns, embedded in the tufa wall of the *cella* – the room that housed the image of the god. Nearby is the small circular Temple of Hercules. It is often referred to as the Temple of Vesta because of its similarity to the one in the Forum.

Luminous interior of Santa Sabina

Santa Sabina ⑨

Piazza Pietro d'Illiria 1.
Map 8 E2. **Tel** 06-5794 0600.
23, 280, 716. **M** Circo Massimo.
Open 6.30am–12.45pm, 3–7pm
daily (to 6pm winter).

High on the Aventine stands
an early Christian basilica,
founded by Peter of Illyria in
AD 425 and restored to its
original simplicity in the early
20th century. Light filters
through 9th-century windows
upon a wide nave framed by
white Corinthian columns
supporting an arcade decorated
with a marble frieze. Over the
main door is a 5th-century blue
and gold mosaic dedicatory
inscription. The pulpit, carved
choir and bishop's throne
date from the 9th century.

The church was given to the
Dominicans in the 13th century
and in the nave is the magnificent mosaic tombstone of one
of the first leaders of the order,
Muñoz de Zamora (died 1300).

The side portico has 5th-
century panelled doors carved
from cypress wood, representing scenes from the Bible,
including one of the earliest
Crucifixions in existence.

Santi Bonifacio e Alessio ⑩

Piazza di Sant'Alessio 23. **Map** 8 D2.
Tel 06-574 3446. 23, 280, 716. **M**
Circo Massimo. **Open** 9–11.45am,
3.30–6.30pm (to 6pm winter) daily.

The church is dedicated to
two early Christian martyrs,
whose remains lie under the
main altar. Legend has it that

Alessio, son of a rich senator
living on the site, fled East to
avoid an impending marriage
and became a pilgrim.
Returning home after many
years, he died as a servant,
unrecognized, under the stairs
of the family entrance hall,
clutching the manuscript of
his story for posterity.

The original 5th-century
church has undergone many
changes over time. Noteworthy
are the 18th-century façade
with its five arches, the restored
Cosmati doorway and pave-
ment, and the magnificent
Romanesque five-storey bell
tower (1217).

An 18th-century Baroque
chapel by Andrea Bergondi
houses part of the famous
staircase. Other relics include
the well from Alessio's family
home and the glowing
Byzantine Madonna of the
Intercession brought from
Damascus to Rome at the end
of the 10th century.

Piazza dei Cavalieri di Malta ⑪

Map 8 D2. 23, 280, 716.
M Circo Massimo.

Surrounded by cypress trees,
this ornate walled piazza
decorated with obelisks and
military trophies was designed
by Piranesi in 1765. It is named
after the Order of
the Knights of
Malta (Cavalieri
di Malta), whose
priory (at No. 3)
is famous for the
bronze keyhole
through which
there is a miniature
view of St Peter's,
framed by a tree-
lined avenue. The
priory church, Santa
Maria del Priorato,
was restored in
Neo-Classical style
by Piranesi in the
18th century. To
visit the church,
ask permission in
person at the
Order's building at
48 Via Condotti. At
the southwest cor-
ner of the square
is Sant'Anselmo,

the international Benedictine
church, where Gregorian
chant may be heard on
Sundays (see p356).

**Doorway of the Priory of the
Knights of Malta**

Monte Testaccio ⑫

Via Galvani. **Map** 8 D4. **M** Piramide.
23, 95, 673. 3. **Open** by appt
only; call 06-0608.

From about 140 BC to AD
250 this hill was created
by dumping millions of testae
(hence Testaccio) – pieces of
the amphorae used to carry
goods to nearby warehouses.
The full archaeological significance of this 36-m (118-ft) high
artificial hill was not realized
until the late 18th century.

Façade of Santi Bonifacio e Alessio

Protestant Cemetery ⑬

Cimitero Acattolico, Via Caio Cestio 6.
Map 8 D4. **Tel** 06-574 1900. 23,
95, 280. 3. Ⓜ Piramide. **Open**
9am–5pm Mon–Sat, 9am–1pm Sun
(last adm: 30 mins before closing).
Donation expected.

The peace of this well-tended
cemetery beneath the Aurelian
Wall is profoundly moving.
Non-Catholics, mainly English
and German, have been
buried here since 1738. In the

oldest part are the
graves of John Keats
(died 1821), whose
epitaph reads:
"Here lies One
Whose Name was
writ in Water", and
his friend Joseph
Severn (died 1879);
not far away are
the ashes of Percy
Bysshe Shelley
(died 1822).
Goethe's son
Julius is also
buried here.

Tombstone of John Keats

Pyramid of Caius Cestius ⑭

Piazzale Ostiense. **Map** 8 E4. 23,
95, 280. 3. Ⓜ Piramide.

Memorial pyramid of Caius Cestius

Caius Cestius, a wealthy
praetor (senior Roman
magistrate), died in 12 BC.
His one claim to fame is his
tomb, an imposing pyramid
faced in white marble set in
the Aurelian Wall near Porta
San Paolo. It stands 36 m
(118 ft) high and, according
to an inscription, took 330 days
to build. Unmistakable as a
landmark, it must have looked
almost as incongruous when
it was built as it does today.

Detail of carving on sarcophagus in the portico of San Saba

San Saba ⑮

Via di San Saba. **Map** 8 F3. **Tel** 06-
6458 0140. 75, 175, 673. 3.
Open 8.30am–noon, 4–6.30pm Mon–
Sat; 9.30am–1pm, 4–6.30pm Sun.

Tucked away in a residential
street on the Little Aventine
hill, San Saba began life as an
oratory for Palestinian monks
fleeing from Arab invasions in
the 7th century. The existing
church dates from the 10th
century and has undergone
much restoration. The portico
houses a fascinating collection
of archaeological remains.

The church has three naves
in the Greek style and a short
fourth 11th-century nave to
the left with vestiges of 13th-
century frescoes of the life of
St Nicholas of Bari. Particularly
intriguing is a scene of three
naked young ladies lying in
bed, who are saved from

penury by the gift of a bag of
gold from St Nicholas, the
future Santa Claus. The
beautiful marble inlay in the
main door, the floor and the
remains of the choir are all
13th-century Cosmati work.

Circus Maximus ⑯

Via del Circo Massimo.
Map 8 F2. 81, 160, 628, 715.
3. Ⓜ Circo Massimo.

What was once ancient
Rome's largest stadium is
today little more than a long
grassy esplanade. Set in the
valley between the Palatine
and Aventine hills, the Circus
Maximus was continually
embellished and expanded
from the 4th century BC until
AD 549 when the last races
were held. The grandstands
held some 300,000 spectators,
cheering wildly at the horse
and chariot races, athletic
contests and wild animal fights,
betting furiously throughout.

The Circus had a central
dividing barrier (*spina*) with
seven large egg-shaped objects
on it used for counting the
laps of a race. These were
joined in 33 BC by seven
bronze dolphins that served
a similar purpose. In 10 BC
Augustus built the Imperial
box under the Palatine and
decorated the *spina* with the
obelisk that now stands in the
centre of Piazza del Popolo
(*see p137*). A second obelisk,
which was added in the 4th
century by Constantine II, is
now in Piazza di San Giovanni
in Laterano (*see pp178–9*).

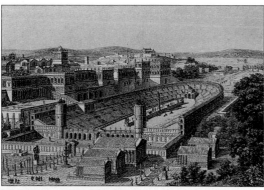

Reconstruction of the Circus Maximus in its heyday

TRASTEVERE

The proud and aggressively independent inhabitants of Trastevere, the area "across the Tiber", consider themselves the most authentic Romans. In one of the most picturesque old quarters of the city, it is still possible to glimpse scenes of everyday life that seem to belong to bygone centuries. There are, however, signs that much of the earthy, proletarian character of the place may soon be destroyed by the proliferation of fashionable restaurants, clubs and boutiques. Some of Rome's most fascinating medieval churches lie hidden away in the patchwork of narrow, cobbled backstreets, the only clue to their location an occasional glimpse of a Romanesque bell tower. Santa Cecilia was built on the site of the martyrdom of the patron saint of music, San Francesco a Ripa commemorates St Francis of Assisi's visit to Rome, and Santa Maria in Trastevere is the traditional centre of the spiritual and social life of the area.

Romanesque bell tower

SIGHTS AT A GLANCE

Churches
San Crisogono ⑥
San Francesco a Ripa ⑩
Santa Cecilia in Trastevere ⑧
Santa Maria della Scala ③
Santa Maria in Trastevere pp212–13 ⑤

Museums and Galleries
Sant'Egidio and Museo di Roma in Trastevere ④

Historic Buildings
Casa della Fornarina ①
Caserma dei Vigili della VII Coorte ⑦
San Michele a Ripa Grande ⑨

Bridges
Ponte Sisto ②

Parks and Gardens
Villa Sciarra ⑪

SEE ALSO

- *Street Finder*, maps 4, 7, 8, 11
- *Where to Stay* pp306–7
- *Restaurants* pp324–5
- *Tiber Walk* pp274–5

KEY

▨	Street-by-Street map
ℹ	Tourist information
---	City Wall

GETTING THERE

The most convenient way is to take tram 8 which starts from Largo di Torre Argentina, crosses the river and runs along the broad, busy Viale di Trastevere. The H bus follows the same route but starts at Stazione Termini. From the Vatican it is best to take a 23 or 280 along Lungotevere.

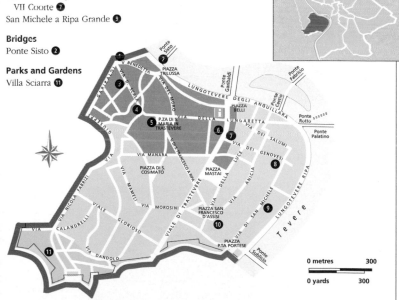

◁ A typical *vicolo* (narrow alleyway) between the densely packed buildings of Trastevere

Street-by-Street: Trastevere

All year round Trastevere is a major attraction both for its restaurants, clubs and cinemas, and for its picturesque maze of narrow cobbled alleyways. On summer evenings the streets are packed with jostling groups of pleasure-seekers, especially during the noisy local festival, the Festa de' Noantri *(see p59)*. Everywhere café and restaurant tables spill out over pavements, especially around Piazza di Santa Maria in Trastevere and outside the pizzerias along Viale di Trastevere. There are also kiosks selling slices of watermelon and *grattachecca*, a mixture of syrup and grated ice. It is usually easier to appreciate the antique charm of Trastevere's narrow streets in the more tranquil atmosphere of the early morning.

Casa della Fornarina
Raphael's beautiful mistress is said to have lived here. There is now a flourishing restaurant in the back garden ❶

Santa Maria dei Sette Dolori
This church (1643) is a minor work by Borromini.

Santa Maria della Scala
The church's unassuming façade conceals a rich Baroque interior ❸

Sant'Egidio and Museo di Roma in Trastevere
This 17th-century fresco of Sant' Egidio by Pomarancio decorates the left-hand chapel in the church. The convent next door is a museum of Roman life and customs ❹

★ Santa Maria in Trastevere
The church is famous for its mosaics by Pietro Cavallini but it also has earlier works such as this mosaic of the prophet Isaiah to the left of the apse ❺

STAR SIGHT

★ Santa Maria in Trastevere

KEY

– – – Suggested route

0 metres	75
0 yards	75

The fountain of Piazza di Santa Maria in Trastevere by Carlo Fontana (1692) is a popular meeting place. At night it is floodlit and dozens of young people sit on the steps around its octagonal base.

Ponte Sisto
This bridge was built on the orders of Sixtus IV in 1474 to link Trastevere to central Rome ❷

LOCATOR MAP
See Central Rome Map pp14–15

Piazza Belli is named after Giuseppe Gioacchino Belli (1791–1863), who wrote satirical sonnets in Roman dialect rather than academic Italian. At the centre of the piazza stands a statue of the poet (1913).

Vicolo del Piede is one of the picturesque narrow streets lined with restaurant tables leading off Piazza di Santa Maria in Trastevere.

The Torre degli Anguillara (13th century) is the only survivor of the many medieval towers that once dominated the Trastevere skyline.

Caserma dei Vigili della VII Coorte
The courtyard of this antique Roman fire station still stands ❼

San Crisogono
The Romanesque bell tower dates from the early 12th century. The plain portico is a later addition (1626), but is in keeping with the spirit of this ancient church ❻

Casa della Fornarina ❶

Via di Santa Dorotea 20.
Map 4 D5 & 11 B5.
🚌 23, 280.

Not much is known about Raphael's model and lover, La Fornarina, yet over the centuries she has acquired a name, Margherita, and even a biography. Her father was a Sienese baker (*la fornarina* means the baker's girl) and his shop was here in Trastevere near Raphael's frescoes in the Villa Farnesina (*see pp220–21*).

Margherita earned a reputation as a "fallen woman" and Raphael, wishing to be absolved before dying, turned her away from his deathbed. After his death she took refuge in the convent of Santa Apollonia in Trastevere.

She is assumed to have been the model for Raphael's famous portrait *La Donna Velata* in the Palazzo Pitti in Florence.

Ponte Sisto ❷

Map 4 E5 & 11 B5. 🚌 23, 280.

Named after Pope Sixtus IV della Rovere (reigned 1471–84), who commissioned it, this bridge was built by Baccio Pontelli to replace an ancient Roman bridge. The enterprising pope also built the Sistine Chapel (*see pp244–7*), the Hospital of Santo Spirito (*see p226*) and restored many churches and monuments. This put him in great financial difficulties and he had to sell personal collections in order to finance his projects.

Another method of financing projects was to levy a tax on the city's prostitutes. Several popes are known to have resorted to this unpopular form of taxation.

Pope Sixtus IV

Gilded Baroque altar of Santa Maria della Scala

Santa Maria della Scala ❸

Piazza della Scala 23. **Map** 4 D5 & 11 B5. *Tel* 06-580 6233. 🚌 23, 280. **Open** 9am–noon, 3.30–7pm daily. ✝

This church belongs to a time of great building activity that lasted about 30 years from the end of the 16th to the early 17th century. Its simple façade contrasts with a rich interior decorated with multicoloured marbles and a number of spirited Baroque altars and reliefs. In 1849, the church was used as a hospital to treat Garibaldi's soldiers (*see pp38–9*).

Sant'Egidio and Museo di Roma in Trastevere ❹

Piazza Sant'Egidio 1. **Map** 7 C1.
🚌 H, 23, 280. 🚊 8.
Church *Tel* 06-58 56 61. **Open** 10am–12.30pm Sat. **Museo di Roma in Trastevere** *Tel* 06-581 6563. **Open** 10am–7pm Tue–Sun. ♿

Built in 1630, Sant'Egidio was the church of the adjoining Carmelite convent, one of many founded in the area to shelter the poor and destitute. The convent is now a museum, containing a wealth of material relating to the festivals, pastimes, superstitions and customs of the Romans when they lived under papal rule.

There are old paintings and prints of the city and tableaux showing scenes of everyday life in 18th- and 19th-century Rome, including reconstructions of shops and a tavern.

The museum also has manuscripts by the much-loved poets Belli and Trilussa who wrote in local dialect.

Watercolour of public scribe (1880) in the Museo di Roma in Trastevere

Santa Maria in Trastevere ❺

See pp212–13.

San Crisogono ❻

Piazza Sonnino 44. **Map** 7 C1.
Tel 06-5810 0076. 🚌 H, 23, 280, 780. 🚊 8. **Open** 7am–noon, 4.15–7.30pm, Mon–Sat; 8.30am–1pm, 4.15–7.30pm Sun.
Adm charge for excavations. ✝ ♿

This church was built on the site of one of the city's oldest *tituli* (private houses used for Christian worship). An 8th-century church with 11th-century frescoes can still be seen beneath the present church. This dates from the early 12th century, a period of intense building activity in Rome. San Crisogono was decorated by Pietro

Apse mosaic in San Crisogono

Cavallini – the apse mosaic remains. Most of the church's columns were taken from previous buildings, including the great porphyry ones of a triumphal arch. The mosaic floor is the result of recycling precious marble from various Roman ruins.

Caserma dei Vigili della VII Coorte **7**

Via della VII Coorte
Map 7 C1. *Tel* 06-0608. H, 23, 280, 780. 8. *Closed* for restoration work; call for details.

Not all Roman ruins are Imperial villas or grand temples; one that illustrates the daily life of a busy city is the barracks of the guards of the VII Coorte (7th Cohort), the Roman fire brigade. It was built in Augustus's reign, in the 1st century AD, and the excavated courtyard is where the men would rest while waiting for a call out.

Santa Cecilia in Trastevere **8**

Piazza di Santa Cecilia.
Map 8 D1. *Tel* 06-589 9289. H, 23, 44, 280. 8. *Open* 9.30am–12.30pm, 4–6.30pm daily. **Adm charge** for excavations. **Cavallini fresco** can be seen 10am–12.30pm Mon–Sat.

St Cecilia, aristocrat and patron saint of music, was martyred here in AD 230. After an attempt at scalding her to death, she was beheaded. A church was founded – perhaps in the 4th century – on the site of her house. (The house, beneath the church with the remains of a Roman tannery, is well worth a visit.) Her body turned up in the Catacombs of San Callisto *(see p265)* and was buried here in the 9th century by Pope Paschal I, who rebuilt the church. A fine apse mosaic survives from this period.
    The altar canopy by Arnolfo di Cambio and the fresco of *The Last Judgment* by Pietro Cavallini, reached through the adjoining convent, date from the 13th century, one of the few periods when Rome had

Detail of 13th-century fresco by Pietro Cavallini in Santa Cecilia

a distinctive artistic style of its own. In front of the altar is a statue of St Cecilia by Stefano Maderno, who used her miraculously preserved remains as a model when she was briefly disinterred in 1599.

San Michele a Ripa Grande **9**

Via di San Michele. **Map** 8 D2. *Tel* 06-584 31. 23, 44, 75, 280. **Open** for special exhibitions only.

This huge, imposing complex, now housing the Ministry of Culture, stretches 300 m (985 ft) along the river Tiber. It was built on the initiative of Pope Innocent XII and contained a home for the elderly, a boys' reform school, a woollen mill

and various chapels. Today contemporary exhibitions are occasionally held here.

San Francesco a Ripa **10**

Piazza San Francesco d'Assisi 88.
Map 7 C2. *Tel* 06-581 9020. H, 23, 44, 75, 280. 8. **Open** 7am–noon, 4–7.30pm Mon–Sat; 7am–1pm, 4–7pm Sun.

St Francis of Assisi lived here in a hospice when he visited Rome in 1219 and his stone pillow and crucifix are preserved in his cell. The church was rebuilt by his follower, the nobleman Rodolfo Anguillara, who is portrayed on his tombstone wearing the Franciscan habit.
    Entirely rebuilt in the 1680s by Cardinal Pallavicini, the church is rich in sculptures. Particularly flamboyant are the 18th-century Rospigliosi and Pallavicini monuments in the transept chapel.
    The Paluzzi-Albertoni chapel (fourth on the left, along the nave) contains Bernini's breathtaking *Ecstasy of Beata Ludovica Albertoni*.

Villa Sciarra **11**

Via Calandrelli 35. **Map** 7 B2. 44, 75. **Park open** 9am–sunset daily.

In Roman times the site of this small, attractive public park was a nymph's sanctuary. It is especially picturesque in spring when its wisterias are in full bloom. The paths through the park are decorated with Romantic follies, fountains and statues, and there are splendid views over the bastions of the Janiculum.

Bernini's *Ecstasy of Beata Ludovica Albertoni* (1674) in San Francesco a Ripa

Santa Maria in Trastevere ❺

Probably the first official Christian place of worship to be built in Rome, this basilica became the focus of devotion to the Virgin Mary. According to legend, the church was founded by Pope Callixtus I in the 3rd century, when Christianity was still a minority cult. Today's church is largely a 12th-century building, remarkable for its mosaics, in particular those by Pietro Cavallini. The 22 granite columns in the nave were taken from the ruins of ancient Roman buildings. Despite some 18th-century Baroque additions, Santa Maria has retained its medieval character. This friendly church has strong links with the local community.

Piazza Santa Maria in Trastevere
The piazza in front of the church is the traditional heart of Trastevere. Today it is surrounded by lively bars and restaurants. Carlo Fontana built the octagonal fountain in the late 17th century.

The floor, relaid in the 1870s, is a recreation of the Cosmatesque mosaic floor of the 13th century.

The bell tower was built in the 12th century. At the top is a small mosaic of the Virgin.

★ Façade Mosaics
The 12th-century mosaic shows Mary feeding the baby Jesus and ten women holding lamps. Eight of the lamps are lit, symbolizing virginity; the veiled women whose lamps have gone out are probably widows.

STAR FEATURES

★ Façade Mosaics

★ Cavallini Mosaics

MODEST DONORS

Many of Rome's mosaics include a portrait of the pope or cardinal responsible for the building of the church. Often the portrait is dwarfed by the rest of the picture, which glorifies the saint to whom the church is dedicated. On the façade of Santa Maria, two tiny unidentified figures kneel at the Virgin's feet. Were they to stand up, the men would barely reach her knees.

Façade mosaic, detail

The portico was remodelled in 1702 by Carlo Fontana. Statues of four popes decorate the balustrade above.

Front entrance

15th-century wall tabernacle by Mino del Reame

Apse Mosaic
The 12th-century mosaic in the basin of the apse shows the Coronation of the Virgin. She sits on Christ's right hand, surrounded by saints.

VISITORS' CHECKLIST

Via della Paglia 14c, Piazza Santa Maria in Trastevere.
Map 7 C1. **Tel** 06-581 4802.
H & 780 to Piazza S. Sonnino, 23 & 280 along Lungotevere Sanzio. 8 from Largo Argentina.
Open 7.30am–8pm daily.
9am & 5.30pm daily.

★ Cavallini Mosaics
The details in the six mosaics of the Life of the Virgin (1291) display a touching realism.

Madonna della Clemenza
The life size icon probably dates from the 7th century. A replica is displayed above the altar of the Cappella Altemps.

Tomb of Cardinal Pietro Stefaneschi
The last of his line, Pietro Stefaneschi died in 1417. His tomb is by an otherwise unknown sculptor called Paolo.

TIMELINE

AD 217–22 Church founded by Pope Callixtus I	*Pope Innocent II*	**1291** Pietro Cavallini adds mosaics of scenes from the life of the Virgin for his patron, Bertoldo Stefaneschi	**1617** Domenichino designs coffered ceiling with octagonal panel of the Assumption of the Virgin	
30 BC	**AD 200**	**1400**	**1650**	**1900**
38 BC Jet of mineral oil spouts from the ground on this site. Later interpreted as a portent of the coming of Christ	**c1138** Pope Innocent II starts rebuilding the church	**1580** Martino Longhi the Elder restores church and builds family chapel for Cardinal Marco Sittico Altemps	**1702** Pope Clement XI has portico rebuilt **1866–77** Church restored by Virginio Vespignani	

JANICULUM

Overlooking the Tiber on the Trastevere side of the river, the Janiculum hill has often played its part in the defence of the city. The last occasion was in 1849 when Garibaldi held off the attacking French troops. The park at the top of the hill is filled with monuments to Garibaldi and his men. A popular place for walks, the park provides a welcome escape from the densely packed streets of Trastevere.

Puppets in the park at the top of the Janiculum hill

You will often find puppet shows and other kinds of amusements for children. In medieval times most of the hill was occupied by monasteries and convents. Bramante built his miniature masterpiece, the Tempietto, in the convent of San Pietro in Montorio. The Renaissance also saw the development of the riverside area along Via della Lungara, where the rich and powerful built beautiful houses such as the Villa Farnesina.

SIGHTS AT A GLANCE

Churches and Temples
San Pietro in Montorio ❼
Sant'Onofrio ❻
Tempietto ❽

Museums and Galleries
Palazzo Corsini and Galleria Nazionale d'Arte Antica ❷

Historic Buildings
Villa Farnesina pp220–21 ❶

Fountains
Fontana dell'Acqua Paola ❾

Monuments
Garibaldi Monument ❺

Arches and Gates
Porta Settimiana ❸

Parks and Gardens
Botanical Gardens ❹

SEE ALSO

- *Street Finder*, maps 3, 4, 7, 11
- *Restaurants* p325

GETTING THERE

The Janiculum (Il Gianicolo) is not the easiest part of Rome to reach by public transport. It can be approached either from the Vatican area (*see p223*) or from Trastevere (*see p207*). There is only one bus, the 870, that goes up to the top of the hill, but the 44 will take you from Piazza Venezia to Via Giacinto Carini from where you can start your walk up. For sights along Via della Lungara, take the 23 or 280, which go along Lungotevere.

KEY

■ Tour of the Janiculum map

--- City Wall

0 metres   300
0 yards   300

◁ **The staircase fountain in the Botanical Gardens**

A Tour of the Janiculum

The long hike to the top of the Janiculum is rewarded
by wonderful views over the city. The park's monuments include a lighthouse and statues of Garibaldi and
his wife Anita. There is also a cannon which is fired
at noon each day. In Via della Lungara,
between the Janiculum and the Tiber,
stand Palazzo Corsini with its national
art collection and the Villa Farnesina,
decorated by Raphael for his friend
and patron, the fabulously wealthy
banker Agostino Chigi.

Tasso's Oak is a
memorial to the
poet Torquato
Tasso, who liked
to sit here in the
days before he
died in 1595. The
tree was struck by
lightning in 184

The Manfredi Lighthouse,
built in 1911, was a gift to
the city of Rome from
Italians in Argentina.

**The Monument to Anita
Garibaldi** by Mario Rutelli
was erected in 1932. The
great patriot's Brazilian
wife lies buried
beneath the
statue.

PIAZZALE
GIUSEPPE GARIBALDI

**The view from Villa
Lante,** a beautiful
Renaissance summer
residence, gives a
magnificent panorama
of the whole city.

ROMA O MORTE

Garibaldi Monument
*The inscription on the base
of the equestrian statue
says "Rome or Death"* ⑤

Botanical Gardens
*These were established in
1883 when part of the
grounds of Palazzo
Corsini was given
to the University
of Rome* ④

★ **Palazzo Corsini**
*This 15th-century triptych by
Fra Angelico hangs in the
Galleria Nazionale
d'Arte Antica* ②

LOCATOR MAP
See Central Rome Map pp14–15

★ **Villa Farnesina**
*The suburban villa of the
banker Agostino Chigi is
celebrated for its frescoes
by Raphael, Baldassarre
Peruzzi and other
Renaissance masters* ①

Porta Settimiana
*Looking through this
Renaissance gateway from
Via della Lungara, you catch
a glimpse of Trastevere's
warren of narrow streets* ③

KEY

– – – Suggested route

0 metres   75
0 yards   75

STAR SIGHTS

★ Palazzo Corsini and
Galleria Nazionale
d'Arte Antica

★ Villa Farnesina

Villa Farnesina ❶

See pp220–21.

Palazzo Corsini and Galleria Nazionale d'Arte Antica ❷

Via della Lungara 10. **Map** 4 D5 & 11 A5. **Tel** 06-6880 2323. 🚌 23, 280. **Open** 8.30am–7pm Tue–Sun (call in advance to check). **Closed** 1 Jan, 1 May, 15 Aug & 25 Dec. **Adm charge.** 🖼 🛈 🕭 🎦 www.galleriaborghese.it

Queen Christina's bedroom in the Palazzo Corsini

The history of Palazzo Corsini is intimately entwined with that of Rome. Built for Cardinal Domenico Riario in 1510–12, it has boasted among its many distinguished guests Bramante, the young Michelangelo, Erasmus and Queen Christina of Sweden, who died here in 1689. The old palazzo was completely rebuilt for Cardinal Neri Corsini by Ferdinando Fuga in 1736. As Via della Lungara is too narrow for a good frontal view, Fuga designed the façade so it could be seen from an angle.

Palazzo Corsini houses the Galleria Nazionale d'Arte Antica, also known as Galleria Corsini. This outstanding collection includes paintings by Rubens, Van Dyck, Murillo, Caravaggio and Guido Reni, together with 17th- and 18th-century Italian regional art. The palazzo is also home to the Accademia dei Lincei, a learned society founded in 1603, which once included Galileo among its members.

In 1797 Palazzo Corsini was the backdrop to momentous events: French General Duphot (the fiancé of Napoleon's sister Pauline) was killed here in a skirmish between papal troops and Republicans. The consequent French occupation of the city and the deportation of Pope Pius VI led to the proclamation of a short-lived Roman Republic (1798–9).

Porta Settimiana ❸

Between Via della Scala and Via della Lungara. **Map** 4 D5 & 11 B5. 🚌 23, 280.

This gate was built in 1498 by Pope Alexander VI Borgia to replace a minor passageway in the Aurelian Wall. The Porta Settimiana marks the start of Via della Lungara, a long straight road built in the early 16th century.

Botanical Gardens ❹

Largo Cristina di Svezia 24, off Via Corsini. **Map** 4 D5. **Tel** 06-4991 7107. 🚌 23, 280. **Open** Apr–Sep: 9am–6.30pm Mon–Sat (Oct–Mar to 5.30pm). **Closed** public hols. **Adm charge.** 🎦 (phone to book).

Sequoias, palm trees and splendid collections of orchids and bromeliads are housed in Rome's Botanical Gardens *(Orto Botanico)*. These tranquil gardens contain more than 7,000 plant species from all over the world. Indigenous and exotic species are grouped to illustrate their botanical families and their adaptation to different climates and eco-systems. There are also plants such as the ginkgo that have survived virtually unchanged from earlier eras. The gardens were originally part of the Palazzo Corsini, but since 1983 have belonged to the University of Rome.

Garibaldi Monument ❺

Piazzale Giuseppe Garibaldi. **Map** 3 C5. 🚌 870.

Base of the Garibaldi Monument

This huge equestrian statue is part of a commemorative park, recalling the heroic events witnessed on the Janiculum when the French army attacked the city in 1849. Garibaldi's Republicans fended off the greatly superior French forces for weeks, until the Italians were overwhelmed. Garibaldi and his men escaped. The monument, erected in 1895, was the work of Emilio Gallori. Around the pedestal are four smaller sculptures in bronze showing battle scenes and allegorical figures.

Steps and tiered fountains at the Botanical Gardens

Courtyard of Sant'Onofrio

Sant'Onofrio **❻**

Piazza di Sant'Onofrio 2.
Map 3 C4. **Tel** 06-686 4498.
870. **Open** 9am–1pm Mon–Fri.
Closed Aug, except saint's feast day
on 12 Aug. **Museum open** by
appt only. **Tel** 06-682 8121.

Beato Nicola da Forca Palena,
whose tombstone guards the
entrance, founded this church
in 1419 in honour of the
hermit Sant'Onofrio. It retains
the flavour of the 15th
century in the simple shapes
of the portico and the cloister.
In the early 17th century the
portico was decorated with
frescoes by Domenichino.
   The monastery next to the
church houses a small museum
dedicated to the 16th-century
Italian poet Torquato Tasso,
who died there.

San Pietro in Montorio **❼**

Piazza San Pietro in Montorio 2.
Map 7 B1. **Tel** 06-581 39 40. 44,
75. **Open** 8.30am–noon daily, 3–4pm
(4–6pm summer) Mon–Fri. If closed,
ring bell at door to right of church.

San Pietro in Montorio – the
church of St Peter on the
Golden Hill – was founded in
the Middle Ages near the spot
where St Peter was presumed
to have been crucified. It was
rebuilt by order of Ferdinand
and Isabella of Spain at the
end of the 15th century, and
decorated by outstanding
artists of the Renaissance.
   The façade is typical of a
time when clean, geometric
shapes derived from Classical
architecture were in vogue.
The single nave ends in a deep
apse that once contained

Raphael's *Transfiguration*, now
in the Vatican. Two wide
chapels, one on either side of
the nave, were decorated by
some of Michelangelo's most
famous pupils. The left-hand
chapel was designed by one
of the few artists Michelangelo
openly admired, Daniele da
Volterra, also responsible
for the altar painting, *The
Baptism of Christ*. The chapel
on the right was the work of
Giorgio Vasari, who included
a self-portrait (in black, on
the left) in his altar painting,
The Conversion of St Paul.
   The first chapel to the right
of the entrance contains a
powerful *Flagellation*, by the
Venetian artist Sebastiano del
Piombo (1518); Michelangelo
is said to have provided the
original drawings. Work by
Bernini and his followers can
be seen in the second chapel
on the left and in the flanking
De Raymondi tombs.

Tempietto **❽**

Piazza San Pietro in Montorio (in court
yard). **Map** 7 B1. **Tel** 06-581 2806.
44, 75. **Open** 9.30am–12.30pm,
2–4.30pm (4–6pm summer) Tue–Sat.
See **The History of Rome** pp32–3.

Around 1502 Bramante com-
pleted what many consider to
be the first true Renaissance
building in Rome – the Tempietto. The name means simply "little temple". Its circular
shape echoes early Christian
martyria, chapels
built on the site of
a saint's martyr-
dom. This was
believed to be the
place where St
Peter was crucified.
   Bramante chose
the Doric order for
the 16 columns
surrounding the
domed chapel.
Above the columns
is a Classical frieze
and a delicate bal-
ustrade. Though
the scale of the
Tempietto is tiny,
Bramante's master-
ly use of Classical
proportions creates
a satisfyingly har-
monious whole.

The Tempietto illustrates the
great Renaissance dream that
the city of Rome would once
again relive its ancient glory.

Fontana dell'Acqua Paola **❾**

Via Garibaldi. **Map** 7 B1. 44, 75.

Fontana dell'Acqua Paola

This monumental fountain
commemorates the reopening
in 1612 of an aqueduct originally built by Emperor Trajan
in AD 109. The aqueduct was
renamed the "Acqua Paola"
after Paul V, the Borghese
pope who ordered its restoration. When it was first built,
the fountain had five small
basins, but in 1690 Carlo Fontana altered the design, adding the huge basin you can
see today. Despite many laws
intended to deter them, generations of Romans used this
convenient pool of fresh
water for bathing and washing their vegetables.

Bramante's round chapel, the Tempietto

Villa Farnesina ❶

The wealthy Sienese banker Agostino Chigi, who had established the headquarters of his far-flung financial empire in Rome, commissioned the villa in 1508 from his compatriot Baldassarre Peruzzi. The simple, harmonious design, with a central block and projecting wings, made this one of the earliest true Renaissance villas. The decoration was carried out between 1510 and 1519 and this has been restored. Peruzzi frescoed some of the interiors himself. Later, Sebastiano del Piombo, Raphael and his pupils added more elaborate works. The frescoes illustrate Classical myths, and the vault of the main hall, the Sala di Galatea, is adorned with astrological scenes showing the position of the stars at the time of Chigi's birth. Artists, poets, cardinals, princes and the pope himself were entertained here in magnificent style by their wealthy and influential host. In 1577 the villa was bought by Cardinal Alessandro Farnese. Since then, it has been known as the Villa Farnesina.

North Façade
The Loggia of Cupid and Psyche looks out on formal gardens that were used for parties and putting on plays.

Entrance

The Wedding of Alexander and Roxanne by Sodoma
Cherubs are shown helping the bride Roxanne to prepare for her marriage.

★ **Triumph of Galatea by Raphael**
The beautiful sea nymph Galatea was one of the 50 daughters of the god Nereus.

THE ARCHITECT

Baldassarre Peruzzi, painter and architect, arrived in Rome from Siena in 1503 aged 20 and became Bramante's chief assistant. Although his architectural designs were typical of Classicism, his painting owes more to Gothic influences, as his figurework is very highly stylized. On Raphael's death, he became Head of Works at St Peter's, but was captured in the Sack of Rome *(see p33)*, exiled to Siena until 1535, and died in 1536.

Baldassarre Peruzzi

Frescoes in the Room of Galatea
Perseus beheads Medusa in a scene from one of Peruzzi's series of mythological frescoes.

★ Salone delle Prospettive
Peruzzi's frescoes create the illusion of looking out at views of 16th-century Rome through a marble colonnade.

VISITORS' CHECKLIST

Via della Lungara 230.
Map 4 D5 & 11 A5.
🚌 23, 280 to Lungotevere
Farnesina. **Tel** 06-6802 7268.
Open 9am–1pm Mon–Sat.
Closed Aug. 🚫 📷 ♿
Adm charge.

Fresco from the Salone delle Prospettive
This scene shows the Torre delle Milizie (see p90) as it looked in the 1500s.

★ Loggia of Cupid and Psyche
The model for the figure on the left in Raphael's painting of The Three Graces *was Agostino Chigi's mistress, the courtesan Imperia.*

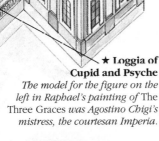

Lunette in the Room of Galatea
This giant monochrome head by Peruzzi was once attributed to Michelangelo.

STAR FEATURES

★ Triumph of Galatea by Raphael

★ Salone delle Prospettive

★ Loggia of Cupid and Psyche

VATICAN

As the site where St Peter was martyred and buried, the Vatican became the residence of the popes who succeeded him. Decisions taken here have shaped the destiny of Europe, and the great basilica of St Peter's draws pilgrims from all over the Christian world. The papal palaces beside St Peter's house the Vatican Museums. With the added attractions of Michelangelo's Sistine Chapel and the Raphael Rooms, their wonderful

Nuns in St Peter's Square

collections of Classical sculpture make them the finest museums in Rome. The Vatican's position as a state within a state was guaranteed by the Lateran Treaty of 1929, marked by the building of a new road, the Via della Conciliazione. This leads from St Peter's to Castel Sant' Angelo, a monument to a far grimmer past. Built originally as the Emperor Hadrian's mausoleum, this papal fortress and prison has witnessed many fierce battles for control of the city.

SIGHTS AT A GLANCE

Churches and Temples
Santa Maria in Traspontina ⑨
Santo Spirito in Sassia ④
St Peter's pp230–33 ①

Museums and Galleries
Vatican Museums pp234–47 ②

Historic Buildings
Castel Sant'Angelo pp248–9 ⑬
Hospital of Santo Spirito ⑤
Palazzo dei Convertendi ⑦

Palazzo dei Penitenzieri ⑧
Palazzo del Commendatore ⑥
Palazzo di Giustizia ⑭
Palazzo Torlonia ⑫

Gates
Porta Santo Spirito ③

Historic Streets and Piazzas
The Borgo ⑩
Vatican Corridor ⑪

GETTING THERE
The quickest way to reach the area is by Metro line A to Ottaviano S. Pietro. The 40 and 64 buses run regularly from Piazza dei Cinquecento, in front of Termini station, although the 62 is the only bus which runs along Via della Conciliazione. Other routes that serve the area include the 81 and 492, which stop in Piazza del Risorgimento.

SEE ALSO

• *Street Finder* maps 3, 4

• *Where to Stay* pp307–8

• *Restaurants* pp325–6

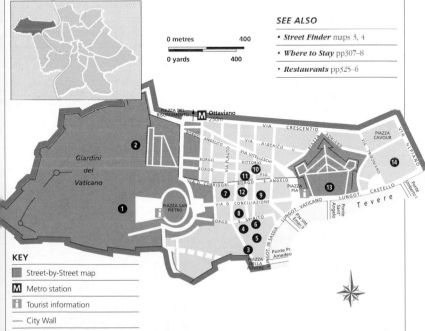

KEY

▨	Street-by-Street map
M	Metro station
ℹ	Tourist information
---	City Wall

◁ **Dome of St Peter's dominating the Vatican skyline**

A Tour of the Vatican

The Vatican, a centre of power for Catholics all over the world and a sovereign state since February 1929, is ruled by the pope. About 1,000 people live here, staffing the Vatican's facilities. There are a post office and shops, Vatican radio, broadcasting to the world in over 20 languages, a daily newspaper (*l'Osservatore Romano*), Vatican offices and a publishing house.

The Madonna of Guadalupe shows the miraculous image of the Madonna which appeared on the cloak of a Mexican Indian in 1531.

Papal heliport

The Grotto of Lourdes is a replica of the grotto in the southwest of France, where in 1858 the Virgin appeared to St Bernadette.

The Vatican Railway Station, opened in 1930, connects with the line from Rome to Viterbo, but is now used only for freight.

Radio Vatican is broadcast from this tower, part of the Leonine Wall built in 847.

The Papal Audience Chamber, by Pier Luigi Nervi, was opened in 1971. It seats up to 12,000.

The information office gives details of tours of the Vatican Gardens.

★ **St Peter's**
The Chapel of St Peter is in the Grottoes under the basilica. The rich marble decoration was added by Clement VIII at the end of the 16th century ❶

Piazza San Pietro was laid out by Bernini between 1656 and 1667. The narrow space in front of the church opens out into an enormous ellipse flanked by colonnades.

The obelisk was erected here in 1586 with the help of 150 horses and 47 winches.

STAR SIGHTS

★ St Peter's

★ Vatican Museums

The Eagle Fountain was built to celebrate the arrival of water from the Acqua Paola aqueduct at the Vatican. The eagle is the Borghese crest.

LOCATOR MAP
See Central Rome Map pp14–15

The Casina of Pius IV is a delightful summerhouse in the Vatican Gardens built by Pirro Ligorio in the mid-16th century.

Entrance to Vatican Museums

★ Vatican Museums
Raphael's Madonna of Foligno *(1513) is just one of the Vatican's many Renaissance masterpieces* ❷

The Galleon Fountain is a perfect scale model of a 17th-century ship in lead, brass and copper. It was made by a Flemish artist for Pope Paul V.

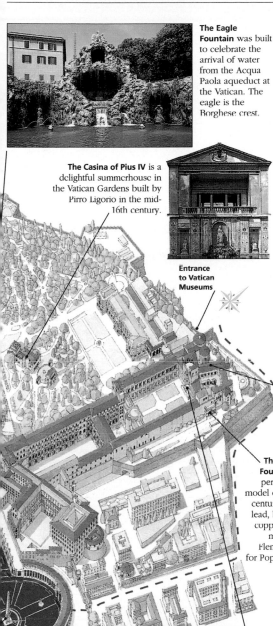

The Cortile della Pigna is mostly the work of Bramante. The niche for the pine cone, once a Roman fountain, was added by Pirro Ligorio in 1562.

To Via della Conciliazione

KEY

— — — Suggested route

0 metres   75

0 yards   75

St Peter's ❶

See pp230–33.

Vatican Museums ❷

See pp234–47.

Porta Santo Spirito ❸

Via dei Penitenzieri. **Map** 3 C3.
23, 34, 46, 62, 64, 98, 870, 881, 982.

This gate is situated at what was the southern limit of the "Leonine City", the area enclosed within walls by Pope Leo IV as a defence against the Saracens who had sacked Rome in AD 845. The walls measure 3 km (2 miles) in circumference.

Work on the walls started in AD 846. Pope Leo supervised the huge army of labourers personally, and thanks to his encouragement, the job was completed in 4 years. He then consecrated his massive feat of construction.

Since the time of Pope Leo the walls have needed much reinforcement and repair. The gateway visible today at Porta Santo Spirito was built by the architect Antonio da Sangallo the Younger in 1543–4. It is framed by two huge bastions that were added in 1564 by Pope Pius IV Medici. Sadly,

Sangallo's design for a monumental entrance to the Vatican was never completed; the principal columns come to an end somewhat abruptly in a modern covering of cement.

Santo Spirito in Sassia ❹

Via dei Penitenzieri 12. **Map** 3 C3.
Tel 06-687 9310. 23, 34, 46, 62, 64, 98, 870, 881, 982. **Open** 7.30am–noon (9.30am–1pm Sun), 3–7.30pm daily.

Nave of Santo Spirito in Sassia

Built on the site of a church erected by King Ine of Wessex, who died in Rome in the 8th century, the church is the work of Antonio da Sangallo the Younger. It was rebuilt (1538–44) after the

Sack of Rome had left it in ruins in 1527. The façade was added under Pope Sixtus V (1585–90). The nave and side chapels are decorated with a series of light, lively frescoes. The pretty bell tower, is earlier, dating from the reign of Sixtus IV (1471–84). It was probably the work of the pope's architect, Baccio Pontelli, who also built the Hospital of Santo Spirito, and the Ponte Sisto *(see p210)* further down the River Tiber.

Sixtus V's arms over door of Santo Spirito

Hospital of Santo Spirito ❺

Borgo Santo Spirito 2. **Map** 3 C3. 23, 34 46, 62, 64. **Complex & chapel open** for tours 10am & 3.30pm Mon (call 06-6821 0854). **Adm charge.**

The oldest hospital in Rome, this is said to have been founded as a result of a nightmare experienced by Pope Innocent III (1198–1216). In the dream, an angel showed him the bodies of Rome's unwanted babies dredged up from the River Tiber in fishing nets. As a result, the pope hastened to build a hospice for sick paupers.

Fresco of an angel in the octagonal chapel of the Hospital of Santo Spirito

In 1475 the hospital was reorganized by Pope Sixtus IV to care for the poor pilgrims expected for the Holy Year. Sixtus's hospital was a radical building. Cloisters divided the different types of patients; one area is still reserved for orphans and their nurses.

Unwanted infants were passed through a revolving barrel-like contraption called the *rota*, still visible to the left of the central entrance in Borgo Santo Spirito, to guarantee anonymity. Martin Luther, who visited in 1511, was shocked by the number of abandoned children he saw, believing them to be "the sons of the pope himself".

In the centre, under the hospital's conspicuous drum, is an octagonal chapel, where mass was said for patients. This room can be visited while the rest of the building still functions as a hospital.

Rusticated doorway of the Palazzo dei Convertendi

The *rota* of Santo Spirito, where mothers left unwanted babies

Palazzo del Commendatore ●

Borgo Santo Spirito 3. **Map** 3 C3. 23, 34, 46, 62, 64. **Closed** for restoration; call 06-6821 0854 for information.

As director of the Hospital of Santo Spirito, the Commendatore not only oversaw the running of the hospital, he was also responsible for its estates and revenues. This important post was originally given to members of the pope's family.

The palazzo, built next door to the hospital, has a spacious 16th-century frescoed loggia appropriate to the dignity and sobriety of its owners. The frescoes represent the story of the founding of the Hospital of Santo Spirito. To the left of the entrance is the Spezieria, or Pharmacy. This still has the wheel used for grinding the bark of the cinchona tree to produce the drug quinine, first introduced here in 1632 by Jesuits from Peru as a cure for malaria.

Above the courtyard is a splendid clock (1827). The dial is divided into six; it was not until 1846 that the familiar division of the day into two periods of 12 hours was introduced in Rome by Pope Pius IX.

Palazzo dei Convertendi ●

Via della Conciliazione 43. **Map** 3 C3. 23, 34, 62, 64. **Not open** to public.

With the building of Via della Conciliazione in the 1930s, Palazzo dei Convertendi was taken down and later moved to this new site nearby. The house, partly attributed to the architect Bramante, is where the artist Raphael died in 1520.

Palazzo dei Penitenzieri ●

Via della Conciliazione 33.
Map 3 C3. **Tel** 06-682 8121.
23, 34, 62, 64.
Open by appt (fax to 06-6880 2298).
Adm charge (donation) for groups.

Della Rovere arms

The palazzo owes its name to the fact that the place was once home to the confessors *(penitenzieri)* of St Peter's. Now the Hotel Columbus, it was originally built by Cardinal Domenico della Rovere in 1480. The palazzo still bears the family's coat of arms, the oak tree *(rovere* means oak), on its graceful courtyard wellhead. On the cardinal's death, the palazzo was acquired by Cardinal Francesco Alidosi, Pope Julius II della Rovere's favourite. Suspected of treason, the cardinal was murdered in 1511 by the pope's nephew, the Duke of Urbino, who took over the palazzo. A few of the rooms of the palazzo still contain beautiful frescoes.

View of the Tiber and the Borgo between Castel Sant'Angelo and St Peter's by Gaspare Vanvitelli (1653–1736)

Santa Maria in Traspontina ❾

Via della Conciliazione 14. **Map** 3 C3. **Tel** 06-6880 6451. 🚌 23, 34, 62, 64. **Open** 7am–noon, 4–7pm daily. 🕇 ⅙

The façade of the Carmelite church of Santa Maria in Traspontina

The church occupies the site of an ancient Roman pyramid, believed in the Middle Ages to have been the Tomb of Romulus. The pyramid was destroyed by Pope Alexander VI Borgia, but representations of it survive in the bronze doors at the entrance to St Peter's and in a Giotto triptych housed in the Vatican Pinacoteca *(see p240)*.

The present church was begun in 1566 to replace an earlier one which had been in the line of fire of the cannons defending Castel Sant'Angelo during the Sack of Rome in 1527. The papal artillery officers insisted that the dome of the new church should be as low as possible, so it was built without a supporting drum. The first chapel to the right is dedicated to the gunners' patron saint, Santa Barbara, and is decorated with warlike motifs. In the third chapel on the left are two columns, popularly thought to be the ones which SS Peter and Paul were bound to before going to their martyrdom nearby.

The Borgo ❿

Map 3 C3. 🚌 23, 34, 40, 62.

The Borgo's name derives from the German *burg*, meaning town. Rome's Borgo is where the first pilgrims to St Peter's were housed in hostels and hospices, often for quite lengthy periods. The first of these foreign colonies, called "schools", was founded in AD 725 by a Saxon, King Ine of Wessex, who wished to live a life of penance and to be buried near the Tomb of St Peter. These days hotels and hostels have made the Borgo a colony of international pilgrims once again. Much of the area's character was lost after redevelopment in the 1930s, but it is still enjoyable to stroll the old narrow streets on either side of Via della Conciliazione.

Vatican Corridor ⓫

Castel Sant'Angelo to the Vatican. **Map** 3 C3. 🚌 23, 34, 40, 62. **Closed** to public.

Clement VII, who used the Vatican Corridor to evade capture in 1527

Locally known as the Passetto (small corridor), this long passageway was built into the fortifications during medieval times. Intended as a link between the Vatican and the fortress of Castel Sant'Angelo, it constituted a fortified escape route which could also be used to control the strategic Borgo area. Arrows and other missiles could be fired from its bastions onto the streets and houses below. The corridor was used in 1494 by Pope Alexander VI Borgia when Rome was invaded by King Charles VIII of France. In 1527 it enabled Pope Clement VII to take refuge in Castel Sant'Angelo, as the troops commanded by the Constable of Bourbon began the Sack of Rome.

Palazzo Torlonia ⑫

Via della Conciliazione 30.
Map 3 C3. 🚌 23, 34, 40, 62, 64.
Not open to the public.

The palazzo was built in the late 15th century by the wealthy Cardinal Adriano Castellesi, in a style closely resembling Palazzo della Cancelleria *(see p149)*. The cardinal was a much-travelled rogue, who collected vast revenues from the bishopric of Bath and Wells which he was given by his friend King Henry VII of England. In return he gave Henry his palazzo for use as the seat of the English ambassador to the Holy See. Castellesi was finally stripped of his cardinalate by Pope Leo X Medici and disappeared from history.

Pope Leo X

Since then the palazzo has had many owners and tenants. In the 17th century it was rented for a time by Queen Christina of Sweden. The Torlonia family, who acquired the building in 1820, owed its fortune to the financial genius of shopkeeper-turned-banker Giovanni Torlonia. He lent money to the impoverished Roman nobility and bought up their property during the Napoleonic Wars.

Palazzo Torlonia (1496), unaffected by changes to the surrounding area

Castel Sant'Angelo ⑬

See pp248–9.

Palazzo di Giustizia ⑭

Piazza Cavour. **Map** 4 E3. 🚌 34, 49, 70, 87, 186, 280, 492, 913, 926, 990, **Not open** to the public.

The monumental Palazzo di Giustizia (Palace of Justice) was built between 1889 and 1910 to house the national law courts. Its riverside façade is crowned with a bronze chariot and fronted by giant statues of the great men of Italian law.

The building was supposed to embody the new order replacing the injustices of papal rule, but it has never endeared itself to the Romans. It was soon dubbed the Palazzaccio (roughly, "the ugly old palazzo") both for its appearance and for the nature of its business. By the 1970s the building was collapsing under its own weight, but it has now been restored.

The ornate travertine façade of the Palazzo di Giustizia

St Peter's ●

The centre of the Roman Catholic faith, St Peter's draws pilgrims from all over the world. Few are disappointed when they enter the sumptuously decorated basilica beneath Michelangelo's vast dome.

A shrine was erected on the site of St Peter's tomb in the 2nd century and the first great basilica, ordered by the Emperor Constantine, was completed around AD 349. By the 15th century it was falling down, so in 1506 Pope Julius II laid the first stone of a new church. It took more than a century to build and all the great architects of the Roman Renaissance and Baroque had a hand in its design.

★ Dome of St Peter's
Designed by Michelangelo, though not finished in his lifetime, the spectacular cupola, 136.5 m (448 ft) high, gives unity to the majestic interior of the basilica.

The nave's total length is 218 m (715 ft).

Papal Altar
The present altar dates from the reign of Clement VIII (1592–1605). The plain slab of marble found in the Forum of Nerva stands under Bernini's baldacchino, overlooking the well of the confessio, the crypt where St Peter's body is reputedly buried.

Baldacchino
This magnificent canopy of gilded bronze, supported on spiral columns 20 m (66 ft) high, was designed by Bernini in the 17th century.

TIMELINE

AD 61 Burial of St Peter		**1506** Julius II lays first stone	**1547** Michelangelo named as chief architect of St Peter's		**1626** New basilica of St Peter's consecrated
324 Constantine builds basilica	**1452** Nicholas V plans restoration			**1593** Dome completed	

AD 60	800	1500	1550	1600

	200 Altar built marking grave of St Peter	**1503** Pope Julius II chooses Bramante as architect for new basilica	**1538** Antonio da Sangallo the Younger made director of works	**1606** Carlo Maderno extends basilica	**1614** Maderno finishes the façade
	800 Charlemagne crowned Emperor of Romans in St Peter's		**1514** Raphael director of works	**1564** Death of Michelangelo	

★ View from the Dome
The superb symmetry of Bernini's colonnade can be appreciated from the dome.

VISITORS' CHECKLIST

Piazza San Pietro. **Map** 3 B3. **Tel**
*06-6988 3712 (sacristy), 06-6988
1662 (tourist information).* 62
*to Via della Conciliazione. 23, 49,
81, 492, 990 to Piazza del Risorgimento. 64 to Largo di Porta Caval-
leggeri* **M** *Ottaviano S. Pietro.*
Basilica open *7am–7pm*
(Oct–Mar: 6pm).
Treasury open *8am–6.50pm*
(Oct–Mar: 5.50pm). **Vatican
Grottoes open** *7am–5.40pm*
(Oct–Mar: 4.40pm). **Dome open**
*8am–5.45pm daily (Oct–Mar:
4.45pm).* **Adm charge** *Treasury
and Dome.* **Pre-Constantinian
Necropolis** *can be visited by appt;
call 06-6988 5318 well in advance.*
Papal audiences: *Regular public
audiences, usually Wed morning in
Papal Audience Chamber or Piazza
San Pietro. Tickets (free) are in
great demand. Ring 06-6988
3114 or check availability at office
through bronze doors on right of
colonnade (9am–1pm). Appearances also at noon on Sundays at
library window to bless the crowd.
No bare knees or shoulders.*

The two minor cupolas at the corners of the transept are by Vignola.

Pope Urban VIII's Keys
At the base of the columns of the baldacchino, the coat of arms of Pope Urban VIII features the keys to the Kingdom of Heaven.

Façade by Carlo Maderno (1614)

Stairs to the dome

Filarete Door
Finished in 1445, Antonio Averulino's bronze door came from the original basilica.

Entrance

Piazza San Pietro
On Sundays and re-ligious occasions the Pope blesses the crowds from his balcony above the square.

STAR FEATURES

★ Dome of St Peter's

★ View from the Dome

A Guided Tour of St Peter's

The vast basilica's 187-m (615-ft) long, marble-encrusted interior contains 11 chapels and 45 altars in addition to a wealth of precious works of art. Some were salvaged from the original basilica and others commissioned from late Renaissance and Baroque artists, but much of the elaborate decoration is owed to Bernini's work in the mid-17th century. The two side aisles are 76 m (250 ft) long and converge under Michelangelo's enormous dome. The central focus of the building is the Papal Altar beneath Bernini's great baldacchino, filling the space between the four piers which support the dome. From the basilica you can visit the Grottoes, where the late Pope John Paul II is buried, the Treasury and St Peter's Sacristy, or the terrace for panoramic views.

⑤ **Baldacchino by Bernini**
Commissioned by Pope Urban VIII in 1624, the extravagant Baroque canopy dominates the nave and crowns the Papal Altar, at which only the pope may celebrate mass.

Bernini's Monument to Urban VIII

④

④ **Throne of St Peter in Glory**
In the domed apse, look up to the window above Bernini's Baroque sculpture of 1656–65. It lights the image of the Holy Spirit, shown as a dove amid clouds, rays of sunlight and flights of angels.

Entrance to Treasury and Sacristy

③

HISTORICAL PLAN OF THE BASILICA OF ST PETER'S

Entrance to Necropolis

St Peter was buried c.AD 64 in a necropolis near his crucifixion site at the Circus of Nero. Constantine built a basilica on the burial site in AD 324. In the 15th century the old church was found to be unsafe and had to be demolished. It was rebuilt in the 16th and 17th centuries. By 1614 the façade was ready, and in 1626 the new church was consecrated.

③ **Monument to Pope Alexander VII**
Bernini's last work was finished in 1678 and is in an alcove on the left of the transept. The pope sits among the figures of Truth, Justice, Charity and Prudence.

② **Monument to Leo XI**
On the left beneath the aisle arch is Alessandro Algardi's white marble 1650 monument to Leo XI, whose reign as pope lasted only 27 days.

KEY

■	Circus of Nero
■	Constantinian
■	Renaissance
□	Baroque

KEY

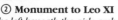

– – – Tour route

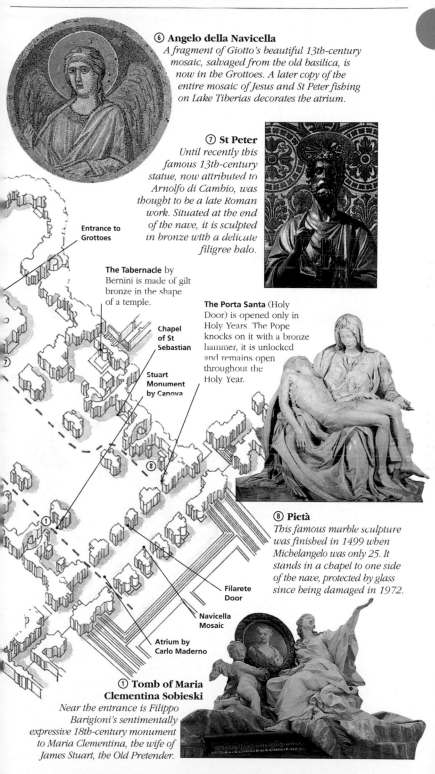

⑥ Angelo della Navicella

A fragment of Giotto's beautiful 13th-century mosaic, salvaged from the old basilica, is now in the Grottoes. A later copy of the entire mosaic of Jesus and St Peter fishing on Lake Tiberias decorates the atrium.

⑦ St Peter

Until recently this famous 13th-century statue, now attributed to Arnolfo di Cambio, was thought to be a late Roman work. Situated at the end of the nave, it is sculpted in bronze with a delicate filigree halo.

Entrance to Grottoes

The Tabernacle by Bernini is made of gilt bronze in the shape of a temple.

Chapel of St Sebastian

Stuart Monument by Canova

The Porta Santa (Holy Door) is opened only in Holy Years. The Pope knocks on it with a bronze hammer, it is unlocked and remains open throughout the Holy Year.

⑧ Pietà

This famous marble sculpture was finished in 1499 when Michelangelo was only 25. It stands in a chapel to one side of the nave, protected by glass since being damaged in 1972.

Filarete Door

Navicella Mosaic

Atrium by Carlo Maderno

① Tomb of Maria Clementina Sobieski

Near the entrance is Filippo Barigioni's sentimentally expressive 18th-century monument to Maria Clementina, the wife of James Stuart, the Old Pretender.

Vatican Museums ②

The buildings that house one of the world's finest art collections were once papal palaces built for Renaissance popes such as Sixtus IV, Innocent VIII and Julius II. The long courtyards and galleries, linking Innocent VIII's Belvedere Palace to the other buildings, are by Donato Bramante and were commissioned for Julius II in 1503. Most of the later additions to the buildings were made in the 18th century, when priceless works of art were first put on show. This complex of museums also houses the Sistine Chapel and the Raphael Rooms, and should not be missed. Note that no bare knees or shoulders are allowed.

★ Atrium of the Four Gates
Built by Camporese in 1792–3, this vast domed edifice was the original entrance to the Vatican Museums.

The Belvedere Palace was commissioned in the late 15th century by Pope Innocent VIII.

★ Cortile della Pigna
This huge bronze pine cone, part of an ancient Roman fountain, once stood in the courtyard of old St Peter's. Its niche was designed by Pirro Ligorio.

Cortile della Biblioteca

Cortile del Belvedere

Apartment of Pius V

Sistine Chapel

Borgia Tower

Borgia Apartment

Raphael Loggia

Cortile di San Damaso

STAR FEATURES

★ Atrium of the Four Gates

★ Cortile della Pigna

★ Bramante Stairway

Spiral Ramp

The spectacular stair-way leading down from the museums to the street was designed by Giuseppe Momo in 1932.

Entrance

VISITORS' CHECKLIST

Città del Vaticano. Entrance in Viale Vaticano. **Map** 3 B2. **Tel** *06-6988 3860.* 49 to entrance, 23, 81, 492, 990 to Piazza del Risorgimento or 62 to St Peter's. Cipro Musei Vaticani, Ottaviano S. Pietro. **Open** *9am–6pm (last adm: 4pm) Mon–Sat, 9am–2pm (last adm: 12.30pm) last Sun of each month.* **Closed** *public & relig hols. Special permit needed for Raphael Loggia, Vatican Library, Lapidary Gallery & Vatican Archives.* **Adm charge,** *free last Sun of month.* special routes. **Temp exhibitions, lectures.** Gardens and tours: *06-6988 4019. Tickets can be bought in advance via the website.* **www.**vatican.va

Simonetti Stairway

Built in the 1780s with a vaulted ceiling, the stairs were part of the conversion of the Belvedere Palace into the Pio-Clementine Museum.

Cortile Ottagonale

The inner court of the Belvedere Palace was given its octagonal shape in 1773.

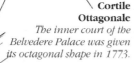

★ Bramante Stairway

Pope Julius II built the spiral staircase within a square tower as an entrance to the palace. The staircase could be ridden up on horseback in case of emergency.

Braccio Nuovo

TIMELINE

1000	1500	1600	1700	1800
1198 Innocent III creates papal palace	**1503** Bramante lays out Belvedere Courtyard **1509** Raphael begins work on Rooms	**1655** Bernini designs Scala Regia	**1756** Foundation of Christian Museum	**1800–23** Chiaramonti Museum founded **1837** Etruscan Museum founded
1473 Pope Sixtus IV builds Sistine Chapel	**1503–13** Pope Julius II starts Classical sculpture collection	*Bramante (1444–1514)*	**1758** Museum of Pagan Antiquities founded **1776–84** Pius VI enlarges museum	**1822** Braccio Nuovo is opened **1970** Pope Paul VI opens Gregorian Museum of Pagan Antiquities

Exploring the Vatican Museums

Four centuries of papal patronage and connoisseurship have resulted in one of the world's great collections of Classical and Renaissance art. The Vatican houses many of the great archaeological finds of central Italy including the *Laocoön* group, discovered in 1506 on the Esquiline, the *Apollo del Belvedere* and the Etruscan bronze known as the *Mars of Todi*. During the Renaissance, parts of the museums were decorated with wonderful frescoes commissioned for the Sistine Chapel, the Raphael Rooms and the Borgia Apartment.

Mars of Todi

Gallery of the Candelabra
Once an open loggia, this gallery of Greek and Roman sculpture has a fine view of the Vatican Gardens.

Roc the

Gallery of Tapestries

Etruscan Museum

Siege of Malta
The Gallery of Maps is an important record of 16th-century history and cartography.

Upper floor

Raphael Loggia

Modern Religious Art

Sistine Chapel

Raphael Rooms

GALLERY GUIDE
Visitors have to follow a one-way system. It is best to concentrate on a single collection or to choose one of the four suggested itineraries. These are colour-coded so that you can follow them throughout the museums. They vary in length from 90 minutes to 5 hours. If you are planning a long visit, make sure you allow plenty of time for resting. Conserve your stamina for the Sistine Chapel and the Raphael Rooms; they are 20–30 minutes' walk from the entrance, without allowing for any viewing time along the way.

Sala dei Misteri
This is one of the rooms of the Borgia Apartment, richly decorated with Pinturicchio frescoes.

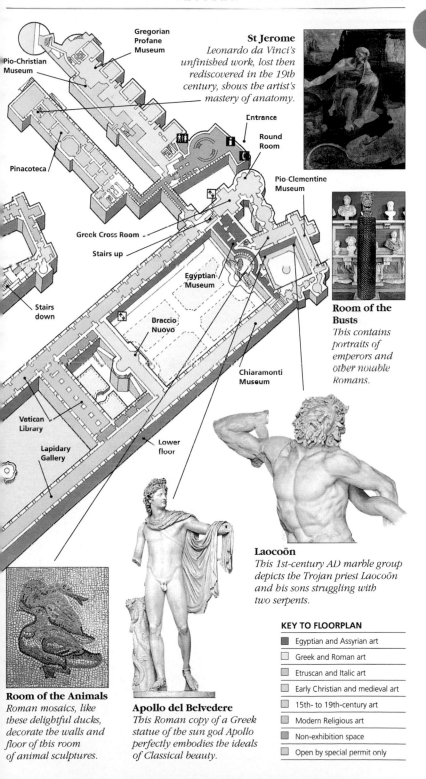

Gregorian Profane Museum

Pio-Christian Museum

St Jerome
Leonardo da Vinci's unfinished work, lost then rediscovered in the 19th century, shows the artist's mastery of anatomy.

Entrance

Round Room

Pinacoteca

Pio-Clementine Museum

Greek Cross Room

Stairs up

Egyptian Museum

Room of the Busts
This contains portraits of emperors and other notable Romans.

Stairs down

Braccio Nuovo

Chiaramonti Museum

Vatican Library

Lower floor

Lapidary Gallery

Laocoön
This 1st-century AD marble group depicts the Trojan priest Laocoön and his sons struggling with two serpents.

Room of the Animals
Roman mosaics, like these delightful ducks, decorate the walls and floor of this room of animal sculptures.

Apollo del Belvedere
This Roman copy of a Greek statue of the sun god Apollo perfectly embodies the ideals of Classical beauty.

KEY TO FLOORPLAN

- Egyptian and Assyrian art
- Greek and Roman art
- Etruscan and Italic art
- Early Christian and medieval art
- 15th- to 19th-century art
- Modern Religious art
- Non-exhibition space
- Open by special permit only

Exploring the Vatican's Collections

The Vatican's greatest treasures are its Greek and Roman antiquities. These have been on display since the 18th century. The 19th century saw the addition of exciting discoveries from Etruscan tombs and excavations in Egypt. In the Pinacoteca (art gallery) there is a small, choice collection of paintings, including works by Raphael, Titian and Leonardo. Works by great painters and sculptors are also on view throughout the older parts of the museums in the form of sumptuous decorations commissioned by the Renaissance popes.

Coloured bas-relief from an Egyptian tomb (c.2400 BC)

EGYPTIAN AND ASSYRIAN ART

The Egyptian collection contains finds from 19th- and 20th-century excavations in Egypt and statues which were brought to Rome in Imperial times. There are also Roman imitations of Egyptian art from Hadrian's Villa *(see p269)* and from the Campus Martius district of ancient Rome. Egyptian-style statuary from Hadrian's Villa was used to decorate the Greek Cross Room, the entrance to the new wing built in 1780 by Michelangelo Simonetti.

The genuine Egyptian works, exhibited on the lower floor of the Belvedere Palace, include statues, mummies, mummy cases and funerary artifacts. There is also a large collection of documents written on papyrus, the paper the ancient Egyptians made from reeds. Among the main treasures is a colossal granite statue of Queen Tuia, the mother of Rameses II, found on the site of the Horti

Sallustiani gardens *(see p251)* in 1714. The statue, which dates from the 13th century BC, may have been brought to Rome by the Emperor Caligula (reigned AD 37–41), who had an unhealthy interest in pharaohs and in his own mother, Agrippina.

Also noteworthy are the head of a statue of Montuhotep IV (21st century BC), the beautiful mummy case of Queen Hetepheres, and the tomb of Iri, the guardian of the Pyramid of Cheops (26th century BC).

The Assyrian Stairway is decorated with fragments of reliefs from the palaces of the kings of Nineveh (8th century BC). These depict the military exploits of King Sennacherib and his son Sargon II, and show scenes from Assyrian and Chaldean mythology.

ETRUSCAN AND OTHER PRE-ROMAN ART

This collection comprises artifacts from pre-Roman civilizations in Etruria and Latium, from Neolithic times to the 1st century BC, when these ancient populations were assimilated into the Roman state. Pride of place in the Gregorian Etruscan Museum goes to the objects found in the Regolini-Galassi tomb, excavated in 1836 at the necropolis of Cerveteri *(see p271)*. The tomb was found intact and yielded numerous everyday household objects, plus a throne, a bed and a funeral cart, all cast in bronze, dating from the 7th century BC. Beautiful black vases, delightful terracotta figurines and bronze statues such as the famous *Mars of Todi*, displayed in the Room of the Bronzes, show the Etruscans to have been a highly civilized, sophisticated people.

A number of Greek vases that were found in Etruscan tombs are on display in the Vase Collection. The Room of the Italiot Vases contains only vases produced locally in the Greek cities of Southern Italy and in Etruria itself. These date from the 3rd to the 1st century BC.

Etruscan gold clasp (fibula) from the 7th century BC

Head of an athlete in mosaic from the Baths of Caracalla

GREEK AND ROMAN ART

The greater part of the Vatican Museums is dedicated to Greek and Roman art. Exhibits line connecting corridors and vestibules; walls and floors display fine mosaics; and famous sculptures decorate the main courtyards.

The first serious organization of the collection took place in the reign of Julius II (1503–13) around Bramante's Belvedere Courtyard. The prize pieces form the nucleus of the 18th-century Pio-Clementine Museum. In the pavilions of the Octagonal Courtyard and in the surrounding rooms are sculptures considered among the greatest achievements of Western art. The *Apoxyomenos* (an athlete wiping his body after a race) and the *Apollo del Belvedere* are high-quality Roman copies of Greek originals of about 320 BC. The magnificent *Laocoön*, sculpted by three artists from Rhodes, had long been known to exist from a description by Pliny the Elder. It was rediscovered near the ruins of the Domus Aurea *(see p175)* in 1506. Classical works such as these had a profound influence on Michelangelo and other Renaissance artists.

The much smaller Chiaramonti Museum, named after Pope Pius VII Chiaramonti, was laid out by Canova in the early 19th century. It includes a striking colossal head of the goddess Athene. The Braccio Nuovo, an extension of the Chiaramonti, decorated with Roman floor mosaics, contains a statue of Augustus from the villa of his wife Livia at Prima Porta. Its pose is based on the famous *Doryphoros* by the Greek sculptor Polyclitus, of which there is a Roman copy on display opposite.

Exhibits in the Vase Rooms range from the Greek geometric style (8th century BC) to black-figure vases from Corinth, such as the famous vase by Exekias, with Achilles and Ajax playing a game similar to draughts (530 BC), and the later red-figure type, such as the *kylix* (a wide shallow cup) with Oedipus and the Sphinx from the 5th century BC. A stairway links this section to the Gallery of the Candelabra and the Room of the Biga (a two-horse chariot). The horses and harness were added in the 18th century.

The Gregorian Profane Museum, housed in a new wing, charts the evolution of Roman art from dependence upon Greek models to a recognizably Roman style.

The *Doryphoros* or spear-carrier, a Roman copy in marble of an original Greek bronze

Original Greek works include large marble fragments from the Parthenon in Athens. There is also a Roman copy of *Athene and Marsyas* by Myron, which was part of the decoration of the Parthenon. Totally Roman in character are two reliefs known as the *Rilievi della Cancelleria*,

Marble relief of the Emperor Vespasian

because they were discovered beneath the Palazzo della Cancelleria *(see p149)* in the 1930s. They show military parades of the Emperor Vespasian and his son Domitian. This section also has fine Roman floor mosaics. There are two from the Baths of Caracalla *(see p197)*, depicting athletes and referees. They date from the 3rd century AD. Most striking of all is a mosaic that creates the impression of an unswept floor, covered with debris after a meal. Away from the main Classical collections, in one of the rooms of the Vatican Library, is the *Aldobrandini Wedding*, a beautiful Roman fresco of a bride being prepared for her marriage, dating from the 1st century AD.

Floor mosaic from the Baths of Otricoli in Umbria, in the Chiaramonti Museum

Detail from Giotto's *Stefaneschi Triptych*

EARLY CHRISTIAN AND MEDIEVAL ART

The main collection of early Christian antiquities is in the Pio-Christian Museum, founded in the last century by Pope Pius IX and formerly housed in the Lateran Palace. It contains inscriptions and sculpture from catacombs and early Christian basilicas. The sculpture consists chiefly of reliefs decorating sarcophagi, though the most striking work is a free-standing 4th-century statue of the *Good Shepherd*. The sculpture's chief interest lies in the way it blends Biblical episodes with pagan mythology. Christianity adopted Classical images so that its doctrines could be understood in clear visual terms. The idealized pastoral figure of the shepherd, for example, became Christ himself, while bearded philosophers turned into the Apostles. At the same time, Christianity laid claim to be the spiritual and cultural heir of the Roman Empire.

The first two rooms of the Pinacoteca are dedicated to late medieval art, mostly tempera-painted wooden panels which served as altarpieces. The outstanding work is Giotto's altarpiece dating from about 1300, known as the *Stefaneschi Triptych*. It expresses much the same theme as the early Christian works: the continuity between the Classical world of the Roman Empire and the new order of Christian Europe. The crucifixion of St Peter takes place between two landmarks of ancient Rome, the Pyramid of Caius Cestius *(see p205)*, and the pyramid known in the Middle Ages as the Tomb of Romulus, which stood near the Vatican. The triptych, which decorated the main altar of old St Peter's, includes portraits of Pope St Celestine V (reigned 1294), and of the donor, Cardinal Jacopo Stefaneschi, shown offering the triptych to St Peter.

The Vatican Library has a number of medieval treasures exhibited rather haphazardly in showcases; these include woven and embroidered cloths, reliquaries, enamels and icons. One of the aims of the 18th-century reorganization of the Vatican collections was to glorify Christian works by contrasting them with earlier pagan creations. In the long Lapidary Gallery over 3,000 stone tablets with Christian and pagan inscriptions are displayed on opposite walls. The world's greatest collection of its kind, it may be visited only with special permission.

15TH- TO 19TH-CENTURY ART

The Renaissance popes, many of whom were cultured connoisseurs of the arts, considered it their duty to sponsor the leading painters, sculptors and goldsmiths of the age.

***Pietà* by the Venetian artist Giovanni Bellini (1430–1516)**

RAPHAEL'S LAST PAINTING

When Raphael died in 1520, the *Transfiguration* was found in his studio, almost complete. The wonderful luminous work was placed at the head of the bier where the great artist's body lay. It depicts the episode in the Gospels in which Christ took three of the Apostles to the top of a mountain, where He appeared to them in divine glory. In the detail shown here Christ floats above the ground in a halo of ethereal light.

MODERN RELIGIOUS ART

Modern artists exhibited in the Vatican Museums face daunting competition from the great works of the past. Few modern works are displayed conspicuously, the exceptions being Momo's spiral staircase of 1932, which greets visitors as they enter the museums, and Giò Pomodoro's abstract sculpture in the centre of the Cortile della Pigna.

In 1973 a contemporary art collection was inaugurated by Pope Paul VI. Housed in the Borgia Apartment, it includes over 800 exhibits by modern artists from all over the world, donated by collectors or the artists themselves. Works in a great variety of media show many contrasting approaches to religious subjects. There are paintings, drawings, engravings and sculpture by 19th- and 20th-century artists, as well as mosaics, stained glass, ceramics and tapestries. Well-known modern painters such as Georges Braque, Paul Klee, Edvard Munch and Graham Sutherland are all represented. There are also drawings by Henry Moore, ceramics by Picasso and stained glass by Fernand Léger. Projects for modern church ornaments include Matisse's decorations for the church of St Paul de Vence, Luigi Fontana's models for the bronze doors of Milan cathedral, and Emilio Greco's panels for the doors of Orvieto cathedral.

The galleries around the Cortile del Belvedere were all decorated by great artists between the 16th and the 19th centuries. The Gallery of Tapestries is hung with tapestries woven in Brussels to designs by students of Raphael; the Apartment of Pope Pius V has beautiful 15th-century Flemish tapestries; and the Gallery of Maps is frescoed with 16th-century maps of ancient and contemporary Italy. When you go to visit the Raphael Rooms (*see pp242–3*), you should not overlook the nearby Room of the Chiaroscuri and Pope Nicholas V's tiny private chapel, frescoed by Fra Angelico between 1447 and 1451. Similarly, before reaching the Sistine Chapel (*see pp244–7*), visit the Borgia Apartment, frescoed in a decorative, flowery style by Pinturicchio and his students in the 1490s. The contrast with Michelangelo's Sistine Chapel ceiling, begun in 1508, could hardly be greater. Another set of fascinating frescoes decorates the Loggia of Raphael, but this requires special permission to visit.

Many important works by Renaissance masters are on show in the Pinacoteca (art gallery). Highlights among the works by 15th-century painters are a fine *Pietà* by the Venetian Giovanni Bellini and Leonardo da Vinci's unfinished *St Jerome*. Of the great 16th-century works, do not miss the fine altarpiece by Titian, the *Crucifixion of St Peter* by Guido Reni, the *Deposition* by Caravaggio and the *Communion of St Jerome* by Domenichino. Raphael has a whole room dedicated to his work. It contains the beautiful *Madonna of Foligno* and the *Transfiguration* as well as eight tapestries made to his designs.

Lunette of the *Adoration of the Magi* by Pinturicchio in the Room of the Mysteries in the Borgia Apartment

Town with Gothic Cathedral by Paul Klee (1879–1940)

Raphael Rooms

Pope Julius II's private apartments were built above those of his hated predecessor, Alexander VI, one of the Borgias, who died in 1503. Julius was impressed with Raphael's work and chose him to redecorate the four

Detail from *The Expulsion of Heliodorus from the Temple,* showing Pope Julius II watching the scene from his litter

rooms *(stanze).* Raphael and his pupils began the task in 1508, replacing existing works by several better-known artists, including Raphael's own teacher, Perugino. The work took over 16 years and Raphael himself died before its completion. The frescoes express the religious and philosophical ideals of the Renaissance. They quickly established Raphael's reputation as an artist in Rome, putting him on a par with Michelangelo, then working on the ceiling of the Sistine Chapel.

Cortile del Belvedere

KEY TO FLOORPLAN

① Hall of Constantine

② Room of Heliodorus

③ Room of the Segnatura

④ Room of *The Fire in the Borgo*

HALL OF CONSTANTINE ①

The frescoes in this room were started in 1517, three years before Raphael's death, but Raphael himself probably had little hand in their execution. As a result they are not held in the same high regard as those in the other rooms. The work was completed in 1525 in the reign of Pope Clement VII by Giulio Romano and two other former pupils of Raphael, Giovanni Francesco Penni and Raffaellino del Colle.

The theme of the decoration is the triumph of Christianity over paganism. The four major frescoes show scenes from the life of Constantine and include his *Vision of the Cross* and his victory over his rival Maxentius at *The Battle of the Milvian Bridge*, for which Raphael had provided a preparatory sketch. In both *The Baptism of Constantine* and *The Donation of Constantine*, the figure of Pope Sylvester *(see p170)* was given the features of Clement VII.

ROOM OF HELIODORUS ②

This private antechamber was decorated by Raphael between 1512 and 1514. The main frescoes show the miraculous protection granted to all the Church's ministers, doctrines and property. The room's name refers to the fresco on the right, *The Expulsion of Heliodorus from the Temple.* This shows a story from Jewish history, in which a thief called Heliodorus is felled

Swiss guards waiting with papal chair in *The Mass at Bolsena*

by a horseman as he tries to make off with the treasure from the Temple of Jerusalem. The scene is witnessed by the pope, borne on a litter by courtiers. The incident is also a thinly veiled reference to Julius II's success in driving foreign armies out of Italy. In *The Meeting of Leo I and Attila* Raphael pays a similar compliment to the pope's political skill. Pope Leo was originally given the face of Julius II, but after his death, Raphael substituted the features of Julius's successor, Leo X.

The Mass at Bolsena depicts a miracle that occurred in 1263. A priest

The Battle of the Milvian Bridge, completed by one of Raphael's assistants

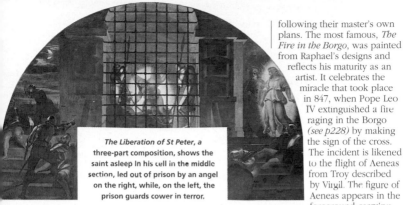

The Liberation of St Peter, a three-part composition, shows the saint asleep in his cell in the middle section, led out of prison by an angel on the right, while, on the left, the prison guards cower in terror.

who doubted that the bread and wine really were the body and blood of Christ suddenly saw the host bleed while he was celebrating mass. Julius II appears in this fresco, accompanied by a colourful group of Swiss guards.

Julius appears yet again as St Peter in *The Liberation of St Peter*. This fresco is remarkable for its dramatic lighting effects, achieved despite the painting's awkward shape and its position above a window.

ROOM OF THE SEGNATURA ③

The name is derived from a special council which met in this room to sign official documents. The frescoes here were completed between 1508 and 1511. The scheme Raphael followed was dictated by Pope Julius II. It reflects the Humanist belief that there could be perfect harmony between Classical culture and Christianity in their mutual search for truth.

The Dispute over the Holy Sacrament, the first fresco completed by Raphael for Pope Julius, represents the triumph of religion and spiritual truth. The conse-crated host is shown at the centre of the painting. This links the group of learned scholars, who discuss its significance, to the Holy Trinity and the saints floating on clouds up above.

On the opposite wall, *The School of Athens (see p232)* is a bustling scene

centred around the debate on the search for truth between Greek philosophers Plato and Aristotle. It also features portraits of many of Raphael's contemporaries, including Leonardo da Vinci, Bramante and Michelangelo. The other works include a portrait of the bearded Pope Julius II, who in 1511 vowed not to shave until he managed to rid Italy of all usurpers.

ROOM OF *THE FIRE IN THE BORGO* ④

This was originally the dining room, but when the deco-ration was completed under Pope Leo X, it became a music room. All the frescoes exalt the reigning pope by depicting events in the lives of his namesakes, the 9th-century popes Leo III and IV. The main frescoes were finished by two of Raphael's assistants between 1514 and 1517,

following their master's own plans. The most famous, *The Fire in the Borgo*, was painted from Raphael's designs and reflects his maturity as an artist. It celebrates the miracle that took place in 847, when Pope Leo IV extinguished a fire raging in the Borgo *(see p228)* by making the sign of the cross. The incident is likened to the flight of Aeneas from Troy described by Virgil. The figure of Aeneas appears in the foreground carrying his father on his back. This borrowing of an event from Classical legend shows a new willingness to experiment on the part of Raphael. Sadly, his pupils did not always follow his designs faithfully and this, combined with some poor restoration, has spoilt the work.

Detail from *The Fire in the Borgo*, showing Aeneas, the Trojan hero, with his father on his back, fleeing from the fire

The Dispute over the Holy Sacrament, the first fresco completed in the Rooms

Sistine Chapel: The Walls

The massive walls of the Sistine Chapel, the main chapel in the Vatican Palace, were frescoed by some of the finest artists of the 15th and 16th centuries. The 12 paintings on the side walls, by artists including Perugino, Ghirlandaio, Botticelli and Signorelli, show parallel episodes from the life of Moses and of Christ. The decoration of the chapel walls was completed between 1534 and 1541 by Michelangelo, who added the great altar wall fresco, *The Last Judgment*.

KEY TO THE FRESCOES: ARTISTS AND SUBJECTS

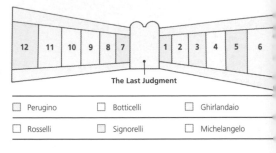

| 12 | 11 | 10 | 9 | 8 | 7 | | 1 | 2 | 3 | 4 | 5 | 6 |

The Last Judgment

☐ Perugino   ☐ Botticelli   ☐ Ghirlandaio

☐ Rosselli   ☐ Signorelli   ☐ Michelangelo

1 Baptism of Christ in the Jordan
2 Temptations of Christ
3 Calling of St Peter and St Andrew
4 Sermon on the Mount
5 Handing over the Keys to St Peter
6 Last Supper
7 Moses's Journey into Egypt
8 Moses Receiving the Call
9 Crossing of the Red Sea
10 Adoration of the Golden Calf
11 Punishment of the Rebels
12 Last Days of Moses

THE LAST JUDGMENT BY MICHELANGELO

Revealed in 1993 after a year's restoration, *The Last Judgment* is considered to be the masterpiece of Michelangelo's mature years. It was commissioned by Pope Paul III Farnese, and required the removal of some earlier frescoes and two windows over the altar. A new wall was erected which slanted inwards to stop dust settling on it. Michelangelo worked alone on the fresco for seven years, until its completion in 1541.

The painting depicts the souls of the dead rising up to face the wrath of God, a subject that is rarely used for an altar decoration. The pope chose it as a warning to Catholics to adhere to their faith in the turmoil of the Reformation. In fact the work conveys the artist's own tormented attitude to his faith. It offers neither the certainties of Christian orthodoxy, nor the ordered view of Classicism.

In a dynamic, emotional composition, the figures are caught in a vortex of motion. The dead are torn from their graves and hauled up to face Christ the Judge, whose athletic, muscular figure is the focus of all the painting's movement. Christ shows little sympathy for the agitated saints around him, clutching the instruments of their martyrdom. Neither is any pity shown for the damned, hurled down to the demons in hell. Here Charon, pushing people off his boat into the depths of Hades, and the infernal judge Minos, are taken from Dante's *Inferno*. Minos has ass's ears, and is a portrait of courtier Biagio da Cesena, who had objected to the nude figures in the fresco. Michelangelo's self-portrait is on the skin held by the martyr St Bartholomew.

Souls meeting the wrath of Christ in Michelangelo's *Last Judgment*

WALL FRESCOES

Detail from Botticelli's fresco
Temptations of Christ

When the Sistine Chapel was built, the papacy was a strong political power with vast accumulated wealth. In 1475 Pope Sixtus IV was able to summon some of the greatest painters of his day to decorate the chapel. Among the artists employed were Perugino, who was Raphael's master and is often credited with overseeing the project, Sandro Botticelli, Domenico Ghirlandaio, Cosimo Rosselli and Luca Signorelli. Their work on the chapel's frescoes took from 1481 to 1483.

Although frequently overlooked by visitors who concentrate on Michelangelo's work, the frescoes along the side walls of the chapel include some of the finest works of 15th-century Italian art. The two cycles of frescoes represent scenes from the lives of Moses and Christ. Above them in the spaces between the windows are portraits of the earliest popes, painted by various artists, including Botticelli.

The fresco cycles start at the altar end of the chapel, with the story of Christ on the right-hand wall and that of Moses on the left. Originally there were two paintings, *The Birth of Christ* and *The Finding of Moses*, on the wall behind the altar, but these were both destroyed to make way for Michelangelo's *Last Judgment*.

The final paintings of the two cycles are also lost. They were on the entrance wall, which collapsed during the 16th century. When the wall was restored, they were replaced with poor substitutes.

As was customary at the time, each fresco contains a series of scenes, linked thematically to the central episode. Hidden meanings and symbols connect each painting with its counterpart on the opposite wall, and there are also many allusions to contemporary events.

The elaborate architectural details in the frescoes include familiar Roman monuments. The Arch of Constantine *(see p91)* provides the backdrop for the *Punishment of the Rebels* by Botticelli, the fifth panel in the cycle of Moses, in which the artist himself appears as the last figure but one on the right. Two similar arches appear in the painting opposite, Perugino's *Handing over the Keys to St Peter*.

Moses was both spiritual and temporal leader of his people. He called down the wrath of God on those who challenged his decisions, thus

The crowd of onlookers in the *Calling of St Peter and St Andrew* by Ghirlandaio

setting a precedent for the power exercised by the pope. In *Handing over the Keys to St Peter*, Christ confers spiritual

and temporal authority on St Peter by giving him the keys to the Kingdoms of Heaven and Earth. The golden-domed building in the centre of the vast piazza represents both the Temple of Jerusalem and the Church, as founded by Peter, the first pope. The fifth figure on the right is thought to be a self-portrait by Perugino.

Botticelli's *Temptations of Christ* includes a view of the

The central episode in Botticelli's *Punishment of the Rebels*

Hospital of Santo Spirito, rebuilt in 1475 by Sixtus IV *(see p226)*. Here the devil is disguised in the habit of a Franciscan monk. Portraits of both Botticelli and Filippino Lippi are visible in the left hand corner. A portrait of the pope's nephew, Girolamo Riario, appears in the painting of the *Crossing of the Red Sea* by Rosselli, in which the sea is literally red. This painting also commemorates the papal victory at Campomorto in 1482.

Perugino's *Handing over the Keys to St Peter*

Sistine Chapel: The Ceiling

Michelangelo frescoed the ceiling for Pope Julius II between 1508 and 1512, working on specially designed scaffolding. The main panels, which chart the Creation of the World and Fall of Man, are surrounded by subjects from the Old and New Testaments – except for the Classical Sibyls who are said to have foreseen the birth of Christ. In the 1980s the ceiling was restored revealing colours of an unsuspected vibrancy.

Libyan Sibyl
The pagan prophetes reaches for the Boo of Knowledge. Li most female figures Michel-angelo painted the beautiful Libyan Sibyl was probably modelle on a man.

Illusionistic architecture

Creation of the Sun and Moon
Michelangelo depicts God as a dynamic but terrifying figure commanding the sun to shed light on the earth.

KEY TO CEILING PANELS

▢ **GENESIS: 1** God Dividing Light from Darkness; **2** Creation of the Sun and Moon; **3** Separating Waters from Land; **4** Creation of Adam; **5** Creation of Eve; **6** Original Sin; **7** Sacrifice of Noah; **8** The Deluge; **9** Drunkenness of Noah.

▢ **ANCESTORS OF CHRIST: 10** Solomon with his Mother; **11** Parents of Jesse; **12** Rehoboam with Mother; **13** Asa with Parents; **14** Uzziah with Parents; **15** Hezekiah with Parents; **16** Zerubbabel with Parents; **17** Josiah with Parents.

▢ **PROPHETS: 18** Jonah; **19** Jeremiah; **20** Daniel; **21** Ezekiel; **22** Isaiah; **23** Joel; **24** Zechariah.

▢ **SIBYLS: 25** Libyan Sibyl; **26** Persian Sibyl; **27** Cumaean Sibyl; **28** Erythrean Sibyl; **29** Delphic Sibyl.

▢ **OLD TESTAMENT SCENES OF SALVATION: 30** Punishment of Haman; **31** Moses and the Brazen Serpent; **32** David and Goliath; **33** Judith and Holofernes.

Original Sin
This shows Adam and Eve tasting the forbidden fruit from the Tree of Knowledge, and their expulsion from Paradise. Michelangelo represents Satan as a snake with the body of a woman.

The Ignudi are athletic male nudes whose significance is uncertain.

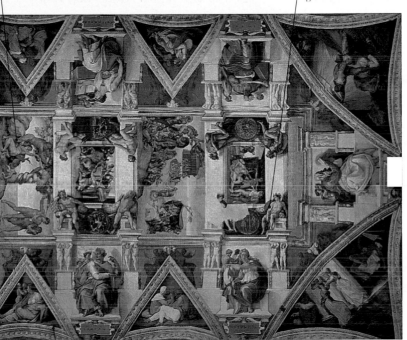

The lunettes are devoted to frescoes of the ancestors of Christ, like Hezekiah.

RESTORATION OF THE SISTINE CEILING

Restorers used computers, photography and spectrum analysis to inspect the fresco before cleaning began. They were therefore able to detect and remove the changes previous restorers had made to Michelangelo's original work. Analysis showed that the ceiling had been cleaned with materials ranging from bread to retsina wine. The restoration then revealed the familiarly dusky,

A restorer cleaning the Libyan Sibyl

eggshell-cracked figures to have creamy skins, lustrous hair and to be dressed in brightly coloured, luscious robes: "a Benetton Michelangelo" mocked one critic, claiming that a layer of varnish which the artist had added to darken the colours had been removed. However, after examining the work, most experts agreed that the new colours probably matched those painted by Michelangelo.

Castel Sant'Angelo ⑬

The massive fortress of Castel Sant'Angelo takes its name from the vision that Pope Gregory the Great had of the Archangel Michael on this site. It began life in AD 139 as Emperor Hadrian's mausoleum. Since then it has had many roles: as part of Emperor Aurelian's city wall, as a medieval citadel and prison, and as the residence of the popes in times of political unrest. From the dank cells in the lower levels to the fine apartments of the Renaissance popes above, a 58-room museum covers all aspects of the castle's history.

Mausoleum of Hadrian
This artist's impression show the tomb before Aurelian fortified its walls in AD 270–75

Courtyard of Honour
Heaps of stone cannonballs decorate the courtyard, once the castle's ammunition store.

The Treasury was probably the original site of Hadrian's burial chamber.

Hall of the Columns

Loggia of Paul III

Hall of the Library

PROTECTING THE POPE

The Vatican Corridor leads from the Vatican Palace to Castel Sant'Angelo. It was built in 1277 to provide an escape route when the pope was in danger. The pentagonal ramparts built around the castle during the 17th century improved its defences in times of siege.

The Rooms of Clement VIII are inscribed with the family crest of the Aldobrandini pope (1592–1605).

The Hall of Justice is decorated with a fresco of *The Angel of Justice* by Domenico Zaga (1545).

The spiral ramp was the entrance to the mausoleum.

■ Walls and fortifications
□ Vatican Corridor

★ **View from Terrace**
The castle's terrace, scene of the last act of Puccini's Tosca, offers splendid views in every direction.

The Chamber of the Urns housed the ashes of members o Hadrian's family.

STAR FEATURES

★ View from Terrace

★ Sala Paolina

★ Staircase of Alexander VI

VISITORS' CHECKLIST

Lungotevere Castello 50. **Map** 4 D3 & 11 A1. **Tel** 06-681 9111. 🚌 23, 34, 62 to Lungotevere Vaticano; 34, 49, 87, 280, 492, 926, 990 to Piazza Cavour. **Open** 9am–7pm (last adm: 6:30pm) Tue–Sun. **Closed** 1 Jan, 25 Dec. **Adm charge.** 🔲 🔘 ♿ 🎫 🗾 **Exhibitions** www.castelsantangelo.com

Bronze Angel
The gigantic statue of the Archangel Michael is by the 18th-century Flemish sculptor Pieter Verschaffelt.

The Round Hall houses the original model from which Verschaffelt's angel was cast.

★ **Sala Paolina**
The illusionistic frescoes by Perin del Vaga and Pellegrino Tibaldi (1546–8) include one of a courtier entering the room through a painted door.

Hall of Apollo
The room is frescoed with scenes from mythology attributed to the pupils of Perin del Vaga (1548).

Ventilation shaft

★ **Staircase of Alexander VI**
This staircase cuts right through the heart of the building.

Bridge

TIMELINE

AD 100	500	1000	1500

AD 139 Mausoleum completed by Antoninus Pius

590 Legendary date of appearance of Archangel Michael above the castle

1493 Pope Alexander VI restores Vatican Corridor

1390 Pope Boniface IX remodels the castle

Façade of Castel Sant'Angelo

271 Tomb is incorporated into Aurelian Wall and fortified

AD 130 Hadrian begins family mausoleum

Cannonballs in the Courtyard of Honour

1527 Castle withstands siege during Sack of Rome

1542–9 Sala Paolina and apartments built for Pope Paul III

1557 Ramparts built to protect the castle

1870 Castle used as barracks and military prison

VIA VENETO

In Imperial Rome, this was a suburb where rich families owned luxurious villas and gardens. Ruins from this era can be seen in the excavations in Piazza Sallustio, named after the most extensive gardens in the area, the Horti Sallustiani. After the Sack of Rome in the 5th century, the area reverted to open countryside. Not until the 17th century did it recover its lost splendour, with the building of Palazzo Barberini and the now-vanished Villa Ludovisi.

Film director Federico Fellini

When Rome became capital of Italy in 1870, the Ludovisi sold their land for development. They kept a plot for a new house, but tax on the profits from the sale was so high, they had to sell that too. By 1900, Via Veneto had become a street of smart modern hotels and cafés. It featured prominently in Fellini's 1960 film *La Dolce Vita*, a scathing satire on the lives of film stars and idle rich, but since then has lost its position as the meeting place of the famous.

SIGHTS AT A GLANCE

Churches and Temples
Santa Maria della
   Concezione ❸
Santa Maria della Vittoria ❽
Santa Susanna ❼

Historic Buildings
Casino dell'Aurora ❷
Palazzo Barberini ❻

Famous Streets
Via Veneto ❶

Fountains
Fontana del Tritone ❺
Fontana delle Api ❹

SEE ALSO

- *Street Finder*, map 5

- *Where to Stay* pp308–9

- *Restaurants* pp326–7

0 metres   200

0 yards   200

GETTING THERE

This is one of the easiest parts of Rome to reach by public transport. Barberini and Repubblica Metro stations on line A are very handy, and Stazione Termini is only 10–15 minutes' walk away. The Via Veneto itself starts at Piazza Barberini, well served by buses from all parts of the city. The 95 goes the whole length of Via Veneto to Porta Pinciana. Other useful routes include the 52, 53, 63, 80, 116 and 119.

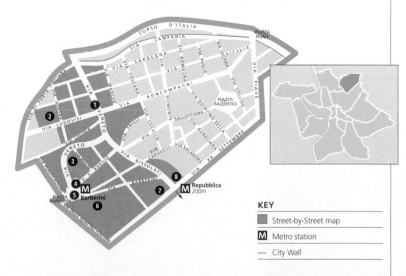

KEY

Street-by-Street map

Ⓜ Metro station

— City Wall

◁ **The onset of autumn in Via Veneto**

Street-by-Street: Via Veneto

The streets around Via Veneto, though within the walls of ancient Rome, contain little dating from before the unification of Italy in 1870. With its hotels, restaurants, bars and travel agencies, the area is the centre of 21st-century tourism in the way that Piazza di Spagna was the hub of the tourist trade in the Rome of the 18th-century Grand Tour. However, glimpses of the old city can be seen among the modern streets. These include Santa Maria della Concezione, the church of the Capuchin friars, whose convent once stood in its own gardens. In the 17th century Palazzo Barberini was built here for the powerful papal family. Bernini's Fontana del Tritone and Fontana delle Api have stood in Piazza Barberini since it was the meeting place of cart tracks entering the city from surrounding vineyards.

Casino dell'Aurora
A pavilion is all that remains of the great Ludovisi estate that once occupied most of this quarter of Rome ❷

Santa Maria della Concezione
This church is best known for the macabre collection of bones in its crypt ❸

Fontana delle Api
Bernini's drinking fountain is decorated with bees, emblem of his Barberini patrons ❹

Barberini station

Fontana del Tritone
Bernini's muscular sea god has been spouting water skywards for 350 years ❺

PIAZZA BARBERINI Ⓜ

VIA VENETO

VIA DI SAN BAS

VIA DI SAN NICOLA DA TOLENTINO

VIA BARBERINI

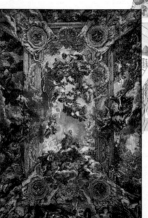

★ **Palazzo Barberini**
Pietro da Cortona worked on his spectacular ceiling fresco The Triumph of Divine Providence *between 1633 and 1639* ❻

VIA XX SETTEMBRE

The Porta Pinciana
was built in AD 403.
Only the central
arch of white
travertine is
original.

LOCATOR MAP
See Central Rome Map pp14–15

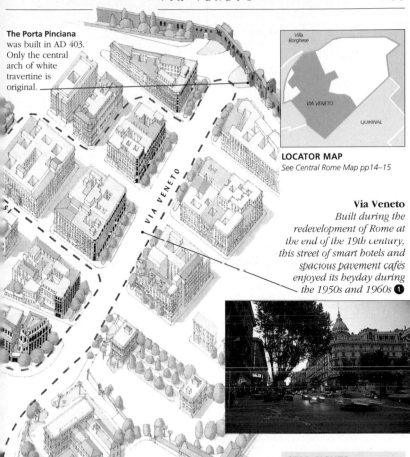

Via Veneto
*Built during the
redevelopment of Rome at
the end of the 19th century,
this street of smart hotels and
spacious pavement cafés
enjoyed its heyday during
the 1950s and 1960s* ❶

Santa Susanna
*This church is
dedicated to a
martyr executed
during Diocletian's
persecution of
Christians in the
3rd century AD* ❼

STAR SIGHTS

★ Palazzo Barberini

★ Santa Maria
della Vittoria

KEY

– – – Suggested route

0 metres	75
0 yards	75

**★ Santa Maria
della Vittoria**
*The highlight of this
Baroque church is
the Cornaro Chapel,
designed to resemble a
theatre. The centre of
the stage is occupied
by Bernini's thrilling
sculpture of* The
Ecstasy of St Teresa ❽

Pavement café in Via Veneto

Via Veneto ❶

Map 5 B1. 🚌 *52, 53, 63, 80, 95, 116, 119 and many routes to Piazza Barberini.* Ⓜ *Barberini.*

Via Veneto descends in a lazy curve from the Porta Pinciana to Piazza Barberini, lined in its upper reaches with exuberant late 19th-century hotels and canopied pavement cafés. It was laid out in 1879 over a large estate sold by the Ludovisi family in the great building boom of Rome's first years as capital of Italy. Palazzo Margherita, intended to be the new Ludovisi family palazzo, was completed in 1890. It now houses the American embassy.

In the 1960s this was the most glamorous street in Rome, its cafés patronized by film stars and plagued by the paparazzi. Most of the people drinking in the cafés today are tourists, as film stars now seem to prefer the livelier bohemian atmosphere of Trastevere.

Palazzo Margherita, the US embassy

Casino dell'Aurora ❷

Via Lombardia 46. **Map** 5 B2. *Tel 06-8346 7000.* 🚌 *52, 53, 63, 80, 95, 116, 119.* Ⓜ *Barberini.* **Open** by appt only. Ring above number, then email aurorapallavicini@saita.it.

The Casino (a stately country residence) was a summer-house on the grounds of the

Ludovisi palace. It was built by Cardinal Ludovisi in the 17th century, and frescoed by Guercino. The ceiling fresco creates the impression that the Casino has no roof, but lies open to a cloudy sky, across which horses pull the carriage of Aurora, the goddess of dawn, from the darkness of night towards the light of day.

Santa Maria della Concezione ❸

Via Veneto 27. **Map** 5 B2. *Tel 06-487 1185.* 🚌 *52, 53, 61, 62, 63, 80, 95, 116, 119, 175.* Ⓜ *Barberini.* **Open** *7am–noon, 3–7pm daily.* **Crypt open** *9am–noon, 3–6pm daily.* **Donation expected.* 🚻

Pope Urban VIII'S brother, Antonio Barberini was a cardinal and a Capuchin friar. In 1626 he founded this plain, unassuming church at what is now the foot of the Via Veneto. When he died he was buried not, like most cardinals, in a grand marble sarcophagus, but below a simple flagstone near the altar, with the bleak epitaph in Latin: "Here lies dust, ashes, nothing".

The grim reality of death is illustrated even more graphically in the crypt beneath the church, where generations of Capuchin friars decorated the walls of the five vaulted chapels with the bones and skulls of their departed brethren. In all, some 4,000 skeletons were used over about 100 years to create this macabre *memento mori* started in the late 17th century. Some of the bones are wired together to form Christian symbols such as crowns of thorns, sacred hearts and crucifixes. There are also some complete skeletons, including one of a Barberini princess who died as a child. At the exit, an inscription in Latin reads: "What you are, we used to be. What we are, you will be." **Pope Urban VIII**

Fontana delle Api ❹

Piazza Barberini. **Map** 5 B2. 🚌 *52, 53, 61, 62, 63, 80, 95, 116, 119, 175.* Ⓜ *Barberini.*

The fountain of the bees – *api* are bees, symbol of the Barberini family – is one of Bernini's more modest works. Tucked away in a corner of Piazza Barberini, it is quite easy to miss. Dating from 1644, it pays homage to Pope Urban VIII Barberini, and features rather crab-like bees which appear to be sipping the water as it dribbles down into the basin. A Latin inscription informs us that the water is for the use of the public and their animals.

Bernini's Fontana delle Api

Fontana del Tritone ❺

Piazza Barberini. **Map** 5 B3. 🚌 *52, 53, 61, 62, 63, 80, 95, 116, 119, 175.* Ⓜ *Barberini.*

In the centre of busy Piazza Barberini is one of Bernini's liveliest creations, the Triton Fountain. It was created for Pope Urban VIII Barberini in 1642, shortly after the completion of his palace on the ridge above. Acrobatic dolphins stand on their heads, twisting their tails together to support a huge scallop shell on which the sea god Triton kneels, blowing a spindly column of water up into the air through a conch shell. Entwined artistically among the dolphins' tails are the papal tiara, the keys of St Peter and the Barberini coat of arms.

The Triton and his conch shell in Bernini's Fontana del Tritone

Palazzo Barberini ⊙

Via delle Quattro Fontane 13. **Map** 5 B3. **Tel** 06-482 4184. 52, 53, 61, 62, 63, 80, 95, 116, 175, 492, 590. Barberini. **Open** 8.30am–7pm Tue–Sun (last adm 30 mins before closing). **Closed** public hols. **Adm charge.** www.galleriaborghese.it

When Maffei Barberini became Pope Urban VIII in 1623 he decided to build a grand palace for his family on the fringes of the city, overlooking a ruined temple. The architect, Carlo Maderno, designed it as a typical rural villa, with wings extending into the surrounding gardens. Maderno died in 1629 and Bernini took over, assisted by Borromini. The peculiar pediments on some of the top floor windows, and the oval staircase inside, are almost certainly by Borromini.

Of the many sumptuously decorated rooms, the most striking is the Gran Salone, with a dazzling illusionistic ceiling fresco by Pietro da Cortona. The palazzo also houses paintings from the 13th to the 16th centuries, part of the Galleria Nazionale d'Arte Antica, with important works by Filippo Lippi, El Greco and

Caravaggio. There is also a Holbein portrait of King Henry VIII of England dressed for his wedding to Anne of Cleves. Of greater local significance are Guido Reni's *Beatrice Cenci*, the young woman executed for planning her father's murder *(see p152)*, and *La Fornarina*, traditionally identified as a portrait of Raphael's mistress *(see p210)*, although not necessarily painted by him.

Santa Susanna ⊙

Via XX Settembre 14. **Map** 5 C2. **Tel** 06-4201 4554. 60, 61, 62, 84, 175, 492, 910. Repubblica. **Open** 9am–noon, 4–7pm daily (to 5.30pm Sun).

Façade of Santa Susanna

Santa Susanna's most striking feature is its vigorous Baroque façade by Carlo Maderno, finished in 1603. Christians have worshipped on the site since at least the 4th century. In the nave, there are four huge frescoes by Baldassarre Croce (1558–1628), painted to resemble tapestries. These depict scenes from the life of Susanna, an obscure Roman saint who was martyred here, and the rather better-known life of the Old Testament Susanna, who was spotted bathing in her husband's garden by two lecherous judges.

Santa Susanna is the Catholic church for Americans in Rome and holds services in English every day.

Santa Maria della Vittoria ⊙

Via XX Settembre 17. **Map** 5 C2. **Tel** 06-4274 0571. 60, 61, 62, 84, 492, 910. Repubblica. **Open** 9am–noon, 3.30–6.30pm Mon–Sat; 3.30–6pm Sun.

Santa Maria della Vittoria is an intimate Baroque church with a lavishly decorated candlelit interior. It contains one of Bernini's most ambitious sculptural works, *The Ecstasy of St Teresa* (1646), centrepiece of the Cornaro Chapel, built to resemble a miniature theatre. It even has an audience: sculptures of the chapel's benefactor, Cardinal Federico Cornaro, and his ancestors sit in boxes, as if watching and discussing the scene occurring in front of them.

Visitors may be shocked or thrilled by the apparently physical nature of St Teresa's ecstasy. She lies on a cloud, her mouth half open and her eyelids closed, with rippling drapery covering her body. Looking over her with a smile, which from different angles can appear either tender or cruel, is a curly-haired angel holding an arrow with which he is about to pierce the saint's body for a second time. The marble figures are framed and illuminated by rays of divine light materialized in bronze.

Bernini's astonishing *Ecstasy of St Teresa*

FURTHER AFIELD

The more inquisitive visitor to Rome may wish to try a few excursions to the large parks and some of the more isolated churches on the outskirts of the city. With a day to spare, you can explore the villas of Tivoli and the ruins of the ancient Roman port of Ostia. Traditional haunts of the

Dish (3rd century BC) in Villa Giulia

Grand Tour (see p130), such as the catacombs and the ruined aqueducts of Parco Appio Claudio, still offer glimpses of the rapidly vanishing Campagna, the countryside around Rome. More modern sights include the suburb of EUR, built in the Fascist era, and the memorial at the Fosse Ardeatine.

SIGHTS AT A GLANCE

Towns and Areas
EUR **15**
Tivoli **19**

Historic Roads
Via Appia Antica **9**

Churches
San Lorenzo fuori le Mura **8**
San Paolo fuori le Mura **16**
Sant'Agnese fuori le Mura **7**
Santa Costanza **6**

Museums and Galleries
Centrale Montemartini **17**
MAXXI **4**
Museo di Arte Contemporanea di Roma **5**
Museo e Galleria Borghese pp260–61 **2**
Villa Giulia pp262–3 **3**

Ancient Sites
Hadrian's Villa **20**
Ostia Antica **22**

Parks and Gardens
Villa Borghese **1**
Villa d'Este **19**
Villa Doria Pamphilj **18**
Villa Gregoriana **21**

Tombs and Catacombs
Catacombs of Domitilla **12**
Catacombs of San Callisto **10**
Catacombs of San Sebastiano **11**
Fosse Ardeatine **13**
Tomb of Cecilia Metella **14**

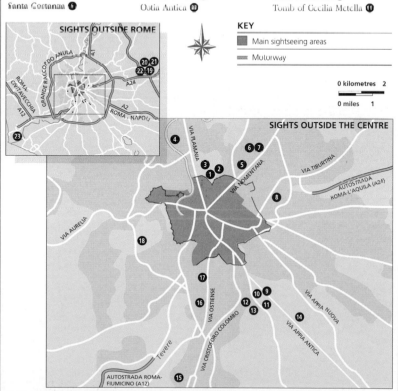

SIGHTS OUTSIDE ROME

KEY

■ Main sightseeing areas
━ Motorway

0 kilometres 2
0 miles 1

SIGHTS OUTSIDE THE CENTRE

◁ Caryatids beside the canal of the Canopus at Hadrian's Villa

Villa Borghese ❶

Map 2 E5. ▦ *52, 53, 88, 95, 116, 490, 495.* ▦ *3, 19.* **Park open** *dawn to sunset.* **Bioparco** *Viale del Giardino Zoologico 20.* **Map** 2 E4. **Tel** *06-360 8211.* ▦ *52.* ▦ *3, 19.* **Open** *daily.* **Closed** *25 Dec.* ♿ ▯ ▯ ▯ **Galleria Nazionale d'Arte Moderna** *Viale delle Belle Arti 131.* **Map** 2 D4. **Tel** *06-3229 8221.* ▦ *3, 19.* **Open** *8.30am–7.30pm Tue–Sun (last adm 6.45pm).* **Closed** *1 May.* ♿ ▯ ▯ ▯ ▯ **Museo Carlo Bilotti** *Viale Fiorello La Guardia.* **Map** 2 D5. **Open** *9am–7pm Tue–Sun.* **Closed** *1 Jan, 1 May, 25 Dec.* **Adm charge.** ▯

British School at Rome, designed by Edwin Lutyens in 1911

The villa and its park were designed in 1605 for Cardinal Scipione Borghese, nephew of Pope Paul V. The park was the first of its kind in Rome. It contained 400 newly-planted pine trees, garden sculpture by Bernini's father, Pietro, and dramatic waterworks built by Giovanni Fontana. The layout of the formal gardens was imitated by other prominent Roman families at Villa Ludovisi and Villa Doria Pamphilj.

In the early 19th century Prince Camillo Borghese assembled the family's magnificent art collection in the Casino Borghese, now the home of the Galleria and Museo Borghese.

In 1901 the park became the property of the Italian state. Within its 6-km (4-mile) circumference there are now museums and galleries, foreign academies and schools of archaeology, a zoo, a riding school, a grassy amphitheatre, an artificial lake, an aviary and an array of summer-houses, fountains, Neo-Classical statuary and exotic follies.

There are several ways into the park, including a monumental entrance on Piazzale Flaminio, built for Prince Camillo Borghese in 1825 by Luigi Canina. Other conveniently-sited entrances are at Porta Pinciana at the end of Via Veneto and from the Pincio Gardens *(see p136).*

Piazza di Siena, a pleasantly open, grass-covered amphitheatre surrounded by tall umbrella pines, was the inspiration for Ottorino Respighi's famous symphonic poem *The Pines of Rome,* written in 1924. Near Piazza di Siena are the so-called Casina di Raffaello, said to have been owned by Raphael, and the 18th-century Palazzetto dell' Orologio. These were summerhouses from which people enjoyed the beautiful vistas across the park. Many buildings in the park were

Statue of the English poet Byron by Thorvaldsen

originally surrounded by formal gardens: the Casino Borghese and the nearby 17th-century Casino della Meridiana and its aviary *(uccelliera)* have both kept their geometrical flowerbeds.

Throughout the park the intersections of paths and avenues are marked by fountains and statues. West of Piazza di Siena is the Fontana dei Cavalli Marini (the Fountain of the Seahorses) added during the villa's 18th-century remodelling. Walking through the park you will encounter statues of Byron, Goethe and Victor Hugo, and a gloomy equestrian King Umberto I.

Dotted about the park are picturesque temples made to look like ruins, including a circular Temple of Diana between Piazza di Siena and Porta Pinciana, and a Temple of Faustina, wife of Emperor Antoninus Pius, on the hill north of Piazza di Siena. The nearby medieval-looking Fortezzuola by Canina contains the works of the sculptor Pietro Canonica, who lived in the building and died there in 1959. In the garden stands Canonica's *Monument to the Alpino and his Mule,* which honours the humblest protagonists in Italy's alpine battles against Austria in World War I.

In the centre of the park is the Giardino del Lago, its main entrance marked by an

Neo-Classical Temple of Diana

Ionic temple dedicated to Aesculapius, built on the lake island

of importance is the Palazzina of Pius IV, close to the Via Flaminia entrance, designed by the architect Vignola in 1552. It now houses the Italian embassy to the Holy See.

Named after its principal benefactor, the Museo Carlo Bilotti is situated in the centre of the Villa Borghese. This former orangery has been transformed into a modern art gallery boasting works by Giorgio de Chirico, Andy Warhol and Gino Severini.

Museo e Galleria Borghese ❷

See pp260–61.

Villa Giulia ❸

See pp262–3

MAXXI (National Museum of 21st Century Arts) ❹

Map 1 A2. 🚌 *53, 217, 225, 910.* 🚋 *2.* **Open** *9am–7pm Tue–Sun (11am–10pm Thu).* **Closed** *1 May, 25 Dec.* **Tel** *06-320 2438.* ♿ 🍽 📷 **Adm charge** *(free up to age 14).* 🌐 www.*maxxibeniculturali.it*

Along with the nearby Parco della Musica *(see p358)*, MAXXI, the National Museum of 21st Century Arts, has put Rome on the contemporary arts map. Located in a stunning building designed by architect Zaha Hadid, it showcases emerging Italian and international artists. An impressive amount of space is also given over to architecture.

18th-century copy of the Arch of Septimius Severus. The garden has an artificial lake complete with an Ionic temple to Aesculapius, the god of healing, by the 18th-century architect Antonio Asprucci. Rowing boats and ducks make the lake a favourite with children, banana trees and bamboo grow around the shore, and clearings are studded with sculptures.

Surrounded by flowerbeds south of the lake is the Art Nouveau Fontana dei Fauni, one of the garden's prettiest sculptures. In a clearing close to the entrance on Viale Pietro Canonica are the original Tritons of the Fontana del Moro in Piazza Navona *(see p120)* – they were moved here and replaced by copies in the 19th century.

From the northwest the park is entered by the Viale delle Belle Arti, where the Galleria Nazionale d'Arte Moderna houses a good collection of 19th- and 20th-century paintings. The Art Nouveau character of the area dates from the International Exhibition held here in 1911, for which pavilions were built by many nations, the most

impressive being the British School at Rome, by Edwin Lutyens, with a façade adapted from the upper west portico of St Paul's Cathedral in London. It is now a research institute for Classical studies, history and the visual arts. Nearby statues include one of Simon Bolivar and other liberators of Latin America.

In the northeastern corner of the park lie the Museo Zoologico and a small zoo, the Bioparco, where the emphasis is on conservation. Nearby, the pretty 16th-century Villa Giulia houses a world-famous collection of Etruscan and other pre-Roman remains. Another Renaissance building

MAXXI, the National Museum of 21st Century Arts, designed by Zaha Hadid

Museo e Galleria Borghese ❷

The villa and park were laid out by Cardinal Scipione Borghese, favourite nephew of Paul V, who had the house designed for pleasure and entertainment. The hedonistic cardinal was also an extravagant patron of the arts and he commissioned sculptures from the young Bernini which now rank among his most famous works. Scipione also opened his pleasure park to the public. Today the villa houses the superb private Borghese collection of sculptures and paintings in the Museo and Galleria Borghese.

MUSEUM GUIDE

The museum is divided into two sections: the sculpture collection (Museo Borghese) occupies the entire ground floor and the picture gallery (Galleria Borghese) is on the upper floor. The Galleria Borghese has reopened to the public after extensive restoration work.

Façade of the Villa Borghese
This painting (1613) by the villa's Flemish architect Jan van Santen shows the highly ornate façade of the original design.

★ Rape of Proserpine
One of Bernini's finest works shows Pluto (Hades) abducting his bride. The sculptor's amazing skill with marble can be seen clearly in the twisting figures.

Sleeping Hermaphrodite
This is a marble Roman copy of the Greek original by Polycles, dated around 150 BC. The head and mattress were added by Andrea Bergondi in the 17th century.

The Egyptian Room
Frescoes show episodes in Egyptian history and Egyptian motifs.

TIMELINE

1613 15-year-old Bernini sculpts *Aeneas and Anchises*	**Early 1800s** Statues and reliefs are considered too ornate and stripped from the villa's façade	**1809** Much of the collection is sold by Prince Camillo Borghese to France and goes to Louvre	**1902** Villa, grounds and collection bought by the state
1622–5 Bernini sculpts *The Rape of Proserpine*			
1625	**1725**	**1825**	
1622–5 Bernini sculpts *Apollo and Daphne*		**1805** Canova sculpts the semi-nude, reclining Pauline Borghese	**Early 1900s** Balustrade round the forecourt is bought by Lord Astor for the Cliveden estate in England
1613–15 The Flemish architect Jan van Santen designs and builds Villa Borghese	*Daphne's fingers turning into leaves*		

★ Apollo and Daphne
Bernini's most famous masterpiece depicts the nymph Daphne fleeing the sun god Apollo at the moment of Daphne's dramatic transformation into a tree.

Rear entrance

David is captured the moment before he slays Goliath in the sculpture by Bernini, who modelled his face on his own.

VISITORS' CHECKLIST

Villa Borghese, Piazzale Scipione Borghese 5. **Map** 2 F5.
Tel 06-328 10 (reservations).
52, 53, 116, 910 to Via Pinciana.
3, 19 to Viale delle Belle Arti.
Open 9am–7pm Tue–Sun (last adm 6.30pm). **Closed** 1 Jan, 1 May, 25 Dec. **Adm charge**.
Advance booking recommended weekdays and obligatory Sat, Sun & for special exhibitions.
www.galleriaborghese.it

★ Galleria Borghese
The gallery has old master paintings, such as Titian's Sacred and Profane Love *(detail) dating from 1514.*

★ Pauline Borghese
Napoleon's sister Pauline posed as Venus for this sculpture. Once the statue was finished, her husband locked it away, even from its sculptor Canova.

Front entrance

Gladiator Mosaic
The floor is decorated with the fragments of a 4th-century AD mosaic from a villa in Torrenova.

KEY TO FLOORPLAN
☐ Exhibition space
■ Non-exhibition space

STAR SCULPTURES

★ Rape of Proserpine by Bernini

★ Apollo and Daphne by Bernini

★ Galleria Borghese

★ Pauline Borghese by Canova

Villa Giulia ❸

This villa was built as a country retreat for Pope Julius III, and was designed for entertaining rather than as a permanent home. It once housed an impressive collection of statues – 160 boatloads were sent to the Vatican after the pope died in 1555. The villa, gardens, pavilions and fountains were designed by exceptional architects: Vignola (designer of the Gesù), Vasari and the sculptor Ammannati. Michelangelo also contributed. The villa's main features are its façade, the court-yard and garden and the *nymphaeum*. Since 1889 Villa Giulia has housed the Museo Nazionale Etrusco, with its out-standing collection of pre-Roman antiquities from central Italy.

★ Ficoroni Cist
Engraved and beautifully illustrated, this fine bronze marriage coffer dates from the 4th century BC.

Chigi Vase
Battle and hunting scenes adorn this Corinthian vase from the 6th century BC

★ Sarcophagus of the Spouses
This 6th-century BC masterpiece, from Cerveteri, shows a dead couple at the eternal banquet.

MUSEUM GUIDE

*This is the most important Etruscan museum in Italy, housing artifacts from most of the major exca-vations in Tuscany and Lazio. Rooms **1–10** and **23–34** are arranged by site and include Vulci, Todi, Veio and Cerveteri, while private collections are in rooms **11–22**.*

Votive Offering
The religious Etruscans made artifacts, such as this model of a boy feeding a bird, in their gods' honour.

TIMELINE

1550	1650	1750	1850	1950
1550 Work begins on Villa Giulia under Pope Julius III	**1655** Queen Christina of Sweden stays in villa as Vatican guest	**Late 1700s** First large-scale studies of Etruscan artifacts	**1889** Etruscan museum founded	**1919** Castellani private collection donated to museum
Late 1500s First chance finds of Etruscan artifacts raise some scholastic interest			**1908** Barberini private collection bought by the state	**1972** Pesciotti private collection bought by the state
1555 Villa completed	*Corner decoration of bronze chariot used to burn incense*			

Façade
The villa's façade dates from 1551. The entrance is designed in the form of a triumphal arch.

VISITORS' CHECKLIST

Piazzale di Villa Giulia 9.
Map 1 C4.
Tel 06-322 6571.
🚌 52, 926 to Viale Bruno Buozzi, 88, 95, 490, 495 to Viale Washington.
🚊 3, 19 to Piazza Thorwaldsen.
Open 8.30am–7.30pm Tue–Sun (last adm 6.30pm).
Closed 1 Jan, 25 Dec.
Adm charge.
🎧 with seven days' notice.
🏠 📷 📁 🔊 🚫

★ Reconstruction of an Etruscan Temple
Count Adolfo Cozza built the Temple of Alatri here in 1891. He based his design on the accounts of Vitruvius and 19th-century excavations.

Nymphaeum
Literally, the "area dedicated to the nymphs", this is a sunken courtyard decorated with Classical mosaics, statues and fountains.

STAR EXHIBITS

★ Sarcophagus of the Spouses

★ Ficoroni Cist

★ Reconstruction of an Etruscan Temple

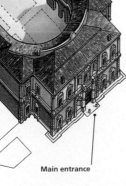

Faliscan Crater of the Dawn
This ornate vase, painted in the free style of the 4th century BC, shows Dawn rising in a chariot.

Main entrance

KEY TO FLOORPLAN

☐ Ground floor

☐ First floor

☐ Non-exhibition space

Museo di Arte Contemporanea di Roma ❺

Via Reggio Emilia 54. **Map** 6 E1.
Tel 06-6710 70400. ▥ 36, 60, 84,
90. **Open** 9am–7pm Tue–Sun.
Adm charge. ▢ ▢
www.macro.roma.museum

The historic Peroni beer factory on Via Reggio Emilia is now home to MACRO, the city's gallery of contemporary art. Apart from a permanent collection of late 20th-century art, featuring artists such as Carla Accardi, Achille Perilli and Mario Schifano, there are interesting exhibitions showcasing the latest developments on the local and national scene.

Interior of Santa Costanza

Santa Costanza ❻

Via Nomentana 349. **Tel** 06-861
0840. ▥ 36, 60, 84, 90. **Open**
9am–noon, 4–6pm Mon–Sat, 4–6pm
Sun. **Adm charge.** ▵ ▨

The round church of Santa Costanza was first built as a mausoleum for Emperor Constantine's daughters Constantia and Helena, in the early 4th century. The dome and its drum are supported by a circular arcade resting on 12 magnificent pairs of granite columns. The ambulatory that runs around the outside of the central arcade has a barrel-

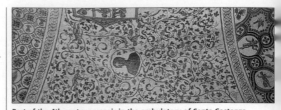

Part of the 4th-century mosaic in the ambulatory of Santa Costanza

vaulted ceiling decorated with wonderful 4th-century mosaics of flora and fauna and charming scenes of a Roman grape harvest. In a niche on the far side of the church from the entrance is a replica of Constantia's ornately carved porphyry sarcophagus. The original was moved to the Vatican Museums in 1790.

Constantia's sanctity is debatable – she was described by the historian Marcellinus as a fury incarnate, constantly goading her equally unpleasant husband Hannibalianus to violence. Her canonization was probably the result of some confusion with a saintly nun of the same name.

Sant'Agnese fuori le Mura ❼

Via Nomentana 349. **Tel** 06-861
0840. ▥ 36, 60, 84, 90.
Open 7.30am–noon, 4–7.45pm
daily. **Adm charge** to catacombs.
▵ ▨

The church of Sant'Agnese stands among a group of early Christian buildings which includes the ruins of

a covered cemetery, some extensive catacombs and the crypt where the 13-year-old martyr St Agnes was buried in AD 304. Agnes was exposed naked by order of Emperor Diocletian, furious that she should have rejected the advances of a young man at his court, but her hair miraculously grew to protect her modesty (see p121).

The church is said to have been built at the request of the Emperor Constantine's daughter, Constantia, after she had prayed at the Tomb of St Agnes for delivery from leprosy.

Though much altered over the centuries, the form and much of the structure of the 4th-century basilica remain intact. In the 7th-century apse mosaic St Agnes appears as a bejewelled Byzantine empress in a stole of gold and a violet robe. According to tradition she appeared like this eight days after her death holding a white lamb. Every year on 21 January two lambs are blessed on the church altar and a vestment called the *pallium* is woven from their wool. Every newly appointed archbishop is sent a *pallium* by the pope.

Apse mosaic in Sant'Agnese, showing the saint flanked by two popes

Cloister, San Lorenzo fuori le Mura

San Lorenzo fuori le Mura ❽

Piazzale del Verano 3. **Tel** 06-49 15 11. ⊟ 71, 492. 🚋 3, 19. **Open** 7.30am–noon, 4–7pm daily. ♿

Just outside the eastern wall of the city stands the church of San Lorenzo. Roasted slowly to death in AD 258, San Lorenzo was one of the most revered of Rome's early Christian martyrs. The first basilica erected over his burial place by Constantine was largely rebuilt in 576 by Pope Pelagius II. Close by stood a 5th-century church dedicated to the Virgin Mary. The intriguing two-level church we see today is the result of these two churches being knocked into one. This process, started in the 8th century, was completed in the 13th century by Pope Honorius III, when the nave, the portico and much of the decoration were added. The remains of San Lorenzo are in the choir of the 6th-century church (beneath the 13th-century high altar).

Romanesque bell tower of San Lorenzo

Via Appia Antica ❾

🚌 118, 218. See **Walks** pp284–5.

The first part of the Via Appia was built in 312 BC by the Censor Appius Claudius Caecus. When it was extended to the ports of Benevento, Taranto and Brindisi in 190 BC, the road became Rome's link with its expanding empire in the East. It was the route taken by the funeral processions of the dictator Sulla (78 BC) and Emperor Augustus (AD 14) and it was along this road that St Paul was led a prisoner to Rome in AD 56. Gradually abandoned during the Middle Ages, the road was restored by Pope Pius IV in the mid-16th century. It is lined with ruined family tombs and collective burial places known as columbaria. Beneath the fields on either side lies a vast maze of catacombs. Today the road starts at Porta San Sebastiano (see p196). Major Christian sights include the church of Domine Quo Vadis, built where St Peter is said to have met Christ while fleeing from Rome, and the Catacombs of San Callisto and San Sebastiano. The tombs lining the road include those of Cecilia Metella (see p266) and Romulus (son of Emperor Maxentius) who died in 309. The ancient Villa dei Quintilli is nearby, at Via Appia Nuova 1092 (phone 06-481 5576).

Catacombs of San Callisto ❿

Via Appia Antica 126. **Tel** 06-5130 1580. 🚌 118, 218. **Open** 9am–noon, 2–5pm Thu–Tue. **Closed** 1 Jan, Feb, Easter Sun & 25 Dec. **Adm charge**. 🔼 🚫 💷 🖵 📷 www.catacombe.roma.it

In burying their dead in underground cemeteries outside the city walls, the early Christians were obeying the laws of the time: it was not because of persecution. So many saints were buried that the catacombs became shrines and places of pilgrimage.

The vast Catacombs of San Callisto are on four different levels and only partly explored.

The rooms and connecting passageways are hewn out of volcanic tufa. The dead were placed in niches, known as *loculi*, which held two or three bodies. The most important rooms were decorated with stucco and frescoes. The area that can be visited includes the Crypt of the Popes, where many of the early popes were buried, and the Crypt of Santa Cecilia, where the saint's body was discovered in 820 before being moved to her church in Trastevere (see p211).

Catacombs of San Sebastiano ⓫

Via Appia Antica 136. **Tel** 06-785 0350. 🚌 118, 218. **Open** 9am–noon, 2–5pm Mon–Sat. **Closed** 1 Jan, mid-Nov–mid-Dec, 25 Dec. **Adm charge.** 🔼 🚫 📷 www.catacombe.org

The 17th-century church of San Sebastiano, above the catacombs, occupies the site of a basilica. Preserved at the entrance to the catacombs is the *triclia*, a building that once stood above ground and was used by mourners for taking funeral refreshments. Its walls are covered with graffiti invoking St Peter and St Paul, whose remains may have been moved here during one of the periods of persecution.

Cypresses lining part of the Roman Via Appia Antica

Catacombs of Domitilla ⑫

Via delle Sette Chiese 282.
Tel 06-511 0342. 🚌 *218, 716.*
Open 9am–noon, 2–5pm Wed–Mon.
Closed first 3 wks Jan, Easter Sun,
25 Dec. Adm charge. 🚫 📷

This network of catacombs is the largest in Rome. Many of the tombs from the 1st and 2nd centuries AD have no Christian connection. In the burial chambers there are frescoes of both Classical and Christian scenes, including one of the earliest depictions of Christ as the *Good Shepherd.* Above the catacombs stands the basilica of Santi Nereo e Achilleo. After rebuilding and restoration, little remains of the original 4th-century church.

Bronze entrance gates to the Fosse Ardeatine by Mirko Basaldella

Fosse Ardeatine ⑬

Via Ardeatina 174. *Tel 06-513 6742.*
🚌 *218, 716. Open 8:15am–3:15pm*
Mon–Fri, 8:15am–4:15pm Sat, Sun.
Closed public hols.

On the evening of 24 March 1944, Nazi forces took 335 prisoners to this abandoned quarry south of Rome and shot them at point blank range. The execution was in reprisal for a bomb attack that had killed 32 German soldiers. The victims included various political prisoners, 73 Jews and ten other civilians, among them a priest and a 14-year-old boy. The Germans blew up the tunnels where the massacre had taken place, but a local peasant had witnessed the scene and later helped

find the corpses. The site is now a memorial to the values of the Resistance against the Nazi occupation, which gave birth to the modern Italian Republic *(see p185).* A forbidding bunker-like monument houses the rows of identical tombs containing the victims.

Beside it is a museum of the Resistance. Interesting works of modern sculpture include *The Martyrs,* by Francesco Coccia, and the gates shaped like a wall of thorns by Mirko Basaldella.

Tomb of Cecilia Metella ⑭

Via Appia Antica, km 3. *Tel 06-3996*
7700. 🚌 *118, 660. Open 9am–1 hr*
before sunset Tue–Sun.

One of the most famous landmarks on the Via Appia Antica is the huge drum-shaped tomb built for the noblewoman Cecilia Metella. Her father and husband were rich patricians and successful generals of late Republican Rome, but hardly anything is known about the woman herself. Byron muses over her unknown destiny in his poem *Childe Harold.*

In 1302 Pope Boniface VIII donated the tomb to his family, the Caetani. They incorporated it in a fortified castle that blocked the Via Appia, allowing them to control the traffic on the road and exact high tolls.

The marble facing of the tomb was pillaged by another pope, Sixtus V, at the end of the 16th century.

Fragments of marble relief on the Tomb of Cecilia Metella

EUR's Palazzo della Civiltà del Lavoro, the "Square Colosseum"

EUR ⑮

🚌 *170, 671, 714 and other routes .*
Ⓜ *EUR Fermi, EUR Palasport.* **Museo della Civiltà Romana** Piazza G.
Agnelli 10. *Tel 06-5422 0919. Open*
9am–2pm Tue–Sat (to 1:30pm Sun);
last adm: 1 hr before closing. Closed
1 Jan, 1 May, 25 Dec. Adm charge.

The Esposizione Universale di Roma (EUR), a suburb south of the city, was built for an international exhibition, a kind of "Work Olympics", that was planned for 1942, but never took place because of the war. The architecture was intended to glorify Fascism and the style of the public buildings is very overblown and rhetorical. The eerie shape of the Palazzo della Civiltà del Lavoro (The Palace of the Civilization of Work) is an unmistakable landmark for people arriving from Fiumicino airport.

The scheme was completed in the 1950s. In terms of town planning, EUR has been quite successful and people are still keen to live here. The great marble halls house several government offices and museums.

The Museo della Civiltà Romana displays a vast scale model of Rome at the time of Constantine and casts of the reliefs on Trajan's Column. These, and the interesting planetarium, make the museum well worth a visit.

To the south is a lake and park, and the huge domed Palazzo dello Sport built for the 1960 Olympics.

San Paolo fuori le Mura 16

Via Ostiense 186. **Tel** 06-541 0341.
23, 128, 170, 670, 707, 761,
769. M San Paolo. **Open** 7am–
6.30pm daily. **Cloister** 9am–6pm
daily

Today's church is a faithful
reconstruction of the great
4th-century basilica destroyed
by fire on 15 July 1823. Few
fragments of the original
church survived. The triumphal arch over the nave is
decorated on one side with
restored 5th-century mosaics.
On the other side are mosaics
by Pietro Cavallini, originally
on the façade. The splendid
Venetian apse mosaics (1220)
depict the figures of Christ
with St Peter, St Andrew, St
Paul and St Luke.

The fine marble canopy
over the high altar is signed
by the sculptor Arnolfo di
Cambio (1285) "together
with his partner Pietro",
who may have been Pietro
Cavallini. Below the altar is
the *confesso*, the tomb of
St Paul. To the right is an
impressive Paschal candlestick by Nicolò di Angelo
and Pietro Vassalletto.

The cloister of San Paolo,
with its pairs of colourful

19th-century mosaic on façade of San Paolo fuori le Mura

inlaid columns supporting
the arcade, was spared
completely by the fire.
Completed around 1214, it
is considered one of the
most beautiful in Rome.

Centrale Montemartini 17

Via Ostiense 106. **Tel** 06-574 8042.
769, 23. **Open** 9am–7pm Tue–
Sun (last adm. 6.30pm). **Closed** public
hols. **Adm charge.**

An enormous old industrial
site has been restored to
house the ACEA art centre.
Originally, the building was
used as Rome's first power

station and its two huge
generators still occupy the
central machine room
creating quite an intriguing
contrast to the exhibitions.
On display are Roman statues
and artifacts belonging to the
Capitoline Museums *(see
pp70–73)*. Many of the statues
were discovered during
excavations in the late 19th
and early 20th centuries but
were kept in storage until
fairly recently.

**Casino del Bel Respiro, summer
residence in Villa Doria Pamphilj**

Villa Doria Pamphilj 18

Via di San Pancrazio. 31, 44,
75, 710, 870. **Park** open dawn–
dusk daily.

One of Rome's largest public
parks, the Villa Doria Pamphilj was laid out in the mid-
17th century for Prince
Camillo Pamphilj. His uncle,
Pope Innocent X, paid for the
magnificent summer resi-
dence, the Casino del Bel
Respiro, and the fountains
and summerhouses, some of
which still survive.

Statue in Centrale Montemartini, former power plant turned art centre

Day Trips around Rome

Tivoli, a favourite place to escape the heat of the Roman summer

Tivoli ⑲

Town is 31 km (20 miles) northeast of Rome. **FS** *from Tiburtina.* ▣ *COTRAL from Ponte Mammolo (on Metro line B).*

Tivoli has been a popular summer resort since the days of the Roman Republic. Among the famous men who owned villas here were the poets Catullus and Horace, Caesar's assassins Brutus and Cassius, and the Emperors Trajan and Hadrian. Tivoli's main attractions were its clean air and beautiful situation on the slopes of the Tiburtini hills, its healthy sulphur springs and the waterfalls of the Aniene – the Emperor Augustus said these had cured him of insomnia. The Romans' luxurious lifestyle was revived in Renaissance times by the owners of the Villa d'Este, the town's most famous sight.

Detail of Fontana dell'Organo at Villa d'Este

In the Middle Ages Tivoli suffered frequent invasions as its position made it an ideal base for an advance on Rome. In 1461 Pope Pius II built a fortress here, the Rocca Pia, declaring: "It is easier to regain Rome while possessing Tivoli, than to regain Tivoli while possessing Rome."

After suffering heavy bomb-damage in 1944, Tivoli's main buildings and churches were speedily restored. The town's cobbled streets are still lined with medieval houses. The Duomo (cathedral) houses a beautiful 13th-century life-size wooden group representing the *Deposition from the Cross.*

Villa d'Este ⑳

Piazza Trento 5, Tivoli. **Tel** *0774-31 2070.* ▣ *COTRAL from Ponte Mammolo (on Metro line B).* **Open** *8.30am–1 hr before sunset Tue–Sun.* **Closed** *1 Jan, 1 May, 25 Dec.* **Adm charge.** ▣ www.villadestetivoli.info

The villa occupies the site of an old Benedictine convent. In the 16th century the estate was developed by Cardinal Ippolito d'Este, son of Lucrezia Borgia. A palace was designed by Pirro Ligorio to make the most of its hilltop situation, but the villa's fame rests more on the terraced gardens and fountains laid out by Ligorio and Giacomo della Porta.

The gardens have suffered neglect in the past, but the grottoes and fountains still give a vivid impression of the great luxury which the princes of the church enjoyed. From the great loggia of the palace you descend through the privet-lined paths to the Grotto of Diana and Bernini's Fontana del Bicchierone. Below to the right is the Rometta (little Rome), a model of Tiber Island with allegorical figures

and the legendary she-wolf. The Rometta is at one end of the Viale delle Cento Fontane, 100 fountains in the shapes of grotesques, obelisks, ships and the eagles of the d'Este coat of arms. Other fountains are now being restored to their former glory. The Fontana dell'Organo is a water-organ, in which the force of the water pumps air through the pipes. The garden's lowest level has flower beds and fountains as well as some splendid views out over the plain below.

Terrace of 100 Fountains in the gardens of Villa d'Este

Villa Gregoriana ㉑

Largo Sant'Angelo, Tivoli. **FS** ▣ *Tivoli, then short walk.* **Tel** *06-3996 7701.* **Open** *10am–6.30pm Tue–Sun (to 2.30pm Mar, 16 Oct–30 Nov).* **Closed** *Dec–Feb.* ▣ ▣

The main attractions of this steeply sloping park are the waterfalls and grottoes created by the River Aniene. The park is named after Pope Gregory XVI, who in the 1830s ordered the building of a tunnel to ward against flooding. When the tunnel was completed, it created a new waterfall, called the Grande Cascata, which plunges 160 m (525 ft) into the valley behind the town.

The Canopus, extensively restored, with replicas of its original caryatids lining the bank of the canal

Hadrian's Villa ②

Villa Adriana, Via Tiburtina. Site is 6 km (4 miles) southwest of Tivoli.
Tel 0774-53 02 03. **FS** Tivoli, then local bus No. 4. **=** COTRAL from Ponte Mammolo (on Metro line B).
Open 9am–1 hr before sunset daily (last adm 1 hour before). **Closed** 1 Jan, 1 May, 25 Dec. **Adm charge**.

Built as a private summer retreat between AD 118 and 134, Hadrian's Villa was a vast open-air museum of the finest architecture of the Roman world. The grounds of the Imperial palace covered an area of 120 hectares (300 acres) and were filled with full-scale reproductions of the emperor's favourite buildings from Greece and Egypt. Although excavations on this site began in the 16th century, many of the ruins lying scattered in the surrounding fields have yet to be identified with any

certainty. The grounds of the villa make a very picturesque site for a picnic, with scattered fragments of columns lying among olive trees and cypresses.

For an idea of how the whole complex would have looked in its heyday, study the scale model in the building beside the car park. The most important buildings are signposted and several have been partially restored or reconstructed. One of the most impressive is the so-called Maritime Theatre. This is a round pool with an island in the middle, surrounded by columns. The island, reached by means of a swing bridge, was probably Hadrian's private studio, where he withdrew from the cares of the Empire to indulge in his two favourite pastimes, painting and architecture. There were also theatres, Greek and Latin libraries, two bathhouses, extensive housing for guests and the palace staff, and formal gardens with fountains, statues and pools.

Hadrian also loved Greek philosophy. One part of the gardens is thought to have been Hadrian's reproduction of the Grove of Academe,

Fragment of marble mosaic pavement in the Imperial palace

where Plato lectured to his students. He also had a replica made of the Stoà Poikile, a beautiful painted colonnade in Athens, from which the Stoic philosophers took their name. This copy enclosed a great piazza with a central pool. The so-called Hall of the Philosophers close to the Poikile was probably a library.

The most ambitious of Hadrian's replicas was the Canopus, a sanctuary of the god Serapis near Alexandria. For this a canal 119 metres (130 yards) long was dug and Egyptian statues were imported to decorate the temple and its grounds. This impressive piece of engineering has been restored and the banks of the canal are lined with caryatids.

Another picturesque spot in the grounds is the Vale of Tempe, the legendary haunt of the goddess Diana with a stream representing the river

Pair of Ionic columns in the vaulted baths of Hadrian's Villa

Peneios. Below ground the emperor even built a fanciful recreation of the underworld, Hades, reached through underground tunnels, of which there were many linking the various parts of the villa.

Plundered by barbarians who camped here in the 6th and 8th centuries, the villa fell into disrepair. Its marble was burned to make lime for cement and Renaissance antiquarians contributed even further to its destruction. Statues unearthed in the grounds are on show in museums around Europe. The Vatican's Egyptian Collection (see p238) has many fine works that were found here.

Ostia Antica

Viale dei Romagnoli 717. Site is 25
km (16 miles) southwest of Rome.
Tel 06-5635 8099. **M** *Piramide, then
train from Porta San Paolo station.*
Excavations and museum open
*8.30am–6pm Tue–Sun (to 4pm
Nov–Feb, to 5pm Mar).* **Closed**
1 Jan, 25 Dec. **Adm charge.** ◻ ◻
♿ www.ostiantica.info

In Republican times Ostia
was Rome's main commercial
port and a military base
defending the coastline and
the mouth of the Tiber. The
port continued to flourish
under the Empire, despite
the development of Portus,
a new port slightly to the
northwest, in the 2nd century
AD. Ostia's decline began in
the 4th century, when a
reduction in trade was combined with the gradual silting
up of the harbour. Then
malaria became endemic in
the area and the city, whose
population may have been
nearly 100,000 at its peak,
was totally abandoned.

Buried for centuries by
sand, the city is remarkably
well preserved. The site is
less spectacular than Pompeii
or Herculaneum because
Ostia died a gradual death,
but it gives a more complete
picture of life under the
Roman Empire. People of all
social classes and from all
over the Mediterranean lived
and worked here.

Visitors can understand
the layout of Ostia's streets
almost at a glance. The main
road through the town, the
Decumanus Maximus, would
have been filled with hurrying
slaves and citizens, avoiding
the jostling carriages and
carts, while tradesmen

Ruins of shops, offices and houses near Ostia's theatre

pursued their business under
the porticoes lining the street.
The floorplans of the public
buildings along the road are
very clear. Many were bathhouses, such as the Baths of
the Cisiarii (carters) and the
grander Baths of Neptune,
named after their fine black-
and-white floor mosaics.
Beside the restored theatre,
three large masks, originally part of the decoration of
the stage, have been mounted on large blocks of tufa.
Beneath the great brick
arches that supported the
semicircular tiers of seats
were taverns and shops.
Classical plays are put on
here in the summer.

The Tiber's course has
changed considerably since
Ostia was the port of Rome. It
once flowed past just to the
north of Piazzale delle

**Mask decorating
the theatre**

Corporazioni, the square
behind the theatre. The
corporations were the guilds
of the various trades involved
in fitting out and
supplying ships:
tanners and rope-
makers, ship-
builders and
timber merchants,
ships' chandlers
and corn weighers.
There were some
60 or 70 offices
around the square.
Mosaics showing
scenes of everyday
life in the port and
the names and
symbols of the
corporations can
still be seen.

There were also offices used
by ship-owners and their
agents from places as far
apart as Tunisia and the south
of France, Sardinia and Egypt.
In one office, belonging to
a merchant from the town
of Sabratha in North Africa,
there is a delightful mosaic
of an elephant.

The main cargo coming into
Rome was grain from Africa.
Much of this was distributed
free to prevent social unrest.
Although only men received
this *annona* or corn dole,
at times over 300,000 were
eligible. In the centre of the
square was a temple, probably

Mural from Ostia of merchant ship being loaded with grain

dedicated to Ceres, goddess of the harvest. Among the buildings excavated are many large warehouses in which grain was stored before it was shipped on to Rome.

The Decumanus leads to the Forum and the city's principal temple, erected by Hadrian in the 2nd century AD and dedicated to Jove, Juno and Minerva. In this rather romantic, lonely spot, it is hard to imagine the Forum as a bustling centre, where justice was dispensed and officials

Floor mosaic of Nereid and sea monster in the House of the Dioscuri

Detail of floor mosaic in the Piazzale delle Corporazioni

met to discuss the city's affairs. In the 18th century it was used as a sheepfold.

Away from the main street are the buildings where Ostia's inhabitants lived. The great majority were housed in rented apartments in blocks three or four storeys high known as *insulae*. These varied considerably in their comfort and decoration. The House of Diana was one of the smarter ones, with a balcony around the second floor, a private bathhouse and a central courtyard with a cistern where tenants came to collect their water. Around the ground floor of the block were shops, taverns and bars selling snacks and drinks. In the bar at the House of Diana you can see the marble counter used by customers buying their sausages and hot wine sweetened with honey.

For the wealthy there were detached houses *(domus)* such as the House of the Dioscuri, which has fine mosaics, and the House of Cupid and Psyche, named after a statue there. This is now in the site's Museo Ostiense, near the Forum, along with other sculptures and reliefs found in Ostia.

Among the houses and shops there are other fascinating buildings including a laundry and the firemen's barracks. The religions practised in Ostia reflect the cosmopolitan nature of the port. There are also no fewer than 18 temples dedicated to the Persian god Mithras, as well as a Jewish synagogue dating from the 1st century AD and a Christian basilica. A plaque records the death of St Augustine's mother in a hotel here in AD 387.

ALSO WORTH SEEING

Anagni FS *from Termini (c.60 min), then local bus (infrequent) or long walk.*
Picturesque hill-town with papal palace and famous cathedral.

Bracciano FS *from Ostiense (c.70 min).* 🚌 *from Lepanto, on Metro line A (bus c.90 min).*
Volcanic lake with villages and wooded hills. Nice for walks or a visit to Orsini Castle. Swimming in summer.

Cerveteri FS *from Termini, Tiburtina or Ostiense to Cerveteri-Ladispoli, then local bus (c.70 min).* 🚌 *from Lepanto, on Metro line A (bus c.80 min).*
One of the greatest Etruscan cities. Necropolis with complete streets and houses.

Nemi 🚌 *from Anagnina, on Metro line A (bus c.60 min).*
Charming village at volcanic lake in the Castelli Romani. Famous for its wine and strawberries.

Palestrina 🚌 *from Anagnina, on Metro line A (bus c.70 min).*
Impressive Roman sanctuary to goddess Fortuna. Museum and the Mosaic of the Nile.

Pompeii FS *to Naples, then change to local train (c.130 min).* 🚌 *Special bus tours from tourist agents.*
Excavations of the wealthy and bustling Roman city where the busy daily life was put to a sudden end by the eruption of Vesuvius in AD 79.

Subiaco 🚌 *from Ponte Mammolo, on Metro line B (bus c.110 min).*
Birthplace of St Benedict. Two monasteries to visit.

Tarquinia FS *from Termini or Ostiense plus local bus (c.100 min).* 🚌 *from Lepanto, on Metro line A. Change at Civitavecchia (c.150 min).*
Outstanding collection of Etruscan objects and frescoes from Tarquinia's necropolis.

Viterbo FS *from Ostiense (c.110 min) or train from Roma Nord, Piazzale Flaminio, on Metro line A (c.120 min).* 🚌 *from Saxa Rubra reached by the train above (bus c.90 min).*
Medieval quarter, papal palace and archaeological museum within 13th-century walls.

NINE GUIDED WALKS

Rome is an excellent city for walking. The distances between major sights in the historic centre are easily covered on foot and many streets are pedestrianized. When you get tired, there are plenty of pavement cafés in wonderful settings, such as Piazza Navona and Campo de' Fiori. If you are interested in archaeology, then a walk across the Forum *(see pp76–87)* and over the Palatine *(see pp96–101)* takes you away from the roaring traffic of modern Rome to a different world of scattered ruins and shady pine trees.

The first of the nine suggested walks takes in picturesque quarters on either side of the Tiber. The second walk, along the perfectly straight Via Giulia, gives a vivid impression of the Renaissance city. The next

Bernini angel on Ponte Sant'Angelo

three walks each follow a particular theme. You can savour the glory of ancient Rome through the triumphal arches of the emperors, tour early Christian churches with well-preserved mosaics and explore the great contribution of Bernini to the appearance of the city.

The sixth walk is outside the centre along the best-known of all Roman roads, the Via Appia Antica, parts of which are still intact after more than 2,000 years of use.

The seventh walk explores some macabre points of interest, including a park said to be haunted by the emperor Nero. The next couples Trastevere's atmospheric backstreets with the romantic viewpoints of the Janiculum. Lastly, there is a tour of churches and ancient ruins on and around the tranquil, leafy Aventine.

CHOOSING A WALK

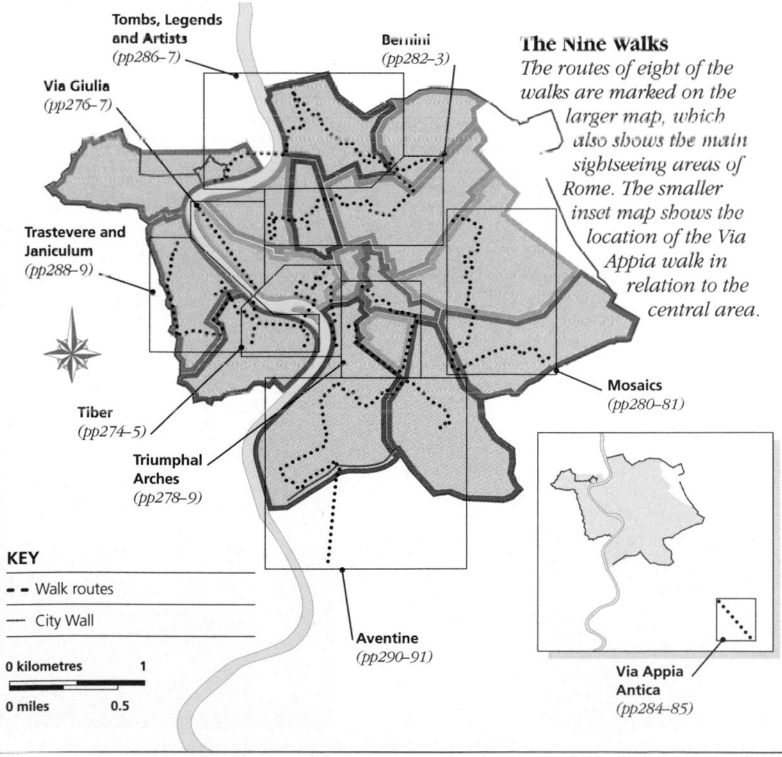

Tombs, Legends and Artists
(pp286–7)

Via Giulia
(pp276–7)

Bernini
(pp282–3)

Trastevere and Janiculum
(pp288–9)

The Nine Walks
The routes of eight of the walks are marked on the larger map, which also shows the main sightseeing areas of Rome. The smaller inset map shows the location of the Via Appia walk in relation to the central area.

Tiber
(pp274–5)

Triumphal Arches
(pp278–9)

Mosaics
(pp280–81)

KEY

- - Walk routes

— City Wall

| 0 kilometres | 1 |
| 0 miles | 0.5 |

Aventine
(pp290–91)

Via Appia Antica
(pp284–85)

◁ **Pedestrians strolling across Ponte Sant'Angelo**

A Two-Hour Walk by the River Tiber

Rome owes its very existence to the Tiber; the city grew up around an easy fording point where a market place developed. The river could also be a hazard; shallow and torrent-like, it flooded the city every winter up to 1870, when work began on the massive Lungotevere embankments that run along both sides of the river. These provide many fine views from points along their avenues of plane trees. The walk also explores the neighbourhoods along the riverside, in particular the Jewish Ghetto and Trastevere, which have preserved much of their character from earlier periods in the colourful history of Rome.

Santa Maria in Cosmedin ①

From the old port of Rome to Via dei Funari

Starting from the church of Santa Maria in Cosmedin ① *(see p202)*, cross the piazza to the Temples of the Forum Boarium ② *(see p203)*. This was the cattle market that stood near the city's river port. The river here has preserved two less obvious structures from ancient Rome: the mouth of the Cloaca Maxima ③, the city's great sewer, and one arch of a ruined bridge, known as the Ponte Rotto ④. In Via Petroselli stands the rather extraordinary medieval Casa dei Crescenzi ⑤ *(see p203)*, decorated with fragments of Roman temples. Passing the modern Anagrafe (public records office) ⑥, built on the site of the old Roman port, you come to San Nicola in Carcere ⑦ *(see p151)*.

You are now in the Foro Olitorio, Rome's ancient vegetable market. To the east stand the ruins of a Roman portico and the medieval house of the Pierleoni family. Head for the massive Theatre

of Marcellus ⑧ *(see p151)*, and look for the three Corinthian columns of the Temple of Apollo beside it. Turn into Piazza Campitelli and walk up to Santa Maria in Campitelli ⑨ *(see p151)*. The church honours a miraculous image of the Virgin credited with halting the plague in 1656. The 16th-century piazza was the home of Flaminio Ponzio, its architect, who lived at No. 6. Take Via dei Delfini to Piazza Margana where you should look up at the 14th-century tower of the Margani family ⑩. Retrace your steps, then go up Via dei Funari (Street of the Ropemakers) to the 16th-century façade of Santa Caterina dei Funari ⑪.

The Ghetto

From Piazza Lov-atelli take Via Sant'Angelo in Pescheria, which

leads to the ruined Portico of Octavia ⑫ *(see p152)* in the Jewish Ghetto *(see p152)*. The Roman portico, once Rome's fish market, houses the church of Sant'Angelo in Pescheria. Find the marble plaque on the façade: fish longer than this slab were given to the city's *conservatori* (governors). Turn into the Ghetto: two column stumps belonging to the Portico stand in front of a patched-up doorway made of fragments of Roman sculpture. The cramped buildings and streets around Via del Portico

Arch of the Ponte Rotto ④

Main altar of Santa Maria in Campitelli ⑨

d'Ottavia are typical of old Rome: see the Casa di Lorenzo Manilio ⑬ (see p152), and turn down Via del Progresso, past Palazzo Cenci ⑭ (see p152), towards the river. On Lungotevere walk past the Synagogue ⑮ (see p152) to the small church of San Gregorio ⑯. Here stood the Ghetto's gates, which were locked at sundown.

Across the river to Trastevere

Crossing to Tiber Island (see p153) by Ponte Fabricio, with its two ancient

Classical relief of Medusa above the doorway of Palazzo Cenci ⑭

much of the spirit of old Trastevere. Walk up to the start of Viale di Trastevere at Piazza Belli. After crossing the road

Santa Maria in Trastevere, don't miss the old-fashioned chemist's shop at No. 7. The piazza itself, in front of the magnificent church of Santa Maria in Trastevere ㉒ (see pp212–13), has a cheerful atmosphere, and the fountain steps are a favourite meeting place. Go back a little way to Via del Moro. This leads to Piazza Trilussa, dominated by the fountain of the Acqua Paola ㉓, where you emerge on to the bank of the river again. Note the lifelike statue, near the fountain, of Roman poet Trilussa, who wrote in the local dialect. From Ponte Sisto ㉔ (see p210), look back to Tiber Island and, beyond it, to the medieval bell tower of Santa Maria in Cosmedin, set against the pine trees on the summit of the Palatine.

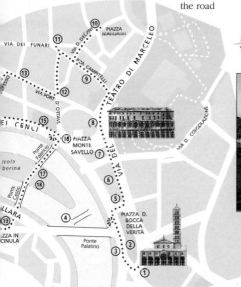

The western tip of Tiber Island

0 metres	250
0 yards	250

stone heads on the parapet, you can enjoy a good view of the river in both directions. On the island itself, you should not miss the Pierleoni Tower ⑰ or the church of San Bartolomeo all'Isola ⑱.

Trastevere

As you cross into Trastevere, you can see the medieval house of the powerful Mattei family ⑲, with its fragments of ancient sculpture. Beyond it, Piazza in Piscinula and the surrounding streets retain

look back at the medieval tower of the Anguillara ⑳ and the statue honouring the poet Gioacchino Belli ㉑ (see p209). As you go down Via della Lungaretta to Piazza

Piazza in Piscinula, old Trastevere

KEY

• • • Walk route

🔆 Good viewing point

TIPS FOR WALKERS

Starting point: Piazza della Bocca della Verità.
Length: 3.5 km (2 miles).
Getting there: The 23, 44, 81, 160, 280, 628, 715 and 716 buses stop near Santa Maria in Cosmedin.
Best time for walk: This walk can be very romantic in the evening but is enjoyable at any time.
Stopping-off points: Piazza Campitelli and Piazza Margana have elegant Roman restaurants, and Via del Portico d'Ottavia has restaurants and a bakery. Tiber Island has a bar and the famous Sora Lella restaurant (see p320). In Viale Trastevere there are bars and pizzerias. Piazza Santa Maria in Trastevere has lively bars and restaurants with outdoor tables.

A One-Hour Walk along Via Giulia

Laid out by Bramante for Pope Julius II in the early 16th century, Via Giulia was one of the first Renaissance streets to slice through Rome's jumble of medieval alleys. The original plan included new law courts in a central piazza, but this project was abandoned for lack of cash. The street now is dominated by antiques shops and furniture restorers. On summer evenings, hundreds of oil lamps light the street while cloisters and courtyards provide romantic settings for a special season of concerts.

Baroque capital on the façade of Sant'Eligio degli Orefici ⑦

From Lungotevere to Largo della Moretta

Starting from Lungotevere dei Tebaldi ① at the eastern end of Via Giulia, you will see ahead of you an archway ② spanning the road. This was the start of Michelangelo's unrealized project linking Palazzo Farnese and its gardens (see p147) with the Villa Farnesina (see pp220–21) on the other side of the river.

Just before you reach the archway, you will see to your left the curious Fontana del Mascherone ③, in which an ancient grotesque mask and granite basin were combined to create a Baroque fountain.

Beyond the Farnese archway on the left is the lively Baroque façade of the church of Santa Maria dell'Orazione e Morte ④ (see p147). A bit further along on the same side of the road stands Palazzo Falconieri ⑤, enlarged by Borromini in 1650. Note its two stone falcons glowering at each other across the width of the façade. On the other side of the road you pass the yellowish façade of Santa Caterina da Siena ⑥, church of the Sienese colony in Rome, which has pretty 18th-century reliefs. The figures of Romulus and Remus symbolize

Relief of Romulus and Remus on Santa Caterina da Siena ⑥

Rome and Siena – there is a legend that the city of Siena was founded by the less fortunate of the twins. After passing the short street that leads down to Sant'Eligio degli Orefici ⑦ (see p148) and the façade of Palazzo Ricci ⑧ (see p149), you come to an area of half-demolished buildings around the ruined church of San Filippo Neri ⑨, called Vicolo della Moretta. If you look to the left down to the river, you

Fontana del Mascherone ③

can see Ponte Mazzini and the huge prison of Regina Coeli on the other side of the Tiber. At this point you may like to make a small detour to the right to the beginning of Via del Pellegrino, where there is an inscription ⑩, defining the *pomerium*, or boundary, of the city in the time of the Emperor Claudius.

From Largo della Moretta to the Sofas of Via Giulia

Further on, facing the narrow Vicolo del Malpasso are the imposing prisons, the Carceri

Nuove ⑪, built by Pope Innocent X Pamphilj in 1655. When first opened, they were a model of humane treatment of prisoners, but were replaced by the Regina Coeli prison across the river at the end of the 19th century. The buildings now house offices of the Ministry of Justice and a small Museum of Crime.

At the corner of Via del Gonfalone, a small side street running down to the river,

KEY

• • • Walk route

☆ Good viewing point

| 0 metres | 250 |
| 0 yards | 250 |

Farnese archway across Via Giulia, built to a design by Michelangelo ②

Plaque honouring Antonio da Sangallo on Palazzo Sacchetti ⑮

the traditional distribution of bread to the poor that took place on the saint's feast day.

On the corner there are more travertine blocks belonging to the foundations of Julius II's projected law courts, known because of their curious shape as the "Sofas of Via Giulia".

The Florentine Quarter

Your next stop should be the imposing Palazzo Sacchetti at No. 66 ⑮. Originally this was the house of Antonio da Sangallo the Younger, the architect of Palazzo Farnese, but it was greatly enlarged by later owners. The porticoed courtyard houses a 15th-century Madonna and a striking Roman relief of the 3rd century AD. Just opposite Palazzo Sacchetti, note the beautiful late Renaissance portal of Palazzo Donarelli ⑯. The 16th-century house at No. 93 is richly decorated with stuccoes and coats of arms ⑰. No. 85 is another typical Renaissance palazzo with a heavily rusticated ground floor ⑱. There is a tradition

that, like many houses of the period, it once belonged to Raphael. Palazzo Clarelli ⑲ was built by Antonio da Sangallo the Younger as his own house. The inscription above the doorway bears the name of Duke Cosimo II de' Medici, whose family later bought the palazzo.

This whole area used to be inhabited by a flourishing Florentine colony, which had its own water-mills built on pontoons along the Tiber. Their national church is San Giovanni dei Fiorentini ⑳ (see p153), the final great landmark at the end of Via Giulia. Many Florentine artists and architects had a hand in its design, including Sangallo and Jacopo Sansovino.

Coat of arms of Pope Paul III Farnese on the façade of Via Giulia No. 93 ⑰

you can see part of the foundations of Julius II's planned law courts. Just down the street stands the small Oratorio di Santa Lucia del Gonfalone ⑫, which is often used for concerts.

The next interesting façade is Carlo Rainaldi's 17th-century Santa Maria del Suffragio ⑬ on the left. On the same side is San Biagio degli Armeni ⑭, the Armenian church in Rome. It is often referred to by local people as San Biagio della Pagnotta (of the loaf of bread). The nickname originates from

Detail on the side of the door of Santa Maria del Suffragio ⑬

TIPS FOR WALKERS

Starting point: Lungotevere dei Tebaldi, by Ponte Sisto.
Length: 1 km (1,100 yds).
Getting there: The 116 goes to and along Via Giulia, or you can take 46, 62 or 64 to Corso Vittorio Emanuele II, then walk down Via dei Pettinari, or take a 23 or 280 along Lungotevere.
Best time for walk: On summer evenings oil lamps light the street. At Christmas, there are cribs on display in many shop windows.
Stopping-off points: There are bars in Via Giulia, at Nos. 18 and 84. Campo de' Fiori has better bars, with outdoor tables, and a wide choice of places to eat. These include a fried fish restaurant in Piazza Santa Barbara dei Librai (closed Sun).

A 90-Minute Tour of Rome's Triumphal Arches

Rome's greatest gift to architecture was the arch, and the Roman people's highest tribute to its victorious generals was the triumphal arch. In Imperial times, arches were erected to honour an emperor's campaign victories almost as a matter of course, promoting his personal cult and ensuring his subsequent deification. Spectacular processions passed through these arches. Conquering generals, cheered by rapturous crowds, rode in their chariots to the Capitol, accompanied by their legions bearing spoils from their campaigns.

Part of the Via Sacra, once spanned by the Arch of Augustus ③

Arches of the Forum

This walk through the Forum and around the base of the Palatine takes in Rome's three great surviving triumphal arches and two arches of more

Relief of barbarian captives on the Arch of Septimius Severus ①

humble design that were used simply as places of business. It starts from the Arch of

TIPS FOR WALKERS

Starting point: The Roman Forum, entrance Largo Romolo e Remo, on Via dei Fori Imperiali.
Length: 2.5 km (1.5 miles).
Getting there: The nearest Metro station is Colosseo on line B. Buses 84, 85, 87, 117, 175, 186, 810, 850 stop in Via dei Fori Imperiali, near Forum entrance.
Best time for walk: Any time of day during Forum opening hours (see p82) is suitable.
Stopping-off points: Several bars and restaurants overlook the Colosseum. There is a small bar in Via dei Cerchi and a smarter one behind San Giorgio in Velabro, in Piazza San Giovanni Decollato (closed Sun). For a meal, try Alvaro al Circo Massimo (closed Mon) in Via di San Teodoro.

Emperor Septimius Severus ① and his sons Geta and Caracalla (see p83) in the Forum. Erected in AD 203, it celebrates a successful campaign in the Middle East. Eight years later, when Caracalla had his brother killed, all mention of Geta was removed from the inscription.

Look up at the reliefs showing phases of the campaigns. Set in tiers, they are probably the sculptural counterparts of the paintings illustrating the general's feats that were borne aloft in the triumphal procession. On the right, the inhabitants of a fortified city surrender to the Romans' siege machines. Below are smaller friezes showing the triumphal procession itself.

Heading east, make your way through the Forum to the ruins of the Temple of Julius Caesar ②. The temple was built by Augustus in 29 BC, on the site where Caesar's body was cremated after Mark Antony's famous funerary oration. A nearby sign marks the ruins of one of the arches dedicated to Augustus ③, spanning the Via Sacra between the Temple of Castor and Pollux ④ (see p84) and the Temple of Caesar. This arch, erected after Augustus had defeated Mark Antony and Cleopatra, was finally demolished in 1545, and its

Capital from Temple of Castor and Pollux ④

materials were used in the new St Peter's. From here, proceed uphill towards the elegant Arch of Titus ⑤ (see p87). Compared with Septimius Severus's arch, it shows an earlier, simpler style. Look up at the beautiful lettering of the inscription before

KEY

· · · Walk route

⅍ Good viewing point

Ⓜ Metro station

0 metres   250
0 yards   250

Arch of Titus in a 19th-century watercolour by the English artist Thomas Hartley Cromek ⑤

excavated in the 18th and 19th centuries. Many of the carts that passed through the arch would have been carrying building materials quarried from the Forum's many ruined monuments.

Arch of Constantine

Leave the Forum by heading down the hill towards the Colosseum ⑥ (see pp92–5) and the nearby Arch of Constantine ⑦ (see p91.) This arch, hastily built to commemorate the emperor's victory over his rival Maxentius in AD 312, is a patchwork of reliefs from different periods. Stand on the Via di San Gregorio side and compare

Arches of Domitian's extension to the Claudian Aqueduct ⑨

you examine the inner bas-reliefs. These show Roman legionaries carrying the spoils looted from the conquest of Jerusalem, heralds holding plaques with the names of vanquished peoples and cities, and Titus riding in triumph in his chariot.

The medieval Frangipane family turned the Colosseum into a vast impregnable stronghold and incorporated the Arch of Titus into their fortifications. Notice the wheelmarks scratched on the inside walls of the arch by generations of carts; they indicate the steady rise in the level of the Forum floor before it was eventually

the earlier panels at the top (AD 180–193) with the hectic battle scenes just above the smaller arches, sculpted in AD 315. In the curious dwarf-like soldiers, you can see the transition from Classicism to a cruder medieval style of sculpture.

Now take Via di San Gregorio, which runs the length of the valley between the Palatine and Celian hills. This was the ancient route taken by most triumphal processions. Passing the entrance to the Palatine ⑧ and the well-preserved arches of the Claudian Aqueduct ⑨

on the right, you come to Piazza di Porta Capena ⑩, named after the gate that stood here to mark the beginning of the Via Appia (see p284). After rounding the back of the Palatine, follow Via dei Cerchi, which runs alongside the grassy area that preserves, in an oval outline, all that remains of the Circus Maximus ⑪ (see p205).

Arches of the Forum Boarium

When you reach the church of Sant'Anastasia ⑫, turn right up Via di San Teodoro, then first left down Via del Velabro. Straddling the street is the four-sided Arch of Janus ⑬ (see p202), erected in the 3rd century AD. This is not a triumphal arch but a covered area where merchants could take shelter from the sun or rain when discussing business. Like the Arch of Titus, it became part of a fortress built by the Frangipane family during the Middle Ages.

Tucked away beside the nearby church of San Giorgio in Velabro ⑭ (see p202) is what looks like a large rectangular doorway. This is the Arco degli Argentari, or Moneychangers' Arch ⑮. Look up at the inscription, which says that it was erected by local silversmiths in honour of Septimius Severus and his family in AD 204. As in the emperor's triumphal arch, the name of Geta has been obliterated by his brother and murderer, Caracalla. Geta's figure has also been removed from among the portraits on the panels inside the arch. Triumph in Imperial Rome could be very short-lived.

Four-sided Arch of Janus in the Forum Boarium ⑬

A Three-Hour Tour of Rome's Best Mosaics

In imitation of the audience chambers of Imperial palaces, Rome's early Christian churches were decorated with colourful mosaics. These were pieced together from cubes of marble, coloured stone and fragments of glass. To create a golden background, gold leaf was placed between pieces of glass. These were then heated so that they fused. The glorious colours and subjects portrayed gave the faithful a glimpse of the heavenly court of the King of Kings. This walk concentrates on a few of the churches decorated in this wonderful medium.

Apse mosaic in the Chapel of Santa Rufina ③

San Giovanni

Start from Piazza di Porta San Giovanni, where you can visit the heavily restored mosaic of the Triclinio Leoniano *(see p179)*. Originally in the banqueting hall of Pope Leo III (795–816) ①, it shows Christ among the Apostles. On the left are Pope Sylvester and the Emperor Constantine, on the right, Pope Leo and Charlemagne just before he

Obelisk and side façade of San Giovanni in Laterano ②

was crowned Emperor of the Romans in AD 800. Inside the basilica of San Giovanni in Laterano ② *(see pp182–3)*, the 13th-century apse mosaic shows Christ as he appeared miraculously during the consecration of the church. In the panels by the windows, look for the small figures of two Franciscan friars; these are the artists Jacopo Torriti (left) and Jacopo de Camerino

(right). Leave by the exit on the right near the splendid 16th-century organ and head for the octagonal Baptistry of San Giovanni ③, where the Chapel of Santa Rufina has a beautiful apse mosaic, dating from the 5th century. In the neighbouring Chapel of San Venanzio, there are golden 7th-century mosaics, showing the strong influence of the Eastern Church at this time.

Santo Stefano Rotondo to San Clemente

Leave the piazza by the narrow road that leads to the round church of Santo Stefano Rotondo ④ *(see p185)*. One of its chapels contains a 7th-century Byzantine mosaic honouring two martyrs buried here. Further on, in Piazza della Navicella, is the church of Santa Maria in Domnica ⑤ *(see p193)*. It houses the superb mosaics commissioned by Pope Paschal I, who gave new impetus to Rome's mosaic production in the 9th century. He is represented kneeling beside the Virgin. On leaving the church, notice the façade of San Tommaso in Formis ⑥, which has a charming mosaic of Christ flanked by two freed slaves, one black and one white, dating from the 13th

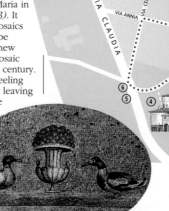

Ceiling mosaic, Baptistry of San Giovanni ③

Interior of Baptistry of San Giovanni ③

century. From here, head up the steep hill, past the forbidding apse of Santi Quattro Coronati ⑦ *(see p185)*, to the fascinating church of San Clemente ⑧ *(see pp186–7)*. Its 12th-century apse mosaic shows the cross set in a swirling pattern of acanthus leaves. San Clemente also has a fine 12th-century Cosmatesque mosaic floor.

The Colle Oppio
Passing the old entrance to the church, cross Via Labicana and walk up the hill to the small Colle Oppio park ⑨. This has fine views of the Colosseum and contains the ruins of the Domus Aurea ⑩ *(see p175)* and the Baths of Trajan ⑪. Across the park lie San Martino ai Monti ⑫ *(see p170)*, which has a 6th-century mosaic portrait of Pope St Sylvester near the crypt, and Santa Prassede ⑬ *(see p171)*. Here the Chapel of St Zeno contains the most important Byzantine mosaics in Rome, reminiscent of the fabulous mosaics of Ravenna. Pope Paschal I erected the chapel as a mausoleum for his mother Theodora. The apse and triumphal arch of the church itself also have fine mosaics. When you move on to Santa Maria Maggiore ⑭ *(see pp172–3)*, go to the column in the centre of the piazza in front of the church to see the beautiful 14th-century façade mosaics by Filippo Rusuti. Inside, the 5th-century mosaics in the nave depict Old Testament stories, while the triumphal arch has scenes relating to the birth of Christ, including one of the Magi wearing striped stockings. In the apse there is a *Coronation of the Virgin* by Jacopo Torriti (1295).

On leaving Santa Maria, pass the obelisk ⑮ in the piazza behind the church and go downhill to Via Urbana and Santa Pudenziana ⑯ *(see p171)*. The figures in the apse mosaic, one of the oldest in Rome (AD 390), are remarkable for their naturalism. The two women with crowns are traditionally identified as Santa Prassede and Santa Pudenziana. When you leave the church, you can either retrace your steps to Santa Maria Maggiore or walk down Via Urbana to Via Cavour Metro station.

Mosaic saint in Santa Prassede ⑬

11th-century frieze above the doorway of Santa Pudenziana ⑯

PIAZZA DI S. GIOVANNI IN LATERANO

PIAZZA DI PORTA S. GIOVANNI

San Giovanni Ⓜ

KEY

• • • Walk route

— City Wall

❖ Good viewing point

Ⓜ Metro station

0 metres 250
0 yards 250

TIPS FOR WALKERS

Starting point: Piazza di Porta San Giovanni.
Length: 3.5 km (2 miles).
Getting there: The nearest Metro station is San Giovanni, on line A, in Piazzale Appio, just outside Porta San Giovanni. The 16, 81, 85, 87, 650 and 850 buses and the 3 tram stop in front of San Giovanni in Laterano, while 117 and 218 stop around the corner on Piazza San Giovanni in Laterano.
Best time for walk: Go in the morning, in order to appreciate the mosaics in the best light.
Stopping-off points: The bars and restaurants in Piazza del Colosseo are popular with tourists. In the Parco del Colle Oppio there is a café kiosk with tables. There are several bars around Santa Maria Maggiore, some with outdoor tables.

A Two-Hour Walk around Bernini's Rome

Gian Lorenzo Bernini (1598–1680) is the artist who probably left the strongest personal mark on the appearance of the city of Rome. Favourite architect, sculptor and town planner to three successive popes, he turned Rome into a uniquely Baroque city. This walk traces his enormous influence on the development and appearance of the centre of Rome. It starts from the busy Largo di Santa Susanna just north of Termini station, at the church of Santa Maria della Vittoria.

Façade of Santa Maria in Via ⑬

Quirinale. The long wing of the Palazzo del Quirinale ⑦ *(see p158)*, nicknamed the *Manica Lunga* (long sleeve), is by Bernini. On the other side of the road is the façade of Sant'Andrea al Quirinale ⑧ *(see p161)*, one of Bernini's greatest churches. When you reach the Piazza del Quirinale ⑨, note the doorway of the palazzo, attributed to Bernini. From the piazza, go down the

composer Donizetti lived at No. 77 and turn into Via di Santa Maria in Via, where the church ⑬ has a fine Baroque

Bernini's Fontana del Tritone ②

Through Piazza Barberini

Santa Maria della Vittoria ① *(see p255)* houses the Cornaro Chapel, the setting for one of Bernini's most revolutionary and controversial sculptures, *The Ecstasy of St Teresa* (1646). From here take Via Barberini to Piazza Barberini. In its centre is Bernini's dramatic Fontana del Tritone ② *(see p254)* and at one side stands the more modest Fontana delle Api ③ *(see p254)*. As you go up Via delle Quattro Fontane, you catch a glimpse of Palazzo Barberini ④ *(see p255)* built by Bernini and several other artists for Pope Urban VIII. The gateway and cornices are decorated with the bees that made up part of the Barberini family crest. Next make your way to the crossroads, decorated by Le Quattro Fontane ⑤ *(see p162)*, to enjoy the splendid views in all four directions.

Passing the diminutive San Carlo alle Quattro Fontane ⑥ *(see p161)*, built by Bernini's rival Borromini, take Via del

stairs to Via della Dataria, and into Vicolo Scanderbeg which leads to a small piazza with the same name ⑩. Scanderbeg was the nickname of the Albanian prince Giorgio Castriota (1403–68), the "Terror of the Turks". His portrait is preserved on the house where he lived.

The Trevi Fountain

Go along the narrow Vicolo dei Modelli ⑪, where male models waited to be chosen by artists, then turn towards the Trevi Fountain ⑫ *(see p159)*. Its energy is clearly inspired by Bernini's work, a tribute to his lasting influence on Roman taste. Leave the piazza along Via delle Muratte where the

Neptune Fountain at the north end of Piazza Navona ⑱

façade by Bernini's follower Carlo Rainaldi. At the top of this street, turn left down to Via del Corso. On the other side of the road, you will see the towering Column of Marcus Aurelius ⑭ *(see p113)* in Piazza Colonna. Beyond this is Palazzo Montecitorio ⑮, begun in 1650 by Bernini and now the home of the Italian parliament *(see p112)*.

Pantheon to Piazza Navona

Via in Aquiro leads you to the Pantheon ⑯ *(see pp110–11)*. Refusing Pope Urban VIII's request for him to redecorate

Statue of the River Nile from the Fontana dei Quattro Fiumi

the dome, Bernini said that although St Peter's had a hundred defects, the Pantheon did not have any. From the Pantheon, make a small detour to Piazza della Minerva where you can see the bizarre Bernini obelisk, supported by a small elephant, by the church of Santa Maria sopra Minerva ⑰ *(see p108)*. Then retrace your steps and take Salita dei Crescenzi to

KEY

••• Walk route

∿ Good viewing point

Ⓜ Metro station

| 0 metres | | 250 |
| 0 yards | | 250 |

Angel on Ponte Sant'Angelo

Quattro Fiumi *(see p120)*, was by Bernini, though the figures symbolic of the four rivers were sculpted by other artists. The central figure in the Fontana del Moro, however, is by Bernini himself. Bernini's contemporaries were fascinated by the innovative use of shells, rocks and other natural forms in his fountains, and his expert handling of water to create constant movement.

An extended walk

More energetic walkers may like to head towards the river to see the Ponte Sant'Angelo and its Bernini angels, and then on to St Peter's *(see pp230–33)* where they can admire Bernini's great colonnaded piazza in front of the church, the papal tombs, his altar decorations and the bronze baldacchino.

TIPS FOR WALKERS

Starting point: *Largo di Santa Susanna.*
Length: *3.5 km (2 miles).*
Getting there: *Take Metro line A to Repubblica or any bus to Termini, then walk. Buses 61, 62, 175 and 492 stop in Via Barberini.*
Best time for walk: *Go either between 9am and noon for good lighting conditions in the churches, or between 4pm and 7pm.*
Stopping-off points: *The Piazza Barberini and Fontana di Trevi areas have lots of bars and pizzerias. The many elegant cafés en route include the famous Caffè Giolitti (see p109) and outdoor cafés and restaurants are plentiful around Piazza della Rotonda and Piazza Navona.*

reach the fabulous Piazza Navona ⑱ *(see p120)* which was remodelled by Bernini for Pope Innocent X Pamphilj. The design for the central fountain, the Fontana dei

A 90-Minute Walk along the Via Appia Antica

Lined with cypresses and pines as it was when the ancient Romans came here by torchlight to bury their dead, the Via Appia is wonderfully atmospheric. The fields are strewn with ruined tombs set against the picturesque background of the Alban hills to the south. Although the marble or travertine stone facings of most tombs have been plundered, a few statues and reliefs survive or have been replaced by copies.

Tomb of Sixtus Pompeus the Righteous ⑨

Capo di Bove

Start from the Tomb of Cecilia Metella ① *(see p266)*. In the Middle Ages this area acquired the name Capo di Bove (ox head) from the frieze of festoons and ox heads still visible on the tomb. On the other side of

Gothic windows in the church of San Nicola ②

the road you can see the ruined Gothic church of San Nicola ②, which, like the Tomb of Cecilia Metella, was part of the medieval fortress of the Caetani family.

Proceed to the crossroads ③, where there are still many original Roman paving slabs, huge blocks of extremely durable volcanic basalt. Just

The ruined church of San Nicola ②

past the next turning (Via Capo di Bove), you will see on your left the nucleus of a great mausoleum overgrown with ivy, known as the Torre di Capo di Bove ④. Beyond it,

on both sides of the Appia, are other tombs, some still capped with the remains of the medieval towers that were built over them. On the right after passing some private villas, you come to a military zone around the Forte Appio ⑤, one of a series of forts built around the city in the 19th century. On the left, a little further on, stand the ruins of the Tomb of Marcus Servilius ⑥, showing fragments of reliefs excavated in 1808 by the Neo-Classical sculptor Antonio Canova. He was one of the first to work on the principle that excavated tombs and their inscriptions and reliefs should be allowed to remain in situ. On the other side of the road stands a tomb with a relief of a man, naked except for a short cape, known as the

"Heroic Relief" ⑦. On the left of the road are the ruins of the so-called Tomb of Seneca ⑧. The great moralist Seneca owned a villa near here, where he committed suicide in AD 65 on the orders of Nero.

The next major tomb is that of the family of Sixtus Pompeus the Righteous, a freed slave of the 1st century AD ⑨. The verse inscription records the father's sadness at having to bury his own children, who died young.

Artist's impression of how the mausoleums and tombs lining the Via Appia looked in the 2nd century AD

Section of the Via Appia Antica, showing original Roman paving stones

From Via dei Lugari to Via di Tor Carbone

Just past Via dei Lugari on the right, screened by trees, is the Tomb of Pope St Urban (reigned 222–230) ⑩. Set back from the road on the left stands a large ruined podium, probably part of a Temple of Jupiter ⑪. The next stretch was excavated by the architect Luigi Canina early in the 19th century. On the right is the Tomb of Caius Licinius ⑫, followed by a smaller Doric tomb ⑬ and the imposing Tomb of Hilarius

Fuscus ⑭, with five portrait busts in relief of members of his family. Next comes the Tomb of Tiberius Claudius Secondinus ⑮, where a group of freedmen of the Imperial household were buried in the 2nd century AD.

Passing a large ruined columbarium, you reach the Tomb of Quintus Apuleius ⑯ and the reconstructed Tomb of the Rabirii freed slaves (1st century BC) ⑰. This has a frieze of three half-length figures above an inscription.

The figure on the right is a priestess of Isis. Behind her you can see the outline of a *sistrum*, the metal rattle used at ceremonies of the cult.

The majority of the tombs are little more than shapeless stacks of eroded brickwork. Two exceptions in the last stretch of this walk are the Tomb of the Festoons ⑱, with its reconstructed frieze of festive putti, and the Tomb of the Frontispiece ⑲, which has a copy of a relief with four portraits. The two central figures are holding hands.

When you reach Via di Tor Carbone, the Via Appia still stretches out ahead of you in a straight line and, if you wish to extend your walk, there are many more tombs and ruined villas to visit along the way.

KEY

• • •	Walk route
⚘	Good viewing point

0 metres 250

0 yards 250

Figure on the Tomb of the Heroic Relief ⑦

TIPS FOR WALKERS

Starting point: *Tomb of Cecilia Metella.*

Length: *3 km (2 miles).*

Getting there: Taking a taxi is the easiest way to reach the tomb. Alternatively, take the 118 from Piazzale Ostiense or the 660 from Colli Albani on Metro Line A.

Best time for walk: *Go fairly early, before it becomes too hot.*

Stopping-off points: *There is a bar near the church of Domine Quo Vadis?, before the start of the walk, but it is advisable to take your own refreshment. There are also several well-established restaurants on the first stretch of the Appia, including the Cecilia Metella, Via Appia Antica 129, tel 06-513 6743 (closed Mon).*

A Two-Hour Tour of Roman Tombs, Legends and Artists

The northern half of central Rome with its air of mystery is a great place for families to explore. Following this trail of creepy places and famous deaths interspersed with glimpses of the city's historic artists' centre, visitors can see Imperial mausoleums, a death mask and a crypt decorated with monks' bones. This is also a Rome where art isn't just in the museums – it's everywhere – so you'll see working art studios, pass Rome's Gallery of Fine Arts and wander down the famous "artists' row".

Frieze from Ara Pacis

exterior of his studio ⑧ at No. 16, a corner building studded with ancient statues and carvings. Turn left onto Via del Corso ⑨, Rome's High Street. This is 1.5 km (just under a mile) of palazzi and shops that has hosted parades, carnivals, races and processions for centuries and still functions as the main drag for Rome's evening stroll, the *passeggiata*. As you pass on your left the Ospedale di San Giacomo (founded in 1339 as a hospice for pilgrims), you'll see on the right Chiesa

Castel Sant'Angelo, site of the Emperor Hadrian's tomb ①

Imperial Tombs

Begin at Emperor Hadrian's tomb, deep in the heart of the papal Castel Sant'Angelo ① (*see pp248–9*). From the castle's riverside entrance, turn left then left again along the star-shaped walls, before turning right into Piazza Cavour, surrounded on the south by the huge, ostentatious Palazzo di Giustizia ② (*see p229*), slowly sinking under its own weight since 1910. Turn right down Via Colonna to cross the Tiber on Ponte Cavour. Once across the busy Lungotevere, turn left to go into the church of San Rocco ③ (*see p141*). Just beyond it lies the Mausoleum of Augustus ④ (*see p141*), sprouting a miniature grove of cypresses. To its left sits the ancient altar, Ara Pacis ⑤ (*see p140*).

of Via Canova, is the church of Santa Maria Portae Paradisi ⑦, designed in 1523 by Antonio Sangallo the Younger with a 1509 *Madonna and Child* by sculptor Sansovino. The octagonal interior dates to 1645. Turn right down Via Canova (named after the sculptor Antonio Canova), to see the

The Tridente

Continue heading north up Via di Ripetta. On your left is the graffiti-covered courtyard of the Accademia di Belle Arti ⑥, Rome's fine art academy, designed in 1845 by Pietro Camporese. On the right, at the corner

0 metres   200

0 yards   200

KEY

••• Suggested route

Ⓜ Metro

Baroque magnificence inside the Chiesa di Gesù e Maria ⑩

The Piazza di Spagna and the famous Spanish Steps, usually busy with visitors but quiet on rare occasions ⑱

TIPS FOR WALKERS

Starting point: Castel Sant'Angelo.

Length: 3.6 km (2.2 miles).

Getting there: Take bus 30, 34, 40, 49, 62, 70, 87, 130, 186, 224, 280, 492, 913, 926 or 990.

Best time for walk: Go in the afternoon, when the area starts to come alive.

Stopping-off points: Piazza del Popolo is flanked by two great Roman cafés with clear political affiliations – leftist Rosati (see p329) on the west side, right-wing Canova on the east. The Spanish Steps area has some great eateries as well as the usual fast food chains (see pp318–19).

di Gesù e Maria ⑩, Carlo Rinaldi's 1675 Baroque masterpiece. Further along, at No. 18, is the Casa di Goethe ⑪ *(see p136)*. The Corso ends in the dramatic Piazza del Popolo ⑫ *(see p137)*. The square is named after the church on its north end, Santa Maria del Popolo ⑬ *(see pp138–9)*. The church, which is full of art treasures, gets its name "St Mary of the People" because it was built to help exorcise the ghost of Nero from a walnut grove on this site, once Nero's family estate where the disgraced emperor was secretly buried. The estate once continued to stroll up the slopes of what are now the Pincio Gardens ⑭ *(see p136)*, above the piazza to the east, and locals declare that the ravens' screams are those of the dead emperor. Leave Piazza del Popolo from the southeast corner to stroll down Via del Babuino ⑮, lined with art galleries

hawking everything from Old Master Madonnas to Modernist abstracts. Take the third left, then right onto quiet Via Margutta ⑯, home of artists' studios and galleries for centuries. Turn right again down Via Orto di Napoli to return to Via del Babuino, then left. On your right, reclining on a fountain and surrounded by various graffiti and placards, is one of the ugliest – and most respected – statues in Rome. The Babuino ⑰ (like the famous Pasquino) has served as a soapbox for political and social dissent for centuries. Via del Babuino ends in Piazza di Spagna ⑱ *(see p133)*, usually thronged with tourists. The pink house to the right of the Spanish Steps is the Keats-Shelley Memorial House ⑲ *(see p134)*. Take a look inside to see Keats' death mask.

The Spanish Steps to the Capuchin Crypt

Go up the famed Spanish Steps ⑳ *(see p134–5)* to Trinità dei Monti ㉑

(see p135). Turn right down Via Gregoriana to No. 28, where painter Frederico Zuccari turned the door and window frames of his Palazzetto Zuccari ㉒ into monsters. At the bottom of Via Gregoriana, turn left up to Via F. Crispi, then right down Via Sistina into Piazza Barberini ㉓, noting Bernini's fountain *(see p252)*. Turn left up the square, cross Via V. Veneto, and left again. A few dozen paces up on the right is the staircase to the church of Santa Maria della Concezione. To finish, stop at the first landing to enter the creepy Capuchin Crypt ㉔ *(see p254)*, where there are four chapels decorated with mosaics and skeletal displays. When you leave the crypt head for Piazza Barberini and the Metro station.

Bones and skulls from monks in the Capuchin Crypt ㉔

A Two-Hour Walk around Trastevere and Janiculum Hill

This walk begins in the warren of cobbled, medieval streets of Trastevere, which is becoming ever more popular, and shows you the neighbourhood's hidden gems rather than its major sights. In the morning enjoy the mosaics and frescoes in the local churches before pausing for lunch in central Trastevere. Then go for a gentle climb up the Gianicolo, or Janiculum Hill. This long crest parallels the Tiber, and is blessed with the best panoramic views in Rome. At sunset, couples find it a romantic place to go for a stroll.

cafés and bars. A short staircase at No. 9 leads to the Museo di Roma in Trastevere ⑨ *(see p210)*, devoted to the history of everyday Roman life. Exit the piazza at the northwest corner and cross Vicolo del Cedro to continue straight on Via della Scala, past shops

The high altar of San Benedetto ③

Southern Trastevere
Start at Santa Cecilia in Trastevere ① *(see p211)*, a church that hides its best – the basement excavations of St Cecilia's house and Pietro Cavallini's sole surviving Roman fresco inside the cloistered convent – behind a bland 18th-century interior. Turn left out of the church, left again onto Via dei Salumi, then right on Via in Piscinula into Piazza in Piscinula ②, named for the remains of a bathing pool underneath. On the piazza's south side, below an 11th-century belltower, sits the tiny church of San Benedetto in Piscinula ③, (ring the doorbell for entry). It contains parts of a beautiful Cosmati mosaic pavement, 13th-century frescoes, and the saint's cell. Head west along Via della Lungaretta and cross the Viale di Trastevere to visit the excavations of a 5th-century basilica and fragments of its later frescoes below San Crisogono ④ *(see p210)*.

Central Trastevere
Turn left out of the church and left again to continue along Via della Lungaretta to Piazza Santa Maria in

Trastevere ⑤, a communal outdoor parlour, busy with cafés, guitar-strumming backpackers on the fountain steps, and visitors to the gorgeous Santa Maria in Trastevere ⑥ *(see p212–13)*. Exit the square on the south side into tiny Piazza San Callisto, and take the right fork down Via di San Cosimato into the large triangular Piazza di San Cosimato ⑦, bustling (until 2pm) with an open-air food market. Backtrack to Piazza Santa Maria in Trastevere. Along the square's north side you'll see a tiny street called Fonte d'Olio, entrance into the twisting maze of alleys and ivy-covered buildings at the heart of Trastevere. The street bends sharply left, then turn right onto Vicolo del Piede to arrive at the diminutive Piazza de' Renzi, lined with medieval houses. Turn left to follow Via della Pelliccia, then left again at the pedestrian intersection. This will bring you into the elongated triangle of Piazza di Sant'Egidio ⑧, alive with

Piazza Santa Maria in Trastevere and its enchanting church ⑤

Raphael's *Galatea* in the Villa Farnesina ⑬

0 metres 150
0 yards 150

the Porta Settimiana ⑫ *(see p218)*. Instead of frescoing the Villa Farnesina ⑬ *(see pp220–21)*, just up Via della Lungara, he spent so much time with his lover that, unlike the famed *Galatea* in the dining room, the "Raphael" work in the Loggia of Cupid and Psyche was executed largely by his assistants. Across from the Farnesina squats the Palazzo Corsini and the Galleria Nazionale d'Arte Antica ⑭ *(see p218)*. Tucked behind the gallery – accessible by back-tracking down Via della Lungara and turning right on Via Corsini – are the Botanical Gardens ⑮ *(see p218)*.

The Gianicolo

Continue back south on Via della Lungara through the Porta Settimiana, and turn right up Via G. Garibaldi to climb Janiculum Hill. After the road makes a sharp left turn, veer right up a set of steps to San Pietro in Montorio, home

TIPS FOR WALKERS

Starting point: Santa Cecilia in Trastevere.
Length: 4.7 km (2.9 miles).
Getting there: Take bus 23, 44 or 280.
Best time for walk: Weekdays (to see the Cavallini fresco), starting mid-morning while the churches of southern Trastevere are still open.
Stopping-off points: Trastevere is the most restaurant-intensive district in Rome, so it has plenty of eateries and bars (see pp324–5).

to Bramante's Tempietto ⑯ *(see p219)*. Go on up Via G. Garibaldi to the broad basin of the Fontana dell'Acqua Paola ⑰ *(see p219)*. Continue along Via G. Garibaldi to the 1644 Porta San Pancrazio ⑱, which had to be rebuilt in 1849 due to cannon damage *(see pp36–7)*. Turn right onto Passeggiata del Gianicolo to enter the park, where the first wide space with a panoramic vista over Rome is Piazzale Garibaldi with its

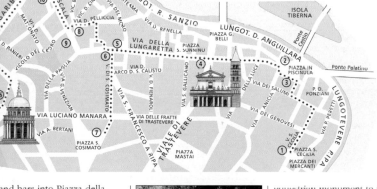

and bars into Piazza della Scala, where the Carmelite convent of Santa Maria della Scala ⑩ *(see p210)* has an ornate interior.

Northern Trastevere

The far northern part of Trastevere, between the Gianicolo and the river, is where the artist Raphael dallied with a baker's daughter at the Casa della Fornarina ⑪ *(see p210)*, on the right just before

KEY

• • • Suggested route
☼ Good viewing point

Steps at the tranquil Botanical Gardens ⑮

equestrian monument to the general ⑲ *(see p218)*. Here, paths are lined with marble busts of other Risorgimento heroes. When you reach the Lighthouse of Manfredi ⑳ *(see p216)*, the dome of St Peter's appears to the north. Continue down the steps at the Passeggiata's first bend to see the 400-year-old remains of Tasso's Oak ㉑ *(see p216)*. At the foot of the steps, rejoin the Passeggiata. Beyond it, a few steps up, finish at the lovely church of Sant'Onofrio ㉒ *(see p219)*. From Viale Aldo Fabrizi you can catch bus No. 870 back to the city centre.

A Two-Hour Walk around the Aventine

Rising just across the Circus Maximus from the Palatine, the residential Aventine Hill has served as a leafy haven of villas and mansions since Imperial times. This southernmost of Rome's legendary seven hills is still an oasis where traffic noise all but disappears. Yet few visitors walk here – despite the lure of fine old churches, lovely city panoramas, and rarely visited ancient ruins. You'll also explore Testaccio, a fine area for authentic restaurants, and see a Roman pyramid.

The gymnasium at the northwest side of the Baths of Caracalla ①

The Aventine

Begin at one of Rome's most magnificent ancient sites, the massive Baths of Caracalla ① *(see p197)*, where plebeian and patrician alike once bathed (and, much later, where the poet Shelley found inspiration for *Prometheus Unbound*). Just outside the Baths' entrance sits the church of SS Nero e Achilleo ② *(see p194)*, with 9th-century mosaics. Across Viale delle Terme di Caracalla lies tiny San Sisto Vecchio ③, first home of the Dominican nuns *(see p193)*. Turning northwest up Viale delle Terme di Caracalla, take the first right onto Via di Valle delle Camene, a tree-lined avenue parallel to the main road. Angle right up Salita di San Gregorio and ascend the imposing staircase of San Gregorio Magno ④ *(see p192)* for great views of the Palatine. Look for the third-century marble table (in the St Barbara chapel, on the left side of the church) at which St Gregory the Great shared meals with the poor and,

once, an angel in disguise. Turn left down Via di San Gregorio and cross wide Piazza di Porta Capena, keeping the long dusty oval of the Circus Maximus ⑤ *(see p205)* on your right. At the start of Viale Aventino you'll see the modernist bulk of FAO ⑥, originally intended to be the Ministry of Italian Africa when Mussolini was launching his ill-fated conquest of the Horn of Africa. Since its 1952 completion, it has housed the UN's Food and Agriculture Organization.

Across the Aventine

Turn right on Via del Circo Massimo, and immediately left onto Via della Fonte di Fauno to start climbing the Aventine Hill. This leads you to a small piazza before the church of Santa Prisca ⑦, built in the third century atop the house where the martyred saint's

parents hosted St Peter. The current church dates largely to a Renaissance-era remodelling, and includes a Passignano altarpiece. Continue north up Via di Santa Prisca, angle left through Largo Arrigo VII, turn left on Via Eufemiano, and immediately right onto Via Sant'Alberto Magno. This leads right into Parco Savello ⑧, a garden of orange trees with a panoramic river view over Trastevere. Leaving the

The apse of Santa Prisca ⑦

0 metres   300

0 yards   300

park, turn right onto Via di Santa Sabina to the gorgeous basilica of Santa Sabina ⑨ (see p204), where its rare, 5th-century wooden doors incorporate one of the earliest Crucifixion representations. Continue along Via di Santa Sabina to see the fine Cosmati work in SS Bonifacio e Alessio ⑩ (see p204). The street ends in the Piazza dei Cavaliere di Malta ⑪ (see p204), where you get a tiny view of St Peter's dome through the keyhole at

Keats' gravestone at the Protestant Cemetery on Via Caio Cestio ⑮

TIPS FOR WALKERS

Starting point: The Baths of Caracalla entrance on Viale delle Terme di Caracalla 52.
Length: 5.3 km (3.3 miles).
Getting there: You can walk from the Circo Massimo Metro stop, or take bus 118 or 628.
Best time for walk: Start in the morning, timing your walk so that you can lunch in Testaccio.
Stopping-off points: You're spoilt for choice as fantastic and authentic local eateries abound in and around Piazza Testaccio, from cheap pizza places to some of Rome's finest restaurants.

have long burrowed into its flanks to take advantage of the terracotta's constant, cool temperature for storing wine. Turn left through Piazza Orazio

number 3.
Turn left down Via di Porta Lavernate, passing the façade of Sant' Anselmo ⑫. Built in 1900, the church houses a 3rd-century mosaic scene of Orpheus found during excavations. From Piazza dei Servili turn right on Via Asinio Pollione to go down off the Aventine.

Testaccio and South
Cross Via Marmorata and continue down Via Galvani. As you cross Via Nicola Zabaglia, the ground on your left rises to form Monte Testaccio ⑬ (see p204), an ancient rubbish tip made up entirely of potsherds. It is lined with various restaurants that

Giustiniani to continue skirting the hill along Via di Monte Testaccio. Across the street, you'll see the blind arcades of the Ex-Mattatoio ⑭, a defunct abattoir whose workers were paid, in part, with the day's offal. They would carry this *quinto quarto* (fifth quarter) of the animal across the street to one of Testaccio's early eateries,

where it would be turned into such (now) classic Roman delicacies as oxtail stew and *pajata* (calf intestines). Continue along Via di Monte Testaccio, which becomes Via Caio Cestio, to the Protestant Cemetery ⑮ (see p205) where such luminaries as Keats and Shelley lie in peace. At Via Marmorata, turn right to pass the Porta San Paolo ⑯, a city gate dating to AD 402. As you walk through the remains of the Aurelian Wall into Piazzale Ostiense, you can't miss on your right the Pyramid of Caius Cestius ⑰ (see p205). The final leg is a long stroll down Via Ostiense or, alternatively, hop on the bus (Nos. 23, 271, or 769) to see the wonderfully weird Centrale Montemartini ⑱, an early Industrial Age power plant now stuffed with ancient sculptures. Bus numbers 23 and 769 will take you back to within walking distance of Piramide Metro.

KEY

••• Suggested route

Ⓜ Metro

☆ Good viewing point

Ancient sculptures on display in the Centrale Montemartini ⑱

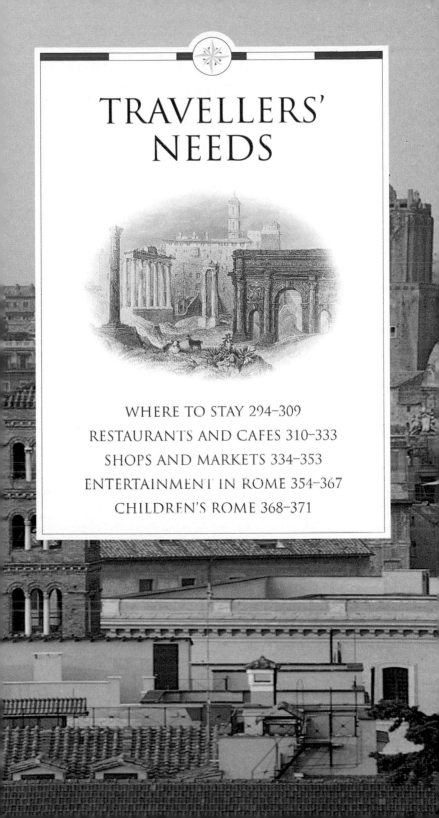

TRAVELLERS'
NEEDS

WHERE TO STAY

Rome has been a major tourist centre since the Middle Ages, when pilgrims from all over Europe came to visit the home of Catholicism and its relic-packed churches. The nostalgic can still sleep in a 15th-century hotel, or stay around the Campo de' Fiori market, where visiting ecclesiastics were entertained by courtesans in the Renaissance era. Those who prefer their history a little less raffish could opt for an ex-monastery or convent, or stay in a still-functioning religious house. Romantics could sleep in the house once occupied by Keats, while stargazers could stay

Porter at the Majestic Hotel

in former palaces graced by celebrities of the past and present. Rome can offer the full range of accommodation, mostly in historical buildings, very little purpose-built. *Pensione* (guesthouse) is no longer an official category, but in practice many retain the name and more personal character that has made them so popular with travellers. Other possibilities include hostels, residential hotels and self-catering accommodation.

The hotels are organized in the listings *(pp300–9)* according to their price category and area while the symbols provide an at-a-glance guide to the facilities available.

WHERE TO LOOK

Around the Spanish Steps and Piazza di Spagna lies the traditional heartland of foreign visitors, with some of the most exclusive smaller hotels. Similar places can be found all over the centre, to the west of Via del Corso.

While moderately priced accommodation is rare in central Rome, the advantages of staying right on the doorstep of the city's many ancient sights cannot be over-estimated; you can walk to the major areas of interest and easily return at midday for a shower and siesta. If the less

expensive hotels we have recommended in the centre are full, try the Borgo – close to the Vatican – or the lively quarter of Trastevere.

Those in search of glamour should head for Via Veneto, which has many grand and luxurious hotels.

If you're looking for a peaceful retreat, try the area around the Aventine, or one of the high-class hotels next to the Villa Borghese park.

Although many of the streets immediately around Termini station are rather seedy, the area is nonetheless a convenient stopover for travellers and there's a

concentration of cheap hotels, with some decent (if basic) ones among them. The hotels recommended lie in a fairly safe area on the east side of the station. The approach to the centre from Termini has a number of good hotels that are particularly suitable for the business traveller.

HOTEL PRICES

Although Rome may still offer less expensive accommodation than other large cities like London or New York, rates for comparable establishments have caught up. Prices are set by the state, and hotels should display the official rate on the door of each room. VAT (*IVA* in Italian) is usually included, and has been taken into account in the price categories on page 297.

Hotels in Rome generally have low and high season rates. April to June, September and October are high season. Double-check tariffs when booking hotels at other times of year as you may initially be quoted the higher rate. Excepting Christmas and New Year, there are some real bargains to be had between November and February, and also in July and August. Many hotels also offer special Internet booking deals. Discounts for long-stay visitors and groups are often negotiable.

The Verdi Room in Via Veneto's Majestic Hotel *(see p308)*

◁ **Rome from the rooftops – a panoramic cityscape**

Grand Hotel de la Minerve *(see p301)*

Rooms without a bathroom can cost about 30 per cent less. Single travellers are badly catered for, and though it is possible to find a single room for 60 per cent of the price of a double, on average you'll pay as much as 70 per cent, and occasionally even more.

HIDDEN EXTRAS

Even if the price of your room includes service, you are frequently expected to tip bellboys and for room service.

Rates are often not inclusive of breakfast, especially at some luxury hotels, where it may cost up to 50 euros. Hotels usually add hefty surcharges to international phone calls, and may charge for parking and air conditioning. The cost of drinks in minibars can be high – you can buy a cheaper supply from local shops.

FACILITIES

Hotel standards have improved in recent years – you can expect Internet access, air conditioning and bathrooms with hair dryers in middle-range establishments and phones in middle to lower price rooms, although budget travellers staying in cheaper hotels shouldn't expect much more than a clean room.

Because most hotels occupy

The Portoghesi Hotel *(see p301)*

historic buildings, room sizes can vary dramatically even within the same establishment (and this is often reflected in the pricing), so don't be afraid to ask to see your room before you check in. For the same reason, swimming pools are few and far between, but roof terraces or gardens are common across the range of hotels.

Top-class hotels will usually have some soundproofing, otherwise noise levels can be dreadful, in which case ask for a room facing away from the road.

Parking in central Rome is a problem, though a few hotels have a limited number of parking spaces of their own.

Business visitors to the capital are well catered for, with hotel facilities ranging from internet access to meeting rooms.

HOW TO BOOK

The Italian postal service tends to be unreliable, so it is safer to book by phone, fax or through the hotel website. You should do this at least two months in advance if you want a particular hotel in May, June, September or October; Easter and Christmas are also busy. If you require any particular features, such as a terrace or a view, insist on confirmation in writing to ensure that you get on arrival what you have been promised.

If a deposit is required you can usually pay by credit card. Under Italian law a booking is valid as soon as the deposit is paid, so you could lose money if you pull out.

Double-check bookings prior to departure. Many hotels have a fierce cancellation policy and if you are not happy with the accommodation, or it is not what you booked, there is every chance that you will be charged for at least one night,

Villa San Pio garden *(see p306)*

even if you decide not to stay. Another reason for checking your booking carefully is that some hotels deliberately overbook and then offer unsatisfactory alternative accommodation.

If you arrive by train, touts may descend on you at the station with offers of accommodation. They can be of some use if you are looking for a budget hotel, but you should exercise the usual caution. A better bet if you have not booked anywhere in advance is to head for one of the tourist board offices *(see p297)*. Here, staff will reserve you a room within the price range you specify.

The Locarno *(see p302)*

CHECKING IN AND OUT

Italian hoteliers are legally obliged to register you with the police, which is the reason they always ask for your passport. They usually hold on to it for a while, but you need it if you are going to change money. Everyone in Italy is supposed to carry with them some sort of identification.

In some of Rome's cheaper *pensioni,* do not be surprised if you are asked to pay on arrival. To speed up the checking out process, mention in advance if you intend to pay by credit card. A tax dodge used by many hotels is to ask for payment in cash; you are entitled to refuse.

DISABLED TRAVELLERS

Provision for disabled travellers is poor. Hotels that occupy parts of buildings often start their rooms up several flights of stairs, while others can only accommodate disabled guests on the ground floor. Ramps, wide doorways and bathroom handrails are rare.

Our entries for wheelchair access in the hotel listings rely on the establishments' own assessments; any specific requirements should be checked before booking.

There is a useful website (www.romapertutti.it) dedicated to mobility within Rome, while the Lazio region provides advice on accessibility further afield (800 27 1027). Public transportation authority **Trambus** offers a pick-up service and bus tourism for travellers with disabilities and must be reserved in advance.

TRAVELLING WITH CHILDREN

Italians love children and they are usually welcome across the range of hotels. Most hotels can provide cots or small beds, but high chairs, children's meals and babysitting services are rare. Those hotels in the listings below that do offer facilities for children carry a symbol to indicate so. In practice, though, many establishments – especially smaller, family-run ones – go out of their way to be helpful.

Many hotels do not have special rates for children and charge a standard rate if you require an extra bed in a room, whether for a baby or an adult, which can add anything from a few euros to 40 per cent on to the price. For a family with older children, two-room suites are sometimes available. Contact the hotel in advance for information on family rates and suite accommodation as high-end hotels may be more flexible.

BED & BREAKFAST

A growing sector for visitors to Rome is bed & breakfast accommodation. Availability can be anything from a spare

The reception area of the Regina Hotel Baglioni *(see p309)*

room in an apartment to something that feels more like a small hotel. Breakfast can also vary depending on the owner. Some invite you into their own kitchen while others set up a large, more continental style breakfast buffet. Contact the **Bed & Breakfast Association of Rome** for a selection of rooms and apartments, **Rome Bed & Breakfast** in the US, or visit Rome's tourist board website *(see p297)*.

RESIDENTIAL HOTELS

If you want the comfort and privacy of your own apartment coupled with the services of a hotel, you could opt to stay in a *residenza*. Prices range from around €300 to over €3,000 for a week in a two-bedded room, though some *residenze* are only available for fortnightly or monthly lets. A full list is available from tourist board offices; some of the most central are listed in the directory on page 297.

Bedroom at the Residenza Cellini *(see p305)*

RELIGIOUS INSTITUTIONS

If you do not mind an early curfew, quite a few religious institutions take in paying guests. All religions are welcome and you do not have to be a practising Catholic. Book well in advance as all of the following places cater for groups of students and pilgrims. **Casa Il Rosario** convent is located near the Colosseum, while **Nostra Signora di Lourdes** and the **Casa di Santa Brigida** are in the centre of Rome. Prices are in the same range as for the cheaper hotels.

BUDGET ACCOMMODATION

Even if you are travelling on a shoestring, it is possible to find a decent room in Rome. More and more mid-range options are now available and dormitory accommodation can be found at rock-bottom prices in simple establishments, such as the **Ottaviano**. Youth hostels are also a good option. At the **Ostello del Foro Italico** bed, breakfast and shower can all be had at a very reasonable cost. **Fawlty Towers** has good facilities for the price, including a roof terrace; like **Stargate**, it is located near Termini station.

Women can get rooms at the **Foresteria Orsa Maggiore** in Trastevere or at the **Young Women's Christian Association** (YWCA) near Termini (those arriving in Termini at night should take care). There are also several budget hotels in the city centre offering clean rooms and often a free breakfast. See websites like www.venere.com and www.eurocheapo.com for more options.

SELF-CATERING APARTMENTS

Independent apartments are a good alternative and allow you more freedom. Apartments range from luxury locations with a daily cleaning service to smaller basic facilities. Most come equipped with cooking utensils, towels and bed linens. **RetRome Bed & Breakfast** *(see p305)* provides apartments at three locations around town.

CAMPING

Camping has come a long way since the simple tent and trailer. Campsites around Rome offer everything from fully-equipped cabins (with private bath) to Jacuzzis and on-site

The pool in the Aldrovandi Palace garden *(see p309)*

discos. Most campsites are located quite far out of town but offer a shuttle service, as well as airport transport; **Flaminio Village** is one exception, at only 6 km (4 miles) north of the centre. Like many sites it has a pool, coffee bar, restaurant and Internet access.

TOURIST BOARDS

Provincial and city tourist boards can provide advice on accommodation. **Hotel Reservation** is a booking service with offices at Termini station, as well as both of the city's airports.

DIRECTORY

DISABLED TRAVELLERS

Trambus
*Tel 800-469 540
(call between 8am 1pm Mon–Fri).*
www.atac.roma.it

BED & BREAKFAST

Bed & Breakfast Association of Rome
Via A. Pacinotti 73.
Tel 06-5530 2248.
Fax 06-5530 2259.
www.b-b.rm.it

Rome Bed & Breakfast
Tel 1-800 872 2632.
Fax 1-619-531 1686.
www.romebandb.com

RESIDENTIAL HOTELS

Di Ripetta
Via di Ripetta 231, 00186.
Tel 06-323 1144.
Fax 06-320 3959.
www.ripetta.it

In Trastevere
Vicolo Moroni 35–36, 00153.
Tel 06-808 3375.
www.romerenting.com

Residence Babuino
Via del Babuino 172, 00187.
Tel/Fax 06-361 1663.

Vittoria
Via Vittoria 60-64, 00187.
Tel 06-679 7533.
Fax 06-679 2185.

RELIGIOUS INSTITUTIONS

Casa di Santa Brigida
Piazza Farnese 96, 00186.
Tel 06-6889 2596.

Casa Il Rosario
Via Sant'Agata dei Goti 10, 00184.
Tel 06-679 2346.

Nostra Signora di Lourdes
Via Sistina 113, 00187.
Tel 06-474 5324.

BUDGET ACCOMMODATION

Associazione Italiana Alberghi per la Gioventù
(Youth Hostels Association)
Via Cavour 44, 00184.
Tel 06-487 1152.
Fax 06-488 0492.
www.aighostels.com

Fawlty Towers
Via Magenta 39, 00185.
Tel 06-445 0374.
Fax 06-4543 5942.
www.fawltytowers.org

Foresteria Orsa Maggiore
Via di San Francesco di Sales 1A, 00165.
Tel 06-689 3753.
www.casainternazionale
delledonne.org

Ostello del Foro Italico
Viale delle Olimpiadi 61, 00194. *Tel 06 323 6267.*
Fax 06-324 2613.
www.hihostels.com

Ottaviano
Via Ottaviano 6, 00192.
Tel 06-3973 8138.
www.pensione
ottaviano.com

Stargate
Via Palestro 88, 00185.
Tel 06-445 7164.
Fax 06-4938 4134.
www.stargatehotels.net

YWCA
Via C. Balbo 4, 00184.
Tel 06-488 3917.
Fax 06-487 1028.
www.ywca-ucdg.it

SELF-CATERING APARTMENTS

RetRome Bed & Breakfast
www.retrome.net

CAMPING

Flaminio Village
Via Flaminia Nuova 821, 00189. *Tel 06-333 2604.*
Fax 06-333 0653.
www.camping
flaminio.com

TOURIST BOARDS

Rome Provincial Tourist Board (APT)
Terminal 3 (arrivals),
Leonardo da Vinci Airport,
Fiumicino.
Open 9am–6pm daily.

Rome City Tourist Board
Termini Station 00185.
Tel 06-0608 (open 8am–8.30pm daily).
www.060608.it

Hotel Reservation
Tel 06-699 1000 (open 7am–10pm daily).
www.hotelreservation.it

Rome's Best: Hotels

Roman hotels range from frescoed palaces and *fin-de-siècle* bastions of faded glamour to family-run guesthouses. Most are close to restaurants, shops and transport. Whatever the price level, all the hotels shown on this map have something special to offer, whether it is a chic location, or a roof terrace with soaring views across the city. The only drawback is that these places and all those on pages 300–9 are exceptions to the many unremarkable hotels in the city, so you should book well in advance. The hotels shown here are the best of their kind or price range.

Locarno
This intimate Art Deco hotel is a step away from Piazza del Popolo and some of Rome's best shopping. (See p302.)

Raphael
Behind its ivy-veiled exterior, the Raphael is full of antiques and art, from ceramics by Picasso in the lobby to Renaissance pieces in some bedrooms. It offers a convenient central location. (See p301.)

Hotel Raphaël

0 metres 500
0 yards 500

Vatican

Piaz
Nav

Janiculum

Tras

Campo de' Fiori
Central Rome's best bargain offers small, well-furnished rooms and terrific views from the sixth-floor roof terrace. (See p303.)

Grand Hotel de la Minerve
Smart, post-modern interiors grace this international standard hotel. (See p301.)

Sant'Anselmo
To be sure of getting a room you need to book well in advance at this peacefully located Roman villa. An added bonus for guests is the lovely secluded garden. (See p306.)

Hassler Roma
*Luxurious suites and an air
of faded grandeur remind
visitors of the Hassler's heyday.
The rooftop restaurant is
Rome's most famous.*
(See p303.)

Hotel Eden
*One of the oldest and most exclusive hotels
in Rome, the Eden offers elegant decor and
truly innovative cuisine.* (See p308.)

Boscolo Aleph
*The audacious, red-tinged decor of the
lobby sets the tone at this sumptuously
luxurious and yet highly unconventional
hotel.* (See p308.)

Via Veneto

Quirinal

Capitol

Esquiline

Forum

Palatine

Lateran

Caracalla

St Regis Grand Hotel
*Good service and extensive
facilities are the main
features of this old-
fashioned, luxury hotel.*
(See p305.)

Fontana
*The fabulous location opposite the
Trevi fountain, and a charming
roof terrace, make this former
monastery a popular choice with
visitors.* (See p304.)

Choosing a Hotel

The choice of rooms selected in this guide is based on the quality of accommodation and service as well as location. The list of hotels covers all the areas and price categories with additional information to help you choose a hotel that best meets your needs. Hotels within the same price category are listed alphabetically.

PRICE CATEGORIES
For a double room per night, including breakfast, tax and service:

€ up to €100
€€ €101–180
€€€ €181–280
€€€€ €281–380
€€€€€ over €380

FORUM

Nicolas Inn
€€
Via Cavour 295, Scala A, Int. 1, 00184 **Tel** *06-9761 8483* **Rooms** *4*
Map *5 B5*

A small B&B run by an American-Italian couple, a brief stroll away from the Forum and Piazza Venezia. The friendly managers offer good-sized rooms, all en suite with WiFi and central heating. Breakfast vouchers are issued for the bar next door and the reception is open from 8am to 4pm. Not for children under five. **www.nicolasinn.com**

Paba
€€
Via Cavour 266, 2nd Floor, 00184 **Tel** *06-4782 4902* **Fax** *06-4788 1225* **Rooms** *7*
Map *5 B5*

Run by a charming lady, this tiny *pensione* is on the second floor of an elegant building, a short walk away from Piazza Venezia and the Forum. The clean, spacious, sound-proofed and well-furnished rooms have parquet floors, WiFi, fridges and kettles for making hot drinks. **www.hotelpaba.com**

Forum
€€€
Via Tor de' Conti 25, 00184 **Tel** *06-679 2446* **Fax** *06-678 6479* **Rooms** *80*
Map *5 B5*

A former convent, with old-fashioned elegance and unbeatable views over the Forum and Trajan's Market. Buffet breakfast is served on the sunny rooftop terrace, which also hosts a bar and a good restaurant. Rooms are exceptionally clean and spacious. The lobby is bedecked with antiques. **www.hotelforumrome.com**

Hotel Celio
€€€
Via SS Quattro 35C, 00184 **Tel** *06-7049 5333* **Fax** *06-709 6377* **Rooms** *20*
Map *9 A1*

Hotel Celio has sumptuous decor, a great location and a cordial staff. Bedrooms are furnished with flair, distinguished by frescoes in the style of Renaissance painters, such as Titian and Cellini. Upper-floor rooms have Jacuzzis and the suite has a private panoramic terrace. There's also a roof garden. **www.hotelcelio.com**

Lancelot
€€€
Via Capo d'Africa 47, 00184 **Tel** *06-7045 0615* **Fax** *06-7045 0640* **Rooms** *60*
Map *9 A1*

A popular place to stay near the Colosseum with very friendly, helpful staff. Rooms are spacious and charming. Some have private terraces with views, and two are specially adapted for guests with disabilities. Half-board option is available and a hearty breakfast is served in the patio garden. **www.lancelothotel.com**

PIAZZA DELLA ROTONDA

Mimosa
€€
Via di Santa Chiara 61, 00186 **Tel** *06-6880 1753* **Fax** *06-683 3557* **Rooms** *11*
Map *4 F4, 12 D3*

Friendly, family-run hotel with simple, spacious rooms, five en suite with air conditioning. Cheaper rooms are also available with shared bathrooms. Popular with those travelling on a budget, the location couldn't be better for visiting the surrounding area. Breakfasts are continental style. **www.hotelmimosa.net**

Pantheon View B&B
€€
Via del Seminario 87, 00186 **Tel/Fax** *06-699 0294* **Rooms** *3*
Map *4 F4, 12 D3*

A pleasant B&B, the Pantheon is cosy and friendly, with beautifully furnished rooms, two of which have a small balcony where guests can sit outside. Whilst the view of the Pantheon is really a sliver, the location is excellent. It's on the fourth floor of a residential palazzo, with a tiny lift. **www.pantheonview.it**

Cesari
€€€
Via di Pietra 89a, 00186 **Tel** *06-674 9701* **Fax** *06-6749 7030* **Rooms** *47*
Map *12 E2*

The historic, four-storey Cesari is located on a lovely romantic square, steps away from the Pantheon beside the Temple of Hadrian. Established as a hotel in 1787, it has been in the same family since 1899. A favourite of Stendhal's, rooms are elegant and spacious. No-smoking floors, roof terrace and free Internet access. **www.albergocesari.it**

Key to Symbols *see back cover flap*

Rinascimento

⬆🔲♿ €€€

Via del Pellegrino 112, 00186 **Tel** *06-6880 9556* **Fax** *06-6821 2410* **Rooms** *15* **Map** *4 E4, 11 B3*

Well-located, this small, family hotel offers old-fashioned comfort for either a long or short stay. Bedooms vary in size and rates, but all have been beautifully refurbished. One small double has a lovely terrace and one of the superior rooms has a sitting area. **www.hotelrinascimento.com**

Santa Chiara

⬆🔲 €€€

Via di Santa Chiara 21, 00186 **Tel** *06-687 2979* **Fax** *06-687 3144* **Rooms** *96* **Map** *4 F4, 12 D3*

A substantial family-run hotel in an apricot-washed palazzo. Beyond the elegant marble lobby with glass chandeliers, bedrooms are comfortable with parquet flooring and subdued, old-fashioned decor. Three of the upper rooms are small apartments with terraces. **www.albergosantachiara.com**

Albergo del Senato

⬆🔲♿🅆 €€€€

Piazza della Rotonda 73, 00186 **Tel** *06-678 4343* **Fax** *06-6994 0297* **Rooms** *57* **Map** *4 F4, 12 D3*

A rather grand, noble old hotel with a side view of the Pantheon and the Piazza. Bedrooms are elegant and service is old-fashioned and reserved. Some rooms have a bath or private terrace and the suite has a beautifully frescoed ceiling. Windows are soundproofed and there's a delightful roof garden. **www.albergodelsenato.it**

Grand Hotel de la Minerve

⬆🅿🍴🎬🔲♿ €€€€€

Piazza della Minerva 69, 00186 **Tel** *06-695 201* **Fax** *06-679 4165* **Rooms** *135* **Map** *4 F4, 12 D3*

Favoured by Italy's first Grand Tourists, with generations following ever since, the charismatic Minerve is a fusion of old-world elegance and contemporary styling. Marble and chandeliers abound, as do wonderful frescoes, tastefully blended with cutting-edge design. Excellent rooftop bar and restaurant. **www.grandhoteldelaminerve.com**

PIAZZA NAVONA

Due Torri

⬆🔲 €€€

Vicolo del Leonetto 23, 00186 **Tel** *06-687 6983* **Fax** *06-686 5442* **Rooms** *26* **Map** *4 E3, 11 C1*

Hidden away on a quiet, cobble-stoned road towards the river, Due Torri is decorated with red velvet and brocade against golden yellow walls, marble and parquet. Once the home of cardinals, it is cosy and friendly, with smallish rooms, some with private terraces, and some with lovely balconies with views. **www.hotelduetorriroma.com**

Fontanella Borghese

⬆🔲 €€€

Largo Fontanella Borghese 84, 00186 **Tel** *06-6880 9504* **Fax** *06-686 1295* **Rooms** *29* **Map** *4 F3, 12 D1*

Due Torri's sister, and run by the same owner, it has larger rooms, though not as prettily decorated. On the second and third floors of a noble palazzo, once owned by the Borghese family, all rooms have modern facilities. Some face the quiet courtyard, others are noisier with street views. **www.fontanellaborghese.com**

Portoghesi

⬆🔲🅆 €€€

Via dei Portoghesi 1, 00186 **Tel** *06-686 4231* **Fax** *06-687 6976* **Rooms** *27* **Map** *4 E3, 11 C2*

North of the Piazza, just off Via della Scrofa, the little Portoghesi is unobtrusively tucked into the corner of the street, in a perfect location for sightseeing. Rooms are fairly small but comfortable with modern features, although the decor is uninspiring. Service is friendly and the roof terrace delightful **www.hotelportoghesiroma.com**

Teatro Pace

🔲 €€€

Via del Teatro Pace 33, 00186 **Tel** *06-687 9075* **Fax** *06-6819 2364* **Rooms** *23* **Map** *11 C3*

Just around the corner from the Piazza, the Teatro Pace opened in 2004. A beautiful ochre palazzo, lovingly restored, its original features – wooden beams, stucco and spiral stone staircase – are intact. Rooms vary but are all spacious and stylishly decorated. The suite has a tiny terrace. Good service. **www.hotelteatropace.com**

Raphael

⬆🅿🍴🔲🅆 €€€€

Largo Febo 2, 00186 **Tel** *06-682 831* **Fax** *06-687 8993* **Rooms** *59* **Map** *11 C2*

A lovely burnt-sienna palazzo, strewn with ivy and fairy lights just off the Piazza, Raphael is romantic and stylish. There are breathtaking views from its roof terrace, where meals are served in summer. Rooms are well-appointed, if fairly small. The lobby is filled with art, including a Picasso porcelain collection. **www.raphaelhotelrome.com**

PIAZZA DI SPAGNA

Erdarelli

⬆🔲 €

Via Due Macelli 28, 00187 **Tel** *06-679 1265* **Fax** *06-679 0705* **Rooms** *28* **Map** *5 A3, 12 F1*

Erdarelli is a small, family-run hotel, halfway between the Trevi Fountain and Piazza di Spagna. Ideal for those on a budget, desiring a central location away from the station. Bedrooms are basic but extremely clean. Air conditioning is available on request as a supplement and some rooms have balconies. **www.erdarelliromehotel.com**

Hotel Suisse
🗐   €€

Via Gregoriana 54, 00187 **Tel** *06-678 3649* **Fax** *06-678 1258* **Rooms** *12*   **Map** *5 A2, 12 F1*

Near the top of the Spanish Steps, the Suisse is a very quiet, distinguished *pensione* run by the same family since the 1920s. Most rooms face an internal courtyard, ideal for a good night's rest after a long day's sightseeing. Parquet floors and antique furniture abound. Breakfast is served in your room. **www.hotelsuisserome.com**

Panda
🗐 W   €€

Via della Croce 35, 00187 **Tel** *06-678 0179* **Fax** *06-6994 2151* **Rooms** *28*   **Map** *5 A2*

Panda is an appealing little hotel with a faithful clientele, offering unpretentious, cheap accommodation in one of Rome's most expensive areas. Clean rooms with or without bathrooms, but all with air conditioning, telephone and Internet access. A couple of the rooms feature original 19th-century frescoes. Friendly staff. **www.hotelpanda.it**

Art
🖪 🍴 🎦 🗐   €€€

Via Margutta 56, 00187 **Tel** *06-328 711* **Fax** *06-3600 3995* **Rooms** *46*   **Map** *4 F1, 5 A2*

The stylish and contemporary Art is located on one of Rome's most famous bohemian streets where Fellini lived in the 1950s. It has an internal garden and brightly coloured sculptural furniture. There's a lively, popular restobar for brunch and snacks in a converted chapel. Rooms, though on the small side, are very smart. **www.hotelart.it**

Casa Howard
🗐 W   €€€

Via Capo le Case 18, 00187 **Tel** *06-6992 4555* **Fax** *06-679 4644* **Rooms** *5*   **Map** *5 A3, 12 F1*

Close to the Spanish Steps, this extremely fashionable boutique hotel is English-owned and designed by Tommaso Ziffer. Rooms have dramatic individual themes, though small and not all en suite. Guests are mollycoddled by an expert concierge. Extras are available, including use of a sauna and *hammam*. **www.casahoward.com**

Concordia
🖪 🗐   €€€

Via Capo le Case 14, 00187 **Tel** *06-679 1953* **Fax** *06-679 5409* **Rooms** *24*   **Map** *5 A3, 12 F1*

Owned by an amicable family, the Concordia has many years of experience and loyal guests. Rooms are compact and clean, with a lovely breakfast room and an enchanting little roof terrace. Well placed for both the Spanish Steps and the Trevi Fountain. A good-value place, with a caring staff. **www.concordiahotel.it**

Hotel Madrid
🖪 🏃 🗐 W   €€€

Via Mario de Fiori 93–95, 00187 **Tel** *06-699 1510* **Fax** *06-679 1653* **Rooms** *26*   **Map** *12 F1*

Situated in the heart of the designer shopping area, the Madrid offers tastefully furnished rooms, some of which are ideal for small families. Rooms for non-smokers are also available and there is free WiFi access. The hotel has a superb roof terrace where breakfasting guests enjoy splendid views across the city. **www.hotelmadridroma.com**

La Lumière di Piazza di Spagna
🗐   €€€

Via Belsiana 72, 00187 **Tel** *06-6938 0806* **Fax** *06-6929 4231* **Rooms** *10*   **Map** *4 F2*

La Lumière lies on the corner with Via Condotti and the bedrooms are spacious and beautifully appointed. The suite has a private terrace. Bathrooms are a little on the small side, although some are fitted with a Jacuzzi. Breakfast is served on the roof terrace in summer. **www.lalumieredipiazzadispagna.com**

Locarno
🖪 P 🗐 W   €€€

Via della Penna 22, 00186 **Tel** *06-361 0841* **Fax** *06-321 5249* **Rooms** *66*   **Map** *4 F1*

A gorgeous Art-Deco hotel, with many original fittings intact in public spaces and bedrooms, the Locarno is a step away from Piazza del Popolo. More than just a place to rest your head, the hotel has a pleasant sitting room with a log fire and a sunny flower-filled patio and roof garden. Bikes on loan. **www.hotellocarno.com**

Parlamento
🖪 🗐   €€€

Via delle Convertite 5, 00187 **Tel/Fax** *06-6992 1000* **Rooms** *23*   **Map** *12 E1*

A delightful hotel on the top floors of a building, just off the bustling Corso. The affable, elegantly dressed owner keeps a very tight ship, offering spacious, old-fashioned rooms with heavy wooden furniture and nicely appointed bathrooms. Air conditioning is on request. Pleasant roof terrace. **www.hotelparlamento.it**

Relais Pierret
🖪 🏃 🗐 W   €€€

Piazza di Spagna 20, 00187 **Tel** *06-6919 0237* **Fax** *06-6978 4592* **Rooms** *6*   **Map** *5 A2*

This hotel enjoys a superb location in the historic Palazzo Pierret at the foot of the Spanish Steps. The six suites (some sleeping up to four people) are spacious and elegantly furnished while the ensuite bathrooms are ultra modern. Breakfast is not available but there is no shortage of good bars on the doorstep. **www.relaispierret.com**

San Carlo
🖪 🗐   €€€

Via delle Carozze 93, 00187 **Tel** *06-678 4548* **Fax** *06-6994 1197* **Rooms** *50*   **Map** *5 A2*

On a charming street just off the Corso and a short walk from the Spanish Steps, in the thick of Rome's shopping mecca, San Carlo is good value for its location, which can be a bit noisy for some. Rooms vary; superior rooms on the upper floors are of a higher standard, while some offer a terrace. Helpful staff. **www.hotelsancarloroma.com**

De Russie
🖪 P 🍴 🎦 🏃 🎦 🗐 W   €€€€€

Via del Babuino 9, 00187 **Tel** *06-328 881* **Fax** *06-3288 8888* **Rooms** *122*   **Map** *4 F1*

One of Rome's top hotels, De Russie is perfectly located off Piazza del Popolo. Guests love its lavish gardens, tranquil spa and romantic restaurant. Rooms, painted in relaxing colours, have original Mapplethorpe flower photos on the walls; bathrooms are mosaic or marble havens. Excellent concierge service. **www.hotelderussie.it**

Key to Price Guide *see p300* **Key to Symbols** *see back cover flap*

Hassler Roma 🖼️🅿️🍴🎾📺📋 €€€€€
Piazza Trinità dei Monti 6, 00187 **Tel** *06-699 340* **Fax** *06-678 9991* **Rooms** *95* **Map** *5 A2*

At the top of the Spanish Steps, this is the glitterati's choice and the *grande dame* of Rome's hotels. Service is impeccable and public spaces are luxurious with marble, chandeliers and wood panelling. Bedrooms and suites are plush, styled individually and mostly with views. Legendary roof restaurant. **www.hotelhasslerroma.com**

Portrait Suites 🖼️📋 €€€€€
Via Bocca di Leone, 00187 **Tel** *06-6938 0742* **Fax** *06-6919 0625* **Rooms** *14* **Map** *5 A2*

This boutique hotel is the baby of designer Salvatore Ferragamo and his group, Lungarno Hotels. Portrait Suites is made up of 14 luxury townhouses, three of which offer terrace views over Piazza di Spagna and the surrounding area, while the rooftop terrace is accessible to all guests. **www.lungarnohotels.com**

CAMPO DE' FIORI

Casa Banzo 📋 €€
Via Monte di Pietà 30, 00186 **Tel** *06-683 3909* **Fax** *06-686 4575* **Rooms** *6* **Map** *4 E5*

This family-run bed and breakfast is housed in a 15th-century palazzo. From the frescoed portico entrance to the formal parlour, the place exudes historic elegance. Each guestroom is unique and all are packed with luscious antiques. Quiet location but just a stone's throw from a great bar scene. **www.casabanzo.it**

Sole 📺🖼️🅿️ €€
Via del Biscione 76, 00186 **Tel** *06-6880 6873* **Fax** *06-689 3787* **Rooms** *59* **Map** *11 C4*

Another popular budget hotel near the Campo. Some rooms are en suite, others have shared bathrooms. A small internal garden and a meandering roof terrace keep the place cool. Rooms are fairly large with pleasant, if dated, furnishing and decor. One of the doubles has a private terrace. **www.solealbiscione.it**

Smeraldo 🖼️📋♿🅆 €€
Vicolo dei Chiodaroli 9, 00186 **Tel** *06-687 5929* **Fax** *06-6880 5495* **Rooms** *50* **Map** *12 D4*

Smeraldo is located in a lovely spot, halfway between the Campo and Largo Argentina. The refurbished rooms are small but charming; one of them has facilities for the disabled. The rooftop terrace, though noisy, is a nice place for an alfresco drink (bring your own). Breakfasts are hearty and staff cordial. **www.smeraldoroma.com**

Campo De' Fiori €€€
Via del Biscione 6, 00186 **Tel** *06-6880 6865* **Fax** *06-687 6003* **Rooms** *21* **Map** *4 E4, 12 D4*

Housed in a lovely pink palazzo right on the corner off the Campo de' Fiori, this hotel boasts a lovely roof terrace with pretty views. Only half of the rooms are en suite and it can be noisy, as the square is very lively. Rooms vary in size and decor. There are 15 apartments for rent in the vicinity. **www.hotelcampodefiori.com**

Locanda Cairoli 🖼️📋 €€€
Piazza Benedetto Cairoli 2, 00186 **Tel** *06-6880 9278* **Fax** *06-6889 2937* **Rooms** *15* **Map** *12 D4*

Hidden away in an old palazzo, not far from Largo Argentina, the Cairoli offers a unique experience to business travellers and tourists alike. Each of the 15 bedrooms is individually decorated with antiques, original modern art and colour. A butler service is available for particularly demanding guests. Excellent breakfast. **www.locandacairoli.it**

Ponte Sisto 🖼️🅿️🍴📋♿ €€€
Via dei Pettinari 64, 00186 **Tel** *06-686 3100* **Fax** *06-6830 1712* **Rooms** *103* **Map** *4 A5, 11 C5*

Ideally placed for both Campo de' Fiori and Trastevere, Ponte Sisto is particularly accessible for wheelchair users. A converted monastic complex, the hotel is modern in feel, with abundant terraces and a lovely cloister with restaurant and bar. The Belvedere suite on the top floor books up fast. **www.hotelpontesisto.com**

Residenza Argentina 🖼️📋 €€€
Via di Torre Argentina 47, 00186 **Tel** *06-6819 3267* **Fax** *06-6813 5794* **Rooms** *6* **Map** *12 D4*

Accessed from a tiny courtyard, just off one of Rome's main squares, the Residenza Argentina boasts minimal, boutique-hotel style interiors. Original beamed ceilings have been retained and bathrooms are equipped with hydromassage units. A substantial continental breakfast is served in the reception area. **www.argentinaresidenza.com**

Residenza Farnese 📋♿🅆 €€€
Via del Mascherone 59, 00186 **Tel** *06-6821 0980* **Fax** *06-8032 1049* **Rooms** *31* **Map** *4 E4, 11 B4*

Small and lovely, Residenza Farnese is located on a quiet side street running behind Piazza Farnese towards the Tiber. A Renaissance palazzo, the public rooms are grand; there's a billiards table in the bar. Breakfast is served on charmingly mismatched china. Nicely decorated rooms. Good service. **www.residenzafarneseroma.it**

Suore di Santa Brigida 🖼️🍴📋 €€€
Piazza Farnese 96, 00186 **Tel** *06-6889 2596* **Fax** *06-6889 1573* **Rooms** *20* **Map** *4 E4, 11 C4*

The nuns at this discreetly appealing hotel offer double rooms en suite to paying guests. B&B or half board options are also available. Internet access, air conditioning and access to the chapel and library are other pluses. Unlike many religious institutions, there is no curfew. Right on the prestigious Piazza Farnese. **www.brigidine.org**

Teatro di Pompeo

€€€

Largo del Pallaro 8, 00186 **Tel** *06-687 2812* **Fax** *06-688 05531* **Rooms** *12*   **Map** *11 C4*

A lovely little hotel built on the remains of the ancient theatre of the same name, where Julius Caesar is said to have met his destiny. Rooms are large and comfortable with wooden beams and dark wood furniture. Breakfast is served in the basement under a Roman vault. **www.hotelteatrodipompeo.it**

Hotel Saint George

€€€€€

Via Giulia 62, 00186 **Tel** *06-686 611* **Fax** *06-6866 1230* **Rooms** *64*   **Map** *11 B4*

The opulent rooms blend contemporary lines and soft colours with a timeless elegance appropriate to the Renaissance-era palazzo housing the hotel. Ideally located in the heart of the historic centre, this five-star hotel features a deluxe spa facility and excellent restaurant and lounge. **www.stgeorgehotel.it**

QUIRINAL

B&B Fellini

€€

Via Rasella 55–6, 00187 **Tel** *06-4274 2732* **Fax** *06-4239 1648* **Rooms** *6*   **Map** *5 B3*

Run by a Frenchman, this B&B is a great option. With high ceilings, rooms have parquet or marble flooring and green or gold decor, and all come with private bathrooms and air conditioning. Guests can enjoy a buffet breakfast with a view of the Quirinal. **www.fellinibnb.com**

Daphne Inn

€€

Via degli Avignonesi 20, 00187 **Tel** *06-8745 0087* **Fax** *06-2332 4997* **Rooms** *9*   **Map** *5 B3*

Daphne Inn runs over two locations, Trevi and Veneto, a short walk apart. Rooms vary in size and price, those with en suite bathrooms are in particularly high demand. All rooms, stylishly decorated and furnished, come with comfortable beds. Guests find the concierge service very helpful. **www.daphne-rome.com**

Giardino

€€

Via XXIV Maggio 51, 00187 **Tel** *06-679 4997* **Fax** *06-679 5155* **Rooms** *11*   **Map** *5 B4*

A pleasant stroll from the Trevi Fountain and the Forum, Giardino shares a street with the Quirinal Palace, the residence of the president of the Republic. Rooms are spacious and well furnished. Air conditioning is available as a supplement. Breakfast is served in a pretty room overlooking a little patio garden. **www.hotel-giardino-roma.com**

Julia

€€

Via Rasella 29, 00187 **Tel** *06-488 1637* **Fax** *06-481 7044* **Rooms** *33*   **Map** *5 B3*

A friendly little hotel in a good location on a quiet street, Julia is a short walk from the Trevi Fountain. Rooms are cheerful, featuring parquet floors, yellow walls and modern frescoes. Two apartments with superior rooms – the Domus Julia – are also available. **www.hoteljulia.it**

Fontana

€€€

Piazza di Trevi 96, 00187 **Tel** *06-678 6113* **Fax** *06-679 0024* **Rooms** *25*   **Map** *12 F2*

This fabulous hotel stands opposite the Trevi Fountain. Before becoming a hotel in the 1700s, the building was a monastery and rooms reflect this: not all have air conditioning. It's old-fashioned with charismatic service and a lovely roof terrace. The crowds below may be noisy, but there are great views. **www.hotelfontana-trevi.com**

Tritone

€€€

Via del Tritone 210, 00187 **Tel** *06-6992 2575* **Fax** *06-678 2624* **Rooms** *43*   **Map** *5 A3, 12 F1*

Near Piazza Barberini and the Trevi Fountain, Tritone has comfortable rooms and fine decor. Superior rooms feature stylish wood-veneered walls, a flat-screen TV and MP3 and plush bathrooms with power showers. A panoramic roof terrace is used for breakfast in summer. **www.tritonehotel.com**

TERMINI

Beehive

€

Via Marghera 8, 00185 **Tel** *06-4470 4553* **Rooms** *8*   **Map** *6 E3*

Probably best suited to cat-lovers, Beehive is run by a feline-loving American couple. A friendly budget travellers' haven, with its own small vegetarian eatery, stylish decor with lots of modern art and a lovely patio. No en suite rooms are available; the hotel also has some apartments for rent near Termini station. Non-smoking. **www.the-beehive.com**

Italy B&B

€

Via Palestro 49, 00185 **Tel** *06-445 2629* **Fax** *06-445 7416* **Rooms** *3*   **Map** *5 E2*

Raved about by fomer guests, the Sicilian Restivo family have moved house and opened a small B&B around the corner from their old *pensione*. Standards remain high with extremely clean, well-maintained rooms, with or without en suite bathrooms. Special deals for students include longer stays. **www.italybnb.it**

Key to Price Guide *see p300* **Key to Symbols** *see back cover flap*

RetRome Guesthouse ▤ €

Via Marghera 13, 00185 **Tel** *339-139-6667* **Rooms** *15*

Map *6 E3*

An energized and young staff owns and runs this funky little bed and breakfast in the vicinity of the train station. The rooms have distinctive 1950s and 1960s decor, with an eclectic mix of vintage finds and clever design. Shared bathrooms are spotlessly clean. Independent apartments are also available. **www.retrome.net**

Canada ▤▤▥ €€

Via Vicenza 58, 00185 **Tel** *06-445 7770* **Fax** *06-445 0749* **Rooms** *70*

Map *6 E2*

A Best Western hotel, with lovely rooms and excellent service, Canada originally housed officers from the nearby barracks. Bedrooms vary in size but all have tiled floors and antique furniture and some have ceiling frescoes. Deluxe rooms are romantic with an eye for detail. Very convenient for the station. **www.hotelcanadaroma.com**

Des Artistes ▤▤ €€

Via Villafranca 20, 00185 **Tel** *06-445 4365* **Fax** *06-446 2368* **Rooms** *40*

Map *6 E2*

A very cheerful hotel with accommodation to suit all pockets. The bedrooms here are decorated with warm fabrics and modern art and have mahogany furniture. Both en suite and communal bathrooms available. Young and helpful staff. There's also a roof terrace. **www.hoteldesartistes.com**

Fiori ▤▤ €€

Via Nazionale 163, 00184 **Tel** *06-679 7212* **Fax** *06-679 5433* **Rooms** *19*

Map *5 B4*

On a busy road, but well placed for the Forum and other sightseeing, Fiori is a small and pleasing hotel with old-fashioned decor. The breakfast room overlooks the nearby gardens of Villa Aldobrandini. Rooms are soundproofed, spacious and very clean. Air conditioning is available on request. **www.travel.it/roma/hotelfiori**

Hotel Art Deco ▤▥▤▥ €€

Via Palestro 19, 00185 **Tel** *06-445 7588* **Fax** *06-444 1483* **Rooms** *70*

Map *6 D2*

True to its name, this Best Western hotel has Art Deco features throughout – some original, some not. Rooms are large, comfortable and charmingly decorated, with heavy wood furniture and individual touches. Many of the bathrooms have Jacuzzi bathtubs. Located in an upmarket area near Termini. **www.travel.it/roma/artdeco**

Oceania ▤▤ €€

Via Firenze 38, 00184 **Tel** *06-482 4696* **Fax** *06-488 5586* **Rooms** *9*

Map *5 C3*

Small, yet very popular, Oceania has a nice location opposite Rome's opera house. Large, immaculate rooms are brightly decorated. All are en suite, with private heating and air conditioning. There is also a garage available to guests. Caring staff. **www.hoteloceania.it**

Palladium Palace ▤▤ €€

Via Gioberti 36, 00185 **Tel** *06-446 6917* **Fax** *06-446 6937* **Rooms** *81*

Map *6 D4*

Conveniently placed for Termini and public transport the Palladium is a short stroll away from Santa Maria Maggiore and the Esquiline Hill. Rooms are large and tastefully decorated. Superior rooms feature Jacuzzi bathtubs. There's also a roof terrace. Excellent staff. **www.hotelpalladiumpalace.it**

Hotel Columbia ▤▤▥ €€€

Via del Viminale 15, 00185 **Tel** *06-488 3509* **Fax** *06-474 0209* **Rooms** *43*

Map *5 C3*

This quiet gem of a hotel is found in one of Rome's busiest neighbourhoods. Dark wood and light coloured fabrics give the rooms an airy, Mediterranean feel; ask for one with a balcony. The buffet breakfast can be enjoyed on the pretty roof terrace. Close to Termini, there is good transport for sightseeing. **www.hotelcolumbia.com**

Radisson ▤▤▥▤▤▤ €€€

Via Filippo Turati 171, 00185 **Tel** *06-444 841* **Fax** *06-4434 1396* **Rooms** *232*

Map *6 E4*

The Radisson is a fabulous hotel, resplendent in glass, wood and steel, with multicoloured lighting at night. From its trendy rooftop bar and restaurant, beside an outdoor swimming pool (with gym and spa), it feels like an ocean liner. Modern rooms. Located beside Termini station. **www.radissonblue.com**

Residenza Cellini ▤▤ €€€

Via Modena 5, 00185 **Tel** *06-4782 5204* **Fax** *06-4788 1806* **Rooms** *6*

Map *5 C3*

Close to Piazza della Repubblica, the Cellini is an absolute find, though it may look unpromising from the outside. Romantic and utterly endearing, this *pensione* has six bedrooms, each decorated with great care: antiques, fresh flowers and every detail you could ask for. Wonderfully caring staff. **www.residenzacellini.it**

Boscolo Exedra ▤▤▥▤▤▤ €€€€€

Piazza Repubblica 47, 00185 **Tel** *06-489 381* **Fax** *06-4893 8000* **Rooms** *240*

Map *5 C3*

On Piazza della Repubblica, Boscolo Exedra hotel has a wonderful roof terrace with prime views over the Diocletian Baths and the Fountain of the Naiads. Rooms are pleasingly luxurious and modern in design. It also has one of Rome's few hotel pools as well as a spa. Very responsive staff. **www.boscolohotels.com**

St Regis Grand Hotel ▤▤▥▤▤▤▥ €€€€€

Via Vittorio Emanuele Orlando 3, 00185 **Tel** *06-470 91* **Fax** *06-474 7307* **Rooms** *161*

Map *5 C3*

As grand as its name, this hotel was built in 1894 as the first deluxe hotel in Rome. Now completely restored, it is one of the world's finest hotels and attracts heads of state, celebrities, royalty and industry moguls. Its restaurant, Vivendo, is cited as Rome's finest. Sumptuous rooms and impeccable service. **www.starwoodhotels.com/stregis**

AVENTINE

Hotel Santa Prisca

⟳ P ⑪ 📋 📶 W   €€

Largo M. Gelsomini 25, 00153 **Tel** *06-574 1917* **Fax** *06-574 6658* **Rooms** *49*   **Map** *8 E3*

This mid-range hotel has an inner garden and quiet peaceful rooms just minutes from the bustling Testaccio and some of the city's most famous nightclubs. Rooms are decorated in blue and yellow schemes with fanciful wall paintings and modest furniture. **www.hotelsantaprisca.it**

Sant'Anselmo

⟳ W   €€

Piazza di Sant'Anselmo 2, 00153 **Tel** *06-570 057* **Fax** *06-578 3604* **Rooms** *34*   **Map** *8 D2*

This pretty villa is on a peaceful square half way up the Aventine hill. The refurbished interior boasts elegant themed rooms, some with terraces and four-poster beds, and bathrooms are inlaid with marble and have Jacuzzi bathtubs. The lounge looks on to the hotel's garden. Warm service. **www.aventinohotels.com**

Domus Aventina

⟳ W   €€€

Via di Santa Prisca 11b, 00153 **Tel** *06-574 6135* **Fax** *06-5730 0044* **Rooms** *26*   **Map** *8 E2*

Domus Aventina is an immaculate hotel, occupying a 14th-century convent at the foot of the Aventine hill. Rooms are large and simply decorated in pastel tones. There are wonderful views of the Celian hill from many of the rooms and from the huge terrace. **www.hoteldomusaventina.com**

FortySeven

⟳ ⑪ 🍴 W ♿ W   €€€

Via Petroselli 47, 00186 **Tel** *06-678 7816* **Fax** *06-6919 0726* **Rooms** *61*   **Map** *8 E1*

FortySeven overlooks the Temple of Hercules and the lovely church of Santa Maria in Cosmedin. Modern but very stylish with lots of modern art on display and a wonderful panoramic roof terrace and bar. Rooms are spacious with lots of luxurious touches. Very friendly staff. **www.fortysevenhotel.com**

Villa San Pio

⟳ P W   €€€

Via di Santa Melania 19, 00153 **Tel** *06-570 057* **Fax** *06-574 1112* **Rooms** *78*   **Map** *8 E3*

Villa San Pio is set in a garden graced with statues. The entrance hall is furnished with velvet and brocade chairs as well as 18th-century tapestries. Some rooms have flower-stencilled furniture. Bathrooms are of marble, many with a Jacuzzi tub. Several of the rooms have terraces. **www.aventinohotels.com**

Kolbe Hotel

⟳ W ♿ W   €€€€

Via di San Teodoro 44, 00186 **Tel** *06-6992 4250* **Fax** *06-679 4975* **Rooms** *72*   **Map** *8 E1*

Perfectly placed for visiting the Palatine and Forum, this former Franciscan monastery has been lavishly restored and elegantly furnished along clean, minimalist lines. Some rooms look onto the Palatine, though those facing the internal garden and cloisters are quieter. Charming outdoors area. **www.kolbehotelrome.com**

TRASTEVERE

Cisterna

⟳ W W   €€

Via della Cisterna 7–9, 00153 **Tel** *06-581 7212* **Fax** *06-581 0091* **Rooms** *19*   **Map** *7 C1*

In the heart of Trastevere, Cisterna is a comfortable hotel with a little stone courtyard and a quiet roof terrace. Rooms are quite spacious and although basic, all have air conditioning and are en suite. Furnishings are adequate if uninspiring, but service is friendly. **www.cisternahotel.it**

Domus Tiberina

P W   €€

Via in Piscinula 37, 00153 **Tel/Fax** *06-580 3033* **Rooms** *10*   **Map** *8 D1*

Not far from the river and the Isola Tiberina, Domus Tiberina provides air conditioning, bathrooms and a 24-hour reception service in its ten flats. The rooms are cosy and richly decorated, with gold brocade bedspreads, warm yellow walls and original wooden beams in the ceiling. **www.hoteldomustiberina.it**

Hotel Trastevere

W   €€

Via Luciano Manara 24a, 00153 **Tel** *06-581 4713* **Fax** *06-588 1016* **Rooms** *9*   **Map** *7 B1*

An old hotel with a new name, the Trastevere offers airy and simply decorated rooms, with tiled floors, sturdy furniture and white walls. Facing the square of San Cosimato, all are en suite, with air conditioning in double rooms. The hotel also owns a neighbourhood restaurant, Carlo Menta, and offers half board. **www.hoteltrastevere.net**

San Francesco

⟳ P W W   €€

Via Jacopa de' Settesoli 7, 00153 **Tel** *06-5830 0051* **Fax** *06-5833 3413* **Rooms** *24*   **Map** *7 C2*

A lovely little hotel, away from the crowds, with the perfect roof terrace. Very stylish, modern rooms in a converted Franciscan convent. Professional and friendly staff. A tiny shuttle bus on the adjacent square takes you to the heart of Trastevere and a tram takes you across the river to the centre. **www.hotelsanfrancesco.net**

Key to Price Guide *see p300* **Key to Symbols** *see back cover flap*

Villa della Fonte

🔲 W   €€

Via della Fonte dell'Olio 8, 00153 **Tel** *06-580 3797* **Fax** *06-580 3796* **Rooms** *5*   **Map** *7 C1*

A delightful B&B overseen by a charming owner, Villa della Fonte is a minute's walk from Piazza Santa Maria di Trastevere. Rooms are pretty with en suite bathrooms and air conditioning. Breakfast is served on a lovely flower-strewn patio, where guests can relax through the day. **www.villafonte.com**

Santa Maria

P 🔲 ♿ W   €€€

Vicolo del Piede 2, 00153 **Tel** *06-589 4626* **Fax** *06-589 4815* **Rooms** *19*   **Map** *7 C1*

An oasis of calm in an area relatively untouched by the onslaught of time, Santa Maria has rooms around a charming courtyard filled with citrus trees, all on the ground floor with tables and chairs outside, creating a relaxed ambience. A wine bar serves snacks and drinks. One room is adapted for disabled guests. **www.hotelsantamaria.info**

VATICAN

Colors

🔲   €

Via Boezio 31, 00192 **Tel** *06-687 4030* **Fax** *06-686 7947* **Rooms** *7*   **Map** *4 D2*

Colors is an extremely popular budget option, ideally located for the Vatican. Dorm rooms, rooms with shared bathroom and en suite rooms are available. Decor is bright and cheerful with playful use of colour throughout. Kitchen facilities are provided and there is a roof terrace. Helpful staff. **www.colorshotel.com**

Lady

↕   €

Via Germanico 198, 00192 **Tel** *06-324 2112* **Fax** *06-324 3446* **Rooms** *7*   **Map** *3 C1*

An old-fashioned and very clean *pensione* with rustic decoration, Lady has wooden-beamed ceilings and lovely old doors in some rooms. While most rooms come with shared bathroom and have a lower rate, those en suite are more expensive. Fans are provided. Breakfasts are good. Near Lepanto Metro station. **www.hotelladyroma.it**

Adriatic

↕ 🔲   €€

Via Vitelleschi 25, 00193 **Tel** *06-6880 8080* **Fax** *06-689 3552* **Rooms** *42*   **Map** *3 C2*

In a quiet street, just three blocks away from St Peter's, Adriatic offers rooms with or without en suite bathroom at a very reasonable price. Rooms are carpeted and brightly coloured. Suites, which cost slightly more, have balconies. Air conditioning is available with a small supplement. There's also a sunny patio. **www.adriatichotel.com**

Florida

↕ 🔲   €€

Via Cola di Rienzo 243, 00192 **Tel** *06-324 1872* **Fax** *06-324 1857* **Rooms** *18*   **Map** *3 C2*

A quiet place to rest your head, Florida is on the second floor of a residential building, very close to St Peter's. Comfortable decor at very good prices, especially off-season. Rooms with or without bathrooms are on offer. All en suite rooms have air conditioning but breakfast is not included. **www.hotelfloridaroma.it**

Il Gattopardo Relais

🔲   €€

Viale G Cesare 94, 00192 **Tel** *06-3735 8480* **Fax** *06-3750 1019* **Rooms** *6*   **Map** *3 C1*

The Relais is a lovely little hotel near Ottaviano Metro station and a five-minute walk from the Vatican. Named after Sicilian islands, bedrooms are individually decorated, combining old-fashioned elegance with modern facilities. Delicious breakfasts using organic produce. **www.ilgattopardorelais.it**

La Rovere

↕ 🔲 W   €€

Vicolo Sant'Onofrio 4, 00165 **Tel** *06-6880 6739* **Fax** *06-6880 7062* **Rooms** *20*   **Map** *3 C4*

The quiet, family-run La Rovere is located just south of Piazza Rovere, on the lower slopes of the Janiculum, midway between the Vatican and Trastevere. Rooms are charming with wood-panelled ceilings and parquet. Roof terrace in summer. It is a short walk across the nearby bridge to the *centro storico*. **www.hotellarovere.com**

Pensione Paradise

↕   €€

Viale G Cesare 47, 00192 **Tel** *06-3600 4331* **Fax** *06-3609 2563* **Rooms** *10*   **Map** *4 D1*

Run by the same team as the Panda *pensione* near the Spanish Steps, this small hotel is beside Lepanto Metro station. Rooms are very clean and all with TV and radio. Guests can opt for en suite rooms or sharing a bathroom. Extremely good value for money. **www.pensioneparadise.com**

Residenza dei Quiriti

↕ 🔲   €€

Via Germanico 198, 00192 **Tel** *06-3600 5389* **Fax** *06-3679 0487* **Rooms** *10*   **Map** *3 C1*

A perfectly reasonable mid-range option, this small hotel is on the fourth floor of a residential building. Bedrooms are elegant; bathrooms are a little dated but some come with bathtubs. Situated midway between two Metro stations and a short stroll away from the Vatican.

Sant'Anna

↕ 🔲   €€

Borgo Pio 133, 00193 **Tel** *06-6880 1602* **Fax** *06-6830 8717* **Rooms** *20*   **Map** *3 C3*

A burnt-orange, 15th-century building houses this lovely family hotel. Bedrooms are romantic and beautifully decorated, with pastel-toned *trompe l'oeil* and marble bathrooms. Upper rooms have terraces. Breakfast is served in a cellar with cheerful murals or on the delightful sunny patio. On a charming street. **www.hotelsantanna.com**

Bramante

Vicolo delle Palline 24, 00192 **Tel** *06-6880 6426* **Fax** *06-6813 3339* **Rooms** *16*   **Map** *3 C3*

€€€

Very conveniently placed for St Peter's and beating the queues at the Vatican, Bramante was the first to open in the area, in the late 1870s. Housed in a lovely 16th-century building, bedrooms are very comfortable and elegant, all with modern facilities. In a quiet street. **www.hotelbramante.com**

Dei Mellini

Via Muzio Clementi 81, 00193 **Tel** *06-324 771* **Fax** *06-3247 7801* **Rooms** *80*   **Map** *4 E2*

€€€

A comfortable hotel with a boutique ambience, Dei Mellini mixes copious modern art with old-fashioned elegance. Rooms are spacious with lovely marble bathrooms, some with a bathtub. A delightful roof terrace with a bar. Breakfasts are ample. Situated near Castel Sant Angelo and near good public transport. **www.hotelmellini.com**

Farnese

Via A Farnese 30, 00192 **Tel** *06-321 2553* **Fax** *06-321 5129* **Rooms** *23*   **Map** *4 D1*

€€€

Conveniently placed for Lepanto Metro station and a short walk from the Vatican, Farnese is a smart, small hotel with wooden parquet floors, custom-made walnut furniture and particularly nice bathrooms. A beautiful roof terrace offers unparalleled views of the dome of St Peter's. **www.hotelfarnese.com**

Palazzo Cardinal Cesi

Via della Conciliazione 51, 00193 **Tel** *06-684 0390* **Fax** *06-6819 3333* **Rooms** *30*   **Map** *3 C3*

€€€

This former cardinal's palace is owned by a cultural association whose aim is to organize cultural events and provide lodging close to the Basilica. The palace is an absolute gem, decorated in warm crimson and sienna with parquet flooring. Rooms have modern facilities. **www.palazzocesi.it**

Spring House

Via Mocenigo 7, 00192 **Tel** *06-3972 0948* **Fax** *06-3972 1047* **Rooms** *54*   **Map** *3 A1*

€€€

The very modern Spring House is only a short walk from the Vatican Museums, and is ideally located for those wishing to beat the queues. Its public spaces are bright and cheerful and bedrooms have simple decor in swathes of colour. Rooms partially adapted for the disabled are available. Good transport links. **www.hotelspringhouse.com**

VIA VENETO

La Residenza

Via Emilia 22, 00187 **Tel** *06-488 0789* **Fax** *06-485 721* **Rooms** *29*   **Map** *5 B2*

€€

High on the Via Veneto hill, not far from the Villa Borghese or the Spanish Steps, and in a quiet side street, this small hotel offers good, old-fashioned service and pleasant rooms, some with balconies. A relative bargain in this prestigious area. Breakfasts are generous and there's a nice roof garden. **www.hotel-la-residenza.com**

Lilium

Via XX Settembre 58a, 00187 **Tel** *06-474 1133* **Fax** *06-2332 8387* **Rooms** *14*   **Map** *6 D2*

€€

On the third floor of a residential building midway between Termini and Via Veneto, Lilium is a charming little hotel. Each of its small, beautifully decorated rooms is named after a flower and painted to match. The breakfast and sitting rooms are pretty with fresh flowers. Excellent staff. **www.liliumhotel.it**

Oxford

Via Boncompagni 89, 00187 **Tel** *06-420 3601* **Fax** *06-4281 5349* **Rooms** *58*   **Map** *5 C1*

€€€

Oxford is located on a quiet residential road off Piazza Fiume, and a short stroll from Via Veneto. The hotel also offers two apartments for brief or long stays. There's a good restaurant and a friendly bar. Bedrooms are comfortable. The stylish public rooms with sofas encourage relaxation. **www.hoteloxford.com**

Boscolo Aleph

Via di San Basilio 15, 00187 **Tel** *06-422 901* **Fax** *06-4229 0000* **Rooms** *96*   **Map** *5 B2*

€€€€

This extremely trendy hotel off Piazza Barberini has an intriguing theme: heaven and hell. From its red-lit entrance onwards, the aim is to seduce guests with life's pleasures. Its spa is lauded and the experience is indeed one of expensive decadence. Perhaps not to everyone's taste, but certainly memorable. **www.boscolohotels.it**

Hotel Eden

Via Ludovisi 49, 00187 **Tel** *06-478 121* **Fax** *06-482 1584* **Rooms** *121*   **Map** *5 B2*

€€€€€

One of Rome's historic hotels with an illustrious guestbook, the Eden is beautifully decorated and works like clockwork. Its rooms and suites gleam and the concierge service is impeccable. The roof garden has a wonderful view with an acclaimed Michelin star restaurant. All at a very high price, however. **www.edenroma.com**

Majestic

Via Veneto 50, 00187 **Tel** *06-421 441* **Fax** *06-488 5657* **Rooms** *93*   **Map** *5 B2*

€€€€€

Founded in 1889, this is the oldest hotel in the area and has played host to celebrities such as Pavarotti and Sylvester Stallone. Most of the furniture and much of the decor in the public rooms are original. Bedrooms and corridors are decorated in a bold, bright style. There's also a state-of-the-art fitness centre. **www.hotelmajestic.com**

Key to Price Guide *see p300* **Key to Symbols** *see back cover flap*

Regina Hotel Baglioni

⬚ P 🍽 🏃 ☰ ♿ Ⓦ €€€€€

Via Veneto 72, 00187 **Tel** *06-421 111* **Fax** *06-4201 2130* **Rooms** *143*   **Map** *5 B2*

With an exuberant Liberty (Italian Art Nouveau) styling, the Baglioni is plush with marble, tapestries, carpets and gold. The reception area has a fabulous wrought-iron staircase guarded by a statue of Neptune, the sea god. There's also a lovely Art-Deco suite. Cosy rooms, excellent service and a good location. **www.baglionihotels.com**

Westin Excelsior

⬚ P 🍽 🏃 🍽 ☰ ♿ Ⓦ €€€€€

Via Veneto 125, 00187 **Tel** *06-470 81* **Fax** *06-482 6205* **Rooms** *319*   **Map** *5 B2*

Exotically sculpted balconies with caryatid figures announce the presence of this extravagant hotel on Via Veneto. Inside are boutiques, a wonderful spa with pool, excellent panoramic restaurants and bar and even a children's club. Rooms are sumptuous throughout with classic decor. **www.excelsior.hotelinroma.com**

VILLA BORGHESE

Buenos Aires

⬚ P ☰ €€

Via Clitunno 9, 00198 **Tel** *06-855 4854* **Fax** *06-841 5272* **Rooms** *54*

A small hotel in the heart of residential Parioli, Buenos Aires is a little further north of the Villa Borghese, but only a 10-minute walk away. Rooms are very smart and have every convenience. With many corporate clients, weekend leisure rates are often available. Transport links are good. **www.hotelbuenosaires.it**

Degli Aranci

⬚ P 🍽 🍽 ☰ Ⓦ €€

Via Barnaba Oriani 11, 00197 **Tel** *06-807 0202* **Fax** *06-807 0704* **Rooms** *58*   **Map** *2 D2*

In Parioli, an area bordering on the Villa Borghese, Degli Aranci is set in a pretty garden with holm oaks, orange trees and a trickling fountain. Rooms are very comfortable with antiques, a soothing colour palette and modern facilities. Some bedrooms have a Jacuzzi or balcony. **www.gruppoloan.it**

The Duke Hotel

⬚ P 🍽 🏃 ☰ Ⓦ €€€

Via Archimede 69, 00197 **Tel** *06-367 221* **Fax** *06-3600 4104* **Rooms** *78*   **Map** *1 C3*

Popular with visiting musicians and film actors, the Duke offers guests a peaceful stay far from the madding crowd. All three classes of room are comfortable and stylishly furnished and the ensuite bathrooms boast marble basins. Efficient service and an abundant buffet breakfast. A free shuttle runs to and from the city centre. **www.thedukehotel.com**

Villa Mangili

⬚ ☰ €€€

Via G Mangili 31, 00197 **Tel** *06-321 7130* **Fax** *06-322 4313* **Rooms** *12*   **Map** *2 D4*

In a pleasant, quiet part of Parioli, Villa Mangili is close to the Villa Borghese park near the auditorium and the Villa Giulia. Although small, it has spacious and beautifully decorated rooms with wooden parquet floors. Breakfast is served in a lovely garden. The hotel exhibits and sells the works of new artists. **www.hotelvillamangili.it**

Aldrovandi Palace

⬚ P 🍽 🍽 ☰ Ⓦ €€€€

Via Aldrovandi 15, 00197 **Tel** *06-322 3993* **Fax** *06-322 1435* **Rooms** *108*   **Map** *2 E4*

For those who prefer to stay away from the frenzy of central Rome, this relaxing luxurious hotel has a prime spot beside the Villa Borghese gardens. Rooms are elegantly decorated in subdued tones. However, the main attractions are its delightful swimming pool and the wonderful restaurant, Baby (*see p327*). **www.aldrovandi.com**

Sofitel Villa Borghese

⬚ P 🍽 ☰ €€€€

Via Lombardia 47, 00187 **Tel** *06-478 021* **Fax** *06-482 1019* **Rooms** *111*   **Map** *5 B2*

Part of the sophisticated French Sofitel chain, the Villa Borghese has classically elegant rooms with luxury facilities; many have views over the park. The much talked about contemporary dining at Le 49 restaurant is a big draw. Both the restaurant and top floor bar overlook the city. **www.sofitel.com**

TIVOLI

Palazzo Maggiore

▤ 🏃 €

Via Domenico Giuliani 89 **Tel** *393-104 4937* **Rooms** *3*

Located in the historic heart of Tivoli, the 16th-century Palazzo Maggiore offers tastefully-furnished rooms at budget rates. A two-roomed apartment is also available, sleeping up to six. The continental breakfast can be enjoyed in rooms, on the small terrace or in the owner's kitchen. Rome is just over an hour away by train. **www.palazzomaggiore.com**

Adriano

P 🍽 ☰ €€

Largo Yourcenar 2, 00010 **Tel** *0774-535 028* **Fax** *0774-535 122* **Rooms** *10*

With an illustrious clientele, Adriano is an exceedingly comfortable hotel with a fine restaurant beside Hadrian's Villa. One of the suites has romantic, privileged views directly over the Roman complex. Breakfast is served in a lovely room inside or outside on the patio and includes home-made preserves. **www.hoteladriano.it**

RESTAURANTS AND CAFES

In Rome, eating out can be both a joy and an entertainment. On warm summer evenings tables flow out into every conceivable open space and diners dedicate long hours to the popular social activity of people watching (and of being noticed and admired themselves) in a confusion of passers-by, buskers, rose sellers and traffic. Although Romans have always loved to linger at the table, the lavish feasts of ancient Rome have slimmed down and today's cooking is based on simplicity, freshness and good quality local raw ingredients in

Waiter at Alberto Ciarla (see p325)

what is essentially a seasonal cuisine. Fast food is gradually arriving, but it is fundamentally alien to the Roman temperament and way of life.

The restaurants reviewed in this chapter have been selected from the best that Rome can offer across all price ranges. Their descriptions, together with symbols providing an at-a-glance guide to facilities, will help narrow down your choice. The section on *Light Meals and Snacks* featured on pages 328–33 has details of recommended cafés, pizzerias, wine bars and other places for more casual eating.

WHERE TO FIND GOOD RESTAURANTS

Every area of the city has its own culinary delights, although certain pockets are known for more authentic Roman cooking. In Testaccio, the area surrounding the old slaughterhouse, you will find long-term neighbourhood establishments and no-frills *trattorias* serving the truest Roman fare. The Jewish quarter (the Ghetto), near Campo de'Fiori, serves Roman-Jewish cuisine, which many consider to have greatly influenced the culinary canons of the city. Around the university, in San Lorenzo, northeast of the city centre, you will find lots of cheap pizzerias and *trattorias*.

The interior of Sapori del Lord Byron (see p327)

Near Termini station there is a good selection of African – particularly Ethiopian and Eritrean – restaurants, as well as Indian and Pakistani specialities. Quartiere Monti (between Via Nazionale and Via Cavour) is also packed with multi-ethnic restaurants as well as wine bars and take-aways. For dining outdoors, which often means in beautifully secluded piazzas, or in impressively ancient parts of the city, try the restaurants in the narrow streets of Trastevere

Fresh artichokes, a Roman speciality

(the old artists' quarter), around Campo de' Fiori, or along the old Via Appia Antica.

TYPES OF RESTAURANTS

In general, a *trattoria* is an unassuming, family-run establishment with good home cooking, while a *ristorante* is more up-market, more elegant and thus more expensive.

Many eating places – where paper table-cloths give a clue to low prices – simply have no name. They offer an open doorway and, more often than not, excellent,

basic home cooking. Some of them offer a great deal more than that, and your chances of finding authentic Roman cooking are higher in the best of these establishments than in expensive restaurants.

There will probably be times when you do not want a full-blown restaurant meal, and Rome offers a huge variety of places for more casual eating *(see pp328–33).* One type of place offering snacks or more substantial dishes is the *enoteca,* which doubles as a well-stocked wine shop for browsers and connoisseurs.

Other places for a sit-down, informal lunch or dinner are *birrerie,* which are not only for beer drinkers, but also offer pizzas and even four-course meals.

There is always plenty of interesting takeaway food for sale – *pizza rustica* or *pizza al taglio* (pizza by the slice) is available all over the city. For full-size pizzas, choose places with wood stoves *(forno a legna)* for better results than from electric ovens. Other takeaways such as whole roast chicken, *pomodori al riso* (tomatoes stuffed with rice), potatoes or *supplì* (fried rice croquettes) can be had from *rosticcerie.* A self-service *tavola calda* will serve an impressive array of hot food and is ideal for lunchtimes.

VEGETARIAN FOOD

Purely vegetarian restaurants are few and far between in Rome, but everywhere you will find pasta and rice dishes (*risotto*). Most menus include an extensive list of vegetable-based side dishes (*contorni*) which could be anything from artichokes (stewed – *alla Romana* or fried – *alla giudia*), grilled or au gratin vegetables, and sautéed spinach, chard or chicory. Vegetables stuffed with rice then baked in the oven are also menu staples. Most menus are very adaptable, as dishes are prepared to order. Tell your waiter that you are *vegetariano* (female: *vegetariana*) and he will advise you accordingly.

THE PRICE OF A MEAL

What you pay will clearly depend on your choice of establishment. In a *tavola calda* or Roman pizzeria, for example, you can still eat for as little as €10 a head. A local *trattoria* costs perhaps €20, whereas in a smarter restaurant reckon on around €30 and up. Bottled wine, as opposed to a jug or carafe of house wine (*vino della casa*), commands higher prices but should offer a more interesting range of tastes (*see p314*). House wine can be a hit-or-miss affair.

READING THE MENU

Not every restaurant automatically provides a menu – the waiter will often tell you the day's specialities (*piatti del giorno*), usually not mentioned

Outdoor café life in the piazza outside Santa Maria in Trastevere

on the standard menu but almost always worth ordering. If you are not sure about these, you can always ask for *la lista* (the menu) and then allow your-self to be guided.

A meal could begin with *antipasti* (appetizers) or *primi piatti* – the latter consisting of *pasta asciutta* (pasta with some kind of sauce), *pasta in brodo* (clear broth with pasta in it), *pasta al forno* (baked pasta), risotto or a substantial soup. You then move on to the *secondi*, the main meat or fish course, for which you will usually need to order vegetables (*contorni*) separately if you would like them. Afterwards you have *formaggi* (cheeses), *frutta* (fruit) or *dolci* (desserts). Romans do not usually eat cheese as well as a sweet dish. Strong espresso coffee, and perhaps a liqueur (*amaro* or *digestivo*) rounds off the meal (*see p315*). You may want to skip the first course, or you may prefer to choose a salad or vegetable dish or substitute the main course with an *antipasto*. Pasta alone tends not to be seen as a full meal.

OPENING TIMES

Restaurants are generally open from about noon to 3pm and from 8pm to 11pm or much later. The busiest times tend to be 9pm–9.30pm for dinner and 1pm–1.30pm at lunchtime. Dinner is generally the preferred time for dedicated, relaxed eating, particularly in summer, when it will begin and end late as the heat of the day subsides. Bars are open all day, often from the early hours, serving all kinds of drinks (alcohol can be sold at any time of

day) and snacks. The quietest month is August, when many restaurant owners take their annual holiday (shown by *chiuso per ferie* signs).

BOOKING A TABLE

Booking (*prenotazione*) is generally advisable. Sunday is the main lunch date of the week when you should definitely book; the same usually goes for Saturday evening. Check the weekly closing day if you do not book. Many places are closed on Mondays, and Sunday evening can also be difficult.

In summer try to book a shady table outside, since air conditioning is not universal.

WHEELCHAIR ACCESS

Rome is becoming more solicitous towards those in wheelchairs, but a call to the restaurant in advance will help secure the right table.

TAKING CHILDREN ALONG

Children are made very welcome, particularly in family-run places. You can usually order half-portions, or just ask for an extra plate. High chairs (*seggioloni*) may also be available.

SMOKING

In 2005 regulations came into force and now restaurants and bars must provide separate no-smoking areas or face a fine. Smokers who light up in no-smoking areas are also liable to a fine. At cafés and restaurants that do not provide sealed-off areas, smoking is limited to outside tables.

One of many Trastevere cafés

The Flavours of Rome

There are few more enduring pleasures than lingering over a leisurely alfresco meal in a piazza in the Eternal City. Roman food is tasty, nutritious, simple and extremely varied. Menus tend to be seasonal and there are even specialities eaten on specific days of the week. Traditionally, Thursday is *gnocchi* day, Friday is for salted cod *(baccalà)* and Saturday for tripe. Food is redolent of aromatic herbs, olive oil, garlic and onion, and there are many signature dishes, including pasta. But much authentic Roman cuisine takes its origins from offal, and slow, inventive cooking transforms these tradtionally "poor" cuts into rich and flavoursome dishes.

Olives and olive oil

Pasta being made by hand in traditional style

CUCINA ROMANA

Traditional Roman cuisine originated in the Testaccio area, near the old slaughter-house whose butchers *(vaccinari)* were paid partly in cash and partly in meat – or rather offal. The "fifth quarter" *(quinto quarto)* included head, trotters, tail, intestines, brain and other unmentionable bits of the beast which, when carefully cooked and richly flavoured with herbs and spices, are transformed into culinary delight. These robust dishes, such as *coda alla vaccinara* (literally, "oxtail cooked in the style of the slaughter-house butcher") still feature on the menus of many of Rome's top restaurants.

For more squeamish carnivores, lamb is popular, often served simply roasted. Veal is another speciality, as is piglet flavoured with herbs.

Authentic *Cucina Sromana* also has roots in the Jewish cuisine of the Ghetto area. Local globe artichokes are fried whole in olive oil *(carciofi alla giudia)* or served *alla romana*, with oil, garlic and Roman mint. Courgette (zucchini) flowers are also deep-fried, as are Jewish-style salt cod fillets *(filetti di baccalà)*.

Seafood and fish restaurants are among the best in Rome, although they can be very

Marinated artichokes · Roast peppers · Sun-blush tomatoes · Sweet baby peppers · Olives · Marinated mushrooms

Selection of delicious, typically Roman *antipasti* (appetizers)

REGIONAL DISHES AND SPECIALITIES

As an appetizer, *bruschetta* (Roman dialect for "lightly burnt bread") may be topped with a selection of intense flavours. Other *antipasti* include crispy-fried or marinated vegetables. A favourite pasta dish is *bucatini all'amatriciana* – pasta tubes in a spicy tomato and sausage or bacon sauce, sprinkled with grated tangy pecorino cheese. Veal is a great favourite and delicacies include *rigatoni alla pajata* (pasta with milk-fed veal intestines). Lamb is also very popular, in dishes such as *abbacchio al forno* (roasted milk-fed lamb) or *alla cacciatore* ("huntsman's style" with anchovy sauce). The generic word for offal is *animelle* and Roman delicacies include *cervelle* (calves' brains), *pajata* (veal intestines) and *trippa* (tripe).

Bruschetta

Supplì *These tasty fried rice croquettes are stuffed with mozzarella cheese that oozes out when they are cut.*

Selecting fresh vegetables at a market in central Rome

LA DOLCE VITA

For those with a taste for "the sweet life", nuts, fruits and versatile ricotta cheese are often combined in mouthwateringly delicious sweets. Ice cream is an art form in Rome, where some parlours offer over 100 flavours of home-made *gelati*. Types vary from the classic *crema* and *frutta* to *grattachecca* (water ice), from *semifreddo* (a half-frozen sponge pudding, similar to *tiramisù* in consistency) to *granità* (ice shavings flavoured with fruit syrups). Glorious *gelato* is one of the great pleasures here, to be enjoyed at any time of the day or night.

expensive. Everything is available, from sumptuous seafood platters to small fish caught off the Lazio coast and served fried or used in soups, as well as superb sea bass cooked Roman-style with porcini mushrooms.

PASTA, PASTA

Pasta is the mainstay of the Roman meal, especially spaghetti. *Spaghetti alla carbonara*, made with *pancetta* (cured bacon) or *guanciale* (pig's cheek), egg yolks and cheese, is a classic Roman dish, as is *spaghetti alle vongole*, with clams. There is even, uniquely, a museum devoted to pasta in Rome. The National Pasta Museum (Museo Nazionale delle Paste Alimentari) *(see p160)* charts the history and shapes of, at a conservative estimate, one type of pasta for every day of the year. Many have wonderfully descriptive or poetic names, such as *capelli d'angelo* (angel's hair) or *ziti* (bridegrooms) whose shape is best left to the imagination. The museum's motto is *la pasta è gioia di vivere* – "pasta is the joy of living".

Huge wheels of pecorino cheese ready to be cut and enjoyed

ON THE MENU

Abbacchio alla cacciatora Lamb simmered in Castelli Romani wine with anchovies, garlic, rosemary and olive oil.

Bruschetta Toasted bread rubbed with garlic, drizzled with olive oil, may be served with a variety of toppings

Gnocchi alla romana Little semolina dumplings served with a tomato or *ragù* sauce, or just with butter.

Pecorino romano The traditional Roman cheese, made from ewe's milk.

Spigola alla romana Sea bass with *porcini* mushrooms, shallots, garlic, Castelli Romani wine and olive oil.

Spaghetti alla carbonara *The creamy sauce thickens as the hot pasta mixes into the egg yolks and cheese.*

Saltimbocca alla romana *Veal slices are rolled with prosciutto and sage. Saltimbocca means "jump in the mouth".*

Crostata di ricotta *This rich, baked cheesecake is made using ricotta and flavoured with Marsala and lemon.*

What to Drink in Rome

Roman mosaic showing bird and vines

Italy is one of Europe's most significant wine-producing countries, keeping up a tradition started in the hills around Rome over 2,000 years ago. Today, wine is usually drunk with meals as a matter of course, and knowing the difference between *rosso* (red) and *bianco* (white) may be all the vocabulary you need to get by. Beer is widely available too, as well as good ranges of apéritifs and digestifs. Rome's drinking water, another debt to the ancient Romans, is particularly good, fresh and sweet, and in abundant supply.

The vineyards of Frascati, southeast of Rome

WHITE WINE

Orvieto   Frascati

Vines thrive in the warm climate of Lazio, the region around Rome, producing abundant supplies of inexpensive dry white wine for the city's cafés and restaurants. It is usually sold by the carafe. Of local bottled wines, Frascati is the best-known, but Castelli Romani, Marino, Colli Albani and Velletri are very similar in style. All are made from one grape variety, the Trebbiano, though better quality versions contain a dash of Malvasia for perfume and flavour. Other central Italian whites worth trying are Orvieto and Verdicchio. Quality white wines from all over Italy, including fine whites from Friuli in the northeast, are widely available in Rome.

Calcaia comes from Barberani, a reliable producer of Orvieto.

Bigi produce good quality Orvieto, especially the single-vineyard Torricella.

WINE TYPE	GOOD VINTAGES	GOOD PRODUCERS
WHITE WINE		
Friuli (Pinot Bianco, Chardonnay, Pinot Grigio, Sauvignon)	The most recent	Gravner, Jermann, Puiatti, Schiopetto, Volpe Pasini
Orvieto/ Orvieto Classico	The most recent	Antinori, Barberani, Bigi, Il Palazzone
RED WINE		
Chianti/ Chianti Classico/ Chianti Rufina	2001, 2000, 99, 97, 95, 90, 88, 85	Antinori, Castello di Ama, Castello di Cacchiano, Castello di Volpaia, Felsina Berardenga, Fontodi, Frescobaldi, Isole e Olena, Il Palazzino, Riecine, Rocca delle Macie, Ruffino, Vecchie Terre di Montefili, Villa Cafaggio
Brunello di Montalcino/ Vino Nobile di Montepulciano	2001, 99, 97, 95, 90, 88, 85	Altesino, Avignonesi, Biondi Santi, Caparzo, Case Basse, Lisini, Il Poggione, Poliziano, Villa Banfi
Barolo/Barbaresco	2006, 2004, 2000, 99, 98, 97, 95, 90, 89, 88	Aldo Conterno, Altare, Ceretto, Clerico, Gaja, Giacomo Conterno, Giacosa, Mascarello, Ratti, Voerzio

Casal Pilozzo is an easy-drinking white wine from Frascati producers, Colli di Catone. Choose the youngest vintage.

Colle Gaio, with its rich, fruity flavour, stands out among the dry white Frascatis.

Tuscan table wine   Barolo

RED WINE

Though some local red wine is made, most of the bottled red wine in Rome comes from other parts of Italy. Regions like Tuscany and Piedmont produce very good everyday drinking as well as top-class wines like Barolo. Price should reflect quality – try Dolcetto, Rosso di Montalcino or Montepulciano for good-value reds.

READING THE LABEL

Italy has a two-tier system for labelling quality wine. DOC *(denominazione di origine controllata)* means you can be sure the wine is from the region declared on the label and is made from designated grape varieties. A higher classification – DOCG *(denominazione di origine controllata e garantita)* – is given to top wines such as the reds Barolo, Barbaresco, Chianti Classico and Brunello di Montalcino.

Chianti Classico

Montepulciano d'Abruzzo, a rich and juicy red wine, is always good value. It is produced in the Abruzzi region east of Rome.

Chianti Classico Riserva is older and stronger than a normal Chianti Classico.

Torre Ercolana is produced in small quantities and is generally regarded as one of Lazio's best red wines. It is made from Cesanese and Cabernet grapes and requires at least five years' ageing

APÉRITIFS AND OTHER DRINKS

Bitter, herb-flavoured drinks like Martini, Campari or Aperol are the most popular apéritifs. (Ask for an *analcolico* if you prefer a non-alcoholic one.) Italians drink their apéritifs neat or with ice and soda. Strong after-dinner drinks, known as *digestivi* or *amari*, are worth trying, as is aniseed *sambuca*, served with coffee beans. Italian brandy and grappa can be very fiery and Italian beer is made in lager style.

Campari

SOFT DRINKS

Italian fruit juices are good and most bars squeeze fresh orange juice *(spremuta di arancia)* on the spot. Iced coffee and fruit-flavoured tea, such as peach, are popular.

Refrigerated storage for wine and beer

DRINKING WATER

Unlike many Mediterranean cities, Rome benefits from a constant supply of fresh drinking water, piped down from the hills through a system of pipes and aqueducts which has changed little from ancient Roman times. Only if there is a sign saying *acqua non potabile* is the water not safe to drink.

One of Rome's many fresh water drinking fountains

Coffee is almost more important to Roman life than wine. Take espresso for neat strong black coffee at any time of day, milky cappuccino for breakfast or mid-afternoon, caffè latte for extra milk.

Espresso

Cappuccino

Caffè latte

Choosing a Restaurant

The restaurants in this guide have been selected for their good value, good food and attractive interiors. The chart below lists restaurants in Rome by area, and the entries are alphabetical within each price category. For more information, see *Light Meals and Drinks* on pages 328–33.

PRICE CATEGORIES
For a three-course meal for one, half a bottle of house wine, and all unavoidable extra charges such as cover, service, tax:
€ up to €25
€€ €26–44
€€€ €45–64
€€€€ €65–80
€€€€€ over €80

PIAZZA DELLA ROTONDA

Enoteca Corsi
€

Via del Gesù 87/88, 00186 **Tel** *06-679 0821*
Map *4 F4, 12 E3*

A friendly wine bar in informal surroundings, Enoteca Corsi has wooden shelves straining under the weight of wine bottles. The charming staff explain the daily specials written on a blackboard. *Pasta e fagioli, zuppa di farro* (spelt soup), *orecchiette pasta con carciofi* (artichokes) or *pollo con peperoni* (chicken with peppers) are typical dishes.

Alle Due Colonne
€€

Via del Seminario 122, 00186 **Tel** *06-678 1449*
Map *4 F4, 12 D3*

Evocative of ancient Rome, the decor of this restaurant includes two imperial columns, from which it gets its name, and a fountain. The cuisine is rich in Mediterranean flavours, with most dishes cooked on the spot. The *spigola alla griglia* (grilled sea bass) and grilled buffalo mozzarella *con radicchio* are particularly good.

Boccondivino
€€

Piazza Campo Marzio 6, 00186 **Tel** *06-6830 8626*
Map *4 F3, 12 D2*

The "Divine Mouthful" offers pan-Italian cuisine with specialities such as *tonnarelli con gamberi* (fresh pasta with prawns). Equal attention is paid to food and decor, which is decidedly modern with zebra-striped chairs. Specific dishes are seasonal, but there is something for everyone here.

Da Gino
€€

Vicolo Rosini 4, 00186 **Tel** *06-687 3434*
Map *4 F3, 12 D1*

Da Gino is an extremely friendly restaurant, packed to the gills with politicans and journalists. The frescoed, old-fashioned interior opens on to a charming pergola in favourable weather. Classic Roman dishes include *spaghetti alla carbonara, l'abbacchio alla cacciatora* (a lamb dish), *seppie con piselli* (cuttlefish with peas), and rabbit.

Grano
€€

Piazza Rondanini 53, 00186 **Tel** *06-6819 2096*
Map *12 D2*

Near the Pantheon, Grano offers classic Mediterranean cuisine to a varied clientele. Large platters of local staples, such as *spaghetti alla carbonara* and *bucatini alla amatriciana* (a spicy bacon and tomato sauce) are served as first courses, followed by roast suckling pig. In warmer months, alfresco dining is available.

La Matricianella
€€

Via del Leone 2–4, 00186 **Tel** *06-683 2100*
Map *4 F3, 12 D1*

A mere stroll away from the Parliament, Matricianella is surrounded by tourist traps. It's an old *trattoria*, known for its traditional food, relaxed atmosphere and prompt service. The extremely reliable and typically Roman menu features fried sweetbreads, *fettuccine* with liver and lamb stew. Good wines and cheeses. Tables outside in summer.

L'Eau Vive
€€

Via Monterone 85, 00186 **Tel** *06-688 01095*
Map *12 D3*

Prepared and served by friendly lay sisters from a French religious order, L'Eau Vive offers classic French cuisine with all profits going to missions in Africa and India. *Quiche lorraine, escargots* (snails), French onion soup and *duck à l'orange* are standards but couscous and international dishes also feature. Beautiful, frescoed dining rooms.

Maccheroni
€€

Piazza delle Coppelle 44, 00186 **Tel** *06-6830 7895*
Map *12 D2*

This attractive restaurant adds modern cool to a retro trattoria base. The food is a similar successful blending of traditional Roman dishes (the *spaghetti alla carbonara* is very good) and some more unusual dishes like *fettuccine al tartufo* (with truffles). The grilled meats are good choices for main courses. Great for alfresco dining but book at weekends.

Clemente alla Maddalena
€€€

Piazza della Maddalena 4/5, 00186 **Tel** *06-683 3633*
Map *4 F3, 12 D2*

A 16th-century palazzo opposite the Maddalena church, it has charming wood-panelled dining rooms and a nice terrace in summer. Its creative cooking features *taglioni* (fresh egg pasta) with clams and artichokes, fillet of Chianino beef with porcini mushrooms and chestnut cake with orange sauce. Excellent wine list and attentive service.

Key to Symbols *see back cover flap*

Fortunato al Pantheon ▤ €€€
Via del Pantheon 55, 00186 **Tel** *06-679 2788* **Map** *4 F4, 12 D2*

Fortunato al Pantheon's excellent cuisine and location attract politicans from the nearby Parliament buildings despite its outdated decor. Rather than sit on its laurels, this long-standing restaurant constantly revives its menu, offering splendid, seasonal fare from a traditional repertoire at reasonable prices.

Il Bacaro ▤ €€€
Via degli Spagnoli 27, 00186 **Tel** *06-687 2554* **Map** *4 F3, 12 D2*

In a little alley, the tiny, romantic Il Bacaro boasts an imaginative cuisine. Dishes include risotto with Castelmagno cheese and red wine, pasta with a *carbonara* and asparagus sauce, fillet steak in Merlot sauce and grouper fish *carpaccio* with oregano and tomato. Chocolate mousse with hot chocolate sauce is a favourite dessert. Book ahead.

La Campana ⚹▤ €€€
Vicolo della Campana 18, 00186 **Tel** *06-686 7820* **Map** *12 D1*

A historic *trattoria*, this is Rome's oldest, established in 1518. Its exterior, though somewhat unpromising, camouflages a gem inside. Dishes, such as chicken *galantina*, pasta with broccoli and sting-ray broth, tripe and peppery chicken are followed by lovely cooked cherries with ice cream. Excellent service and a good wine list.

Riccioli Café ▤& €€€
Via delle Coppelle 13, 00186 **Tel** *06-6821 0313* **Map** *2 F3*

This youthful, trendy hotspot features seafood galore. The menu combines a fusion of Mediterranean classics, *sushi* and *sashimi*, and there's even an oyster bar. Some good meat dishes are also available, and you can choose from an ample international wine list. Riccioli opens for breakfast, lunch, happy hour and dinner.

Sangallo ▤ €€€
Via dei Coronari 180, 00186 **Tel** *06-686 5549* **Map** *4 E3*

An elegant restaurant, Sangallo has a daily menu, often including dishes based on the catch of the day. Sangallo is renowned, however, for its buffalo meat and cheese dishes: pasta with buffalo ragù, *carpaccio*, *stracotto* (a type of stew), not to mention various cheese dishes, all bear witness to the restaurant's southern Lazio roots.

Trattoria ⚹▤ €€€
Via del Pozzo delle Cornacchie 25, 00186 **Tel** *06-6830 1427* **Map** *12 D2*

A fresh take on Sicilian inspired cuisine that focuses on dishes flavoured with herbs, citrus zest and nuts; examples include meatballs with pistachios and almonds, or scallops with oranges and nuts. The restaurant has a contemporary design and the wine list is rigorously Sicilian.

La Rosetta ▤ €€€€€
Via della Rosetta 8, 00186 **Tel** *06-6830 8841* **Map** *4 F3, 12 D2*

Booking is imperative at La Rosetta, Rome's finest fish restaurant. Internationally acclaimed, it can be fiendishly expensive, although a cheaper menu is available at lunchtime. Ingredients, such as oysters, tuna, cuttlefish and grouper, are guaranteed to be the freshest. Food is simple, but expertly cooked. Excellent wine.

PIAZZA NAVONA

Da Tonino ▨⚹ €
Via del Governo Vecchio 18, 00186 **Tel** *333-587 0779* **Map** *4 E4*

The quintessential neighbourhood *trattoria*, this no-frills eatery serves heaped portions of home-style Roman cuisine, including one of the city's best *carbonaras*, at rock bottom prices. The atmosphere is cosy, warm and truly authentic. Order house wine and save room for *tiramisu* or ricotta *crostata* with pine nuts.

Fraterna Domus ⚹▤& €
Via di Monte Brianzo 62 (corner of Via del Cancello), 00186 **Tel** *06-6880 2727* **Map** *11 C1*

A small hostel, run by a group of friendly nuns, Fraterna Domus serves three-course meals at set lunchtime and dinner-time sittings. Try the minestrone or *pollo arrosto* (roast chicken) – if they figure on the menu – for a fraction of the price of other *centro storico* eateries. Book in advance. All credit cards, except AmEx, accepted. Closed on Thursdays.

Da Luigi ⚹▤& €€
Piazza Sforza Cesarini 24, 00186 **Tel** *06-686 5946* **Map** *11 B3*

On Da Luigi's impressive, verdant square, the chef offers traditional Roman cooking. The restaurant's crowd-pleasing menu is extremely comprehensive. On offer are various salads and fish *carpaccio*, fresh oysters, pastas, grilled fish and meat dishes, in addition to standards such as fried brains and baked lamb.

Cul de Sac ▤ €€
Piazza Pasquino 73, 00186 **Tel** *06-6880 1094* **Map** *4 E4, 11 C3*

With over 30 years of experience, Cul de Sac is Rome's oldest wine bar. While the wine list offers thousands of wines, from Italy and beyond, the food menu also has an equally wide choice. The smoked swordfish, creamed red lentils, sundried tomatoes, chickpea sausages, cheese, *salumi* and pâtés make for a substantial meal.

Etabli' Restaurant & Wine Bar

Vicolo delle Vacche 9a, 00186 **Tel** *06-9761 6694*   €€

                                                               Map *4 E4*

This wine bar and restaurant is a sophisticated blend of classic and creative. The menu spans Italy and the Mediterranean with dishes like fish tartare and couscous alongside more traditional cheese and meat plates. The restaurant has rich pastel tones, antique furniture and a long wine list.

La Focaccia

Via della Pace 11, 00186 **Tel** *06-6880 3312*   €€

                                                               Map *11 C3*

On a beautiful lane behind Piazza Navona, La Focaccia is a stylish and busy place, with an impressive dining room and tables outside in summer. Simple cuisine is on offer. *Zeppole* (fritters), pasta and grilled meats are typical fare. A great place for people-watching, it mainly draws a cosmopolitan clientele.

Il Cantuccio

Corso Rinascimento 71, 00186 **Tel** *06-6880 2982*   €€€

                                                  Map *4 E3, 11 C2*

Dazzling at night with candlelight and mirrors, Il Cantuccio is celebrated by the rich and the famous. Try the potato soup, flavoured with cod roe and pecorino cheese or the baked turbot in a potato and courgette crust. End with home-made *profiteroles* or *Vin Santo* with *cantuccini* biscuits. Great service and open till after midnight.

Hostaria dell'Orso

Via dei Soldati 25c, 00186 **Tel** *06-6830 1192*   €€€€€

                                                  Map *11 C2*

A smart restaurant inside a historic 14th-century palazzo, it offers superb food, excellent service and an extensive wine list. There's also an elite piano bar and nightclub below. A four-course tasting menu is available. Home-made *tortellini* and hay-steamed sea bass with pesto sauce are typical dishes. Open only in the evening.

PIAZZA DI SPAGNA

Tad Café

Via del Babuino 155a, 00187 **Tel** *06-9506 1482*   €

                                                  Map *5 A2*

Perfectly located, near Piazza del Popolo, this modern and stylish café with a picturesque patio garden serves daily specials and light meals. Extremely popular after a morning's window-shopping by well-heeled Romans, the food combines Italian and Eastern inspiration. Particularly recommended for lunches.

Buca di Ripetta

Via di Ripetta 36, 00186 **Tel** *06-321 9391*   €€

                                                  Map *4 F1*

Beyond the wine and food shop, Buca di Ripetta has a few tables, surrounded by wooden shelves heaving with wine and beautiful wrought-iron chandeliers. Wine is by the glass or bottle and there are delicious daily specials such as fillet steak in Barolo, in addition to the menu of salads, pastas and cheese or *salumi* platters. Efficient staff.

Edy

Vicolo del Babuino 4, 00187 **Tel** *06-3600 1738*   €€

                                                  Map *4 F1*

Edy is a friendly and, at times, noisy place to eat in a nice location. Prices, given the area, are very reasonable. The blackboard at the door indicates daily specials, such as *fettuccine ai funghi porcini*, *scamorza* (smoked cheese) *al prosciutto*, grilled prawns or veal cutlets. The service is relaxed.

Fiaschetteria Beltramme

Via della Croce 39, 00187   €€

                                                  Map *5A2*

This delightful hostelry was set up in 1886 and has maintained its fascination. The atmosphere is convivial and informal, though a little cramped at times, with walls full of paintings. You cannot make a reservation and may have to share a table. Fish is served on Friday. The cuisine is typically Roman.

'Gusto

Piazza Augusto Imperatore 9, 00186 **Tel** *06-322 6273*   €€

                                                  Map *4 F2*

A family-owned emporium, with a wine bar, *osteria*, pizzeria and restaurant to choose from, 'Gusto is extremely popular. The food is of a very high standard and you may have to queue. Open every day, all year round. The Sunday brunch offers particular value. There's a sun trap, with tables outside. Young and very friendly staff.

Il Giardino

Via Zucchelli 29, 00187 **Tel** *06-488 5202*   €€

                                                  Map *5 B3*

A stroll away from Piazza Barberini, beyond the dining rooms lies the pretty garden that gives the restaurant its name. You can sit here in summer and winter. The menu offers excellent pasta dishes such as *spaghetti con vongole veraci* (clams) and *linguini al limone*. Reasonable prices for the area and reliable cuisine.

Margutta Vegetariana

Via Margutta 118, 00187 **Tel** *06-3265 0577*   €€

                                                  Map *4 F1*

A colourful, plant-filled dining room with modern art in profusion and a jazz soundtrack, this is Rome's first and finest vegetarian eatery. It also offers a special rate buffet lunch and an excellent value Sunday brunch. The adjacent restaurant prepares vegetarian meals with creative flair at much higher prices.

Key to Price Guide *see p316* **Key to Symbols** *see back cover flap*

Palatium
Via Frattina 94, 00187 **Tel** *06-6920 2132*

🔲 ⓩ   €€

Map 5 A2

This wine bar and restaurant is unique – sponsored by the Lazio region, it showcases the best products from the countryside around Rome, including wines, cheeses, cold cuts and even Lazio's own olive oils and mineral waters. Hot dishes include chickpea soup served with *baccalà* (salt cod) and *abbacchio alla scottadito* (fried lamb cutlets).

La Penna d'Oca
Via della Penna 53, 00126 **Tel** *06-320 2898*

🔲 ⓩ   €€€

Map 4 F1

A short stroll from Piazza del Popolo, La Penna d'Oca is an appealing *trattoria* with a cosy, elegant dining room and a pleasant terrace in summer. Creative Roman Mediterranean cooking, friendly service and an excellent wine list are the attractions. *Farro* and goose tart, *risotto alle ostriche* (oyster risotto), or turbot and basil are typical choices.

Le Sorelle
Via Belsiana 30, 00187 **Tel** *06-679 4969*

🔲   €€€

Map 4 F2

Run by two sisters, Le Sorelle has attracted a loyal following, with a second branch in the Lateran. The atmosphere is cosy and the cuisine is creative Mediterranean. Scrambled egg with truffles, cream of *porcini* mushrooms in a pastry crust and ravioli with gorgonzola and walnuts are typical dishes.

Nino dal 1934
Via Borgognona 11, 00187 **Tel** *06-679 5676*

🔲 ⓩ   €€€

Map 5 A2, 12 E1

A family restaurant with elegant surroundings, Nino serves genuine Tuscan cooking, drawing prestigious regulars. Try the delicious spinach, bean and tomato soup, *salumi* or pasta for starters, Fiorentina steaks, seasonal game and catch of the day for seconds. Old-fashioned service. Italian-only wine list with a heavy Tuscan bias.

Casina Valadier
Piazza Bucarest, 00187 **Tel** *06-6992 2090*

🔲 ⓩ 🔳   €€€€

Map 5 A1

The Casina Valadier is a restored historic palace set within the Villa Borghese, just a 10-minute walk from the top of the Spanish Steps. The food is creative Italian, served in the dining rooms on two floors. There's a nice, spacious terrace, with spectacular views.

Dal Bolognese
Piazza del Popolo 1, 00187 **Tel** *06-361 1426*

🔲   €€€€

Map 4 F1

With a convenient location and potential for easy pickings, this long-established restaurant serves extremely good Emilian cuisine. The menu features seasonal dishes, such as *tagliatelle al tartufo* (truffle) and *pappardelle* with duck *ragù*. Favoured by politicians and Italian celebrities. Service is prompt and the wine list impressive.

Hassler Roof Garden Imagò
Piazza Trinità dei Monti 6, 00187 **Tel** *06-6993 4726*

🔲 ⓩ 🔳 🔳   €€€€€

Map 5 A2

On the top floor of Hotel Hassler Roma, this restaurant overlooks the Spanish Steps, with a bird's-eye view of the roofs of old Rome. With impeccable service and delicious Italian food with a creative twist, it is ideal for a romantic meal or a moment of pure folly.

Le Jardin du Russie
Via del Babuino 9, 00187 **Tel** *06 3288 8870*

⭐🔲 ⓩ   €€€€€

Map 4 F1

Surrounded by beautiful gardens, Le Jardin serves Italian food that does not disappoint. The changing menu offers tantalizing fare such as *foie gras* with tangerine chutney, *fettuccine* with *porcini* mushrooms, John Dory with endive and truffle, and honey with pears in red wine. There's also a children's menu.

CAMPO DE' FIORI

Insalata Ricca
Via dei Chiavari 85, 00186 **Tel** *06-6880 3656*

🔳🔲   €

Map 11 C4

Of the several Insalata Riccas in the city, this flagship branch has the edge. While pasta eaters are catered for, the restaurant is best known for its abundant, reasonably-priced bowls of salad. Over 30 exotically-named combinations grace the menu, from standard Niçoise to house favourite *Baires* (gorgonzola, apple and walnut).

Sora Margherita
Piazza delle Cinque Scole 30, 00186 **Tel** *06-687 4216*

🔲   €

Map 12 D5

This unmarked trattoria is a local institution. Traditional Roman Jewish dishes such as *carciofi alla giudia* (deep-fried artichokes) are served alongside classics like *pasta cacio e pepe* (pasta with pecorino cheese and pepper) and *ossobuco* (stewed oxtail). Be prepared to share a table and fill in a membership card (a licensing arrangement).

Al Pompiere
Via S. M. de' Calderari 38, 00186 **Tel** *06-686 8377*

🔲   €€

Map 4 F5, 12 D5

Located on the first floor of Palazzo Cenci in the Ghetto, Al Pompiere has an attractive dining room with frescoes and wooden beams. The authentic Roman-Jewish menu features *carciofi alla giudia* (twice-fried artichokes), *rigatoni con la coda* (oxtail sauce), beef stew with citron and baby lamb. Desserts include *ricotta fritta* (deep-fried ricotta cheese).

Ar Galletto

📋♿ €€

Piazza Farnese 102, 00186 **Tel** *06-686 1714*

Map 11 C4

The main attraction at this popular trattoria is the location. In warmer months you can dine out in a corner of the Piazza Farnese overlooking the fountains and the vast Farnese Palace. The menu features straightforward but tasty Italian dishes; their *penne all'arrabbiata* (pasta with a spicy tomato sauce) deserves a special mention.

Da Pancrazio

🚶 €€

Piazza del Biscione 92, 00186 **Tel** *06-686 1246*

Map 11 C4

The main attraction here is the underground dining area, once part of the ancient Pompey's Theatre, where Julius Caesar met his destiny. The menu is classically Roman: *pasta alla amatriciana* (a spicy bacon and tomato sauce), *saltimbocca* (veal escalopes with Parma ham and sage) and roast *abbacchio* (lamb). Closed Wed.

Ditirambo

🚶📋 €€

Piazza della Cancelleria 74–75, 00186 **Tel** *06-687 1626*

Map 11 C4

This popular restaurant sources organic produce for its original takes on classic Italian cuisine. The cold cuts and cheeses are safe bets, but the more adventurous will opt for dishes such as the *ravioli alla zucca* (pumpkin ravioli) or specialities like the *baccalà* (salt cod) in a thyme and sesame-seed crust. Service is brisk. Book ahead.

Il Gonfalone

€€

Via del Gonfalone 7, 00186 **Tel** *06-6880 1269*

Map 11 A3

A Renaissance palazzo, just off Via Giulia, Il Gonfalone is especially pretty in summer when you can dine alfresco. It is a beautiful setting with candlelit tables in the evening, and the menu is accompanied by an extensive wine list. The chef serves creative Neapolitan cuisine prepared with fresh seasonal ingredients. Pizza is also available.

Monserrato

📋 €€

Via Monserrato 96, 00186 **Tel** *06-687 3386*

Map 4 D4, 11 B4

Popular and well-located, with outdoor tables in summer, Monserrato is renowned for the quality of its fish and seafood. Service is impeccable and the fish arrives fresh every day. *Bigoli* with prawns and asparagus and sea bass in salt are excellent. Appetizing steaks and meat dishes are also available.

Thien Kim

🚶📋 €€

Via Giulia 201, 00186 **Tel** *06-6830 7832*

Map 4 E5, 11 C5

This Vietnamese restaurant has been here since 1974 and serves authentic food, which has attracted a faithful following. Spring rolls, noodle and rice dishes, with pork, prawn, chicken, duck and beef are on offer, flavoured with lemon grass, chilli and coconut milk. Only open in the evening.

Da Giggetto

📋 €€€

Via Portica d'Ottavia 21, 00186 **Tel** *06-686 1105*

Map 4 F5, 12 D5

An old-fashioned place, Da Giggetto offers an attentive service. In summer there are lovely tables outside, overlooking the Portica d'Ottavia. Cooking follows the Roman-Jewish tradition: the *carciofi alla giudia* (deep-fried artichokes) are the restaurant's pride and joy. Popular with tourists and locals.

Il Drappo

📋♿ €€€

Vicolo del Malpasso 9, 00186 **Tel** *06-687 7365*

Map 4 D4, 11 B3

The small, intimate Drappo is decorated with ceiling drapes (hence the name), plants and candlelight inside and a welcoming patio garden and terrace outside. It serves authentic Sardinian cuisine, with choices from *terra e mare*. Staples include ricotta, spinach and mint ravioli, *aragosta* (lobster) *alla catalana* and duck with apples or blueberries.

Sora Lella

🚶📋 €€€

Via Ponte Quattro Capi 16, 186 **Tel** *06-686 1601*

Map 8 D1

In an enviable location, on the enchanting Isola Tiberina, the impressive Sora Lella was founded by the famous actress Lella Fabrizi in 1959. Excellent classic dishes such as *tonnarelli alla cuccagna* (fresh pasta with sausage, ham and walnuts) are staples. There are also delicious vegetarian and fish menus. Friendly service.

Piperno

📋♿ €€€€

Via Monte de' Cenci 9, 00186 **Tel** *06-6880 6629*

Map 4 F5, 12 D5

A restaurant has been here since the mid-1800s, though the original Piperno is long gone. His name still carries great kudos, however, as one of the finest in Roman-Jewish cooking. Pasta is made fresh every day; the fish arrives daily. The house wine is a delicious Frascati. Don't miss the *carciofi alla giudia* (twice-fried artichokes). Book ahead.

Camponeschi

📋 €€€€€

Piazza Farnese 50, 00186 **Tel** *06-687 4927*

Map 4 E5, 11 C4

One of Rome's finest restaurants, Camponeschi offers wonderful views of the Piazza Farnese. Its creative Italian and Mediterranean cuisine is extremely refined. Superb fish and meat dishes. Its *cantina* (cellar) contains over 400 wines, including its own prestigious label from the family vineyard. Open in the evenings only.

Il Pagliaccio

📋♿ €€€€€

Via dei Banchi Vecci 129A, 00186 **Tel** *06-6880 9595*

Map 11 A3

Located in a 16th-century building with elegant decor, this top restaurant offers inventive Italian cuisine. Incorporating various international influences, dishes include *sogliola in crosta de riso* (sole in a saffron risotto crust) served with a seafood soup, and desserts are exceptional. Booking essential. Closed Mon, Sun, 1–10 Jan, three weeks in Aug.

Key to Price Guide *see p316* **Key to Symbols** *see back cover flap*

QUIRINAL

Antica Birreria Peroni
🚶‍♂️ 🎵   €
Via di San Marcello 19, 00187 **Tel** *06-679 5310*   **Map** 5 A4, 12 F3

Crowded at lunchtime, and popular with large groups, this Art-Nouveau beer house offers good food and generous portions. Cheese and *salumi* platters, salads, pasta, sausages, hamburgers and goulash are typical fare and the Peroni beer is excellent. Service is efficient. Convenient location.

Il Cuore di Napoli
🚶‍♂️ 📋   €
Via Cernaia 31, 00185 **Tel** *06-4434 0252*   **Map** 6 D2

Not far from Termini, this unpretentious *trattoria* and pizzeria offers classic cuisine from Naples. The seafood antipasti and buffalo mozzarella are worth trying. There's a good choice of pasta dishes, grilled fish of the day and pizzas. Try the delicious *babà* for dessert. Wine is from the Campania region. Bargain set menus at lunchtimes.

Abruzzi ai SS Apostoli
🚶‍♂️ 📋 ♿   €€
Via del Vaccaro 1, 00187 **Tel** *06-679 3897*   **Map** 12 F3

An old-style restaurant with classic Abruzzese cuisine and forthcoming service, this eatery is located very close to the Church of the Holy Apostles. The *pasta amatriciana* (tomatoes and *pancetta*) and risotto with herbs are very good. Fresh fish and pork dishes are also specialities. Try a typical orange *amaro* after your meal.

Colline Emiliane
📋   €€
Via degli Avignonesi 22, 00187 **Tel** *06-481 7538*   **Map** 5 B3

Quiet and elegant, Colline Emiliane is a family *trattoria* on an unlikely street. It's reputed for its excellent food and wine originating from the gourmet's region of Emilia-Romagna. Staples include handmade *tortellini* with pumpkin and fine Parmesan, hand-sliced Parma ham, delicious boiled or roasted meats and home-made desserts. Booking recommended.

Ristorante del Giglio
🚶‍♂️ 📋 ♿   €€
Via Torino 137, 00184 **Tel** *06-488 1606*   **Map** 5 C3

Conveniently located near the Opera House and Via Nazionale, this old-time family restaurant is a gem. Efficient service, good wines and classic cuisine. Dishes include *Fettucine alla Tosca*, with ricotta and fresh tomato; *sfogliatine di manzo al radicchio* (thin slices of beef with red radicchio salad); and turbot, oven-baked with potato and tomato.

Al Moro
📋   €€€
Vicolo delle Bollette 13, 00187 **Tel** *06-678 3495*   **Map** 5 A3, 12 F2

A typical *trattoria* since 1929, Al Moro serves expertly prepared traditional Roman food. As in many restaurants in Rome, certain dishes are offered on a rotation system – for instance, *gnocchi* on Thursdays, baked lamb or salt cod on Fridays. The *spaghetti alla carbonara* is excellent, and the fish and seafood dishes are renowned.

F.I.S.H.
📋   €€€
Via dei Serpenti 16, 00184 **Tel** *06-4782 4962*   **Map** 5 B4

One of Rome's trendiest eateries, F.I.S.H. is run by two Italian brothers who spent several years in Oceania. Decked out in black and red, L'Aqua Bar is a fine place for an apéritif with oysters. The Sushi Bar offers Japanese beer with sushi and sashimi and the Grill Lounge prepares temptingly fresh fish, cooked to perfection. Evenings only.

Al Presidente
🚶‍♂️ 📋   €€€€
Via in Arcione 95, 00187 **Tel** *06-679 7342*   **Map** 5 A3

One of the city's best restaurants, Al Presidente has wonderful, modern cuisine, elegant decor and fine wine. Only a short walk from the Trevi Fountain, it also has a great outdoor terrace. Ingredients are expertly researched, with the predominantly fish-based menu changing accordingly. Good value at lunch; taster menus at dinner.

TERMINI

Da Vincenzo
🚶‍♂️ 📋 ♿   €€
Via Castelfidardo 4/6, 00185 **Tel** *06-484 596*   **Map** 6 D2

Fish is the speciality at Da Vincenzo, a timeless neighbourhood restaurant, near Termini. Start with the excellent seafood antipasti or smoked swordfish. For the pasta course, try *tonnarelli all'astice* (pasta with lobster), then baked seabass or turbot with potatoes. There's also *bucatini alla amatriciana* (tomatoes and *pancetta*). Delicious home-made desserts.

Vivendo
🚶‍♂️ 📋 ♿ 🍴   €€€€€
Via V Emanuele Orlando 3, 00185 **Tel** *06-4709 2736*   **Map** 5 C3

The stylish, modern and unstuffy Vivendo is one of Rome's top restaurants. The food is Italian and international – a delicious combination of traditional dishes with unusual ingredients. There is a tasting menu available and also a children's menu. Service is wonderful and the wine list extensive.

ESQUILINE

La Gallina Bianca
Via Antonio Rosmini 9, 00184 **Tel** *06-474 3777*

€   **Map** 6 D4

Very convenient for Termini, La Gallina Bianca has a nice terrace outside and a spacious dining room. It is particularly popular for its Neapolitan thick-crust pizzas, cooked in a wood-fired oven. Service is quick and friendly and there's a very good antipasti buffet, pasta and excellent steaks too. Desserts are home-made: try the *tiramisù*.

Baires
Via Cavour 315, 00184 **Tel** *06-6920 2164*

€€   **Map** 5 B5

Baires promises traditional Argentinian food, South American wine and beer and live music on Monday and Thursday evenings. Typical dishes include *empanadas* (meat pasties), *pollo all'escabeche* (chicken in a spicy sauce), *matambre* (stuffed beef) and perfect charcoal-grilled steaks. The "express" lunch menus offer great value for money.

Cavour 313
Via Cavour 313, 00184 **Tel** *06-678 5496*

€€   **Map** 5 B5

Cavour, a friendly, wood-panelled *enoteca*, lies at the far end of Via Cavour, very near the Forum. Its extensive menu tempts you with salads, *carpaccio*, cheeses and *salumi* (many from famed producers) and the various hot specials prepared each day. Ingredients are well-researched and, naturally, the extensive wine list is excellent. Good-natured staff.

Monti
Via di San Vito 13a, 00185 **Tel** *06-446 6573*

€€   **Map** 6 D4

Justly popular, this family-run *trattoria* offers seasonal cuisine from the Marche. Typical dishes are vegetable *lasagnette*, rabbit or chicken cooked with herbs and turkey in balsamic vinegar. The service is competent, the wine list excellent and the desserts delicious. Fresh fish from the Adriatic is served on Fridays. Booking is recommended.

Oppio Café & Oppio Grill
Via delle Terme di Tito 72, 00184 **Tel** *06-474 5262*

€€   **Map** 5 C5

This all-purpose café and cocktail bar has added a restaurant and grill to its facilities. The fare consists of locally-sourced meat, fish and vegetables. The bar is open late and serves great mixed drinks to the tune of varied DJ sets. The terrace offers a magnificent view of the Colosseum.

Urbana 47
Via Urbana 47, 00184 **Tel** *06-4788 4006*

€€   **Map** 5 C4

In line with the alternative feel of the Monti area, everything, even the chair you are sitting on, is for sale in this restaurant. Pan-Mediterranean cuisine is made from local and organic (when possible) produce, and wines are all local Lazio labels. The retro-style furniture is designed and produced at the neighbouring store, ZOC, just around the corner.

Agata e Romeo
Via Carlo Alberto 45, 00185 **Tel** *06-446 6115*

€€€€€   **Map** 6 D4

Originally a *trattoria*, this is now an internationally-renowned restaurant. The chef, Agata, uses the finest ingredients in an ever-innovative menu, based on Roman and southern Italian dishes. Her husband, Romeo, an expert *sommelier*, ensures the wines perfectly complement each dish. The taster menu (with or without wine) is exceptional.

LATERAN

I Clementini
Via San Giovanni in Laterano 106, 00184 **Tel** *06-454 26395*

€   **Map** 9 B1

Popular with Irish trainee priests from nearby San Clemente, as well as locals, Il Clementini is a friendly, old neighbourhood *trattoria* serving classic Roman cuisine. *Spaghetti alla carbonara*, *bucatini all'amatriciana* (a spicy tomato and bacon sauce), *carciofi alla romana* (artichokes with mint), and rabbit or lamb are typical dishes.

Arancia Blu
Via Prenestina 396E, 00171 **Tel** *06-445 4105*

€€

In the Prenestina district, east of Termini, Arancia Blu offers largely vegetarian dishes, using mostly organic produce. Risotto with Gorgonzola and saffron; potato and mint ravioli; vegetable balls with spicy tomato sauce and aubergine *cannelloni* are typical dishes. Good wine list.

Roberto e Loretta
Via Saturnia 18–24, 00183 **Tel** *06-7720 1037*

€€   **Map** 10 D3

Roberto and Loretta's *trattoria* has a pavement pergola for outdoor eating. The dining room is unfashionable, yet charming. Regional cooking – using seasonal produce – and served in ample portions offers excellent value for money. Fish and meat dishes available. Very friendly service.

Key to Price Guide *see p316* **Key to Symbols** *see back cover flap*

SAID dal 1923

€€

Via Tiburtina 135, 00185 Tel 06-446 9204

Map 6 F4

A chocolate factory since 1923, and today also a restaurant, SAID offers a complete change of scenery. The dinner menu is traditional Italian along with some creative dishes such as the flagship *fettuccine di Said* (with pear, pecorino cheese, chilli and bitter chocolate). Not to miss is the home-made hazelnut chocolate cream to spread on fresh bread.

San Lollo

€€

Via dei Sabelli 51, 00185 Tel 06-494 0726

Map 6 F4

The owner of this Sicilian *trattoria* comes from Palermo and serves pizza, grilled meats and some classic dishes with a creative touch. Daily specials and staples feature *caponata* (ratatouille), *vermicelli con la molluca* (anchovies, orange rind and breadcrumbs) and *paccheri alla norma* (pasta with ricotta). Excellent desserts.

Tram Tram

€€

Via dei Reti 44–46, 00185 Tel 06-490 416

Decorated like the interior of an old tram, opposite the tram lines in the heart of the San Lorenzo district, Tram Tram is a boisterous, fun place to eat, far from the tourist trail. Influenced by Puglia and Sicily, the cuisine here mostly features fish and seafood dishes as well as great steaks and meaty pastas. There's also a good wine list.

Charly's Saucière

€€€

Via San Giovanni in Laterano 270, 00184 Tel 06-7049 5666

Map 9 B1

A long-established Swiss-French restaurant, Charly's Saucière is especially tempting on a cold winter's evening. An appealing interior with candlelit tables, delicious food and mostly French wines. Goose liver pâté, sherry *consommé*, cheese soufflé, Swiss fondue, *boeuf bourguignonne, crêpes suzette* and French cheeses are typical fare.

CARACALLA

Tramonti & Muffati

€€

Via di Santa Maria Ausiliatrice 105, 00181 Tel 06-780 1342

Map 10 F4

This pleasant *enoteca* is located near the Via Appia and Furio Camillo Metro station. Excellent wines complement the daily specials and the meticulously-researched *salumi* and cheeses. Creative use of local products works exceedingly well. Open only in the evening. Booking is strongly advised.

AVENTINE

Da Oio a Casa Mia

€€

Via Galvani 43, 00153 Tel 06-578 2680

Map 8 D3

This reliable, family-run *trattoria* offers typical Roman cuisine. Its menu, one of Testaccio's best, includes *bucatini alla amatriciana, alla gricia* (bacon and pecorino) and *alla carbonara; tonnarelli cacio e pepe* (pecorino and pepper); *rigatoni con la pajata* (veal stomach); *coda alla vaccinara* (oxtail); and *abbacchio* (lamb). Good range of wines

Divinare

€€

Via A Manunzio 13, 00153 Tel 06-5725 0432

Map 8 D3

Occupying almost a whole block in the Testaccio quarter, Divinare is a relatively upmarket wine bar and restaurant. *Spuntini* (snacks), platters of *formaggi e salumi* (cheese and cured meats) or salads accompany a delicious glass of wine from the vast, tempting wine list. There are also hot daily specials on offer.

Felice

€€

Via Mastro Giorgio 29, 00153 Tel 06-574 6800

Map 8 D3

A deservedly popular restaurant, Felice has the upper hand when it comes to serving traditional Roman cuisine. The *spaghetti alla carbonara*, or *cacio e pepe* (with cheese and pepper) are excellent starters, while the *abbacchio arrosto* (roast lamb) and *torta di ricotta* (ricotta and candied peel cake) complete the feast. Closed Sun evening and 3 weeks in Aug.

Né Arte Né Parte

€€

Via Luca della Robbia 15–17, 00153 Tel 06-575 0279

Map 8 D3

An unpretentious *trattoria* that offers Roman classics such as *saltimbocca* (veal and Parma ham cooked with sage and wine) as well as more adventurous regional dishes such as *zuppa di fave* (broad bean soup) and their signature dish of pasta with courgettes and smoked cheese. The ample *antipasto* buffet is a good option for a light lunch.

Tuttifrutti

€€

Via Luca della Robbia 3a, 00153 Tel 06-575 7902

Map 8 D3

Run by a Testaccio cultural association, Tuttifrutti is a lively, youthful place to eat, with honest prices, forthcoming service and creative local and pan-Italian cuisine. The antipasti are very good and the pasta, meat and fish dishes change daily. Busy, occasionally with live music, the restaurant is only open in the evening.

Checchino dal 1887

🔥 €€€€

Via di Monte Testaccio 30, 00153 **Tel** *06-574 6318*

Map *8 D4*

Checchino dal 1887 specializes in traditional *cucina romana*, using the *quarto quinto* (offal). Originally discarded in the slaughterhouses opposite, it became a delicacy in working-class cuisine. The menu includes *rigatoni alla pajata* (calf intestines), *coda alla vaccinara* (oxtail) and *carciofi alla romana*, as well as pig's trotter salad. Good value set menus.

TRASTEVERE

Artù Café

📋 €

Largo M. D. Fumasoni Biondi 5, 00153 **Tel** *06-588 0398*

Map *7 C1*

A halfway house between Anglo-Saxon and Italian cultures, this friendly gastropub offers superb food in the evenings with sandwiches, pasta, steaks and a good buffet at apéritif time. Built inside the former presbytery of Santa Maria di Trastevere, with stained-glass windows, dark wood panelling and very good beer on tap.

Da Lucia

🍴🚹 €

Vicolo del Mattonato 2b, 00153 **Tel** *06-580 3601*

Map *7 B1*

A small family *trattoria*, on one of Trastevere's loveliest alleys, Da Lucia has only a few tables and outside dining in summer. The cuisine is excellent, though with a limited choice of dishes each day. Typical fare is *alici al limone* (anchovies in lemon juice); pasta with broccoli and stingray; and rabbit, tripe or beef in onion.

Alle Fratte di Trastevere

🚹📋 €€

Via delle Fratte di Trastevere 49, 00153 **Tel** *06-583 5775*

Map *7 C1*

In the heart of Trastevere, this family-run restaurant reveals a Roman-Neapolitan inspiration in the kitchen as well as further afield. Pasta, fish and meat dishes, such as octopus antipasto, oven-roasted sea bream, as well as the simple bruschetta, feature on the expansive menu. Popular and unpretentious, with generous portions.

Il Boom

📋 €€

Via dei Fienaroli 30a, 00153 **Tel** *06-589 7196*

Map *7 C1*

A lively, evenings-only bistro with a highly original and cheerful decor. The multi-coloured chairs, large black-and-white photos of Rome in the Swinging Sixties and an old juke box with Italian music of the era are a delight. The young Calabrian chef uses his southern flair in the kitchen, with a menu that changes from day to day and from season to season.

Isole di Sicilia

🚹📋🔥 €€

Via Garibaldi 68/69, 00153 **Tel** *06-5833 4212*

Map *7 B1*

A sunny Sicilian wine bar, Isole di Sicilia is located near the foot of the road leading up to the Janiculum. Wooden tables and Caltagirone ceramics combine with a warm welcome and excellent Sicilian cuisine to make it an extremely popular choice. With over 250 Sicilian wines, as well as *sfizi* (snacks), salads and *focacce* in abundance.

Ripa 12

📋🔥 €€

Via di San Francesco a Ripa 12, 00153 **Tel** *06-580 9093*

Map *7 C2*

In southern Trastevere, far from the tourist trail, Ripa 12 serves excellent Mediterranean cuisine, with the focus firmly on fish. Marinated raw sea bass *carpaccio* is the house starter, followed by fresh fish of the day or a platter of fried seafood. Very much a locals' favourite.

Vizi Capitali

📋 €€

Vicolo della Renella 94, 00153 **Tel** *06-581 8840*

Map *7 C1*

Vizi Capitali has an elegant dining room with seven oil paintings depicting the seven deadly sins. Fish and seafood specialities include octopus served with marinated fruit, though there may also be savoury flan of *pecorino* cheese served with *bresaola* (cured beef) and chestnut honey; and warm chocolate tart with caramelised fruit.

Antica Pesa

🚹📋 €€€

Via Garibaldi 18, 00153 **Tel** *06-580 9236*

Map *4 D5, 7 B1, 11 B5*

Inside the 17th-century former customs house of the Papal State, Antica Pesa has a pretty patio garden, once a popular bowling alley in the 19th century. The excellent cuisine is Mediterranean with a menu that changes with the whim of the chef and the seasons. Extensive wine list. A delightful place to eat and relax.

Asinocotto

📋 €€€

Via dei Vascellaro 48, 00153 **Tel** *06-589 8985*

Map *8 D1*

Situated in the quieter reaches of Trastevere, Giuliano Brenna's elegant but friendly restaurant offers a creative take on Italian cuisine. The menu changes with the season and includes specialities such as home-made pasta with duck *ragù*, followed by an excellent rack of lamb or roast honey-glazed pigeon. Evenings only.

Enoteca Ferrara

📋🔥 €€€

Via del Moro 1a, 00153 **Tel** *06-5833 3920*

Map *4 E5, 11 B5*

Within a 17th-century palazzo, tucked behind Piazza Trilussa, Enoteca Ferrara is situated near Ponte Sisto. This wine bar, shop and restaurant offers an excellent, welcoming service in its five rooms. The cuisine is extremely good and creative, complemented by a wine list with over 1,000 labels.

Key to Price Guide *see p316* **Key to Symbols** *see back cover flap*

Somo
田目 €€€

Via Goffredo Mameli 5, 00153 **Tel** *06-588 2060*
Map *7 B1*

Sleek and über-modern, this Japanese-fusion restaurant is further evidence of the Trastevere area's contemporary edge. The menu runs the gamut of traditional Japanese fare, from sushi and sashimi to creative twists on rice and noodle dishes. Prized Kobe beef is also served. Fine Italian wines are on offer along with expert cocktails.

Alberto Ciarla
目& €€€€

Piazza San Cosimato 40, 00153 **Tel** *06-581 8668*
Map *7 C1*

A marvellous place to eat fresh fish, this legendary restaurant remains hugely popular. Rooted in classic cuisine, Ciarla uses considerable creative flair to concoct delicious new dishes. Three taster menus are on offer as well as an *à la carte*, complemented by an exceptional range of wines. A fanciful dining room and terrace. Evenings only.

JANICULUM

Lo Scarpone
田 €€

Via San Pancrazio 15, 00152 **Tel** *06-581 4094*
Map *7 A1*

Halfway between town and country, from the top of the Janiculum hill you have the whole of Rome at your feet. The garden inside this elegant, noble restaurant is very pleasant in summer. Inside, the decor is endearingly rustic. Good traditional food with fish and grilled meat specialities.

VATICAN

Borgo Antico
目 €€

Borgo Pio 21, 00193 **Tel** *06-686 5967*
Map *3 C3*

A 17th-century tavern, Borgo Antico serves platters of *salumi* and *formaggi*, cooked with great flair and originality. Old recipes are prepared with the finest of produce. Dishes range from cheese fondue to their own speciality *La Papalina* (potato and truffle). Wonderful bruschette, home-made pastas and polenta. Excellent wines, served by the glass or bottle.

Da Cesare
目 €€

Via Crescenzio 13, 00193 **Tel** *06-686 1227*
Map *4 D2*

Established in 1966, this restaurant offers classic cuisine and the finest of ingredients. The elegant dining room has vaulted ceilings, service is attentive and the wine list satisfying. Delicacies include smoked fish, boar or venison *prosciutto*; fish soup, lobster or fresh fish; and Italy's finest beef from Val di Chiana. Good set menu.

Il Bar Sotto il Mare
目 €€

Via Tunisi 27, 00192 **Tel** *06-3972 8453*
Map *3 B2*

The menu at Il Bar Sotto il Mare is dominated by seafood. Shellfish and crustaceans reign as antipasti, followed by inventive pasta dishes and excellent grilled fish. A family restaurant, with a young, friendly service, it's located almost directly opposite the Vatican museums.

La Piccola Irpinia
田目 €€

Via Muzio Clementi 69–75, 00193 **Tel** *06-320 4508*
Map *4 E2*

Close to Piazza Cavour and Castel Sant'Angelo, La Piccola is run by a family from Irpinia, in the province of Avellino, near Naples. The menu features dishes from both *terra e mare*, prepared with great care; the home-made pasta is especially recommended. Seasonal produce is used – look out for Montella chestnuts.

Osteria dell'Angelo
目目 €€

Via G Bettolo 24–32, 00195 **Tel** *06-372 9470*
Map *3 B1*

Dell'Angelo serves timeless cuisine in the quintessential *trattoria* – informal and bustling. *Spaghetti cacio e pepe* (pecorino and pepper) or *alla gricia* (pecorino and bacon), anchovy tart, *baccalà* (salt cod) and other staples from the Roman repertoire, followed by *Vin Santo* and biscuits. Excellent menu at a bargain price. Booking is essential.

Taverna Angelica
目 €€

Piazza A. Capponi 6, 00193 **Tel** *06-687 4514*
Map *3 C2*

Creative regional cuisine is served in this modern restaurant, with specialities including home-made pasta with prawns and pumpkin; potato *gnocchi* with a seafood sauce; and breast of goose or guinea fowl. Desserts, such as citrus fruit cheesecake, will tempt even the hardiest souls.

Da Benito e Gilberto
目 €€€

Via del Falco 19, 00193 **Tel** *06-686 7769*
Map *3 C2*

A small, elegant restaurant with walls hung with paintings. The food is very good, serving only the freshest of seafood and fish, displayed in a chilled cabinet. Dishes are simply but lovingly prepared, the wine list is good and the service is extremely cordial. Booking recommended. Closed Sun & Mon.

Dal Toscano ▣ €€€
*Via Germanico 58, 00192 **Tel** 06-3972 5717* **Map** 3 B2

An exceedingly popular and ever-reliable restaurant, Dal Toscano has outside tables in summer and a wood-panelled dining room. You can expect old-fashioned service, exquisitely cooked meat dishes and excellent red wines. The menu includes *Pappardelle pasta sulla lepre* (hare sauce), polenta and *porcini* mushrooms or *bistecca alla Fiorentina*.

Siciliainbocca 🏃▣ €€€
*Via E Faà di Bruno 26, 00195 **Tel** 06-3751 2485*

A delightful Sicilian restaurant, Siciliainbocca is painted sunshine yellow and decorated with Caltagirone ceramics. Excellent dishes hail from all over Sicily: *pasta alla Norma* (with aubergine, tomato and ricotta) or *pasta con le sarde* (sardines, fennel and pine nuts). Main dishes consist of meat and fish. Desserts are exquisite.

Velando ▣🕭 €€€
*Borgo Vittorio 26, 00193 **Tel** 06-6880 9955* **Map** 3 C3

Combining traditional and *nouvelle cuisine* from the Lombard region of Val Camonica, this minimalist restaurant offers a menu full of surprises and excellent service. Risotto with wild strawberries, freshwater fish, guinea fowl with pear, as well as dishes made with chestnuts, cheeses and *funghi* from the region. Delicious desserts and good set menu options.

Veranda ▣🕭 €€€€
*Hotel Columbus, Borgo Santo Spirito 73, 00193 **Tel** 06-687 2973* **Map** 3 C3

Veranda offers hotel dining in the elegant Palazzo della Rovere. The dining room ceiling has exquisite Pinturicchio frescoes. Service is attentive and the cuisine is creative Italian, with a changing menu. Typical dishes are chestnut flour pasta with lamb *ragù* or Argentine fillet steak with *foie gras* and a marsala *jus*. Set lunch menu.

La Pergola ▣🕭🎵 €€€€€
*Via A Cadlolo 101, 00136 **Tel** 06-3509 2152*

A taxi-ride away, in the hills above the Vatican, La Pergola is Rome's finest restaurant, run by celebrated German chef Heinz Beck. The superlative food, served on a wonderfully panoramic roof terrace, humbles even the sternest critics. There is an excellent tasting menu and the wines harmonize perfectly with the food.

VIA VENETO

Cantina Cantarini €€
*Piazza Sallustio 12, 00187 **Tel** 06-485 528* **Map** 5 C2

A long-established venue that is the epitome of the Italian *trattoria* – tightly-packed tables, bustling staff and copious plates of Roman and regional food, including dishes such as *coniglio alla cacciatore* (rabbit with garlic and rosemary). From Monday to Thursday lunchtime meat predominates, while fish takes pride of place Thursday evening to Saturday.

Da Giovanni 🏃▣ €€
*Via Antonio Salandra 1, 00187 **Tel** 06-485 950* **Map** 5 C2

On the corner of Via XX Settembre and Via Salandra, Da Giovanni is a typical family restaurant with classic cuisine. The *agnolotti* and cannelloni are worth a try. Meat dishes, such as *pollo arrosto* (roast chicken) and veal escalope are delicious. The fish of the day is prepared to order, grilled or steamed and deboned at the table.

Taverna Flavia ▣ €€
*Via Flavia 9, 00187 **Tel** 06-474 5214* **Map** 5 C2

Off Via XX Settembre, the old and celebrated Taverna Flavia evokes nostalgia, with autographed photos of Hollywood film stars covering its walls. Elizabeth Taylor and Richard Burton regularly ate here while filming *Cleopatra*. The food remains excellent and highly sought-after, with dishes named after famous muses.

Asador Café Veneto ▣🕭 €€€
*Via V Veneto 116, 00187 **Tel** 06-482 7107* **Map** 5 B2

An elegant Argentinian steakhouse, Café Veneto procures beef from the owner's own cattle on his estate in the Pampas. Beef, duck, lamb and sausages are prepared *sulla parrilla* (on the grill). Cosmopolitan and ideal for people-watching on the Via Veneto, it offers a good menu and an impeccable service at high prices.

Edoardo ▣🎵 €€€
*Via Lucullo 2, 00187 **Tel** 06-486 428* **Map** 5 C2

This elegant restaurant is popular with tourists and businessmen alike, the ever-changing menu combining traditional staples with inspired ingredients. Cherry *risotto*, *fusilli ai carciofi* (pasta with artichokes), grilled fish and rabbit with apricots do not disappoint. Lunchtime prices are cheaper. A piano bar on Friday and Saturday evenings. Lovely terrace.

Girarrosto Fiorentino ▣🕭 €€€
*Via Sicilia 46, 00187 **Tel** 06-4288 0660* **Map** 5 C1

An elegant restaurant with over 30 years' experience, the Fiorentino serves classic fish and meat dishes from Tuscany. *Salumi toscano* and hand-sliced *prosciutto crudo* are excellent, as are the *ribollita* (Tuscan bread soup) or *zuppa senese*, with *porcini* mushrooms. The trademark dish remains the steak Fiorentina.

Key to Price Guide *see p316* **Key to Symbols** *see back cover flap*

Papà Baccus   📋   €€€
*Via Toscana 36, 00187 **Tel** 06-4274 2808*   **Map** 5 C1

One of the best addresses in the city for bona fide Tuscan cuisine. From the classic *ribollita* (a soup of beans, vegetables and bread) to the various cuts of Chianina beef, every option here is a good one. The simply seared fillet steak reigns supreme, though the baked *rombo* (turbot) and *baccalà* (salt cod) should satisfy fish eaters.

Brunello Lounge & Restaurant   📋🏃♿🇹   €€€€€
*Via Vittorio Veneto 70A, 00187 **Tel** 06-4890 2867*   **Map** 5 B2

Presented in a warm, exotic Moroccan style with wrought iron lanterns, tapestries and an exposed wine cellar, the restaurant and lounge of the Baglioni Regina Hotel serves ornate takes on Mediterranean specialities. Fare is accompanied by an exclusive wine list, which includes over 500 labels and specializes in Sassicaia Super Tuscan wines.

Cantina La Terrazza, Hotel Eden   📋♿🇹   €€€€€
*Via Ludovisi 49, 00187 **Tel** 06-4781 2752*   **Map** 5 B2

With a breathtaking view of the city, La Terrazza is undoubtedly one of Rome's most alluring restaurants and, to some people, worth the elevated prices alone. Service is top-notch and the young chef combines international cuisine with Mediterranean flair. A tasting menu with wine included.

Mirabelle   📋♿🇹   €€€€€
*Via di Porta Pinciana 14, 00187 **Tel** 06-4216 8838*   **Map** 5 B1

On the seventh floor of an elegant hotel, near the top of Via Veneto, Mirabelle has a panoramic terrace, a pleasing dining room and expert service. The well-compiled wine list complements memorable cuisine such as risotto with saffron and asparagus *ragù*, duck with orange or *spigola al vapore* (sea bass). Book ahead for the terrace.

VILLA BORGHESE

Caffè delle Arti   🏃♿   €€
*Via A Gramsci 73, 00197 **Tel** 06-3265 1236*   **Map** 1 B4

A serene place to pause and rest awhile, this café-restaurant is located in the grounds of the Museum of Modern Art at the top of Villa Borghese. The delightful dining rooms and gardens are not only perfect for a coffee or an apéritif, they also have good light snacks and daily specials available all day. Good Sunday brunch.

Duke's   📋♿   €€€
*Viale Parioli 200, 00197 **Tel** 06-8066 2455*   **Map** 2 E3

Attracting crowds of Rome's beautiful people every night, Duke's is a bar for an apéritif with nibbles, a late-night venue as well as an excellent restaurant. The cooking is decidedly Californian fusion, with influences from the Orient, Mexico and the Mediterranean. Service is very professional and the outside terrace is arresting.

Al Ceppo   🏃📋♿   €€€€
*Via Panama 2, 00198 **Tel** 06-841 9696*   **Map** 2 F3

Established over 35 years ago by two sisters from the Marche region, this restaurant has not lost its sparkle and still attracts regulars. The menu changes regularly and the service is impeccable. Typical dishes include vegetable strudel with *speck* and ricotta; *pappardelle* with duck *ragù*; and rabbit. Excellent wine list.

Sapori del Lord Byron   📋🇹   €€€€
*Via Giuseppe de Notaris 5, 00197 **Tel** 06-322 0404*   **Map** 2 D4

In one of Parioli's top-notch hotels, on the edge of the Villa Borghese, this picturesque restaurant serves *haute cuisine* at somewhat high prices. This is Italian cuisine with international inspiration, creative twists on traditional dishes. The service is efficient, the surroundings beautiful and the wine list prize-winning.

Baby   📋♿🇹   €€€€€
*Via U Aldrovandi 15, 00197 **Tel** 06-321 6126*   **Map** 2 D4

Baby, housed in the Aldrovandi Palace hotel (*see p309*), is run by the renowned husband-and-wife team of Don Alfonso (one of Italy's finest restaurants) on the Amalfi Coast. Outstanding Neapolitan-inspired cuisine is served in a delightful dining room and terrace at one of Rome's top hotels.

TIVOLI

Adriano   📋♿   €€€
*Largo Yourcenar 2, 00010 **Tel** 0774-382 235*

A charming restaurant, perfectly placed for visits to Villa Adriana and other Tivoli delights. Booking is recommended. Set in a garden, the cuisine is traditional and wines are from local vineyards. *Fettuccine* with aromatic herbs makes for an excellent first course, whereas filleted rabbit casserole is a typical main course. Try the adjacent café for lunch.

Light Meals and Drinks

Rome can delight the most demanding gourmet and satisfy the keenest appetite, whatever the hour. An enticing array of *gelaterie, pasticcerie, pizzerie, enoteche, rosticcerie* and *gastronomie* means that good food and drink are, literally, around the corner.

Hotel breakfasts often aren't up to scratch and you would be better off starting the day with a genuine Italian breakfast at your local stand-up bar: a cappuccino or latte with a hot *cornetto* (croissant) or *fagottino* (similar to a *pain au chocolat*). If you are in Italy during late winter, when blood-red oranges from Sicily are in season, order a *spremuta,* a freshly squeezed orange juice.

A heavy morning's sightseeing may leave you ready for a coffee or an apéritif in one of Rome's elegant 19th-century bars, followed by lunch at a wine bar or Roman-style fast food joint. Later, enjoy tea in a tearoom or coffee and cakes at a *pasticceria*. Once the sun starts to set, there are several places where you can sip a drink, linger over an ice cream and ponder upon another wonderful day in the city.

PIZZERIAS

Roman *pizzerias* are an obvious choice if you feel like an informal meal: they are noisy, convivial and great fun. Many, however, open only in the evening. Look out for the *forno a legno* (wood-burning oven) sign – electric ovens simply don't produce the same results. In the best *pizzerias* you can sit in view of the vast marble slabs where the *pizzaioli* flatten the dough and whip the pizzas in and out of the oven on long-handled pallets. The turnaround is fast and queues are common so you may not be encouraged to linger after you have eaten.

The running order is fairly straightforward: you might have a *bruschetta* (toasted tomato or garlic bread) to start with, some *supplì* (fried rice croquettes) or *fiori di zucca* (courgette flowers in batter, filled with hot mozzarella and a single anchovy). Alternatively, try the *filetti di baccalà* (battered cod fillets) or perhaps a plate of *cannellini* beans in oil. Follow this with a crisp *calzone* (folded-over pizza) or the classic Roman pizza – round, thin and crunchy – with a variety of toppings: the basic *margherita* (tomato, mozzarella), *napoletana* (tomato, anchovies, mozzarella),

capricciosa (ham, artichokes, eggs, olives) or anything else the *pizzaiolo* fancies. Draught beer or *birra alla spina* is the classic drink, but wine is always available, even if limited in choice and quality. You should expect to pay around €14 a head for a meal.

The most representative Roman *pizzerias*, from all points of view, are **Da Baffetto** which can be easily found by looking for the queue outside, and its offspring, **La Montecarlo**. **Remo** in Testaccio and **Dar Poeta** and **Pizzeria Ivo** in Trastevere, where tables line the road in summer, are also typically Roman. Another place not to be missed is **Panattoni – I Marmi**, where a huge variety of customers patiently queue for a pavement seat on Viale Trastevere in summer, or clamour for one of the marble-topped tables (which gives it its nickname "the mortuary") inside. For slick interiors and Neapolitan-style (high-rise) pizza, try **'Gusto** or **Squisito**, but once again, be prepared to queue.

ENOTECHE

Enoteche or wine bars offer a very fine selection of wines, mainly from Italy, but often from around the world. Usually run by experts, keen to share their knowledge

and advise on the best combinations of wine and food, many are simply shops for browsing and buying wine. Others, such as **Achilli al Parlamento** *(see p351)* and **Bevitoria Navona**, offer the traditional *mescita* – wine and champagne tasting by the glass, accompanied by snacks and canapés. Prices are fairly reasonable: about €3 for a glass on tap, €4 upwards for a quality wine, to about €5 for *prosecco* or *spumante*, Italian champagne. **La Vineria** *(see p350)* in Campo de' Fiori is a typical spot for *mescita*, especially at night. Nearby, **L'Angolo Divino** *(see p362)* and the beautiful **Il Goccetto**, with original painted ceilings, serve excellent wines and delicious food.

Some of the oldest wine bars are inside historic buildings, such as **Caffè Novecento**, which serves excellent food, mainly vegetarian. The **Antica Locanda** is nestled within a 17th-century palazzo whilst **La Curia di Bacco** is a candlelit cave dating back to 70 BC.

For more substantial food for around €15–20 per head, try the bistro- or restaurant-style *enoteche*, open from lunch until late. Particularly recommended are the innovative **Cul de Sac**, **Trimani** *(see p351)*, **Il Tajut** serving specialities from Friuli, and **Cavour 313**. Food emporium **'Gusto** *(see p351)* has a wine bar with a gourmet cheese selection, while the speciality at **Al Bric** is *sarcofage bretone* – beef stroganoff with Barolo and a Jerusalem artichoke. The **Antico Forno Roscioli** is particularly creative, with great dishes such as pasta with *radicchio* and orange peel and pear pastry with coconut.

Enoteche are often tucked away near famous sights or in unlikely places. **Vinando** is extremely convenient for the Capitol, whilst the Tuscan **Vineria Il Chianti** is near the Trevi Fountain. Over in Testaccio, **Divinare** offers fine labels alongside top quality preserves and chocolate. There are a growing number of wine bars across the river.

Crowds at **Enoteca Trastevere** spill on to the pavement outside, while **Cantina Paradiso** is a quieter venue with a reasonable evening menu. When night falls, try the lively **In Vino Veritas Art Bar** at the foot of the Janiculum hill.

BIRRERIE

Roman *birrerie* or beer houses had their heyday in the early 1900s, often with sumptuous interiors and abundant stained glass. Although many subsequently closed, thanks to their growing popularity with most Italian teenagers they are today undergoing something of a revival. Many British- and Irish-style pubs have also opened. At German-style beer houses you can still enjoy beer and substantial snacks in traditional wood-panelled rooms. The **Old Bear** pub is a jewel inside a 17th-century convent, with romantic candlelight and excellent food and beer. **Löwenhaus** is bedecked in old oil paintings depicting typical Bavarian scenes, again with low lighting for a mellow evening. The ever crowded **Birreria Peroni**, serving classic beer-drinkers' fare, is also well worth a visit for its local beer and lovely decor. Attracting Italians and foreigners alike is the **Birreria Viennese/Wiener Bierhaus** with its excellent Transylvanian specialities, which come generously heaped on a wooden plate. If you eat here, or at the equally charming **L'Oasi della Birra**, expect to pay about €25. Other beer houses with a great atmosphere, food and late closing times are **The Fiddler's Elbow**, often with live music, **La Pace del Cervello** – meaning, peace of mind – or **Trinity College**, a favourite with expats and Romans.

FAST FOOD

The term "fast food" in Rome encompasses a cornucopia of choice. The most prolific establishments are *pizza a taglio* shops where slices of freshly baked pizza are available for €1 or €2 – these are sold by weight. Many of these places also sell spit-roasted chickens *(pollo allo spiedo)*, *supplì* and other fried fare. **Frontoni's** and **Forno La Renella** in Trastevere are two of the finest. Pizza with fig and ham or potato and rosemary are typical toppings. At **La Pratolina**, near the Vatican, pizza with sausage, potato and truffle is on the menu. **Chagat**, in the Ghetto, prepares tasty kosher food, while **Rosticceri**, with branches in Testaccio and near Piazza Navona, specializes in classic Roman take-away with an inventive twist.

Rosticcerie and *gastronomie* also offer roast chicken and potatoes, as well as ready-made pasta dishes, cooked vegetables *sott'olio* (in oil), salads and desserts – useful for takeaway picnics. Many offer stools and narrow bars where you can also devour your purchases on the spot. Near the Vatican are some of the finest: **Franchi** *(see p350)*, **Volpetti Più** and **Ercoli dal 1928**.

For a sit-down snack, bars with a *tavola calda* (hot table) have a similar selection, especially at lunch time. One of the most elegant is **Caffetteria Nazionale**. For a taste of traditional deep-fried fast food, try **Cose Fritte** near Piazza del Popolo. In the **Galleria Alberto Sordi**, opposite the Piazza Colonna, there are two excellent cafés, offering hot and cold food until 10pm.

Most *alimentari* (food stores) or *salumerie* (delicatessens) will make you a *panino* (filled roll). Especially delicious are **Lo Zozzone's** hot plain pizza pockets stuffed with choices from the shop's counters, where you can also sip a glass of wine. Try a typical local speciality if you see the sign *porchetta* – whole aromatic roast pig with crackling, sliced into *rosette* (rolls) or thick country-bread sandwiches. A good place to try this is the stall at the tram stop in Viale Carlo Felice opposite San Giovanni in Laterano. Alternatively, go to the hole-in-the-wall **Er Buchetto**, where you can sit down in (relative) comfort with a glass of wine. For a really typical Roman snack, make a late-afternoon detour to **Filetti di Baccalà** serving, as the name suggests, fried cod fillets.

For cheese, go to **Obiká** near the Pantheon. This bar offers a vast choice of fresh buffalo and cow mozzarella; eat it as it should be – unadulterated – or prepared in a variety of creative ways.

Termini now has two good options for those waiting or rushing for trains – the self-service restaurant **Chef Express** or **Vyta** *(see p350)*, which makes up gourmet sandwiches to go.

BARS, CAFES AND TEAROOMS

Roman bars are the city's lifeline: places to meet, eat, drink, buy milk or coffee, make phone calls or find a toilet. Some are small, stand-up, basic one-counter bars for grabbing a quick *cornetto* and cappuccino; some may be more luxurious, doubling as a cake shop, ice cream parlour, tearoom or *tavola calda*; or a combination of all these. Most open early at about 7.30am and close late, particularly at weekends, at around midnight or 2am. If you sit down you will be served by a waiter and pay for the privilege. At busy times, or at popular bars, the crowds at the counter will be large and you will have to wait your turn. If you choose to stand you pay for your drink at the till beforehand. A small tip (5 or 10 cents per drink) may increase your chances of speedy service. In summer, tables cover all the available outdoor space, and the fight for a place in the shade is never ending.

Traditionally elegant – and expensive – bars for peoplewatching are the admirably located **Rosati** and **Doney**, as well as **Caffè Greco**, the 19th-century haunt of artists, writers and composers *(see p133)*, or the carefully restored **La Caffettiera**, near the Pantheon. Other popular and well-established bars are the **Antico Caffè della Pace** and **Café Romano**; both these places are recommended for late-night drinks. **Zodiaco** on Monte Mario pulls in the crowds for its panoramic views as does **Oppio Café** near the Domus Aurea. For sheer decadence go to **Stravinsky** at the Hotel de Russie for wonderful martinis or a relaxed cup of coffee.

Tearooms are becoming increasingly popular. **Babington's Tea Rooms** *(see p134)* on Piazza di Spagna serves an outrageously expensive cup of tea and scones in genteel surroundings, while **Dolci e Doni** is more relaxed. Much better value can be found at **Il Giardino del Te** and **Makasar**. For serious luxury, you can have a full afternoon tea at the **Grand Bar** in the St Regis Grand *(see p299)*.

Coffee fiends should try a *gran caffè speciale* at the counters of **Caffè Sant'Eustachio**, or one of Rome's best espressos at **La Tazza d'Oro** *(see p104)*. Less familiar to tourists, however, are the excellent **Antico Caffè del Brasile** *(see p351)*, **Bar del Cappuccino**, **Ciamei** or **Spinelli**. **Ciampini al Café du Jardin** with its garden setting and roof-top views is unbeatable in summer, particularly at the apéritif hour, as is the **Caffè Parnaso** in Parioli. Gradually becoming the norm in Rome are bookshop cafés – **Caffè la Feltrinelli** and **Biblioteq** are two examples – and museum cafés. The **Caffetteria D'Art al Chiostro del Bramante** is in an art gallery on the upper loggia of a beautiful cloister. The bar at the Capitoline Museums has breathtaking views if average food, whilst the café in the **Palazzo delle Esposizioni** *(see p164)* is open throughout the day with an attractive selection of snacks and drinks.

PASTICCERIE

On Sunday mornings you will often see the Romans emerging from the local pastry shop or *pasticceria* with a beautifully wrapped package. This can contain dainty individual pastries, whole cakes or tarts, traditional Easter *colombe* (doves) or the Christmas *panettoni* – huge cakes with raisins and candied peel – all for consumption by large gatherings of friends or family after lunch. The window displays of cake shops are often fantastic. These, and the aroma of brewing coffee, will tempt even those who claim not to have a sweet tooth. The selection is vast from a hot *cornetto* or *brioche* in the early morning, a midday *pizzetta* or savoury tart at lunch, or a choux pastry or fruit tart in the afternoon. **Cipriani** *(see p347)*, open since 1906, has delicious biscuits, ricotta cake and apple tart. Nearby **Regoli** has wonderful *mille feuilles* and *torta con crema e pinoli* (pine kernels). **Dagnino** prepares hundreds of Sicilian specialities every day whilst **Josephine's Bakery** sells beautiful iced cakes that are delicious works of art. As well as cakes, numerous shops offer handmade chocolates. At some, such as **Rivendita dei Ciococolati e Vino** *(see p350)*, you can pause over a cup of coffee or glass of wine while deciding which you like best.

GELATERIE

Ice cream *(gelato)* is one of summer's main delights and at Rome's ice-cream parlours, you are certainly in for a lavish treat. Look for the word *artigianale,* if you want to savour the best. The choice is endless – water-ices made with a phenomenal variety of fruit; lemon and coffee *granite* (crushed ice); as well as more exotic ice-cream specialities such as rice pudding, *zuppa inglese* (English trifle), *zabaglione* and *tiramisù*. Choose as many varieties as the size of your cone or cup will hold, ask for an optional topping of cream *(panna)* and go for a sensation-filled stroll. Or take a seat and rest awhile – you will be served an obscenely-sized creation at the table (at a price). *Gelaterie* are open all day, many until late at night, and are very much an integral part of Roman socializing. **Tre Scalini** in Piazza Navona is a famous spot for enjoying the pricey, yet so heavenly, chocolate *tartufo* (truffle), while a summer evening in EUR, especially with children, nearly always ends in a trip to **Giolitti**, a historic ice-cream name. The strategically placed, crowded original near the Pantheon deserves at least one visit too. Gourmet fans of *gelato* should not miss **San Crispino**, which offers home-made delicacies made with the best ingredients. Its *zabaglione* is made with 20-year-old barrel-aged Marsala. In summer try the mouth-watering *susine* (yellow plum) flavour and in winter, the *arancia selvatica* (wild orange) should not be missed.

Adults may prefer to pick their night-time treat at **Chalet del Lago**, again in EUR, while sitting beside the lake. If you come across a small kiosk with the sign *grattachecche* (most likely in Trastevere and Testaccio), try one of Rome's oldest traditions – ice grated by a gloved hand on the spot and enlivened with a variety of classic flavourings.

Everyone has their own favourite flavours and preferred *gelateria*, but the quest for perfection is an ongoing pleasure. For top *zabaglione*, try **Fiocco di Neve**, **Giolitti** of Via Vespucci or **Petrini dal 1926**. **Palazzo del Freddo** makes an exceptionally wonderful rice pudding flavour and its own *La Caterinetta* – one of the secret ingredients is honey. **Al Settimo Gelo**, a witty play on words (*settimo* is seventh, *cielo* is heaven and *gelo* is ice), creates exciting chestnut sorbet, chocolate with *pepperoncino*, ginger and ice cream made from Greek yoghurt. For those with dairy allergies, visit the Sicilian *gelateria*, **Gelarmony**, which also uses soya milk and has 14 different flavours on offer. At **Fior di Luna** in Trastevere, all ingredients are organic. **Duse**, in Parioli, is famed for its white or dark *(fondente)* chocolate. Less familiar, however, is its baby nettle leaf *(ortica)*, which is usually available in very early spring.

DIRECTORY

CAPITOL

BARS, CAFES AND TEAROOMS

Caffè Capitolino
Piazzale Caffarelli.
Map 12 F5.

PIAZZA DELLA ROTONDA

PIZZERIAS

Barroccio
Via dei Pastini 13.
Map 12 D2.

Er Faciolaro
Via dei Pastini 123.
Map 12 D2.

La Sagrestia
Via del Seminario 89.
Map 12 E3.

ENOTECHE

Achilli al Parlamento
Via dei Prefetti 15.
Map 12 D1.

Corsi
Via del Gesù 88.
Map 12 E3.

BIRRERIE

Trinity College
Via del Collegio Romano
6. **Map** 12 E3.

FAST FOOD

Obikà
Piazza Firenze 28.
Map 12 D1.

BARS, CAFES AND TEAROOMS

Caffè Sant'Eustachio
Piazza Sant'Eustachio 82.
Map 12 D3.

La Caffettiera
Piazza di Pietra 65.
Map 12 E2.

Ciampini
Piazza S. Lorenzo in Lucina
29. **Map** 12 D1.

La Tazza d'Oro
Via degli Orfani 82/84.
Map 12 D2.

Teichner
Piazza San Lorenzo in
Lucina 15–17.
Map 12 D1.

Vitti
Piazza San Lorenzo in
Lucina. **Map** 12 E1.

GELATERIE

Fiocco di Neve
Via del Pantheon 51.
Map 12 D2.

Giolitti
Via degli Uffici del
Vicario 40.
Map 12 D2.

PIAZZA NAVONA

PIZZERIAS

Da Baffetto
Via del Governo Vecchio
114. **Map** 11 B3.

Da Francesco
Piazza del Fico 29.
Map 11 B2.

La Montecarlo
Vicolo Savelli 12/13.
Map 11 C3.

ENOTECHE

Bevitoria Navona
Piazza Navona 72.
Map 11 C2.

Caffè Novecento
Via del Governo Vecchio
12. **Map** 11 B3.

Cul de Sac
Piazza Pasquino 73.
Map 11 C3.

Giulio Passami l'Olio
Via di Monte Giordano 28.
Map 11B2.

Il Piccolo
Via del Governo Vecchio
74–75. **Map** 11 C3.

BIRRERIE

Old Bear
Via dei Gigli d'Oro 2.
Map 11 C2.

FAST FOOD

Lo Zozzone
Via del Teatro Pace 32.
Map 11 B3.

BARS, CAFES AND TEAROOMS

Antico Caffè della Pace
Via della Pace 5.
Map 11 C3.

Caffeteria D'Art al Chiostro del Bramante
Via della Pace.
Map 11 C2.

PASTICCERIE

La Deliziosa
Vicolo Savelli 50.
Map 11 B3.

GELATERIE

Bar Navona
Piazza Navona 67.
Map 11 C3.

Da Quinto
Via di Tor Millina 15.
Map 11 C3.

Tre Scalini
Piazza Navona 28.
Map 11 C3.

PIAZZA DI SPAGNA

PIZZERIAS

PizzaRé
Via di Ripetta 14.
Map 4 F1.

'Gusto
Piazza Augusto
Imperatore 9.
Map 4 F2.

ENOTECHE

Antica Enoteca di Via della Croce
Via della Croce 76B.
Map 5 A2.

Il Brillo Parlante
Via della Fontanella 12.
Map 4 F1.

Buccone
Via di Ripetta 19.
Map 4 F1.

'Gusto
See Pizzerias.

BIRRERIE

Birreria Viennese/ Wiener Bierhaus
Via della
Croce 21.
Map 5 A2.

Löwenhaus
Via della
Fontanella 16B.
Map 4 F1.

FAST FOOD

Cose Fritte
Via di Ripetta 3.
Map 4 F1.

Difronte A
Via della Croce 38.
Map 4 F2.

Fratelli Fabbi
Via della Croce 27.
Map 4 F2.

BARS, CAFES AND TEAROOMS

Babington's Tea Rooms
Piazza di Spagna 23.
Map 5 A2.

Café Romano
Via Borgognona 4.
Map 12 E1.

Caffè Greco
Via Condotti 86.
Map 5 A2.

Ciampini al Café du Jardin
Viale Trinità
dei Monti.
Map 5 A2.

Dolci e Doni
Via delle Carrozze 85D.
Map 4 F2.

Rosati
Piazza del Popolo 5.
Map 4 F1.

Stravinsky Bar
Hotel de Russie,
Via del Babuino 9.
Map 5 A2.

GELATERIE

Caffetteria-Gelateria Barcaccia
Piazza di Spagna 71.
Map 5 A2.

CAMPO DE' FIORI

PIZZERIAS

Acchiappafantasmi
Via dei Cappellari 66.
Map 11 B3.

ENOTECHE

Al Bric
Via del Pellegrino 51.
Map 11 B3.

Antico Forno Roscioli
Via dei Giubbonari 21.
Map 11 C4.

La Curia di Bacco
Via del Biscione 79.
Map 11 C4.

DIRECTORY

Il Goccetto
Via dei Banchi Vecchi 14.
Map 11 B3.

L'Angolo Divino
Via dei Balestrari 12.
Map 11 C4.

Vinando
Piazza Margana 23.
Map 12 E4.

La Vineria
Piazza Campo de' Fiori 15.
Map 11 C4.

FAST FOOD

Chagat
Via Santa Maria del Pianto
66. **Map** 12 D5.

Da Benito
Via dei Falegnami 14.
Map 12 D4.

Filetti di Baccalà
Largo dei Librari 88.
Map 11 C4.

**Forno Campo de'
Fiori**
Piazza Campo de' Fiori 22.
Map 11 C4.

Pizza Florida
Via Florida 25. **Map** 12 D4.

BARS, CAFES AND TEAROOMS

Alberto Pica
Via della Seggiola 12.
Map 12 D5.

Bar del Cappuccino
Via Arenula 50.
Map 12 D4.

Bernasconi
Piazza Cairoli 16.
Map 12 D4.

Bibliotèq
Via dei Banchi Vecchi 124.
Map 11 B3.

Caffè la Feltrinelli
Largo Torre Argentina 5.
Map 12 D4.

PASTICCERIE

Boccione
Via del Portico d'Ottavia 1.
Map 12 E5.

Josephine's Bakery
Piazza del Paradiso 56–57.
Map 11 C4.

La Dolceroma
Via del Portico d'Ottavia
20B. **Map** 12 E5.

GELATERIE

L'Angolo dell'Artista
Largo dei Librari 86.
Map 11 C4.

Blue Ice
Via dei Baullari 130 and
141. **Map** 11 C4.

QUIRINAL

PIZZERIAS

Al Giubileo
Via Palermo 7.
Map 5 B4.

Est! Est! Est!
Via Genova 32. **Map** 5 C4.

ENOTECHE

Antica Locanda
Via del Boschetto 83–4.
Map 5 B4.

Cavour 313
Via Cavour 313. **Map** 5 B5.

Vineria Il Chianti
Via del Lavatore 81.
Map 12 F2.

BIRRERIE

The Albert
Via del Traforo 132.
Map 5 B3.

Birreria Peroni
Via San Marcello 19.
Map 12 F3.

FAST FOOD

Caffetteria Nazionale
Via Nazionale 26–27.
Map 5 C3.

Er Buchetto
Via Viminale 2. **Map** 5 C3.

Fior di Pizza
Via Milano 33. **Map** 5 B4.

**Galleria Alberto
Sordi**
Via del Corso. **Map** 12 E2.

BARS, CAFES AND TEAROOMS

**Antico Caffè del
Brasile**
Via dei Serpenti 23.
Map 5 B4.

Il Giardino del Tè
Via del Boschetto 112A.
Map 5 B4.

**Palazzo delle
Esposizioni**
Via Milano 15–17.
Map 5 B4.

Spinelli
Piazza del Viminale 18.
Map 5 C3.

PASTICCERIE

Dagnino
Galleria Esedra, Via
Vittorio Emanuele Orlando
75. **Map** 5 C2.

GELATERIE

San Crispino
Via della Panetteria 42.
Map 12 F2.

TERMINI

PIZZERIAS

La Bruschetta
Via Sardegna 39.
Map 5 B1.

Formula Uno
Via degli Equi 13.
Map 6 F4.

ENOTECHE

Enoteca Chirra
Via Torino 132–133.
Map 5 C3.

Trimani
Via Cernaia 37B.
Map 6 D2.

FAST FOOD

Chef Express
Galleria Termini – Exit
Via Marsala. **Map** 6 D3.

Vyta
Galleria Termini – Exit
Via Marsala. **Map** 6 D3.

Wok
Stazione Termini (Lower
Level). **Map** 6 D3.

BARS, CAFES AND TEAROOMS

Grand Bar
St Regis Grand
Via Vittorio Emanuele
Orlando 3. **Map** 6 C3.

ESQUILINE

BIRRERIE

**The Fiddler's
Elbow**
Via dell'Olmata 43.
Map 6 D4.

Old Marconi
Via di Sante Prassede 9C.
Map 6 D4.

FAST FOOD

Panella
Via Merulana 54.
Map 6 D5.

BARS, CAFES AND TEAROOMS

Ciamei
Via Emanuele Filiberto 57.
Map 6 E5.

Oppio Café
Via delle Terme di Tito 72.
Map 5 C5.

PASTICCERIE

Cipriani
Via C. Botta 21. **Map** 6 D5.

Regoli
Via dello Statuto 60.
Map 6 D5.

GELATERIE

Palazzo del Freddo
Via Principe Eugenio
65/67. **Map** 6 E5.

LATERAN

BIRRERIE

La Pace del Cervello
Via dei SS Quattro 63.
Map 9 A1.

ENOTECHE

Il Tajut
Via di San Giovanni in
Laterano 244.
Map 9 B1.

FAST FOOD

Porchetta Stall
Viale Carlo Felice.
Map 10 D1.

PASTICCERIE

Paci
Via dei Marsi 35.
Off **Map** 6 F4.

GELATERIE

Gelateria Fantasia
Via La Spezia 100/102.
Map 10 E1.

San Crispino
Via Acaia 56.
Map 9 C4.

AVENTINE

PIZZERIAS

Remo
Piazza Santa Maria
Liberatrice 44.
Map 8 D3.

BIRRERIE

L'Oasi della Birra
Piazza Testaccio 41.
Map 8 D3.

ENOTECHE

Divinare
Via Manunzio 13.
Map 8 D3.

FAST FOOD

Farinando
Via Luca della Robbia 30.
Map 8 D3.

Rosticcerì
Piazza Testaccio 24–5.
Map 8 D3.

Volpetti Più
Via Alessandro Volta 8.
Map 8 D3.

GELATERIE

Café du Parc
Piazza di Porta San Paolo.
Map 8 E4.

Giolitti
Via Vespucci 35. **Map** 8 D3.

TRASTEVERE

PIZZERIAS

Da Vittorio
Via di S. Cosimato 14A.
Map 7 C1.

Dar Poeta
Vicolo del Bologna 45.
Map 11 B5.

Panattoni – I Marmi
Viale Trastevere 53.
Map 7 C1.

Pizzeria Ivo
Via S. Francesco a Ripa
158. **Map** 7 C1.

ENOTECHE

Cantina Paradiso
Via San Francesco
a Ripa 73. **Map** 7 C2.

Ferrara
Via del Moro 1A.
Map 7 C1.

Trastevere
Via della Lungaretta 86.
Map 7 C1.

FAST FOOD

Forno La Renella
Via del Moro 15.
Map 7 C1.

Frontoni
Viale Trastevere 52.
Map 7 C1.

BARS, CAFES AND TEAROOMS

Caffè Settimiano
Via di Porta Settimiana 1.
Map 11 B5.

PASTICCERIE

Innocenti
Via della Luce 21A.
Map 7 C2.

Pasticceria Trastevere
Via Natale del Grande 49.
Map 7 C1.

**Rivendita di
Cioccolata e Vino**
Vicolo del Cinque 11A.
Map 11 B5.

GELATERIE

Fior di Luna
Via della Lungaretta 96.
Map 7 C1.

La Fonte della Salute
Via Cardinale Marmaggi
2–4. **Map** 7 C1.

JANICULUM

ENOTECHE

**In Vino Veritas Art
Bar**
Via Garibaldi 2A.
Map 11 B5.

VATICAN

PIZZERIAS

Napul'è
Viale Giulio Cesare 91.
Map 3 C1.

Pizzeria San Marco
Via Tacito 29. **Map** 4 D2.

ENOTECHE

Costantini
Piazza Cavour 16.
Map 4 E2.

Del Frate
Via degli Scipioni 118.
Map 3 C1.

Il Pane e Le Rose
Via Quirino Visconti 61A.
Map 4 E2.

BIRRERIE

Cantina Tirolese
Via Vitelleschi 23.
Map 3 C2.

The Proud Lion
Borgo Pio 36. **Map** 3 C3.

FAST FOOD

Ercoli dal 1928
Via Montello 26.
Off **Map** 1 A5.

Franchi
Via Cola di Rienzo 200.
Map 4 D2.

La Pratolina
Via degli Scipioni 248.
Map 3 C1.

BARS, CAFES AND TEAROOMS

Art Studio Café
Via dei Gracchi 187A.
Map 4 D2.

Faggiani
Via G. Ferrari 23.
Map 1 A5.

Makasar
Via Plauto 33. **Map** 3 C3.

PASTICCERIE

Antonini
Via Sabotino 19–29.
Just off **Map** 1 A5.

Gran Caffè Esperia
Lungotevere Mellini 1.
Map 4 E1.

GELATERIE

Al Settimo Gelo
Via Vodice 21A.
Just off **Map** 1 A5.

Gelarmony
Via Marcantonio Colonna
34. **Map** 4 D1.

VIA VENETO

PIZZERIAS

Squisito
Via Lucullo 22.
Map 5 C2.

BARS, CAFES AND TEAROOMS

Café de Paris
Via Veneto 90. **Map** 5 B2.

Cine Caffè
Largo M. Mastroianni 1.
Map 5 B1.

Doney
Via Veneto 141. **Map** 5 B2.

EUR

ENOTECHE

La Cave des Amis
Piazzale Ardigò 27–29.

BARS, CAFES AND TEAROOMS

Palombini
Piazzale Adenauer 12.

PASTICCERIE

Dulcis In Fundo
Via Tommaso
Odescalchi 13–15.

GELATERIE

Chalet del Lago
Lake, EUR

Giolitti
Casina dei Tre Laghi,
Viale Oceania 90.

FURTHER AFIELD

PIZZERIAS

**Al Forno della
Soffitta**
Via Piave 62.
Map 6 D1.

BARS, CAFES AND TEAROOMS

Caffè Parnaso
Piazza delle Muse 22.
Map 2 E2.

Zodiaco
Viale Parco Mellini 88–92.
Off **Map** 3 A1.

PASTICCERIE

Euclide
Via Filippo Civinini 119.
Map 2 D3.

Mondi
Via Flaminia 468.
Off **Map** 1 A1.

GELATERIE

Duse
Via Eleonora Duse 1B.
Map 2 F2.

Petrini dal 1926
Piazza dell'Alberone 16A.
Map 10 F4.

SHOPS AND MARKETS

Rome has been a thriving centre for design and cosmopolitan shopping since ancient times. In the heyday of the Empire the finest craftsmen were drawn to Rome, and artifacts and produce of all kinds, including gold, furs, wine and slaves, were imported from far-flung corners of the Empire to service the needs of the wealthy Roman population. Shopping in Rome today in many ways reflects this diverse tradition. Italian designers

Stylish window display

have an international reputation for their luxuriously chic style in fashion, knitwear and leather goods (especially shoes and handbags) as well as in interior design, fabrics, ceramics and glass. The artisan-craftsman tradition is strong and the love of good design filters through into the smallest items. Rome is not a city for bargains (although it is often better value than Florence or Milan), but the joys of window shopping here will offer plenty of compensation.

BEST BUYS

Leather goods of all kinds, including shoes and bags, are a strong point. Ready-to-wear Italian designer clothes are not cheap, but they are certainly less expensive than in other countries. Armani jeans are a good example *(see p339)*. You are also likely to find designer lighting fixtures, for example, at lower prices here. Both modern and traditional Italian ceramics and handicrafts can be very beautifully made and, if you have time to wander around the back streets, really unusual and individual gifts can often be found.

SALES

Bargain hunters may like to visit Rome during sale time *(saldi)*, from mid-July to mid-September and the period from just after Christmas

to the first week in March. Top designers *(see p338)* can slash prices by half, but their clothes are still very expensive even then. Good bargains can be found in the young designer-wear shops *(see p339)* and good-quality small and large shoe sizes are sold off very cheaply. In general, though, sales in Rome tend to offer moderate rather than huge discounts.

Both the original and the sale price should be quoted on each reduced item. *Liquidazioni* (closing-down sales) are usually genuine and can sometimes be worth investigating. However, other signs in shop windows such as *vendite promozionali* (special introductory prices) and *sconti* (discounts) are often only lures to get you into the shop. The sign on the door saying *entrata libera* means "browsers welcome".

Antiques at Acanto *(see p348)*

WHEN TO SHOP

Shops are generally open from 9am to 1pm and from 3.30pm to 7.30pm (4pm to 8pm in the summer months). Some of the shops in the centre stay open all day from 10am to 7.30pm.

Most shops are closed on Sunday (except immediately before Christmas). Shops are also closed on Monday morning, apart from most food stores, which close on Thursday afternoons in winter and Saturday afternoons in high summer.

August brings the city to a virtual standstill as Roman families escape the heat to the sea or the mountains, but this is gradually changing, with Romans taking shorter summer holidays. Most shops close for at least 2 weeks around 15 August, the national holiday.

Flower stalls in Piazza Campo de' Fiori *(see p352)*

SHOPPING ETIQUETTE

Apart from a few department stores, most Roman shops are small, specializing in just one field. Browsing at leisure may at first seem daunting if you are used to large shopping centres. Customers will almost always receive better attention if they dress smartly – the emphasis on *fare una bella figura* (making a good impression) is taken seriously.

Sizes are not always uniform, so it is wise to try clothes on if possible before buying, since refunds and exchanges are not always given.

Stylish leather gloves on display

HOW TO PAY

Most shops now accept all the major credit cards, whose signs are displayed on the shop window. Some will also accept foreign currency, though the exchange rate may not be good. When you make a purchase you are bound by Italian law to leave the shop with a *scontrino fiscale* (receipt). You can try asking for a discount if paying cash and you may be lucky, though many shops have a *prezzi fissi* (fixed prices) sign.

VAT EXEMPTION

Value Added Tax – VAT (IVA in Italy) – ranges from 12 per cent on clothing to 35 per cent on luxury items such as jewellery and furs. Marked or advertised prices normally include the IVA. It is possible for non-European Union

One of many designer shops around Piazza di Spagna

residents to obtain an IVA refund for individual purchases that exceed about 155 euros, but be prepared for a long and bureaucratic process. The simplest method is to shop at a place displaying the "Euro Free Tax" sign. Present your passport when you make your purchase and ask for a **Global Refund Italia** cheque. On leaving Italy, show your new purchases and receipts at customs and get the cheque stamped. You can either collect your refund at Fiumicino airport or send the cheque to Global Refund who will reimburse you.

If you wish to buy something from a shop which is not part of the "Euro Free Tax" scheme, you must get the Italian customs to stamp the vendor's receipt at your departure, showing them the purchased article, then post the receipt back to the shop, who should then send you a refund.

Mercato delle Stampe (see p352)

DEPARTMENT STORES AND SHOPPING CENTRES

Department stores, known as *grandi magazzini,* are few and far between in Rome, but they tend to have longer opening hours than smaller shops. **La Rinascente** and **Coin** are good for ready-to-wear clothes, both for men and women, household linens and haberdashery, and have well-stocked perfume counters. The **Oviesse** and **Upim** chain stores offer moderately priced medium-quality clothes and a variety of household goods.

Another alternative for the zealous shopper is to head for one of Rome's shopping malls. **Cinecittà Due Centro Commerciale**, built in 1988, offers around 100 shops plus bars, banks and

Bargains in Via Sannio *(see p353)*

restaurants within easy reach of the centre by Metro (line A to Cinecittà).

Cinecittà Due Centro Commerciale
Viale Palmiro Togliatti 2.
Tel 06-722 0910.

Coin
Piazzale Appio 7. **Map** 10 D2.
Tel 06-708 0020.

Via Cola di Rienzo 173. **Map** 3 C2.
Tel 06-3600 4298.

Global Refund Italia
Via Carlo Noè 33, Gallarate 21013.
Tel 0331-177 8000.
www.globalrefund.com

La Rinascente
Galleria Alberto Sordi.
Map 12 E2.
Tel 06-678 4209.

Piazza Fiume. **Map** 6 D1.
Tel 06-884 1231.

Oviesse
Viale Trastevere 62. **Map** 7 C2.
Tel 06-5833 3633.

Via Appia Nuova 181–5.
Map 10 D2.
Tel 06-702 3214.

Upim
Via del Tritone 172. **Map** 5 A3.
Tel 06-678 3336.

Termini Station. **Map** 6 D3.
Tel 06-4782 5909.

Piazza Santa Maria Maggiore.
Map 6 D4.
Tel 06-446 5579.

Rome's Best: Shopping Streets and Markets

The most interesting shops in Rome are in the old centre, so shopping is easy to combine with sightseeing. The shops are often housed in medieval or Renaissance buildings and their window displays can be exquisite. Just like shopkeepers in past centuries, traders tend to specialize in one type of merchandise. Street names often refer to the old tradesmen: locksmiths in Via dei Chiavari, leather jerkin makers in Via dei Giubbonari and chairs in Via dei Sediari. Today, antique merchants have taken over from the rosary sellers on Via dei Coronari. The top names in fashion and modern design dominate the Via Condotti area, and the artisan-craftsman tradition is still strong around Campo de' Fiori and Piazza Navona.

Via dei Coronari

Art Nouveau and antiques enthusiasts will love browsing in the shops that line this charming street just northwest of Piazza Navona. But be prepared for high prices as most of the items are imported.

Via Cola di Rienzo

Situated close to the Vatican Museums, this long wide street has the finest food shops and is also good for clothes, books and gifts.

Via del Pellegrino

Book and art shops abound here next to working artisans in the historic centre. Do not miss the mirror-lined alley near Campo de' Fiori.

Via dei Cappellari

This narrow, medieval street is a great place for watching furniture restorers and other artisans plying their crafts in the open air.

Porta Portese

You can buy anything from antiques to a tin whistle at Trastevere's Sunday morning flea market. (See p353.)

Vatican

Piazza Navona

Janiculum

T I B E R

Tras

Via Margutta
Up-market antique shops mix with genteel restaurants on this peaceful, cobbled street.

Via del Babuino
This street is renowned for designer furniture, lighting and glass, as well as interesting antique and fashion shops.

DESIGNER SHOPPING

All the well-known stars of the Italian fashion scene, plus exclusive jewellers, gift shops, shoe designers and tailors, are concentrated in this cluster of chic and stylish shopping streets by the Spanish Steps (see pp338–43). Romans love to stroll here in the early evening.

Via Veneto

set

Quirinal

Capitol

Esquiline

Forum

Palatine

Caracalla

Lateran

Via Borgognona
Crowds flock here to buy, or just gaze at, high-fashion clothes, shoes, leather bags and other accessories.

| 0 metres | 500 |
| 0 yards | 500 |

Testaccio Market
A visual feast of fruit and vegetables greets the eye in this lively market. (See p352.)

Men's and Women's Fashion

Italy is one of the leading lights in high-class fashion, or *alta moda*. Many of the most famous designers are based in Milan, but Rome is home to a cluster of sophisticated and internationally distinguished fashion houses. There is also a wonderful selection of *alta moda* shops. Boutiques displaying an eclectic mix of designer goods rub shoulders with showrooms devoted to single collections. But even for those of us unable to splash out on genuine designer-wear, much fun can be gained from a stroll down the glittering streets that radiate out from the Piazza di Spagna, as some of the window displays are truly spectacular.

The "atelier" made-to-measure fashions are beyond most pockets, but the designers also offer ready-to-wear alternatives in their boutiques. These are not cheap, but cost far less than a tailor-made garment.

WOMEN'S HIGH FASHION

Rome's most famous designer internationally is probably **Valentino**, who retired in 2008 but whose boutique on Piazza di Spagna is still a mecca for the younger fashionista. Just up the Spanish Steps, in chic Via Sistina, is the Rome branch of **Gattinoni**, which showcases the subtly extravagant haute couture and ready-to-wear designs of Guillermo Mariotto.

The equally impressive **Fendi** occupies a 19th-century palazzo in Largo Goldoni. Fendi made its name with high-fashion furs, then branched out into leather goods, accessories and ready-to-wear, collaborating with Karl Lagerfeld who designed the coveted double-F logo which emblazons its very collectable products. Third-generation family members design the younger, less expensive Fendissime line.

For well over a decade, **Laura Biagiotti** has reigned as Rome's queen of discreet, conservative couture. From her headquarters in a castle just outside Rome, she designs a range of timelessly elegant knitwear and silk separates for women who don't want to sacrifice style for comfort. She is famous for her use of cashmere and white as well as her creative use of fabrics and quality of finish. Her flagship showroom in Via Borgognona stocks her complete collection, which now includes hosiery, perfumes, swimwear and leather goods. Her scarves make wonderful presents, and are often reduced in price during sales; other items from previous collections are available in the shop all year round at very good discounts. Meanwhile, in nearby Via Condotti, there is the temple to the creations of **Salvatore Ferragamo**.

Other internationally known Rome-based designers include **Renato Balestra**, who produces tailored suits and glamorous evening wear and **Roberto Capucci**, who uses wonderful textures and fabrics in classy suits.

Milan's miraculous fashion house **Prada** has an alluring branch on Via Condotti, featuring clothes, shoes and accessories in unmistakable style. The window display is always worth a look. Other luminaries of Italian fashion who have shops in Rome include **Giorgio Armani**, **Gianni Versace**, **Trussardi** and **Dolce & Gabbana**.

An affirmed star in ready-to-wear is **Roberto Cavalli**, whose design team produces some coolly imaginative and stylish collections.

If you're looking for clothes from more unconventional designers, **Gente** is the place to go – its Roman showrooms have exclusive rights to the original couture collections of avant-garde stylists such as Dolce & Gabbana, Moschino, and Jean-Paul Gaultier.

MaxMara also has a number of branches here. Chic suits and separates are the mainstays of this popular label. The quality of fabric and finish is superb and, with suits available for around €500, its prices are much lower than other *alta moda* couture designers' ready-to-wear lines.

MEN'S TAILORS AND DESIGNER WEAR

Italian men are every bit as fashion conscious as the women, and there is no shortage of choice in Rome for the well-dressed man. Suits generally begin at around €620, jackets €415 and trousers €155.

Most of the "star" designers of women's *alta moda* have a shop for men, like **Valentino**, **Prada** and **Gianni Versace**. The designs are generally less dramatic than the women's, with the accent on understated sophistication and casual sportiness. Valentino's distinctive monogrammed accessories are relatively affordable.

VALENTINO

One of the high priests of Italian fashion, **Valentino Garavani**, opened the doors of his Roman studio in 1959 to a distinguished clientele which included Sophia Loren, Audrey Hepburn and Jackie Kennedy, and has never looked back. He has created some of the most dramatic and flattering evening dresses of the last four decades. In the 1970s he began designing ready-to-wear lines for both men and women alongside his *alta moda* collections, and you can now find his very distinctive "V" logo on a wide range of accessories. Valentino's headquarters is in a huge palazzo in Piazza Mignanelli, and he also has a separate ready-to-wear boutique nearby (see p342).

Battistoni is probably the most prestigious designer concentrating on menswear. Giorgio Battistoni and family's fine custom-made shirts and suits have been in demand with film stars and top society for 50 years. **Etro** sells classically cut clothes and accessories for men and women in exotic Italian-designed printed fabrics.

Ermenegildo Zegna is housed in a Baroque palazzo setting. It offers elegant ready-to-wear, and the master tailor Gaetano will also make to measure. **Davide Cenci** has been a mecca for those in search of the English country gentleman look since 1926. **Brioni** offers traditional tailor-made and own-label ready-to-wear men's clothing, **Trussardi** sells beautifully tailored classics, and **Testa** has impeccably tailored suits that appeal to younger Romans. **Degli Effetti** stocks more avant-garde designers such as Romeo Gigli and Jean-Paul Gaultier.

YOUNG DESIGNER WEAR

There is a huge choice for the young. Top designers Valentino and Armani offer their particular styles trans-lated into more affordable lines at **Valentino Sport** and **Emporio Armani** (Armani jeans are good value at around €90). **Fendi** has its Fendissime line, **Ermanno Scervino** also has a boutique at Piazza di Spagna not far from **Gianfranco Ferré**'s youth-inspired label. Targeted at the younger set, these are good places to pick up stylish, sporty numbers.

Timberland is another casual label very popular with young Italians. Average prices are in the region of €52 for a shirt and €210 for raincoats.

Energie is a big hit and has some of the best window displays in Rome. Teenagers flock here for jeans and T-shirts, both the shop's own and other labels. Trussardi's casual line is found at **Tru Trussardi**, and **Aria**, **Diesel**, and **SBU** are also

very popular. **Eventi** represents the more avant-garde styles – *dark*, as they call it here – fusing Gothic, New Age and punk influences which can result in some out-rageous window displays. For women, Via del Governo Vecchio is the place to head for. **Arsenale**, **Luna e L'altra** and **Maga Morgana** offer some unconventional design-er clothes in a pleasant, friendly atmosphere.

HIGH STREET FASHION

Rome is not a good place to look for everyday wear, since there is a distinct lack of mid-price shops bridging the huge gap between the dazzlingly priced *alta moda* designer exclusives and the ultra-cheap goods sold in markets *(see pp352–3)*. Lower-budget shops do exist, but quality is often poor. If you have the stamina, you may find a bargain along Via del Corso, Via del Tritone, Via Nazionale, Via Cavour, Via Cola di Rienzo, Via Ottaviano or the Via dei Giubbonari.

The most convenient places to shop are department stores like La Rinascente, Coin and Upim *(see p335)*. They may not sound exciting, but you can browse at leisure and occasionally find nice things. It is also worth trying shops mentioned under Young Designer Wear – particularly the *alta moda* designers' cheaper lines such as **Emporio Armani**. At the different branches of **Discount dell'Alta Moda** you can find end-of-season designer labels at 50 per cent less than the boutique prices. And while you don't need to come all the way to Rome to shop at **Benetton**, there are many shops here, which sell the authentic garments in their universal colours.

KNITWEAR

Knitwear is a particular strength in Italian design, and in Rome there are plenty of specialist shops. **Laura Biagiotti** is celebrated for her luxurious cashmere separates, and

Missoni for spectacular kalei-doscopic patterns and colours.

Krizia no longer has a shop in Rome but sophisti-cated knitwear can be purchased at **Liz**.

Gallo has a wide range of colourful tights and socks in wool and cashmere. Other shops, such as the **Luisa Spagnoli** outlets, offer a wider selection, including lower-priced items.

LINGERIE

This is another Italian speciality excelling in both style and quality, with lines like La Perla exported world-wide. Lingerie is traditionally sold in top household linen shops *(see p345)* – **Cesari**, for example, has its own complete range. There are also boutiques specializing in lingerie and swimwear.

Liberblu has a range of swimwear that's ideal for Ital-ian beaches, as well as linge-rie and women's night attire. **Brighenti** is said to be where film stars go for their lingerie. **Schostal** has more traditional underwear with a very good men's section.

SECOND-HAND CLOTHES

Those who are willing to browse will find a wide variety of second-hand clothes, whether inspired by a collec-tor's interest in vintage clothes or a low budget. Apart from Via Sannio and Porta Portese markets *(see p353)*, which have many second-hand clothes stalls, the mecca is Via del Governo Vecchio. Among the best shops in this ancient street near Piazza Navona is **Mado**, which has mostly 1920s dresses and some hats and jewellery.

Le Gallinelle offers a marvellous selection of second-hand and vintage clothes, as well as their own line. At **Daniela e Daniela** in Via Mastro Giorgio, Testaccio, there is an excellent range of women's clothes, mostly sporting designer labels. Via del Pellegrino is also a good street for shops selling second-hand clothes and for independent stores.

Shoes and Accessories

Italy's leather industry is renowned all over the world, and shoes, bags and belts are a good buy in Rome. Accessories in general are not just an afterthought but an integral part of an outfit for the well-dressed Roman. The choice of stylish jewellery, scarves, ties and other accessories is excellent.

SHOES

Rome is full of shoe shops, ranging from high-quality stores in the Via Condotti area (where prices tend to start at €170) to the more economical shops around the Trevi fountain, and every big market has its bargain shoe stalls on its fringes.

Probably the best-known shop is **Salvatore Ferragamo** – one of the world's top shoe shops. It stocks classic yet fashion-conscious shoes, as well as women's clothing and leather goods. The silk signature scarves are famous.

Fratelli Rossetti is a close contender for the number one position. Founded by brothers Renzo and Renato some 50 years ago, this company produces classic men's shoes and beautiful, dressy low-heeled shoes for women that reflect the most up-to-the-minute trends. Along with **Campanile** in Via Condotti it represents the epitome of elegance. The prices, of course, are sky-high but why not buy something small, and at least you'll have the bag!

Barrilà, which is located near Piazza San Lorenzo in Lucina, sells more affordable women's shoes.

Boccanera's retail outlets, over in Testaccio, offer the latest men's and women's shoe styles from top Italian and British designers, with prices to match.

Silvano Lattanzi is one of the longer-lived shoe shops in Rome, having been in business for almost two decades, but it can't compete with **Domus**, which opened in 1938. Silvano Lattanzi sells made-to-measure footwear for both men and women, particularly shoes for special occasions and to customers' personal specifications. Domus sells a selection of high-quality footwear, specializing in classic shoes for women. They also stock a limited range of leather bags and accessories. **De Bach** has colourful shoe styles for women.

Via Frattina has several more great shoe shops such as **Pollini**, which makes boots and bags for both men and women in trendy and imaginative styles. Native designer **Fausto Santini** stocks original, stylish, colourful designs for younger people. More moderate prices can be found at **Cervone**, which specializes in highly colourful women's shoes.

Borini stocks simple and elegant, low-heeled designs. The **Mr Boots** chain of shops stocks a wide range of trendy boots and casual shoes for men and women, while **Nuyorica** sells quirky, smart footwear for women alongside its select clothes range.

LEATHER BAGS AND ACCESSORIES

The most famous of Rome's leather shops is the super-trendy **Gucci**, a dandy's paradise selling shoes, suitcases, handbags, wallets, belts and other accessories. It has a fashion boutique for men and women and is well-known for its silk ties and scarves. **Fendi** also has exquisite leather goods as well as some lower-priced lines in synthetic materials and a range of gift items. Although their famous "stripe" line of leather-finished synthetic handbags cost €130 (and their all-leather ones start at €155), they are at least cheaper to buy here than abroad. **Skin**, situated around the Via Sistina area, is also quite pricey. Located a short walk to the south of Skin, near the Trevi Fountain, is **La Sella**. It sells all things leather, including a range of shoes, bags, purses and belts.

Mandarina Duck's brightly coloured fabric bags and range of luggage are very much in fashion and make an attractive (and vegetarian) alternative to the more traditional leather styles. For sleek, utterly fashionable handbags check out the latest creations from **Furla** or go for one of **Alviero Martini**'s famous "map" bags.

For a more unusual men's present, try **La Cravatta** in Trastevere. In addition to their selection of classy handmade ties, they also manufacture ties to customers' specifications. You can choose the design, material, length and shape of the tie to create the perfect gift.

CLASSIC JEWELLERY

What Cartier is to Paris, Tiffany & Co is to New York and Asprey's is to London, **Bulgari** is to Rome. This internationally revered jeweller's has passers-by glued to the windows gazing at its large fat gemstones. These "windows" are rather curious small boxes inserted into a wall with one or two pieces of jewellery in each of them, which adds to the feeling of looking at precious items in a case at a museum. Bulgari's watches, especially the men's, are popular and very elegant, as are the famous mesh necklaces. It specializes in large, colourful stones in High Renaissance-style settings but also produces a selection of contemporary designs. This was one of Andy Warhol's favourite shops, and it is definitely the most palatial shop on Via Condotti. Inside, the shop's atmosphere is one of almost religious awe and contemplation.

Buccellati is an offshoot of the famous Florentine dynasty, which was begun by Mario Buccellati in the 1920s and patronized by the poet Gabriele D'Annunzio. Its delicately engraved designs are inspired by the Italian Renaissance, and are real classics, displaying superb craftsmanship.

Ansuini designs are fashionable yet classic with strong, imaginative themes being introduced for each new collection. **Massoni**, founded in 1790, is one of Rome's oldest jewellery houses. Its refined one-offs and brooches are quite outstanding.

At **Moroni Gioielli** you will also find imaginative, unique pieces of the highest-quality workmanship.

Peroso is an old-fashioned shop which has been going since 1891 and specializes in antique jewellery and silverware. **Boncompagni Sturni** sells traditional designs with the emphasis on quality and craftsmanship. You have to ring the bell to be admitted to both of these shops, and they are extremely expensive.

Tiffany & Co sells its classic designs in jewellery, watches, accessories and gifts at an exquisite outlet on elegant Via del Babuino.

COSTUME JEWELLERY

For less conventional tastes, there are several shops selling innovative, avant-garde pieces, often using semi-precious metals and stones. **Via dei Coronari 193** is worth trying.

Tempi Moderni has an interesting collection of Art Deco and Liberty (Art Nouveau) period jewellery including Bakelite brooches. There is also a range of designer pieces from the fifties and sixties.

Danae makes interesting pieces using silver and precious stones, inspired by Coco Chanel, while **Paola Volpi** uses industrial materials and is one of the most interesting designers of modern jewellery in Italy.

TRADITIONAL GOLDSMITHS AND SILVERSMITHS

The mainstay of Rome's jewellery industry is still the traditional artisan goldsmith

and silversmith, working to order in tiny studio workshops. These are concentrated in the old Jewish Ghetto area by the Tiber river, Campo de' Fiori, Ponte Sisto near Via Giulia, and in Montepietà (which is also where the city pawn-brokers are situated).

Artisan jewellery can also be found in Via dei Coronari, Via dell'Orso and Via del Pellegrino. The jewellers create individual pieces to their own designs and have often learned their profession from their parents and grand-parents. They will also do repair work, or take old gold jewellery, melt it down and make it into something to the customer's order.

Gioie d'Arte produces some traditional artisan jewellery and always works to customers' commissions.

GLOVES, HATS AND HOSIERY

If you're looking for top quality, you will find an expensive line in gloves at **Di Cori** and **Sermoneta**, both of which stock every imaginable kind.

To find smart leather gloves to match your new shoes and handbags, whatever their colour, make a visit to **Settimio Mieli** which is sure to have something suitable, and at a reasonable price.

Catello d'Auria specializes in gloves and hosiery. **Borsalino** is a good place to go for all sorts of hats, including its namesake.

Calzedonia has several branches in the city and will serve you with almost any colour or pattern of tights and stockings that you could wish for.

SIZE CHART

For Australian sizes follow British and American convention.

Children's clothing

Italian	2-3	4-5	6-7	8-9	10-11	12	14	14+ (years)
British	2-3	4-5	6-7	8-9	10-11	12	14	14+ (years)
American	2-3	4-5	6-6x	7-8	10	12	14	16 (size)

Children's shoes

Italian	24	25½	27	28	29	30	32	33	34
British	7	8	9	10	11	12	13	1	2
American	7½	8½	9½	10½	11½	12½	13½	1½	2½

Women's dresses, coats and skirts

Italian	38	40	42	44	46	48	50
British	8	10	12	14	16	18	20
American	6	8	10	12	14	16	18

Women's blouses and sweaters

Italian	81	84	87	90	93	96	99 (cms)
British	31	32	34	36	38	40	42 (inches)
American	6	8	10	12	14	16	18 (size)

Women's shoes

Italian	36	37	38	39	40	41
British	3	4	5	6	7	8
American	5	6	7	8	9	10

Men's suits

Italian	44	46	48	50	52	54	56	58 (size)
British	34	36	38	40	42	44	46	48 (inches)
American	34	36	38	40	42	44	46	48 (inches)

Men's shirts (collar size)

Italian	36	38	39	41	42	43	44	45 (cms)
British	14	15	15½	16	16½	17	17½	18 (inches)
American	14	15	15½	16	16½	17	17½	18 (inches)

Men's shoes

Italian	39	40	41	42	43	44	45	46
British	6	7	7½	8	9	10	11	12
American	7	7½	8	8½	9½	10½	11	11½

DIRECTORY

WOMEN'S HIGH FASHION

Dolce & Gabbana
Via Condotti 51–52.
Map 5 A2.
Tel 06-6992 4999.

Fendi
Largo Goldoni 419.
Map 12 E1.
Tel 06-69 66 61.

Gattinoni
Via Sistina 44.
Map 5 A2.
Tel 06-678 3972.

Gente
Via del Babuino 81.
Map 4 F1.
Tel 06-320 7671.
Also: Via Frattina 69.
Map 5 A2.
Tel 06-678 9132.

Gianni Versace
Via Bocca di Leone 26–27.
Map 5 A2.
Tel 06-678 0521.

Giorgio Armani
Via Condotti 77.
Map 5 A2.
Tel 06-699 1461.
Also: Via del Babuino 140.
Map 4 F1.
Tel 06-3600 2197.

Laura Biagiotti
Via Borgognona 43–44.
Map 5 A2.
Tel 06-679 1205.

Max & Co
Via Condotti 46.
Map 5 A2.
Tel 06-678 7946.

MaxMara
Via Frattina 28. **Map** 5 A2.
Tel 06-679 3638.

Prada
Via Condotti 92–95.
Map 5 A2.
Tel 06-679 0897.

Renato Balestra
Via Abruzzi 3. **Map** 5 C1.
Tel 06-482 1723.

Roberto Capucci
Via Gregoriana 56.
Map 5 A2.
Tel 06-679 5180.

Roberto Cavalli
Via Borgognona 25.
Map 5 A2.
Tel 06-6992 5469.

Salvatore Ferragamo
Via Condotti 73–74.
Map 5 A2.
Tel 06-679 1565.

Trussardi
Via Condotti 49–50. **Map** 5 A2. *Tel 06-679 2151.*

Valentino
Via Condotti 15.
Map 5 A2.
Tel 06-673 9420.

MEN'S TAILORS AND DESIGNER WEAR

Battistoni
Via Condotti 61A.
Map 5 A2.
Tel 06-697 6111.

Brioni
Via Condotti 21A.
Map 5 A2.
Tel 06-678 3428.

Davide Cenci
Via Campo Marzio 1–7.
Map 4 F3 & 12 D2.
Tel 06-699 0681.

Degli Effetti
Piazza Capranica 79 & 93.
Map 4 F3 & 12 D2.
Tel 06-679 0202.

Ermenegildo Zegna
Via Borgognona 7E.
Map 5 A2.
Tel 06-678 9143.

Etro
Via del Babuino 102.
Map 5 A2.
Tel 06-678 8257.

Gianfranco Ferré
Via Borgognona 7A.
Map 12 E1.
Tel 06-6920 0815.

Gianni Versace
Via Bocca di Leone 26–27.
Map 5 A2.
Tel 06-678 0521.

Gucci
Via Condotti 8. **Map** 5 A2.
Tel 06-679 0405.

Testa
Via Borgognona 13.
Map 12 E1.
Tel 06-679 0660.
Also: Piazza Euclide 27.
Map 2 D2.
Tel 06-807 0118.

Trussardi
See Women's High Fashion.

Valentino
Via Bocca di Leone 15.
Map 5 A2.
Tel 06-673 9430.

YOUNG DESIGNER WEAR

Aria
Via Nazionale 239.
Map 5 C3.
Tel 06-48 44 21.

Arsenale
Via del Governo Vecchio 64. **Map** 4 E4 & 11 B3.
Tel 06-686 1380.

Diesel
Via del Corso 186.
Map 4 F3 & 12 E1.
Tel 06-678 3933.

Emporio Armani
Via del Babuino 140.
Map 4 F1.
Tel 06-3600 2197.

Energie
Via del Corso 486.
Map 4 F2.
Tel 06-322 7046.

Ermanno Scervino
Piazza di Spagna 82–83.
Map 5 A2.
Tel 06-679 2294.

Eventi
Via dei Serpenti 134.
Map 5 B4.
Tel 06-48 49 60.

Gianfranco Ferré
Piazza di Spagna 70. **Map** 5 A2. *Tel 06-679 1451.*

Luna e L'Altra
Piazza Pasquino 76.
Map 4 E4 & 11 C3.
Tel 06-6880 4995.

Maga Morgana
Via del Governo Vecchio 27 & 98. **Map** 4 E4 & 11 C3.
Tel 06-687 9995.

SBU
Via S. Pantaleo 68.
Map 11 C3.
Tel 06-324 3363.

Timberland
Via del Corso 488.
Map 4 F2.
Tel 06-324 3363.

Tru Trussardi
Via Frattina 42.
Map 5 A2.
Tel 06-6938 0939.

Valentino
Via del Babuino 61.
Map 4 F1.
Tel 06-3600 1906.

HIGH STREET FASHION

Benetton
Via del Corso 422.
Map 12 E1.
Tel 06-6810 2520.

Discount dell'Alta Moda
Via di Gesù e Maria 14 & 16A. **Map** 4 F2.
Tel 06-361 3796.
Also: Via de Pretis 88.
Map 5 C3.
Tel 06-4782 5672.

Emporio Armani
See Young Designer Wear

Zara
Galleria Alberto Sordi.
Map 12 E2.
Tel 06-6992 5401.

KNITWEAR

Gallo
Via Vittoria 63.
Map 4 F2.
Tel 06-3600 2174.

Laura Biagiotti
See Women's High Fashion.

Liz
Via Appia Nuova 90.
Map 10 D2.
Tel 06-700 3609.

Luisa Spagnoli
Via del Tritone 30.
Map 5 A3 & B3 & 12F1.
Tel 06-6992 2769.
Also: Via Vittorio
Veneto 130.
Map 5 B1.
Tel 06-4201 1281.
Also: Via Frattina 84B.
Map 5 A2.
Tel 06-699 1706.

Missoni
Piazza di Spagna 78.
Map 5 A2.
Tel 06-679 2555.

LINGERIE

Brighenti
Via Frattina 7–8.
Map 5 A2.
Tel 06-679 1484.
Also: Via Borgognona 27.
Map 5 A2.
Tel 06-678 3898.

Cesari
Via del Babuino 195.
Map 5 B3.
Tel 06-638 1241.

Liberblu
Via del Tritone 101.
Map 12 F1.
Tel 06-488 2246.

Schostal
Via del Corso 158.
Map 4 F3 & 12 E1.
Tel 06-679 1240.

SECOND-HAND CLOTHES

Daniela e Daniela
Via Mastro Giorgio 79B.
Map 8 D3.
Tel 06-5728 5208.

Le Gallinelle
Via Panisperna 61.
Map 5 B4.
Tel 06-488 1017.

Mado
Via del Governo Vecchio
89A. **Map** 4 E4 & 11 B3.
Tel 06-687 5028.

SHOES

Barrilà
Via del Leone 17.
Map 12 D1.
Tel 06-687 1009.

Boccanera
Via Luca della Robbia
34–36. **Map** 8 D3.
Tel 06-575 6804.

Borini
Via dei Pettinari 86–87.
Map 4 E5 & 11 C5.
Tel 06-687 5670.

Campanile
Via Condotti 58.
Map 5 A2.
Tel 06-679 0731.

Cervone
Via del Corso 99.
Map 4 F2.
Tel 06-678 3522.

De Bach
Via del Babuino 123.
Map 4 F1.
Tel 06-678 3384.

Domus
Via Belsiana 52. **Map** 4 F2.
Tel 06-678 9003.

Fausto Santini
Via Frattina 120.
Map 5 A2.
Tel 06-678 4114.

Ferragamo
Via Condotti 73–74.
Map 5 A2.
Tel 06-679 1565.
Also: Via Condotti 66.
Map 5 A2.
Tel 06-678 1130.

Fratelli Rossetti
Via Borgognona 5A.
Map 5 A2.
Tel 06-678 2676.

Mr Boots
Piazza Re di Roma 10.
Map 10 D3.
Tel 06-7720 8672.
Also: Via A Brunetti 2.
Map 4 F1.
Tel 06-321 5733.

Nuyorica
Piazza della Pollarola 36–7.
Map 11 C4.
Tel 06-6889 1243.

Pollini
Via Frattina 22–24.
Map 5 A2 & 12 E1.
Tel 06-679 8360.

Silvano Lattanzi
Via Bocca di Leone 59.
Map 5 A2.
Tel 06-678 6119.

LEATHER GOODS

Alviero Martini
Via Frattina 116.
Map 5 A2.
Tel 06-6992 3381.

Furla
Via Condotti 56.
Map 5 A2.
Tel 06-679 1973.

Gucci
Via Borgognona 7D. **Map**
5 A2. **Tel** 06-6920 2077.

Mandarina Duck
Via Due Macelli 59F/G.
Map 12 F1.
Tel 06-678 6414.

La Sella
Via del Lavatore 56.
Map 5 A3 & 12 F2.
Tel 06-679 6654.

Skin
Via Capo le Case 41
Map 5 A3 & 12 F1.
Tel 06-678 5531.

CLASSIC JEWELLERY

Ansuini
Corso Vittorio Emanuele
151.
Map 4 E4 & 11 C3.
Tel 06-689 2193.

Boncompagni
Via Vittoria 4A.
Map 4 F2.
Tel 06-321 3950.

Buccellati
Via Condotti 31. **Map**
5 A2. **Tel** 06-679 0329.

Bulgari
Via Condotti 10. **Map**
5 A2. **Tel** 06-679 3876.

Massoni
Via Margutta 74.
Map 4 F1.
Tel 06-321 6916.

Moroni Gioielli
Via Belsiana 32A. **Map**
4 F2. **Tel** 06-678 0466.

Peroso
Via Sistina 29A.
Map 5 B3.
Tel 06-474 7952.

Tiffany & Co
Via del Babuino 118.
Map 5 A2.
Tel 06-679 0717.

COSTUME JEWELLERY

Danae
Via della Maddalena 40.
Map 12 D2.
Tel 06-679 1881.

Granuzzo
Via dei Coronari 193.
Map 4 E3 & 11 B2.
Tel 06-6880 1503.

Paola Volpi
Piazza dei Satiri 55.
Map 11 C4.
Tel 06-687 3366.

Tempi Moderni
Via del Governo
Vecchio 108.
Map 4 E4 & 11 B3.
Tel 06-687 7007.

TRADITIONAL GOLDSMITHS AND SILVERSMITHS

Gioie d'Arte
Via de' Gigli d'Oro 10.
Map 4 E3 & 11 C2.
Tel 06-687 7524.

GLOVES, HATS AND HOSIERY

Borsalino
Piazza del Popolo 20.
Map 4 F1.
Tel 06-3265 0838.
Also: Via Sistina 58A.
Map 5 B2.
Tel 06-6994 1223.

Calzedonia
Via del Corso 106.
Map 4 F2.
Tel 06-6992 5436.

Catello d'Auria
Via dei Due Macelli 55.
Map 5 A2 & 12 F1.
Tel 06-679 3364.

Di Cori
Piazza di Spagna 53.
Map 5 A2.
Tel 06-678 4439.

La Cravatta
Via di Santa Cecilia 12.
Map 8 D1.
Tel 06-8901 6941.

Fendi
See Women's High Fashion.

Sermoneta
Piazza di Spagna 61.
Map 5 A2.
Tel 06-679 1960.

Settimio Mieli
Via San Claudio 70.
Map 5 A3 & 12 E2.
Tel 06-678 5979.

Interior Design

Italian design belongs to a long-established tradition based on the skills of the master craftsman, and some firms have a history going back hundreds of years. Rome's stylish interior design shops are worth seeking out, even if it is only to look around and enjoy the ambience. You might well pick up some design ideas for your home, or find some interesting or unusual things to buy. They are an excellent place to buy souvenirs and presents to take home.

FURNITURE

Italy is well-known for its stylish, well-made furniture. Although there is no distinct area of Rome that is renowned for its furniture shops, many of the top stores are located to the north of the city centre.

In the heart of the historic centre, on Via dei Banchi Vecchi, is **Bernardini**. This small shop is filled with its trademark slick, elegant designs, from wood and steel furniture to more affordable household items.

Decoration 2000 dazzles with its sensible prices and its covetable Tuscan wrought iron and Venetian painted furniture in sun-drenched or delicate hues.

Spazio Sette, near Largo Argentina, is worth visiting for the building itself. The store has a spectacular showroom on three levels in the Palazzo Lazzaroni, a former cardinal's palace. Spazio Sette is one of Rome's premier home furnishing stores and, as well as furniture, the shop stocks plenty of items that would make interesting gifts. The furniture, including modern, laminated stack-up chairs and the vases, glass, bowls and kitchen equipment, are jumbled together in a fascinating display.

Nearby, on Piazza Cairoli, stands **Confalone**, a furniture shop that specialises in well-upholstered sofas and armchairs, though dining tables and chairs also crowd the display area. The shop's wide range of classical designs suits any interior.

Benedetti, which occupies a line of shops on the Via Marmorata, offers a range of fine modern wood furniture, while **Fattorini**, on Via Arenula, gives a modern Italian take on 1970s retro styling.

LIGHTING FIXTURES

Lighting fixtures are one of the most popular and more easily transportable items, and there are several superb showrooms in Rome that are worth a visit.

Flos is a merger of two design houses whose Roman showroom displays its lights as if they were museum exhibits. The design style is chic and minimalist, with plenty of black and white, chrome and steel.

Nearby **Artemide** is, like Flos, a design house in its own right, and is similarly well-known abroad. Its showroom in Rome is elegant, with expensive, hi-tech lighting design. **Borghini** sells less famous names, and is therefore more economical.

To see examples of light fittings from all of Italy's leading producers, head to **Obor**, where high-tech items are displayed alongside more traditional designs.

Some independent craftsmen take a lead when it comes to lampshade design. **Paolo Marj**, for instance, is a sculptor working in mixed media such as glass, wood and plastics to create lamps that are original works of art in themselves. Also on sale is a variety of original sculptures by the artist.

Italian lighting and other electrical equipment is designed for 220–240 volts. If you are going to use it in countries with lower voltage always ask the shop whether the product needs a transformer, as this can depend on the model.

Lighting fixtures generally take screw-bulbs, although some designer models can be ordered with fittings for bayonet-bulbs.

KITCHENS AND BATHROOMS

Although you won't be able to take one home with you, you may like to take a look at the ultra-modern hi-tech kitchen designs in Rome.

For an overview of the latest smart, steel designs, visit **Arclinea**, near Ponte Garibaldi, for its select display of state-of-the-art kitchens. Equally inspiring are the kitchens on display at **Emporio Cucina**, just off Piazza Navona.

Italian bathroom shops concentrate almost exclusively on modern designs, some of which are luxuriously decadent. **Ravasini** has very decorative floral fixtures with some matching accessories. **Materia** is another bathroom shop that sells all the latest styles.

TILES

The Italian ceramic tile tradition is an ancient one. A great variety of tiles is displayed in kitchen and bathroom showrooms, but there are also one or two specialist shops.

Ceramiche Musa specializes in modern tiles incorporating decorative floral and ancient Roman motifs, which are popular, especially with foreign visitors.

GLASS

Decorative glass objects are a popular buy in Rome. **Murano Più**, just behind Piazza Navona, sells Murano and other glass items at reasonable prices. This shop is one of the few that open on Sundays – which can be useful for visitors on short trips to Rome.

Archimede Seguso also specializes in Murano glass

but includes smaller pieces and also offers a range of gift-sized items.

Arteque is a very beautiful shop which has a more traditional flavour.

For less expensive gifts, try **Stilvetro**. It is the ideal place for pasta bowls, glass and ceramics.

An added advantage is that shipment abroad can usually be arranged at any of these glass establishments so you can make your purchase without worrying about transporting it home.

FABRICS

Beautiful fabrics and wallpapers to order are offered by **Il Sigillo** which has a rich assortment of samples.

At **Celsa** you can find all manner of fabrics, some at bargain discount prices. If you are looking for further bargains, take a walk round the old Jewish quarter, Il Ghetto, that runs from Largo Argentina down to the Tiber; the area contains numerous fabric shops such as **Paganini**. During sale times (see p334), remnants of fabrics (scampoli) are always sold off cheaply, and if you are lucky you could find just the right fabric for just the right price.

HOUSEHOLD LINEN AND KITCHENWARE

Shops selling household goods abound. For a selection of lovely sheets head to **Frette**.

If you enjoy designer kitchenware, don't miss **C.u.c.i.n.a**. tucked away in No. 65 Via Mario de' Fiori.

The shop stocks kitchen utensils from all over the world, as well as pots and pans in both rustic and hi-tech styles and countless space-saving kitchen accessories.

Right next to Piazza Venezia, **House & Kitchen** specializes in articles for the table and kitchen, selling every gadget imaginable.

The Roman pizzeria **'Gusto** (see p331) also offers an interesting range of kitchen utensils and essentials in its ground-floor shop.

Finally, there is **Limentani**, whose basement shop in the old ghetto area is well stocked with interesting gift ideas. Here, you will find an extraordinary array of household and kitchenware, including silver, china and crystal items.

DIRECTORY

FURNITURE

Benedetti
Via Marmorata 141.
Map 8 D3.
Tel 06-574 6610.

Bernardini
Via dei Banchi Vecchi 109.
Map 4 D4 & 11 A3.
Tel 06-6880 4622.

Confalone
Piazza Cairoli 110.
Map 12 D4.
Tel 06-6880 3684.

Decoration 2000
Piazza Nicosia 33.
Map 11 C1.
Tel 06-6839 2064.

Fattorini
Via Arenula 55.
Map 12 D5.
Tel 06-6813 6615.

Spazio Sette
Via dei Barbieri 7.
Map 4 F5 & 12 D4.
Tel 06-6880 4261.

LIGHTING FIXTURES

Artemide
Via Margutta 107.
Map 4 F1.
Tel 06-3600 1802.

Borghini
Via Belsiana 87–89.
Map 4 F2.
Tel 06-679 0629.

Flos
Via del Babuino 84.
Map 5 A2.
Tel 06-320 7631.

Obor
Piazza San Lorenzo
in Lucina 28.
Map 12 E1.
Tel 06-687 1496.

Paolo Marj
Piazza del Fico 21A.
Map 11 B3.
Tel 06-6880 7707.

KITCHENS AND BATHROOMS

Arclinea
Lungotevere
dei Cenci 4B.
Map 4 F5 & 12 D5.
Tel 06-686 5104.

Emporio Cucina
Piazza delle Cinque Lune
74. **Map** 11 C2.
Tel 06-6880 3685.

Materia
Corso Vittorio Emanuele II
189.
Map 11 C3.
Tel 06-686 1896.

Ravasini
Via di Ripetta 69–71.
Map 4 F2.
Tel 06-322 7096.

TILES

Ceramiche Musa
Via Campo Marzio 39.
Map 4 F3 & 12 D1.
Tel 06-687 1242.

GLASS

Archimede Seguso
Via dei Due Macelli 56.
Map 5 A2.
Tel 06-679 1781.

Arteque
Via Giulia 13. **Map** 4 D4 &
11 A3. **Tel** 06-687 7388.

Murano Più
Corso Rinascimento
43–45.
Map 4 E3.
Tel 06-6880 8038.

Stilvetro
Via Frattina 56. **Map** 5 A2.
Tel 06-679 0258.

FABRICS

Celsa
Via delle Botteghe Oscure
44. **Map** 12 E4.
Tel 06-6994 0872.

Paganini
Via Aracoeli 23.
Map 4 F5 & 12 E4.
Tel 06-678 6831.

Il Sigillo
Via Laurina 15.
Map 4 F1
Tel 06-361 3247.

HOUSEHOLD AND KITCHENWARE

C.u.c.i.n.a.
Via Mario de' Fiori 65.
Map 5 A2.
Tel 06-679 1275.

Frette
Piazza di Spagna 10.
Map 5 A2.
Tel 06-679 0673.

'Gusto
Piazza Augusto
Imperatore 7.
Map 4 F2.

House & Kitchen
Via del Plebiscito 103.
Map 12 E3.
Tel 06-679 4208.

Limentani
Via del Portico D'Ottavia 48.
Map 12 E5.
Tel 06-6880 6949.

Books and Gifts

Rome offers huge scope for gift buying, both in the well-established tourist stores in the *centro storico* (historic centre) and smaller shops in less frequented parts of the city. Seeking out the smaller shops can be an adventure in itself, as many are in attractive parts of the city that you might not otherwise visit.

Unusual artisan ceramics, wonderful books on Italian art and architecture, paper products, vintage Italian film posters, beautiful prints of historic views of Rome and specialist sweets and cakes make ideal souvenirs to take home. While masterpieces by Michelangelo, Raphael and Caravaggio are popular icons for T-shirts, statuettes and postcards, religious artifacts are also readily available in the city that hosts the papal seat.

BOOKSHOPS

Rome is rich in bookshops, from the encyclopedic to the very specialized. Italian books, both hardback and softback, are generally very attractive but also tend to be expensive.

As Italy's largest and most renowned bookshop chain, **Feltrinelli** dedicates its endless shelf space to both modern and classic Italian literature, and also houses a wide selection of non-fiction titles. **Feltrinelli International** in Via Emanuele Orlando has an excellent range of foreign-language fiction and specialist non-fiction, covering various subjects including art, cookery, travel and history. It also stocks some superb photographic, art and cinema posters. Magazines and stationery are available as well and the notice-board is a lifeline for information on rooms for rent and Italian language courses.

Specialist English bookstores include **The Lion Bookshop** and the **Anglo-American Book Co.**, both of which are located near Piazza di Spagna. In Trastevere, the **Almost Corner Bookshop**, though small, has probably the most extensive selection of English language fiction in the capital, as well as non-fiction titles – from ancient Rome to modern Italian culture and politics.

The **Libreria del Viaggiatore** is jam-packed with maps and travel guides (some in English). **Libreria Godel** is good for browsing and **Remainder** sells half-price

bargains and games for children. For prospective chefs, fantastic recipe books on Italian and international cuisine can be found at **Emporio Libreria 'Gusto** (*see p351*) in Piazza Augusto Imperatore.

As an alternative to traditional bookstores, there are lots of cut-price deals at the second-hand book stalls in Via delle Terme di Diocleziano and in Largo della Fontanella di Borghese.

MULTIMEDIA AND MUSIC

The newly-opened **Feltrinelli** in Galleria Alberto Sordi on Via del Corso and its sister store in Largo Argentina, represent the closest Rome gets to a multimedia megastore. At both these stores, in addition to their stock of fiction and non-fiction titles, there is a reasonable selection of CDs and DVDs that cover mainstream tastes.

For harder-to-find albums visit **Ricordi**, which is considered Rome's biggest specialist music store. Besides the fine collection of records, cassettes and CDs, it sells musical instruments and musical scores in its four central outlets.

STATIONERY AND PAPER CRAFTS

Near the Pantheon, the Florentine **Il Papiro** sells a great range of illustrious paper-based products that include notebooks, diaries, envelopes and beautiful seal and wax sets that make for

an ideal gift. In a similar vein, a wide selection of pretty marbled notebooks, writing papers, and files and boxes in various sizes are also on offer at **Laboratorio Scatole**. **Pineider**, stationery suppliers to the Roman gentry, will print sets of exquisite visiting cards for you. The more modern **Vertecchi** is filled with original paper gifts, including boxes of every shape and size, while **Fabriano** has its own fabulous line of stationery and notebooks.

POSTERS AND PRINTS

Near Piazza Navona, **L'Image** has an extensive range of artistic, photographic and film posters on sale, as well as a decent range of stationery, souvenirs and calendars. Geared more towards antiques, **Galleria Trincia** sells good quality and reasonably priced prints of 17th-century panoramic paintings of Rome, as well as watercolours. It also undertakes restoration work.

For superb posters on past exhibitions as well as stylish souvenirs and postcards, visit Rome's museum shops, for example, **Il Chiostro del Bramante** near Piazza Navona, or **Complesso del Vittoriano** next to the Forum.

ARTISAN HANDICRAFTS AND DESIGN

The central Via del Pellegrino is a street crammed with small specialist outlets such as **Le Tre Ghinee**, which sells ceramics and glass objects. **La Chiave** is a good choice for gifts, selling all things ethnic with the emphasis on bright furnishings and original jewellery.

If you are more interested in contemporary design, visit the **Palazzo delle Esposizioni** (*see p164*) where a wide range of objects by famous designers is available. For a really original gift, try **Bottega del Marmoraro**, a workshop that reproduces ancient Roman and Pompeian inscriptions on marble. The owner will recreate any design you choose to order.

SOUVENIRS AND RELIGIOUS ARTIFACTS

Most of the tobacconists in central Rome sell postcards, stamps and a variety of souvenirs. Cheap and sometimes appealingly kitsch souvenirs are also found at the mobile stalls around the major tourist attractions.

Bookshops near the main basilicas, such as **Libreria Belardetti**, sell souvenirs and religious mementos. Other shops specialize in religious articles for both the clergy and the layperson. Facing the Vatican gates in Via di Porta Angelica there are several shops, such as **Al Pellegrino Cattolico**, selling artifacts to visiting pilgrims.

SWEETS AND BISCUITS

In addition to the several bars and cafés that sell cakes and biscuits to take away *(da portare via)*, there are a number of specialist stores in Rome well worth taking the time to visit.

Near Piazza Navona in the centre, **La Deliziosa** *(see p331)*, though small, offers a great range of classic Italian desserts and cakes; the ricotta-based variety deserves a special mention. Further afield, at the top of Via Gregorio XII that runs alongside the Vatican City walls, **Siciliana Svizzera** is renowned in Rome as the best place for sugary Sicilian delicacies, such as *cannoli* and *cassate*.

For a wonderful range of fresh and appetizing Italian biscuits to suit all occasions and every whim, head for **Cipriani** *(see p330)* in Esquilino near Termini station or **Innocenti** *(see p331)*, a historic *pasticceria* famed for its elaborate biscuits made with varied ingredients including almonds, pine kernels and honey. Innocenti is situated across the Tiber from the *centro storico* in Trastevere.

DIRECTORY

BOOKSHOPS

Almost Corner Bookshop
Via del Moro 45. **Map** 7 C1. **Tel** 06-583 6942.

Anglo-American Book Co.
Via della Vite 102. **Map** 12 E1. **Tel** 06-679 5222.

Emporio Libreria 'Gusto
Piazza Augusto Imperatore 7. **Map** 4 F2.
Tel 06-323 6363.

Feltrinelli
Largo Argentina 5A. **Map** 4 F4. **Tel** 06-6880 3248.
Also: Galleria Alberto Sordi 31–35. **Map** 12 E2.
Tel 06-6975 5001.

Feltrinelli International
Via E. Orlando 84–86. **Map** 5 C3. **Tel** 06-482 7878.

Libreria del Viaggiatore
Via del Pellegrino 78.
Map 11 B3.
Tel 06-6880 1048.

Libreria Godel
Via Poli 46. **Map** 12 F2.
Tel 06-679 8716.

The Lion Bookshop
Via dei Greci 33–36.
Map 4 F2.
Tel 06-3265 4007.

Remainder
Piazza San Silvestro 28.
Map 12 E1.
Tel 06-679 2824.

MULTIMEDIA AND MUSIC

Feltrinelli
See bookshops.

Ricordi
Via del Corso 506.
Map 12 E1.
Tel 06-361 2370.

STATIONERY AND PAPER CRAFTS

Fabriano
Via del Babuino 173.
Map 4 F2.
Tel 06-3260 0361.

Laboratorio Scatole
Via della Stelletta 27.
Map 12 D2.
Tel 06-6880 2053.

Il Papiro
Via del Pantheon 50
(leading to Via Degli Orfani). **Map** 12 D2.
Tel 06-679 5597.

Pineider
Via dei Due Macelli 68.
Map 12 F1.
Tel 06-679 5884.

Vertecchi
Via della Croce 70.
Map 4 F2.
Tel 06-332 2821.

POSTERS AND PRINTS

Il Chiostro del Bramante
Via della Pace 5. **Map** 11 C2. **Tel** 06-880 9098.

Complesso del Vittoriano
Via San Pietro In Carcere.
Map 5 A5.
Tel 06-678 0664.

Galleria Trincia
Via Laurina 12. **Map** 4 F1.
Tel 06-361 2322.

L'Image
Via della Scrofa 67.
Map 12 D2.
Tel 06-686 4050.

ARTISAN HANDICRAFTS AND DESIGN

Bottega del Marmoraro
Via Margutta 53B.
Map 5 A2.
Tel 06-320 7660.

La Chiave
Largo delle Stimmate 28.
Map 12 D4.
Tel 06-6830 8848.

Le Tre Ghinee
Via del Pellegrino 90.
Map 11 B3.
Tel 06-687 2739.

Palazzo delle Esposizioni
Via Milano 15–17.
Map 5 B4.
Tel 06-4891 3361.

SOUVENIRS AND RELIGIOUS ARTIFACTS

Al Pellegrino Cattolico
Via di Porta Angelica 83.
Map 3 C1.
Tel 06-6880 2351.

Libreria Belardetti
Via della Conciliazione 4A.
Map 3 C3.
Tel 06-686 5502.

SWEETS AND BISCUITS

Cipriani
Via C. Botta 21.
Map 6 D5.
Tel 06-7045 3930.

La Deliziosa
Vicolo Savelli 50.
Map 11 B3.
Tel 06-6880 3155.

Innocenti
Via della Luce 21A.
Map 7 C2.
Tel 06-580 3926.

Siciliana Svizzera
Piazza Pio XI 10 *(at the end of Via Gregorio VII)*.
Tel 06-637 4974.

Art and Antiques

Rome's art and antique shops range from exclusive establishments to contemporary art galleries. In response to a fashion for collecting early 20th-century artifacts, new dealers and galleries are springing up throughout Rome – Venini's Murano glass is popular, as are lighting and furniture. Many more sell general bric-à-brac and jewellery. Copies of antique prints can be picked up for a fraction of the original's price. Rome is not good for antique bargains, but it is worth looking in shops along Via dei Cappellari and Via del Pellegrino or going to the Porta Portese Sunday market *(see p353)*.

ANTIQUES AND OLD MASTER PAINTINGS

There are antique shops dotted all over the centre of Rome, though the cream tend to be concentrated in distinct areas. Discreet haggling in the shops is accepted practice, but even if you get a reduction in price, make sure the dealer provides you with the relevant export documents.

The famous Via del Babuino, and to a lesser extent Via Margutta, which is better known for its art galleries, are home to around 30 of Rome's grandest showrooms for antique furniture, Old Master paintings and *objets d'art*.

Cesare Lampronti is owned by the top dealer of that name. Aided and complemented by his partner Carlo Peruzzi, he sells 16th- to 18th-century European paintings, with an emphasis on Roman and Italian works in general.

Alberto di Castro, situated in Piazza di Spagna, is a fourth-generation dealer specialising in statues, paintings and other precious objects from the medieval to the Neo-Classical periods.

Via Giulia *(see p153)* has over 20 high-quality antique shops to choose from. Definitely worth a visit is **Antichità Cipriani**, which is a temple to owner Paola Cipriani's love of simply elegant Neo-Classical furniture and paintings. She also sells the occasional modern piece. Another shop not to miss on Via Giulia is **Antiquariato Valligiano**. This is the only place in Rome

where you can find 19th-century Italian country furniture, a rustic antidote for those overpowered by the grandiose Baroque.

Via Monserrato, running parallel, is worth scouring for slightly lower-quality pieces at more attainable prices. The area just to the north of Via Giulia is also a good hunting ground. **Mario Prilli**, on Via Banchi Nuovi, is tiny, but don't let that deter you. With every inch of space occupied by a wide variety of antiques, this fascinating shop is worth a look even if you are only browsing.

Via dei Coronari is almost exclusively devoted to antiques, with over 40 shops lining both sides of the street. Quality is very high – as are the prices. It is a good place for Baroque and Empire elaborate inlaid vases, secretaries and consoles. **Ad Antiqua Domus** is a treasure trove of antique Italian furniture. Pieces dating from ancient Rome through to the 19th century are on sale.

L'Art Nouveau specializes in high-quality Art Nouveau (usually called *Liberty* here). The **Art Deco Gallery** sells furniture and sculpture from that period.

Piero Taloni has a superb collection of lighting fixtures from the Baroque through to Art Deco periods. **Antichità Arredamenti** also specializes in Italian light fittings and candlesticks.

Slightly further away is Via della Stelletta, which is home to a handful of unusual and fascinating shops. **Acanto** is an inexpensively priced

Aladdin's cave with an eclectic mix of *objets d'art*. It is the perfect place to search for religious memorabilia, Italian curiosities and prints.

Bilenchi is yet another specialist, this time in exquisite, early 20th-century lamps.

Another relatively undiscovered area is the one around Via del Boschetto and Via Panisperna. Shops around here tend to specialize in early 20th-century artifacts, with some English Victorian pieces thrown in.

Tad is a fairly good place to come and browse, with a large collection of weird and original design items from all around the world.

Of course there are many perennial favourites apart from these streets. The best way to discover them is through word of mouth or just by chance as you stroll along. **Antichità Carnovale** is a shop full of interesting 19th- and 20th-century canvases, while **Galleria dei Cosmati** is one of the oldest antique shops in Rome, and definitely one of the largest. It offers an impressive collection of European antiques.

Anticaja e Petrella has an eccentric collection of used junk and printed ephemera stored under Sant'Andrea della Valle *(see p123)*.

MODERN ART

Rome is rich in avant-garde galleries exhibiting paintings by recognized Modern Masters through to the up-and-coming generation of young, mainly Italian, artists.

Rome's art galleries are usually open 10am–1pm and 5–8pm Tue–Sat. Some open only in the afternoon; others also stay open on Monday afternoon. The best times to visit are afternoons and early evenings.

As with Rome's antique shops, the art galleries tend to be concentrated in a couple of distinct areas. The largest of these covers the triangular area between Via del Babuino and Via di Ripetta and adjoining streets, known locally as the Trident. Via Margutta is also home to several prestigious private galleries.

The **Galleria Valentina Moncada** exhibits contemporary Italian and international art and also showcases 20th-century photography, while **Monogramma Arte Contemporanea** deals with promising young artists from Italy and abroad.

One of this area's highlights is the Via Margutta art fair (see p353), which usually takes place around Christmas and in springtime.

The enterprising **Fontanella Borghese** gallery shows works by foreign artists such as Sam Francis and Andy Warhol. Also on view at the gallery are Italian artists like Boetti, Festa and Turcato.

Via Giulia and its surroundings is the next area to investigate: **Galleria Giulia** is a gallery-cum bookshop with works by artists such as Argeles, Boille, Cano, Cascella, Echaurren, Erba and Lionni, as well as by Bauhaus artists

and German Expressionists. Fabio Sargentini at **L'Attico** follows the latest trends in Italian art from Del Giudice to Corsini and Fabiani.

Another innovative venture in the centre is **Galleria Bonomo** (owned by Alessandra Bonomo), which spotlights Italian and foreign painters such as Schifano, Boetti, Twombly, Nunzio, Tremlett, LeWitt and Dokoupil.

On the other side of the Tiber, the **Galleria Lorcan O'Neill** showcases contemporary Italian and international art. In 2010 the gallery hosted its third exhibition of Tracey Emin's work.

ANTIQUE PRINTS AND PHOTOGRAPHS

The justifiably celebrated **Nardecchia**, named after its erudite owner Plinio, is the cream of Rome's print dealers. Look out for originals by the 18th-century engraver Piranesi, as well as views of the city

and depictions of ancient Roman life.

Another Roman institution, **Casali**, has been trading for over 100 years. The family now runs two shops specializing in 16th- to 19th-century drawings and engravings of Roman scenes ranging from museum-standard Piranesi down to relatively inexpensive unknown and delightfully decorative floral scenes.

The Florence-based **Alinari** family is renowned for its old sepia photographs of Italy from 1890 onwards, including shots of Rome a century ago. At its Roman outlet, prices of photographs from the original plates start at around €30 and mounted prints at €280. Larger sizes can be mounted on wood or card.

Another place definitely worth heading for in search of that perfect print of old Rome and some enjoyable, relaxing and maybe persuasive browsing is the **Mercato delle Stampe** (see p352).

DIRECTORY

ANTIQUES AND OLD MASTER PAINTINGS

Acanto
Via della Stelletta 10.
Map 4 F3 & 12 D2.
Tel 06-686 5481.

Ad Antiqua Domus
Via dei Coronari 39–43.
Map 4 E3 & 11 B2.
Tel 06-686 1100.

Alberto di Castro
Piazza di Spagna 5.
Map 5 A2.
Tel 06-679 2269.

Anticaja e Petrella
Via Monte della Farina 62.
Map 4 F5 & 12 D4.

Antichità Arredamenti
Via dei Coronari 218. **Map** 4 E3. *Tel 06-6880 1254.*

Antichità Carnovale
Via del Governo Vecchio 71.
Map 11 C3.
Tel 06-686 4850.

Antichità Cipriani
Via Giulia 122. **Map** 4 D4 & 11 A3. *Tel 06-6830 8344.*

Antiquariato Valligiano
Via Giulia 193. **Map** 4 E5 & 11 B5. *Tel 06-686 9505.*

Art Deco Gallery
Via dei Coronari 14.
Map 4 E3 & 11 C2.
Tel 06-686 5330.

L'Art Nouveau
Via dei Coronari 221.
Map 4 E3 & 11 C2.
Tel 06-6880 5230.

Bilenchi
Via della Stelletta 17.
Map 4 F3 & 12 D2.
Tel 06-687 5222.

Cesare Lampronti
Via del Babuino 174–75.
Map 4 F1. *Tel 06-322 7194.*

Galleria dei Cosmati
Piazza Borghese 1. **Map** 12 D1. *Tel 06-687 3632.*

Mario Prilli
Via dei Banchi Nuovi 42.

Map 4 D3 & 11 A2.
Tel 06-686 8816.

Piero Taloni
Via dei Coronari 135.
Map 4 E3 & 11 B2.
Tel 06-687 5450.

Tad
Piazza Adriana 10A. **Map** 4 D2. *Tel 06-683 3303.*
Also: Via del Babuino 155A. **Map** 4 F1.
Tel 06-3269 5125.

MODERN ART

L'Attico
Via del Paradiso 41.
Map 4 E4 & 11 C4.
Tel 06-686 9846.

Fontanella Borghese
Via Fontanella Borghese 31.
Map 12 D1. *Tel 06-687 3741.*

Galleria Bonomo
Via del Gesù 62. **Map** 12 E3. *Tel 06-6992 5858.*

Galleria Giulia
Via della Barchetta 13.
Map 4 D4 & 11 B4.
Tel 06-686 1443.

Galleria Lorcan O'Neill
Via Orti D'Alibert 1E. **Map** 4 D4. *Tel 06-6889 2980.*

Galleria Valentina Moncada
Via Margutta 54. **Map** 5 A2. *Tel 06-320 7956.*

Monogramma Arte Contemporanea
Via Margutta 57. **Map** 5 A2. *Tel 06-3265 0297.*

ANTIQUE PRINTS AND PHOTOGRAPHS

Alinari
Via Alibert 16A. **Map** 5 A2.
Tel 06-679 2923.

Casali
Piazza della Rotonda 81A/82. **Map** 4 F4 & 12 D3. *Tel 06-678 3515.*
Also: Via dei Coronari 115.
Map 11 B2.
Tel 06-687 3705.

Nardecchia
Piazza Navona 25.
Map 4 E4 & 11 C3.
Tel 06-686 9318.

Food and Drink

Having sampled the local cuisine during your stay in Rome, you may be tempted to take home some irresistible delicacies that are typical of Italy. The traditional Italian food stores, *alimentari*, offer an extensive range of goods and are a great place to start. However, specialist shops are also well worth a visit. Shop around and choose from many typically Italian products such as pecorino romano cheese, Parma ham, extra-virgin olive oil, dried porcini mushrooms, sun-dried tomatoes, olives and grappa as well as superb wines from Lazio and elsewhere. If coffee or chocolate feature on your list, then there's plenty of opportunity to satisfy those cravings too.

Do bear in mind, however, that customs restrictions can apply to certain foodstuffs. Also, when on your shopping sprees, a decent pocket-sized dictionary can be very useful in helping you unravel the unfathomable.

ALIMENTARI

The well-stocked **Fratelli Fabbi**, near Piazza di Spagna, has an exceptional selection of delicious cold meats and cheeses from every corner of Italy, as well as carefully chosen quality wines and sparkling wines to accompany them. A few doors down Via della Croce, **Focacci** is a stiff competitor with its wonderful array of Italian delicacies, while nearby **Cambi** caters to its loyal clientele with similarly first-rate fare.

Elsewhere in the centre, near Campo de' Fiori, the renovated **Roscioli** *(see p328)*, with a reputation for quality and friendly service, is a favourite among locals.

Further afield, **Franchi** *(see p329)* in Prati is recognized as one of the best delicatessens in the capital for its tempting window display of seafood platters, pâtés, regional cheeses and cold meats that continue to pull in the crowds. The historic but expensive **Volpetti** in Testaccio is synonymous with great service and uncompromising quality. Aside from specializing in unusual cheeses, olive oils, vinegars and a fabulous selection of food hampers it also stocks a variety of Italian lard and caviar – you can even try before you buy. Nearby is the well-stocked **La Fromagerie**, though those who favour organic produce may prefer to head for **Canestro**.

The **Ferrara Store** in Trastevere sells almost everything from fresh pasta to chocolate, in addition to an amazing range of hams and cheeses, and great wines to complement them. In the vicinity of Via Veneto is **Carlo Gargani**, with its elaborate variety of food items.

A saviour for commuters and tourists is **Vyta** *(see p329)* located inside Termini station; you can choose from a selection of appetizing sandwiches or wines by the glass *(alla mescita)* and enjoy them at the bar. You can even make a last-minute gift purchase from the wide array of preserves, pasta and wines at your disposal. Vyta opens its doors on Sundays too.

CHEESE SPECIALISTS

For the ultimate cheese lover, a wider choice of regional and national cheeses, including the best buffalo mozzarella in town, can be found in a select number of specialist shops. In the Pinciano district, the **Casa dei Latticini Micocci** sells a comprehensive range of cheeses from even the most remote regions of Italy. While in Trastevere, the family-run store **Antica Caciara Trasteverina** also has a vast assortment of local and regional products, which include sheep's ricotta and the Piemontese *toma del fen*. Branches of **Cisternino** sell well-priced local cheeses.

CHOCOLATE SPECIALISTS

The capital now hosts a number of specialist shops designed to fulfil the needs of the ever-expanding luxury food market. In the *centro storico*, **Chocolat** sells brand name and home-made chocolate and also organizes occasional tastings and dinners for connoisseurs. In Santa Croce, **La Bottega del Cioccolato** is known for its creativity – try their chocolate Colosseums. Elsewhere, close to the Pantheon, the landmark **Moriondo e Gariglio** has been in operation since 1850, serving up strictly Piedmontese treats. Across the Tiber in Trastevere, **Dolce Idea** produces bizarre but interesting concoctions such as white chocolate with lemon liqueur filling and dark chocolate laced with ginger. **Rivendita di Cioccolato e Vino** *(see p330)* can also be recommended for its selection.

ENOTECHE

Although most *alimentari* and supermarkets stock a decent selection of reasonably priced Italian wines, Rome's many *enoteche (see p328)* represent a more characteristic and gratifying alternative. As well as being wine bars and sometimes even restaurants, they also sell carefully selected wines, after-dinner liqueurs, spirits and beers to take away.

In the centre, the cramped but friendly **Mr Wine** displays a superb range of mainly Italian and a few French wines, as well as a host of sparkling wines, whiskies, grappa, rum, liqueurs and some classic Italian food. **La Vineria** *(see p328)* in Campo de' Fiori, while maintaining its status as an institution for many bohemian drinkers, also successfully doubles up as a well-stocked and competitively priced wine shop.

Better known for its Neapolitan pizza parlour, chic restaurant and lively wine bar, **'Gusto** (see p328) in Piazza Augusto Imperatore offers an outstanding assortment of wines for sale too. Don't pass by the shop either, as it is full of designer kitchen accessories and specialist cookbooks with recipes for both Italian and international cuisine.

The central **Achilli Enoteca al Parlamento** (see p328) and **L'Angolo Divino** both warrant a visit for a refined alternative, especially if you want to relax with an apéritif while you select wines to carry home. **Ferrazza** (see p362) in San Lorenzo and **Il Vinaietto**

near Campo de' Fiori also deserve special mentions for their extensive wine lists and memorable ambience.

In Trastevere, the well-stocked off-licence **Bernabei** is good value for money as is the family-run **Trimani** (see p328) near Termini, which has an astounding variety of wines and spirits.

Others that should not be overlooked include the impressive **Costantini** in Piazza Cavour, the beer-oriented **Palombi** in Testaccio and **Marchetti** in Pinciano, which is the wine experts' not so closely guarded secret.

COFFEE SPECIALISTS

Italian brand coffee has been internationally available for many years but if you are looking for something rarer or more exotic then make your way to **Antico Caffè del Brasile** (see p330) in Monti for four mouth-watering blends, from Brazilian gem (the 90 per cent pure variety) to economy and family mixes. In the shadow of the Pantheon, the historic **Tazza d'Oro** (see p104) also offers a fantastic selection of blends, including the Queen of Coffees and Jamaican Blue Mountain.

DIRECTORY

Street Markets

Rome's open-air markets are essential to visit if you are interested in soaking up the bubbling exuberance and earthiness for which Romans are renowned. They are wonderfully vivid experiences too, as Italian stallholders have raised the display of even the humblest vegetable to an art form.

The city is dotted with popular, small local food markets, and there are several fascinating well-established markets near the centre, along with the famous flea market over in Trastevere.

It is important to keep your wits about you in markets because pickpockets work with lightning speed in the bustling crowds. But this said, Roman markets provide a vibrant source of entertainment and it would be a shame to let such caveats deter you from joining in.

The street fairs that take place throughout the year are fun to go to, if they coincide with your visit, as they normally sell a good variety of local produce, handicrafts and clothes. Seasonal fairs also occur, especially around Christmas, when you can stock up on Italian specialities.

Campo de' Fiori

Piazza Campo de' Fiori. **Map** 4 E4 & 11 C4. 40, 46, 62, 64, 70, 81, 116, 492, 628. 8. **Open** 7am–1.30pm Mon–Sat. See p146.

Right in the heart of the old city, Rome's most picturesque market is also its most historical. Its name, Campo de' Fiori, which translates as field of flowers, sometimes misleads people into expecting a flower market. In fact the name is said to derive from Campus Florae (Flora's square) – Flora being the lover of the great Roman general Pompey. A market has actually been held in this beautiful piazza for many centuries. Every morning, except Sunday, the piazza is transformed by an array of stalls selling fruit and vegetables, meat, poultry and fish. One or two stalls specialize in pulses, rice, dried fruit and nuts and there are also flower stalls situated near the fountain. But the huge open baskets of broccoli and spinach, chopped vegetables and freshly prepared green salad mixes are the main attraction for visitors. They provide a real visual display as well as an edible feast.

The excellent delicatessen shops on the square, and bread shops nearby, complement the market. They make it a great place to stock up for an impromptu picnic if the weather turns out fine and you are tempted to do some alfresco dining in one of Rome's many parks. The market gets extremely busy on Saturdays, so be prepared to fight your way through the crowds.

Mercato delle Stampe

Largo della Fontanella di Borghese. **Map** 4 F3 & 12 D1. 81, 116, 117, 492, 628. **Open** 7am–1pm Mon–Sat.

This market is a veritable haven for lovers of old prints, books (both genuine antiquarian and less-exalted second-hand), magazines and other printed ephemera. The quality varies, but it is a good deal more specialized than the banche or stalls near Termini station which are a more obvious tourist trap. Italian-speaking collectors can enjoy a field day leafing through back issues of specialist magazines. Other visitors might prefer the wonderful selection of illustrated art books and old prints of Rome. It is a good place to pick up that Piranesi print of your favourite Roman vista, ruin or church – but be prepared to bargain hard.

Mercato dei Fiori

Via Trionfale. **Map** 3 B1. Ottaviano S. Pietro. 23, 51, 70, 490. **Open** 10.30am–1pm Tue.

Essentially a trade market, the Flower Market, just north of Via Andrea Doria, is open to the public only on Tuesdays. Housed in a covered hall, it has two floors brimming over with cut flowers upstairs and all kinds of pot plants on the lower floor. Anyone who has an interest in flowers will enjoy this wonderful array of Mediterranean blooms, which are on sale at giveaway prices.

Mercato Andrea Doria

Via Andrea Doria. **Map** 3 B1. Ottaviano S. Pietro. 23, 70, 490. **Open** 7am–1.30pm Mon–Sat.

The market used to stretch the whole length of this wide avenue. It has now been transferred to a modern, covered state-of-the-art building. Apart from the magnificent displays of fruit and vegetables, it has numerous stalls selling meat, poultry, fish and groceries, as well as an interesting clothes and shoe section. Situated northwest of the Vatican Museums, it is a little off the normal beaten track and has remained very much a Roman market that caters for the needs of the large local population.

Nuovo Mercato Esquilino

Via Principe Amedeo. **Map** 6 E5. Vittorio Emanuele. 105. **Open** 7am–2pm Mon–Sat. See p174.

Bustling Piazza Vittorio was, until recently, perhaps the most Roman of the city's larger markets.

Now rechristened, it has moved to new covered premises, but it is still the place where bargain-hunting popolari, Rome's bustling shoppers, buy their food. Stallholders offer cheap prices if you buy by the kilo, but watch out for bad fruit.

Lately it has become more international and now features African and Asian food stalls which cater to the area's many ethnic groups. Definitely a place to go to to capture the atmosphere of a traditional but changing city.

Mercato di Testaccio

Piazza Testaccio. **Map** 8 D3. Piramide. 23, 75, 280. 3. **Open** 7.30am–1.30pm Mon–Sat.

The covered market at Testaccio occupies the central area of its eponymous piazza. The few cheap clothing and shoe stalls skirting the outside are unremarkable, but the inside is well worth a visit. Lined with butchers, grocers and fishmongers, the whole central area is given over to fruit and vegetables – a theatre-set array of seductive colours and textures. Very popular with local residents, it offers super-fresh, high-quality produce and reasonable prices. Much of this market's charm for visitors lies in its compact size and relaxed, friendly atmosphere.

Porta Portese

Via Portuense & Via Ippolito Nievo.
Map 7 C3. 🚌 H, 23, 44, 75. 🚋 3, 8. **Open** 6.30am–2pm Sun.

The *mercato delle pulci* or flea market is a relatively new market in Roman terms. Established shortly after the end of World War II, it is said to have grown out of the thriving black market that operated at Tor di Nona opposite Castel Sant'Angelo during those lean years. Stallholders come from as far away as Naples and set up shop in the early hours of the morning – if you are strolling in that direction after a late night in Trastevere, it is well worth pausing just to watch them.

Anything and everything seems to be for sale, piled high on stalls in carefully arranged disorder – clothes, shoes, bags, luggage, camping equipment, linen, towels, pots, pans, kitchen utensils, plants, pets, spare parts, cassettes and CDs, old LPs and 78s.

Furniture stalls tend to be concentrated around Piazza Ippolito Nievo along with what they call "antiques", though you may have to sort through an awful lot of junk before finding a real one. And then you will have to bargain for it. The technique is to offer them half the asked price and then walk away. A lot of people go just for the fun of it and always end up buying something.

There are also second-hand clothes – leather or sheepskin coats and jackets go for €10 – with many of the Via Sannio stall-holders relocating here for the Sunday trade. In recent years Porta Portese has become much frequented by customers belonging to the various immigrant groups in the capital. If you have a Sunday morning to spare, a visit to the market is now one of the most cosmopolitan experiences that the city offers.

Mercato di Via Sannio

Via Sannio. **Map** 9 C2. Ⓜ San Giovanni. 🚌 16, 81, 87. **Open** 8am–1pm Mon–Fri, 8am–6pm Sat.

In the 1960s and 1970s this used to be Italy's answer to Carnaby Street. Today, at first glance, it seems not to have anything very special to offer – random stalls selling inexpensive casual clothes, shoes, bags, belts, jewellery, toys, kitchen utensils and music cassettes. But towards the end of the street there is a large covered section which extends back to the Aurelian Wall *(see p196)* with many stalls piled high with second-hand clothes at very low prices for those who like to rummage.

There is also a section that sells military-style goods plus some camping and fishing equipment.

Some of these stalls move their wares to Porta Portese on a Sunday morning.

Local markets

Generally open 7am–1pm Mon–Sat.

Piazza delle Coppelle (map 4 F3 & 12 D2), near the Pantheon, is probably the most picturesque of the food markets sprinkled around the city. A tiny market devoted to food and fruit and flowers, it offers a charming splash of colour in the heart of the city.

Piazza San Cosimato (map 7 C1) in Trastevere hosts another lively local market with some tempting cheeses and salami.

There is a fairly big market on **Via Alessandria** (map 6 D1) in Nomentana, and other smaller ones in **Via della Pace** (map 4 E4 & 11 C3) near Piazza Navona, and in **Via Balbo** (map 5 C4) and **Via Milazzo** (map 6 E3) near Termini station.

All markets usually have at least one stall selling household goods and basic Italian kitchen gadgets.

STREET FAIRS

A special and interesting feature of shopping in Rome is the street fair:

The **Tevere Expo** exhibition starts each year between mid-June and mid-July on both sides of the river bank between the Sant'Angelo and Cavour bridges. Its stalls display Italian regional arts and crafts and also sell pasta, jam, olive oil, wines and liqueurs. Some items are cheaper than in the shops. The exhibition opens in the evening (6pm–1am). The entrance fee occasionally includes ferry transport across the Tiber.

There are two antiques fairs, both known as the **Fiera dell'Antiquariato**, that take place in Via dei Coronari. The first starts in the second half of May, 10am–1pm and 4–11pm daily. It makes a memorable event at night when lighted torches line the carpeted street. The second goes along Via dell'Orso as well and normally occurs in mid-October (but has also started in late September), Mon–Thu 3–11pm & Fri–Sun 10am–11pm. Stalls also sell leatherwork, jewellery and gifts.

The **Via Margutta Art Fair** usually takes place around Christmas and in springtime. Set in one of the most charming and exclusive streets of the city, this is an event not to be missed, although it is more for browsing as prices are very high.

The utterly glamorous **Spanish Steps Alta Moda Fashion Show** is a fairly new event and does not have a set date. The limited seating space is filled by invitation only. However, the public can squeeze in behind to enjoy this display of all-Italian designer fashion. So far it has been held mid- to late July.

The traditional **Christmas Fair** held in Piazza Navona from mid-December until 6 January is now rather down-at-heel, but still fascinating for those who have not seen it before or for children. Stalls selling clay statues for nativity scenes and sweets that look like pieces of coal are the main attraction.

Natale Oggi is a well-established event taking place near Christmas at the Fiera di Roma in the Portuense district, and worth visiting to have a look at the Italian Christmas treats.

Via Giulia hosts art fairs now and then, and open evenings when the antique and art galleries stay open late offering food and wine to all visitors.

Every year Trastevere hosts its very own carnival, the **Festa de Noantri**, in late July, when Viale Trastevere is overrun with the typical *porchetta* stalls *(see p355)*, party lights, gift stalls and people.

The details given here may change, so check the local listings, the tourist office or ring the tourist call centre *(see p377)*.

ENTERTAINMENT IN ROME

There's a particular excitement attached to Roman entertainment. Football and opera, for example, are both worth experiencing for sheer atmosphere alone, whether or not you are a fan. The jazz scene is especially good with international stars appearing alongside local talent. And concerts and films take on an added dimension when performances take place beneath the stars in the many open-air arenas spread

across the city. Unexpectedly, given the general shutdown among shops and restaurants, the summer remains Rome's liveliest time for live music and other cultural events. Rome's graceful Renaissance squares, vast parks, villa gardens, Classical ruins and other open spaces host various major arts festivals. If you prefer sport, or want to try out some Roman nightclubs, there's plenty on offer too.

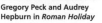

Gregory Peck and Audrey Hepburn in *Roman Holiday*

PRACTICAL INFORMATION

A good source of information about what's on is *Trova-Roma,* the weekly Thursday supplement to *La Repubblica* newspaper. It has a day-by-day rundown of what's on and where, and covers music, exhibitions, theatre, cinemas,

Saxophonist at Alpheus *(see p358)*

guided tours, restaurants and children's entertainment. The weekly listings magazine *Roma c'è* has an English section. Daily newspapers like *Il Messaggero, Il Manifesto* and *La Repubblica* usually list that evening's entertainment.

The magazine *Wanted in Rome,* found at Via Veneto newsagents or English bookshops, provides less detailed listings in English. Also worth getting hold of is *L'Evento,* a free booklet that is available from tourist information offices around the city *(see p377).* Published every two months, it gives details in English of classical music, festivals, theatre, exhibitions and more in the city and surroundings. Up-to-date

information can also be found on various websites.

Punctuality is not what Italians are renowned for, so don't be surprised if events start later than advertised.

BOOKING TICKETS

Booking in advance is not part of Italian lifestyle, though this is slowly changing. Two ticket agencies that will book tickets for some performances for you (for a small fee) are **Orbis** and the Internet-based **Ticketeria.** Many theatres themselves do not accept telephone bookings – you have to visit the box office in person. They will charge you a *prevendita* supplement (about 10 per cent of the normal price) for any tickets sold in advance. The price of a theatre ticket can be anything between €8 and €52.

Tickets for classical concerts are usually sold on the spot, and are sometimes for that night only, an arrangement that favours the last-minute

decision to go. Opera is the exception. Tickets are sold months in advance, with just a few held back until two days before the performance.

Stage at Caffè Latino *(see pp358–9)*

It is usually easier (and also a bit cheaper) to get tickets for the open-air summer performances.

The **Teatro dell'Opera** box office *(see p357)* handles sales for both summer and winter seasons, and they have a high-tech booking system, with a computer which colour-codes unsold seats.

Tickets for most big rock and jazz events can be bought at **Orbis** and at larger record shops such as **Ricordi**.

Remember that if you are trying to get hold of a ticket for a particular performance that has already sold out, you are extremely unlikely to be able to obtain one from

Member of contemporary dance group Momix *(see p357)*

unofficial sources – there are very few ticket touts in Rome, except at major football matches such as important finals.

REDUCED-PRICE TICKETS

Theatres and concert venues tend not to offer discounts directly, although there is a centralized service (**Sportello Last Minute**) offering up to 50 per cent off seats on the day of performance.

Cinemas occasionally offer people aged over 60 and disabled people a 30 per cent reduction on weekdays. Many cinemas also have cheaper ticket prices for weekday afternoon screenings and for all shows on Wednesdays.

Some clubs offer reductions: look out for *due per uno* coupons in local bars that allow two people entrance for the price of one.

FACILITIES FOR THE DISABLED

Few Roman venues provide easy access for people with restricted mobility, and any disabled visitors and their companions are likely to find the lack of provision for them very frustrating.

The situation does improve a little in summer, however,

Singers performing the Barber of Seville

when a great many performances in the city are held at open-air venues. The classical concerts held in the beautiful gardens of Villa Giulia *(see pp262–3)* have wheelchair access.

For more general information on provision for disabled people visiting Rome, see pages 376–7.

Summer night outdoor performance among Roman ruins

OPEN-AIR ENTERTAINMENT

Open-air opera, cinema, classical music and jazz concerts fill the calendar from late June until the end of September. These performances outdoors can be wonderful, with spectacular settings and enthusiastic audiences. Some of them are grand affairs, but small events may be just as evocative – a guitar recital in the cloisters of Santa Maria della Pace *(see p121)*, for example, or jazz in the beautiful gardens of Villa Celimontana *(see p193)*.

Some cinemas roll back their ceilings in summer for open-air screenings, or else move to outdoor arenas, and there are also annual open-air cinema festivals. The Cineporto along the Tiber and the Festival di Massenzio offer films, food and small exhibitions in July and August. Theatre, too, moves outside in summer. Greek and Roman plays are staged at Ostia Antica *(see p270)* and other shows take place at the Anfiteatro del Tasso *(see p361)*.

Rome's most important autumn performing arts festival is RomaEuropa, with occasional performances in the grounds of the Villa Medici. There are other, smaller festivals too, but times and venues change from year to year, so it is best to consult

listings in newspapers, magazines or websites *(see p354)* or watch for posters around the city for the most up-to-date information. More traditional is Trastevere's community festival, Festa de Noantri *(see p59)*, with music, fireworks and processions. This religious festival begins on the Saturday after 16 July but celebrations continue into August. The Festa dell' Unità, run by the DS (the former Communist Party), but not limited to politics, is generally held in summer. The programme includes games, stalls, food and drink.

Finally, if you like your entertainment less structured, do as the Romans do and take part in the *passeggiata* (early evening stroll) – the city's favourite spots are Piazza Navona *(see p120)* and along Via del Corso.

TICKET AGENCIES

Box Office (inside Feltrinelli)
Largo Argentina 5A.
Map 4 F4. *Tel* 06-6830 8596.
Classical music, rock, pop and jazz concerts and some sporting events.

Orbis
Piazza dell'Esquilino 37.
Map 6 D4. *Tel* 06-474 4776.

Sportello Last Minute
Largo Corrado Ricci 1. **Map** 5 B5.
Tel 06-4891 6614. *Open* 11am–8pm Tue–Sat, 11am–4pm Sun.

USEFUL WEBSITES

www.helloticket.it
www.listicket.it
www.romaturismo.it
www.ticketeria.it

The Teatro dell'Opera *(see p356)*

Classical Music and Dance

Classical concerts take place in a surprising number of venues: tickets for opera premieres may be hard to get, but soloists, groups or orchestras playing in gardens, churches, villas or ancient ruins are more accessible. World-renowned soloists and orchestras make appearances throughout the year; past visitors have included Luciano Pavarotti and Placido Domingo, the Berlin Philharmonic and prima ballerina Sylvie Guillem.

Programmes are generally international in scope but sometimes you will find a festival dedicated to one of Italy's own, like Palestrina, the great 16th-century master of polyphonic church music, or Arcangelo Corelli, inventor of the Baroque *concerto grosso*.

MUSIC IN CHURCHES

One of Rome's main attractions for classical music is the rich repertoire in the city's churches. Always sacred in theme (by decree of Pope John Paul II), music is mainly performed as concerts rather than during services.

Programmes are posted around the city and outside the churches. You will often find very good musicians playing in the main churches, while the smaller, out-of-the-way churches frequently have young musicians and amateur choirs as well.

St Peter's *(see p230)* hosts one major RAI (national broadcasting company) concert on 5 December attended by the Pope and free for the general public. It has two established choirs. The Coro della Cappella Giulia sing at the 10.30am mass and 5pm vespers on Sunday. The Coro della Cappella Sistina sing whenever the Pope celebrates mass here, as on 29 June (St Peter and St Paul's day).

Important choral masses also take place on 25 January in **San Paolo fuori le Mura** *(see p267)*, when the Pope attends, on 24 June in **San Giovanni in Laterano** *(p182)* and on 31 December at the **Gesù** *(pp114–5)* where the *Te Deum* is sung. The church of **Sant'Ignazio di Loyola** *(p106)* is another favourite venue for choral concerts.

Plainsong and Gregorian chant can be heard in **Sant' Anselmo** *(p204)* every Sunday (Oct–Jul) at the 8.30am mass and 7.15pm vespers.

Easter and the Christmas festivities are a great time for cheap and chilly concerts.

ORCHESTRAL, CHAMBER AND CHORAL MUSIC

Without doubt, the arts event of the decade was the opening of the Renzo Piano-designed **Parco della Musica** on the Via Flaminia in spring 2002. Up to then the **Auditorium Conciliazione** and the **Teatro dell'Opera** had been Rome's two main auditoriums, with their own resident orchestras and choirs. Both offer varied seasons that include visiting groups and soloists from all over the world. It remains to be seen how the Orchestra e Coro dell'Accademia di Santa Cecilia, formerly housed in Via della Conciliazione, fares in its new home.

The season at the **Teatro Olimpico** usually offers good chamber music, some orchestral concerts and ballet with at least one concert a week.

Although a variety of classical concerts take place at the **Accademia Filarmonica Romana**, the emphasis is on chamber and choral music, with an internationally renowned series of concerts running from mid-October to mid-May. Performances take place in the Sala Casella, which seats around 180.

Ticket prices for classical concerts depend a lot on performers and venue. The **Auditorium del Foro Italico** sells tickets for most concerts for under €15; a ticket for the **Teatro Olimpico** costs

between €15–€25, but seats for an important concert at **Teatro dell'Opera** may cost as much as €80.

The Associazione Musicale Romana, dedicated to Renaissance and Baroque music, organizes three annual festivals in the **Palazzo della Cancelleria** *(see p149)*: the Festival Internazionale di Cembalo (harpsichord festival) in March; Musica al Palazzo in May; and the Festival Internazionale di Organo in September. Classical music fans should also watch out for performances by the Orchestra di Roma e del Lazio at **Teatro Argentina** or **Teatro Valle** *(see p361)*.

It is always worth checking which musicians are due to be playing at the **Teatro Ghione**, the **Oratorio del Gonfalone** and especially the **Aula Magna dell'Università La Sapienza**, which has one of the most innovative programmes of classical and contemporary music.

OPEN-AIR SUMMER CONCERTS

In the summer music lovers can enjoy concerts in cloisters, palazzo courtyards and ancient ruins. Concerts can be one-offs or part of a festival programme, regular fixtures or impromptu. Do as the Romans do, wait until the last moment and keep an eye on the posters and listings pages *(see p354)*.

Open-air opera and dance once had their home in the Baths of Caracalla, but this venue is seldom used. Classical concerts are often part of festivals like Roma-Europa *(see p355)* but there are also open-air festivals and concert series dedicated to classical music. Among the more interesting is the Stagione Estiva dell'Orchestra dell'Accademia di Santa Cecilia held at the Ninfeo *(nympheum)* in the grounds of **Villa Giulia** *(see p263)*. Also listed as the Concerti a Villa Giulia, the concerts take place in July and tickets are around €12.

The Associazione Musicale Romana organizes Serenate in Chiostro – a lively and varied programme of concerts during July in the cloisters of **Santa Maria della Pace** *(see p121)* with tickets at reasonable prices. The Concerti del Tempietto are a real summer treat with concerts held almost every evening from July to September in the **Area Archeologica del Teatro di Marcello** *(see p151)* or in the park of the Villa Torlonia.

Festival Villa Pamphilj in Musica, in July, is a series of concerts in the gardens of **Villa Doria Pamphilj** *(see p267).* Programmes range from comic opera to jazz and 20th-century classical music.

Brass bands can be heard in the **Pincio Gardens** *(see p136)* on Sunday mornings from the end of April until mid-July – they usually strike up at around 10.30am.

CONTEMPORARY MUSIC

The Parco della Musica and the Accademia Filarmonica Romana (usually at the **Teatro Olimpico**) often include contemporary pieces in their programmes but these are less popular than the classical pieces and there is no set venue with a regular contemporary programme.

International names appear on festival programmes and at one-off concerts at the **Aula Magna dell'Università La Sapienza**. The most interesting contemporary music festival is organized by the Nuova Consonanza in the autumn. Modern Italian composers are performed in the Rassegna Nuova Musica Italiana concert series two or three times a year. Also worth keeping an eye out for are performances by scholars of the French Academy at **Villa Medici** *(see p135).*

OPERA

Italy and opera are to many people synonymous. Critics will tell you (justifiably) that Rome's opera is not up to the standard of Milan's La Scala or Naples's San Carlo. But that doesn't mean it is not worth visiting – world-class singers do appear here *(see p40),* mainly in premières or solo recitals. However you judge the quality of the performances, the surroundings in which they take place are often incomparable. In summer the visual spectacle of *Aida,* say, performed in the open air, is simply magnificent.

The season starts late at **Teatro dell'Opera**, between November and January. In recent years programmes have concentrated on the great popular operas, rather than staging experimental productions. Tickets range from €17 to €130.

The Teatro dell'Opera moves outdoors in July and August to stage opera and ballet in the ancient Baths of Caracalla *(see p197).* Popular works by Verdi and Puccini are performed, and although the acoustics are not perfect, the unique setting makes up for it.

BALLET AND DANCE

Opportunities to watch ballet or contemporary dance can be limited in Rome. The opera house's resident company Corpo di Ballo del Teatro dell'Opera di Roma performs the great classics as well as Roland Petit-style modern choreographies. Performances are staged at **Teatro dell'Opera**.

Contemporary dance is best seen during the Equilibrio Festival in February or at summer festivals, but foreign companies also perform at **Teatro Olimpico**. American modern dance groups of the Moses Pendleton school – Pilobolus, Momix, ISO and Daniel Ezralow – are popular visitors. **Teatro del Vascello** is another venue noted for its experimental dance performances.

In late summer and autumn, entertaining performances are organized during the **RomaEuropa Festival**.

DIRECTORY

For information about festivals and open-air concerts, see Trovaroma or similar listings (see pp354 & 375).

ORCHESTRAL, CHAMBER AND CHORAL MUSIC

Accademia Filarmonica Romana
Via Flaminia 118. **Map 1** A1. **Tel** 06-320 1752.
www.filarmonicaromana. org

Auditorium Conciliazione
Via della Conciliazione 4. **Map 3** C3. **Tel** 800-904 560. **www**.auditorium conciliazione.it

Aula Magna dell'Università La Sapienza
Piazzale Aldo Moro 5. **Tel** 06-361 0051.
www.concertiiuc.it

Oratorio del Gonfalone
Via del Gonfalone 32A. **Map** 4 D4 & 11 A3. **Tel** 06-687 5952.

Parco della Musica
Viale de Coubertin 30. **Map** 1 C2. **Tel** 06-8024 1281 *(for information);* **Tel** 892 982 *(for credit card sales).* **www**.auditorium.com

Sant'Anselmo
Piazza Cavalieri di Malta 5. **Map** 8 D2. **Tel** 06-579 11.

Teatro Ghione
Via delle Fornaci 37. **Map** 3 B4. **Tel** 06-637 2294. **www**.teatroghione.it

Teatro Olimpico
Piazza Gentile da Fabriano 17. **Tel** 06-326 5991. **www**.teatroolimpico.it

OPERA

Teatro dell'Opera
Piazza Beniamino Gigli 1. **Map** 5 C3. **Tel** 06-4816 0255. **www**.operaroma.it

BALLET & DANCE

RomaEuropa Festival
Via dei Magazzini Generali 20A. **Tel** 06-4555 3000. **http**://romaeuropa.net

Teatro Olimpico
Piazza Gentile da Fabriano 17. **Tel** 06-326 5991.

Teatro dell'Opera
Piazza Beniamino Gigli 1. **Map** 5 C3. **Tel** 06-4816 0255.

Teatro Vascello
Via G Carini 78. **Map** 7 A2. **Tel** 06-588 1021. **www**.teatrovascello.it

Rock, Jazz, Folk and World Music

Rome's non-classical music scene is unpredictable and subject to vast seasonal changes, but there is a huge variety of music at the many clubs and stadiums, with visiting foreign and home-grown stars. Recent years have seen the emergence of many new Italian bands who are well worth seeing. Summer months bring excellent open-air rock, jazz and world music festivals.

The music sections of *Trova-Roma* and *Roma c'è (see p354)* give a good idea of what's on, and ticket agencies at Orbis and Feltrinelli will have details of the latest tours. For smaller venues you might need to buy a *tessera* (monthly or annual membership card) costing anything from €2 to €11, which often includes the entrance fee for smaller bands.

ROCK MUSIC

Big-name rock concerts are held in sports venues at the **Palalottomatica** and the legendary **Stadio Olimpico**. The **Palladium** and Testaccio's **Villaggio Globale** at the Ex-Mattatoio (a converted abattoir) are other large-scale venues for concerts and other events, while the new **Parco della Musica** also hosts top acts. Entrance can cost above €25, but there are plenty of opportunities for smaller pockets. If you're in Rome for 1 May, join the crowds at the massive open-air concert which is usually held at Piazza San Giovanni. Bands also play for free during the European Festival of Music celebrations on and around 21 June. For all mega-concerts it is always a good idea to turn up an hour or so before the act gets under way to be sure of a good place.

Not far from the Vatican, **Fonclea** and **The Place** are also worth checking out.

One of the city's most interesting venues is **Forte Prenestino**, a former prison taken over by squatters a few years ago and turned into a social centre with a characteristically alternative feel. It now hosts rock concerts, debates and art exhibitions. Nearer the centre of town is the enterprising **Akab-Cave** which usually has a season full of interesting rock and ethnic fixtures. Meanwhile,

Locanda Atlantide, with its low entrance fee and central location, is a place where many up-and-coming Roman bands and soloists cut their teeth. **Init** is also worth checking out.

Discos often double as live music venues too, so check to see if there are any mid-week surprises at **Piper** or weekend concerts at the **Circolo degli Artisti** and the slightly more alternative **Brancaleone**.

JAZZ

Rome's taste for jazz has developed over the years as a result of visits from American and other foreign musicians. Miles Davis played one of his last concerts here and other jazz gurus such as Pat Metheny, Michael Brecker, Sonny Rollins and Joe Zawinul's Syndicate are all frequent visitors.

On no account should aficionados miss a visit to the excellent **Casa del Jazz**. Top musicians also play at **Alexanderplatz** and Trastevere's **Big Mama** club, one of the city's legendary addresses for important names, offering punters everything from trad r'n'b to progressive jazz and rock. It is also worth checking out what's on at **Gregory's**, **Boogie Club** and **Be Bop** jazz and blues club. **Alpheus** is unique in offering separate concert halls and interesting festivals featuring high-quality ensembles. Otherwise check local listings to see what's on at **Caffè Latino** or **Caruso –**

Café de Oriente. Some of Rome's smaller venues, like **Charity Cafè**, also showcase formidable new talent.

If you want to mix music with your meal, then try **'Gusto**, a slick pizzeria / restaurant in the city centre with live jazz performances on most nights. If Creole cuisine is more to your taste, then book a table in advance at Alexanderplatz.

Local names to look out for include pianist Antonello Salis, who mingles jazz and Caribbean rhythms, and respected soul-singer Fulvio Tomaino. Other leading lights on the blues scene are Roberto Gatto and Maurizio Gianmarco, frequent visitors at Big Mama.

The Roman summer abounds in jazz. The principal event is the Alexanderplatz Jazz Image festival in June and July with nightly alfresco performances at the Villa Celimontana park, just behind the Colosseum. Tickets cost around €10 and are available at the park itself. Another important fixture is the yearly Autumn Roma Jazz Festival with big names from the Italian and international jazz scene visiting the Parco della Musica.

FOLK MUSIC

Since the sad demise of Rome's historic Folkstudio, there is no single venue for folk aficionados in the city, though those prepared to scour the listings may uncover a country evening at **Four Green Fields**, an interesting acoustic set at **Caffè Latino** or a soulful soloist at **Lettere Caffè**.

Traditional Roman folk music has been more or less reduced to tourist-diluted serenades at outdoor restaurants; besides, young locals tend to favour the folk music of other regions and countries. Many bands from various parts of Italy, such as Mau Mau and Agricantus, have found success by drawing on regional rhythms and singing in dialect.

Italians' love of all things Irish also means that strains of the fiddle and drum can be heard in many of the Irish pubs dotted throughout the city. If you have to choose one, then make it the Guinness-enriched **Fiddler's Elbow** near Santa Maria Maggiore.

WORLD MUSIC

As capital of a Latin country which has strong links with other Mediterranean cultures, Rome is a place where world music flourishes. Whether you are looking for South American salsa, African rhythms or Arab cadences, you are unlikely to be disappointed.

Latin American music is no passing fad, as the well-established festivals,

dance-schools and sell-out tours by the likes of Brazilian mega-star Caetano Veloso testify. Many venues offer opportunities to enjoy Latin American music throughout the year. **Arriba Arriba** serves up a choice menu of strictly spicy Latin rhythms. Check too what's on at **Caruso – Café de Oriente** in Testaccio, where you can enjoy a cocktail or two along with the predominantly Cuban music.

But it is summer when Latin American music really comes into its own. The two-month Fiesta festival at the **Ippodromo delle Capannelle** has become by far the most popular feature of the long list of Roman Summer events, clocking up in excess of one million ticket sales.

If your tastes are more eclectic, there's also the excellent "Roma Incontra Il Mondo". This summer festival of world music takes place at **Villa Ada**, a large park north of the city centre, from mid-June to early August. Fans gather each evening to appreciate the talents of names like Angelique Kidjo and South African pianist Abdullah Ibrahim.

World music is also well-served at the aptly-named **Villaggio Globale**, which hosts regular concerts. For a rather more eclectic experience, try **Lettere Caffè**, Rome's first literary café, which offers a variety of world music on Fridays with performances of anything from Australian aborigine to Greek syrtaki sounds.

DIRECTORY

Akab-Cave
Via di Monte Testaccio 69.
Map 8 D4.
Tel 06-5725 0585.

Alexanderplatz
Via Ostia 9. **Map** 3 B1.
Tel 06-5833 5781.

Alpheus
Via del Commercio 36–8.
Map 8 D5.
Tel 06-574 7826.

Arriba Arriba
Via delle Capannelle 104.
Tel 06-721 3772.

Be Bop
Via Giulietti 14. **Map** 8 E4.
Tel 340 556 0112.

Big Mama
Vicolo San Francesco
a Ripa 18. **Map** 7 C2.
Tel 06-581 2551.

Boogie Club
Via Gaetano Astolfi 63
(southeast of Stazione
Trastevere).
Tel 06-6066 4283.

Brancaleone
Via Levanna 13 (in
Monte Sacro).
Tel 06-8200 4382.

Caffè Latino
Via di Monte Testaccio 96.
Map 8 D4.
Tel 06-5728 8556.

**Caruso –
Café de Oriente**
Via di Monte Testaccio 36.
Map 8 D4.
Tel 06-574 5019.**Casa
del Jazz**
Viale di Porta Ardeatina 55.
Map 9 A4.
Tel 06-704 731.

Charity Cafè
Via Panisperna 68.
Map 5 C4.
Tel 06-4782 5881.

Circolo degli Artisti
Via Casilina Vecchia 42.
Map 10 F1.
Tel 06-7030 5684.

Fiddler's Elbow
Via dell'Olmata 43.
Map 6 D4.
Tel 06-487 2110.

Feltrinelli
Galleria Alberto Sordi
31–35.
Map 12 E2.
Tel 06-679 4957.

Fonclea
Via Crescenzio 82A.
Map 3 C2.
Tel 06-689 6302.

Forte Prenestino
Via F. Delpino (east of city,
along Via Prenestina).
Tel 06-2180 7855.

Four Green Fields
Via Morin 40.
Map 3 B1.
Tel 06-372 5091.

Gregory's
Via Gregoriana 54D.
Map 5 A2.
Tel 06-679 6386.

'Gusto
Via della Frezza 23.
Map 4 F2.
Tel 06-322 6273.

Init
Via della Stazione
Tuscolana 133.
Map 10 F3.
Tel 06-9727 7724.

**Ippodromo delle
Capannelle**
Via Appia Nuova 1245
(km 12).
Tel 06-718 2139.

Lettere Caffè
Via San Francesco
a Ripa 100.
Map 7 C1.
Tel 06-9727 0991.

Locanda Atlantide
Via dei Lucani 22B
(San Lorenzo district).
Tel 06-4470 4540.

Orbis
Piazza Esquilino 37.
Map 6 D4.
Tel 06-474 4776.

Palalottomatica
Piazzale dello Sport,
EUR. *Tel* 199 128 800.

Palladium
Piazza B. Romano 8 (to the
south of Stazione Ostiense).
Tel 06-5706 7761.

Parco della Musica
Viale de Coubertin 15.
Map 1 C2.
Tel 06-8024 1281.
www.auditorium.com

Stadio Olimpico
Viale dei Gladiatori (northwest of city centre, across
the Tiber by Monte Mario).

The Place
Via Alberico II 27.
Map 3 C2.
Tel 06-6830 7137.

Villa Ada
Via Salaria 197 (north of
the city centre).
Tel 06-4173 4712.

Villaggio Globale
Ex-Mattatoio, Lungotevere
Testaccio 2.
Map 8 D4.
Tel 334 1790 006.

Cinema and Theatre

Cinema-going is very popular in Rome, with around 40 films on show during the week. The excellent Casa del Cinema and high profile International Festival of Cinema reflect the city's enduring love of the big screen.

The great majority of Roman cinemas are *prima visione* (first run) and show the latest international films in dubbed versions. The smaller art cinemas are more likely to show subtitled versions of foreign films.

Theatre productions are performed in Italian whether the plays are national classics or by foreign playwrights. The main theatres offer a selection by great Italian playwrights. There are also performances of traditional cabaret, avant-garde theatre and dance theatre. Theatre tickets cost between €8 and €50 and can be booked in advance by visiting the theatre box office, or through the last-minute booking service *(see p355)*.

PRIMA VISIONE

There are over 80 *prima visione* cinemas in the city. The best cinemas for decor and comfort are the **Fiamma** (two screens) and **Barberini** (three screens).

Foreign films are usually dubbed. Films in the original language are shown at the **Metropolitan** and the **Nuovo Olimpia** (daily) and on Mondays at the **Alcazar**.

Tickets for new films cost around €7, but a few cinemas listed as *prima visione* charge less, namely **Farnese** and **Reale**. Over 60s and disabled people are normally entitled to a 30 per cent reduction on weekdays. Tickets are reduced in many cinemas on weekday afternoons and on Wednesdays. Check the newspaper or listings such as *Trova-Roma* or *Roma c'è* for details *(see p354)*.

ART CINEMAS

True film buffs flock to Rome in October for the International Festival of Cinema (www.romacinemafest.it) with events centring on the **Parco della Musica**.

There are two main types of art cinema in Rome: the *cine-clubs* and the *cinema d'essai*. Both are good if you're interested in catching older classics and new foreign films as well as films by contemporary Italian directors.

The *d'essai* cinemas now and then show films in the original language (indicated

by *v.o.* for *versione originale* in the listings). Try the **Azzurro Scipioni** (one of the few to be open throughout summer), **Filmstudio** or Nanni Moretti's **Nuovo Sacher**. Some of the smaller cinemas are called *cine-clubs* and require membership.

The **Palazzo delle Esposizioni** shows interesting series of international films though you should head for the **Casa del Cinema** for the real art-house experience.

Cartoons and children's favourites are shown at **Dei Piccoli**, in the leafy surrounds of the Villa Borghese.

ENGLISH-LANGUAGE FILMS

In addition to occasional undubbed showings of British, American and Australasian films in art cinemas and at the **Nuovo Olimpia** and **Warner Village Moderno**, the excellent **Casa del Cinema** has a policy of screening all films in their original language.

SUMMER CINEMA

Some Roman cinemas have roll-back ceilings which are in use during the summer, while the others close down. The **Nuovo Sacher** has an outdoor arena. Rome also has various summer cinema festivals: Cineporto and Massenzio to name but two. These show several films each night from 9pm until the small hours, with food

and drinks on sale and often live music during the intervals. Cineporto takes place in the Parco della Farnesina nightly between July and September, but Massenzio moves around *(see listings)*.

Sci-fi enthusiasts should keep an eye out for the Fantafestival (early June), a science fiction, fantasy and horror film festival. The Venezia a Roma event in September gives film buffs the chance to see movies presented at the summer Venice Film Festival.

The listings pages *(see p354)* have details on retrospectives and avant-garde film seasons at the **Azzurro Scipioni** and the open-air arts festivals like RomaEuropa *(see p355)* and Festa dell'Unità *(see p355)*.

MAINSTREAM THEATRE

The backbone of Rome's theatrical repertoire are Luigi Pirandello's dramas and comedies by 18th-century Venetian Carlo Goldoni and 20th-century Neapolitan Eduardo de Filippo. Major foreign playwrights are also performed from time to time.

The best classic productions are staged at the **Teatro Argentina**, **Teatro Quirino**, **Teatro Valle**, **Teatro Eliseo** and **Teatro Piccolo Eliseo**. **Teatro Argentina** is state-owned and home of Rome's permanent theatre company. Its sister theatre, **Teatro India**, stages more innovative works. The **Quirino** and **Valle** host productions from other Italian cities. The latter shows both great Italian classics by famous companies to lesser known modernist works, and occasionally hosts prestigious foreign companies. Plays at the **Quirino** often feature famous Italian actors. The **Eliseo** and **Piccolo Eliseo** are among the city's best private theatres.

At **Teatro Sistina** and **Teatro Brancaccio** you can see hit musicals by visiting foreign companies and shows by popular Italian actors, while **Teatro Vittoria** goes in for plays by Noël Coward or Neil Simon.

CONTEMPORARY THEATRE

The home of contemporary theatre is the ever-dynamic **Vascello**, the **Orologio** and, beyond these well-known names, in a host of small theatres, ingeniously rigged up in cellars, garages, small apartments or even tents.

The **Colosseo** hosts some alternative fringe-type productions (known here as *teatro off*) while the **Palladium** and the **Vascello** tend to stage works by contemporary authors and occasional avant-garde productions. Some of them, like **Teatro India** and Orologio, also put on foreign-language productions.

FOLK, CABARET AND PUPPET THEATRE

Roman and Neapolitan folk songs and cabaret can be enjoyed in Trastevere's tourist-trade restaurants, like **Meo Patacca**, while **Tina Pika Village** offers more alternative cabaret.

Puppet theatre is another Roman tradition. Shows take place early in the evening at weekends, and sometimes during the week, at **Teatro Verde** and **Teatro Mongiovino**. In the Villa Borghese, the **Teatro San Carlino** also presents plays with the younger audience in mind. Among the most popular are the adventures of *Pulcinella* (the Italian Punch).

OPEN-AIR THEATRE

The open-air summer theatre season usually features Greek and Roman plays at **Ostia Antica** *(see pp270–71)*.

The **Anfiteatro Quercia del Tasso** in the Janiculum park takes its name from the oak tree under which 16th-century poet Tasso used to sit. Comedy shows are staged here in July to September, when the weather permits. In winter the company performs at the **Teatro Anfitrione**.

Nearby is a Neapolitan street puppet theatre booth featuring *Pulcinella* (the Italian original of Punch). Shows are usually on in the afternoons, with morning shows on Sundays

DIRECTORY

PRIMA VISIONE

Alcazar
Via Card. Merry del Val 14.
Map 7 C1.
Tel 06-588 0099.

Barberini
Piazza Barberini 24.
Map 5 B3.
Tel 06-482 1082.

Farnese
Piazza Campo de' Fiori 56.
Map 4 E5.
Tel 06-686 4395.

Fiamma
Via Bissolati 47.
Map 5 C2.
Tel 06-485 526.

Metropolitan
Via del Corso 7. **Map** 4
F1. *Tel* 06-320 0933.

Nuovo Olimpia
Via in Lucina 16. **Map** 12
E1. *Tel* 06-686 1068.

Reale
Piazza Sonnino 7.
Map 7 C1.
Tel 06-5810 234.

Warner Village Moderno
Piazza della Repubblica 45.
Map 5 C3.
Tel 06-4777 9202.

ART CINEMAS

Azzurro Scipioni
Via degli Scipioni 82.
Map 3 C2.
Tel 06-3973 7161.

Casa del Cinema
Largo M. Mastroianni 1.
Map 5 B1.
Tel 06-423 601.
www.casadelcinema.it

Dei Piccoli
Viale della Pineta 15. **Map**
5 B1. *Tel* 06-855 3485.

Filmstudio
Via degli Orti d'Alibert 1C.
Map 4 D4
Tel 06-4543 9775.

Nuovo Sacher
Largo Ascianghi 1. **Map** 7
C2. *Tel* 06-581 8116.

Palazzo delle Esposizioni
Via Nazionale 194. **Map** 5
B4. *Tel* 06-3996 7500.
www.palaexpo.com

Parco della Musica
Viale de Coubertin 30.
Map 1 C2.
Tel 06-8024 1281.
www.romacinemafest.org

MAINSTREAM THEATRE

Teatro Argentina
Largo Argentina 56. **Map**
4 F4. *Tel* 06-68400 0311.
www.teatrodiroma.net

Teatro Brancaccio
Via Merulana 244. **Map** 6
D5. *Tel* 06-9826 4500.

Teatro Eliseo
Via Nazionale 183. **Map**
5 B4. *Tel* 06-488 2114.
www.teatroeliseo.it

Teatro India
Via L. Pierantoni 6. **Map** 7
C5. *Tel* 06-684 000 311.

Teatro Piccolo Eliseo
Via Nazionale 183. **Map**
5 B4. *Tel* 06-488 2114.

Teatro Quirino
Via delle Vergini 7.
Map 5 A4 & 12 F2.
Tel 06-679 4585.
www.teatroquirino.it

Teatro Sistina
Via Sistina 129. **Map** 5 B2.
Tel 06-420 0711.

Teatro Valle
Via del Teatro Valle 21.
Map 4 F4 & 12 D3.
Tel 06-6880 3794.
www.teatrovalle.it

Teatro Vittoria
Piazza S. Maria Liberatrice
8. **Map** 8 D3.
Tel 06-574 0598.

CONTEMPORARY THEATRE

Palladium
Piazza B. Romano 8 (south
of Stazione Ostiense).
Tel 06-5706 7761.

Teatro Anfitrione
Via di San Saba 24. **Map**
8 E3. *Tel* 06-575 0827.

Teatro Colosseo
Via Capo d'Africa 29A.
Map 9 A1.
Tel 06-700 4932.

Teatro dell'Orologio
Via dei Filippini 17A. **Map**
11 B3. *Tel* 06-687 5550.

Teatro Olimpico
Piazza Gentile da Fabriano
17 (off Via Guido Reni).
Map 1 A2. *Tel* 06-326
5991.

Teatro Vascello
Via G. Carini 72. **Map** 7
A2. *Tel* 06-588 1021.

FOLK, CABARET, PUPPET THEATRE

Meo Patacca
P. dei Mercanti 30. **Map**
8 D1. *Tel* 06-581 6198.

Teatro Mongiovino
Via Genocchi 15.
Tel 06-513 9405.

Teatro San Carlino
Viale dei Bambini (Pincio).
Map 4 F1.
Tel 06-6992 2117.

Teatro Verde
Circonvall. Gianicolense 10.
Map 7 B4. *Tel* 06-588 2034.

Tina Pika Village
Via Fonteiana 57
(Monteverde district).
Tel 06-588 5754.

OPEN-AIR THEATRE

Anfiteatro Quercia del Tasso
Passeggiata del Gianicolo.
Map 3 C5.
Tel 06-575 0827.

Nightlife

Rome's nightlife has never been as diverse or vibrant as it is today. Recent years have witnessed a sharp rise in the number of bar and club openings that cater for an ever more demanding clientele. Where once the choice was limited to the Irish theme bars near Termini, the few well-established but crowded bars in the centre and the hugely popular clubs in Testaccio, the capital now offers a wide range of options designed to satisfy all tastes and budgets. Depending on your mood, head first for a stylish pre-clubbing bar and then on to one of the centre's exclusive clubs, or simply relax with friends and a bottle of good wine in an earthy wine bar in one of the historic centre's breathtaking squares. For a memorable first stop, enjoy spectacular views with an apéritif from a rooftop terrace bar.

On the downside, despite the greater number of bars and clubs, prices have soared in Rome since the euro was introduced – today you can be charged up to €10 for a cocktail! For cheaper alternative nights out, away from the tourist traps, visit a bar in San Lorenzo.

WHAT'S ON

As in any major city, Rome's nightlife is constantly evolving. Roman club-goers are an extremely varied group and most clubs arrange different nights to appeal to the diverse range of tastes – so it is essential to keep up-to-date on what's happening by checking listings magazines (see p354) that hit the newsstands every Thursday.

Flyers for many nightclubs are handed out in some of the busier squares in and around the centre, such as Campo de' Fiori and Piazza del Fico. They are also distributed inside the many pre-clubbing bars dotted around Testaccio such as Il Seme e La Foglia.

PRACTICALITIES

Preferred clubbing nights are Friday and Saturday, when the cars and scooters of revellers block the streets of the city centre. Queues at the most popular venues can be very long at peak entrance time (around midnight), so it is advisable to get there an hour or so earlier. However, if you are unable do so, and don't feel like waiting, try ringing up in advance and charming your way onto the guestlist.

Instead of an entrance fee, some smaller clubs require a *tessera*, a monthly or yearly membership card, which you can buy and fill out on the spot. If you're paying just to get through the door that night, hold on to your entrance ticket as it usually entitles you to a free first drink (*la consumazione*); your second could be expensive and cost as much as €15.

As a general rule, remember that all-male groups are rarely welcome, and in some exclusive clubs neither are unaccompanied men. Also, to enter any of the more select venues you'll need both an introduction from one of the regulars and clothes that aim to impress.

BARS

Despite increased competition, especially from the revitalized rustic wine bar Il Nolano, La Vineria (see p328) in Campo de' Fiori has maintained its cult status among Romans of all ages and backgrounds for unpretentious, lively drinking at reasonable prices. Just around the corner, L'Angolo Divino (see p328) is less well-known, and consequently not as bustling. It nonetheless remains a perfect spot for socializing over great wines and heart-warming food.

Another landmark in the *centro storico* (historic centre), though for a more well-to-do and fashion-conscious crowd, is the in-vogue Antico Caffè della Pace, a popular choice near Piazza Navona for those who want to see and be seen. Fluid, on Via del Governo Vecchio, is much livelier and has made its mark in the capital as the perfect venue to get you in the mood for late-night clubbing. A few doors down but really a world away, the comfortable and candlelit Mimì e Cocò is a great place to relax (alfresco or inside) and linger over subtle wines, served with a smile. Just off the top end of the same street, moving away from Corso Vittorio Emanuele II, is Giulio Passami l'Olio, a warm, welcoming and animated *enoteca*, tucked away from the usual *passaggiate* (promenade) routes. Closer to Piazza di Spagna, the striking interior and extensive choice of wines by the glass make the Antica Enoteca di Via della Croce a favourite spot for wine connoisseurs. Although it's definitely not cheap, the impressive bar buffet is well worth sampling.

In Trastevere, too, the romantic streets are full of tiny bars aimed at diverse crowds. Find a table if you can outside Ombre Rosse in the wonderful Piazza Sant'Egidio and watch the world go by. If Ombre Rosse is too crowded, Caffè della Scala, just a few minutes' walk away, is a good alternative. Other bars in the area include the sophisticated Beige and Friends Art Café, which is a perfect spot to enjoy a refreshing, though expensive apéritif with complimentary but elaborate snacks – a growing trend in the Eternal City. The simple, but vintage, Bar San Callisto, located just off Piazza Santa Maria, draws strictly non-conventional patrons.

Elsewhere in the city, the sophisticated Ferrazza

(see p351), in San Lorenzo, serves up exceptional wines for more sophisticated customers, while the monumental student bar **Rive Gauche** does great business as the biggest pub in the area. The slick surf-bar **Duke's** in Parioli is slightly away from the centre, but is worth it for star-spotting. Duke's has tried to curb its soaring popularity by closing on Saturday nights, but to no avail. It remains the number one place to be seen in north Rome.

Finally, and not just for hopeless romantics, breathtaking views of Rome can be had at the lavish rooftop terrace bars at **Hotel Eden** (see p308), near Via Veneto, and the **Radisson Hotel** (see p305) near Termini. At dusk, particularly after a sunny day, these stunning venues offer a great place to start an unforgettable evening out.

CLUBS

To brush shoulders with TV starlets and parliamentary under-secretaries, head for **Gilda**. Its glitzy dance-floor and restaurant have made it a favourite with the Roman jet set and hangers-on. The famous Sixties nightclub, **Jackie O**, revamped in lavish style, with a lush interior, a piano bar and an expensive eatery, draws an international, thirty-something crowd.

Bòeme is a safe option for commercial music among Roman twenty-somethings, though **Heaven** is slightly funkier with its marked preference for house. More challenging is the eclectic **Micca Club** with the chance to hear live sets while the more traditional disco is at its best at **Piper**, which changes look each season and organizes imaginative floor shows and other events. There are a few disco-pubs in the city centre which offer a compromise between a straightforward bar and an all-out club. **The Nag's Head** is one that is especially worth noting.

In and around Testaccio, the undisputed clubbing heart of Rome, you'll find it difficult to decide which club to visit. **Akab-Cave** is cool and unashamedly commercial; the stylish **Caruso – Café de Oriente** concentrates on Latin, R&B and salsa sounds, while the multi-functional **Distillerie Clandestine** and **Joia** clubs are the places for eating, drinking, relaxing and dancing. Still on the crest of the 70s revival wave is the trendy **La Saponeria**, while the **Neo** is a strong-hold of underground music. Saturday night at **Big Bang** signifies all things dark and new wave, while at the equally alternative **Alpheus**, you can drift between three rooms offering three completely different DJ sets. Last but by no means least, the legendary **Goa** remains the champion of Roman clubs, attracting the best of Italian as well as international DJs.

The wine bar at **'Gusto** offers live music and the chance to explore the venue's various restaurant areas while enjoying a glass of wine from the vast selection available. On the other side of Corso Vittorio Emanuele, the select **La Maison** attracts a slightly older crowd with its less commercial music and elegant ambience. However, if you're in the mood for a mainstream alternative that is free of charge and easier to gain entry to, then head to the upbeat **Habana Café** for a continuous programme of live music and DJ sets every evening.

For something a little different, the **Radio Café** is a multi-functional venue with a lounge, café, disco and meeting spaces frequented by a trendy media set.

GAY SCENE

Rome is no longer the provincial backwater it once was. This is clearly reflected both in the rise in the number of gay bars and clubs and their increasing popularity. While some are exclusively gay, others attract a mixed clientele.

Across the river from the *centro storico* in Trastevere is the exclusive **Il Giardino dei Ciliegi**, a living-room-style bar that specializes in cocktails. It also stocks a wide variety of teas and serves exciting salads and an excellent Sunday brunch – even on public holidays. For livelier social drinking, head for **Anfiteatro My Bar** and **Coming Out**, between San Giovanni and the Colosseum, to mingle with a mixed crowd that usually spills out onto the street. Nearby, the men-only bar **Hangar** continues to pack them in.

When it comes to clubbing, the ever-growing number of gay one-nighters in both alternative and mainstream clubs in many ways present the best venues for drinking and dancing until the early hours. **Goa**, just off Via Ostiense, occasionally hosts gay nights such as the women-only Venus Rising once a month; Mucca Assassina (quite literally "homicidal cow") pulls in the crowds every Friday at the monumental **Qube** in Tiburtino; the rival Omogenic crew take over the **Circolo degli Artisti** on the same evening, while the **Alpheus** hosts the Gorgeous one-nighters every Saturday. These clubs are in addition to the justly famous gay-friendly disco **Alibi** in Testaccio with its explosive mix of house music and retro classics.

Pride Week, a yearly event held at the end of June/early July, is a time when gay Romans hit the streets for seven days of non-stop partying. The programme and date change from year to year, so it is wise to consult listing magazines for full details.

In summer, as with most clubs, Rome's gay venues move outdoors in an attempt to beat the stifling heat. In recent years, many of these have been hosted at

Gay Village, a summer-long outdoor beanfeast. This is yet another important indication that gay culture is finally beginning to be accepted on the mainstream entertainment scene.

CENTRI SOCIALI

Centri sociali, or illegally occupied buildings that have been converted into centres for the arts and entertainment, give an alternative edge to Rome's vivacious nightlife and cultural scene. While some centres are run on a professional basis and are able to successfully compete with many of the capital's swankier and established venues, others have continued to maintain their staunch anti-establishment stance.

Top billing must go to **Brancaleone** in north Rome, which regularly features progressive Italian and international DJs for the very best in electronic and house tunes. This well-run establishment is also home to an organic café and shop, superb art exhibitions and a cinema club.

Near the Baths of Caracalla, the **Angelo Mai Centre** regularly organizes a multitude of cultural events, including exhibitions and showings of art house films – sometimes even in their original non-dubbed version. At weekends, the venue dedicates its space primarily to club nights, covering a spectrum of tastes from underground and ethnic live bands to wild DJ sets. They also boast their own eatery.

Further away from the centre, the abandoned fort, **Forte Prenestino**, is a magical maze of spooky rooms and endless corridors and represents the most bizarre of Rome's social centre venues. Famous for its anti-establishment Labour Day concert – the official and free rock concert is held in Piazza San Giovanni in Laterano – it also holds theatre productions, film festivals and club nights throughout the year for a young but alternative crowd. Closer to the centre, **Villaggio Globale**, situated on a vast area of

DIRECTORY

BARS

Angelo Mai
Viale delle Terme di
Caracalla 55A. **Map** 9 A2.
Tel 329 448 1358.

L'Angolo Divino
Via dei Balestrari 12–14.
Map 11 C4.
Tel 06-686 4413.

**Antica Enoteca di
Via della Croce**
Via della Croce 76B.
Map 4 F2.
Tel 06-679 0896.

**Antico Caffè
della Pace**
Via della Pace 3–7.
Map 11 C3.
Tel 06-686 1216.

Bar San Callisto
Piazza San Callisto 3–4.
Map 7 C1.
Tel 06-583 5869.

Beige
Via dei Politeama 13.
Map 11 C5.
Tel 06-5833 0686.

Caffè della Scala
Via della Scala 4.
Map 7 C1.
Tel 06-580 3610.

Duke's
Viale Parioli 200.
Map 2 D1.
Tel 06-8066 2455.

Ferrazza
Via dei Volsci 59.
Map 6 F4.
Tel 06-490 506.

Fluid
Via del Governo Vecchio
46/47.
Map 11 C3.
Tel 06-683 2361.

Friends Art Café
Piazza Trilussa 34.
Map 4 E5.
Tel 06-581 6111.

**Giulio Passami
l'Olio**
Via di Monte
Giordano 28.
Map 11 B2.
Tel 06-6880 3288.

Hotel Eden
Via Ludovisi 49.
Map 5 B2.
Tel 06-478 121.

Mimì e Cocò
Via del Governo
Vecchio 72.
Map 11 C3.
Tel 06-6821 0845.

Il Nolano
Campo de' Fiori
11/12. **Map** 11 C4.
Tel 06-687 9344.

Ombre Rosse
Piazza Sant'Egidio 12.
Map 7 C1.
Tel 06-588 4155.

Radisson Hotel
Via Filippo Turati 171.
Map 6 D4.
Tel 06-444 841.

Rive Gauche
Via dei Sabelli 43.
Map 6 F4.
Tel 06-445 6722.

Il Seme e la Foglia
Via Galvani 18.
Map 8 D4.
Tel 06-574 3008.

La Vineria
Campo de' Fiori 15.
Map 11 C4.
Tel 06-6880 3268.

CLUBS

Akab-Cave
Via di Monte Testaccio 69.
Map 8 D4.
Tel 06-5725 0585.

Alpheus
Via del Commercio 36/8.
Map 8 D5.
Tel 06-574 7826.

Big Bang
Via Monte Testaccio 22.
Map 8 D4.
Tel 392 901 1993.

Bòeme
Via Velletri 13.
Map 6 D1.
Tel 06-841 2212.

**Caruso –
Café de Orient**
Via di Monte Testaccio 36.
Map 8 D4.
Tel 06-574 5019.

**Distillerie
Clandestine**
Via Libetta 7.
Tel 06-5730 5102.

Gilda
Via Mario de' Fiori 97.
Map 12 F1.
Tel 06-678 4838.

Goa
Via Libetta 13.
Tel 06-574 8277.

'Gusto
Via delle Frezza 23.
Map 4 F2.
Tel 06-322 6273.

open space at the edge of Testaccio, has a very similar philosophy and range of services. In summer, it regularly hosts open-air concerts, occasionally beating off the competition to feature big name Italian bands such as Tiromancino.

JAZZ, SALSA AND AFRICAN SOUNDS

Rome offers countless venues for jazz, from trad and swing to modern fusion *(see p358)*. Several jazz and Latin American clubs combine live music with dancing, eating and drinking. For South American style music, **Fonclea** and **Arriba Arriba** *(see p359)* or **Alpheus** all pay homage to Latin

American and world music, although **Caffè Latino** in Testaccio is by far and away the best place to check out at the weekend.

CLUBBING IN SUMMER

At the height of the sweltering summer, when virtually everything closes down in the capital, **Art Cafè** in Villa Borghese stands out as the supreme club venue for the fun-loving, young and hip. A number of floating venues open up on the Tiber too, while some of the bigger clubs hit the coast from July through to December – most notably in Ostia and in Fregene, where the legendary **Gilda On The Beach** is a permanent fixture. Also

worth checking out is the sophisticated **Singita** beach club, where they hold a special sunset ceremony accompanied by a DJ set.

AFTER HOURS

Most Roman clubs stay open until 2am or 3am. However, night-owls may find one or two dance havens that see in the dawn, especially during the beach-party season. Before heading off to bed, you could join the other die-hard clubbers for a final drink at one of the city's 24-hour watering holes, or else make for one of the early-morning bakers and feast on sweet breakfast *cornetti* straight from the oven.

DIRECTORY

Habana Café
Via dei Pastini 120.
Map 12 D2.
Tel 06-678 1983.

Heaven
Viale di Porta Ardeatina 119. **Map** 9 B5.
Tel 06-574 3772.

Jackie O
Via Boncompagni 11
Map 5 B2.
Tel 06-4288 5457.

Joia
Via Galvani 20. **Map** 8 D4.
Tel 06-574 0802.

La Maison
Vicolo dei Granari 4.
Map 11 C3.
Tel 06-683 3312.

Micca Club
Via P. Micca 7A.
Map 6 F5.
Tel 06-8744 0079.

The Nag's Head
Via IV Novembre 138B.
Map 5 A4.
Tel 06-679 4620.

Neo
Via degli Argonauti 18
(to the south of Stazione Ostiense).
Tel 06-5728 7330.

Piper
Via Tagliamento 9
(north of the city centre).
Tel 06-855 5398.

Radio Café
Via Principe Umberto 67.
Map 6 E5.
Tel 06-4436 1110.

La Saponeria
Via degli Argonauti 20
(to the south of Stazione Ostiense, off Via Ostiense).
Tel 06-574 6999.

GAY SCENE

Alibi
Via di Monte Testaccio 39–44. **Map** 8 D4.
Tel 06-574 3448.

Alpheus
See clubs.

Anfiteatro My Bar
Via San Giovanni in Laterano 12.
Map 9 A1.
Tel 06-700 4425.

Circolo degli Artisti
Via Casilina Vecchia 42.
Map 10 F1.
Tel 06-7030 5684.

Coming Out
Via San Giovanni In Laterano 8. **Map** 9 A1.
Tel 06-700 9871.

Gay Village
Phone or check website
for venue.
Tel 06-513 4741.
www.gayvillage.it

Il Giardino dei Ciliegi
Via dei Fienaroli 4.
Tel 06-580 3423.

Goa
See clubs.

Hangar
Via in Selci 69.
Map 5 C5.
Tel 06-488 1397.

Qube
Via di Portonaccio 212
(north of the city centre).
Tel 06-541 3985.

CENTRI SOCIALI

Brancaleone
Via Levanna 11
(in Montesacro).
Tel 06-8200 4382.

Forte Prenestino
Via F. Delpino (in Prenestino).
Tel 06-2180 7855.

Villaggio Globale
Lungotevere Testaccio 2/
Via di Monte Testaccio 22.
Map 7 4C.
Tel 334 967 2699.

JAZZ, SALSA AND AFRICAN SOUNDS

Alpheus
See clubs.

Arriba Arriba
Via delle Capannelle 104.
Tel 06-721 3772.

Caffè Latino
Via di Monte Testaccio 96.
Map 8 D4.
Tel 06-5728 8556.

Fonclea
Via Crescenzio 82A.
Map 3 C2.
Tel 06 689 6302.
www.fonclea.it

CLUBBING IN SUMMER

Art Cafè
Viale del Galoppatoio, 33 (Villa Borghese).
Map 5 A1.
Tel 06-3600 6578.

Gilda on the Beach
Lungomare di Ponente 11, Fregene.
Tel 06-6656 0649.

Singita
Villaggio dei Pescatori Fregne.
Tel 06-6196 4921.

Sport

Do not be surprised if the peace of a Sunday afternoon in Rome is interrupted by the honking of cars and people shouting. It simply means that one of the home football teams has won at the stadium and the whole city will vibrate with the excitement.

Football is Italy's national sport but other sports also attract a large following and Roman sports fans are never at a loss for varied events and activities.

You will find times and venues for most spectator sports listed in *Trova-Roma or Roma c'è (see p354)*, as well as the local sections of *La Gazzetta dello Sport* or *Corriere dello Sport*.

FOOTBALL

An Italian soccer match is an experience not to be missed for the quality of the play and the fun atmosphere, though hooliganism has begun to raise its ugly head.

Rome has two teams, Roma and Lazio, and they take it in turns to play at the **Stadio Olimpico** on a Sunday afternoon at 3pm, in the Campionato Italiano (Italian championship league).

Seats can be scarce, so get tickets in advance from the stadium (€15 to €80) from noon onwards on the day itself, or through club web-sites (www.sslazio.it and www.asroma.it). The cheapest seats are in the Le Curve stand; the middle-range and most expensive are in Le Gradinate and La Tribuna respectively.

On Wednesday evenings there may be international competitions – the UEFA cup or the Coppa dei Campioni (European Championship Cup). In between these, teams battle it out for the national Coppa Italia.

TENNIS

A major event, the Inter-national Championships go on at **Foro Italico** for two weeks in May. The world's top tennis stars thrash it out on clay courts at 1pm and 8.30pm from Tuesday to Friday, and at 1pm only at weekends. Buy tickets in advance either directly from the Foro Italico or from a ticket agency.

If you wish to play yourself, there are now more than 350 tennis clubs in Rome. It is often essential to book at least a week in advance and there is usually a moderate court fee.

Clubs where membership is not required include **Tennis Club Nomentano** and the **Circolo Tennis della Stampa** in northern Rome and the **Oasi di Pace**, just off the Via Appia Antica. The big hotels offer tennis for a reasonable price. The **Crowne Plaza** requires a small annual membership fee on top of the court price, which includes the gym and the pool (in the summer).

HORSE-RACING, TROTTING AND LEISURE-RIDING

Important races include the Derby in May and the Premio Roma in November. There are trotting races at the **Ippodromo di Tor di Valle** and both flat races and steeplechases at the **Ippodromo delle Capannelle**.

The International Horse Show is held in May in Piazza di Siena, Villa Borghese *(see p258)*. It is organized by the Federazione Italiana Sport Equestri (**FISE**) and is one of the most important social and sporting events in the calendar. The setting makes it a great attraction.

Through the FISE, it may be possible to find a riding club that will take you on a hack in the countryside around Rome, but most do not accept short-term members.

GOLF

Even the most elite golf clubs will accept a touring golfer with a home membership and handicap. Most clubs are shut on Mondays and at the weekend when they host competitions, and when guests cannot play. Prices range from €55 to €100.

The **Olgiata Golf Club** is open to everybody from Tuesday to Sunday, though it is best to phone first if you want to play at the weekend. **Country Club Castel Gandolfo** is the newest club and **Circolo del Golf di Roma Acquasanta** the oldest and most prestig-ious. Within the city ring road is the course at the **Sheraton Golf Hotel** (closed Tuesdays).

One of the many important competitions on the various golf courses around Rome is the Circolo Golf Roma Coppa d'Oro (Gold Cup) in April.

CAR AND MOTORBIKE RACING

Formula 1 and Formula 3 races take place on Sundays at **Vallelunga**; be prepared for some expensive entrance fees. Frequently on Saturdays official trials are open to spectators, and on some non-racing Sundays Italy's car designers show new models.

RUGBY

Rugby has taken off in Italy recently, particularly since Italy joined the Six Nations tournament. This means that in winter (usually Feb–Mar) there are a couple of inter-national matches in Rome. The home team is drawn against two other member "nations" each year: France, England, Scotland, Ireland or Wales.

ROWING

In mid-June an Oxbridge crew challenges the historic Aniene crew to a race taking place alternately on the Thames and the Tiber. The best place to view this from is between the Margherita and the Sant'Angelo bridges. The race usually starts at around 6pm. Another event is the battle between the Roma and Lazio crews, from Ponte Duca d'Aosta to Ponte Risorgimento, on the same variable date as the Roma-Lazio football derby.

SWIMMING

Swimming pools are few and definitely not geared to the short-term visitor. It is often necessary to pay an expensive membership plus a monthly tariff. Most pools also require you to produce a medical certificate assuring your good health, and have lane-only swimming, so check to see if free swimming *(nuoto libero)* is possible. The state-owned pools can be slightly cheaper, but you still have to pay an initial membership fee.

The **Shangri-La Hotel** opens its pool to non-residents in the summer months, as does the **Cavalieri Rome Hotel**, for a higher entrance fee. The best deal is on a Sunday when the sports club and swimming pool **La Margherita** opens to non-members 10am–1pm, for a reasonable entrance charge. **Piscina delle Rose** in EUR is an Olympic-sized pool open from June to September 9am–5.30pm during the week, 9am–7pm at weekends.

HEALTH CLUBS

Like the swimming pools, Roman health clubs usually require both a membership fee and monthly payments. For a short stay in Rome, it is more sensible to try the facilities in your hotel, or, if you are willing to pay, head for one of the private clubs. Use of club facilities may well be negotiable.

The **Roman Sport Center** welcomes daily members for a reasonable price (€30) and you can use the pools, the gym and the sauna. The facilities are open 7am–10.30pm on weekdays (until 8:30pm Saturday, 9am–3pm Sunday). Any shorts worn must be made of lycra.

JOGGING AND CYCLING

Rome's perfect climate and stunning scenery attract thousands of well dressed joggers and cyclists into the city's many parks. Early on weekday mornings or at any time on a Sunday you'll find the more popular locations looking more like a high-speed fashion show than sweat tracks. Each March, however, more serious runners take part in the Rome Marathon.

Villa Doria Pamphilj *(see p267)* is an extensive park situated above the Janiculum, where you can choose from various spaces, plenty of open spaces and a network of paths. **Villa Borghese** *(see p258)* is another vast popular place with a running track.

Alternatively, jog under the acacia trees and palms at Villa Torlonia, on the spot-lit track at Villa Glori, or combine sport with culture by running the **Via Appia Antica** *(see p265)* branching off into Parco Caffarella. Other favourite places are Viale delle Terme di Caracalla, Circo Massimo, Parco degli Aquedotti and Parco di Colle Oppio.

All of the above are also ideal for cyclists, and you can hire bikes from many places including **Collalti** and **Treno e Scooter Rent**.

DIRECTORY

FOOTBALL

Stadio Olimpico
Via Foro Italico.
Tel 06-368 51.

TENNIS

Circolo Tennis della Stampa
Piazza Mancini 19.
Map 1 A2.
Tel 06-323 2454.

Crowne Plaza
Via Aurelia Antica 415.
Tel 06-663 1572.

Foro Italico
Viale dei Gladiatori 31.
Tel 06-3685 4140.
http://ctforoitalico.coni.it

Oasi di Pace
Via degli Eugenii 2.
Tel 06-718 4550.

Tennis Club Nomentano
Viale Rousseau 124.
Tel 06-8680 1888.
www.clubnomentano.it

HORSE-RACING AND RIDING

FISE
Viale Tiziano 74. **Map** 1 A1. *Tel 06-3685 8326.*
www.fise.it

Ippodromo delle Capannelle
Via Appia Nuova 1255.
Tel 06-71 67 71.

Ippodromo di Tor di Valle
Via del Mare km 9. *Tel 06-524 761.* http://tordivalle.
ippocity.com

GOLF

Circolo del Golf di Roma Acquasanta
Via Appia Nuova 716A.
Tel 06-780 3407.

Country Club Castel Gandolfo
Via di Santo Spirito 13, Castelgandolfo.
Tel 06-931 2301.

Olgiata Golf Club
Largo dell'Olgiata 15.
Tel 06-3088 9141.

Sheraton Golf Hotel
Viale Salvatore Rebecchini 39. *Tel 06-655 3477.*
www.golfparcode
medici.com

MOTOR RACING

Vallelunga
Autodromo di Roma, Via Cassia km 34.5. *Tel 06-901 550.* www.vallelunga.it

RUGBY

Federazione Italiana Rugby
Curva Nord, Stadio Olimpico, Viale dei Gladiatori. *Tel 06-4521 3117.* www.federugby.it

SWIMMING

ARCA Swimming Club
Via Monti Tiburtini 511.
Tel 06-451 0552.

Cavalieri Rome Hotel
Via Cadlolo 101. *Tel 06-350 91.* www.rome
cavalieri.com

Piscina delle Rose
Viale America 20.
Tel 06-5422 0333. www.
piscinadellerose.com

Shangri-La Hotel
Viale Algeria 141.
Tel 06-591 6441.

HEALTH CLUBS

Roman Sport Center
Via del Galoppatoio 33.
Map 5 A1.
Tel 06-320 1667.

JOGGING AND CYCLING

Collalti
Via del Pellegrino 82. **Map** 4 E4. *Tel 06-6880 1084.*

Maratona di Roma
Tel 06-406 5064.
www.maratonadiroma.it

Treno e Scooter Rent
Termini Station. **Map** 6 D3. *Tel 06-4890 5823.*

Via del Corso
Piazza S. Lorenzo in Lucina.
Map 4 F3 & 12 E1.

CHILDREN'S ROME

Italians love having children around, and you can be sure yours will be made welcome wherever they go. But there are few special facilities for children, and the heat, crowds and lack of clean public loos mean that Rome is not an ideal city for a holiday with babies or under-sevens. It does, however, have plenty to offer slightly older children, especially those who are keen on history

Renaissance cherub from the Villa Farnesina

or art. The temptation may be to wear yourself and your children out by packing too many sights into one day. Plan in advance and leave plenty of time to wander around the city: looking at the quirkier fountains and monuments, watching knife-grinders at work in the markets, and spending hours agonizing over the choice of ice-cream flavours and special pizza toppings.

PRACTICAL ADVICE

If you are planning to bring your children to Rome, try to come in early spring or late autumn, when the weather is good, but not too hot. Easter is best avoided, as the city is more crowded than usual, and you're constantly jostled on packed buses and streets. Where you stay is crucial. A hotel near the Villa Borghese park will give your children plenty of chance to relax and let off steam, though you may end up spending a lot of time and money to get to and from the town centre. A hotel in the old centre is ideal, as you can easily pop back during the day for a rest and a clean bathroom.

Jogging in Villa Borghese

As hygienic toilets and changing facilities are rare within the city, it is really not advisable to bring a baby to Rome unless you are visiting friends or family. As with many historic cities, Rome may not instantly appeal to all children, but there is plenty to inspire their imaginations. Use this book to make the buildings and history come alive. Children might also enjoy learning a few Italian words and phrases so they can order food and buy things by themselves.

If lingering over drinks on the café terraces is what you enjoy best, bring your off-spring something to keep them busy once they have finished with their treat: crayons and paper, a computer game or a Walk-man. Alternatively, most other adults are very tolerant of children running around and making a noise while they relax and, if yours are reasonably outgoing, they could join in with the local children playing ball games in early evenings on piazzas like Campo de' Fiori.

If you feel the need for a total break, most hotels will be able to provide a baby-sitter or help you to contact a qualified childminding agency.

In the event of bad luck, see pages 378–9 for information on what to do and a list of emergency numbers.

Fairground in the Villa Borghese park

GETTING AROUND

Bumpy cobbles, narrow streets without pavements and over-crowded buses make pushing children around in pushchairs tiring work. Mothers with young children are, however, usually allowed to jump queues. Outside rush hours, the Metro is often less busy. Kids under 1 m (3 ft 3 in) tall travel free on public transport.

Although the city is not good for cyclists, families with older children could hire bikes to ride along the Tiber on the cycle tracks to the north of the city, or to take on a regional train into the country. The bikes, tandems and rickshaws for hire in Villa Borghese are good fun, and the bike hire hut in the Pincio gardens has free baby seats.

Anyone over the age of 14 is permitted to ride a scooter under 50 cc, although Rome is not the best place for novices *(see p394)*.

A hire bike with free baby seat

Pony-pulled trains in the Villa Borghese park

EATING OUT

Children are normally warmly welcomed in neighbourhood pizzerias and trattorias, and high chairs are often available for toddlers and babies. If there is no high chair, be prepared for the waiters to improvise for you with armloads of cushions or telephone directories. Most places are perfectly happy to serve half portions, or to let children share meals.

In trattorias it can sometimes be difficult to be exactly sure what a certain dish contains (especially when there is no menu and the dishes of the day are reeled off, usually at top speed, by the waiter), so faddy eaters are likely to be happier in pizzerias *(see pp328–33)*. Here they can choose their own topping (remember

that *prosciutto,* which is usually translated in menus as ham, is cured). The most entertaining pizzerias for kids are the old-fashioned ones where they can watch the chefs pound, stretch and flip the pizza dough. Restaurants open in the evening at or soon after 7pm and the best places get busy from around 8.30pm, so it is wise to go early to avoid having to queue.

PICNICS

Picnics in the parks are ideal, and shopping for the food is often half the fun. There is no problem finding small cartons of fruit juice and branded canned drinks, but these are expensive unless you go to a supermarket – the branch of Oviesse on Viale Trastevere is the most convenient.

Water from the drinking fountains is potable, so it is worth carrying plastic cups around with you.

As well as picnic food from bakeries and markets, there are lots of scrumptious takeaway foods. Many of them are appealingly messy, so it is wise to take paper tissues. Try deep-fried fruit and vegetables from Cose Fritte on Via di Ripetta and *supplì al telefono,* rice croquettes with a gooey string of mozzarella inside, from *pizza al taglio* or *pizza rustica* outlets. A *tramezzino* comes quite close to an English sandwich and if your kids are miserable without Marmite, you can find it (and other foreign foods) at Castroni on Via Cola di Rienzo.

Feeding pigeons on Piazza Navona

ICE CREAM

Rome, of course, is famous for ice cream; you and your children are likely to be tempted at every turn. Real ice-cream fans may even want to plan their day's sight-seeing round one of the best *gelaterie (see pp330–33)*. It is far cheaper to buy either a cone or tub of ice cream to eat in the street, but in some of the more traditional places it is worth paying to sit down. At Fassi, they have an old-fashioned ice cream-making machine on display and at Giolitti, you can enjoy gargantuan sundaes in the elegant parlour *(see p109)*.

Investigating some of the hundreds of Italian ice-cream flavours

Sightseeing with Children

Entrance to the Villa Borghese Zoo

GENERAL TIPS

Rome does not have many museums with the sort of hands-on exhibits that many other cities lay on for children. However, Bernini's marble elephant *(see p108)* and the fat *facchino*, or porter *(p107)*, appeal to kids. The Capuchin cemetery at Santa Maria della Concezione *(p254)*, the cata-combs *(pp264–6)* and the Mamertine Prison *(p91)* will grab the more ghoulish imagi-nations, and children will enjoy putting their hands into the Bocca della Verità *(p202)*.

Look for details like the dirty toenails on figures in Caravaggio's paintings, the Etruscan votives, which were offered to the gods, at the Villa Giulia *(pp262–3)*, and the illusory collapsing ceiling in the Chiesa Nuova as well as the fake dome of Sant' Ignazio di Loyola *(see p106)*.

Museums your children will enjoy include **Museo Explora**, full of interesting hands-on exhibits for children, and the Museo delle Mura, which explores a short length of the Aurelian Wall *(p196)*. Among the churches, St Peter's *(see p230)* and San Clemente *(see pp186–7)* are the most fun.

At the Vatican children will like the animal statues and mosaics in the Animal Gallery and also the Sistine Ceiling *(p246)*, especially once they know that Michelangelo had to paint it hunched up on a scaf-folding platform. Remember that Vatican dress etiquette *(see p231)* applies to kids too.

Museo Explora
Via Flamino 82. **Map** 1 C5. **Tel** 06-361 3776 *(book ahead)*. **www**.mdbr.it

ANCIENT RUINS

The ancient ruins best appreciated by children are the Colosseum *(see pp92–5)*, and Trajan's Markets *(see pp88–9)*. You can still make out what both these buildings looked like from their remains. The scant ruins of the Forum and Palatine, on the other hand, may not appeal so strongly. Ostia Antica, where the remains include a theatre, shop and 20-seater public toilet, is much more likely to interest them *(see pp270–71)*.

Mosaic from the Vatican

MOSAICS

There are scores of vivid, sometimes quirky, mosaics in buildings all over Rome. Many of these are particularly appealing to children. Details in the mosaics range from brilliantly coloured flowers, leaves, animals and buildings (in the churches of San Clemente, Santa Prassede and Santa Maria in Trastevere, *see p186, p171 and pp212–13*) to the debris of a banquet (in the Vatican's Museo Gregorio Profano, *see pp234–5*).

Miniature trains in Villa Borghese

ENTERTAINMENT

To find out what's on for children in Rome, scour the cinema pages of newspapers and the listings in *Trova-Roma, Roma c'è, Wanted in Rome* and entertainment websites *(see pp354–5)*. For older children, **Time Elevator** presents 3,000 years of Rome's history in an educational yet entertaining way. Most theatres and cinemas have reduced entry fees for children, but shows are often only in Italian.

There are cartoons shown at Villa Borghese's Cinema dei Piccoli and traditional puppet shows every afternoon, except Wednesday, on Janiculum hill.

An appealing time for children to be in Rome is over Christmas, when Piazza Navona hosts

Stall at the Christmas toy fair on Piazza Navona

Resting on the kerb side

a Christmas toy fair, where stalls sell toys and sweets.

Time Elevator
Via SS Apostoli 20. **Map** 5 A4 & 12 F3. **Tel** 06-9774 6243.

PARKS

Villa Borghese *(see p258)* has rowing boats to hire; pony-cart rides; bikes to rent; a mini cinema; a small funfair; and a zoo. Villa Celimontana *(see p193)* has bike trails, and open-air theatre performances in the summer. Technotown, a multimedia playhouse, in the grounds of Villa Torlonia is fun. At EUR *(see p266)* is the Piscina delle Rose, a swimming pool open in the summer *(see p367)*. The Bomarzo Monster Park, 95 km (60 miles) north of Rome, was built in the 16th century for a mad duke.

Children can clamber over its giant stone monsters.

TOYS

A visit to a Roman toyshop can be a lot of fun. **Città del Sole** sells educational toys and games, while **Al Sogno** is a dream come true for kids who love stuffed animals.

Città del Sole
Via della Scrofa 65. **Map** 4 F3 & 12 D2. **Tel** 06-687 5404.

Al Sogno
Piazza Navona 53. **Map** 4 E4 & 11 C3. **Tel** 06-686 4198.

CHILDREN'S CLOTHES

Italians adore dressing their children up, and on Sunday afternoons in particular, you are likely to encounter young children dressed as if they had walked straight out of a costume drama: girls in frills and flounces and boys in velvet breeches or knee-length shorts.

Many shops sell beautifully hand-crafted children's shoes and clothes – the downside is that they can often be expensive and impractical: dry-clean-only clothes are common and shoes are not made for mud.

Lavori Artigianali Femminili sells handmade silk and wool clothes for children up to eight. **Rachele** offers top-quality handmade clothes for children, while **Benetton** has more wallet-friendly smart casuals.

Benetton
Via del Corso 288. **Map** 4 F2. **Tel** 06-6810 2520.

Lavori Artigianali Femminili
Via Capo le Case 6. **Map** 5 A3 & 12 F1. **Tel** 06-679 2992.

Rachele
Vicolo del Bollo 6-7 (off Via del Pelle-grino). **Map** 11 C4. **Tel** 06-686 4975.

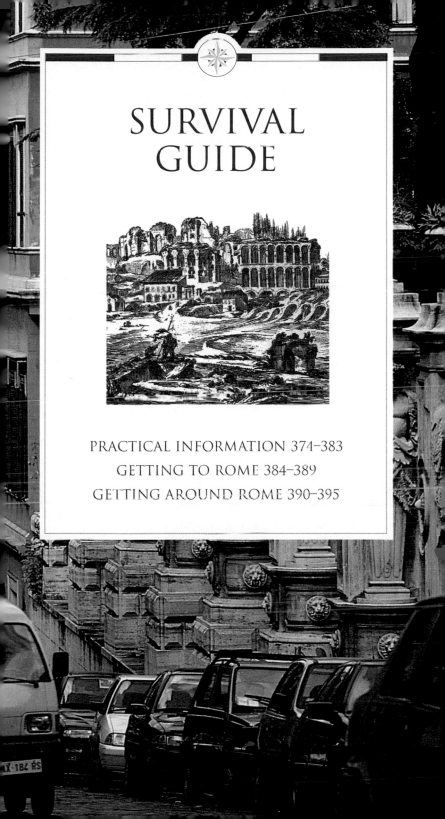

SURVIVAL
GUIDE

PRACTICAL INFORMATION

Romans often seem unconcerned by the priceless art treasures and ancient ruins which lie casually among the buildings and workings of their hectic 21st-century city. However, it's not always easy for visitors to make the most of these wonders; relaxed local attitudes make for dozens of variations in opening hours, and many places – including shops, banks and

Comune di Roma logo

offices – closed for 2 or 3 hours over lunch, reopening in the late afternoon. On a more positive note, most of the main sights are within easy walking distance of one another. Start your day early and wear comfortable shoes. Rome can be a delightfully informal city to visit, but remember to observe dress rules and cover up in churches, since this is one area where regulations are strictly enforced.

Steps heading to Michelangelo's Piazza del Campidoglio

WHEN TO GO

Rome enjoys a Mediterranean climate, with hot, dry summers and mild-to-cold, rainy winters. From late March to June and from September to October, the pleasant, sunny weather allows for plenty of time outdoors. Visitors can expect to pay more to stay during the high season, between March and November. In hot August, most Romans are on holiday and the smaller shops and restaurants are closed, but all tourist sights stay open, the city is quieter, and you can find good hotel deals.

VISAS AND PASSPORTS

Italy is part of the Schengen agreement, which means travellers moving from one Shengen country to another are not subject to border controls, although there are occasional spot checks.

All visitors to Italy must register with the police within

eight working days of arrival. If you are staying in a hotel, this will be done for you. Otherwise, contact the local *questura* (police station). European Union nationals and citizens of the US, Canada, Australia and New Zealand do not need visas for stays of up to three months.

Anyone wishing to stay for more than three months (eight working days for citizens from countries other than those mentioned above) will have to obtain a *permesso di soggiorno* (permit to stay). European Union citizens can apply for a permit at any main police station. Non-EU citizens must apply in advance in their home country for a permit to stay; it is very difficult for non-EU citizens to obtain a work permit. If you lose your passport contact your embassy *(see p377)*.

CUSTOMS INFORMATION

Duty-free allowances are as follows: non-EU citizens can bring into Italy: 200 cigarettes or 50 cigars or 100 cigarillos or 250 grams of tobacco, 1 litre of spirits or 2 litres of wine and 50 grams of perfume. EU residents do not need to declare goods, but random checks are often made to guard against any drugs traffickers. To find out what you can take back from Italy to a non-EU country, contact that country's customs department. The refund system for Value Added Tax (IVA in Italy) for non-EU residents is very complex *(see p335)*.

TOURIST INFORMATION

Information kiosks run by the Comune di Roma have English-speaking staff who provide free maps, leaflets

Tourist information sign

and advice. Alternatively ring their **Rome City Council Tourist Information Call Center** for information in English. The Center's useful website has detailed information on all the sights as well as on current exhibitions, events and hotels in the city. The **Italian Government Tourist Board (ENIT)** and the **American Express** office can also be helpful to visitors. A privately run company called **Enjoy Rome** has an informative website and offices situated close to the Termini railway station. A word of warning:

◁ **Heavy traffic in Via delle Quattro Fontane**

admission prices and opening times change often and sights can be closed for what seems to be unbelievably long periods for restoration (*chiuso per restauro*) or because of a strike (*sciopero*).

OPENING HOURS AND ADMISSION PRICES

Museums are generally open all day, although most close on Mondays and on some public holidays. Open-air sights such as the Forum are open daily year-round, closing 1 hour before sunset.

The three-day **Roma Pass** costs €25 and allows free transport within Rome, free entrance to two museums or archaeological sites, and discounts for various exhibitions, events and services. National and city museums offer entrance free of charge to EU passport-holders who are under 18 and over 65, and discounted entry for those aged between 18 and 25 with a valid student ID card.

Entrance to churches is free and many contain extraordinary works of art: keep in mind that you may be charged a small fee to see a certain area, such as a chapel, cloister or underground ruins.

Some of Rome's sights, such as Nero's Aqueduct and the Vatican gardens, are accessible only on personal application or by written appointment (*see below*). The *Area by Area* section of this guide gives opening times for each sight and tells you whether there is an admission charge.

The weekly supplement *Trova-Roma* (*see p383*) has a small English section with details of current exhibitions.

SIGHTSEEING PERMITS

To visit certain sights in Rome, you need to obtain a written permit and book your visit in advance, particularly for archaeological sites, which may sometimes be closed during excavations. Call the **Rome City Tourist Office** number on page 377, giving your name, the number of people in your party (individual visits are generally not possible) and when you would like to visit. You may then be asked to send written confirmation by email or fax.

SOCIAL CUSTOMS AND ETIQUETTE

Romans are generally courteous and friendly to foreign visitors. Italians are delighted at any effort to speak their language, so it is worth learning a few phrases (*see p447*). Italians tend to drink only with meals and are unlikely to be seen drunk – obvious drunkenness is frowned upon. Smoking is banned on public transport and in restaurants, bars and cafés.

VISITING CHURCHES

Many of Italy's churches are very dark, but they usually have electric, coin-operated light meters to illuminate chapels and works of art. Recorded information in several languages is also often available. Dress codes (*see below*) are firmly upheld in churches and should be respected; St Peter's (*see pp230–33*) is especially strict – you cannot wear shorts.

CATHOLIC SERVICES

For many Catholics, a visit to Rome means an audience with the pope. General audiences are usually held every Wednesday at 10.30am either in St Peter's Square, indoors at

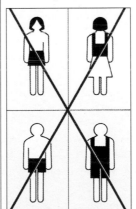
Unacceptable dress in church: both sexes should cover torsos, upper arms and legs

Pope Benedict XVI during an audience in St Peter's Square

the Sala Paolo VI or at Castel Gandolfo. To attend an audience, ring the **Prefettura della Casa Pontificia** (*see p231*) or go in person to the office through the bronze doors on the right of the colonnade in St Peter's Square (9am–1pm). Travel agencies can also arrange an audience as part of a coach tour.

Mass is held daily in the main churches of Rome (High Mass is on Sunday). Confession is heard in St Peter's (*see pp230–33*), San Giovanni in Laterano (*pp182–3*), San Paolo fuori le Mura (*p267*), Santa Maria Maggiore (*pp172–3*), the Gesù (*pp114–15*), Santa Sabina (*p204*) and Sant'Ignazio (*p106*). English-speaking Catholic churches include San Clemente (*see p187*) and Santa Susanna (*see p255*).

For details of non-Catholic services *see p377*.

TIPPING

Service is sometimes included in the bill at restaurants, bars and cafés. Italians usually tip a few euros if the service was good. It is not necessary to tip taxi drivers, though you should round up to the next euro. Keep small change handy for sacristans, cleaners, doormen and porters.

ACCESSIBILITY TO PUBLIC CONVENIENCES

Public toilets are few and far between. There are clean ones by the Colosseum (with facilities for the disabled) and at St Peter's. Most cafés will let you use theirs if you ask.

Disabled access sign at the Vatican

TRAVELLERS WITH SPECIAL NEEDS

Rome is not particularly well organized to cater for disabled visitors. The **Disabled Customer Assistance** centre at Termini station offers help and advice on train travel. Disabled travellers needing assistance getting on and off the train should book a special lift service 12 hours in advance, clearly stating the names of all the stations at which they require help. A limited number of buses and trams have wheelchair access and only a few metro stations have lifts. Ramps, lifts and modified WCs are available in an increasing number of places, including Termini station, although you may find a lift is broken down indefinitely, or a ramp is blocked by an illegally parked car. Some restaurants have wheelchair access to the dining area, but not to the WC.

If you are travelling without an escort to Rome, consider a specially designed package tour, or contact an organization for disabled travellers before you set off.

The Vatican Museums, Sistine Chapel and St Peter's are all accessible by wheelchair.

SENIOR TRAVELLERS

EU citizens over 65 have free entry to many museums, and discounts for *anziani* (elderly citizens) are available at most other sights and on some **Trenitalia** *(see p387)* tickets.

STUDENT INFORMATION

If you are an EU passport holder, it is worth having an International Student Identity Card (ISIC) or a Youth International Educational Exchange Card (YIEE) because you will receive reduced admission prices to national museums. Non-EU members with an ISIC or a YIEE card can also benefit from discounts at some private museums.

Contact the **Centro Turistico Studentesco** for general student information. The **Associazione Italiana Alberghi per la Gioventù** (the Italian YHA) operates four hostels across the city.

International Student Identity Card

GAY & LESBIAN TRAVELLERS

The main venue for Rome's gay community is the gay-friendly bar **Coming Out** *(see p363)*, near the Colosseum. The Gay Pride parade takes place in June. The two-month-long **Gay Village** event (one of Europe's largest gay festivals) begins in July. In Rome, displays of public affection between same sex individuals are not common, and some violence against homosexuals has been reported in the past.

ROME TIME

Rome is 1 hour ahead of Greenwich Mean Time (GMT). Examples of the time difference with Rome for other major cities are as follows: London: -1 hour; New York: -6 hours; Dallas: -7 hours; Los Angeles: -9 hours; Perth: +7 hours; Sydney: +9 hours; Auckland: +11 hours; Tokyo: +8 hours. These figures can vary slightly for brief periods during local changes in summer. For all official purposes, Italians use the 24-hour clock.

CONVERSION TABLE

Imperial to Metric
1 inch = 2.54 centimetres
1 foot = 30 centimetres
1 mile = 1.6 kilometres
1 ounce = 28 grams
1 pound = 454 grams
1 pint = 0.57 litres
1 gallon = 4.6 litres

Metric to Imperial
1 centimetre = 0.4 inches
1 metre = 3 feet 3 inches
1 kilometre = 0.6 miles
1 gram = 0.04 ounces
1 kilogram = 2.2 pounds
1 litre = 1.8 pints

ELECTRICAL ADAPTORS

Electric current in Italy is 220V AC, with two- or three-pin round-pronged plugs. Adaptors can be bought in most countries. Most hotels of three or more stars have hair dryers and shaving points in all bedrooms.

A Gay Pride march passing the Colosseum

RESPONSIBLE TOURISM

Rome is aware of the need to become more "green" and environmental initiatives are taking place across the city. Italian cookery has traditionally placed an emphasis on local seasonal food, but Italians are now also starting to understand the importance of reducing additives and carbon emissions. Choosing to eat local is a good way for visitors to support the area's economy, as well as helping the environment.

Organic shops and restaurants are springing up across Rome. A good place to buy regional food is **Spazio Bio**, inside the Città dell Altra Economia, a large expo space dedicated to the the promotion of an organic and

Shady terrace at Rome's Bed & Breakfast Bio

sustainable lifestyle, fair trade, ethical tourism and recycling (which still needs to improve in Rome). Those dreaming of greener nights can book a room in one of the mini boutique hotels and B&Bs offering an eco-friendly stay.

Two such establishments are **EcoHotel** and **Bed & Breakfast Bio**, both of which guarantee energy- and water-saving rooms, serve organic breakfasts and offer free bicycles for rides in the surrounding parks and natural reserves.

DIRECTORY

TOURIST INFORMATION

American Express
Piazza di Spagna 38.
Map 5 A2. **Tel** 06-676 41.

Enjoy Rome
Via Marghera 8A. **Map** 6 E3. **Tel** 06-445 1843.
www.enjoyrome.com

Italian Government Tourist Board
Via XX Settembre 26.
Map 5 B3. **Tel** 06-421 381. www.aptprovroma.it

Rome City Council Tourist Information Call Center
Termini Station (Platform 24). **Map** 6 D3. **Tel** 06-0608. www.060608.it

OPENING HOURS AND ADMISSION PRICES

Roma Pass
Tel 06-0608.
www.romapass.it

EMBASSIES

Australia
Via A. Bosio 5.
Tel 06-85 27 21.
www.italy.embassy.gov.au

Canada
Via Zara 30.
Tel 06-85 444 2911.
www.canada.it

New Zealand
Via Clitunno 44.
Tel 06-853 7501.
www.nzembassy.com

United Kingdom
Via XX Settembre 80A.
Map 6 D2.
Tel 06-4220 0001.
http://ukinitaly.fco.gov.uk

United States
Via Veneto 119A/121.
Map 5 B2. **Tel** 06-467 41.
www.usembassy.it

RELIGIOUS SERVICES

Anglican
All Saints, Via del Babuino 153. **Map** 4 F2.
Tel 06-3600 1881.

American Episcopal
St Paul's, Via Napoli 58.
Map 5 C3.
Tel 06-488 3339.

Jewish
Sinagoga (Tempio Maggiore), Lungotevere Cenci. **Map** 4 F5 & 12 D5.
Tel 06-684 0061.

Methodist
Via del Banco di Santo Spirito 3. **Map** 4 E3 & 11 A2. **Tel** 06-686 8314.

Muslim
The Mosque (Grande Moschea). Viale della Moschea 85 (Parioli district). **Map** 2 F1.
Tel 06-808 2258.

Prefettura della Casa Pontificia
Città del Vaticano. **Map** 3 B3. **Tel** 06-6988 3114.

Presbyterian
St Andrew's, Via XX Settembre 7. **Map** 5 C3.
Tel 06-482 7627.

TRAVELLERS WITH SPECIAL NEEDS

Disabled Customer Assistance
Termini Station (Platform 1). **Map** 6 D3.
Tel 199-30 30 60.

STUDENT INFORMATION

Associazione Italiana Alberghi per la Gioventù
Via Cavour 44. **Map** 3 D3.
Tel 06-487 1152.
Fax 06-488 0492.
www.aighostels.com

Centro Turistico Studentesco
Via Solferino 6A. **Map** 6 D3. **Tel** 06-462 0431.
Corso Vittorio Emanuele 297 **Map** 4 D3. **Tel** (06-687 2672). www.cts.it

GAY AND LESBIAN TRAVELLERS

Coming Out
Via San Giovanni, Laterano 8. **Map** 9 A1.
Tel 06-700 9871.
www.comingout.it

Gay Village
Parco del Turismo (EUR).
www.gayvillage.it

RESPONSIBLE TOURISM

Bed & Breakfast Bio
Via Cavalese 28.
Tel 335-7151 749.
www.bedandbreakfast bio.com

EcoHotel
Via di Bravetta 91.
Tel 06-6615 6920.
www.ecohotelroma.com

Spazio Bio
Città dell'Altra Economia Largo Dino Frisullo.
Map 8 D4. **Tel** 06-5728 9957. www.cittadellaltra economia.org

Personal Security and Health

FARMACIA
Pharmacy sign

On the whole, Rome is a safe, unthreatening place for visitors, but petty street crime is a problem. Do not carry more money than needed for the day and leave other valuables or documents in a hotel safe. Cameras are less likely to be snatched if they are in a carrier bag rather than an obvious case. Take particular care in crowded places, such as stations, or on full buses, and steer clear of bands of innocent-looking children – they may be skilful professional pickpockets.

Carabinieri in dress uniform

POLICE

There are several different police forces in Rome. The *polizia* (state police) wear blue uniforms with white belts and berets. They deal with all kinds of criminal offences and are the ones who issue *permessi di soggiorno* (residence permits) to foreigners and passports to Italian citizens *(see p374)*.

The *vigili urbani* (municipal police) wear blue uniforms in winter and white in summer, and can issue heavy fines for traffic and parking offences. They can usually be seen patrolling the streets, enforcing laws or regulating traffic.

The *carabinieri* (military police) wear red striped trousers. They deal with everything from fine-art thefts to speeding offences.

The *guardia di finanza* are the tax police and wear grey uniforms. They deal with tax evasion and with customs; you will see them at the airport, behind the "goods to declare" counter.

To report stolen or lost items, go to the nearest police station *(questura)* or *carabinieri* office. If you

believe your car may have been towed away, you should find a member of the *vigili urbani* on the streets or have the Comune put you through to them by calling 06-0606.

WHAT TO BE AWARE OF

Be wary of bag-snatchers on mopeds who operate in quiet streets. Carry your bag at your side away from the road, or carry a discreet money belt or a securely fastened, long-strapped shoulder bag across your body. Equipment like video cameras should be disguised. Pickpockets (sometimes children) adopt highly sophisticated distraction techniques with pieces of card or newspaper while they sever you from your possessions in seconds. Take extra care of your valuables in market places or on public transport. Bus routes 40 and 64, which run between Termini station and the Vatican, are notorious for pickpockets.

Thefts from cars are also rife. Jackets or bags should never be left visible inside a car parked on Rome's streets, and do not carry luggage on a roof rack. The streets to the east and south of Termini station are well-known for prostitution and drug-peddling, and are unsavoury at night.

Women travelling alone (or even in small groups) may need to take extra care. Women without male escorts attract more attention than they do in much of the rest of Europe and North America.

Beware of unauthorized minicab drivers who are probably not insured and frequently overcharge. They operate in particular at the airport and Termini station, waiting to profit from new arrivals. Hotel touts and unofficial tour guides are also best avoided; instead stick to the official tourist agencies *(see p295 and p377)*.

IN AN EMERGENCY

For emergency phone numbers see the Directory. For other medical attention, contact the First Aid *(Pronto Soccorso)* department of a main hospital such as **Policlinico Umberto I**, or **Ospedale di Santo Spirito**, or check the Yellow Pages *(Pagine Gialle)* for a doctor *(medico)* or dentist *(dentista)*. For children, the **Ospedale Pediatrico Bambino Gesù** is renowned. Emergency care in public hospitals is free, even for foreigners.

Municipal policeman directing traffic

Poliziotto – a member of the state police

Carabiniere – a member of the military police

Police car

Ambulance

Fire engine

LOST PROPERTY

For items lost on a bus or on the Metro, contact the numbers in the Directory. Otherwise, ask at a police station. To make an insurance claim, report your loss to a police station and get a signed form. For lost passports, contact your embassy or consulate (see p377); for lost credit cards or traveller's cheques, contact the issuing company's office (see p380).

HOSPITALS AND PHARMACIES

English-speaking doctors can be found at **Rome American Hospital** or by looking in the English Yellow Pages, which is available at some hotel receptions and international bookshops. For access to paediatricians, visit the **Ospedale Pediatrico Bambino Gesù**. The **Ospedale Odontoiatrico G Eastman** can help with serious dental problems.

Pharmacists display late-opening rosters (several stay open all night), and can usually supply the local equivalent of foreign medicines. The **Vatican Pharmacy** stocks some American and British pharmaceutical products. For minor problems, pharmacists can give advice and recommend over-the-counter medications.

MINOR HAZARDS

No inoculations are needed for Rome, but take mosquito repellent and sun screen in the summer. Be sure to wash your hands frequently if you use public transport, especially in winter when colds and flu are passed around easily. The Tiber is polluted but water from taps and potable street fountains is piped straight from the hills, and is fresh and palatable.

TRAVEL AND HEALTH INSURANCE

EU residents are officially entitled to reciprocal medical care, but the bureaucracy involved can be daunting. Before you travel, make sure you obtain the European Health Insurance Card (EHIC) from the UK Department of Health (www.dh.gov.uk) or a post office. The card comes with a booklet of advice and information on the procedure for claiming free medical treatment. All visitors should take out insurance to cover everything. When booking air travel, ask if there are any waivers included in your particular ticket for medical problems, death in the family or other emergencies.

Take out adequate property insurance before you travel (it is difficult to arrange once you are in Italy), and look after your belongings while you are in Rome. Be particularly careful when using public transport and when visiting crowded tourist sights, where pickpocketing is common. If possible, leave valuables at your hotel instead of carrying them around with you. Some hotels provide personal safes in the bedrooms. You can set these with your own memorable number. (Do not use your date of birth; it is on your passport and registration slip.) To be prepared for all

eventualities, it is advisable to keep a separate photocopy of vital documents, such as your passport and air tickets, to minimise the problem of replacing them if they are lost or stolen. It is also useful to take a spare passport-sized photograph or two.

DIRECTORY

IN AN EMERGENCY

Ambulance
Tel 118 (free from any telephone).

Fire
Tel 115 (free from any telephone).

General SOS
Tel 113 (free from any telephone).

Police
Tel 112 (Carabinieri); 113 (Police) (free from any telephone).

Samaritans
Tel 800-860 022.
Line open 1–10pm daily.

Traffic Police
Tel 06-676 91.

LOST PROPERTY

Buses and Trams
Tel 06-6769 3214.

Metro
Line A *Tel* 06-487 4309.
Open 9.30am–12.30pm Mon, Wed, Fri.
Line B *Tel* 06-4695 8165.
Open 7am–7pm Mon–Sat.

HOSPITALS AND PHARMACIES

Ospedale Odontoiatrico G Eastman
Viale Regina Elena.
Map 6 F2. *Tel* 06-844 831.

Ospedale Pediatrico Bambino Gesù
Piazza S. Onofrio 4.
Map 3 C4. *Tel* 06-68 591.

Ospedale di Santo Spirito
Lungotevere in Sassia 1.
Map 3 C3. *Tel* 06-683 51.

Policlinico Umberto I
Viale del Policlinico 155.
Map 6 F2. *Tel* 06-499 71.

Rome American Hospital
Via Emilio Longoni 69.
Tel 06-225 51.

Vatican Pharmacy
Via di Porta Angelica.
Map 3 C2. *Tel* 06-6989 0561.

Banking and Local Currency

Eagle sculpture on the Ministry of Finance

ATMs are easily found across Rome. Many businesses will accept credit cards, but some smaller family-run establishments still only accept cash. Exchanging money and traveller's cheques can involve a lot of paperwork. Banks and post office exchange rates are generally more favourable than those offered in travel agents. Carry some small change, since coins are needed for tips and illuminating works of art and chapels in churches *(see p375)*.

A branch of Banca d'Italia, one of the major Italian banks

BANKS AND BUREAUX DE CHANGE

It is best to have a few euros when you arrive, so you won't have to change money immediately. However, ATMs are found everywhere, including the airports.

For the best exchange rates, change money at a bank (look for the sign *Cambio*). Exchange offices and hotels tend to give poor rates, even if they charge modest commissions. At the Vatican Museums *(see p235)*, you won't be charged any commission. The American Express office *(see p377)* offers good rates and is open on Saturday mornings.

Queues in banks can be long and the form-filling involved in changing money can take up a lot of time. Take some form of identification with you, such as a passport. You may be asked to leave handbags, shopping bags and metal objects in the small lockers outside the bank.

Post offices also give good exchange rates, but queues can be long here as well.

Currency can only be changed at the main post offices, such as the one near Piramide Metro station.

Banks are usually open 8.30am–1.20pm and 3–4.30pm Mon–Fri, but opening times vary. They are always closed on public holidays.

Bureaux de change have more generous opening times, similar to shop hours. The two exchange offices at Termini station *(see p386)* are also open on Sundays.

ATMS

ATM machines (*Bancomat*) can be found throughout the city and accept a wide range of credit and debit cards. The daily limit for withdrawals is usually €250. A fee is charged for each withdrawal. ATM crime (mainly related to card cloning rather than to theft) has been reported in the past. Always use caution at an ATM machine: cover the hand that is typing the code with the other hand, and avoid withdrawing cash from any machine you are unsure about.

CREDIT CARDS AND TRAVELLER'S CHEQUES

Credit cards, which used to be regarded with great suspicion in Italy, are now much more widely accepted in hotels, restaurants and shops. All major credit and charge cards (American Express, MasterCard, Visa, Diners Club) are well known. Banks and cash dispensers are more likely to accept Visa cards for cash advances, but MasterCard is accepted by many retail outlets in Italy. Take both if you have them. Paying for anything in foreign currency will almost always be expensive.

Some restaurants and shops set a minimum expenditure level, below which they will not accept credit card payment. Ask first or check you have some cash just in case.

Traveller's cheques are not as popular as they used to be and tourists are finding it increasingly hard to cash or spend them. If you decide to use them, choose a well-known name such as American Express. Record the traveller's cheque numbers and refund addresses separately from the cheques themselves in case they are stolen.

DIRECTORY

BANKS AND BUREAUX DE CHANGE

Banca Intesa San Paolo
Via Condotti 61A. **Map** 5 A2.
Tel 06-697 6111. **Open** 8.35am–1.35pm, 2.45–4.15pm Mon–Fri.

Banca Nazionale del Lavoro BNL
Via Giovanni Lanza 194.
Map 5 C5. **Tel** 06-487 1955.
Open 8.20am–1.20pm, 3–4.30pm Mon–Fri.

LOST AND STOLEN CREDIT CARDS

American Express
Tel 06-7290 0347 or 800-914 912 (toll free).

Diners Club
Tel 800-864 064 (toll free).

Visa and MasterCard
Tel 800-819 014 (toll free).

THE EURO

The euro (€) is the common currency of the European Union. It went into general circulation on 1 January 2002, initially for 12 participating countries. Italy was one of those 12 countries.

The area comprising the EU member states using the euro as sole official currency is known as the eurozone. Several EU members have opted out of joining this common currency.

Euro notes are identical throughout the eurozone,

each one including designs of fictional architectural structures. The coins, however, have one side identical (the value side), and one side with an image unique to each country. Notes and coins are exchangeable in all participating euro countries.

Euro Bank Notes
Euro bank notes have seven denominations. The €5 note (grey in colour) is the smallest, followed by the €10 note (pink), €20 note (blue), €50 note (orange), €100 note (green), €200 note (yellow) and €500 note (purple). All notes show the stars of the European Union.

€5 note

€10 note

€20 note

€50 note

€100 note

€200 note

€500 note

€2 coin

€1 coin

50 cents

20 cents

10 cents

Coins
The euro has eight coin denominations: €1 and €2; 50 cents, 20 cents, 10 cents, 5 cents, 2 cents and 1 cent. The €2 and €1 coins are both silver and gold in colour. The 50-, 20- and 10-cent coins are gold. The 5-, 2- and 1-cent coins are bronze.

5 cents

2 cents

1 cent

Communications and Media

With the most recent advances in technology, it is easier and cheaper than ever to stay in touch with family and friends while abroad. Even if you don't have a mobile with Internet capabilities, you'll find that Wi-Fi and Internet cafés are everywhere in Rome, and phone cards offering very reasonable call rates abound. You can stay abreast of the news at home through BBC World (most likely available in your hotel) or the English-language publications available at many newsagents in the centre of Rome.

Telephone company logo

INTERNATIONAL AND LOCAL TELEPHONE CALLS

Privately owned "call centres" offer a convenient way of making private long-distance calls. They are equipped with several metered telephones in sound-proofed booths. An assistant will assign you a booth and meter your call. You pay at the desk when you have finished so coins are not needed. Call centres tend to be open from early morning until late night and many also offer fax, Internet and photocopying facilities.

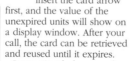

Public telephone sign

REACHING THE RIGHT NUMBER

• The code for Rome is 06 (obligatory also within the city).
• Multilingual directory enquiries is on 1254 (press 2).
• Operator assistance is on 170. Reverse charge and credit card calls are also accepted.
• Italian directory enquiries is on 1254 (press 1).
• To reach the operator in your own country to place a collect or credit card call dial 800 172 then: 441 for the UK; 444 for AT&T, US; 401 for Verizon, US; 405 for US Sprint; 610 for Telstra, Australia; and 611 for Optus, Australia.

In the wake of the mobile phone revolution, demand for public telephones has decreased considerably. However, there are some payphones around the city, mostly at train stations, metro stations and other main hubs. From these you can dial long-distance and most international calls direct. The newest phones take coins; the older ones only take telephone cards (ask for a *scheda telefonica*), available in several denominations. Telephone cards are sold in shops and tobacconists *(tabacchi)*. Break off the marked corner, insert the card arrow first, and the value of the unexpired units will show on a display window. After your call, the card can be retrieved and reused until it expires.

International phone cards, such as the Europa card, are by far the cheapest option if phoning abroad from Italy. They come in either €5 or €10 cards, which give 120 (or more) minutes of calling time. When using, dial the main number on the card, key in the pin code and then dial the number required.

Any Italian landline telephone number dialled needs to have the full relevant local code (including the zero) dialled in front of it, even if you are calling within the same city. Mobile phone number prefixes begin with a 3 and do not require a 0.

Keep in mind that telephone calls from hotel rooms are usually very expensive, sometimes marked up by as much as several hundred per cent.

MOBILE PHONES

If you are staying in Rome for a considerable period of time, it is probably worth buying an Italian SIM card, with its own unique telephone number, to use with your own mobile phone. You must show an official ID (such as a passport) when buying a SIM card. There are four main mobile providers: Vodafone, TIM, Tre and Wind. The SIM cards cost around €15 and usually come with €5 of free credit. They can be purchased, and topped up, from various mobile phone outlets throughout the city.

Once you have the SIM, you can also top up your credit with a scratch-off card *(ricarica)* bought at tobacconist's shops or some newsagents. Some tobacconist's shops have a computerized system where they insert your mobile number and put the credit on your phone for you, which is easier and quicker than following the instructions on the scratch-off card.

Internet café sign

INTERNET ACCESS

Many hotels now offer Internet connection or Wi-Fi access so you can access the Internet and email with your own laptop (often for an extra fee). There are also a number of Internet cafés (Italians call them *Internet point*) throughout Rome where you can go online and use email; some even offer headphones and webcams so customers can use Skype or other chat programs.

There are plenty of Internet cafés, found all around the city centre. Many Internet points have Wi-Fi so you can access the Internet through your laptop with a password provided by the assistant. An anti-terrorism law requires Internet café staff to take your information from an official ID (such as a passport), so staff may want to take a photocopy before allowing customers to use the Internet on their computers. This does not apply to customers using their own laptops.

Post office sign

POSTAL SERVICES

Post offices are multifunctional in Italy, used not only for postal services, but also for paying bills, managing certain bank accounts and more. Lines can be long and disorganized, so if you are just sending a regular letter or postcard, save yourself the exasperation and buy a stamp at a tobacconist's shop. Then drop your letter in the post boxes on walls around the city; most are red, with a slot for mail within Rome (*Roma e provincia di Roma*) and one for mail outside Rome (*per tutte le altre destinazioni*). There are also some blue post boxes exclusively for foreign destinations (marked *estero*).

The post itself is quite reliable and efficient, though it tends to be slower around

Vatican post office sign

Vatican postage stamps

Christmas time. For urgent items, use the post office's express or registered service.

The Italian post office offers a *poste restante* service, where letters and parcels addressed to you can be picked up directly at the post office. Post should be sent care of (*c/o*) *Fermo Posta* and the name of the relevant post office. Print the surname clearly in block capitals and underline it to make sure it is filed correctly. To collect your post, you have to show your passport and pay a small charge.

Regular post office hours are generally from around 8.30am to 2pm (8.30am to noon on Saturdays and on holiday eves), but main offices stay open until well into the evening for some services (such as registered post).

NEWSPAPERS, TV, RADIO

Rome's main newspapers are *La Repubblica* and *Il Messaggero*. British and American newspapers are readily available, with the *International Herald Tribune* and the *Guardian* on sale on the day of issue. The *Trova-Roma* supplement, in the Thursday edition of *La Repubblica*, and the weekly magazine *Roma c'è* are the main guides to what's on. The magazines *Wanted in Rome*, *The Roman Forum* (www.theromanforum.com) and *Where Rome* (www.whererome.it) also have English listings. Some of these publications also have websites full of information.

The state TV channels are RAI Uno, Due and Tre, matched by four private channels. Analogue TV has been replaced by digital across the region, so all TVs

VATICAN POST

The Vatican postal service costs the same as the state post, but is faster. Buy cards and stamps at the post office near the Vatican Museums entrance, or in Piazza San Pietro. Letters bearing Vatican stamps can only be posted within the Vatican city.

Foreign papers at a newsstand

must now have a digital decoder to pick up any channels; with the decoder, you can access these basic Italian networks, plus some other channels including BBC World in English.

Vatican Radio transmits on 93.3MHz and 105MHz (FM) and also broadcasts news in English.

DIRECTORY

INTERNET CAFES

Bibli
Via dei Fienaroli 28. **Map** 7 C1.
Tel 06-581 4534.
Open 5.30pm–midnight Mon, 11am–midnight Tue–Sun.

Internet Café
Via Cavour 213. **Map** 5 C5.
Tel 06-4782 3051.
Open 11am–1am Mon–Fri, 3pm–1am Sat & Sun.

Internet Train
Via Marrucini 12. **Map** 8 F3.
Tel 06-445 4953.
Open 10am–11.30pm Mon–Sat, 3pm–11.30pm Sun.

Interpoint YX
Piazza Sant'Andrea della Valle 3.
Map 12 D4. **Tel** 06-9727 3136.
Open 10am–10pm daily. Also:
Corso Vittorio Emanuele 106.
Map 12 D3. **Tel** 06-4542 9818.
Open 11am–8pm daily.

POST OFFICES

Termini Station, Via Marsala 39.
Map 6 D3. **Tel** 06-488 0673.
Open 8am–7pm Mon–Fri, 8am–1.15pm Sat.

Piazza San Silvestro 19.
Map 5 A3. **Tel** 06-6973 7213.
Open 8am–7pm Mon–Fri, 8am–1.15pm Sat.

GETTING TO ROME

Many national airlines, including Italy's Alitalia, fly direct to Rome from most European cities and several in North America. Fiumicino airport now has a high-security terminal, Terminal 5, for flights to the US and Israel. Ciampino airport is smaller and mainly caters to low-cost airlines flying in from other European cities.

Alitalia aircraft

Rome also has train and coach links with the rest of Europe. These take a lot longer than flights (about 24 hours from London, for example, compared with about 2½ hours by air), but tend to cost about the same, so are only really worthwhile if you want to travel overland. The trains are often crowded during the summer.

ARRIVING BY AIR

If you are flying from the United States, **Delta**, **United**, **US Airways** and **Alitalia** operate regular direct scheduled flights to Rome, with services from New York. Flying time is about 8½ hours. **Air Canada** and **Qantas** operate from Canada and Australia respectively. There are also direct flights from Boston, Atlanta, Miami, Philadelphia and Toronto. However, it may be considerably cheaper for intercontinental travellers to take a budget flight to London, Paris, Athens, Frankfurt or Amsterdam and continue the journey to Rome from there. **British Airways** and Alitalia both operate direct scheduled flights from London Heathrow to Rome (Fiumicino), and you can also fly from Gatwick. **Swiss** and **KLM** also fly to Rome from London and other British cities. A change in Zurich or Amsterdam is usually involved.

Excursion fares generally offer the best value in scheduled flights, but you must purchase them well in advance. They are subject to penalty clauses if you cancel, so it is advisable to take out insurance as soon as you buy your ticket.

In addition to BA and Alitalia, you can book low-cost tickets direct from airlines **easyJet** and **Ryanair**, which have daily flights from London and other locations to Rome. Hotels and car rental can also be booked via these airlines' websites, and both offer their own privately chartered bus to transport incoming passengers from Ciampino airport to Termini.

Alitalia flight tickets

Regular charter flights for Rome's Ciampino airport run all year round. Most leave from Stansted, Gatwick and Luton, but there are also a few flights that leave from Manchester, Glasgow and Birmingham. The price of fares varies, peaking in summer and in Holy Week for the Pope's Easter blessing. In Rome, the American Express travel office (*see p377*) will also book flights.

FIUMICINO AIRPORT

Rome has two international airports. Leonardo da Vinci – known as Fiumicino – is the largest one and handles most scheduled flights, as well as several easyJet routes. It is located about 30 km (18 miles) southwest of the city and has four terminals: 1 for domestic flights, 2 for EU flights, 3 for international flights and 5 for flights to the US or Israel. The vast shopping area inside the airport offers a variety of stores, selling the most important Italian brands.

From Fiumicino there are two types of train to Rome:

Part of the extension to Fiumicino airport

Check-in area at Fiumicino, Rome's main international airport

one (€5.50) runs every 15–30 minutes (5.57am–11.27pm) to Fara Sabina station, stopping at Trastevere, Ostiense, Tuscolana and Tiburtina, but not Termini. The other train, known as the "Leonardo Express", is faster and more expensive (€11), running non-stop to Termini every half-hour (6.36am–11.36pm). If the ticket office is not open, try the automatic ticket machine (you can choose to see the instructions in English). Remember to specify which train you want when buying your ticket.

Ostiense station is linked with Piramide Metro (Line B) where you can catch an underground train to the city centre from 5.30am until 11.30pm daily (to 1.30am Fri and Sat). It can be hard to find a taxi at Ostiense after 9pm, but there are buses (Nos. 95 and 30) to Piazza Venezia. At night there is a coach service from Fiumicino to Tiburtina station. Car rental is available from offices at the airport (see p395).

Train linking Fiumicino airport to Stazione Termini

CIAMPINO AIRPORT

The other airport that serves Rome is Giovanni Battista Pastine Airport, known as Ciampino. It is located approximately 20 km (12½ miles) southeast of the city and used by the majority of charter flights and low-cost airlines. Ciampino airport is always busy and sometimes chaotic, so it is advisable to arrive

Check-in area at Rome's Ciampino airport

there well in advance of your departure time.

Major car hire firms have a rental office at the airport (see p395), though you may find it less harrowing to travel into the city centre on public transport or by taxi.

The swiftest way to get to the centre of Rome is by the private **Terravision**, **Atral/Schiaffini** or **SITBusShuttle** coach services. Coaches go direct to Termini station and tickets cost between €4 and €6 one way. You can buy them on board the bus. A cheaper option is by **COTRAL** bus to Anagnina Metro station, then by underground train to Termini. Tickets (€1, plus €1 for each large bag) can be bought on the bus. A local bus service also links the airport to Ciampino mainline station.

AIRPORT TAXIS

Always use the official white taxis with a "taxi" sign on the roof. They usually line up in the yellow TAXI lanes in front of the airports and stations. The Rome Comune recently established a flat fee for taxi rides from and to the airports: €40 to/from Fiumicino from/to anywhere in the centre (inside the Aurelian walls) and €30 to/from Ciampino from/to the centre. The fare covers a maximum of four people with baggage included. If a taxi refuses to apply the flat fee, you should report the driver by calling 06-6710 70721 and stating the cab number, which is found on both the inside and the outside of the car.

DIRECTORY

ARRIVING BY AIR

Air Canada
Tel 06-8351 4955.
www.aircanada.com

Alitalia
www.alitalia.com

British Airways
Tel 199 712 266.
www.britishairways.com

Delta
www.delta.com

easyJet
www.easyjet.com

KLM
www.klm.com

Qantas
Tel 848 350 010.
www.qantas.com

Ryanair
www.ryanair.com

Swiss
www.swiss.com

United Airlines
www.united.com

US Airways
Tel 8488 13177.
www.usair.com

FIUMICINO & CIAMPINO AIRPORTS

Atral (Ciampino)
Tel 800 700 805 (toll free).
www.atral-lazio.com

COTRAL Spa (both airports)
Tel 800 174 471 (toll free).
www.cotralspa.it

SITBusShuttle (both airports)
Tel 06-5916 826, 06-5923 507.
www.sitbusshuttle.it

Terravision (Ciampino)
www.terravision.eu

Arriving in Rome by Train, Coach or Car

Any overland journey to Rome is fastest by train, though there are coach connections to most major European cities. Within Italy, journeys between large cities are usually also best done by train, but when travelling from towns which are not on the main Intercity rail routes, coaches can be quicker. For drivers, the **Italian Automobile Club** *(see p387)* provides free assistance and excellent maps to members of affiliated automobile clubs from all over the world.

A Eurostar train

The concourse at Stazione Termini

STAZIONE TERMINI

Stazione Termini, Rome's main train station, is also the hub of the urban transport system. Beneath it is the only interchange between the city's two Metro lines, and outside, on Piazza dei Cinquecento, is the central bus terminus. Though it is one of Rome's most stunning 20th-century buildings, it also has some unsavoury aspects, so don't linger longer than necessary at night.

If you do arrive here late, there are usually taxis available (go to the official queue) even in the small hours, and many of the city's night buses start at Termini.

In summer the station gets crowded, and you can expect long queues. Termini has a left luggage office, a police station, a bureau de change, and tourist and travel information offices. Other facilities include many tobacconists and newsagents (where you can buy bus and Metro tickets), as well as various bars and restaurants on the mezzanine floor, with more eateries and shops, including a bookstore, on the lower Termini Forum level. A post office is adjacent to platform 24, as are desks for car-hire firms. There is only one waiting room, located next to platform 1.

Of Rome's other stations, four are most likely to be of interest to tourists. They are Ostiense and Trastevere, for trains to Fiumicino airport and Viterbo *(see p271)*; Tiburtina, for some of the late-night trains on the north-south line through Italy; and Roma Nord, for trains to Prima Porta.

Trenitalia logo

TRAVELLING BY TRAIN

Trenitalia, the Italian State Railway, has several levels of service, including the Regionale trains. These stop at almost every station, often have no air conditioning and are much cheaper than the other trains. Regionale trains have a coach-like seating arrangement, and sometimes first-class seats are "declassed" so second-class ticket holders can sit there. The Eurostar, a newer, cleaner, faster train, offers a first- and second-class service. It runs between Rome and Milan, Turin, Genoa, Bari, Naples and Venice, with an extra fast *(alta velocità)* service called TBIZ operating on the Naples-Rome-Milan line. You have to reserve a seat and you are charged hefty supplements for the privileges of speed and hostess service. Intercity trains, which are for fast long-distance journeys, also charge a supplement. First- and second-class tickets are available from Rome to Venice, Milan, Florence, Naples and other cities. From Rome you can also take international or Eurocity (EC) trains to destinations all over Europe.

Reservations are compulsory on all trains

Termini, the heart of Italy's rail network and Rome's transport system

except the Regionale ones. Tickets for immediate travel can be bought at the station, but you should allow plenty of time to queue.

The Trenitalia website *(see below)* is useful for planning trips, checking scheduled train times and buying tickets. If you book in advance or are a family with a child, you may be able to get a cheaper rate. However, it is easiest to go to a travel agency when trying to book a discounted ticket because Trenitalia's offers and fares change all the time.

An Intercity train

TRAVELLING BY COACH

Long-distance coaches terminate at Tiburtina, which is the city's main coach station. Information and tickets for European coaches to European cities are available from **Lazzi Express**. The **Appian Line** offers regular services within Italy. Its itineraries include Florence, Naples, Capri, Sorrento and Pompei, and, in summer, Venice and Assisi. Local buses, serving villages and towns within the Lazio region, are run by **COTRAL**. All bus stations used by COTRAL in Rome are linked to Metro stations. Tickets are purchased on the spot and cannot be booked in advance. Some day trips from Rome by bus are described on pages 268–71.

Eurolines coach connecting Rome with the rest of Europe

MACHINES FOR TRENITALIA RAIL TICKETS

These machines are easy to use, and most have instructions on screen in a choice of six languages. They accept coins, notes and debit/credit cards.

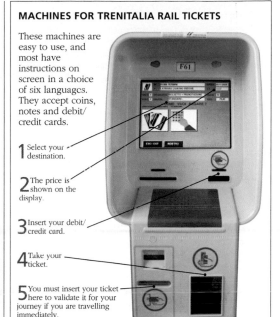

1 Select your destination.

2 The price is shown on the display.

3 Insert your debit/credit card.

4 Take your ticket.

5 You must insert your ticket here to validate it for your journey if you are travelling immediately.

TRAVELLING BY CAR

To drive your own car in Italy you need your driving licence, an international Green Card (for insurance purposes) and the vehicle registration document. A translation of your driving licence, available at Italian tourist offices abroad, is useful. Wearing seatbelts is compulsory in Italy. You must also carry a warning triangle and a reflective orange or yellow vest to wear if you leave your car in case of breakdown. Main routes to Rome connect with the Grande Raccordo Anulare (GRA), Rome's ring-road. Tolls are charged on all Italian motorways. You get a ticket by pressing the red button at the toll booth as you enter the motorway and pay when you leave by presenting the ticket to the person in the booth. Prices vary on the different roads. Official speed limits are 30–50 km/h (18–30 mph) in town, 80–110 km/h (50–70 mph) on two-lane roads outside town, and 130 km/h (90 mph) on motorways.

DIRECTORY

TRAVELLING BY TRAIN

Trenitalia
Tel 89 20 21. www.trenitalia.com

TRAVELLING BY COACH

Appian Line
www.appianline.it

COTRAL
www.cotralspa.it

EUROLINES
www.eurolines.com

Lazzi Express
www.lazziexpress.it

BREAKDOWN SERVICE

Automobile Club d'Italia
Tel 803116.

Arriving in Rome

This map shows the main bus, rail and Metro links used by travellers arriving in Rome. The connections between Rome's two airports and the city centre are shown, as well as links between Rome and the rest of Italy and international rail routes from neighbouring European countries. Travel information, including details of journey times and service frequency, is listed separately in each box.

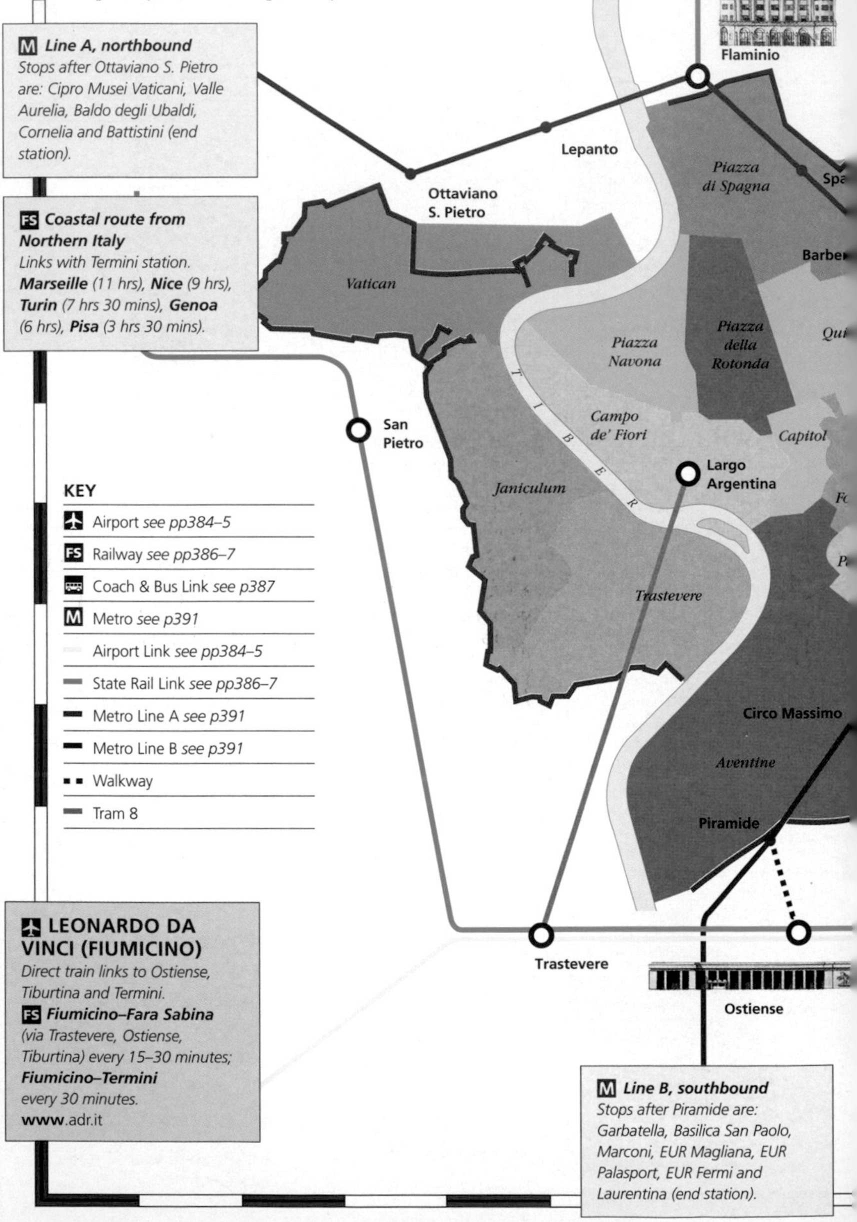

FS National connections
*Links to Flaminio from **Viterbo** (2 hrs), **Bracciano** (70 mins).*

M Line A, northbound
Stops after Ottaviano S. Pietro are: Cipro Musei Vaticani, Valle Aurelia, Baldo degli Ubaldi, Cornelia and Battistini (end station).

FS Coastal route from Northern Italy
*Links with Termini station. **Marseille** (11 hrs), **Nice** (9 hrs), **Turin** (7 hrs 30 mins), **Genoa** (6 hrs), **Pisa** (3 hrs 30 mins).*

Flaminio

Lepanto

Ottaviano S. Pietro

Piazza di Spagna

Spa[...]

Barbe[...]

Vatican

Piazza Navona

Piazza della Rotonda

Qui[...]

San Pietro

Campo de' Fiori

Largo Argentina

Capitol

Janiculum

Fo[...]

Trastevere

P[...]

KEY

✈	Airport *see pp384–5*
FS	Railway *see pp386–7*
🚌	Coach & Bus Link *see p387*
M	Metro *see p391*
	Airport Link *see pp384–5*
	State Rail Link *see pp386–7*
	Metro Line A *see p391*
	Metro Line B *see p391*
▪ ▪	Walkway
	Tram 8

Circo Massimo

Aventine

Piramide

✈ LEONARDO DA VINCI (FIUMICINO)
Direct train links to Ostiense, Tiburtina and Termini.
FS Fiumicino–Fara Sabina
(via Trastevere, Ostiense, Tiburtina) every 15–30 minutes;
Fiumicino–Termini
every 30 minutes.
www.adr.it

Trastevere

Ostiense

M Line B, southbound
Stops after Piramide are: Garbatella, Basilica San Paolo, Marconi, EUR Magliana, EUR Palasport, EUR Fermi and Laurentina (end station).

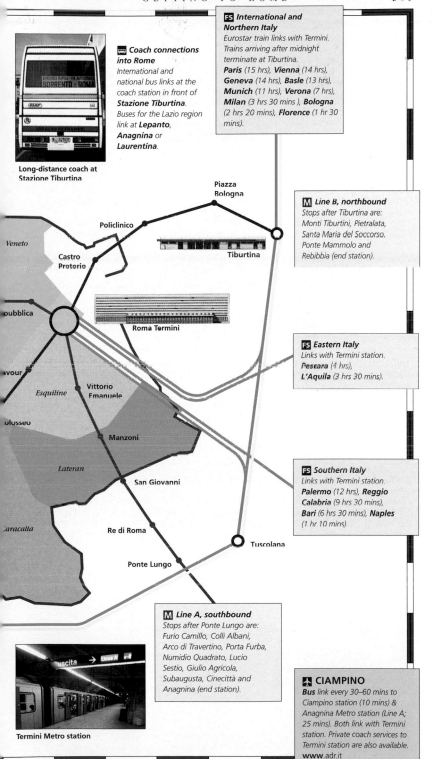

🚌 Coach connections into Rome
International and national bus links at the coach station in front of **Stazione Tiburtina**. Buses for the Lazio region link at **Lepanto**, **Anagnina** or **Laurentina**.

Long-distance coach at Stazione Tiburtina

FS International and Northern Italy
Eurostar train links with Termini. Trains arriving after midnight terminate at Tiburtina. **Paris** (15 hrs), **Vienna** (14 hrs), **Geneva** (14 hrs), **Basle** (13 hrs), **Munich** (11 hrs), **Verona** (7 hrs), **Milan** (3 hrs 30 mins), **Bologna** (2 hrs 20 mins), **Florence** (1 hr 30 mins).

Piazza Bologna

Policlinico

Veneto

Castro Pretorio

Tiburtina

M Line B, northbound
Stops after Tiburtina are: Monti Tiburtini, Pietralata, Santa Maria del Soccorso, Ponte Mammolo and Rebibbia (end station).

Roma Termini

pubblica

avour

Esquiline

Vittorio Emanuele

olosseo

Manzoni

Lateran

San Giovanni

aracalla

Re di Roma

Ponte Lungo

Tuscolana

FS Eastern Italy
Links with Termini station. Pescara (4 hrs), **L'Aquila** (3 hrs 30 mins).

FS Southern Italy
Links with Termini station. **Palermo** (12 hrs), **Reggio Calabria** (9 hrs 30 mins), **Bari** (6 hrs 30 mins), **Naples** (1 hr 10 mins)

M Line A, southbound
Stops after Ponte Lungo are: Furio Camillo, Colli Albani, Arco di Travertino, Porta Furba, Numidio Quadrato, Lucio Sestio, Giulio Agricola, Subaugusta, Cinecittà and Anagnina (end station).

Termini Metro station

✈ CIAMPINO
Bus link every 30–60 mins to Ciampino station (10 mins) & Anagnina Metro station (Line A; 25 mins). Both link with Termini station. Private coach services to Termini station are also available. **www**.adr.it

GETTING AROUND ROME

Rome's centre is compact and, even though walking absolutely everywhere would be over-ambitious, it is a city in which you can spend much of your time on foot. As the main streets in the centre are usually clogged with traffic, driving and cycling cannot be recommended, but courageous motorbike or scooter riders can have great fun buzzing

Scooter riders wearing safety helmets

around on a rented Vespa. Travelling by bus and tram can be very slow, so use overland public transport only when you have a long way to go. The Metro, designed to connect the suburbs with the centre, has no stops in the historic city centre near the Pantheon or Piazza Navona, though it is certainly the swiftest way of crossing the city.

GREEN TRAVEL

As the largest and most advanced city of the ancient world, Rome was the first to face (and combat) air pollution from burning wood. The fight against smog continues today, as many Romans rely exclusively on their cars. Car-sharing schemes, city-owned bicycles and some (but not enough) bike lanes, **electric-car charging stations**, and car-free Sundays (in the springtime) are among the initiatives. Video cameras prevent unauthorized cars from entering the *centro storico*, where many bus lines (three of which are electric) cover almost everything there is to see. Though often busy and chaotic, public transportation is always a better option than driving, and some used bus tickets will buy you discounted entry to selected exhibitions (see instructions

FERMATA

Bus stop listing details of routes served

on the ticket itself). Walking around the centre is pleasant, so if you want to enjoy the warm sunshine and avoid public transport, make sure you wear sturdy, comfortable shoes.

BUSES AND TRAMS

Rome's public transport company is called **ATAC** (Azienda Tramvie e Autobus del Comune di Roma). Scores of buses and a few trams cover most parts of the city. Most run from early morning until midnight, meaning the last bus leaves from the end of the line at midnight. There are also a few night buses.

Apart from some small electric minibuses (like the 116 and 119), no buses can run through the narrow streets of the historic centre. But there are plenty of bus routes to take you within a short walk of the main sights *(see inside back cover)*.

Bus stops list the details of routes taken by all buses using that stop. Night buses are indicated by an "N" before the number.

There are several trams in the city but the only main line of tourist interest is the 8, which runs from Torre Argentina to Casaletto, going through Trastevere and Monteverde.

SPECIAL BUS SERVICES

There are two tourist bus services; the 110 and the Archeobus service. The 110, a red, open-topped double-decker, is a hop-on hop-off service, which passes many of the city's tourist attractions. It leaves from Piazza dei Cinquecento every 20 minutes between 8.30am and 8.30pm. Linking the centre with the catacombs and the monuments on the Via Appia Antica, the Archeobus leaves Piazza Venezia every half-hour between 8.30am and 4pm.

USING BUSES AND TRAMS

The main terminus is on Piazza dei Cinquecento outside Termini station, but there are other major route hubs throughout the city, most usefully those at Piazza del Risorgimento, Piazza San Silvestro and Piazza Venezia. Information on public transport can be obtained from ATAC kiosks, the customer service office or the ATAC website. You should board the bus at the front or the back; the central door is

A modern tram taking passengers through the city

One of Rome's red and grey ATAC buses

reserved for people getting off. You must stamp your ticket in the yellow machine once you get on the bus. Timed tickets, *biglietto integrato a tempo* (BIT), can be used on all means of transport.

TICKETS

Tickets for buses, trams and Metros should be bought in advance and stamped in the appropriate machine as soon as you start your journey. You can buy tickets at bars, some newsagents and tobacconists, as well as in Metro stations and at bus termini. There are automatic ticket machines at main bus stops and Metro stations

that take coins. Some buses have a machine on board for buying tickets, but there is no way of knowing which buses have one, so purchase a ticket before you board.

BIT tickets are valid for 75 minutes, during which time you can take one Metro ride and as many buses and trams as you like. If you are going to make four or more journeys in one day, buy a daily (BIG) ticket. There are also three-day, seven-day and monthly passes. To travel farther afield in Lazio, consider buying a regional DIRO ticket. Fare-dodging incurs a hefty on the spot fine.

Metro logo

METROPOLITANA

Rome's underground system, the Metropolitana, has two lines (A and B) which cross the city in a rough X-shape, converging at Termini station *(see inside back cover)*. Line A (red) leads from Battistini in the west to Anagnina in the southeast of the city, from where buses go to Ciampino airport. Line B (blue) runs from Rebibbia in the northeast, down to EUR in the southwest, where buses leave for the coast. Stations are clearly marked by the Metro logo, a white M on a red background. Among the most useful stations are Colosseo, Spagna, San Giovanni, Ottaviano S. Pietro and Piramide (for trains to Fiumicino). Both lines run from 5.30am until 11.30pm every day (to 1.30am Friday and Saturday). For more details, visit www.atacoroma.it. A third Metro line, C, is scheduled to open in 2015. A fourth line is also planned.

USEFUL BUS ROUTES

This map shows some of the buses that go through interesting parts of Rome with good views of major sights. The 40 Express is always full of tourists, since it goes from Termini to St Peter's and the Vatican. The other routes are likely to be less crowded.

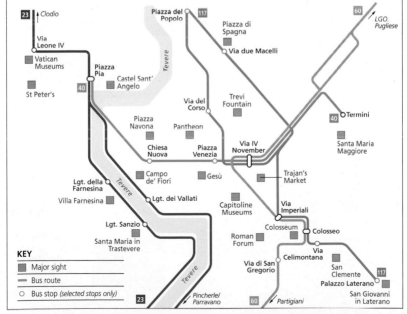

WALKING

Wandering through Rome's old centre is one of the most enjoyable aspects of the city. You can take in the architectural details, absorb the streetlife, make diversions at will, and peek into any church, shop or bar that catches your interest. You can easily visit several of the main tourist sights in a few hours.

Explore the city area by area, using public transport when distances are too far. Although some parts of the historic centre are now pedestrianized, a street which is closed to cars may still be used by cyclists and, illegally, by scooter riders. There have been many plans to create more traffic-free zones, but imposing such measures on a population as insubordinate as Rome's is not easily done.

During the height of summer, you'll have a more enjoyable time if you follow the example of the Italians. Walk slowly on the shady side of the street; have a long lunch followed by a siesta in the hottest part of the day. Continue exploring in the late afternoon, when churches and shops reopen and the streets are at their liveliest. Wandering at night is delightful, as the streets are cool and many façades floodlit.

Passengers sightseeing on an open-top tour bus

lights and pedestrian crossings strictly in your favour, there is sure to be some van or Vespa hurtling toward you with apparently homicidal intent. Fortunately, Roman drivers have quick reactions and accidents are relatively rare. The best tactic is to be as alert and confident as Romans. The roads are very busy. When crossing, you should try to leave as large a gap as possible between yourself and oncoming traffic. Step purposefully into the road, making eye contact with approaching motorists, and don't hesitate or change your course. Once a driver sees that you are determined to cross, he will stop, or at least swerve. Pedestrians must take particular care at night, when the traffic lights are switched to a constantly flashing amber, turning the crossings into free-for-alls.

STREET SIGNS

Theoretically, although it may not always seem to be the case, pedestrians have right of way at crossings when the green *avanti* sign is lit up. The red sign *alt* means you must wait. Underground crossings are indicated by a sign reading *sottopassaggio*.

It is easy to get lost in the maze of streets and piazzas of the historic centre. Until you know your way around you can follow the yellow signs marking routes between the sights

and piazzas of particular interest to tourists. Routes leading to other landmarks are indicated by signs on a brown or grey background.

GUIDED TOURS

Several companies offer guided tours in English; these include American Express (*see p373*), **Green Line Tours**, **Context** and **Carrani Tours**. Full-day city tours including lunch cost around €75; half-day tours around €35. Alternatively the **No. 110 Bus** passes many of the main sights on a 2-hour circuit. Tickets cost around €20 and the bus leaves from Termini every 20 minutes between 8.30am and 8.30pm; the website has further details as well as information on the

Directions for walkers

Nuns walking in Rome's city centre

CROSSING ROADS

First impressions suggest there can be only two sorts of pedestrian in Rome: the quick and the dead. Even if you cross roads by traffic

Avanti: go! Pedestrians have right of way

Alt: stop! Traffic has right of way

Watch out for children

Pedestrian crossing

Archeobus tours of the ancient monuments. Tour guides can often be hired at major sights, such as the Roman Forum *(see pp78–87)*. Employ only official guides and establish the fee in advance; they usually charge around €50 for a half-day tour.

DRIVING

Driving in Rome can be an extremely intimidating experience for visitors. The flamboyant aggression of Italian drivers is notorious, pedestrians step out into the roads without warning, and the one-way system operating in much of the centre makes retaining a sense of direction impossible. You'll also find motorists overtaking on the wrong side, while scooters and Vespas zoom among the lanes of traffic and go the wrong way down one-way streets. One rule to remember is to give way to the right. Additionally, non-resident drivers cannot enter the city centre's ZTL (Limited Traffic Zone) during the day and on some weekend nights. There are cameras at the entrance of the ZTL, and cars without a permit will receive a fine each time they pass in front of the camera. The cameras are very visible, and there is always an electronic sign saying whether access is open to everyone *(varco aperto)* or restricted *(varco chiuso)*. You can call

No stopping

continua

No parking

One-way street

strada senza uscita

No through road

06-570036 or check www.atacmobile.it for ZTL times. Unless you are accustomed to driving in Italian cities and fully aware of the ZTL regulations and zones, leave your car at home – or, failing that, in a guarded car park.

Thefts from cars are rife in Rome, so never leave anything of value in your vehicle, even out of sight: areas such as Campo de' Fiori are patrolled by gangs on the lookout for anyone leaving cameras and other costly items in the car. You should

also remove the car radio and Sat Nav if you can – you won't be the only person carrying these with you.

Take extra care if driving late at night. Not only do traffic lights switch to flashing amber, but some drivers are astonishingly cavalier about driving under the influence of drink or drugs. In case of a breakdown, call the **ACI** *(see pp394 & 395)*.

PARKING

The most convenient car park is below the Villa Borghese. Much of the city centre is reserved for residents with permits but there are around 2,000 metered parking spaces marked with a blue line (from 8am–8pm or 8am–11pm, depending on the area). If you do find a legal place to park, however, you may return and find that you have been hemmed in by double-parked cars. Locations of some of the most useful car parks are listed on page 395.

Beware of illegal parking attendants, found especially at night in busy areas where parking is free, who direct you to a space (sometimes even an unauthorized one) in exchange for some change. This practice is against the law, but Italians often pay, for fear the attendant will damage their car if they don't.

PETROL

Petrol is very expensive. It can be bought from roadside petrol pumps (many of which are self-service, which is cheaper, operated by banknotes or debit/credit cards), as well as from regular garages. Check whether your car uses lead-free petrol *(benzina senza piombo* or *benzina verde)* or not. Late-night petrol stations are listed on page 395. At night, most self-service stations are attended by illegal petrol station attendants, who will put the petrol in for you in exchange for a tip.

zona rimozione fermata consentita per salita e discesa con conducente a bordo

Signpost for a tow-away area *(zona rimozione)*

Agip

The state petrol company logo

ILLEGAL PARKING

Rome's traffic police are vigilant. If you've parked illegally, your car may be clamped or (if it's causing an obstruction) towed away, so phone 06-67 691 or 06-0606 before reporting it stolen. No-parking zones should be clearly marked, but check in case the sign is hidden by a tree.

A tow truck at work

CAR HIRE

Major international firms
(**Avis, Hertz, Europcar**) and
Italy by Car Thrifty have rental
offices at the airports, Termini
station and in the city.
However, you may get a
better deal by booking a car
before you arrive through a
travel agent or online, or by
using a local firm (such as
Maggiore). Check that breakdown service and collision
damage waiver are included.
Prospective renters usually
need to be at least 25 years
old and have held a driving
licence for at least a year. You
will also need to leave a
deposit – a credit card
number is usually enough.
Some firms also ask for an
international licence
(available from your national
automobile association).

Accident rates on Italian
roads are high, so make sure
you are fully insured against
all eventualities. It is a good
idea to join an internationally
affiliated automobile association (such as the AA in Britain
or the AAA in the US) so that
if you do break down, the
ACI (Italian Automobile
Club) will tow your car without charging.

Details of road and traffic
conditions (in Italian) are
available from a special **Road
Conditions** number. For more
information on driving and
parking in the city, as well as
understanding road signs and
buying fuel, *see page 393*.

MOPED AND BICYCLE HIRE

Rome's narrow streets and
heavy traffic, combined with
the seven steep hills on
which it was built, make it a
challenging place for even the
most serious of cyclists. However, there are a few areas,
such as the Villa Borghese,
the banks of the Tiber and
some pockets in the historic
centre (around the Pantheon
and Piazza Navona), where
bike lanes make for a relaxing
way to see the city.

Mopeds (*motorini*) and
scooters – like the classic
Piaggio Vespa, meaning "wasp"
– are good for getting through
the traffic. You may want to
stick to quiet streets to begin
with, though.

Bikes and scooters can be
hired from **Collalti, Scoot-a-
Long** and **Scooters for Rent**.
There are also several **Bike
Rental** spots dotted around
the city. Motorcyclists, scooter
drivers and their passengers
must wear helmets by law;
these can be rented from most
hire shops. You may be asked
to leave a credit card number
or cash as a deposit when you
pick up the vehicle *(see p367)*.

The **Roma Bikesharing**
scheme is good for short rides
in the city centre. You must
first enrol and pay a €10
deposit for an electronic
"smartcard", which can be
topped up. You then have
access to bikes at various
stands across the city.

Taxi on a busy street in Rome's city centre

TAXIS

Official taxis in Rome are
white, say "Comune di Roma"
on the side and bear a "taxi"
sign on the roof. Do not use
the taxis offered by touts at
stations and tourist spots;
official taxi drivers do not tout
for customers. Official taxis
can be hailed at specially
marked taxi ranks or on the
street (drivers are not meant
to stop in the street but many
of them do). You can nearly
always find them at the main
tourist sights, at airports and
at stations (including Termini
and Ostiense). Roman taxi
drivers are not renowned for
their friendliness and may even
refuse to take you if you're
going too far from the lucra-
tive city centre or, conversely,
if the ride is too short.

Taxis are not particularly
cheap, so, unless you have
heavy luggage or screaming
toddlers, public transport is
usually a better option. Taxi
drivers charge supplements
for baggage, night journeys
(10pm–7am), and journeys on
Sundays or public holidays.

Customers should ensure
the meter is turned on and
visible. The meter continues
running while you are at a
standstill, so traffic jams can
become expensive. Drivers
may take suspiciously
circuitous routes. Italians
don't tip taxi drivers; they
simply round up to the
nearest euro. You can phone
for a taxi (but you will pay
from the time the driver gets
the call from the switchboard)
from: **Mondo Taxi, Cooperativa
Autoradiotaxi Romana 35-70**

Motorbikes and scooters, a popular means of transport in Rome

or **La Capitale Radio Taxi**. Taxi rides to and from the city's airports incur a flat fee for up to four passengers and their luggage *(see p385)*.

RIVER TOUR

The service offered by **Battelli di Roma** runs from an embarkation point near the Ponte Sant'Angelo and Tiber Island. Boats depart every half-hour, starting at 10am, and all-day tickets cost €15 (see website for details). There are also dinner cruises on weekends.

HORSE-DRAWN CARRIAGES

You can hire horse-drawn caleches *(carrozzelle)* for a gentle tour of the historic

Horse-drawn carriage offering tours from St Peter's Square

centre. Carriages carry up to five people and can be hired from many points: Piazza di Spagna, the Colosseum, Trevi Fountain, St Peter's, Via Veneto, Villa Borghese, Piazza Venezia and Piazza Navona. Trips last half an hour, an hour, half a day or a day. They tend to be expensive, but prices for longer rides are negotiable; establish the price before you set off and make sure you understand whether the rate is per person, or for the whole carriage.

DIRECTORY

ELECTRIC-CAR CHARGING STATIONS

Via Cola di Rienzo.
Map 4 D5. Piazza Mastai.
Map 7 C1. **www.**
colonnineelettriche.it.

BUSES AND TRAMS

ATAC
Piazza dei Cinquecento.
Map 6 D3. **Tel** 800-43 1784. **www.**atac.roma.it

Customer Service
Via Ostiense 131L (1st floor), to the south of Stazione Ostiense.

GUIDED TOURS

Carrani Tours
Via V. E. Orlando 95.
Map 5 C3. **Tel** 06-474 2501. **www.**carrani.com

Context
Tel 06-9762 5204. **www.**contexttravel.com/rome

Green Line Tours
Via Farini 16. **Map 6** D4.
Map 06-482 7480.
www.greenlinetours.com

No. 110 bus and Archeobus
Piazza dei Cinquecento.
Map 6 D3.
Tel 800-281 281.
www.trambusopen.com

MAIN CAR PARKS

Acqua Acetosa station
Map 2 E1. Also: Lepanto Metro station. **Map 4** D1.
Also: Villa Borghese. **Map 5** A1. Also: Piazzale dei Partigiani. **Map 8** E4.

USEFUL 24-HOUR PETROL STATIONS

Portuense
Piazzale della Radio.
Map 7 B5.

Trastevere
Lungotevere Ripa.
Map 8 D1.

CAR BREAKDOWN SERVICES

ACI Breakdown
Tel 803 116.

Road Conditions
Tel 1518.

CAR HIRE

Avis
Tel 199-100 133
(centralized booking).
Also: Ciampino airport.
Tel 06-7934 0195.
Also: Fiumicino airport.
Tel 06-6501 1531. Also:
Via Sardegna 38A. **Map 5** C1. **Tel** 06-4282 4728.
www.avisautonoleggio.it

Europcar

Tel 199 307 030
(centralized free booking).
Also: Fiumicino airport.
Tel 06-6576 1211. Also:
Stazione Termini. **Map 6** D3. **Tel** 06-488 2854.
www.europcar.it

Hertz
Via Gregorio VII 207.
Tel 06-3937 8807. Also:
Stazione Termini. **Map 6** D3. **Tel** 06-474 0389.
Also: Fiumicino airport.
Tel 06-6501 1553.
www.hertz.it

Italy By Car Thrifty
Stazione Termini. **Map 6** D3. **Tel** 06-474 7825.
Also: Fiumicino airport.
Tel 06-6501 0347.
Also: Ciampino airport.
Tel 06-7934 0137.
www.italybycar.it

Maggiore
Stazione Termini. **Map 6** D3. **Tel** 06-488 0049.
Also: Via Po 8A. **Map 5** C1. **Tel** 06-854 8698.
www.maggiore.it

MOPED AND BICYCLE HIRE

Bike Rental
Piazza del Popolo. **Map 4** F1. Also: Piazza di Spagna.
Map 5 A2.

Collalti

Via del Pellegrino 82.
Map 4 E4 & 11 C4.
Tel 06-6880 1084 (bikes).

Roma Bikesharing
Tel 06-57003.
www.atac-bikesharing.it

Scoot-a-Long
Via Cavour 302. **Map 5** B5. **Tel** 06-678 0206
(mopeds and scooters).

Scooters for Rent
Via della Purificazione 84.
Tel 06-488 5485 (bikes, scooters and mopeds).

TAXI BOOKING NUMBERS

Cooperativa Autoradiotaxi Romana 35-70
Tel 06-35 70.

La Capitale Radio Taxi
Tel 06-49 94.

Mondo Taxi
Tel 06-88 22.

RIVER TRANSPORT

Battelli di Roma
Tel 06-9774 5498.
www.battellidiroma.it

STREET FINDER

ap references given with sights, restaurants, hotels, shops and entertainment venues refer to the maps in this section *(see* How the Map References Work *opposite)*. A complete index of the street names and places of interest marked on the maps follows on pages 398–407. The key map below shows the area of Rome covered by the *Street Finder* only. This includes the sightseeing areas (which are colour-coded) as well as the whole of central Rome with all the districts important for restaurants, hotels and entertainment venues. Because the historic centre is so packed with sights, there is a large-scale map of this area on maps 11 and 12.

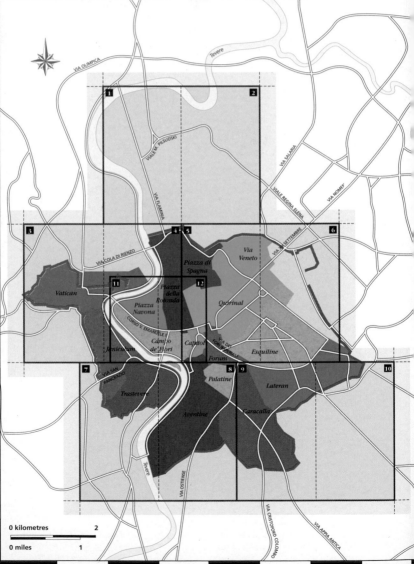

HOW THE MAP
REFERENCES WORK

The first figure tells you which Street Finder map to turn to.

Trevi Fountain **⑦**

Fontana di Trevi. **Map 5** ^3 &
12 F2. 🚌 52, 53, 61, 62, 63, 71, 80,
95, 116, 119.

The letter and number are a grid reference. You will find the letters at the top and bottom of the map and the numbers at the sides.

The second reference refers to the large-scale maps of central Rome (11 & 12). It is read in exactly the same way as the first.

The map continues on map 8 of the Street Finder.

The key to the abbreviations used in the Street Finder is on page 398.

KEY TO STREET FINDER

◼	Major sight
◼	Places of Interest
◼	Railway station
M	Metro station
🚌	Bus terminus
🚋	Tram terminus
P	Main car parks
ℹ	Tourist information office
✚	Hospital with casualty unit
🚓	Police station
✝	Church
✡	Synagogue
⊠	Post office
═	Railway line
▬	Steps
▬	City wall

SCALE OF MAPS 1–10

0 metres	250
▬▬▬▬▬	**1:12,000**
0 yards	250

SCALE OF MAPS 11 & 12

0 metres	150
▬▬▬▬▬	**1:7,600**
0 yards	150

Street Finder Index

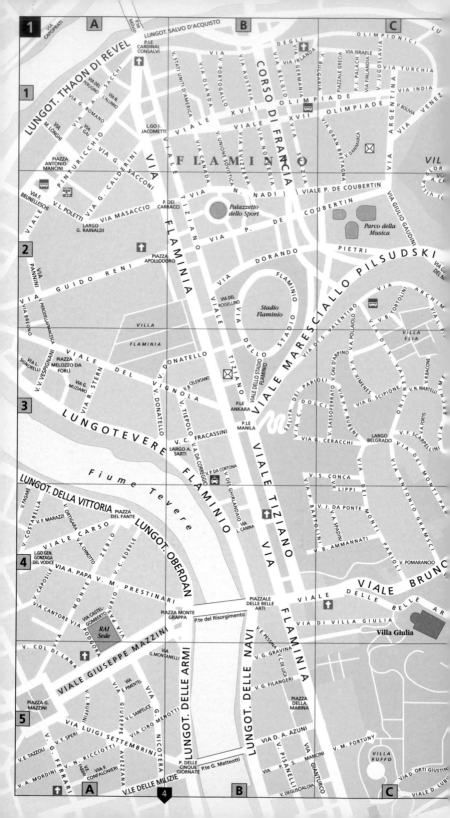

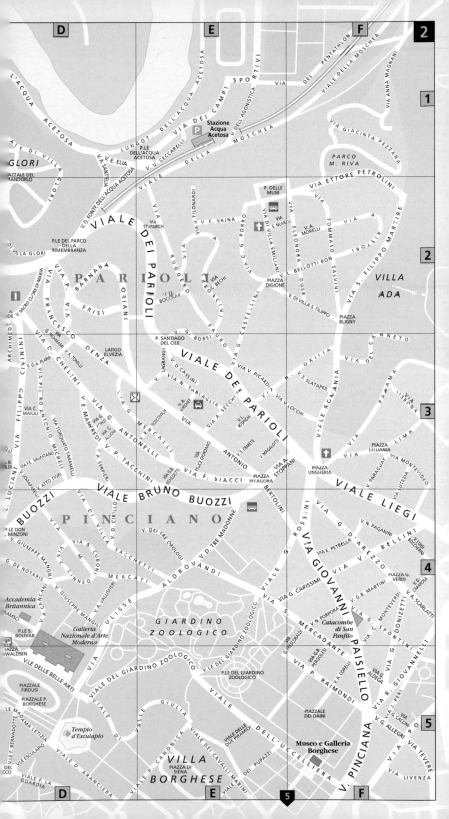

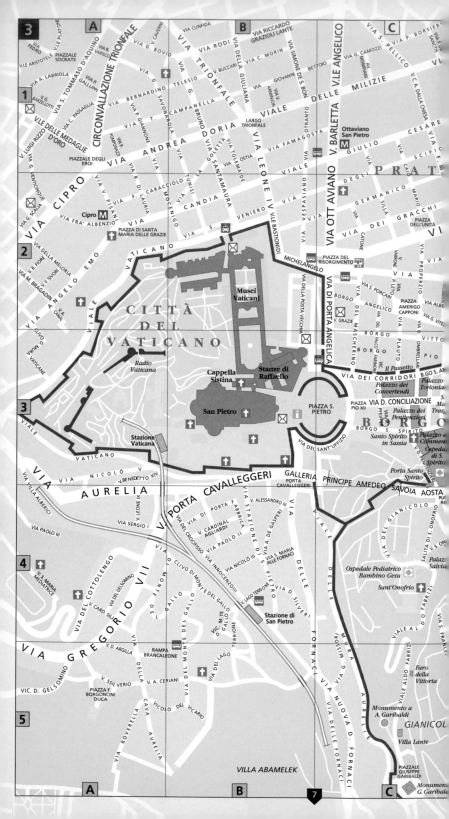

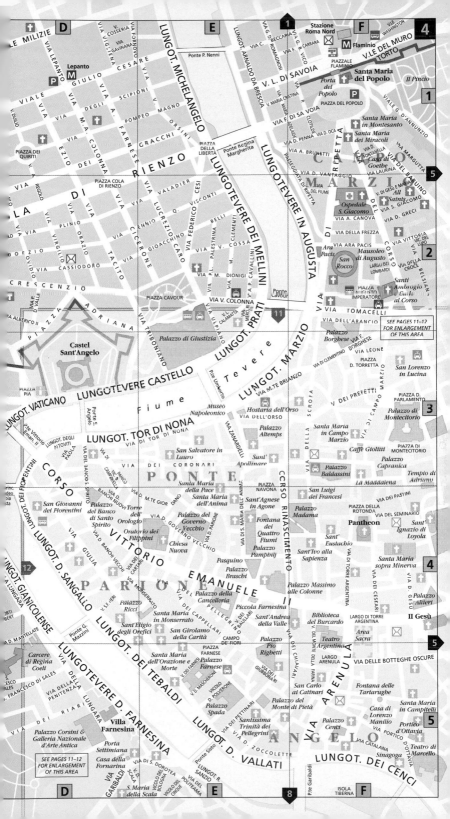

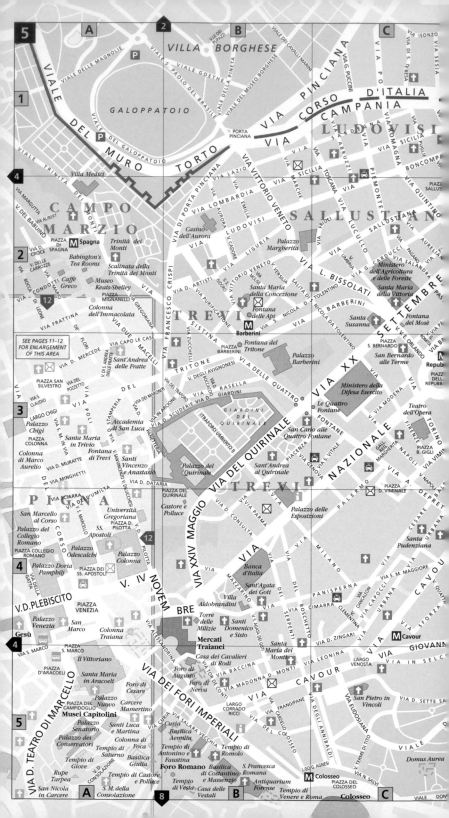

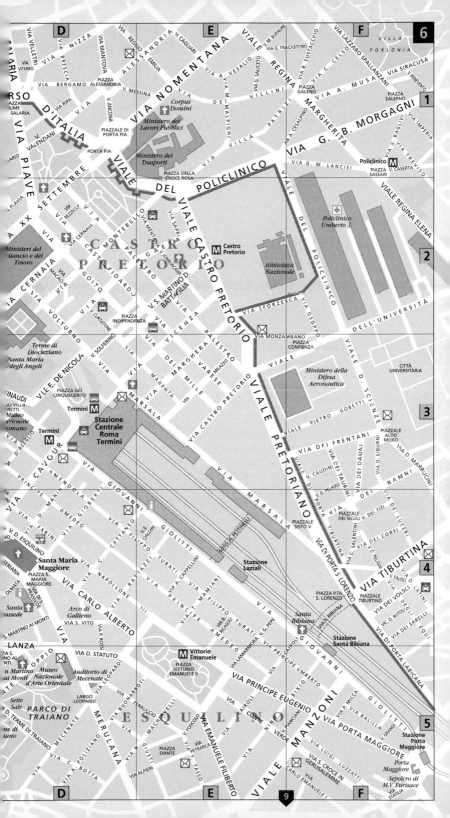

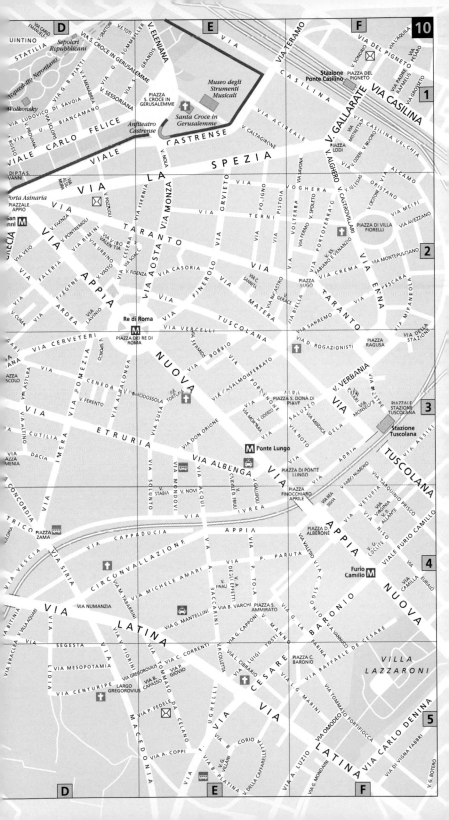

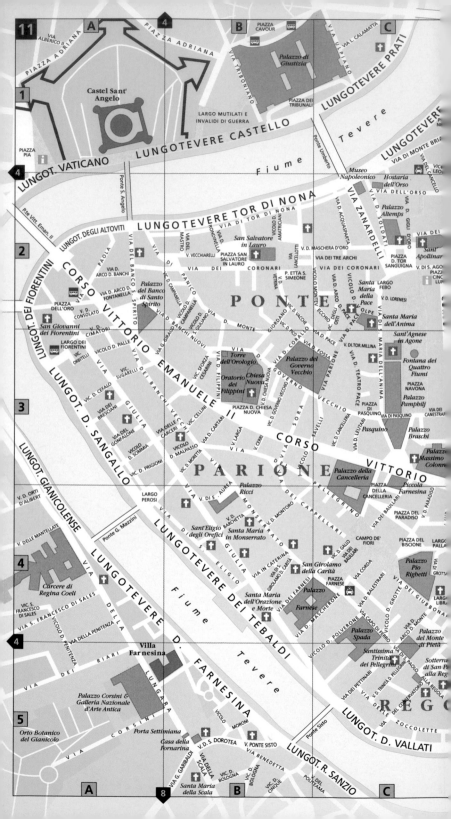

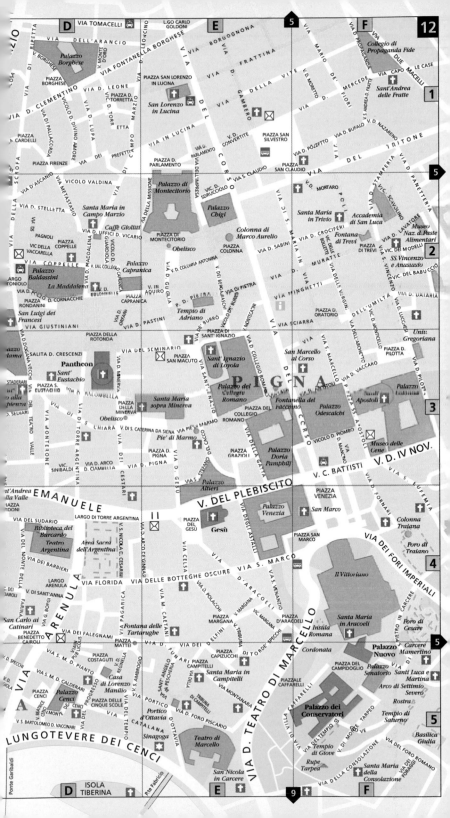

General Index

Acknowledgments

Dorling Kindersley would like to thank the following people whose contributions and assistance have made the preparation of this book possible.

Main Contributors

Olivia Ercoli is an art historian and tour guide, who has lived all her life in Rome. Bilingual in English and Italian, she lectures on art history and writes on a range of subjects for English and Italian publications.

Travel writer Ros Belford conceived the idea of the Virago Woman's Guides, of which she is now series editor, and wrote the *Virago Woman's Guide to Rome*. She has travelled widely in Europe and as well as writing guide books contributes to a variety of publications including *The Guardian*.

Roberta Mitchell heads the editorial section of the UN's Publishing Division in Rome, where she has lived for many years. An experienced writer and editor with extensive knowledge of the city, she has contributed to a number of guides to Rome including the *American Express Guide to Rome*.

Contributors

Reid Bramblett, Sam Cole, Mary Jane Cryan Pancani, Daphne Wilson Ercoli, Laura Ercoli, Lindsay Hunt, Adrian James, Leonie Loudon, Christopher McDowall, Davina Palmer, Rodney Palmer, Pardeep Sandhu, Debra Shipley.

Dorling Kindersley wishes to thank the following editors and researchers at Websters International Publishers: Sandy Carr, Matthew Barrell, Siobhan Bremner, Serena Cross, Valeria Fabbri, Annie Galpin, Gemma Hancock, Celia Woolfrey.

Additional Photography

Max Alexander, Guiseppe Carfagna, Demetrio Carrasco, Andy Crawford, Peter Douglas, Mike Dunning, Philip Enticknap, Steve Gorton, John Heseltine, Britta Jaschinski, Neil Mersh, Ian O'Leary, Poppy, Rough Guides/James McConnachie, Alessandra Santarelli, David Sutherland, Martin Woodward.

Additional Illustrations

Anne Bowes, Robin Carter, Pramod Negi, Gillie Newman, Chris D Orr.

Additional Picture Research

Sharon Buckley.

Cartography

Advanced Illustration (Cheshire), Contour Publishing (Derby), Euromap Limited (Berkshire), Alok Pathak, Kunal Singh. Street Finder maps: ERA Maptec Ltd (Dublin) adapted with permission from original survey and mapping from Shobunsha (Japan).

Cartographic Research

James Anderson, Donna Rispoli, Joan Russell.

Research Assistance

Janet Abbott, Flaminia Allvin, Fabrizio Ardito, Licia Bronzin, Lupus Sabene.

Design and Editorial Assistance

Beverley Ager, Marta Bescos Sanchez, Tessa Bindloss, Kristin Dolina-Adamczyk, Peter Bently, Vandana Bhagra, Hilary Bird, Lucinda Cooke, Michelle Crane, Vanessa Courtier, Claire Edwards, Peter Douglas, Jon Eldan, Simon Farbrother, Karen Fitzpatrick, Anna Freiberger, Vanessa Hamilton, Marcus Hardy, Sasha Heseltine, Sally Ann Hibbard, Paul Hines, Stephanie Jackson, Claire Jones, Steve Knowlden, Priya Kukadia, Mary Lambert, Maite Lantaron, Jude Ledger, Janette Leung, Carly Madden, Shahid Mahmood, Nicola Malone, Jane Middleton, Ian Midson, Fiona Morgan, Jane Oliver-Jedrzejak, Helen Partington, Catherine Palmi, Naomi Peck, Marianne Petrou, Carolyn Pyrah, Pete Quinlan, Salim Qurashi, Rada Radojicic, Pamposh Raina, Ellen Root, Collette Sadler, Sands Publishing Solutions, Mathew Baishakhee Sengupta, Jane Shaw, Clare Sullivan, Rachel Symons, Andrew Szudek, Alka Thakur, Daphne Trotter, Karen Villabona, Diana Vowles, Lynda Warrington, Stewart J. Wild.

Special Assistance

Dottore Riccardo Baldini, Signor Mario di Bartolomeo of the Soprintendenza dei Beni Artistici e Storici di Roma, Belloni, Dorling Kindersley picture department, Peter Douglas, David Gleave MW, Debbie Harris, Emma Hutton and Cooling Brown Partnership, Marina Tavolato, Dottoressa Todaro and Signora Camimiti at the Ministero dell'Interno, Trestini.

Photography Permissions

Dorling Kindersley would like to thank the following for their kind permission to photograph at their establishments: Bathsheba Abse at the Keats-Shelley Memorial House, Accademia dei Lincei, Accanto, Aeroporti di Roma, Aldrovandi Palace, Alpheus, Banco di Santo Spirito at Palazzo del Monte di Pietà,

Rory Bruck at Babington's, Caffè Giolitti, Caffè Latino, Comune di Roma (Ripartizione X), Comunità Ebraica di Roma, Guido Cornini at Monumenti Musei e Gallerie Pontificie, Direzione Sanitaria Ospedale di Santo Spirito, Dottoressa Laura Falsini at the Soprintendenza Archeologica di Etruria Meridionale, Hotel Gregoriana, Hotel Majestic, Hotel Regina Baglioni, Marco Marchetti at Ente EUR, Dottoressa Mercalli at the Museo Nazionale di Castel Sant'Angelo, Ministero dell' Interno, Plaza Minerva, Ristorante Alberto Ciarla, Ristorante Filetti di Baccalà, Ristorante Romolo, Signor Rulli and Signor Angeli at the Soprinten-denza Archeologica di Roma, Soprintendenza Archeologica per il Lazio, Soprintendenza per i Beni Ambientali e Architettonici, Soprintendenza per i Beni Artistici e Storici di Roma, Daniela Tabo at the Musei Capitolini, Villa d'Este, Villa San Pio, Mrs Marjorie Weeke at St Peter's.

Picture Credits

t = top; tl = top left; tc = top centre; tr = top right; cla = centre left above; ca = centre above; cra = centre right above; cl = centre left; c = centre; cr = centre right; clb = centre left below; cb = centre below; crb = centre right below; bl = bottom left; b = bottom; bc = bottom centre; br = bottom right.

Every effort has been made to trace the copyright holders and we apologize for any unintentional omissions. We would be pleased to insert the appropriate acknowledgments in any subsequent edition of this publication.

Works of art have been reproduced with the permission of the following copyright holders: *Town with Gothic Cathedral*, Paul Klee © DACS, London 2006 241b.

The publishers are grateful to the following individuals, companies and picture libraries for permission to reproduce their photographs:

ACCADEMIA NAZIONALE DI SAN LUCA, Rome: 160b; AFE: 57b, 61cr; Sandro Battaglia 59c, 61clb, 61br, 336br; Louise Goldman 157t; G La Malfa 251t; AEROPORTI DI ROMA: 384b, 385tr; AGENZIA SINTESI: 378br, 378cla; AKG-IMAGES: Andrea Jemolo 10br; ALAMY IMAGES: CuboImages srl/Gimmi 395tr; Kathy DeWitt 305tl; Antonella di Girolamo 377c; Lautaro 192c; Marco Marcotulli 376bc; Travel Ink/Jim Gibson 382crb; R Venturi 376bl; Rob Wilkinson 379tl; AGF FOTO: 40–41c; ALDROVANDI PALACE HOTEL: 297tr; ALITALIA: 384t, 385cl; ALLSPORT: David Cannon 41br; ANCIENT ART AND

ARCHITECTURE: 18bl, 22tl, 23tl, 27bc, 36crb, 37tc, 46cl; ARTOTHEK, Städelsches Kunstinstitut Frankfurt, Goethe in the Roman Campagna by JHW Tischbein 136t.

BAGLIONI HOTELS SPA: 296tr; BANCA D'ITALIA: 380cla; BED AND BREAKFAST BIO: 377tr; BIBLIOTECA REALE, Torino: 30–31c; BOSCOLO ALEPH HOTEL: 299cra; BRIDGEMAN ART LIBRARY, LONDON/NEW YORK: 20br, 39tr; Agnew & Sons, London 53tr; Antikenmuseum Staatliches Museum, Berlin 21bl; Biblioteca Publica Episcopal, Barcelona/Index 114bl; Bibliothèque da la Sorbonne 30c; British Museum, London 29ctr; Château de Versailles, France/Giraudon 35tr; Christie's, London 42, 68b, 95t; The Fine Art Society, London 151tr, 279tl; Galleria degli Uffizi, Florence 33bl; Greek Museum, University of Newcastle-upon-Tyne 18br; King Street Galleries, London 35br; Louvre, Paris/Lauros Giraudon 56br; Louvre, Paris/Giraudon 28br; Roy Miles Gallery, 29 Bruton St, London 228t; Musée des Beaux-Arts, Nantes 55t; Museo e Gallerie Nazionali di Capodimonte, Naples, Detail from the predella of San Ludovico by Simone Martini 28tr; Musée Condé, Chantilly f.71v Très Riches Heures, 28tc, Museum of Fine Arts, Budapest 110bl; Museo Archeologico di Villa Giulia 50cl; Palazzo Doria Pamphilj, Rome 107b; Piacenza Town Hall, Italy/Index 29br; Private Collection 21br, 24bl, 26br, 29tr, 178b; Pushkin Museum, Moscow 111t; Sotheby's, London 20bl; Vatican Museums & Galleries 43ca, 237tr.

CAPITOLINE MUSEUMS, ROME: 73cra; CEPHAS PICTURE LIBRARY: Mick Rock 314tr; COMUNE DI ROMA: 374tc; CORBIS: Alessandra Benedetti 375tr; Owen Franken 304cla; Bob Krist 305c; Araldo de Luca 70tr; Reuters/Max Rossi 40cb; CORPO NAZIONALE DEI VIGILI DEL FUOCO: 379cl; VANESSA COURTIER: 371t; CROCE BIANCA ITALIANA: 379cla.

IL DAGHERROTIPO: 118clb, 145cra, 334t, 335bl, 388cla, 393t; Stefano Chieppa 152cl, 289bc, 290bc, 394b; Andrea Getuli 287tl; Museo di Roma/Giorgio Oddi 118b; Stephano Occhibelli inside front cover cl, 116, 286tl, 288cla, 288br; Giorgio Oddi 55cl; Paolo Priori 204tr; Giovanni Rinaldi 196tr, 286cla, 286br, 287br, 290cla, 291tc, 291br, 390t; CM DIXON: 19bl, 26c, 268b, 269t, 269b.

ECOLE NATIONALE SUPERIEURE DES BEAUX-ARTS: 23cr, 24–25, 248t, 284–285b; ENTE NAZIONALE ITALIANO PER IL TURISMO: 374cl, cr; ET ARCHIVE: 16, 19tr, 19clb, 20tr, 21tc, 25t, 29cl, 30tl, 33br, 34br, 39cl, 50tl, 314tl; EUROLINES: 387bl; MARY EVANS PICTURE LIBRARY: 9, 20cl, 25cl, 26cl, 31br, 32cb, 32b, 33t, 36tl, 36cr, 36bl, 56tl, 67bl, 74t, 81b, 91t, 92b, 94bl, 127c, 135t, 213b.

CORALDO FALSINI: 41tl, 354b, 355t, 355c; FERROVIE DELLO STATO: 386clb, 387cl, 387tr; WERNER FORMAN ARCHIVE:

19cr, 22bl, 24tl, 25cr, 25bl, 25br, 49tr, 155t, 163tr, 175c; FOLKLORE MUSEUM, ROME: 210br.

GARDEN PICTURE LIBRARY: Bob Challinor 172cb; GETTY IMAGES: AFP/Andreas Olaro 376br; Andre Thijssen 376tl; Robert Harding World Imagery 116; Stone/ Richard Passmore 1c; GIRAUDON: 17b, 30br, 38br; GRANDI STAZIONI S.P.A: 386b; RONALD GRANT: 54br, 354t.

SONIA HALLIDAY: 21c, 24br, 27cl; Laura Lushington 26bl; ROBERT HARDING PICTURE LIBRARY: 25cra, 34bl, 79cr, 177t, 268c, 369c; Mario Carrieri 37tr; John G Ross 40tl, 59cl, 355b; Sheila Terry 41cl; G White 59br; HOTEL FONTANA-TREVI: 299bc; HULTON DEUTSCH: 38tl, 57cr, 63, 175b, 293c, 373c.

ISTOCKPHOTO.COM: Robert Caucino 116.

KATZ/FSP: 21tr, 27bl, 28bc, 33cl, 56cl, 57cl, 75cl, 75cr, 78tc, 93b, 112c, 122t, 125tr, 126tl, 132br, 133cr, 136bl, 139bl, 139br, 162tr, 172bl, 172 br, 183br, 192bl, 196c, 210c, 220bl, 227cr, 229cr; Alinari 80br, 141bl, 174t, 254b; Anderson 78cr, 138bl, 163tl, 228b.

MAGNUM: Erich Lessing 17t, 19tl, 89br; MARKA: V Arcomano 35cr; Roberto Benzi 337crb; D. Donadoni 11br; Piranha 337cra; Lorenzo Sechi 10cla, 224br; MAXXI: Roberto Galasso 259br; MORO ROMA: 38cl, 39cl, 40br, 41tr, 41bl.

NATIONAL PORTRAIT GALLERY, LONDON: 56tr, 57tr; GRAZIA NERI: Vision/Giorgio Casulich 112br, 156br, 337crc; Vision/Roberta Krasnig 124tr, 283t; © NIPPON TELEVISION NETWORK CORPORATION, Tokyo 1999: 244b and all pictures on 246-7.

LA REPUBBLICA TROVAROMA: 375tl; RESIDENZA CELLINI: 296br; REX FEATURES: Steve Wood 41cr.

SCALA GROUP S.P.A: 94t, 125tl, 278cl, 289tl Casa di Augusto 97t, Chiesa del Gesù 115t, Galleria Borghese 34cla, 260tr, Galleria Colonna 157b, Galleria Doria Pamphilj 48br, 105cr, Galleria Spada 48cl, Galleria degli Uffizi 18–19, 29bl, Museo d'Arte Orientale 174t, 174br, Musei Capitolini 49bl, Museo della Civiltà Romana 50tr, 50b, Museo delle Terme 23tr, Museo Napoleonico 51cr, Museo Nazionale, Napoli 23cl, Museo Nazionale, Ravenna 24cl, Museo del Risorgimento, Milano 38clb, 38–39c, Museo del Risorgimento, Roma 39tl, Palazzo Barberini 252bl,

Palazzo Ducale 8, 21tr, Palazzo della Farnesina 220ct, Palazzo Madama 22cl, Palazzo Venezia 49cr, 66bl, San Carlo alle Quattro Fontane 35cl, Santa Cecilia in Trastevere 34tl, San Clemente 37bl, Santa Costanza 26–27c, Santa Maria Antiqua 26tl, Santa Maria dell'Anima 121t, Santa Maria Maggiore 45tr, Santa Maria del Popolo 139tr, 139c, Santa Prassede 28bl, 30bl, Santa Sabina 27tc, 31cl, Vatican Museums 21bc, 27t, 27cr, 27cra, 29cr, 31tl, 31cr, 32tl, 32ct, 33cr, 33bc, 34cr, 34clb, 43tr, 48tl, 50cr, 51bl, 224bl, 225cr, 235t, 238tl, 238br, 240t, 240b, 241t, 241c, 241b, 242tl, 242c, 242b, 243t, 243c, 243b, 245 (all 4), 289tl; LOURENS SMAK: 11tl; STA TRAVEL GROUP: 376c.

TRAMBUS OPEN S.P.A: 392tr, TOPHAM PICTURE SOURCE: 40cl.

ZEFA: 2, 230cl, 231br, 372–3, 388t; Eric Carle 58t; Kohlhas 231t.

Thanks also to Dottoressa Giulia De Marchi of L'ACCADEMIA NAZIONALE DI SAN LUCA, Rome for 160b, Rettore Padre Libianchi of LA CHIESA DI SANT'IGNAZIO DI LOYOLA for 106t, ENTE NAZIONALE PER IL TURISMO, HASSLER HOTEL, Rome for 299tl, GRAND HOTEL, Rome for 299crb and to LA REPUBBLICA TROVAROMA.

FRONT ENDPAPERS

iStockphoto.com: Roberto Caucino Left page c

MAP COVER

4CORNERS IMAGES: SIME/Maurizio Rellini 999

JACKET

Front – 4CORNERS IMAGES: SIME/Maurizio Rellini. Back – ALAMY IMAGES: JLImages bl; DORLING KINDERSLEY: cla; Mike Dunning Kim Sayer tl. Spine – 4CORNERS IMAGES: SIME/Maurizio Rellini t.

All other images © Dorling Kindersley. For further information see: www.dkimages.com

---

SPECIAL EDITIONS OF DK TRAVEL GUIDES

DK Travel Guides can be purchased in bulk quantities at discounted prices for use in promotions or as premiums. We are also able to offer special editions and personalized jackets, corporate imprints, and excerpts from all of our books, tailored specifically to meet your own needs.

To find out more, please contact:
(in the United States) SpecialSales@dk.com
(in the UK) TravelSpecialSales@uk.dk.com
(in Canada) DK Special Sales at general@tourmaline.ca
(in Australia) business.development@pearson.com.au

Phrase Book

In Emergency

Help!	**Aiuto!**	*eye-yoo-toh*
Stop!	**Fermate!**	*fair-mah-teh*
Call a doctor	**Chiama un medico**	*kee-ah-mah oon meh-dee-koh*
Call an ambulance	**Chiama un' ambulanza**	*kee-ah-mah oon am-boo-lan-tsa*
Call the police	**Chiama la polizia**	*kee-ah-mah lah pol-ee-tsee-ah*
Call the fire brigade	**Chiama i pompieri**	*kee ah-mah ee pom-pee-air-ee*
Where is the telephone?	**Dov'è il telefono?**	*dov-eheel teh-leh-foh-noh?*
The nearest hospital?	**L'ospedale più vicino?**	*loss-peh-dah-leh pee-oovee-chee-noh?*

Communication Essentials

Yes/No	**Sì/No**	*see/noh*
Please	**Per favore**	*pair fah vor-eh*
Thank you	**Grazie**	*grah-tsee-eh*
Excuse me	**Mi scusi**	*mee skoo-zee*
Hello	**Buon giorno**	*bwon jor-noh*
Goodbye	**Arrivederci**	*ah-ree-veh-dair-chee*
Good evening	**Buona sera**	*bwon-ah sair-ah*
morning	**la mattina**	*lah mah-tee-nah*
afternoon	**il pomeriggio**	*eel poh-meh-ree-joh*
evening	**la sera**	*lah sair-ah*
yesterday	**ieri**	*ee-air-ee*
today	**oggi**	*oh-jee*
tomorrow	**domani**	*doh-mah-nee*
here	**qui**	*kwee*
there	**la**	*lah*
What?	**Quale?**	*kwah-leh?*
When?	**Quando?**	*kwan-doh?*
Why?	**Perchè?**	*pair-keh?*
Where?	**Dove?**	*doh-veh*

Useful Phrases

How are you?	**Come sta?**	*koh-meh stah?*
Very well, thank you.	**Molto bene, grazie**	*moll-toh beh-neh grah-tsee-eh*
Pleased to meet you.	**Piacere di conoscerla.**	*pee-ah-chair-eh dee coh-noh-shair-lah*
See you soon.	**A più tardi.**	*ah pee-oo tar-dee*
That's fine.	**Va bene.**	*va beh-neh*
Where is/are ...?	**Dov'è/Dove sono...?**	*dou-eh/doveh soh-noh?*
How long does it take to get to ...?	**Quanto tempo ci vuole per andare a ...?**	*kwan-toh tem-poh chee voo-oh-leh pair an-dar-eh ah...?*
How do I get to ...?	**Come faccio per arrivare a ...?**	*koh-meh fah-choh pair arri-var-eh ah...?*
Do you speak English?	**Parla inglese?**	*par-lah een-gleh-zeh?*
I don't understand.	**Non capisco.**	*non ka-pee-skoh*
Could you speak more slowly, please?	**Può parlare più lentamente, per favore?**	*pwoh par-lah-reh pee-oo len-ta-men-teh pair fah-vor eh*
I'm sorry.	**Mi dispiace.**	*mee dee-spee-ah-cheh*

Useful Words

big	**grande**	*gran-deh*
small	**piccolo**	*pee-koh-loh*
hot	**caldo**	*kal-doh*
cold	**freddo**	*fred-doh*
good	**buono**	*bwoh-noh*
bad	**cattivo**	*kat-tee-voh*
enough	**basta**	*bas-tah*
well	**bene**	*beh-neh*
open	**aperto**	*ah-pair-toh*
closed	**chiuso**	*kee-oo-zoh*
left	**a sinistra**	*ah see-nee-strah*
right	**a destra**	*ah dess-trah*
straight on	**sempre dritto**	*sem-preh dree-toh*
near	**vicino**	*vee-chee-noh*
far	**lontano**	*lon-tah-noh*
up	**su**	*soo*
down	**giù**	*joo*
early	**presto**	*press-toh*
late	**tardi**	*tar-dee*
entrance	**entrata**	*en-trah-tah*
exit	**uscita**	*oo-shee-ta*
toilet	**il gabinetto**	*eel gab-bee-net-toh*
free, unoccupied	**libero**	*lee-bair-oh*
free, no charge	**gratuito**	*grah-too-ee-toh*

Making a Telephone Call

I'd like to place a long-distance call.	**Vorrei fare una interurbana.**	*vor-ray far-eh oona in-tair-oor-bah-nah*
I'd like to make a reverse-charge call.	**Vorrei fare una telefonata a carico del destinatario.**	*vor-ray far-eh oona teh-leh-fon-ah-tah ah kar-ee-koh dell dess-tee-nah-tar-ree-oh*
I'll try again later.	**Ritelefono più tardi.**	*ree-teh-leh-foh-noh pee-oo tar-dee*
Can I leave a message?	**Posso lasciare un messaggio?**	*poss-oh lash-ah-reh oon mess-sah-joh?*
Hold on	**Un attimo, per favore**	*oon ah-tee-moh, pair fah-vor-eh*
Could you speak up a little please?	**Può parlare più forte, per favore?**	*pwoh par-lah-reh pee-oo for-teh, pair fah-vor-eh?*
local call	**la telefonata locale**	*lah teh-leh fon-ah-ta loh-kah-leh*

Shopping

How much does this cost?	**Quant'è, per favore?**	*kwan-teh pair fah-vor-eh?*
I would like ...	**Vorrei ...**	*vor-ray*
Do you have ...?	**Avete ...?**	*ah-veh-teh ..?*
I'm just looking.	**Sto soltanto guardando.**	*stoh sol-tan toh gwar-dan-doh*
Do you take credit cards?	**Accettate carte di credito?**	*ah-chet tah-teh kar-teh dee creh-dee-toh?*
What time do you open/close?	**A che ora apre/ chiude?**	*ah keh or-ah ah-preh/kee-oo-deh?*
this one	**questo**	*kweh-stoh*
that one	**quello**	*kwell-oh*
expensive	**caro**	*kar-oh*
cheap	**a buon prezzo**	*ah bwon pret-soh*
size, clothes	**la taglia**	*lah tah-lee-ah*
size, shoes	**il numero**	*eel noo-mair-oh*
white	**bianco**	*bee-ang-koh*
black	**nero**	*neh-roh*
red	**rosso**	*ross-oh*
yellow	**giallo**	*jal-loh*
green	**verde**	*vair-deh*
blue	**blu**	*bloo*
brown	**marrone**	*mar-roh-neh*

Types of Shop

antique dealer	**l'antiquario**	*lan-tee-kwah-ree-oh*
bakery	**la panetteria**	*lah pah-net-tair-ree-ah*
bank	**la banca**	*lah bang-kah*
bookshop	**la libreria**	*lah lee-breh-ree-ah*
butcher's	**la macelleria**	*lah mah-chell-eh-ree-ah*
cake shop	**la pasticceria**	*lah pas-tee-chair-ee-ah*
chemist's	**la farmacia**	*lah far-mah-chee-ah*
department store	**il grande magazzino**	*eel gran-deh mag-gad-zee-noh*
delicatessen	**la salumeria**	*lah sah-loo-meh-ree-ah*
fishmonger's	**la pescheria**	*lah pess-keh-ree-ah*
florist	**il fioraio**	*eel foe-o-eye-oh*
greengrocer	**il fruttivendolo**	*eel froo-tee-ven-doh-loh*
grocery	**alimentari**	*ah-lee-men-tah-ree*
hairdresser	**il parrucchiere**	*eel par-oo-kee-air-eh*
ice cream parlour	**la gelateria**	*lah jel-lah-tair-ree-ah*
market	**il mercato**	*eel mair-kah-toh*
news-stand	**l'edicola**	*leh-dee-koh-lah*
post office	**l'ufficio postale**	*loo-fee-choh pos-tah-leh*
shoe shop	**il negozio di scarpe**	*eel neh-goh-tsioh dee skar-peh*
supermarket	**il supermercato**	*su-pair-mair-kah-toh*
tobacconist	**il tabaccaio**	*eel tab-bak-eye-oh*
travel agency	**l'agenzia di viaggi**	*lah-jen-tsee-ah dee vee-ad-jee*

Sightseeing

art gallery	**la pinacoteca**	*lah peena-koh-teh-kah*
bus stop	**la fermata dell'autobus**	*lah fair-mah-tah dell ow-toh-booss*
church	**la chiesa la basilica**	*lah kee-eh-zah lah bah-seel-i-kah*
garden	**il giardino**	*eel jar-dee-no*
library	**la biblioteca**	*lah beeb-lee-oh-teh-kah*
museum	**il museo**	*eel moo-zeh-oh*
railway station	**la stazione**	*lah stah-tsee-oh-neh*
tourist information	**l'ufficio turistico**	*loo-fee-choh too-ree-stee-koh*
closed for the public holiday	**chiuso per la festa**	*kee-oo-zoh pair lah fess-tah*

Staying in a Hotel

Do you have any vacant rooms?	Avete camere libere?	ab-veh-teb kah-mair-eb lee-bair-eb?
double room	una camera doppia	oona kah-mair-ab doh-pee-ab
with double bed	con letto matrimoniale	kon let-tob mab-tree-mob-nee-ah-leb
twin room	una camera con due letti	oona kah-mair-ab kon doo-eb let-tee
single room	una camera singola	oona kah-mair-ab sing-gob-lab
room with a bath, shower	una camera con bagno, con doccia	oona kah-mair-ab kon ban-yob, kon dot-chab
porter	il facchino	eel fab-kee-nob
key	la chiave	lab kee-ah-veb
I have a reservation.	Ho fatto una prenotazione.	ob fat-tob oona preb-nob-tab-tsee-oh-neb

Eating Out

Have you got a table for …?	Avete una tavola per … ?	ab-veh-teb oona tah-vob-lab pair …?
I'd like to reserve a table.	Vorrei riservare una tavola.	vor-ray ree-sair-vah-reb oona tah-vob-lab
breakfast	colazione	kob-lab-tsee-oh-neb
lunch	pranzo	pran-tsob
dinner	cena	cheh-nab
The bill, please.	Il conto, per favore.	eel kon-tob pair fab-vor-eb
I am a vegetarian.	Sono vegetariano/a.	soh-nob veh-jeb-tar-ee-ah-nob/nab
waitress	cameriera	kab-mair-ee-air-ab
waiter	cameriere	kab-mair-ee-air-eb
fixed price menu	il menù a prezzo fisso	eel meb-noo ab pret-sob fee-sob
dish of the day	piatto del giorno	pee-ah-tob dell jor-no
starter	antipasto	an-tee-pass-tob
first course	il primo	eel pree-mob
main course	il secondo	eel seb-kon-dob
vegetables	il contorno	eel kon-tor-nob
dessert	il dolce	eel doll-cheb
cover charge	il coperto	eel kob-pair-tob
wine list	la lista dei vini	lab lee-stab day vee-nee
rare	al sangue	al sang-gweb
medium	al puntino	al poon-tee-nob
well done	ben cotto	ben kot-tob
glass	il bicchiere	eel bee-kee-air-eb
bottle	la bottiglia	lab bot-teel-yab
knife	il coltello	eel kol-tell-ob
fork	la forchetta	lab for-ket-tab
spoon	il cucchiaio	eel koo-kee-eye-ob

Menu Decoder

apple	la mela	lab meh-lab
artichoke	il carciofo	eel kar-choff-ob
aubergine	la melanzana	lab meh-lan-tsah-nab
baked	al forno	al for-nob
beans	i fagioli	ee fab-joh-lee
beef	il manzo	eel man-tsob
beer	la birra	lab beer-rab
boiled	lesso	less-ob
bread	il pane	eel pah-neb
broth	il brodo	eel broh-dob
butter	il burro	eel boor-ob
cake	la torta	lab tor-tab
cheese	il formaggio	eel for-mad-job
chicken	il pollo	eel poll-ob
chips	patatine fritte	pab-tab-teen-eb free-teb
baby clams	le vongole	leb von-gob-leb
coffee	il caffè	eel kab-feh
courgettes	gli zucchini	lyee dzoo-kee-nee
dry	secco	sek-kob
duck	l'anatra	lah-nab-trab
egg	l'uovo	loo-ob-vob
fish	il pesce	eel pesh-eb
fresh fruit	frutta fresca	froo-tab fress-kab
garlic	l'aglio	lahl-yob
grapes	l'uva	loo-vab
grilled	alla griglia	ab-lab greel-yab
ham	il prosciutto	eel pro-shoo-tob
cooked/cured	cotto/crudo	kot-tob/kroo-dob
ice cream	il gelato	eel jel-lah-tob
lamb	l'abbacchio	lab-back-kee-ob
lobster	l'aragosta	lab-rab-goss-tab
meat	la carne	la kar-neb

milk	il latte	eel laht-teb
mineral water fizzy/still	l'acqua minerale gasata/naturale	lah-kwab mee-nair-ah-leb gab-zah-tab/ nab-too-rah-leb
mushrooms	i funghi	ee foon-gee
oil	l'olio	loll-yob
olive	l'oliva	lob-lee-vab
onion	la cipolla	lab cbee-poll-ab
orange	l'arancia	lab-ran-chab
orange/lemon juice	succo d'arancia/ di limone	soo-kob dab-ran-chab/ dee lee-moh-neb
peach	la pesca	lab pess-kab
pepper	il pepe	eel peh-peb
pork	carne di maiale	kar-neb dee mab-yah-leb
potatoes	le patate	leb pab-tah-teb
prawns	i gamberi	ee gam-bair-ee
rice	il riso	eel ree-zob
roast	arrosto	ar-ross-tob
roll	il panino	eel pab-nee-nob
salad	l'insalata	leen-sab-lah-tab
salt	il sale	eel sah-leb
sausage	la salsiccia	lab sal-see-chab
seafood	frutti di mare	froo-tee dee mah-reb
soup	la zuppa, la minestra	lab tsoo-pab, lab mee-ness-trab
steak	la bistecca	lab bee-stek-kab
strawberries	le fragole	leb frah-gob-leb
sugar	lo zucchero	lob zoo-kair-ob
tea	il tè	eel teh
herb tea	la tisana	lab tee-zah-nab
tomato	il pomodoro	eel pob-mob-dor-ob
tuna	il tonno	ton-nob
veal	il vitello	vee-tell-ob
vegetables	i legumi	ee leb-goo-mee
vinegar	l'aceto	lab-cheh-tob
water	l'acqua	lah-kwab
red wine	vino rosso	vee-nob ross-ob
white wine	vino bianco	vee-nob bee-ang-kob

Numbers

1	uno	oo-nob
2	due	doo-eb
3	tre	treb
4	quattro	kwat-rob
5	cinque	ching-kweb
6	sei	say-ee
7	sette	set-teb
8	otto	ot-tob
9	nove	noh-veb
10	dieci	dee-eh-cbee
11	undici	oon-dee-chee
12	dodici	doh-dee-cbee
13	tredici	tray-dee-cbee
14	quattordici	kwat-tor-dee-cbee
15	quindici	kwin-dee-cbee
16	sedici	say-dee-cbee
17	diciassette	dee-cbab-set-teb
18	diciotto	dee-chot-tob
19	diciannove	dee-chab-noh-veb
20	venti	ven-tee
30	trenta	tren-tab
40	quaranta	kwab-ran-tab
50	cinquanta	ching-kwan-tab
60	sessanta	sess-an-tab
70	settanta	set-tan-tab
80	ottanta	ot-tan-tab
90	novanta	nob-van-tab
100	cento	chen-tob
1,000	mille	mee-leb
2,000	duemila	doo-eb mee-lab
5,000	cinquemila	ching-kweb mee-lab
1,000,000	un milione	oon meel-yoh-neb

Time

one minute	un minuto	oon mee-noo-tob
one hour	un'ora	oon or-ab
half an hour	mezz'ora	medz-or-ab
a day	un giorno	oon jor-nob
a week	una settimana	oona set-tee-mah-nab
Monday	lunedì	loo-neb-dee
Tuesday	martedì	mar-teb-dee
Wednesday	mercoledì	mair-kob-leb-dee
Thursday	giovedì	job-veb-dee
Friday	venerdì	ven-air-dee
Saturday	sabato	sah-bab-tob
Sunday	domenica	dob-meh-nee-kab

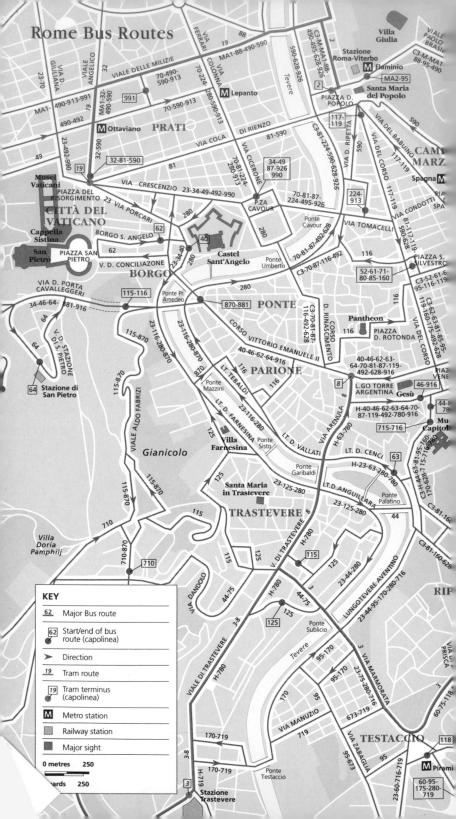